Clean it *fast*
Clean it RIGHT

Clean it *fast*
Clean it RIGHT

The ULTIMATE GUIDE

to Making Absolutely Everything You Own
Sparkle & Shine

Edited by Jeff Bredenberg

RODALE

Library of Congress Cataloging-in-Publication Data

Clean it fast, clean it right : the ultimate guide to making
  absolutely everything you own sparkle and shine / edited by Jeff
  Bredenberg.
      p.   cm.
  Includes index.
  ISBN 0–87596–509–1 hardcover
  ISBN 1–57954–019–8 paperback
  1. House cleaning. I. Bredenberg, Jeff.
TX324.C578 1998
648'.5—dc21   98–4828

Distributed to the book trade by St. Martin's Press

    16 18 20 19 17 15   hardcover
              10   9   paperback

Visit us on the Web at www.rodalestore.com, or call us toll-free at (800) 848-4735.

WE INSPIRE AND ENABLE PEOPLE TO IMPROVE THEIR LIVES AND THE WORLD AROUND THEM

Clean It Fast, Clean It Right Staff

Managing Editor: **Jeff Bredenberg**
Contributing Writers: **Dean King, Diane Kozak, Mark Robinson, Charles Slack, Logan Ward**
Book Project Researcher: **Christine Dreisbach**
Editorial Researchers: **Jennifer A. Barefoot, Jan Eickmeier, Leah B. Flickinger, Jennifer L. Kaas, Nanci Kulig, Mary S. Mesaros, Deanna Moyer, Teresa A. Yeykal**
Copy Editor: **David R. Umla**
Art Director: **Darlene Schneck**
Cover and Interior Designer: **Charles Beasley**
Layout Designer: **Andrew MacBride**
Manufacturing Coordinator: **Melinda B. Rizzo**
Office Manager: **Roberta Mulliner**
Office Staff: **Julie Kehs, Suzanne Lynch**

Rodale Health and Fitness Books

Vice President and Editorial Director: **Debora T. Yost**
Executive Editor: **Neil Wertheimer**
Design and Production Director: **Michael Ward**
Research Manager: **Ann Gossy Yermish**
Copy Manager: **Lisa D. Andruscavage**
Marketing Director: **Janine Slaughter**
Production Manager: **Robert V. Anderson Jr.**
Studio Manager: **Leslie M. Keefe**
Associate Studio Manager: **Thomas P. Aczel**
Book Manufacturing Director: **Helen Clogston**

Contents

Part 1: Clean Living

Part 2: The Dirty Stuff

> ***Shine copper buttons***
> ***with ketchup***
> page 131

Polish alligator handbag with car wax
page 211

*Clean your grill in a
car wash*
page 64

Bathe diamond jewelry in vodka
page 222

Take a shower with your tuba
page 263

Steam-clean your microwave oven
page 256

*Rub out rust stains with
lemon juice*
page 323

*Clean watchbands in the
clothes washer*
page 420

Part 3: Tools and Materials

Grime-Fighters, Choose Your Weapons 443
The Ultimate Primer on Cleaning Implements and Chemicals

Remove decals with vinegar
page 229

Restore a shrunken sweater with hair conditioner

page 439

Introduction

A bemused colleague presented me with a gift the other day, a 1952 volume titled *Housekeeping Made Simple*, part of *The Homemaker's Encyclopedia*. Flip through it and you find photographs of women vacuuming and doing laundry in their pearls and high heels. "Today's lady of the house," we are informed, "is a smart girl who applies the science of saving time and motion to her housework." And as for males, "the man of the house should at least hang up his own clothes and refrain from leaving a trail of ashes in his wake."

Well, the 1950s-style housewife may be extinct, but dust bunnies are not. We still want easy and efficient ways to clean our homes and possessions. So I am happy to present to you the ultimate cleaning book for the real world. Around the house, this book is as handy as a phone book and as versatile as a Swiss Army knife. How you dress while cleaning is strictly your business (although I personally favor sneakers and jeans). And needless to say, this is a gender-neutral publication. Both women and men will find it valuable.

You will not find a more complete and authoritative book on the subject. A top-notch team of how-to journalists interviewed hundreds of scientists, industry professionals, and other cleaning experts to bring you all the cutting-edge information about how to clean your home and all your possessions.

You're about to reap enormous rewards from all of that expertise. Not only will you learn how to make everything you own sparkle and shine. You'll save enormous amounts of time and money by doing it right the first time. You'll learn hundreds of ingenious shortcuts. You'll learn how to safeguard your family from germs that you never knew were lurking. You'll also learn cleaning secrets that will improve your performance at a broad range of activities, including golf, bowling, gardening, cooking, fishing, sewing, and skiing.

What's more, we'll tell you what not to bother cleaning. A soccer ball, for instance, really ought to look a little nicked and smudged. Think of it as a badge of honor. Nobody in the world cares if your fireplace walls are blackened either. And if you clean some items—like rare coins—you're likely to *decrease* their value.

This book is extremely easy to use and understand. Part 1, "Clean Living," is jam-packed with general advice about cleaning—getting motivated, working room to room in the home, conquering clutter, and protecting your health. Part 2, "The Dirty Stuff," is a massive A-to-Z listing of everything in and around your home. You'll find the best cleaning techniques and speed tips for those items, plus cautionary notes so that you'll harm neither yourself nor the things you're cleaning. Wherever possible, we steer you toward the least toxic methods available. Part 3, "Tools and Materials," is a rundown of all the gear you'll need to do this work quickly and effectively.

I suggest that you keep this book in a very handy place. When a guest splashes red wine on your living room rug, you're going to want easy access to the special "Emergency Action" notes. Before you wash any more windows, you're going to want a look at the formulas for homemade cleaners that even outperform commercial products—and cost just pennies to whip up. And before you take one more swipe with that moist kitchen sponge, you'll want to know the hassle-free ways to kill the colony of bacteria hiding inside it.

Finally, you will find this book surprisingly fun to read. For tips on cleaning taxidermy, for instance, we moseyed on over to the Roy Rogers–Dale Evans Museum, where that famous steed Trigger and 200 other creatures are immortalized. On the subject of barbecue grills, we consulted a champion rib-joint proprietor. For sweeping expertise, we consulted the fellow who pushes a broom behind circus elephants for a living. And on the subject of scouring powders, we spoke to a gunnery sergeant who has inspected many a pristine toilet.

If you have trouble thinking of cleaning as anything other than drudgery, then this book will change your life. Done sensibly, cleaning is an easy habit to incorporate into your lifestyle. And the payoffs are monumental—not just visually but also in terms of cost savings, time savings, health, and self-esteem. I'm proud to be putting into your hands a tool that will make your life better and easier. Here's to your sparkling future.

Jeff Bredenberg
Managing Editor

Part 1

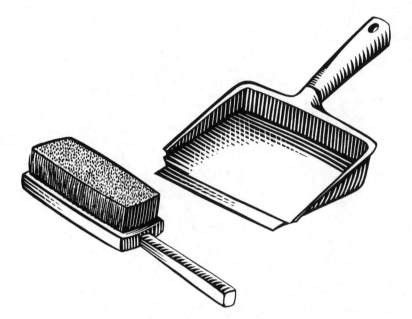

Clean
Living

Get into a Clean Mindset

A Look at the Bright Side: You'll Save Time and Money—And Feel Better, Too

For Snow White, cleaning came easily. Not only did she have an army of cute little forest creatures to help her sanitize the Seven Dwarves' home but also she knew how to clean the house with a smile on her face and a hop in her step. Her secret? Whistling while she worked.

So much for fairy tales. If we could just pucker up and blow our cares away, we'd all be whistling virtuosos. In the real world, cleaning is just not the kind of subject that gets people tapping toes or turning pirouettes.

Still, cleaning around the house is a vital part of daily existence, a practice that provides many rewards—not the least of which are more pleasant surroundings and better health. Who wouldn't want a home that's clean and clutter-free and stays that way with minimum effort? You can have that. But achieving it starts with a positive mindset and some basic motivation skills for both you and your family. Master the advice in this chapter, and you'll be well on your way. You'll realize that keeping your home clean is not such a daunting task after all. And *that* would be something to whistle about.

WHY BOTHER WITH CLEANING AT ALL?

Yes, let's test that basic assumption that cleaning is necessary. Could it be that we scour, mop, and vacuum our lives away for no good reason? After all, fad and fashion have pushed upon us such tortures as bustles and spike heels for no practical reason. Maybe you and your home would manage fine with the grunge look if you could just weather a little disapproval from a few family members and friends. So before we totally commit ourselves to the clean mindset, let's examine the benefits of clean living. If you buy the following arguments, you'll be ready to approach cleaning from the positive side.

Cleaning Saves Money

You know that brushing your teeth can save you thousands of dollars in dental bills. Well, the same thinking applies to all the things you own. Dirty stuff wears out faster than clean stuff. Simple preventive practices, including cleaning, can extend the life of everything from appliances to upholstery and, in turn, spare your pocketbook.

Moreover, regular cleaning makes for easier, less risky cleaning. Regular cleaning is more gentle to household surfaces. It minimizes the need for scrubbing, which causes wear and tear on walls, floors, and furniture.

Cleaning Saves Time

What could save more time than just avoiding the drudgery of cleaning altogether?

By keeping on top of dirt and clutter, you save time and effort. Wipe up a spill on your stove top before dinner and it takes you seconds to clean. Put it off until later and it becomes a dried up mess that requires more time, more effort, and more cleaning products to remove, says Carol Seelaus, a speed-cleaning instructor at Temple University in Philadelphia and owner of Somebody's Gotta Do It, a professional cleaning service.

Cleaning Protects Your Health

A dirty house can make you sick. Whether it's an allergy to the thriving colony of dust mites that reside in your mattress or a case of food poisoning, the risk of illness from exposure to germs in the home is real. An estimated 50 to 80 percent of food-borne illness originates in the home, says Charles Gerba, Ph.D., professor of microbiology at the University of Arizona in Tucson. "People think that they have the 24-hour bug. Well, the truth is that there's no such thing. It's usually food-borne or water poisoning," Dr. Gerba says.

Hot zones around the house that need regular disinfecting include sinks, faucets, doorknobs, cutting boards, the refrigerator handle, and the toilets.

Cleanliness Is Comforting

Cleaning makes things look good and makes us feel good. Forget about company coming. The main reason that people clean, according to a 1996 survey conducted by the Soap and Detergent Association in New York City, is to feel good about themselves.

"I call it house pride," says Seelaus. "The house is an extension of oneself, and if it looks good, it's a good reflection on oneself."

NOW SLIDE INTO A ROUTINE

Motivated to clean now? Don't start just yet—randomly attacking the house won't lead to long-term success. Experts agree: You need a regular cleaning routine. With a systematic approach, you assign the basic cleaning duties to a daily, weekly, monthly, or seasonal schedule—a move that will free you from the burdens of domestic chaos. A cleaning schedule saves time, effort, and frustration.

Look at it this way. You wouldn't think of going on vacation without knowing where you're going and how to get there. So when it comes to planning your housework, think of cleanliness as your destination and your cleaning schedule as the route you follow.

"With housework, the shortest distance between two points—starting and finishing—is a housekeeping schedule," says Deniece Schofield, a home management consultant in Cedar Rapids, Iowa, and author of *Confessions of an Organized Homemaker.* If you're domestically challenged, a schedule puts necessary tasks in writing so that the dirt and clutter do not overwhelm you. If you're a perfectionist, a schedule will keep you from doing tasks more often than they need to be done.

"I think that schedules are so important because housework is never done. But schedules make it feel done. That feeling of accomplishment, of being finished, is vital to housework," says Schofield. And don't think that you'll have to consult your cleaning schedule every day for the rest of your life. The good habits you develop from following a schedule will soon become routine.

Four Steps to Bringing Order to Chaos

There is no magic formula that works for each and every household. Make a schedule that works for you by following these steps.

1. Decide how much time will be spent cleaning. On how many days of the week will you schedule cleaning time? How many hours each day? The number of hours you plan to devote to cleaning (and maintaining) will provide the rough framework for your schedule.

2. For each room or area in your house, make a list of the jobs that need to be done. Include day-to-day jobs, such as picking up, dusting, and vacuuming, as well as once-a-year jobs like cleaning under furniture or appliances.

3. Next to each task write down how often each job needs to be done—daily, weekly, monthly, or seasonally. How often you clean will depend upon the conditions in your house. A bathroom used by several people may need daily cleaning, for instance, while a single person with two bathrooms may only clean once a week. Daily vacuuming might seem excessive to some people and necessary to others.

4. Decide who will be responsible for each job. Post the schedule in a form you are comfortable with—in poster form or on index cards, for example. Until you memorize your routine, you will probably need to consult the schedule frequently.

It's All in the Timing

Here's an example of what your schedule might look like.

Daily: Straighten up, do all dishes, wipe stove and countertops, make beds, hang up clothes, read and dispose of mail, clean up any spots and spills.

Weekly: Vacuum carpets, sweep and mop floors, dust furniture, change beds, clean bathrooms, spot-clean handprints, empty all trash cans.

Monthly: Dust along woodwork, vacuum upholstery and window treatments, wipe kitchen cabinets, clean out refrigerator, sweep garage.

How to Clean Like a Pro

People are often amazed by how much a housekeeper can accomplish in four hours, says Margaret Dasso, owner of the Clean Sweep, a professional cleaning service based in Lafayette, California, and co-author of *Dirt Busters.* You can spend less time cleaning if you approach it the way a professional housecleaner does. "The more nearly you can duplicate these conditions, the more you will accomplish during your own cleaning time," she says.

Work from a list—and prioritize. A professional has a clear idea of what needs to be done. Make a list for yourself of what you will accomplish during your cleaning. Add a list of extra chores to be done if time and energy permit. Then stick to the list. If you see something else that needs to be done, make a mental note and schedule it for another day. "Distraction is your number one enemy when cleaning your own home," says Dasso.

Get the kids out of the house for a few hours. A professional does not have to deal with people underfoot. If possible, clean when there is no one else around. You won't have the distraction of trying to do two jobs at once.

Don't answer the telephone. "Every break in your routine is a time-robber," says Dasso. "Interruptions are far more time-consuming than they seem." Take the phone off the hook or let the answering machine pick up.

Straighten up before you clean. A professional comes into a house that's ready to be cleaned. Get your house ready by picking up clutter the night before.

Set a time limit. Professionals are usually paid by the hour and must work within a certain time frame. Setting a time limit for yourself will keep you moving and on track.

Reward yourself for a job well-done. Professionals are paid for their work. Since no one is going to pay you to clean your own house, doing something nice for yourself does wonders for your motivation. "Whether it's a banana split, a great book, or a leisurely bubble bath, give yourself a treat," says Dasso.

Seasonally (twice a year—at the end of summer and winter): Wash windows, clean chimney, wash walls, clean oven, defrost freezer, clean furnace filters, clean light fixtures, clean window blinds.

MOTIVATION:
RALLYING YOURSELF—AND THE TROOPS

To understand how to motivate yourself, you first have to look at what motivates you to clean. Have you been taking a "dirt-driven" approach to cleaning? That is, do you decide it's time to wash the dishes when the kitchen sink is full? Do you decide to do the laundry when the hamper is overflowing and you've run out of matching socks? Do you find yourself dousing one mess after another but never really getting the whole job done?

The problem with mess-motivated cleaning is that when the mess isn't there, you're not motivated to clean. Instead of controlling the housework, the housework controls you.

What you need is an attitude shift, a shift in what's motivating you to clean. Instead of reacting to a negative situation—a mess—look at cleaning as striving toward something positive—an orderly pleasant environment.

"It takes a lot of motivation to clean a house and keep it that way. That is only gotten by looking at the end result: the beauty of an orderly harmonious home. You have to start at the end and work back," says Sandra Felton, author of *The Messies Manual* and founder of Messies Anonymous, a Miami-based national organization for chronically messy people. Most people would rather have a clean home instead of a disorderly messy one, but they just don't know how to get started. Here's what to do.

Start Small

Before she became a home management consultant, Schofield says that she was overwhelmed by housework and the demands of motherhood. "I had three kids under age four. The house was a mess. I didn't know where to start, so I didn't do anything," she says. "One day I sat down and made a list of everything that was driving me crazy."

The list of neglected household tasks filled an entire sheet of paper. "I said to myself, 'I can't do it all, but I'll choose one thing.' That was the beginning of my freedom."

She started out by scheduling when she would do laundry—on Mondays, Wednesdays, and Fridays. That meant she didn't even think about laundry four days a week. Soon her schedule enabled her to stop feeling overwhelmed and motivated her to accomplish more.

Here are some tips that will set you on the path to an organized cleaning routine, one you'll be motivated to stick with.

Make a wish list. If you're feeling overwhelmed and discouraged by the never-ending task of cleaning, write down everything you would like to change. The list serves two purposes, says Schofield. First, it clears your mind. Once you write it down, stop beating yourself up about it. Then focus on the list itself. It allows you to see in black and white what needs to be done so that you can set priorities.

Take it step-by-step. Working from your list, pick the one cleaning task that you feel most motivated to work on. Develop a routine for that task and live with it for a few weeks before picking another item from the list. Don't burn yourself out by trying to accomplish too much too soon.

Start out with some inspiration. To boost your motivation when cleaning a room, start with a task where you'll see obvious improvements. If you're in the bedroom, for instance, make the bed first. "You'll see an immediate payoff," says Schofield.

With Children, Get Specific

It's unlikely that the desire for a clean, orderly home will motivate children to pick up their dirty socks. You can, however, instill a sense of household responsibility and foster good habits by teaching children basic cleaning skills and rewarding their efforts. Children can learn to make beds, do dishes, and sweep the floor the same way that they learn to walk, ride bikes, and read. Teaching a child a task is a four-step process, according to Elizabeth Crary in her book *Pick Up Your Socks.*

Decide exactly what needs doing. When you say, "Take out the trash," what does that mean? Does it simply mean tying up the garbage bag and placing it in the trash can outside? Should the child empty all the litter receptacles in the house? Should a new trash can liner be placed in the can? When you decide, collect all the material that the child will need.

Introduce the task. Depending on the child's learning style, either show him how to do the task, tell him how to do it, or do it together.

Set a time limit. Unless a time frame is established, children tend to put off their chores until a parent gets angry. Attach a time frame to each task. For instance, set the table by 5:00 P.M., clean your room before talking on the phone, take the trash out before watching television.

Establish standards for the job. Explain exactly how you want the job done. Does making the bed mean making hospital corners or just straightening out the wrinkles and fluffing the pillow?

Use Reminders and Rewards

To keep your new cleaning program from going astray, set up a system of reminders and rewards for your helpers. Here's how.

Post your schedule. Use a chart, index cards, or planning sheets to post a schedule of household responsibilities. The list helps family members remember and greatly reduces your need to prod, pester, and nag. To make them more effective, use your charts or calendars as the basis for some kind of reward. To add a touch of fun, design your chart to look like a game board and fill in squares as each task is completed.

Keep their eyes on a prize. Common rewards for kids cleaning include an allowance, treats, services, time and attention, and praise. To keep the family working together, have a family night out after everyone has done his job for seven days straight.

Mix it up occasionally. Children get bored with same chart and reward system month after month. When you see signs that their interest is waning, it's time for a change.

Keep things age-appropriate. Children have three levels of involvement in household tasks: Can do a task with help, can do it with reminding or supervision, and does the chore as needed. In general, chores such as tidying rooms, hanging up clothing, vacuuming floors, making beds, and taking out the trash can be done with help by children ages 4 to 7, with reminding or supervision for children ages 7 to 11, and unsupervised from about age 12.

Make it fun. Sure, children need to learn responsibility. But injecting some fun into cleanup detail can save a lot of whining. Crank up the stereo—kids love to work to music. Or make pickup time a game. The simpler and sillier, the better. For instance, start out by picking up everything that is red, and then work your way through the rainbow.

Hone Your Cleaning Smarts

How to Get More Sparkle in Less Time with Less Effort

Nobody misses June Cleaver. A lot has changed since the days when the domestic ideal meant cleaning an already-immaculate house in your pumps and pearls. A pristine home is still important to many Americans today. But according to a 1997 survey by the Soap and Detergent Association in New York City, almost 40 percent of us say that it's tough to find the time or energy to keep our homes clean.

Still, no matter how finicky or nonchalant you may be about housekeeping, the prospect of getting it done with a minimum amount of time and effort is alluring indeed. Here's a look at strategies for thorough-but-fast cleaning, and a guide to calling in the reinforcements—professional cleaners—for the really tricky jobs.

ROOM-BY-ROOM STRATEGIES

When you're ready to actually get some cleaning done—to apply dust cloth to vase and mop to linoleum—a few simple guidelines will ensure that you're working efficiently.

- Avoid distractions. Don't get sidetracked by lugging Junior's skates to his closet or stray socks to the laundry room.
- Work your way around the room in an orderly progression. Zipping from one side of the room to another again and again will waste a lot of footwork.
- Take all your cleaning tools with you. You waste time when you're perpetually stopping your work to get more tools from the pantry or basement. Besides, when you work without all the tools you'll need, you get tempted to skip tasks that need attention.

Here's how to apply those principles as you go about your regular housecleaning for both general living areas, like living rooms and bedrooms, and those two notorious hot spots, kitchens and bathrooms.

Make Like a Hotel Housekeeper

The key to cleaning a room fast and efficiently is staying in the room until the cleaning is done, says Deniece Schofield, a home management consultant in Cedar Rapids, Iowa, and author of *Confessions of an Organized Homemaker*. One way to accomplish that is by using a utility cart that you can purchase at janitorial supply stores. They cost anywhere from $180 to $230. Like professional housekeepers in hotels, Schofield wheels her cart from room to room as she cleans. The top of the cart holds a tray with cleaning supplies and cloths. A garbage bag hangs from one side of the cart. A second bag or a pillowcase hangs on the other side of the cart to carry misplaced articles picked up from the room.

Here's how she recommends you work a room: Wheel the cart in. Remove the caddy of cleaning supplies and place all the soiled laundry in the cart. Put all the trash from the room in the garbage bag attached to the cart. Any misplaced items that do not belong in the room should be placed in the second bag. Now clean the room, working your way around the room in a circular fashion. As a general rule, start at the top and work your way down. The floors should be the last thing you do.

If buying a utility cart sounds like too big a step, Schofield suggests that you test the method first. The same technique can be accomplished with a garbage bag and a laundry basket. Use a caddy for your cleaning supplies and cloths. Instead of the cart, place all the soiled laundry in the basket and garbage in the bag. Place any misplaced items outside the door of each room. After you've emptied the laundry basket, use it to tote the articles that need to be put away.

Hey, What Do I Clean First?

Here's an easy-to-remember strategy that will save you loads of grief as you clean a room: Start with the "dry" methods first. Always do as much vacuuming, sweeping, scraping, or dusting as possible before you douse something with water or spray it with cleaner. You wouldn't think of throwing a plate in the dishwasher if half of your dinner was still stuck to it. You'd scrape it off first. The same idea applies to all the surfaces in your home. Remove the bulk of the mess without getting it wet.

Then, when it's time to wield the sprays, sponges, and wet mops, here are a few more basic points to remember. First, of course, you wet the thing you're cleaning with the appropriate cleaning solution. Then, be patient—let the cleaner do its work. Save yourself some elbow grease and give the cleaner time to loosen and dissolve the dirt. Vigorous scrubbing not only takes a lot of energy but also can damage some surfaces. Then it should be easy to wipe the dirt away, using a sponge, cloth, paper towel, or squeegee.

A PRO'S RECIPE FOR THE KITCHEN

The kitchen is one of the two biggest cleaning tasks in any house (the other is the bathroom). To get through it quickly, Margaret Dasso, owner of the Clean Sweep, a professional cleaning service based in Lafayette, California, and co-author of *Dirt Busters*, recommends the following strategies.

- If you have an electric stove with drip pans, remove them (when the burners are cool) and put them in a strong solution of automatic dishwasher detergent in the sink.
- Check floors, counters, and cabinets for any stubborn spots, such as dried-on food. Spray them with all-purpose cleaner and let them soak.
- Clean the spill tray underneath the stove burners by lifting the burners and reaching your hand into the holes with a cloth or sponge where the drip pans were, or lifting up the stove top. Polish the stove top, knobs (make sure that you don't accidentally turn them on), and backsplash with all-purpose cleaner or window cleaner.
- Scour the drip pans that have been soaking with a nylon scrubber or plastic brush. Dry them and place them back in the stove.
- Move to your left or right around the room in an orderly manner. Carry your supplies with you so that you do not have to retrace your steps.
- Polish appliance surfaces with glass cleaner and paper towels. Wipe doors on the inside and outside.
- As you go, clean and polish countertops. Pull items forward, clean behind them, and then slide them back. Also, check cabinets for fingerprints and clean them off with an all-purpose cleaner.
- If you have a windowsill above the sink, wash it.
- Clean the sink. Use a toothbrush around the garbage disposal opening and the lip around the edge of the sink.
- Polish sink fixtures. Use a toothbrush around handles and the base of the fixture.
- Empty the trash.
- Sweep or vacuum the floor.
- Mop the floor.

Now Plunge Into the Bathroom

In the same vein, here are Dasso's suggested strategies for tackling the bathroom.

- Remove throw rugs.
- Sweep or vacuum hair from the counter, sink, and floor. Use a paper towel instead of a wet sponge and save yourself the effort of cleaning the hair off the sponge.

- Spray the bathtub, shower walls, tile, and shower doors or curtain with an all-purpose cleaner.
- Clean the soap dish and any chrome fixtures in the shower.
- Spray a small amount of glass cleaner on the mirror. Wipe until it is completely dry to avoid streaks.
- Spray the sink and counter with cleaner and wipe them dry. Move vanity items to one side, clean the vanity, and then slide them back.
- Clean the toilet, bowl first. Flush. Put the toilet seat up and spray and wipe each side with disinfectant cleaner. Clean the tank, base, handle, and any exposed pipes.
- Wipe the toilet paper holder.
- Go around the perimeter of the room. Wipe towel racks, refold towels, and dust the pictures and shelves. Check for fingerprints on doors and light switches and clean with an all-purpose spray cleaner. Don't spray the light switches directly—spray your cleaning cloth first, then wipe.
- Wash the floor and replace rugs after it dries.

MAKE A CLEAN BREAK FROM MESSY HABITS

Little changes to your daily routine can speed up your cleaning by preventing your house from getting dirty in the first place. "Everyone is time-constrained or energy-constrained when it comes to cleaning," says cleaning consultant Kent Gerard from Oakland, California. "Through daily habits that don't generate filth in the first place, you can keep your house cleaner."

A few seconds or minutes of preventive maintenance can add up to hours of time saved on cleaning day.

11 Preventive Practices

Cleaning experts recommend that you build these 11 practices into your everyday routine. They'll make cleaning day in your home much easier and will help keep bacteria at bay.

1. Ventilate the bathroom. Excess moisture left in the air after bathing or showering promotes the growth of mildew, mold, and fungus. If you have a ventilation fan, use it. If not, open the bathroom window for a few minutes. If you don't have a window or a fan in the bathroom, try opening the window in a nearby room.

2. Close the toilet seat when you flush. Studies from the University of Arizona department of microbiology in Tucson show that when you flush, a mist is propelled from the toilet. The microscopic, bacteria-laden water droplets contaminate surfaces in the

The Basics of Efficient Cleaning

To keep yourself sane and to make maximum use of your cleaning time, cleaning pros recommend that you follow these guidelines.

1. Keep your cleaning supplies together. Before you start, gather your equipment and cleaning products and load them in a tray, apron, or bucket. You won't waste time running from room to room for supplies.

2. If it's not dirty, don't clean it. Don't waste time and energy sanitizing an unused bathroom just because it's cleaning day.

3. Spot-clean whenever possible. Don't clean the entire oven when only the glass door has a grease mark.

4. Don't scrub. Let the cleaning solution do the work for you. Spray tough spots—like a soap-scummed shower wall—with cleaner and let it soak while you clean something else. This way you'll make double use of your time and save elbow grease.

5. Less is more. Use only as much cleaning product as you need. Using too much is a waste of money, and it means more time is spent mopping up the excess.

bathroom, creating the potential for infection.

3. Squeegee the shower walls after use. "It takes a minute and a half, and makes your weekly bathroom cleaning a 15-minute job," says Carol Seelaus, a speed-cleaning instructor at Temple University in Philadelphia and owner of Somebody's Gotta Do It, a professional cleaning service. The three major cleaning problems in bathtubs and showers—soap scum, mildew, and mineral buildup—are caused by allowing water to stand until it evaporates. By drying the walls right away, you prevent all three problems.

"A lot of people have a problem with using a squeegee," says Seelaus. "They say, 'Can't I just dry it with a towel?' The answer is yes, but then you have a soaking wet towel to deal with." One shortcut she recommends is to use liquid soap products instead of bar soaps when bathing. They don't contain the fat that causes soap scum to form.

4. Ban stove-top splatter art. In the kitchen, use bigger pots and pans when cooking. When *Woman's Day* magazine surveyed 1,000 women to find out the household chores that they absolutely hate, cleaning the stove came up as number one.

"A lot of spills and boil-overs are caused by cooking with too small a pan. People say, 'I don't want to wash a big pot,' and then they wind up having to wash the whole stove," says Seelaus.

5. Blow grease and odors away. Use an exhaust fan while you're cooking and you'll eliminate airborne grease that builds up on kitchen surfaces. You'll also reduce cooking odors, which can be absorbed by carpets and upholstery.

6. Don't let germs hitchhike. Use a clean sponge or dishcloth to mop up messes and spills. Everything from countertops to cabinets to refrigerator handles can be blanketed in a coating of thriving bacteria after a swipe with a germ-laden sponge or dishcloth. Moist cellulose sponges provide just the right environment for colony-forming microbes—a surface to cling to, moisture, and a steady supply of nutrients. The same holds true for cotton dishcloths.

"From a microbial standpoint, the cleanest people actually have the dirtiest kitchens because they are always wiping everything down," says Charles Gerba, Ph.D., professor of microbiology at the University of Arizona in Tucson.

7. Empty the dishwasher promptly. If the dishwasher is full of clean dishes, no one can load it with dirty dishes. So the dirty dishes end up in the kitchen sink, creating a mess that has to be cleaned up prior to meal preparation instead of after.

8. Put a mat at each entrance to the home. About 80 percent of the dirt on floors comes in through the door, says Seelaus. If you stop dirt from being tracked in by wiping it off or, better yet, removing your shoes, you'll have cleaner floors and carpets.

Avoid decorative mats, carpet squares, and link mats made of old tires. Instead, purchase a commercial mat from a restaurant supply store or janitorial supply store. They come in various sizes and range in price from $12 to $37. An effective mat can reduce the cleaning time in the average household by 200 hours per year.

Quick Jobs for Those Spare Moments

Put spare minutes to use. Accomplishing little tasks when you have an extra minute or two can add up to hours of cleaning by the end of the week. Here are a few examples, and once you pick up the habit, you'll think of many more, says Carol Seelaus, a speed-cleaning instructor at Temple University in Philadelphia and owner of Somebody's Gotta Do It, a professional cleaning service.

While the coffee is brewing: Clean the refrigerator door or empty the crumb tray in the toaster.

While TV commercials are on: Clean the remote, dust the coffee table, clean the loose change and popcorn out of the couch cushions.

While the laundry is in the dryer: Tidy up your laundry area and cleaning supplies.

While the cookies bake: Clean the knobs on the stove.

While the dishwasher is finishing: Sort the mail or organize the junk drawer.

While your hair is drying: Launder hand washables.

While waiting for water to boil: Spot-clean the floor.

9. Shut dirt out. Keep drawers, cabinets, closets, and furniture closed. In the kitchen, food and crumbs won't end up inside a closed silverware drawer. Dust has a way of infiltrating everything, but items stored away in closets will stay clean longer if the doors are shut.

10. Put things back where they belong. Clutter is the number one cleaning problem in most homes—about half of the housework is caused by junk that's lying around. When clogged with the clutter of carelessly strewn objects, no room can be cleaned fast or efficiently. You waste time and energy picking each object up, deciding where it's supposed to be, and putting it away. Altering this habit is probably the most difficult because clutter is an ongoing battle.

11. Provide plenty of litter receptacles. Another way to avoid clutter is to make sure that there is always a readily available place to throw things away.

CALLING IN THE REINFORCEMENTS

The soap scum in your shower is so thick you can write your name in it. And your in-laws are on their way for their annual visit. Uh-oh.

You might be one of the nearly 10 million Americans each year who decide to pay professionals to clean their homes. Although homes with children under age 18 may need the most cleaning help, the people most likely to hire such help are empty-nesters age 45-plus. Here's how to hire the right pro for the right job.

Choose the Right Helper

If you're looking for a housecleaning service, there are two basic routes to take: Hire a housekeeper, or hire a professional cleaning service. There are a number of factors to consider, says Dasso—cost, reliability, frequency of use, convenience, and the type of cleaning to be done.

The cost of hiring a cleaning person, or housekeeper, can vary from $5 an hour for a college student to more than $12 an hour for a trained professional. In addition to cleaning, housekeepers will often perform more intimate tasks, such as babysitting, folding and putting away laundry, and picking up clutter. If you need this kind of flexibility and personal service, hiring a housekeeper is a good solution, says Dasso.

Professional cleaning services descend on a home with one or more cleaners and whip the place into shape. They are usually hired to do a predetermined, standardized cleaning and are in and out of your home in a very short amount of time, Dasso says. The cost is usually $50 to $85 per visit.

Because their services are strictly cleaning, you'll need to pick up and have things out of the way when professional cleaning services come. If you don't need regular help but have a special event coming up, such as a party, or if you just want to get the spring cleaning out of the way, professional services are a good choice.

When you hire a professional housecleaner, be sure that you both understand the services that will be provided—what is going to be cleaned, how long it will take, how much it will cost, how frequently it will be done.

Put Dry Cleaners to the Test

Dry cleaning is only called dry because clothes are washed in solvents instead of water. Fabrics that can be harmed by contact with water, such as silk or wool, are laundered in a mixture of solvents, soap, and a tiny bit of water in big front-loading washing machines. Remember: The chemical cleaning process is hard on fibers, and frequent cleaning can cause some fabrics, such as wool, to develop a sheen, according to Jennifer Morgan, Ph.D., product technologist for the Wool Bureau in New York City.

Clothing does not need to be dry-cleaned every time it is worn. After wearing, brush the garment off or shake it out to remove surface soils, then let it air out. Inspect the garment for any spills or stains. If the fabric is visibly soiled, take it to the cleaners. Whenever possible, tell the dry cleaner the source of stains and spots—they'll be able to do a better job for you, says Dr. Morgan.

Your clothes should come back from the cleaners looking like new. But that doesn't always happen. If you're shopping for a new cleaner, dry-cleaning experts suggest that you try this test: Pick two garments that you're not too fond of, one in a bright color and the other white. Give them to the prospective cleaner and see how they come back. Ask yourself the following questions, suggests Jerry Levine, associate director of the Neighborhood Cleaners Association International in New York City.

- Does the color look the same as when you sent it? Is the white clean, or dingy looking? Some dry cleaners try to cut corners by not purifying the solvents often enough to remove dissolved stain material. Or they might not replace or regenerate the filters in their machines frequently enough, leaving solids in the solvent that could damage your clothing.
- Where are the tags attached? Garments need to be identified so they do not get lost. The tags, however, should never be stapled to the garment itself, but to the label. Some finer dry cleaners will remove the tags from the garment and attach them to the invoice.

- Did they touch up the ironing, or just machine press it? The cleaner should touch up garments that have special darts or pleats, like a fitted blouse or a pleated skirt, with a hand iron to remove any creases left by the pressing machine. Some try to save on labor costs by skipping this step.
- Are all the stains that can be removed gone? Stains should be taken out by hand. The more training the cleaner has, the more likely that stains will be removed.
- Are all buttons still on the garment? Are any damaged? Some buttons are solvent-soluble. A good dry cleaner should take care to protect buttons from solvents or should recommend removing them before cleaning.

"And remember," says Levine, "don't expect the best quality cleaning for the lowest price. They don't go together. Cheap usually means a lousy cleaner."

For Drapes, Carpets, and Upholstery, Turn Up the Heat

There's actually no steam involved in professional steam cleaning. Dirt and soils are removed from draperies, carpets, and upholstery through a process of hot-water extraction. Special machinery applies a cleaning solution and then suctions the soiled water from the fibers. Although you can rent this type of machine at rental centers and grocery stores for less than $40 a day (cleaning solutions are extra), they usually do not remove water as effectively as professional machinery.

And if you don't remove it, you'll be the one in hot water. "Damage occurs when fibers stay wet for too long," says Claudia Ramirez, former executive vice president of the Association of Specialists in Cleaning and Restoration (ASCR) in Annapolis Junction, Maryland. The longer the fabric is wet, the more likely you are to get dye bleeding, odors, and mildew. "Mildew can start forming in just 24 hours."

Under normal use, carpet should be cleaned once a year and draperies and upholstery every two years, says Ramirez. You may have to clean them more often if you have a smoker, young children, or pets in the home, or if you live in a region with high humidity, extreme cold, or excessive airborne dust.

Here are tips for working with a steam cleaner.

Check out the training. You want a steam-cleaning service that is adequately trained, so contact the Carpet and Upholstery Cleaning Institute at the Association of Specialists in Cleaning and Restoration, 10830 Annapolis Junction Road, Suite 312, Annapolis Junction, MD 20701-1120. Ask for a free list of professional carpet and upholstery cleaners in your region. Members of ASCR are backed up by technical advisors and the organization's laboratory if a cleaning problem comes up.

Walk and talk. Do a walk-through inspection with the contractor. "This is your time to point out any special areas of concern," says Ramirez. "This way, everyone is aware of the expectations."

Watch for the preliminaries. A steam-cleaning contractor should not just enter your house and start cleaning the carpet or upholstery right away. A professional will avoid costly mistakes by inspecting and testing fabrics first.

When Your Ducts Go South

The heating and air-conditioning systems in your home have filters that will trap most dust, pet dander, and other particles and keep them out of your duct system. If you maintain the filter regularly, your ducts should stay reasonably clean.

You may need professional duct cleaning, however, if you've had an unusually high level of contamination in your house—say, remodeling that created large amounts of dust, a furnace malfunction that forced soot into the system, or water damage. Moisture in ducts will promote the growth of mold, mildew, and bacteria.

That's when you'll need to call in a professional duct cleaner, who attaches a vacuum device to your vents to suck out the dust and particles. The procedure is usually priced by the number of vents in your home.

To make sure that you're hiring a competent duct cleaner, follow these tips from the ASCR.

Look for certification. Hire a certified mechanical hygienist (CMH), the highest recognition of competency in the duct-cleaning industry. Contractors who have earned a CMH designation are members of the Mechanical Systems Hygiene Institute, a division of the ASCR. They get ongoing technical updates, continuing accreditation in the latest cleaning techniques, and access to a network of technical advisors at ASCR. To find a CMH in your region, contact the ASCR at the address mentioned above for a free referral.

Expect an inspection. The first thing a duct-cleaning contractor should do is inspect the system visually and provide an assessment of what needs to be done.

For tough jobs only, seal it. Ideally, you want the dirt removed from your duct system. But sometimes contractors will recommend coating the interior of a duct with sealant to reline the system. The sealant is sprayed into the duct on top of existing dirt and dries to a lacquerlike finish to prevent dust from circulating. This may be nec-

Design Dirt out of Your Life

Dirt happens—you can't totally banish it from your life. But you can reduce the amount of time it takes to clean your home by choosing low-maintenance materials when you buy items such as furniture, fixtures, flooring, and carpeting.

An example is a light-colored floor that requires an extra half-hour of sweeping and mopping each week; it will cost you 26 hours of time in the course of a year. Now, that floor is likely to last 10 years, so you'll spend 10 days more cleaning it than you would if you had chosen a darker floor.

Here are some other ways that cleaning professionals say you can design dirt out of your life.

Keep it simple. The more fussy and ornate something is, the more difficult it is to clean, says Carol Seelaus, a speed-cleaning instructor at Temple University in Philadelphia and owner of Somebody's Gotta Do It, a professional cleaning service. Why spend hours working the dirt out of cracks and crevices when a sleek, simple design will do the job? Use the simplicity rule on everything from draperies to faucets.

Go for less surface. Look at design in terms of surface area. Every surface collects dust and dirt and requires cleaning. A louvered surface, like shutter doors, will be much more difficult to clean than a flat surface. Eliminate edges and ledges and textures and grooves. Each is a surface requiring another swipe of the cleaning cloth, so stick with smooth surfaces, Seelaus says.

Camouflage dirt. The idea isn't to wallow in hidden filth but to pick patterns and colors that blend with your lifestyle. If every strand of your dog's white hair shows on your dark blue carpeting, then you'll need to vacuum every day. A lighter color will camouflage the hair so you can stick to a reasonable cleaning routine. Patterns and designs will hide dirt and wear and tear because the eye is distracted. Solid colors, on the other hand, hide very little, cleaning professionals note. Select colors based on the number of kids you have, the color of your pets, or the color of your local soil.

essary in hard-to-reach areas, but the contractor should remove as much dirt buildup as possible before resorting to sealants.

Give your ducts a checkup. To ensure that it is operating efficiently, have your ventilation system inspected annually by a member of the Mechanical Systems Hygiene Institute or by a heating, ventilation, and air-conditioning contractor. Dirt collects in areas where the air moves sluggishly. On air-conditioning systems, clean the condensation drip pan at the base of the unit regularly to prevent growth of molds and fungi. To do this, remove the drip pan from the unit, draining the excess water and washing it with a sponge or cloth in a mild soap and water solution.

Clobber That Clutter

Remove Those Mountains of Junk, and the Cleaning Will Go Like Clockwork

It's guaranteed. No matter what size home you live in, no matter how spacious it seemed when you first moved in, eventually stuff will fill every available inch of space if you don't keep it under control.

Clutter is the by-product of our consumer-driven society. We amass a collection of items that we don't use but that we keep just in case we need them someday—bargains we just couldn't pass up, gifts from well-meaning family and friends, clothing that no longer fits, decorations for the house.

Soon the house that once seemed perfectly adequate is stuffed like Fibber McGee's closet. Cabinets and drawers are disorganized. Tables and counters are littered with objects. On cleaning day, navigating your way through a jumble of possessions robs you of time in several ways.

- It takes longer to find things.
- You have to stop to put items away, or at the very least move them around as you clean.
- All those possessions you have amassed need cleaning themselves, which means added hours of cleaning, dusting, polishing, and maintaining.

"If you are ever going to get control of this beast we call housework, the clutter has to go," says Margaret Dasso, owner of the Clean Sweep, a professional cleaning service based in Lafayette, California, and co-author of *Dirt Busters*.

De-cluttering your home is a simple organizational process that starts with sorting through everything, discarding unneeded items, finding a storage spot for the keepers, and then—the hardest part—developing a workable system to stay on top of it so that you don't have to dig your way out again. Here's how to go about it, says Sandra Felton, author of *The Messies Manual* and founder of Messies Anonymous, a Miami-based national organization for chronically messy people.

TAKE AN UNSENTIMENTAL JOURNEY THROUGH YOUR HOME

There's little room for sentimentality when you embark on a clutter-clearing mission. Prepare yourself for some letting go. Be as ruthless as you can in your assessment of the necessity of each object. If in doubt, throw it out.

Do you really need the ceramic chicken that Aunt Bessie gave you for your anniversary 12 years ago? How about those size 6 jeans that you haven't worn in 10 years, but just might be able to fit into someday? Is the 1976-vintage fondue pot really going to make an appearance at your next party?

To give yourself some momentum, you might want to start with the closet that will be easiest to de-junk, or with the one that bothers you the most. Targets such as those will give you an immediate sense of accomplishment.

The four-container discard-and-sort technique will help you mow right through any mountain of clutter. Here's how to do it. Get three boxes and a large trash can. One box will hold anything that should be kept in another room or closet. One box is for items you plan to sell or give away. Things that you know you should part with, but can't, go in the third box. (Tape this box shut when you're done and put it in the garage. If you haven't missed the contents of the box in six months, get rid of it.) The big trash can is there to encourage you to throw away as much as possible.

Give Every Item the Third Degree

Ask yourself the following questions as you give each item a hard look, recommends Deniece Schofield, a home management consultant in Cedar Rapids, Iowa, and author of *Confessions of an Organized Homemaker.*

1. Do I really need this? "Fear and sentiment are prob-

Stretch Your Storage

What if you've faithfully de-cluttered every corner of your house, and you're still short on space? Don't despair. There are plenty of ways to stretch the space you have, according to Minneapolis household expert Mary Ellen Pinkham in her book *Mary Ellen's Clean House.* When scouting for overlooked space, think about places you can go in, go on, and go under.

- Store extra blankets between the mattress and box spring.
- Use your luggage to store spare bedding, presents, or out-of-season sports equipment.
- Hang narrow shelves from the back of a hallway door.
- Make use of the inside of your kitchen cabinet doors by hanging racks that can hold lids for pots and pans, rolls of aluminum foil, or a spice rack.
- Build a loft below the ceiling of your garage to store little-used items.

ably the two main reasons you hang on to things," Schofield says. "You're afraid you might need them someday." To help yourself overcome that fear, ask yourself, "What's the worst thing that would happen if I got rid of this?" If it's nothing drastic, pitch it.

2. How long has it been since I used this? Things deteriorate with age—clothing, in particular. If you haven't worn something for several months, or if you didn't wear it the last time it was in season, it's doubtful that you'll pull it out to wear again. If you haven't used something for 6 to 12 months, then you can probably live without it.

3. Do I need so many? Duplication of items is common, especially in the kitchen. But ask yourself: Do I really need four can openers? Can I do without 20 bottles of nail polish? "The less you have, the less you have to take care of," says Schofield.

Once you've finished one closet or area of the house, move on to the next. Make a commitment to stick with it until the job is done, whether it takes two weeks or two months.

Variations on the Clutter-Busting Theme

Try these alternative methods to clear clutter.

Use it or lose it. Box up everything that has been cluttering up a given closet, drawer, or cabinet. Put a date on the container. As you need things, pull them from the box and put them away. Whatever remains in the box after six months is given away, sold, or discarded. "This is an interesting method, to say the least, and it works extremely well in the kitchen," says Schofield. "I know a family who does this on a regular basis. They swear by it."

Take it a bite at a time. If you're dealing with major-scale clutter, schedule your de-cluttering sessions in time bites, suggests professional organizer Stephanie Winston, founder and president of the Organizing Principle in New York City, in her book *Stephanie Winston's Best Organizing Tips*. "You do not need to take a deep breath and charge into the mess in one fell swoop," she says. "Setting unrealistic goals can be paralyzing." Instead, work a half-hour a day plowing through the piles. You're more likely to accomplish the task if you schedule regular sessions on your calendar. Try to schedule one time bite per day, or at least two a week. And stick to your schedule.

Managing the Paper Avalanche

As papers make their way into your house sheet by sheet, they are stacked and shuffled, read, and sometimes even filed. But sooner or later, these innocuous little slips add up to piles. "People say, 'Oh, it's only a little piece of paper,'" says Felton. "But paper is the primary clutterer. We are a society glutted with paper. It's not a once and done thing."

Daily preventive maintenance is the key to holding the paper avalanche at bay. Here's how to deal with it.

- Sort the mail daily. Immediately throw away the mail you have no use for, and file your bills. Keep a container for items that you plan to read.
- Stash your newspapers in the recycling bin daily and go through your magazines every two months.
- Use a calendar to record all your activities and engagements. When you receive a notice or invitation, mark it on the calendar, then discard the unnecessary paperwork.
- Set up a filing system for all your important papers. Use bright color-coded folders, with corresponding colored labels on the drawers, to help you spot files quickly.
- To accommodate the volume of papers generated by children in school, designate a drawer or file for each child. Clean it out once or twice a year and only keep things that will be meaningful 10 years from now.

The Pickup Game: Recruit the Entire Family

Keeping a lid on clutter is not a one-person job. Every member of the household over the age of two can pitch in to help maintain order in the home.

"Keeping your house orderly without family cooperation is a little like hanging wallpaper with only one arm," says Dasso. "You can do it, but who would want to?"

She recommends the following strategies for getting the family involved.

- Make this rule number one in your house: "Don't put it down; put it away."
- Insist that every family member over the age of two put their belongings away before dinner is served. Make sure that you're specific about exactly what you mean by "put away."
- Schedule a different family member each night for pickup duty. His or her things must be put away. Other people's possessions must be laid outside the owner's bedroom door.
- Create a "Saturday Box" or a ransom bag, where everyone's wayward objects are collected each day. On Saturday, the owners may regain a possession by doing a chore or paying the ransom for each item that they take out.

STORAGE STRATEGIES

Once your house is de-cluttered, you'll be surprised at how much closet, cabinet, and drawer space you reclaim. Storage, however, is more than just having a place to put things. It's knowing where to find a pair of scissors when you need them. It's being able to put a can of shoe polish away without shifting through stacks of containers. It's user-friendly organization.

"Make it easy to get out and easy to get in," says Felton. "I used to have plastic shoe boxes that you could see in. I thought it was so clever, but it was too hard to get into them when I needed something. Now I use baskets and I label them. They're easy to get into. If it's too much effort, your storage strategy isn't going to work."

Winston estimates that 80 percent of overcrowding in homes is due to poor organization, not insufficient space. There's always more room than you think.

Storing It Where You'll Find It Again

To maximize the storage potential of your home, plan your space with the following tips in mind, says Schofield.

Store like objects together. This commonsense approach to basic organization will save you a lot of hunting-around time. For instance, a container for shoe supplies kept in the utility closet might contain polish, brushes, shoelaces, and odor insoles. If you broke a shoelace, you wouldn't have to rifle through three junk drawers looking for a pair of laces. You'd just go to the "shoe box."

"Grouping will trim hours off your housekeeping time," says Schofield. When things are tucked here and there, family members will only have a vague idea of where to put something away. Things will end up being put away haphazardly and will be more difficult to find the next time you need them.

Keep it where it's used. To decide where to store something, don't ask yourself, "Where can I put this?" Instead say, "Where would I go to get it?" The logical places to look for a pair of scissors, for instance, might be a desk, a sewing basket, or a utility drawer. It wouldn't make much sense to put them in your sock drawer.

Make popular items easy. The more often you use something, the easier it should be to reach. If you have a favorite skillet that you cook with nearly every day, don't store it at the back of the cabinet so that you have to shuffle around a dozen pots and pans to get to it. Don't keep the dustpan and broom out in the garage if you need to sweep up your kitchen floor every day.

Label everything. Make sure that you can read the contents of the container from a clearly visible label. This way you won't waste time rooting through the wrong box to see if it contains last year's tax return. Use this technique on any opaque container—garment bags, cardboard cartons, or plastic storage containers.

Establish a place for everything. "Everything in your house should have such a well-defined place that you are able to find it in the dark," says Schofield. To assign spaces, use drawer dividers in bathroom and dresser drawers as well as your kitchen drawers.

If your kids won't use hangers, install a row of pegs for jackets and school supplies to eliminate day-to-day clutter. Family members are more likely to put things away if they know exactly where the items are supposed to go.

Protect Valuables with the Right Storage

For family heirlooms, precious objects, or important papers, not just any storage container will do. Here's how you can keep such objects accessible yet out from underfoot—and therefore safe, according to Minneapolis household expert Mary Ellen Pinkham in her book *Mary Ellen's Clean House.*

Photos: An easy way to store photos is to place them loose in three- by five-inch or four- by six-inch index card files. You can use the dividers to mark the dates. If you prefer to display photos in albums, use a safe plastic made of nonpolyvinyl chloride that does not contain adhesive on the pages. Some photo albums can damage your photographs. The cardboard backing in magnetic photo albums can stain the photo, and the adhesive may permanently bond the photo to the page. Some plastics give off gases that harm the photos.

Clothes: If you're short on closet space, you may choose to store out-of-season clothing in another area of the house. Always clean clothing before you store it. Residue from spills, such as beverages containing sugar, will discolor with age and create a permanent stain. Soiled clothing is also more likely to attract pests such as moths and carpet beetles.

Wash items in soft water and make sure that they are thoroughly rinsed since detergent residue can cause chemical discoloration. Do not starch prior to storing. Cover clothing with a sheet or muslin cloth to keep out dust, and store it away from dampness, which could promote the growth of mold and mildew. Avoid storing leather or suede in plastic. The lack of air circulation will cause it to dry out.

Clothing depreciates just like cars do. Consider the average life span of an article of clothing before you decide to store it. It may not be worth wearing when you get it out. Shirts, lightweight suits, and dresses will last an average of two years, according to the Neighborhood Cleaners Association International in New York City, a mem-

What Do I Do with All of This Junk?

You've spent weeks purging and paring down your household possessions, and now you're staring at a teetering mountain of boxed-up
castoffs. The little pack-rat voice in the back of your head is urging you to
stuff it all in the crawl space. But that's the approach that got you in trouble
in the first place. You need to get these items out of your life. But how?

The quickest way to dispense of the things that you want to sell is to
give them to a consignment shop, says Deniece Schofield, a home management consultant in Cedar Rapids, Iowa, and author of *Confessions of
an Organized Homemaker*. The fee that they charge for selling an item—
normally 60 percent of the selling price—is worth it compared with the
trouble and expense of advertising and marketing it yourself.

If you have a large number of things, hold a yard sale or garage sale
to put some extra money in your pocket.

Giving away usable items to charitable organizations, such as Good-
will Industries or the Salvation Army, will add up at tax time. The IRS will
allow you to deduct the fair value of your charitable donations. Check at
your local library or ask an accountant for a complete list of allowable
amounts you may claim for your donations.

If you don't want to haul a load of boxes to the donation site, call and
see if the organization has pickup service. Many will arrange an appoint-
ment to pick up donations.

bership organization that offers education for consumers and training
for dry cleaners. Wool blend suits, evening dresses, and cloth coats
look good for about three years, while you can get about four years
of wear out of leather coats and sweaters.

Heirloom items such as wedding and christening gowns should
be stuffed and wrapped in acid-free tissue to minimize wrinkling and
protect the fabric.

Documents: To protect important papers and documents from
theft, fire, or natural disaster, your storage plan should include a bank
safe deposit box, a fireproof strongbox, and a file drawer or cabinet
in your home.

In the safe deposit box, store birth and other certificates; marriage
license; stocks and bonds; legal documents such as your mortgage,
deed, and a copy of your will; military papers; passports; pension
plan; and an inventory of your household goods. In the fireproof
strongbox, store bank documents and insurance policies. In the file
drawer, store bank statements, tax returns, warranties, and photo-
copies of driver's licenses, credit cards, Social Security cards, and any
other identification cards.

A Clean Bill of Health

Make Your Home and Your Planet Safer with Some Sanitation Savvy

Sick of cleaning, you say? Just think how sick you'd be without it. Each year, millions of people develop health problems because of improper or insufficient cleaning. Consider these facts.

- About 20 percent of the yearly 6.5 million cases of food-borne illness originate in the home when hands, utensils, and surfaces are contaminated by bacteria.
- About one in six Americans will be affected by an allergy-related illness sometime in his life.
- Between 1982 and 1994, the prevalence of asthma in the United States increased by 61.2 percent. Among children under age 18, the rate rose 72.3 percent.

Our comfortable homes, with their wall-to-wall carpeting and weather-tight insulation, are the ideal places for allergens, such as dust mites, to live and multiply. If you suffer from allergies, no doubt you've been told to keep your home as clean as possible.

While a clean home may be healthier than a neglected one, the very cleaners that we use to sanitize and sparkle can be hazardous to our health. Cleaning exposes us to harsh chemical compounds that are as hard on humans as they are on the environment. Prolonged contact with many everyday cleaners like liquid household bleach can cause eye and skin irritation, respiratory tract irritation, nausea, and dizziness. Because most cleaners are marketed as friendly, helpful products designed to make our lives easier, it's easy to forget that safety hazards can also come in those perky little packages.

HOW TO HUNT MICROBES

The dirt detection capabilities of a white glove may be perfectly adequate for your coffee table, but in the kitchen and bathroom, unless you have a microscope, there's no way to see if it's clean enough. Dirt that you can't see—germs and bacteria—can make you sick by contaminating food, surfaces, and utensils.

The kitchen is the most germ-laden room in the house. Billions and billions of microbes from raw meat juices, festering dishcloths and sponges, rotting garbage, spoiled food, dirty dishes, and unwashed hands are found on every surface. From a health standpoint, a freshly wiped countertop may be the dirtiest place in your home.

"Clean people are usually the dirtiest because they spread the germs all around. The bachelor who never cleans is usually the cleanest from a germ standpoint," says Charles Gerba, Ph.D., professor of microbiology at the University of Arizona in Tucson.

Arm Yourself with Disinfectant

It's impossible to rid your surroundings of every microbial life form. Your goal shouldn't be to create a sterile environment but to exercise day-to-day cleanliness habits that discourage the growth of germs and bacteria, says Dr. Gerba.

Use a disinfectant cleaner approved for use in the kitchen for your routine kitchen cleaning and for daily cleanup on surfaces that have come in contact with raw meat. Most homemade cleaners, like concoctions made from vinegar or baking soda, or environmentally friendly cleaners have no disinfectant properties at all—they merely move germs around. To be sure that a product kills germs like salmonella, look for a disinfectant with an Environmental Protection Agency registration number on the label. Read the instructions. It may be necessary to leave the cleaner on the surface for a specified period of time in order to kill germs.

Although the bathroom has a reputation for being germ-infested, there are fewer microbes in it that are likely to make you sick than there are in the kitchen. This is probably because people tend to use disinfectants in their bathrooms more often than in their kitchens, Dr. Gerba says. Regular hand-washing with soap and water is the best precaution against sickness or infection.

Six Germ-Stopping Habits

To keep microbes in check, follow these tips recommended by Dr. Gerba.

1. Rub-a-dub, bub. Wash your hands frequently. Your hands and fingers are common transmitters of germs and bacteria. The National Restaurant Association's hand-washing recommendations include using warm soapy water for at least 20 seconds and rinsing thoroughly with clean water. Follow this procedure both before and after preparing foods (especially when you handle raw poultry, meat, or seafood), using the bathroom, and after sneezing, coughing, smoking, eating, or drinking. When washing your hands, the National Restaurant Association suggests that you pay particular attention to the areas underneath your fingernails and between your fingers.

2. Ditch your dishcloth. In a study of sponges and dishcloths, Dr.

Gerba found that dishcloths are contaminated with more fecal coliform bacteria (an indicator of unsanitary conditions) than sponges.

3. Disinfect your sponge. Put your sponge in the dishwasher with the dishes daily. If it develops a pungent odor, discard it. Smell indicates the presence of germs. Sponges should only be used for a month.

4. Do paperwork. Use paper towels to wipe up meat juices. Discard the towels and clean the surface with disinfectant cleaner.

5. Done eating? Get busy. Do your dishes right after meals. Bacteria thrive on unwashed dishes. While a dishwasher will sanitize your dishes and utensils, they don't stay that way. Make sure to wash your hands before you put them away to avoid contaminating the sanitized dishes.

6. Take it outside. Empty the trash every day. Moist, rotting garbage is a haven for germ growth, so make taking out the trash a nightly ritual. When preparing meat, make sure to dispose of the packaging promptly by wrapping it in plastic and putting it in the trash, says cleaning consultant Kent Gerard from Oakland, California. Letting it lie on the counter could spread germs.

SAFE AT HOME

You've been using the same brand of all-purpose cleaner for years, so why would you need to read the label? Because it may be a different product without your knowing it—product formulations change. To get an edge in the glutted market for household cleaners, manufacturers routinely reformulate their products to clean faster or clean better. New product ingredients may mean that additional precautions need to be taken with the product. So do read labels, even on your old favorites.

Remember that although they are user-friendly for the most part, household cleaners are chemical compounds that can be hazardous. And using them improperly can endanger your health or the environment, according to the U.S. Consumer Product Safety Commission (CPSC).

A cleaner is classified as hazardous if it displays one or more of these four properties.

Ignitable: Catches fire easily
Toxic: Can be poisonous or harmful when eaten, absorbed through the skin, or inhaled
Corrosive: Can dissolve or destroy living tissue or materials
Reactive: Can explode or react violently

Hazardous products are required by law to include a warning and description of the hazard on the label, says Wilma Hammett, Ph.D., professor and extension home furnishings specialist at the North Carolina Cooperative Extension Service at North Carolina State University in Raleigh. Words such as *danger, warning,* or *caution* will be printed on the label, indicating the level of the hazard.

Poison: Highly toxic or poisonous
Danger: Extremely flammable, corrosive, or highly toxic
Warning: Moderately or slightly toxic
Caution: Moderately or slightly toxic

The product must also include a statement telling you how to avoid the hazard and how to use the product safely.

Heading Off Accidents

Here's how to handle cleaning products safely.

Keep the original. Always store household cleaning products in their original containers to avoid accidental misuse or poisoning, recommends the CPSC. Labels on the original packaging contain directions for use, safety precautions, and antidote or treatment information. Accidental swallowing is more likely to occur when cleaning products are placed in containers such as cups, soft drink bottles, and milk cartons, which children associate with food and drink. A brightly colored cleaner placed in such a container is a dangerous temptation.

Hide the bottles. Store cleaning compounds and all potentially hazardous household chemicals out of the reach of children and pets. More than one million children age 5 and under were exposed to potentially poisonous substances in 1995, according to the American Association of Poison Control Centers. Use locks or child-resistant latches to secure storage areas. On products that have child-resistant packaging, always re-secure the child-resistant closure before putting it away.

Never mix cleaning products. Combining cleaning products can create hazardous fumes. The classic example is chlorine bleach and ammonia: When mixed together, they form a toxic gas that can cause loss of voice, coughing, feeling of suffocation and burning, and possibly death. Some products—such as automatic dishwasher detergent and liquid cleansers—contain bleach and should not be mixed with ammonia-based products like window cleaners. Also, be careful when using toilet-bowl cleaners. Some contain acids, which can cause a dangerous reaction if mixed with other chemicals, according to the CPSC.

Go for the pump. Exposure to cleaning solutions, air fresheners, oven cleaners, and rug and upholstery cleaners can cause dizziness, nausea, and respiratory tract irritation. To reduce your exposure to potential irritants, use a pump spray instead of an aerosol whenever possible. The fine mist of aerosols is more easily inhaled.

Slow down. Hurrying and plain carelessness are frequently the cause of accidents in the home. According to the National Safety Council, accidental poisoning is second only to falls as the leading cause of death in the home. Take the time to do things the right way.

Here are a few more ways to protect yourself when using hazardous chemicals, says Dr. Hammett.

Stay under cover. Wear protective equipment, like rubber gloves, if recommended by the manufacturer.

Clear the air. Use products in a well-ventilated area. Open windows and use a fan to circulate the air. Take plenty of fresh-air breaks.

Don't work hand to mouth. Traces of chemicals can be carried from your hands to your mouth. So do not eat, drink, or smoke while using hazardous products.

Forget your contacts. Don't wear soft contact lenses when working with solvents and pesticides. Soft contacts can absorb and hold the chemical next to your eyes.

Keep a lid on it. Keep containers tightly closed between applications to avoid spills and make it less accessible to children.

Stay on guard. Do not leave products unattended while using them if there is a chance that a child could handle them.

Savvy Use of Solvents

Some household cleaners contain organic solvents—usually a petroleum product that is added to keep the product in its liquid or paste form or to enable it to dissolve dirt and grease. Products containing organic solvents evaporate readily and quickly fill a room with fumes. The fumes can cause intoxication, drowsiness, disorientation, and headaches. The CPSC requires that hazardous ingredients be identified on the label. Read the label; it's there for your safety.

Long-term exposure to some organic solvents, such as methylene chloride, which is found in some paint strippers, degreasers, and waxes, can damage the nervous system and may cause cancer in humans. For example, 1,1,1 trichlorethane, which is found in drain cleaners, spot removers, and shoe polish, can damage the nervous system.

Very high doses of cleaners containing petroleum distillates or organic solvents—furniture polish and spot remover are among a vast array of products—can lead to lung problems, an irregular heartbeat, and skin rashes.

Cut your risks when using organic solvents by taking these precautions, says the CPSC.

• Use solvents outdoors, if possible. If you must work indoors, open windows and doors and use a fan as you work. Wear a respirator (a mask that comes with special filter cartridges for different types of fumes—be sure that it's made from a material that cannot be permeated by the substance you are handling) and goggles, if necessary. If you decide to wear a respirator, check with your doctor first. You must have good lung function to operate the filter cartridges. And make sure that you get the proper filter and that the mask fits well.

• Don't use more than one solvent product at a time, and don't use one immediately after another.

• Fumes of some solvents tend to sink, so you may inhale more vapors if you are bent over while working.

• Alcoholic beverages can heighten the toxic effects of solvent fumes. Don't drink alcohol if you will be using a solvent that day.

• Many solvents are flammable, so use them away from heat or flames.

GETTING CLEAN, STAYING GREEN

Most households contain dozens of chemical products that have the potential to pollute our soil, air, and water, if improperly used or disposed of carelessly. The average American household generates about 15 pounds of hazardous waste each year and may have more than 100 pounds of it stored away at any one time.

Cleaners aren't the worst of the household polluters. They rank fourth, behind maintenance items like paint, batteries, and personal-care products such as hair spray and deodorant. But cleaners do account for more than 10 percent of all hazardous waste generated per year per household.

Many household cleaners, in the amounts normally used, can be safely washed down the drain if you are served by either a municipal sewer system or a septic system, says Robert Rubin, Ph.D., professor of biological and agricultural engineering at North Carolina State University in Raleigh. This applies to dishwashing and laundry products, bleaches, toilet-bowl cleaners, and all-purpose cleaners. But large quantities can overload either system to the point that its treatment does not meet specific water-quality standards when it is released into lakes, rivers, and streams.

Solvent Disposal: Get with a Program

For the most part, only organic solvent–based cleaning products such as spot removers, paint thinners, metal and furniture cleaners, drain cleaners, and degreasers are considered hazardous to the environment and fit the criteria mentioned above. Unfortunately, many make their way into sewage treatment plants, landfills, and incinerators when people dump them down the drain or simply throw them in the trash. This not only poses a threat to the environment but also can harm sanitation workers.

If you cannot recycle or reuse such a product, store it until you can dispose of it through household hazardous waste collection programs, which are periodically sponsored by many communities. Call your city or county environmental management or waste management division (listed in the government offices section of your phone book) for information.

The most common type of program is a collection day that offers residents a periodic opportunity to take wastes to a central location where they are sorted and then recycled or sent to an appropriate disposal site.

When you want to dispose of solvent-based materials, leave them

Formulas for a Clean Home and a Clean Planet

What good is having a clean home if it means polluting the planet? Here's how to make an Earth-friendly cleaning kit that's devoid of potentially harmful cleaners or toxic chemicals. You'll need just six readily available ingredients: baking soda, white vinegar, lemon juice, olive oil, salt, and borax.

From these common household items, you can make cleaners that are in many cases as effective as commercial products, but are safer and less costly. Here are a few formulas for homemade "green" cleaners.

Fabric softener: Add ¼ cup vinegar during the rinse cycle of your laundry. Clothes will feel softer and smell fresh.

Furniture polish: Mix 2 tablespoons olive oil and 1 tablespoon vinegar in 1 quart warm water. Store it in a spray bottle. (*Note:* This solution works best when kept warm. Let the bottle rest in a bucket of hot water while using.) Apply with a polishing cloth to produce a clean shiny surface.

Glass cleaner: Mix ½ cup vinegar and 1 gallon warm water in a pump spray bottle.

Toilet-bowl cleaner: Pour 1 cup borax and ¼ cup vinegar or lemon juice into the bowl. Let it sit for two hours and then scour thoroughly with a brush.

Drain cleaner: Pour ½ cup baking soda down the drain. Add ¼ cup vinegar and ½ cup salt. Let it sit for 15 minutes (the mixture will bubble and gurgle noisily), then pour a kettle of boiling water down the drain. Be sure to cover your face and hands.

sealed tightly in their original containers. Store them in a well-ventilated location, says Dr. Hammett. If they are flammable, store them away from sources of heat, sparks, or ignition. Be sure that they are not stored with or near corrosive products.

Reduce Your Chemical Dependence

Here are ways to reduce your use of chemical products.

Buy versatile cleaners. Contrary to what manufacturers want you to believe, you do not need a different product to clean each surface in your home, says Dr. Hammett. Multipurpose cleaners will reduce the number of hazardous cleaners in your home and save you money.

Take it easy. Buy the least harmful product available. Learn to identify hazardous products from their labels. Remember the difference between a product labeled "danger" and one that is labeled "caution."

To reduce the danger in your home and the impact on the environment, use cleaners labeled "warning" or "caution." And don't be fooled by the label "nontoxic." That's a marketing term that is not defined by the federal government, so it can be used on products that are indeed toxic.

Buy only what you need. To avoid the need to store or dispose of unused cleaners, buy the smallest amount needed to do the cleaning task.

Five Paths to Cleaning Conservation

You can be kind to our environment simply by using up fewer resources when you clean. Here are five ways to do that, according to cleaning expert Don Aslett in his book *The Cleaning Encyclopedia.*

1. Use concentrated cleaners. They use less packaging and are cheaper, too. Recycle your empties.

2. Clean with reusable products. Use cloths that you can launder when you're through, instead of disposable paper towels. (Be careful when disposing of cloths you have used with hazardous chemicals—read the manufacturer's label for disposal instructions.)

3. Don't put it off. More accumulated dirt means that more energy, cleaning supplies, and water will be needed to do the job.

4. Use energy efficiently. Use cold water when you can—when running the garbage disposal or washing floors, for instance. Make sure that you have a full load before you use the dishwasher, washer, or dryer. Make sure that all the clutter is picked up before you turn on the vacuum cleaner.

SCRUB THIS APPROACH

Septic Systems Are No Match for Chemicals

Septic systems are not designed to handle the disposal of products containing heavy metals, volatile organic compounds, or petroleum-based solvents. While most household chemicals should decompose in time, volatile organic compounds can destroy the microorganisms in a septic system that actually make it work. Both volatile organic compounds and solvents can flow from the system undiluted, polluting the surrounding soil and groundwater.

If you own a septic system, do not allow the following types of products to be flushed down the toilet or poured down your drain: large quantities of liquid household bleach, disinfectants, and mold or mildew treatments, and any quantity of paints, solvents, pesticides, or any product labeled toxic, flammable, or corrosive. Here are some ways to dispose of these chemicals safely, says Wilma Hammett, Ph.D., professor and extension home furnishings specialist at the North Carolina Cooperative Extension Service at North Carolina State University in Raleigh.

Read the fine print. Some household cleaners now have disposal instructions printed on the labels. Follow them carefully.

Use it up. If you use the product up, you won't have to worry about getting rid of large quantities.

Repeat yourself. Recycle what you use—you can reuse paint thinner, for example, if you strain out the solids. Let it settle for a few days, pour off clear liquid, and reuse.

Do a good deed. Donate leftover paint and other products to local charities, theaters, the housing authority, or even friends and neighbors.

Pick up the phone. Call your local environmental management or waste management division. They may be able to take some hazardous products or tell you how to dispose of them.

---

5. Use only what you need. Cleaners (like laundry detergent or floor cleaner) work best when they are mixed with a specific amount of water. Follow the instructions on the package carefully.

COMBATING ALLERGIES

If you're one of the 50 million Americans who suffer from allergies, not only do you have to put up with the sneezing and itching but also you have to go the extra mile with cleaning routines, too. But the effort is worth it because specific cleaning procedures will reduce or eliminate the irritants from your home.

The most common allergy triggers are found in the home in house dust, which is made up of human skin particles, animal dan-

der, and molds. Dust mites and cockroaches also produce allergic reactions. Symptoms, according to the American Academy of Allergy,
Asthma, and Immunology, may include a blocked or runny nose with
sneezing (especially in the morning), watery eyes, itching rashes,
coughing, and wheezing. Many people may not be aware that they
have allergies and may only experience occasional symptoms.

What's Bugging You?

A doctor can determine what you're allergic to by taking a medical history and doing a series of skin tests. Here's a rundown of the
most common household allergens.

Dust mites. Nearly 100,000 of these Lilliputian members of the
spider family can live on a square yard of carpeting. The microscopic mites aren't the cause of the allergic reaction; their waste is.
Dust mites dine on the skin cells that you shed every day. That's
why they thrive wherever you spend the most time—beds, pillows,
or your favorite stuffed chair. They produce about 20 tiny pellets of
waste a day that contain a protein that many people are allergic to.
Mites thrive in humid conditions, especially carpeting placed on a
concrete floor.

Animal dander. It's a common misconception that people are allergic to the fur of an animal. The real cause of the problem is the protein in tiny flakes of pet skin and saliva that float through the air in the
house, irritating your eyes, nose, and respiratory tract. Allergies to cats
are the most common, but other animals can cause allergies as well.

Animal dander is light and remains airborne for a long time before falling to the floor. Vacuuming aggravates the condition by
swirling allergens around the room. It may take over an hour for the
dander to settle back down to the floor.

Mold. Mold thrives in moist areas of the house, such as bathrooms and basements. It's not the black grimy stuff growing on the
tile grout that causes the allergic irritation but the reproductive spores
it produces that are carried through the air.

Cockroaches. More than half of the people afflicted with allergies are allergic to cockroaches and their droppings. If you have
cockroaches, they are normally evident in the kitchen.

Pollen. Pollen allergies are a seasonal problem, normally occurring in the spring and the fall when pollen invades your home
through open doors and windows.

No More Sleeping with the Enemy

Ridding the house of a zillion microscopic particles seems like a
daunting task, but some simple steps will greatly reduce your expo-

sure. With allergic irritants lurking throughout the house, where do you start?

"The bedroom is where you spend the most time," says Gerard, who specializes in clients with allergies. "Where you spend the most time is where you want the least exposure to indoor pollutants."

Here's how the American Academy of Allergy, Asthma, and Immunology recommends that you allergy-proof your bedroom.

- Keep the bedroom uncluttered and easy to clean. Avoid dust collectors such as books, knickknacks, stuffed animals, and televisions.
- Encase the mattress, box springs, and pillows in airtight, zippered plastic covers. Controlling dust mites in mattresses requires either

An Allergy-Busting Schedule

If you have allergies to indoor pollutants like mold or dust mites, you have probably been told to keep your house as clean as possible. Supplement your regular cleaning schedule with the following tasks to keep allergens at bay, says Thomas Platts-Mills, M.D., Ph.D., head of the division of asthma, allergy, and immunology at the University of Virginia Health Sciences Center in Charlottesville and director of its Asthma and Allergic Disease Center.

Daily
- Ventilate the bathroom (using a fan, open window, or air-conditioning) to ensure that walls and curtains get fully dry.

Weekly
- Wash all bedding—sheets, mattress pads, pillowcases, and bed covers—in hot water.
- Bathe pets in soap and water to loosen and remove dander.
- Before vacuuming, dust furniture, windowsills, and crevices with a slightly damp cloth.

Every Two Weeks
- Vacuum plastic mattress, box spring, and pillow covers, then wipe with a slightly damp cloth.

Monthly
- Wash stuffed toys in hot water, or put them in the freezer in a plastic bag overnight to kill dust mites.
- Clean tubs, showers, and shower doors and curtains with a 10 percent solution of disinfectant or liquid household bleach and water (one part disinfectant or bleach and nine parts water) to kill molds. Scrub with a stiff-bristle brush and rinse with clean water. Wear gloves.

regular vacuuming or keeping them in dust-free casings. Covering them is the easiest, most effective solution.

- Wash all bedding regularly in hot water—at least 130°F to kill dust mites. Comforters and pillows should be made of synthetic materials such as Dacron or Orlon so that they can be washed. Pillows should be washed regularly and replaced every two to three years.

These allergy-proofing tips apply not only to the bedroom but to the rest of the house as well.

- Remove carpeting, if possible. All types of allergens are abundant in carpeting. Replace it with hard flooring such as wood or vinyl.
- Keep the humidity low. To reduce the growth of dust mites and mold, keep the indoor relative humidity below 50 percent but above 30 percent. Central air-conditioning is the most effective way of controlling humidity. It cools and cleans indoor air and keeps outdoor air out. Dehumidifiers are useful in basements.
- Keep your pet off bedding and furniture. If he refuses to give up his favorite spot on the sofa, cover the area with a cloth that can be laundered frequently.
- Use the right vacuum. People with allergies should avoid vacuuming. While it cleans dust, it also stirs up dust. If you have to vacuum, wear a dust mask or use a vacuum with a HEPA (high-efficiency particulate air) or the newer ULPA (ultra low penetration air) filter. They're sold by allergy-supply and hospital-supply companies as well as discount stores and drugstores, and good ones can cost from $500 to $1,000. Avoid water vacs that filter dust into a canister of water. They can spew a fine mist of allergens.

Part 2

The Dirty Stuff

Acoustical Tile

You never walk on it. And the laws of gravity haven't been revoked—things still spill reliably downward. So what could possibly be tinting your acoustical tile? The main enemies here are cigar and cigarette smoke, cooking vapors, and other airborne contaminants that rise on warm currents and, over time, soil the light-colored tiles. Dark ugly patches form around heating and air-conditioning ducts, where dust and grime collect. Cleaning must be done gently, especially if your tiles are the type that rest on grids, so as not to dislodge the tiles.

Technique: Most acoustical tiles found in homes are made of highly porous, absorbent fiber, so washing with a lot of water is not an option. Rub grime-darkened areas with a putty wallpaper cleaner called Absorene or a foam-rubber wall-cleaning sponge. Be sure that it is the type that is chemically treated and used by fire restorers to repair soot damage. Wall-cleaning sponges are available at hardware stores, janitorial supply stores, and paint stores. "You use it sort of as an eraser to lift the material off," says Martin L. King, a restoration consultant in Arlington, Virginia, and technical advisor to the National Institute of Disaster Restoration in Annapolis, Maryland. Common kitchen sponges shouldn't be used because they will smear dirt instead of rubbing it away.

To remove remaining grime, use an acoustical-tile cleaner that incorporates bleaches, available at janitorial supply stores. Follow the manufacturer's directions on the container.

Note: Painting acoustical ceiling tile could cause two problems, says Keith Mullen, technical consultant for Armstrong World Industries of Lancaster, Pennsylvania, the maker of Armstrong Ceilings. First, your ceiling could lose its sound-absorbing quality. Second, painting could change the ceiling's fire rating. So check first with your local building inspector before painting ceiling tile in your home, Mullen says. Mineral fiber ceilings can be painted by spraying, brushing, or rolling, Mullen says; but vinyl- or Mylar-laminated ceilings should not be painted. If you do paint your ceiling tile, use a high-quality paint and be careful not to fill in the little perforations in the material.

A resurfacing product called Coustic-Coat will maintain the tile's fire rating, says Gary Becker, owner of a Coustic Glo franchise in Northampton, Pennsylvania. For the location of a Coustic Glo dealer in your area, consult the toll-free telephone directory.

Speed tips: As part of your routine vacuuming chores, vacuum the tiles using a brush attachment, especially around air-conditioning or heating ducts. "The best thing is to have a well-maintained heating system with clean air ducts and to change the furnace filter regularly," King says.

In a pinch: If you can't get to the store for a foam-rubber sponge or putty wallpaper cleaner, you may rub dirty tiles with a hunk of fresh bread rolled into a ball, which will scrub without doing damage, King adds. Or pat the area with sticky tape.

Caution: Always use a drop cloth, preferably canvas because it's easy to slip on a plastic one. Always wear eye protection. Rubber gloves and a filter mask are also a good idea.

Acrylic Fabric

Acrylic fabric is easy to clean, which is one reason that it is used in everything from sweaters to sweat socks to outdoor furniture.

Technique: For garments, machine-wash in warm water, using a fabric softener during the final rinse cycle. Tumble dry on a low temperature setting. Remove quickly from the dryer. Hand-wash delicates in warm water and dry them flat, says the Acrylic Council in New York City.

When cleaning stains from upholstery, remove as much of the stain as you can with a spoon or spatula if it's solid, or, if liquid, blot up as much as you can. Mix powdered laundry detergent without brighteners in warm water. Using a sponge dipped in the suds, work around the stain from the outside in. For greasy or sugary soft-drink stains, do the above steps and then rinse the area with a mixture of half water, half white vinegar. Place towels on the area and cover with a heavy flat object for several hours, according to Solutia, a fiber producer in New York City.

Speed tips: For a quick general cleaning of acrylic upholstery, sponge lightly with water, or use a spot remover such as K2r or Carbona Stain Devils, available at supermarkets, hardware stores, or discount department stores. Use as little cleaning fluid as will get the job done and liberal supplies of absorbent towels. Always read product label for proper usage and any applicable safety precautions.

Caution: If this fabric has an Achilles' heel (an acrylic heel?), it's heat. When ironing acrylic fabric, "you don't want to get it too hot," says Leon Moser, extension specialist and fabric expert at North Carolina State University's College of Textiles in Raleigh. "All things considered, it has a relatively low melting point." Also, be sure to read the product labels for proper usage and safety precautions before ironing.

Air

Scientists first began studying indoor air pollution during the 1960s and are only now beginning to understand its health effects. Indoor air pollution can come from an almost-unlimited variety of sources, so you shouldn't count on one method or product (no matter how fantastic its claims) to clean the air in your home. Improved building methods in recent years have made "tighter" homes that conserve energy but may actually worsen indoor air pollution by allowing less exchange between inside and out. Mechanical air cleaners can help, but simply opening your windows can do wonders. A balanced approach is best, says Leyla McCurdy, director of indoor air programs for the American Lung Association in Washington, D.C.

Technique: Of the three main strategies for improving indoor air quality, the Environmental Protection Agency ranks controlling the source of the pollution as the most effective method. Ventilating your home ranks second, and mechanical cleaners such as HEPA (high-efficiency particulate air) filters and ionizers are third.

Source Control

Ways of controlling pollution sources are as varied as the sources themselves. They may include covering exposed asbestos, dusting and vacuuming rooms frequently to cut down on airborne particles, restricting smoking, and carefully following instructions when using chemical products. Since asbestos is highly carcinogenic, it's best to hire a professional to work with it.

Ventilation

For ventilation, the best way is also the easiest—open windows and doors regularly (weather and security permitting, of course).

The potential drawback with open windows is that if you live in an area with high levels of outdoor air pollution, you may be letting bad stuff in even as you drive bad stuff out. "In certain climates, it may be better to have a tighter house, then control air quality through mechanical ventilation," says McCurdy. For instance, in the tropics,

How Healthy Is Your Home?

Linking health problems to specific pollution sources can be difficult, especially since symptoms caused by bad air in your home may be nearly identical to those for colds, flus, or other common illnesses. But if your symptoms tend to disappear when you leave the house, it may be a clue that your house is making you sick.

Here are some major sources of air pollution in the home, according to the American Lung Association, as well as some suggestions for keeping them in check.

Asbestos

Sources: Asbestos is commonly used in homes, from roofing and flooring materials to insulation. It's rarely a problem unless it's disturbed, as during home renovations, or if it begins to deteriorate with age.

Effects: Asbestos fibers may be inhaled and can cause lung scarring, lung cancer, or other forms of cancer.

Solutions: Exposed asbestos-containing materials should be covered with plastic and duct tape. Any asbestos that is flaking or damaged should be handled by a professional. Doing it yourself increases your exposure and risk.

Asbestos can be difficult to identify unless it's labeled. There's usually no health risk unless the asbestos material is actively flaking or decomposing—that's when particles become airborne, according to the American Lung Association. If you have doubts about a material, go to the phone book and call in an asbestos specialist.

Biological Pollutants

Sources: Biological pollutants include viruses, bacteria, molds, fungi, and mites. They can come from dirty air conditioners, humidifiers, dehumidifiers, and air-cleaning filters. They can also come from plants, pets, and unwashed bedding.

Effects: Biological pollutants can cause fevers, colds, and allergic reactions.

Solutions: Clean your air-filtering appliances regularly, following manufacturers' instructions. Use distilled water in humidifiers. Wash sheets frequently in hot water (at least 130˚F) to kill mites. Keep your home ventilated.

Formaldehyde

Sources: Sources of formaldehyde include cigarette smoke; resins in particleboard, fiberboard, and plywood paneling; some adhesives; carpet

McCurdy says, hot humid air blowing in through open windows and doors can promote mold growth inside.

For additional ventilation, use your bathroom or kitchen exhaust fans as needed. Run your unit air conditioner with the vent control backing; upholstery; and drapery fabrics. It is also found in older foam insulation.

Effects: Formaldehyde can cause headaches, dizziness, lethargy, rashes, nausea, and irritation of the eyes and respiratory tract. High levels may trigger asthma attacks in people with asthma.

Solutions: Restrict smoking. Increase ventilation in your home. Consider replacing or coating particleboard, fiberboard, or foam insulation if it was made prior to the mid-1980s. Since then, many manufacturers have begun making products that emit lower levels of formaldehyde. If you're building a home, specify that you want pressed wood products that emit low levels of formaldehyde.

Nitrogen Dioxide

Sources: Nitrogen dioxide is often a result of poorly vented gas ranges or other appliances, or wood or coal stoves.

Effects: Nitrogen dioxide can cause eye and respiratory tract irritation and, in serious cases, bronchitis.

Solutions: Gas ranges should be fitted with a range hood that vents pollutants outside. Or keep a window open and use an exhaust fan while cooking. Have the gas company regularly inspect your gas furnace, water heater, and clothes dryer to make sure that they are burning efficiently and not emitting gas.

Secondhand Smoke

Sources: Secondhand smoke is a result of cigarettes, pipes, and cigars.

Effects: A proven cancer-causer, secondhand smoke is responsible for about 3,000 lung cancer deaths per year.

Solutions: Don't smoke, and don't allow others to smoke in your home. Or confine smoking to one room and use an exhaust fan there.

Toxic Chemicals in Household Products

Sources: Toxic chemicals include pesticides, heavy cleaning solutions, hobby products, and solvents.

Effects: Effects range from dizziness and nausea to allergic reactions and eye, skin, and respiratory tract irritation.

Solutions: Read and follow all instruction and warning labels carefully. Use toxic chemical products only in well-ventilated areas. Use pump sprays instead of aerosols and, when possible, substitute toxic products with nontoxic products.

open to increase the rate at which air is exchanged from indoor to out. Ventilation is especially important when you're doing anything indoors that may generate pollutants—cooking, painting, using chemicals, using kerosene heaters, or installing new carpet.

Air Cleaners

Mechanical air cleaners include tabletop and floor models as well as larger filters that operate in conjunction with central heating and air-conditioning systems. They come in two general types: filters and ionizers. Mechanical filters, also known as HEPA filters, are generally more effective than ionizers, says McCurdy. HEPA filters are the most efficient mechanical filters for removing small particles that can be breathed deep into the lungs. They operate by drawing air from a room through a series of filters, then expelling cleaned air back into the room. The filters, which must be replaced every few months, depending on how dirty the air is to begin with, are made of tightly woven glass. They trap pollen, mold spores, animal hair, dander, dust mites, dust, and other particles. Many commercial HEPA filters also include a carbon filter to reduce room odors. But HEPA filters are far less effective at removing gases than particles from the air.

Tabletop or room models, sold under brand names such as Holmes, Enviracaire, and Duracraft, range in price from around $99 to nearly $350. In general, the larger the cleaner, the more "air changes per hour" the machine will perform, and the more particles will be removed.

Ionizers are portable devices that charge particles floating in the air so that they stick to walls, floors, tables, drapes, and the like, thus removing them from the air you breathe. The problem with ionizers is that bumping a chair or brushing a curtain can send the particles right back into the air. Also, ionizers do little to remove gases from the air. For gases, ventilation and source control are superior. In addition, some ionizers emit ozone, which may actually add to the air-quality problems in your home.

Colossal Cleanups

Not-So-Heavenly Bodies

The number of man-made objects orbiting the Earth: 7,000 objects larger than a soccer ball. A few hundred of the largest pieces are functioning satellites. The rest are various castoffs—spent rockets, protective shrouds, clamps, fasteners, fragments from space-vehicle explosions, and even an astronaut's silver glove.

Plants

Plants look great and add a touch of the outdoors to your home. But the jury's still out on their air-cleaning prowess. Excessive moisture in the your plants' soil may actually provide a breeding ground for microorganisms that could wind up in your air, says McCurdy.

The Lowdown on Radon

It sounds like something from outer space, but radon is actually a down-to-earth problem. It's an odorless, colorless, radioactive gas that is produced naturally when uranium in soil and rocks breaks down. "People can't see it, can't smell it. It seems unreal," says Leyla McCurdy, director of indoor air programs for the American Lung Association in Washington, D.C.

Radon seeps into homes through cracks in the foundation, floor and wall joints, mortar joints, and even through the water supply. Once in the home, radon concentrates, building to potentially dangerous levels. The surgeon general says that radon is the second leading cause of lung cancer deaths in the United States, with an estimated 14,000 per year. Smoking is first, and smoking in a home with radon problems greatly increases your risk of developing lung cancer.

The Environmental Protection Agency (EPA) estimates that six million American homes have significant radon levels. No state is geographically safe. On a single street, one house may have low levels, while the house next door has significant levels.

Fortunately, methods for testing radon levels and eradicating problems are well-established and reliable. The surgeon general suggests that everyone who lives on the third floor or lower have their homes tested. You may hire a radon tester to do the work, or do it yourself with a test kit available at hardware stores and home and garden centers.

You may want to start with a short-term kit that will test the radon level in as little as two days. Then, if you get a high reading, retest with a longer-term device that will take readings for three months or more. Radon levels are measured in units called picocuries per liter (pCi/l.). Levels higher than 4 pCi/l. are considered significant. The average in U.S. homes is 1.25 pCi/l.

Solving your home's radon problems will cost $500 to $2,500, depending on the level of the problem and the methods used to fix it. The most common solution is to seal cracks and install an exhaust system that sucks radon-laden air from beneath your home's foundation, draws it through a tube, and releases it from an exhaust pipe in your roof. The contractor you select should be well-versed in radon reduction. Choose one who is state-certified or listed in the EPA's Radon Contractor Proficiency program. This means that the contractor has been trained and has passed a comprehensive examination, according to the EPA's pamphlet "Consumer's Guide to Radon Reduction." There are also many effective ways to protect new homes from developing radon problems in the first place. When building or buying a new home, make certain that the contractor has taken antiradon precautions.

Every state has a radon information telephone number, usually operated by the health department, available to answer your radon questions. Check the government listings in the phone book or call information.

Caution: Don't confuse commercial air fresheners with clean air. Spraying air fresheners in a room just masks odors and introduces more foreign particles into the air. For a simple and inexpensive alternative to artificial air fresheners, pour some warmed vinegar into a dish and set it in it in the room until it evaporates and then keep replacing it until the odor is gone, advises the American Lung Association.

Air Conditioners

Air conditioners exchange air from outside to inside your house. Cutting down on dust and other airborne stuff is essential.

Technique: For room air conditioners (window units), filters should be washed before the unit is used for the first time in the season and once a month when the air conditioner is in use. Wash them more frequently if you have pets or a lot of activity in the house. Slide the filters out of the air conditioner and wash them by hand in warm water, with no soap. Be sure to let them dry thoroughly before reinstalling. If the fans in your unit are easily accessible, wipe them periodically with a soft cloth, says Vincent Brackin, spokesman for the Carrier Corporation in Syracuse, New York. With some units, the air conditioner chassis (the mechanical unit) slides into a metal casing or frame that holds the window open. If you have this type, slide the chassis out every few months and brush away twigs, leaves, or other debris from the casing. Lightly dust the exterior surfaces and grille of the air conditioner as part of your routine housecleaning. This will help prevent dust from building up on the filters.

If you have central air-conditioning, "it's wise to clean or change the filter monthly during periods of high use," says Edward W. Dooley, spokesman for the Air-Conditioning and Refrigeration Institute near Washington, D.C. Some central air-conditioning filters are disposable (they're flimsy and are usually marked "disposable" by the manufacturer). Others may be washed. Methods vary with the make of the filter, and it's best to follow the manufacturer's washing instructions. Dust or vacuum duct outlets and registers as part of your regular home-cleaning routine. The ducts themselves shouldn't require cleaning if the outlets and filters are kept clean. Check the outdoor unit regularly for leaves and other debris.

Speed tips: Unit air conditioner filters may be vacuumed instead of washed. Handheld vacuums are best because a too-powerful suction could suck up and misshape the filter, says Brackin.

Caution: Never apply soap or detergents to the coils inside the air-conditioning unit. If you vacuum the coils, do it carefully. "They're fragile; they're made out of aluminum," says Brackin. "If you bend the coils over, you're preventing the heat exchange from occurring." Always unplug the unit before cleaning inside.

Alabaster

Alabaster is a soft stone that can be damaged easily by water, so proceed with caution.

Technique: For most cleaning jobs, dusting with a dry soft cloth should do the trick. For heavier dirt, rub with a slightly damp cloth dabbed with a small amount of mild dishwashing detergent. Or spit on a cotton swab. No kidding—this method is favored by George Wheeler, Ph.D., stone specialist at the Sherman-Fairchilds Center for Objects Conservation with the Metropolitan Museum of Art in New York City, who says that the enzymes in saliva make a safe and effective cleaning substance. For serious spots or stains, rub gently with a cotton swab dabbed with an acetone cleaner such as nail polish remover or mineral spirits, but use it sparingly.

Caution: Never bathe or splash water on alabaster.

Antiques

The most important steps you take in cleaning antiques involve keeping objects out of harm's way—and dirt's way—in the first place. The actual cleaning of objects should be kept to a minimum. "Do-it-yourselfism is very American," says Joyce Hill Stoner, Ph.D., professor of art conservation at the Winterthur/University of Delaware Program in Art Conservation in Newark. "With antiques, we want to quell that as much as possible."

Aggressive cleaning is likely to wipe away history along with the grime. Scour an antique coin or a bronze statue to a shine and you're likely to significantly lessen its value. Go after an old painting with a cloth and a can of cleaning spray and you could destroy the work altogether.

When anything other than the lightest cleaning is required, it's best to let a professional conservator handle it unless you have special knowledge or experience. When in doubt, says Timothy Lennon, conservator of paintings at the Art Institute of Chicago, "leave the thing alone. If it does need attention, get an expert." After all, he adds, "you wouldn't advise people to fill their own teeth."

Technique: The environment in which your antiques sit plays such an important role in their well-being. So establishing an antique-friendly home is key. Fastidious housecleaning will help keep dust and grime from collecting on antiques. Vacuum carpets and rugs and dust other room surfaces frequently to reduce the level of airborne pollutants that might find their way onto your antiques. Air filters can help as well.

Whenever possible, keep valued items away from the kitchen and entrance areas to the kitchen. Cooking near antiques increases their exposure to airborne grime. "I treated a painting at an Italian restaurant that just reeked of oregano and tomato sauce," Dr. Stoner says. "And you can't clean it the way you'd clean a wall." For the same reason, it's best to keep smoking to a minimum.

Other than outright dropping or otherwise damaging a piece, the biggest dangers to antiques come from light and moisture. "You want a clean dry environment with balanced humidity," Lennon says.

Moisture and light can be especially harmful to objects made from organic materials. These include wooden furniture, textiles, paintings, and books. Objects made from stone, metal, or glass are less susceptible, but it's still a good idea to protect those objects from strong light or changes in humidity.

Natural sunlight, with its concentration of ultraviolet rays, is the most damaging. Whenever possible, keep prized objects away from areas that are regularly exposed to direct sunlight. Sunlight can fade colors in paints or dyes, yellow the varnish on a painting, bleach paper, and even weaken textile fabric. Even indirect sunlight over time can do damage, and light damage, like lead poisoning, is cumulative—meaning that it only intensifies over time. Use curtains and blinds liberally.

"In general, try to cluster things of great value and sensitivity in rooms that are less likely to be used, and draw the curtains," says Steven Weintraub, conservation consultant with Art Preservation Services in New York City.

Maintaining an even level of humidity is crucial to protecting antiques. Too much moisture in the air promotes mildew growth and encourages insects. But the opposite extreme is damaging as well. Super dryness can promote cracks in wood, ivory, paint, and other

Not Just Any Old Conservator Will Do

The United States has no formal licensing program for art and antiques conservators. Just about anyone can hang out a shingle.

So if you're looking for a professional to clean an antique item for you, it's not a good idea to simply pick the first name you come across in the phone book.

A good place to start is your local art museum. Many museums set aside a day or two periodically to allow residents to take in their antiques for evaluation by the conservation staff. At any rate, the staff may be able to direct you to good professionals in your area.

If there is more than one museum in your area, call them all. "If the same conservator's name comes up at two different museums, that's good," says Joyce Hill Stoner, Ph.D., professor of art conservation at the Winterthur/University of Delaware Program in Art Conservation in Newark.

If there aren't good museums nearby, or if you simply want more information about finding conservators, you can write to the American Institute for Conservation of Historic and Artistic Works (AIC) at 1717 K Street NW, Suite 301, Washington, DC 20006. The AIC has brochures to help your search and also runs a referral service.

Here are some AIC tips on selecting a conservator.

- Ask potential conservators about their training, length of experience, and whether conservation is their primary activity.
- Ask whether they have experience dealing with the type of objects you own that need attention and whether they belong to conservation organizations.
- Ask for references, including lists of previous clients. Contact some of those clients.
- Expect to receive a written preliminary examination report detailing the condition of the object as well as proposed treatment, the limitations of that treatment, and the cost and duration. A good conservator will notify you of major or unexpected changes in the treatment and will provide written and, in some cases, photographic documentation of the treatment.
- Conservators, like physicians, don't always agree. Don't be shy about getting a second opinion.

materials. Constant fluctuations are as damaging to objects as a moisture-laden or overarid environment. Paper, for example, expands and contracts with the humidity or aridity of the air around it. Too many changes and the paper simply breaks apart.

Use humidifiers and dehumidifiers as needed throughout the year to help maintain a reasonably steady relative humidity level of 30 to 70 percent. Beyond that range, "you can be assured that there's going to be significant risk of damage," Weintraub says. A "thermohygrometer" will measure relative humidity in a given room. These devices can often be purchased for about $100. Contact your local art museum or a local conservator for advice on finding a good thermohygrometer in your area.

Here are general tips for cleaning various types of antiques.

Furniture

Dust most antique furniture surfaces with dry, clean lint-free cloths that are frequently washed. Especially delicate areas may be cleaned with a sable brush with an air bulb attached to the stem for gently blowing dust away. These are available from camera equipment stores.

If extra cleaning is required on wood furniture, the National Committee to Save America's Cultural Collections suggests a solution of 50 parts distilled water to 1 part Murphy Oil Soap. Dip a clean soft cloth in the solution and wring it out so that it is damp rather than wet. Gently wipe the surface of the furniture. Use a cloth dampened with plain water to rinse, then dry with a clean soft cloth.

Caution: Always test the solution on an inconspicuous corner of the furniture before applying widely. Do not use any other cleaning solutions. Never let moist cleaning cloths sit on furniture. Read the product label for proper use and safety instructions.

Metal Objects

You can remove dust and other surface dirt from metal objects using a clean soft brush. To remove fingerprints or oily or greasy deposits from gold, bronze, copper, or brass, dip the brush in a little ethyl alcohol and brush gently.

Caution: Always test the ethyl alcohol using a cotton swab on an inconspicuous corner of the piece to make certain that you aren't damaging the object. Don't attempt to polish antique metal objects. Not only can this erase historically significant marks but also you're rubbing away part of the metal itself. "Every time you polish it, you have less substance there. Every time you polish metal, it's thinner," Dr. Stoner says.

How They Did It: Bath Brick and Soapwort

Ever wonder how people cleaned antiques before they were antiques? Frances Phipps, in her book, *The Collector's Complete Dictionary of American Antiques*, perused some nineteenth-century British and American household care guides and came up with these gems.

Gold: "Dissolve a little sal-ammoniac in urine, boil your soiled gold therein, and it will become clean and brilliant."
—*Thomas Tegg,* Book of Utility, *London, 1828*

Leather: "Mix together 1 lb. of Bath brick, 2 lbs. of pipe clay, 4 oz. of pumice stone powder, and 6 oz. of ox-gall; color it with yellow ochre if desired. It is to be used over the leather by rubbing it with a little water, and when it has remained on to get dry, rub off the loose powder with a hard clothes brush."
—*G. W. Francis,* The Dictionary of Practical Receipts, *London, 1847*

Letters: "The best method of disinfecting letters and other articles coming from places that are supposed to be visited by the plague is to expose them to the fumes of burning sulphur, mixed with saltpetre."
—*G. W. Francis,* The Dictionary of Practical Receipts, *London, 1847*

Rust: "It consists in combining a proportion of quick lime with mutton fat, into balls, which must be rubbed on the utensils till it has entirely obliterated the rust; after their coating has remained for a few days on the metal, it is removed with coarse flannel or other rags; then another composition, made of equal parts of charcoal, red calx of vitriol, and drying oil, is applied by continued friction, till the surface be restored to its pristine brightness."
—The Domestic Encyclopedia, *Philadelphia, 1828*

Soapwort: "A decoction of this plant is used to cleanse and scour woolen cloths; the poorer people use it instead of soap for washing."
—The Domestic Encyclopedia, *Philadelphia, 1828*

Paintings

About the only cleaning you should consider attempting yourself on an old painting is light dusting with a sable brush. Even this must be done with extreme care. Before you dust with the brush, check the painting carefully for loose pieces of frame or lifting paint that may be dislodged by the brush. Any other cleaning or restoration work should be done by a professional art conservator.

Caution: Do not use cleaning solutions or sponges on antique paintings. Don't even use a feather duster, cloth, vacuum brush, or handheld vacuum cleaner. "The danger would be lifting loose paint off the surface," Lennon says. Before using any product, read the label for proper use and safety precautions.

Avoid touching the front or back of the painting. Oils from your fingers can damage the paint or varnish on the painting itself, while finger pressure on the back may promote cracks in the painting. Never lift a painting or other antique unless you've thought out exactly where you're going to put it down.

Avoid old-time, word-of-mouth cleaning prescriptions like the plague. One such prescription calls for rubbing a painting with a raw potato. "This makes a delicious scum for cockroaches," Dr. Stoner says.

Textiles

Textiles, whether they're on display or in storage, should be inspected and vacuumed regularly. This will remove dust and help protect against insect damage. Always work on a padded surface. For example, you can place a mattress pad over your dining-room table and cover it with a clean white sheet. Use a low-power, handheld vacuum cleaner. For added protection of the fabric, place a clean fiberglass window screen over the fabric and vacuum through it.

Caution: Don't eat, drink, or smoke when cleaning textiles. You only increase the chances of a damaging stain, crumbs that will attract insects, or smoke residue.

Aquariums

An aquarium is an inherently unnatural environment for fish. To reduce their stress level, you should compensate by making sure that the stuff you put inside the tank, including cleaning supplies, is as natural as possible.

Technique: You can clean out an aquarium that hasn't been used in a while with a solution of 1 teaspoon aquarium salt (noniodized salt) to ½ gallon water. Wipe the aquarium down with the solution and a clean soft cloth. Then rinse thoroughly with plain water. Use the same method to clean out a new aquarium before using it for the first time.

An older aquarium may have a whitish film on the sides. "This is caused by hard water or calcium deposits," says Lance Reyniers, president of Python Products, a Milwaukee-based manufacturer of aquarium maintenance equipment. If the film is heavy or the grime stubborn, you should use a solution specially made for cleaning aquariums. These solutions, available at aquarium stores, are stronger than the homemade saltwater solution but still safe for fish.

When your aquarium is actually in use, you keep the water clean using a variety of filters and regular water changes. There are three basic types of filters, all of which may be used at the same time to filter out different pollutants. A biological filter, which sits at the bottom of the tank underneath a layer of gravel, screens out ammonia released by fish and other aquatic animals. Mechanical filters remove such debris as uneaten food and solid waste. A chemical filter uses carbon or other substances to screen out chemical pollutants.

There are many filters on the market. The ones you use and the frequency with which you clean and change them will depend on the type and number of fish you have, the size of your tank, and other factors. Get specific advice from your aquarium store.

Every two weeks or so (more often if you have a crowded tank) change 5 to 10 percent of the water in your tank. "Smaller, more frequent water changes are healthier and less stressful for fish," says Reyniers. "In the natural environment they're constantly in new water."

The bottom of the tank is where the dirty water is, so water should always be removed from the bottom of the tank using a siphon. There are a variety of siphoning products and methods available, from sophisticated water change systems made by Python Products and other companies to a simple hose. At the very least, it's a good idea to use a siphon that is equipped with a mesh to prevent gravel from being sucked up.

Use an aquarium thermometer to measure the water temperature before you change the water and while you are replacing it. You can use a hose attached to your faucet or a clean bucket that has not contained cleaning supplies. Adjust the hot and cold knobs on your faucet as needed to make sure that the temperature in your aquarium does not change during the process.

Aquatic plants help clean the water in the tank by removing carbon dioxide and producing oxygen, and they help create a natural environment for the fish.

Caution: Here's one rule that you should remember when cleaning an aquarium: Fish hate soap, be it mild hand soap or harsh detergent. Even traces left behind after you think you've rinsed it all away may be enough to stress or even sicken fish. The bottom line is this: Don't use soap to clean an aquarium. Don't even use buckets or cloths that have had soap on them. Keep soap-free supplies and tools on hand that you use only for your aquarium. Never change the water in your aquarium within 48 hours of a major rainfall or snow melt in your area. These events prompt municipal water systems to increase chlorine levels in the water supply, which can be harmful to fish, says Reyniers.

Ashes

Ashes shouldn't be a problem to clean up—as long as they don't contain a glowing ember hidden inside.

Technique: Ashes are insoluble and therefore won't stain fabric. Most ashes can be easily brushed from clothing or vacuumed from upholstery. (If the ashes do include an ember, and the fabric is burned, see Burns—Cigarette on page 94. See also Soot on page 351.)

Ashtrays

Take no chances with the cigarettes, cigars, matches, and such that collect in ashtrays. To prevent fires, sop them down with water.

"There are two ways to empty an ashtray safely," says Susan Siegel-McKelvey, spokesperson for the National Fire Protection Association in Quincy, Massachusetts. "If you're going to discard the butts into a trash can, you want to make sure that you douse them thoroughly before you throw them out. Just turn on the water and make sure that they're all wet. The second way is to just flush them down the toilet. Always follow one of these methods."

The safest kind of ashtray to use is a heavy, deep sturdy one, Siegel-McKelvey says. "Empty it frequently; you don't want to let butts build up in there," she says.

Technique: Most ashtrays can be rinsed and washed in the dishwasher, or rub them with a paper towel and rubbing alcohol. If the ashtray is made of china or crystal, see China on page 117 or Crystal on page 136.

Asphalt

Asphalt is tough and durable, but removing stains isn't always easy. For a bad stain, you may have to decide between living with it or resurfacing the asphalt.

Technique: To rid an outdoor basketball court or driveway of routine dirt and grime, "a hose with a good nozzle should get most of the stuff up," says Ross Bentsen, education director of the Asphalt Institute in Lexington, Kentucky.

For more serious cleaning jobs, pour some general household

cleaner such as Spic and Span into a bucket of warm water. Using the mixture, scrub the surface with a stiff brush. For mixture amounts, follow the manufacturer's instructions on the cleaner container.

Speed tips: If you've spilled paint on asphalt, you better get it up quickly or be prepared to live with it. If you catch latex paint before it seeps in, it may be removed with plenty of water and the previous cleaning method. Oil-based paint is nearly impossible to remove.

Caution: Use cleaning solutions sparingly on asphalt. Anything you use will inevitably wash its way into your yard, or your neighbor's. When cleaning asphalt, don't use a petroleum-based product such as WD-40 cleaner and lubricant, Bentsen says. Asphalt is an oil-based product, and the cleaner will cut through the asphalt just as it cuts through the stain.

Asphalt Stains

Asphalt is a petroleum-based product, so a petroleum-based product such as WD-40 cleaner and lubricant, which dissolves oil and petroleum stains, will cut it down to size.

Technique: To remove a fresh asphalt stain, such as one picked up on the bottom of your sneakers from a road construction site, rub with a cloth sprayed with WD-40.

Caution: To avoid making a stain worse, always test-clean a small obscure portion of whatever you're cleaning. Always read any product label for proper use and safety precautions.

Attics

Chances are that you won't be throwing any fancy dinner parties up here, so don't subject yourself to a spit-and-polish cleaning routine. What you want is a clean, orderly safe place to store your stuff. Getting your attic into shape consists of two primary steps: cleaning and organizing. Remember that attics may be full of safety hazards. "You have to be careful about walking around up there," says Cliff Zlotnik, owner of Unsmoke/Restorx, a property restoration and cleaning company in Braddock, Pennsylvania, and a member of the Association of Specialists in Cleaning and Restoration in Annapolis Junction, Maryland.

Technique: The first step, if your attic hasn't been cleaned in a while, will be to clear out cobwebs and dust. A soft broom or floor

HOW I DO IT

Everything in Its Place

As a professional organizer, Barbara Hemphill, president of Hemphill and Associates in Raleigh, North Carolina, makes her living helping clients get control of their lives by helping them get control of their things. A past president of the National Association of Professional Organizers, Hemphill practices what she preaches, starting in the attic of her North Carolina home.

"I recently moved into a house that is blessed with a large attic. It contains holiday decorations, furniture on hold for my five children, even an antique sewing machine.

"The attic is evenly divided by a central staircase. On the left I keep things I actually use from time to time. For example, I have a 30-cup coffeepot that I use maybe six times a year. It's a wonderful thing to store in my attic, but not if I have to dig all over to get at it. On the right side of the attic, I keep rarely used memorabilia—things that are just too precious or meaningful to throw away.

"Ample shelves are essential to an organized attic. You can buy cheap shelves at any home or hardware store, or use the planks and cinder block method. I store boxes on the shelves. Each box has a large label with writing in bold markers, letting me know what's inside. I have a different box for each holiday, and I can identify each box without having to move things around.

"Whenever possible, I find a use for storage items. For example, old bookshelves become handy holders for boxes. A stored file cabinet is used to house old tax records. If I need to consult them, they're easy to find.

"I don't advocate throwing everything away—far from it. But it is important to decide what items you can and can't live without, then get rid of what you can. If it's still usable, give it to a friend or relative, or to a charitable group. You'll feel a lot better about getting rid of an object if you know that someone else is using it.

"Finally, when I set out to organize my attic (or attack any other major project), I give myself a specific goal and time limit. It's amazing how much you can accomplish when you set a deadline. I put on some music to help me work and promise myself some small reward when I finish."

brush on a pole is the best tool for cleaning cobwebs from walls, rafters, and ceilings. To remove remaining cobwebs and dust, vacuum all surfaces, including the floor, with a brush attachment. Attics contain a lot of unfinished wood, which can be damaged by excessive moisture. You don't want to use a lot of water when cleaning the surfaces. Dirt and stains should be rubbed with a damp cloth. Insulation is difficult to clean beyond simple vacuuming. If your insulation is really dusty or in bad shape, consider adding an extra layer on top of it, which will improve the appearance and help make the house more snug.

As everybody knows, attics can be stifling, especially in the summer. Attic fans can help by circulating the air. But be sure that the vents on your fans are properly screened to keep out pests.

In a pinch: If your attic is too gloomy to bear, consider spray painting the surfaces in a bright color. Rent an airless paint sprayer and spray the attic with latex paint. This will brighten things up and make the most of the available light.

Caution: Dangers lurk from head to foot. Before traipsing around, check out the flooring to be sure that it's sturdy enough to support you. Watch for beams, pipes, and other tripping hazards. Be careful not to bump your head on beams and slanted ceilings, and watch out for nails. Roofers sometimes drive nails through thin roofs, leaving the business end pointing dangerously inward. If you have a hard hat or helmet, wear it (forget how you look—nobody's going to see you up there anyway).

Always wear a dust mask when cleaning the attic. You can buy them at just about any paint or hardware store. Keep a flashlight handy so that you don't get caught in the dark if a lightbulb goes out. Store a fresh bulb nearby to avoid having to go downstairs for a replacement. Never cover walls or insulation with plastic sheeting or any other air-proof or waterproof material, which can trap heat or moisture. Since houses do much of their "breathing" through the attic, this is like placing cellophane wrap over your mouth and nose, says Zlotnik.

Because an attic gets hot, pace yourself when working there. Keep cool drinks on hand, and use a portable fan.

If you have bats in your attic, hire a professional exterminator to remove them. Contact with their feces can cause serious health problems, including two fatal conditions called histoplasmosis and coccidiosis, if inhaled.

Always read product labels for safety precautions.

Awnings

Most residential awnings are made of woven fabric, either canvas or synthetic fibers. Periodic cleaning will keep them looking good. Awnings should be cleaned every five to seven months to remove dust, grime, and other atmospheric residue. "If you wait a year, the sun bakes it in," says Bob Van Gelder, owner of Awning Care Plus, which has been cleaning awnings in the San Francisco area for more than 20 years.

Technique: For routine cleaning of awnings that are relatively easy to reach, homeowners may do the job themselves. For heavier jobs or on hard-to-reach awnings, the best step is to call a professional, who will attack the problem with a pressurized water cleaner that flushes dirt and grime away.

For routine jobs, Van Gelder swears by a "truck brush." As the name implies, truck brushes (available at janitorial supply stores) are long-handle brushes with soft flexible bristles designed for cleaning the sides of large trucks. Mix 2 ounces mild liquid dishwashing detergent, such as Joy or Ivory, into a gallon of water. Dip the brush in the mixture and gently scrub the awning. For bird droppings use the same cleaning solution, but try a stiffer-bristle brush if the spot doesn't come right off. When you're finished scrubbing, spray the awning thoroughly with a garden hose.

Minor tree sap stains can be removed with acetone. Put a small amount on a sponge mop and rub the sap stain.

Note: For colored awnings, test-clean by applying a small amount of acetone to an inconspicuous corner with a cotton swab. Allow it to dry and check that the color hasn't faded. Extensive sap stains require professional help.

Speed tips: Some awnings may be removed easily from their frames. If you have this type, it may pay to take the awning down and give it a good cleaning on the ground, using the same cleaning methods as above. Some awning services will remove the awnings for you and replace them when they're clean if you want to do the cleaning yourself.

In a pinch: If you can't find a truck brush, any long-handle brush with soft bristles should work.

Caution: How you reach your awnings will of course depend on how they're positioned around your house. Always use caution when working on ladders, and avoid leaning a ladder against an awning frame. Avoid harsh household detergents, which may cause colors to fade. Before starting to clean your awnings, read any product labels for their proper use and safety precautions.

Balls—Leather, Plastic, Rubber

You don't want to get athletic balls too clean. After all, the occasional grass stain is a sign that you've been out there playing the game, a sort of green badge of courage.

Technique: Most soccer balls or volleyballs these days aren't made of leather but of synthetic materials such as polyvinyl chloride, which are easily cleaned. These types of balls should be washed with mild soap, such as Ivory, and water and dried with a soft towel. Rubber balls, such as all-surface basketballs, and plastic balls, should be cleaned the same way. A quick brushing will do the trick for most leather balls. The Chicago-based Wilson Sporting Goods Company, which makes the official ball of the National Football League, recommends a stiff horsehair-type brush that can be found at leather-goods stores. A muddy ball (including the mud) should be allowed to dry completely before being brushed.

In a pinch: Unless the dirt or soil is interfering with the performance of the ball, consider spending your cleaning time on other objects. Most balls are manufactured with heavy use in mind. "When we make a soccer ball, we're planning on you using it outdoors, planning on it getting dirty," says Carrie Fischer, Wilson's communications manager.

Caution: Leather balls should not be washed and do not need to be coated with leather protectants or other coatings. They're made for heavy outdoor use.

Barbecue Grills

Grease, gunk, and crawly things can threaten your outdoor feast.

Technique: On gas grills, the flame coming from the burners should be blue when shaded and invisible in sunlight. If the flame is yellow or orange, it's a good indication that the tubes or burner are dirty. Once a year, brush the burner with a wire brush, and poke each burner hole with a nail or drill bit to clear away gunk. Of course, do this when your grill is cool. Venturi tubes, which transfer gas from the valve to the burner, should be checked at least once a year for spiders. There are either one or two venturi tubes connecting the gas supply to the bottom of the burner. "Spiders love to build nests inside the venturi tubes, and they can block the flow of gas,"

HOW I DO IT

Hog Wild

Mention ribs and places like Texas and Arkansas spring to mind. But Steve Ross, proprietor of Roscoe's Rootbeer and Ribs in Rochester, Minnesota, cooks up a mean enough rack to have won national competitions in 1993, 1994, and 1996. Cooking up to 5,000 pounds of loin back ribs per month, Ross has cleaned an awful lot of secret sauce from his grills and smokers.

"I don't like to use a strong detergent on any cooking surface. Each night, we remove the grill racks and soak them in hot water and mild liquid dishwashing detergent, then in the morning rinse thoroughly and wipe them down. On the sides of the grills and the insides of the smokers, we use wallpaper scrapers to get rid of carbonized meat and sauce. Then we wipe the surfaces with a cloth. Once a week we give all the surfaces an extra-thorough cleaning, getting into all the crevices. You'll never get the cookers completely cleaned, though, and you don't really want to. I'm a firm believer that smokers and grills get seasoned over time.

"When we cook on the road, at competitions, we use a giant portable contraption called a Maxi Barbecue Chicken and Rib Cooker. (It holds 600 chickens or 180 slabs of pork ribs.) To clean this, we spray it inside and out with an organic degreaser called Jungle Jake, then let it sit overnight. In the morning, we take it to a do-it-yourself car wash and hose it down."

says John Bassemier, president of Bassemier's Fireplace and Patio in Evansville, Indiana, and past president of the National Barbecue Association. Dealers sell special venturi-tube brushes, but you can insert a pipe cleaner or plastic straw into the tubes and twist it to collect and clear spiderwebs and nests, Bassemier says.

The basket (the inside of the grill) and the grill grid (the cooking surface) can be cleaned by leaving your grill on high for several minutes after you're through cooking. If it's not a gas grill, let the grid sit over the hot coals after you're finished cooking. Another way to clean the grid is to place it, after it has cooled, on several sheets of newspaper. Coat the grid with an oven cleaner or commercial grill cleaner. Then place more newspaper over the top. Dampen the newspaper with enough water so that the paper clings to the grid, and place weights on top. Let it sit for several hours or overnight; then brush the grids clean with a grill brush and rinse with water. The inside of the grill can be scraped with a grill scraper or a putty knife.

Speed tips: When cleaning a gas grill by flame, place a double thickness of aluminum foil over the grill grids, enough to fully cover them and hang out over the edges. Light the grill and then close the lid. When the cover comes down, the foil sticking out will bend over, creating a seal. Leave on high for a maximum of 30 minutes or until smoking stops, whichever comes first, says Bassemier. The foil will intensify the heat, cleaning better and faster. Never leave the gas on for more than 30 minutes when cleaning with this method. Prolonged heating can warp the grill basket.

In a pinch: If your gas grill has lava rocks, these will become greasy on the top over time. Turn them periodically to allow the grease to burn off.

Caution: Never use a scraper on the inside of your grill if it's made of porcelain. This can cause scratches that can weaken the grill.

Place a double thickness of aluminum foil over the grill grids (long and wide enough to stick out over the edges). Turn on the grill, close the cover to create a seal, and heat on high for a maximum of 30 minutes. *Note:* More than 30 minutes could warp the grill.

Baseboards

Baseboards are usually coated with durable, shiny oil-based paint, which means that they can stand up to fairly aggressive cleaning methods.

Technique: You can use a nylon scrub pad or fine (#00) steel wool with liquid dishwashing detergent or a household cleaner such as Spic and Span, says Martin L. King, a restoration consultant in Arlington, Virginia, and technical advisor to the National Institute of Disaster Restoration in Annapolis, Maryland. For mixture amounts, follow instructions on the cleaner container.

Caution: Occasionally, you will come across baseboards painted with flat paint. These demand a gentler touch. Use a terry towel or sponge with a dilute solution of liquid dishwashing detergent and water.

Basements

How you clean your basement will depend, of course, on whether it is finished or unfinished, carpeted or uncarpeted, and what you use the area for. The biggest and most universal concern with basements, though, is moisture. Keeping basements as dry as possible and cleaning promptly after leaks and flooding are essential to minimizing damage, mildew, and potentially harmful bacteria.

Technique: For general cleaning, the first step for a basement that hasn't been cleaned in a while is to clear out cobwebs. Always start at the top and work down. A soft broom or brush on a pole is the best tool for cleaning cobwebs from walls, pipes, and rafters. A stiff floor brush is good for general cleaning of concrete floors. To keep the dust down, sprinkle the floor with water, sawdust, or a commercial sweeping compound, available at janitorial supply stores or some automotive supply departments. If the floor is grimy enough to warrant more than sweeping, brush with a solution of liquid dishwashing detergent and water, or a household cleaner such as Spic and Span and water. Or use a small amount of trisodium phosphate (TSP) or sodium metasilicate, which are available at hardware stores, in a bucket of warm water. Use whatever proportions the TSP or household cleaner container label recommends for heavy cleaning. Wear long sleeves and rubber gloves and eye protection when using these products. Carefully follow the product label for proper use and all safety precautions.

To keep air in your basement up to snuff, be sure that gas appliances such as ranges, water heaters, and clothes dryers are properly vented to the outside. This will prevent a buildup of harmful nitrogen dioxide, which can contribute to respiratory tissue damage, or carbon monoxide, which can be harmful or even fatal. Have the gas company regularly inspect these appliances, advises the American Lung Association. Basements are a prime entry point for radon, an odorless, colorless radioactive gas that seeps in from surrounding soil and rocks that contain traces of uranium or radium. If you haven't had your home checked for radon, you should do so.

Moisture and Flooding

To help reduce the moisture level in your basement, take advantage of sunny dry days (or any time the air outside is drier than the air in your basement) by opening windows and doors to the basement. Mechanical dehumidifiers also can reduce moisture in the air.

If your basement gets flooded, the first thing you need to determine is the source and cleanliness of the unwelcome water. There are four general types of basement floodwater: clean, gray, black, and riverine.

"I'm a real expert because I've had most of these things happen at my house," says Cliff Zlotnik, owner of Unsmoke/Restorx, a property restoration and cleaning company in Braddock, Pennsylvania, and a member of the Association of Specialists in Cleaning and Restoration in Annapolis Junction, Maryland.

Clean water from burst pipes or a clean sink or tub overflow is, as you might expect, the least damaging. Gray water contains detergents or food—maybe your sink, dishwasher, or clothes washer leaked. Black water is contaminated water such as sewage. Riverine is water from outside flooding, usually containing soil, fertilizers, dirt, and other debris.

Even with clean-water flooding, swift action is required to avoid major damage, Zlotnik says. If the floor is carpeted, remove any furniture. Water may cause furniture stain to bleed onto the carpet. Walk on the carpet as little as possible. The latex adhesive on carpets weakens when immersed in water and too many feet could cause the backing to separate.

Use a water vacuum to suck up as much of the water as you can. You can rent one from any store that rents heavy appliances. You may also want to rent several dehumidifiers and keep them running in the basement. Be careful in using fans, though. Too many fans will simply convert the liquid to water vapor, which may damage furniture, paintings, books, and other objects not directly affected by the flooding. To check whether this is happening, look for signs of condensation on windows and metallic surfaces.

With contaminated floodwater, carpeting will have to be discarded. You will also need to rip out any drywall that has come into contact with sewage. Drywall will soak the sewage up and could pose a health risk. To clean and disinfect a concrete floor that has been exposed to raw sewage, scrub it with a quaternary ammonium compound, available at janitorial supply stores. Wear gloves when using this product, and follow the label instructions. For extra cleaning, you may want to apply the quaternary ammonium solution with a pressure washer, which can be rented.

When the floodwaters have come from outside, as in riverine flooding, you don't want to remove the water in your basement until the water outside has begun to recede. Removing the water while the outside soil is laden with moisture could create uneven pressure and crack your basement walls. The best thing to do is to mark the water level with a crayon, chalk, or a felt-tip marker. After removing some of the water, see if the level returns to your marking. If so, it's best to wait a while.

In a pinch: To reduce air moisture during a flood, calcium chloride is a good alternative or supplement to mechanical dehumidifiers. Calcium chloride, available at hardware stores, is best-known as an ice-melting material but also soaks up moisture from the air. While wearing rubber gloves, fill an old pillowcase with the pellets of calcium chloride and hang it from a pipe or other ceiling fixture, Zlotnik says. Place a large pan or bucket underneath the bag to catch drops of the resulting brine. To dispose of the brine, pour it down the toilet. When the pillowcase is empty, discard it.

Caution: Always wear rubber boots and rubber gloves when working in a flooded basement, and be especially careful of electrical appliances that may be sitting in water. Never unplug an appliance using your bare hands. Instead, wearing boots and gloves, use a wooden stick or pole to unplug the cord.

Baskets

Most baskets are made from reeds. A good dousing every now and then won't just keep them clean—it will also extend their lives. "It keeps the reed flexible and pliable, and the basket will last for years," says Nancy Varner, manager of Basketville in Toano, Virginia, which is near Colonial Williamsburg and is one of the nation's largest stores specializing in baskets. Other baskets are made from wood, usually white oak or white ash, and should be cleaned with much less water.

Technique: You can wash a reed basket in the kitchen sink using the spray attachment, or take it out back and spray it down with your garden hose. Use a little mild dishwashing detergent and a soft-bristle brush to scrub away dirt or stains, and then rinse thoroughly. Let the basket air-dry outdoors in the sun or in a sunny window. Although water is good for the reed, if the basket is allowed to remain wet, it will begin to rot. The basket should dry in a few hours.

For painted baskets, use the same method as above but don't scrub with a brush, which may scratch the paint. Use a soft cloth instead.

Heavy amounts of water may damage wooden baskets. Instead of spraying or immersing them, wipe them down with a soft cloth dampened with plain water.

In a pinch: A white basket that has become stained or scuffed up will look like new with a coat of white spray paint.

Caution: Avoid using harsh detergents, which could mar the surface of the basket. For the same reason, avoid using a brush with metal bristles. Don't put the basket away while still wet.

Bathroom Rugs

Terry bathroom rugs are like heavy-duty towels and usually can be thrown in the same washing machine loads as towels.

Technique: It's best to follow the cleaning instructions on the label. As a general rule, though, bathroom rugs that do not have a latex backing may be machine-washed with similarly colored towels in warm water, then tumble dried or air-dried. Mats that do have a latex backing should be washed separately and tumble dried on low or air-dried, advises Joan Garrison, manager of consumer relations for the bedding and linen company Fieldcrest Cannon in Kannapolis, North Carolina.

Caution: A bathroom rug of a deep color should always be washed before the first use to prevent color from bleeding off onto your feet or the floor. Wash it separately the first time to prevent bleeding onto other items.

Bathtubs

A little routine cleaning on a regular basis will lessen the need for the longer more difficult process of scrubbing away caked-on soap scum.

Technique: After each use, wipe your bathtub with a sponge and rinse it with water. This will prevent soap from building up. About once a week give your tub a more thorough cleaning.

Before you run out and purchase expensive cleansers made specifically for bathrooms, try cleaning your tub with other types of detergents or cleaners already lying around the house. Bon Ami or a mild liquid dishwashing detergent on a sponge makes a good general bathtub cleaner. Bon Ami acts as a polisher, too. A liquid laundry detergent such as Tide, applied with a sponge, does an excellent job of cleaning away grime as well as discoloration caused by hard water, says Neil Pirthipal, a customer service representative at American Standard in Piscataway, New Jersey. If your bathtub has adhesive strips on the bottom to prevent slipping, try scrubbing these with some Bon Ami and a soft nylon-bristle brush. If a grittier cleanser is required, put some baking soda on a damp sponge. It's natural, safe, and won't scrape bathtub surfaces.

In a pinch: Need something a little tougher than a sponge? Try scrubbing the tub with a nylon net ball or pad (available in your grocery store cleaning section). You can even roll up an old nylon stocking into a ball.

Caution: Avoid using abrasive cleansers, pads, or brushes that might scratch or dull the surface of the tub, Pirthipal says. Never use cleansers containing acetone or ethyl alcohol to clean a fiberglass tub. They will damage the fiberglass finish. Never use steel wool instead of a nylon brush to scrub no-slip surfaces. "If pieces get imbedded in the skid-resistant surface, it will cause rust stains," says Pirthipal.

Bats—Aluminum, Wood

You might not be able to hit the ball farther with a shiny bat, but you'll think that you can.

Technique: For a wooden bat, wash with plain water and dry immediately to prevent water from soaking into the wood. This is especially important if the surface of the bat isn't finished, says George Manning, vice president of technical services at Hillerich and Bradsby Company in Louisville, the leading bat-maker in the United States. For an extra shine, apply a floor wax made for wood floors. Use a clear floor wax if your wooden bat has a clear finish. Wash an aluminum bat with soap and water. For extra sparkle, apply a liquid car polish or paste wax. Rubber grips should be scrubbed with a wet bristle brush. Leather grips should not be scrubbed. Instead, wipe with a damp cloth.

Caution: Do not use abrasive cleansers or abrasive pads, which can mar the surface of aluminum or wooden bats.

Beams—Exposed

They're rugged, they're beautiful...they collect dust.

Technique: Vacuum beams periodically with a brush attachment. If the beams are covered with wood stain or paint (as most are), they may be washed with towels and a solution of water and a household cleaner such as Spic and Span. For mixture amounts, follow instructions on the cleaner container. If the wood is untreated, try giving the beams a vigorous brushing. To wash untreated beams, dip a towel in the water and household cleaner but wring out thoroughly before rubbing the beams, says Martin L. King, a restoration consultant in Arlington, Virginia, and technical advisor to the National Institute of Disaster Restoration in Annapolis, Maryland. You don't want too much moisture getting into the wood.

Caution: Always use a fabric drop cloth on the floor when cleaning beams. A plastic one can be slippery.

Bicycles

Cleaning your bicycle is similar to cleaning your car. A thorough going-over periodically, including a good waxing, won't just make your ride sparkle. It will help your bicycle perform better and last longer.

Bikes these days fall into two major categories: mountain bikes and road bikes. Cleaning methods for both are similar, but mountain bikes, with their wide tires made for negotiating muddy trails, are likely to get a lot dirtier and need extra attention.

Technique: For most items, waxing comes at the end of a cleaning process. But your bicycle should be waxed before you take it out and get it dirty in the first place. "The key to protecting the frame is to prepare it for the duty it's going to perform," says Jim Langley, senior technical editor for *Bicycling* magazine, in Soquel, California. "This will go a long way toward making it easy to clean after a muddy or dirty ride." If your bike isn't that dirty, often a wipe down with a clean cloth, followed by waxing, will suffice.

You can find waxes made especially for bicycles at just about any good bicycle store, but car wax will do as well. The key is to find something easy to apply since bike frames have lots of tubes and joints. Liquids are generally easier to work with than pastes. Apply the wax with a clean soft cloth, following the instructions on the container.

Cleaning a bike involves two major areas: the frame and the drivetrain. A bicycle should be supported right side up, off the ground when cleaning. Hang it on an open garage door by hooking the saddle tip on a metal brace, a sturdy tree branch at the right height, a bike stand, or any other place where you can safely secure it. Simple bike stands can be found for under $20 in some bike shops. Or you can invest in a repair stand, which costs $125 to $150.

Drivetrain

The drivetrain includes the chain, pedals, derailleurs, rear hub, and other mechanical parts of the bike. This is a messier job than cleaning the frame and should be done first. These parts should be cleaned about once a month if you ride regularly, or whenever you notice a buildup of grime. Clean the chain a few links at a time by spraying with a degreaser such as WD-40 and wiping with a cloth. When those links are clean, advance the pedals slightly and work on a new section of the chain. Once the chain is clean, use your finger to lift it off the chainring. These are the large metal wheels with teeth that hold the chain. Use a screwdriver to remove gunk from between the teeth. Slide a cloth between the rings, slipping it back and forth like dental floss.

Spray a degreaser such as WD-40 on the derailleurs, crankset, cogs, and pedals, wiping with the cloth as you go. Always spray mechanical parts from the top to avoid getting degreaser inside components and eliminating necessary lubricants. The main goal here is to get rid of any built-up gunk. "You don't want it spotless," Langley says. "You still want it lubed." When you're done, apply drops of bicycle lubricant (available at bike stores) to the chain, pedals, and other parts.

Frame

First use a garden hose without a spray attachment to dribble water over the entire frame. Mix ¼ cup mild liquid dishwashing detergent (enough to create suds) in a bucket of water. Use a sponge to soap down the entire frame, including the handlebars, grips, and seat. While washing, inspect the frame for signs of rust. Minor rust spots can be removed by rubbing with medium fine (#0) steel wool. Significant rust should be checked out by a bike mechanic because it could lead to structural failure of the frame.

Use a nylon-bristle brush to get rid of stubborn, dried-on mud. Use a smaller nylon brush to go after dirt in crevices the sponge can't reach. Then dribble water over the frame until the soap is gone. When you're finished washing, dry the frame with clean soft cloths, then wax.

Wash the wheels and tires with the same solution. Wash the tires slowly and methodically, taking the opportunity to inspect them for signs of damage. Look for nicks or cuts and debris embedded in the tread. The sidewalls of the tires are usually made of fabric. Check them for signs of fraying. If the tires are damaged, they should be replaced.

Speed tips: Instead of applying bike or car wax to your frame, you can use a furniture spray such as Pledge instead. Just spray it on and wipe to a shine. It goes on a lot faster than the waxes. The drawback is that this treatment won't hold up as long—you'll have to do it every few days.

Caution: Never clean a bike while it's standing on the ground without solid support. It might fall over. That's the number one cause of bicycle damage, Langley says.

Don't use a spray attachment to hose your bike down, and don't take it to one of those do-it-yourself car washes with high-pressure hoses. Water will get into crevices and wash away necessary lubricants, which will cause expensive components to wear rapidly. For the same reason, don't wash a bike upside down or spray degreaser directly into drivetrain parts. Don't use a tire protectant, such as Armor All, on your tires. They'll get slippery and you could lose control when riding.

Birdbaths

Because birds are susceptible to bacteria that can breed in birdbaths, the National Audubon Society, in New York City, advises regular cleaning.

Technique: Birdbaths should be scrubbed once a week with a scrub brush or sponge. Change the water every few days. In summer, you may want to change the water daily.

Caution: Always keep birdbaths free of cleaning solutions and other chemicals. If you must use soap, use only a small amount and rinse thoroughly because birds are very sensitive to chemicals.

Bird Feeders

You want to keep bird feeders clean, but you must be careful not to leave soapy residue that can harm your feathered dinner guests.

Technique: Bird feeders should be given a thorough cleaning at least every three months. Wash plastic feeders with water and rinse thoroughly. Wooden feeders should be taken apart (if possible), brushed out, and cleaned with a wire brush. You may even want to sand the surfaces from time to time with a piece of sandpaper. Rinse wooden feeders thoroughly, but do not use soap because it will be impossible to get all the soap out of the wood, says John Bianchi, communications director and spokesman for the National Audubon Society in New York City. Hummingbird feeders should be flushed every few days with very hot water because they can develop molds that hummingbirds are particularly sensitive to. Take down the feeder, pour out any sugar water, and rinse the feeder under very hot water at a sink.

Blankets

Most blankets, even woolen ones, may be machine-washed. Whenever possible, no matter what the blanket is made of, closely follow the cleaning instructions on the care label. And watch how you dry the blanket, or it'll lose its shape.

Technique: With woolen blankets, dry cleaning is most often recommended. But if you have the time and the desire, you can wash them at home, with care. If you choose the home method, machine-wash one blanket at a time in cool water on the gentle cycle. "Friction and heat cause wool to shrink," says Charlotte Hughes, manager of blanket operations for Cascade Woolen Mill in Oakland, Maine. You can wash the blanket by hand by gently swishing it in a tub of cool water with a mild laundry detergent such as Ivory Snow or a teaspoon of mild liquid dishwashing detergent. There are several methods for drying a wool blanket. You can dry it in a machine dryer on the "No Heat" setting. Or you can spread the blanket flat on a picnic table to dry or hang it on a taut line that doesn't bow under the weight of the blanket. If drying outdoors, keep the blanket in the shade. After the blanket has dried, you can fluff it in a machine dryer on the "No Heat" setting.

Vellux blankets are velvetlike synthetic blankets made from two thin layers of polyurethane foam with a surface of flocked nylon that gives it the velvety feel. These can be machine-washed in warm water using your usual laundry detergent. Machine-dry them on medium heat and remove immediately. Washing Vellux blankets twice a year will keep them fluffy and help maintain their thermal properties. Do not spot-clean or dry-clean.

Cotton holds up well to laundry detergent. Cotton blankets may be washed right along with your regular laundry. Loose-knit cotton blankets should be washed on a delicate cycle to avoid pilling. Dry them on a taut line that doesn't bow under the weight of the blanket.

Caution: Hanging your blanket (especially a woolen one) on a droopy line will cause it to dry in the shape of the droop. Make certain that the line is taut, or lay the blanket flat. For wool, find a shady spot for drying because direct sunlight may cause the wool to shrink.

Blinds

More heat and cold is transferred through your windows than through your walls. Because dust and other airborne pollutants are drawn to areas where energy transfer is the greatest, window blinds become virtual dust magnets.

Technique: No matter what your blinds are made of, dusting is the first cleaning step. For routine maintenance, dust venetian or vertical blinds regularly using a lamb's wool duster or a soft house painting brush. Or go over the blinds using a vacuum cleaner with a brush attachment. Close the blinds fully and clean one side, then turn them so the slats are facing the opposite way and clean the other side.

Blinds in or near kitchens can become grimy, and nicotine from smoking may leave a yellowish film on blinds in other rooms. If your blinds are made from a synthetic material such as vinyl or from metal with a baked-on coating, you can wash them with a cleaner like Windex or Formula 409 and a soft cloth. Or you can make your own effective cleaner by mixing a couple of ounces of trisodium phosphate (available at hardware stores) in a bucket of water. Be sure to protect your eyes, wear rubber gloves and a long-sleeve shirt, and follow all safety precautions on the product label. Wipe the blinds with a soft cloth dipped in the mixture, then go over them again with a cloth dipped in plain water. If you have trouble getting between the slats, use a soft clean paintbrush or wrap a tongue depressor–size piece of wood in a terry towel or paper towel.

If wooden blinds need more than just dusting, you can use a cloth dampened with the trisodium phosphate mixture. But be careful not to slop on the water. You don't want to oversaturate wood.

For heavier cleaning of blinds covered with fabric, mix 3 to 4 ounces mild liquid dishwashing detergent in a bucket of water. Beat the mixture into a sudsy froth. Take a damp sponge and skim some foam off the top without dipping into the water. Scrub the fabric with the foam. Then rub with a clean terry cloth. "That extracts the soil, plus it dries the surface," says Cliff Zlotnik, owner of Unsmoke/Restorx, a property restoration and cleaning company in Braddock, Pennsylvania, and a member of the Association of Specialists in Cleaning and Restoration in Annapolis Junction, Maryland.

Vinyl or coated metal mini-blinds can be washed in the bathtub. The Window Covering Safety Council, in New York City, recommends this method. Extend the blind to its full length and remove it from its support brackets. Place it gently in your bathtub with warm water mixed with 1 to 2 cups of powdered automatic dishwasher detergent. There should be enough water to completely submerge the blind. Hold the blind by its headrail and dip the blind up and down in the water several times to loosen dirt and dust. Use a sponge to wash each slat. Wear rubber gloves to avoid irritating your hands in the dishwasher detergent.

When the blind is clean, empty the tub of the soapy water and refill the tub halfway with plain cold water. Dip the blind up and down until soap is off, then drain the tub. If it's necessary to rinse more, refill the tub again halfway. Gather the blind and place it upright in a corner of the tub and allow it to dry for several hours. If the slats are still damp, rehang the blind anyway and wipe slats dry with a soft cloth.

In a pinch: If you don't have time to clean or if your blinds are really dirty, there are professional blind-cleaning services. They use an "ultrasonic bath" method, which uses sound waves vibrating through water to clean the blinds. Often you can get a lower rate if you deliver your blinds to the cleaner and pick them up yourself.

Caution: It's a good idea to test any cleaning solution on an inconspicuous part of your blind before cleaning the whole blind. Just dab some of the solution on with a cotton swab. This is especially advised for fabric or painted wood blinds. Often these are imported, and it's difficult to know what dyes or paints have been used.

Blood Stains

As with most stains, the quicker you get to a blood stain, the better chance you have of getting it out. But work patiently and follow the steps. "There are no quick ways to clean a blood stain," says Jane Rising, instructor in the education department at the International Fabricare Institute in Silver Spring, Maryland.

Technique: First, blot the stain with cool water. Then blot with a mild liquid dishwashing detergent mixed with water. Flush thoroughly with water. If the stain persists, try mixing the detergent and water with a couple of drops of ammonia. Flush thoroughly with water. If the stain still won't go away, and the fabric is colorfast, soak it in an enzyme-containing product such as Shout. Test for colorfastness first in an inconspicuous spot. Flush thoroughly with water.

If all else fails, blot the stain using a bleach containing hydrogen peroxide, as long as the bleach is safe for the color and fabric of your garment. Or soak the cloth in a nonchlorine colorfast bleach, such as Biz, for several hours or overnight. Use ½ scoop Biz in 2 gallons warm water.

If that doesn't work, you can try a rust remover, such as Whink or Rit, and follow the label directions. It's important to flush thoroughly with water between each step so that individual cleaning solutions don't mix on the fabric. Follow the cleaning instructions on the garment. If you have treated the fabric with an aerosol stain protector, such as Scotchgard, reapply it after you've cleaned the fabric.

To remove a blood stain from fabric that has been Scotchgard-treated at the factory, follow the manufacturer's instructions very carefully to protect any warranty. For furniture, read the label under the cushion and check the cleanability code. A "W" means use a water-based cleaner to clean; an "S" means use a cleaning solvent, not water; a "W-S" means use either water or a solvent; and an "X" means use neither, just vacuum. In general, for carpets that have been stain-treated at the factory, the following method can be used to remove a water-based stain such as blood. Blot up as much as you can with paper towel. Mix ¼ teaspoon clear dishwashing detergent and 1 cup lukewarm water.

Don't use laundry detergent because it may contain brighteners and other additives. Blot from the outside to the center of the stain. Blot with plain white paper towels or terry towels until the towel no longer picks up the stain. Rinse with clear water. If the stain is gone, place white paper towels over the area and weight down, changing towels periodically until the area is dry. The paper toweling will wick up stains from deep in the carpet. If the stain is stubborn, try a solution of 2 tablespoons nonsudsing ammonia with 1 cup lukewarm water. Rinse and blot as mentioned previously. Immediately follow with a mixture of 1 cup white vinegar and 2 cups water to neutralize the ammonia. Blot and rinse as mentioned previously, and weight down paper towels over the stain until dry.

In a pinch: If a minor blood stain happens at work or someplace you can't get to cleaning supplies easily, "blot it with water immediately," Rising says. "Often, that will take care of it."

Caution: Never rub or brush a stain because this may spread the stain or damage the fabric. Make certain that you have flushed completely between each cleaning step with clean water. Make sure, if you've used bleach, to flush it completely away. Bleach left on fabric can weaken it. Be sure to test any cleaning method on a small obscure corner of the fabric before attacking the stain, even if you've used the method before, to make sure that the colors and the fabric can withstand the cleaning. Read the labels on clothing for cleaning instructions. Follow the product label carefully for proper use and safety precautions.

Boats

Always start with the gentlest approach when cleaning a boat. Use stronger methods sparingly, and then be sure that they're suitable for your boat's materials.

Technique: Regardless of what your boat is made of, cleaning starts with a bucket of freshwater and mild soap or liquid dishwashing detergent. Soap the boat down thoroughly with a good sponge, then rinse with generous amounts of freshwater.

Wooden Boats

Since wooden boats are painted, "you are essentially cleaning paint, which means that solvents are out. Soap and water is the best routine," says Randy Cobb, plant engineer for Old Town Canoe Company, the venerable maker of canoes and other small boats located in Old Town, Maine. For crusted-on dirt that the sponge won't clean, try one of the least abrasive Scotch-Brite pads, which are white, tan, or beige. Using anything more abrasive may damage the surface.

Of Rats and Men

Ah, to take to the high seas in an old English sailing ship. The excitement! The adventure! The vermin! Well, you had to figure it wasn't *all* excitement and adventure. Among the less glamorous tasks was cleaning the ship of rats and cockroaches after a long sea voyage.

James Horsburgh, a ship captain from the early nineteenth century, describes the following method, which doubled as a way to check for leaks. The description appears in *The Naval Chronicle*, a multivolume British naval journal of that era. First, a large pot filled with red-hot charcoal was lowered onto the ballast in the hold and covered with shakings (pieces of old rope, canvas, and other sweepings) that had been moistened and dipped in tar.

"But in order to make certain of destroying the vermin," Horsburgh writes, "I also placed upon the ballast a small kettle, with sulphur on fire, and immediately closed the hatch, securing it with clay. In a few minutes, the smoke began to issue out at many parts of the ship, which enabled the carpenter to mark them with chalk, by which means a leak was discovered in the stem (the bow), of 10 years standing, or from the time the ship first floated; and many efforts had been made at various times to discover it, without success.

"After 40 hours, the hatches were opened, and the rats were found in a petrified state, but the cockroaches were as lively as ever."

Fiberglass Boats

Start with soap and water. If that doesn't do the trick, go after tough dirt or oily stains with a little mineral spirits (paint thinner), applied sparingly on a soft cloth. Then rinse the boat thoroughly. Don't use lacquer thinner or acetone, which are stronger solvents and can damage fiberglass.

Vinyl-Covered Boats

Many small boats today are made from a vinyl composite material called Royalex. These hulls have a vinyl exterior with a hard plastic layer underneath and a foam plastic core. After soap and water, go after tougher grime with some denatured alcohol, available at hardware stores, on a cloth. These boats have a tendency to mildew, especially if stored in a shed for a long time. Denatured alcohol will clear mildew away without damaging the material. For truly stubborn stains, apply a little acetone—very sparingly. Heavy use of acetone or other solvents may weaken the foam core and will remove some of the vinyl skin.

Colossal Cleanups

Bowled Over
The number of toilets washed each day on board the Carnival Destiny, Carnival Cruise Lines' largest ship: more than 3,000

Polyethylene Boats
Some canoes, kayaks, and small boats are made of this rugged but flexible plastic, somewhat similar to the plastic used for liquid laundry detergent containers. If the boat needs more cleaning after soap and water, apply a limited amount of paint thinner or acetone with a cloth, Cobb says. Small amounts of lacquer thinner may be used as a last resort.

Aluminum Boats
If the aluminum is painted, use the same cleaning method as for wooden boats. Unpainted aluminum boats are rugged; they can withstand any of the aforementioned cleaning methods.

Speed tips: If you use your boat in salt water, hose it down with freshwater thoroughly and as soon as possible after each use. This will prevent a saltwater film from building up and limits corrosion.

Caution: Don't use thinners or other solvents on a painted boat. Use them sparingly on other boats. "You never want to get any more aggressive than necessary," Cobb says. Always rinse cleaning agents thoroughly with water.

Bone

Objects made of bone are porous and frequently brittle. Overclean and you may wind up being bad to the bone.

Technique: Smooth bone, such as handles for knives or letter openers, may be wiped with a slightly dampened cloth or cotton swab. Bone carvings should be dusted with an artist's sable paintbrush, available at art stores. Don't use cloth or swabs on carvings, as you may break off brittle pieces or lodge bits of cloth or cotton in crevices, warns Stephen Koob, a conservation specialist at the Freer Gallery of the Smithsonian Institution in Washington, D.C.

Speed tips: You can vacuum bone pieces instead of dusting. Use a small battery-operated vacuum cleaner, available at electronics stores.

Caution: Never submerge bone in water. Even getting it wet is a bad idea—mold grows easily. Never use soap or wax, both of which can leave a residue that will turn the piece yellow. Bone that you don't want to clean yourself or that is stained or damaged by fire should be taken to a professional conservator. To find one in your area, contact the American Institute for Conservation of Historic and Artistic Works, 1717 K Street NW, Suite 301, Washington, DC 20006.

Books

In cleaning books, as in making the perfect omelet, the best rule is keep to it light and simple.

Technique: "Unless there is a need to clean, just dusting books with a soft cloth is the thing to do," says Karen Muller, executive director of the Association for Library Collections and Technical Services, a division of the American Library Association in Chicago. Food or fingerprint smudges on the cover of a hardcover book or a paperback with a hard finish may be cleaned with a damp, but not wet, sponge or cloth. For smudges on conventional paperbacks, use a very soft eraser and rub gently. Go super gently on colored paper, to make sure that you don't rub off color. For leather-bound books, wipe with a clean dry cloth, or carefully vacuum off the obvious dust.

There is no surefire method for removing the musty smell from old books, but the Northeast Document Conservation Center in Andover, Massachusetts, suggests this nifty (if somewhat involved) method. It requires two clean garbage can–type containers, one small enough to fit into the larger with room to spare. Place the book in the smaller can, and put that in the larger can. Then place some odor-absorbing material such as baking soda, plain charcoal briquettes, or cat litter in the bottom of the larger can, around the base of the smaller. Cover the big can and let it sit for several days, checking periodically. Don't leave your treasure where the trash collector might mistakenly haul it off.

Speed tips: To keep an entire shelf of books looking good, use a vacuum cleaner with a long, soft brush attachment to clean the spines. Then lightly dust the tops and edges of the books. Do not press down because you may damage the tops.

HOW I DO IT

Guarding the Bard

In 1623, seven years after the death of William Shakespeare, two of his actor friends collected and published 36 plays in an edition called the First Folio. Without the remarkable efforts of John Heminges and Henry Condell, at a time when plays were rarely considered literature worth saving, many Shakespearean dramas would have been lost forever. Of the fewer than 300 remaining copies from the original edition, the Folger Shakespeare Library in Washington, D.C., owns 80, the world's largest collection.

"First Folios are worth three-quarters of a million dollars apiece, so we don't just 'clean them,' " says conservation director Frank Mowery.

"Like all of our rare books, they're kept in a walk-in vault with a constant 68°F temperature and 50 percent humidity. Consistency is essential. Paper expands and contracts as it gains and loses moisture. After too many fluctuations it breaks apart, just like a piece of metal that has been bent back and forth. Fifty percent humidity is moist enough to keep the paper from getting brittle but too dry for silverfish and other destructive insects that get their water from what they eat.

"We have sophisticated atmospheric control systems that keep the vault nearly dust-free, but once a year a staff member dusts the books with a lint-free cloth sprayed with a spray-on cleaner and polish, like Endust, or with a static-free Dust Bunny, a cloth that creates a magnetic attraction to dust.

"Scholars are permitted to handle the books, but they must wash and dry their hands thoroughly before doing so. You might think that gloves would be required, but we don't permit them. Even with ultra-thin gloves you lose some of your feel, increasing the chance of tearing a page or dropping a book.

"You may not have access to all this sophisticated climate control machinery, but you can preserve your own books by using humidifiers and dehumidifiers as the climate demands, to stabilize the humidity in your home library."

Caution: For leather books, conservationists no longer recommend leather dressings such as neat's-foot oil or lanolin, as they once did. The current consensus is that dressings may discolor or stain leather books, make them sticky, or absorb into other books or papers. Dressings may also increase the chance of mold.

Boots—Leather, Rubber

Good-quality boots will stand up to years of trekking through the mud and over rough terrain, provided that you treat them nicely once they're safely back home.

Technique: Rubber boots require relatively simple care. Just take them out back and put the hose to them when they get muddy. Even hard caked-on mud should soften after a few moments under the hose. "I'm always in mud with my rubber boots, and it does not take much to get hardened mud off them," says Rocky Rodrigues, footwear representative for L.L. Bean, the venerable outdoors store in Freeport, Maine, that started making and selling boots in 1912. Remove any remaining mud with a soft towel or cloth.

There's not much you can do to prevent cheap or imitation rubber boots from fading and cracking. But you can prolong the life of any rubber boot by storing it out of direct sunlight. If shiny boots are your thing, apply a coat of automotive tire and vinyl protectant such as Armor All for tires once or twice a year, Rodrigues says.

The biggest concern with leather boots is not getting them wet but getting them dry in the right way. Not that you want to soak your boots just for the fun of it, but most full-grain leather work boots or hiking boots can stand up to a hosing if they've gotten really muddy. The important thing is to let them dry at room temperature, away from direct sources of heat. Radiators, ovens, and blow-dryers will certainly dry boots faster, but you run the risk of cracking or warping the leather.

Saddle soap, available in tins at many shoe stores, will do a good job of cleaning routine dirt and stains from leather boots. Just follow the instructions on the can. But saddle soap may wipe away some needed moisture. Remember that leather is a hide and, just like your skin, should be kept soft. If the boots feel dry after using saddle soap, apply a commercial leather conditioner.

Suede and nubuck boots should be brushed as needed to keep them looking good. Suede is made from leather that has been split, with the soft inside turned out. Nubuck is full-grain leather that has been lightly sanded to produce a soft, suedelike exterior. For suede, you can use a brass suede brush. Nubuck has a shorter nap that may be damaged by a metal brush, so use a horsehair or soft nylon brush or similar soft brush instead. Brush against the nap to lift dirt particles. Then brush back into place by stroking in the direction of the nap, says Rodrigues. You can use a block eraser, available at shoe stores, to erase light stains on nubuck. If you want to use a protectant spray on your suede or nubuck shoes, use one that contains fluoropolymers, not silicon.

Note: Commercial waterproofing products, widely available at shoe stores, will help protect your boots against rain and stains. Carefully follow the instructions on the container. Boots should be clean before you apply waterproofing. Also, you may want to wear new boots a few times before waterproofing them. Some manufacturers apply a polish to make boots look great on the shoe-store shelves. This should be allowed to wear away before applying waterproofing.

In a pinch: It's unlikely that dress boots will ever get as dirty or need the type of heavy-duty cleaning as work boots, but you can spot-clean them using clear tap water applied to a clean towel.

Caution: For boots made of exotic hides or materials, carefully follow the instructions of the manufacturer or the store where you purchased them.

Bowling Balls

Dirt and mineral oils (used to coat lanes) gunk up the surface of the ball and can hurt its performance.

Technique: "Cleaning oil off a ball is like cleaning grease off dishes," says Larry Vezina, team leader of the specifications and certification department for Bowling, serving the American Bowling Congress and Women's International Bowling Congress, both in Greendale, Wisconsin. Place the ball in your kitchen sink carefully and wash it with hot water and liquid dishwashing detergent. Some bowlers actually place their ball on the lower rack of the dishwasher and run it through a regular cycle (remove dishes first).

In a pinch: Use a spray glass cleaner and rub with a soft cloth.

Caution: Avoid acetone cleaners (such as nail polish remover), which may soften the ball.

Brass

A shiny alloy of copper and zinc, brass is used in everything from lamps to candlesticks to buttons. General cleaning is simple and easy.

Keeping brass shiny is a different story. How hard you work at it depends on whether the metal is lacquered.

Technique: Dust brass objects regularly using a soft cloth. Old T-shirts are great to use. Occasionally, grease or grime from particles in the air will collect on a brass object. Rub the object with a soft damp cloth. Dry the object right away to prevent water spots. Or rinse in a solution of a rinse agent such as Jet-Dry and water to prevent water spots, and then dry thoroughly.

Most brass objects and fixtures are lacquered to protect them from oxidation, a natural tarnishing process that occurs when oxygen interacts with the metal. Lacquered brass does not need to be polished until the lacquer begins to wear away. "If it's not handled a lot, the lacquer could last 10 years," says James W. McGann, vice president for quality at Virginia Metalcrafters in Waynesboro, which creates all the brass and bronze pieces used at Colonial Williamsburg.

When lacquered brass does finally begin to tarnish, it must be completely removed before you polish or relacquer it. You can use any commercial lacquer thinner, available at hardware stores. Be sure to follow the directions carefully. Stubborn lacquer that has been baked on may have to be removed by a professional metalworker. Relacquering should also be done by a professional. Check your phone book for metal finishers, antique dealers, or lighting repair shops to locate a professional.

Unlacquered brass or brass that has had its lacquer removed will have to be polished regularly to maintain its shine. Doorknobs and other objects that are touched frequently should be polished once a month to stay shiny. Other pieces should be polished every two to three months. You can use any of several dozen commercial brass polishes on the market. One popular brand is Brasso, which is widely used by the U.S. military. Getting a brass piece back to its original shine may be difficult or impossible using the standard home methods. If you're really finicky, a professional metalworker may come closest using a buffing wheel and jeweler's rouge.

Speed tips: To remove wax from a brass candlestick, dampen a soft cloth with warm water, which will melt the wax as you rub.

In a pinch: You can make your own brass polish, says McGann, by mixing 1 tablespoon salt with 1 tablespoon flour. Stir in 1 tablespoon white vinegar. Apply the paste with a soft damp cloth, rub gently, rinse, and wipe dry with a dry soft cloth.

Caution: Never use harsh cleansers or abrasive pads to clean brass. These can scratch the metal. Handle brass pieces as infrequently as possible. Oils from your fingers can leave permanent marks on unlacquered pieces and hasten the deterioration of lacquer. "If you handle a piece of brass with sweaty hands, it'll show fingerprints by tomorrow," McGann says. If you have a piece of brass that you think may be a valuable antique, don't polish it until you've had it examined by a professional conservator. The patina, a fine film that forms naturally on antique brass and other objects, is considered historically significant.

Brick

Because of brick's rough rugged surface, you may be tempted to really apply the pressure when cleaning. But take care—it's more delicate than you think. The trick is to apply the right amount of pressure without damaging the brick or mortar.

Technique: "If it's just general dirt, it could be relatively effective to get out there with a garden hose with a spray attachment," says Brian Trimble, senior engineer for the Brick Institute of America in Reston, Virginia.

For tougher cleaning jobs, mix ½ cup trisodium phosphate (available at hardware stores) with ½ cup dry laundry detergent in 1 gallon water. When using trisodium phosphate, wear eye protection, rubber gloves, and a long-sleeve shirt, and follow safety precautions on the product label. Hose down the bricks thoroughly before washing. Then scrub lightly with the cleaning mixture, using a natural-fiber or nylon brush. Wire brushes can damage sand-coated, hand-molded, or historic brick and leave small metal deposits that can cause rust stains. Oil-based paint stains must be wiped immediately with paint thinner, then rinsed thoroughly with water, or they will be nearly impossible to remove.

Moss does not damage brick, but for aesthetic reasons, you may want to remove moss or algae from shaded brick surfaces. To do so, you may use an organic herbicide, following the package instructions, or you may douse the algae or moss with a mixture of half chlorine bleach and half water instead. Rinse thoroughly with plain water. Then let the area dry, brush away the moss or algae, and follow the same cleaning method as above. Reworking poor drainage or cutting down on shade will keep moss and algae from returning, Trimble advises.

Sometimes brick gets a chalky white stain in patches. This is caused by waterborne salts that have worked their way to the surface of the brick and dried. Usually, these marks will wear away on their own over time. Persistent marks may indicate a drainage leak around your home that should be fixed.

Speed tips: You may rent a pressure washer to clean brick, but make sure that it's one that can be set for 700 pounds per square inch or less, to avoid damage to the bricks or mortar. Be especially careful on sand-coated brick, where pressure washers set too high may leave "bald spots" on the surface.

Caution: You may hear that muriatic acid is good for cleaning brick; professional bricklayers use it to remove fresh mortar. But, Trimble warns, "indiscriminate use can cause staining, kill plants, and etch glass. It's just not something I'd recommend the average homeowner to be doing."

Briefcases

Like a good pair of shoes, a briefcase should be regularly conditioned to prepare it for the outdoor pounding it will take.

Technique: The easiest way to clean a briefcase made of finished leather (as opposed to suede or nubuck) is with a damp sponge and some mild liquid dishwashing detergent or Woolite, says George Mooers, manager of a Tandy Leather and Crafts store in Torrence, California. Squirt a little of the detergent onto the sponge and rub the surface. Then wipe away soap residue with a sponge dampened only with water. If this method fails, try a cleaner specially made for leather, available at most leather stores.

Every three to six months, depending on how often you use the briefcase and whether it is frequently exposed to harsh weather, you should treat the briefcase with a leather conditioner. You can use any good-quality conditioner. Follow the instructions on the container. "Even a boot cream would work," says Mooers. "If you don't treat the leather, the oils will dry out of it."

For briefcases made of vinyl or other imitation materials, use the liquid dishwashing detergent or Woolite. But instead of applying a leather conditioner, protect the surface with an automotive tire and vinyl protectant like Armor All.

Detergent should not be used on suede or nubuck, both of which have a softer brushed feel. Instead, use cleaners and protectants made specifically for those surfaces.

Clean the handle and other fixtures of the briefcase according to

How to Get a Handle on Your Briefcase's Contents

Think of your briefcase as a "mini-desk" rather than as a general repository for all your stuff. That's the advice of Barbara Hemphill, an organizational consultant who has appeared on *Good Morning America*, *The Today Show*, *This Morning*, and other national television shows, and author of *Taming the Paper Tiger*. Hemphill, president of Hemphill and Associates in Raleigh, North Carolina, offers these tips so that your briefcase doesn't turn you into a head case.

- Open your briefcase next to the wastebasket whenever possible. Continually ask yourself, "What's the worst possible thing that would happen if I didn't have this piece of paper?" If you can live without it, toss it.
- Carry a file folder labeled "File" for papers you want to file back at the office. Inside the folder keep an index of your files so that you can determine quickly where you or your assistant should put the papers once you return.
- Carry a set of "action files" with labels such as "Call," "Discuss with _____," "Read," or "Write" for papers that require your action.
- Keep in your briefcase a well-organized store of office supplies that you may need on the road. For example, a small stapler, self-stick removable notes, highlighting marker, stationery, envelopes, and stamps. Keep a supply of return address labels on hand in case you need to mail things to yourself while on the road.

the material of which they're made. (See Brass on page 84 and Chrome on page 119, for example.)

Speed tips: You can remove ink marks caused by ballpoint pens quickly and easily from a finished leather surface by rubbing with a cloth or sponge sprayed with a little hair spray, says Mooers. The chemicals in the hair spray break down the ink. Ink marks may be impossible to remove from suede or nubuck.

In a pinch: You can mask small scrapes or nicks in finished leather by dabbing the area with a magic marker of a color similar to your briefcase's. For tiny scratches that haven't gone through the surface color, you can simply rub them out with your fingertips. The natural oils in your hands will make these disappear. For scuff marks, try rubbing on some shoe polish that is similar in color.

Caution: Never use harsh cleansers or abrasive pads to clean leather.

Brocade

Brocade refers to fabric that has been decorated with a raised woven design, often in an intricate floral pattern. Brocaded fabrics range from silk to synthetic materials and may be used for clothing, drapery, and upholstery. Because of the complex weaves, the best bet is often to leave the cleaning of brocaded fabric to the professionals. "Cleaning brocade yourself is an iffy task at best," says Leon Moser, extension specialist and fabric expert at North Carolina State University's College of Textiles in Raleigh.

Technique: For light cleaning of brocaded upholstery or drapes, vacuum gently using a brush attachment. For heavy soil or stains, take the item to a dry cleaner whom you trust. This is especially advised if the item is old or prized.

Caution: If the brocaded item is an heirloom, be sure to let the dry cleaner know.

Bronze

A cousin of brass, bronze is an alloy of copper and tin, used since ancient times in sculptures and other objects. Left unpolished and unlacquered, bronze quickly develops a greenish patina through oxidation. That's not always bad. In fact, in older pieces patina is considered an important part of the beauty of the object.

Technique: General cleaning of bronze objects is easy and should be done gently. The main thing you want to avoid is scratching the surface. For routine maintenance, just dust with a soft dry cloth such as an old T-shirt. If grime from the air has built up on the piece, dampen the cloth before rubbing the piece. Dry the object right away to prevent water spots.

Some bronze objects are lacquered to protect them from oxidation. Lacquered bronze does not need to be polished until the lacquer begins to wear away. When lacquered bronze does finally begin to tarnish, it must be completely removed before you polish or relacquer it. You can use any commercial lacquer thinner, available at hardware stores. Be sure to follow the directions carefully. Stubborn lacquer that has been baked on may have to be removed by a professional metalworker. Relacquering should also be done by a pro-

A Yard of Prevention

A bronze statue of a seated John Harvard has gazed down on generations of Harvard University students passing through the Yard in Cambridge, Massachusetts. Conservators cite the statue as being particularly well-maintained. That's quite a feat, considering that during football season the statue is a perennial target for pranksters from Yale, Dartmouth, or Brown, who are known to give John Harvard an unwanted coat of paint in their team's colors (blue, green, and brown, respectively).

To prepare the statue for the expected onslaught, workers give it a pre-football season coating of melted beeswax mixed with gum turpentine, explains Merle Bicknell, manager of Harvard Yard. They stir in some burnt umber and burnt sienna coloring to match the statue's dark patina. The mixture is then applied with paintbrushes, and the excess is patted off with cloths. "Basically, that prevents damage from vandalism, even when someone throws paint on it, or whatever," Bicknell says.

When an attack does occur (usually late at night), the university's 24-hour maintenance team springs into action. Workers wash the paint away before it has a chance to dry, using pressure washers and a water-soluble solvent.

fessional. Check your phone book for metal finishers, antique dealers, or even lighting repair shops to find a professional.

Unlacquered bronze will have to be polished as necessary to maintain its shine. Commercial brass polishes such as Brasso work well on bronze, says James W. McGann, vice president for quality at Virginia Metalcrafters in Waynesboro, which creates all the brass and bronze pieces used at Colonial Williamsburg. Home polishes will restore a shine, but getting them to like-new condition may require the skills of a professional metalworker using a buffing wheel and jeweler's rouge.

Speed tips: To add a quick shine to a small piece of bronze or copper, try rubbing it with a little ketchup. "If you want to see how this works, squirt a little bit on a penny," suggests McGann. "It'll brighten it up." Wipe away residue with a damp cloth.

In a pinch: You can make your own polish, says McGann, by mixing 1 tablespoon salt with 1 tablespoon flour. Stir in 1 tablespoon white vinegar. Apply the paste with a soft damp cloth, rub gently, rinse, and wipe dry with a dry soft cloth.

Caution: Never use harsh cleansers or abrasive pads to clean bronze. These can scratch the metal. Handle pieces as infrequently as possible. Oils from your fingers can leave permanent marks. If you have a piece of bronze that you think may be valuable or historically significant, don't polish it until you've had it examined by a professional conservator. If you use moisture when cleaning a bronze piece, dry it thoroughly afterward with a soft dry cloth to prevent spots from forming. Don't use spray waxes or furniture polishes. They'll just dull the shine.

Brushes—Hair

Periodic cleaning will keep your hairbrush from turning into a bird's nest of tangled hair and styling residue.

Technique: Whether your brush has natural or synthetic bristles, the best thing for it is a bath of warm soapy water. First, though, you will want to remove as much hair as possible. The best way to do this is to run a comb through the bristles. "Start pulling hair away from the base of the brush, working out to the tips," says Rebecca Viands, executive vice president of the Potomac Academy of Hair Design and a commissioner of the National Accrediting Commission of Cosmetology Arts and Sciences, both in Falls Church, Virginia.

Then, soak the brush in your sink in a sudsy mixture of warm water and mild liquid dishwashing detergent for 10 to 20 minutes, or long enough to remove hair oils and residue from styling products.

In most instances, particularly if you're the only one using the brush, the above cleaning method should suffice. If you're really finicky, or the brush has been used by multiple people, you may want to sanitize it by soaking it in a commercial bactericide or fungicide solution. These are available at professional beauty supply stores. Be sure to follow the instructions carefully.

Speed tips: Since brushes, combs, and curlers all do well in a warm soapy bath, you can save time and water by washing all these items together.

In a pinch: If a brush has become seriously fouled but you still want to save it, you can disinfect it by soaking it for about 15 minutes in a 10 percent solution of liquid household bleach and water. Then rinse thoroughly with plain water, says Viands.

Caution: Most brush handles are made of plastic, hard rubber, or coated metal and can stand up well to soaking. If you have your doubts, or if the brush is a prized item with a handle made of silver or some other valuable substance, try suspending the brush over a bowl of warm soapy water so that only the bristles are submerged.

Brushes—Paint

If you want to keep house painting brushes in good shape, the cleaning process should begin while you're still painting. Wait too long and your brush will stiffen up, maybe for good.

Technique: Cleaning methods depend on whether you're using oil-based or latex (water-based) paint. Regardless of the paint, though, one indispensable cleaning tool is a brush comb. Brush combs, available at paint stores, have long metal teeth that slip easily between the bristles of a paintbrush. A good brush comb will set you back $10 to $15. (As an inexpensive alternative, try a standard wire brush.) As you work, some paint is bound to get forced up near the heel of the brush, where it can begin to dry even as you paint. Whenever the brush begins to gunk up, run the comb or wire brush through it as if you were combing someone's hair, says Darryl Kaminski, senior product engineer for EZ Paint Corporation in Saint Francis, Wisconsin, one of the nation's largest paintbrush manufacturers.

Latex Paint

As you would expect, latex is easier to clean from brushes than is oil-based paint. Whenever painting with latex, use a synthetic brush. Natural-hair bristles are too absorbent and will become soft and mushy with a water-based paint. The best choice is a nylon-polyester blend, which combines the smooth application of nylon with the low absorbency of polyester.

When you are finished painting, hold the brush under a running tap, working your fingers through the brush, until it is clean. You can also swish the brush in a bucket of water. If you're having trouble getting the brush clean, add ¼ cup powdered laundry detergent such as Tide to the bucket, Kaminski says.

> ## Colossal Cleanups
>
> ### Alaskan Disaster
> The amount of oil spilled by the Exxon *Valdez* tanker in Prince William Sound on March 24, 1989: more than 10 million gallons

When the brush is clean, it's best to spin it dry. You can buy a brush spinner at a paint store or do it by hand. With the bristles pointing down, clasp your hands together with the brush handle between your palms. Then rub your hands back and forth as though trying to keep them warm. The circular motion will do a better job of drying the brush than if you simply shake it. Be sure to do this in a protected sink or bucket to prevent splatters. "That gets the best results. It spreads the bristles out," Kaminski says.

Hang the brush up to store it. The brush should be stored with a paper or cardboard form around the bristles to maintain their shape. If the form that came with your brush is gone, wrap the bristles in a heavy paper—a cut-up grocery bag will do.

Oil-Based Paint

When using oil-based paint, lacquer, or varnish, use a natural-hair brush such as hog's hair or ox hair. Natural brushes also include horsehair, but ox and hog are better because the bristles are naturally tapered, Kaminski says.

When you are finished painting, swish the brush in a pan or pail of recommended solvent or thinner such as one that contains MEK (methyl ethyl ketone) until clean, then rinse with water and a little soap powder and rinse clean. Follow with the same drying and hanging methods as for latex paint.

In a pinch: If a valued paintbrush has become really hardened with paint, it may not be a total loss. You can try dipping the brush in a liquid paint stripper (made for stripping old paint from walls) for about 20 seconds. Then proceed with the appropriate cleaning method for latex or oil. This method may not work. "But it's your last chance to salvage that brush," Kaminski says.

If you're in the middle of painting and get interrupted or need to stop for a break, you can wrap the brush in plastic wrap or aluminum foil and stick it in the freezer to keep it from drying out. Be sure to wrap it carefully to avoid leaks, and don't mistake the brush for a midnight snack.

Caution: Many liquid paint strippers are harsh and may irritate the skin. Wear rubber gloves when dipping the brush, and follow instructions carefully. Never store a brush resting on its bristles.

Don't throw away paint thinner after just one use—it can clean 8 to 10 brushes. Store the unused paint thinner back in the original container or in another jar or can. When discarding, don't wash it down a sink or throw it in the garbage. Instead, call your local recycling center and ask where you can take old thinner, Kaminski suggests.

Burns—Cigarette

Stains from cigarette burns may be reversible as long as the damage from the burn itself isn't too severe.

Technique: On clothing, "if it hasn't actually burned a hole in the fabric, a blot of water may take it out," says Jane Rising, instructor in the education department at the International Fabricare Institute in Silver Spring, Maryland. If plain water doesn't work, blot with mild laundry detergent and water. Rinse thoroughly with water. As a final step, try blotting the stain with a small amount of hydrogen peroxide.

For cigarette burns on carpet, mix ¼ teaspoon liquid dishwashing detergent per cup of lukewarm water. Use it to blot the stain with a white absorbent cloth or white paper towels. As a second step, rinse the area with lukewarm water and blot until dry, changing towels as needed. If these steps don't work, your next alternative is a professional carpet cleaner.

Speed tips: The quicker you attend to this or any stain, the better your chances of removing it.

Caution: Always test-clean an inconspicuous corner before attacking the stain to ensure that the cleaning method is safe for the material. When cleaning carpets, never use a stronger concentration than ¼ teaspoon liquid dishwashing detergent to 1 cup water. Residues of cleaning solutions may cause the carpet to get dirty faster. The stronger the concentration, the more likely residues will remain after rinsing. Never use laundry detergent on carpet. They contain optical brighteners that may dye the fiber. Blot carpet—don't scrub. Scrubbing may distort the pile.

Butcher Block

Like chapped hands, butcher blocks are susceptible to changes in humidity. In addition to regular cleaning, keep butcher blocks well-oiled to extend their life.

Technique: When you are finished preparing food on a butcher block, use a steel scraper or spatula with a wide blade to scrape away any scraps of food. Use a cloth to brush away remaining particles. Then dip a clean dishcloth in hot water mixed with soap or mild liquid dishwashing detergent and rub the surface of the wood. Rinse the

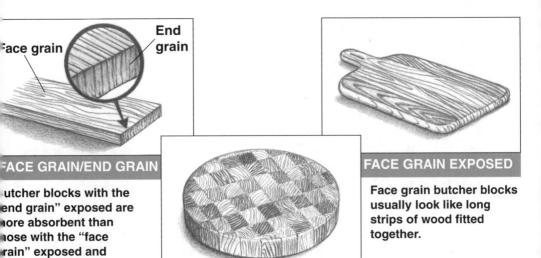

Face grain

End grain

FACE GRAIN/END GRAIN

Butcher blocks with the "end grain" exposed are more absorbent than those with the "face grain" exposed and should be treated with paraffin or beeswax in addition to mineral oil.

END GRAIN EXPOSED

End grain blocks tend to have a checkerboard pattern.

FACE GRAIN EXPOSED

Face grain butcher blocks usually look like long strips of wood fitted together.

cloth thoroughly in clear water, wring it out, and rub again. Use a different dry cloth and go over the surface until it is thoroughly dry, says Ken Ballard Jr., safety and quality engineer for John Boos and Company, a butcher block manufacturer based in Effingham, Illinois.

To prevent stains, clean butcher blocks immediately after using, and don't leave food sitting on the wood for extended periods. If stains do occur, you can gently rub them with a light-grade sandpaper or fine steel wool. Rub with the grain and then re-oil the board as explained later. Any remaining stain marks will eventually dissipate into the wood grain with regular cleaning and maintenance. Don't panic if dark streaks appear in the wood over time. These are caused by natural discoloring of the wood due to mineral deposits in the tree and simply add to the character and individuality of your piece.

Excessive dryness is bad for butcher blocks and, in serious cases, may cause the wood to split. Before the first use and once every several weeks (depending on how often you use the block and how dry the air is), coat the block with a layer of mineral oil. This will help keep the natural moisture in the wood and will also help prevent the wood from absorbing bacteria from raw meat and other food, according to Ballard. Do not use vegetable oil.

Butcher blocks with "face grain" wood on the surface need only mineral oil. Surfaces of "end grain" wood are more absorbent and need mineral oil mixed with melted paraffin. End grain refers to the top or bottom of a board that has been cut lengthwise from a tree. (For example, when a tree is cut down, the circle of exposed wood on the stump is end grain). Face grain refers to the sides of the boards. You can tell the two apart in butcher blocks because face grain surfaces tend to be made of long strips of wood fixed together, while end grain looks more like a checkerboard of wood squares.

To apply mineral oil to face grain, warm some oil by heating it in a microwave oven for 20 to 30 seconds or less. Or you can place the container of oil in a saucepan of very warm water. The amount of oil required depends on the dryness of the wood, but you will need at least six to eight ounces of oil for every two-foot-square section of block. Pour the warm oil over the block and spread it around the entire surface with a horsehair brush or a heavy cloth. Let it sit for four to five minutes. "If it soaks in real fast, you want to apply a second coat," Ballard says. "It's really a judgment call."

For end grain wood, melt some canning wax, or paraffin (available at grocery stores), in with the mineral oil in a ratio of about four parts oil to one part wax. Or buy premixed block oils, which are much easier to use and are available at your hardware store, a chef store, or through a chefs' products catalog. Pour the oil and wax over the block and spread around with a brush. If it soaks right in, add more. When the oil and wax have dried, some of the hardened wax will bead on the surface. Scrape this away with your scraper or metal spatula. To clean the brush, hold it under hot running water for about five minutes or until the oil and wax are removed.

Speed tips: You can help your butcher block stay young and lessen the frequency of oiling by using a humidifier in your home during dry winter months.

Caution: Always be sure to clean your butcher block thoroughly shortly after preparing food. As an added precaution against bacteria, use one block or section of a block for cutting meat, fish, and poultry, and another for cutting vegetables and other foods. Never use harsh detergents or cleansers to clean a butcher block, says Ballard. If your butcher block is installed near a stove or other heat source, be sure that there's proper insulation between them. Don't cut continuously in the same place. Spread your cuts around to even the wear. If you have to alter your butcher block or wooden cutting board by cutting it, immediately oil the cut end to prevent it from drawing in moisture and cracking, says Ballard.

Cabinets—Kitchen

Most solid wood and veneer kitchen cabinets are finished with a protective varnish that makes cleaning straightforward. Laminated surfaces are even easier.

Technique: For general cleaning on solid wood or veneer, simply wipe cabinets with a damp cloth and dry them with a soft dry towel. For grease or heavier grime, dip a cloth lightly in a solution of 1 gallon water mixed with ¼ cup mild soap such as Murphy Oil Soap. Clean up spills as quickly as possible to prevent permanent stains. After cleaning, wipe dry with a clean soft cloth.

Immediately after installation and once every six months, wood cabinets should be waxed. First, wipe with a damp cloth and then dry with a another soft dry cloth. Then give them a light coating of liquid or paste furniture wax that does not contain abrasive cleaners. Working on small areas at a time, rub the wax into the wood quickly (before the wax sets) applying in the direction of the wood grain. If you use a spray wax, spray the wax onto the cloth rather than directly onto the cabinet. "This treatment helps resist excessive moisture and prevents damage to the finish," says Jean Butler, vice president of marketing at Yorktowne Cabinets, a Pennsylvania cabinet manufacturer.

Laminated cabinets should be washed with the water and mild soap solution and a clean soft cloth, as with wood cabinets. Unlike wood cabinets, laminated ones don't need to be waxed.

Caution: Avoid harsh detergents and abrasive soaps or cleaners, all of which may damage the surface. Don't use your dishcloth to wipe cabinets. It may contain residues of detergents or grease. Excessive moisture is the primary enemy of wood products. Spills should be wiped up as quickly as possible. Check areas near sinks and major appliances regularly. Avoid mounting or placing appliances such as coffeemakers or toasters on counters directly under cabinets. Heat from these appliances could damage the cabinets.

Calculators

Computer keyboards are notorious dust collectors. And what's a calculator but a mini-keyboard? So it figures that they would be dust magnets, too. Keeping them clean is as easy as 1, 2, 3.

Technique: Wipe the keys occasionally with a static-free cloth and a cleaning fluid made for computers (both available at electronics and computer stores). Pour the fluid onto the cloth, not directly onto the keys. You can also buy pads that are presoaked.

In a pinch: You may use plain rubbing alcohol to rub down the keyboard and casing of the calculator, says Lisa Fasold, spokeswoman for the Consumer Electronics Manufacturers Association in Arlington, Virginia. But for the display screen it's still best to use an electronics cleaning solution (such as Endust for Electronics) since they're formulated to not damage delicate components.

Caution: Avoid household cleansers such as ammonia, powders, or abrasives, which may damage the calculator.

Camcorders

Sure, camcorders are meant to be used indoors and out. But they're delicate machines that must be protected from dust and moisture as well as extreme heat and cold. Leave the rough stuff to Bruce Willis.

Technique: The casing of the camcorder may be wiped with a soft dry cloth, but don't use any household cleaning products, especially liquids that may seep into the electronics. Wipe the lens periodically, especially if you're filming outdoors. Use a commercial lens cleaner made for cameras or camcorders. To clean the heads (the taping apparatus), use a head cleaner. This is a special cassette that cleans as it runs; it can be purchased at electronics stores.

Speed tips: "One thing every camcorder owner should have is a plastic bag," says Lisa Fasold, spokeswoman for the Consumer Electronics Manufacturers Association in Arlington, Virginia. Wrap the camcorder loosely to keep rain or other moisture from getting in. Thin clear bags such as those that come from the dry cleaner are good. But don't close tightly and leave for extended periods—that will trap moisture inside.

Caution: Never use a spray glass cleaner such as Windex to clean the lens. Never blow into the camcorder to clean out dust. Moisture from your saliva may rust components.

Cameos

True cameos are made of carved shell. Other materials such as coral, agate, or synthetics are sometimes substituted. Cameos, particularly if they are antiques, should be cleaned lightly and with care.

Technique: For general cleaning, rub the cameo gently with a soft damp (not wet) cloth to remove dust or other light dirt. If the item is prized and has a stain that won't come off with the damp cloth, take it to a conservator. "Don't go at it yourself," says Joyce Hill Stoner, Ph.D., professor of art conservation at the Winterthur/University of Delaware Program in Art Conservation in Newark. (For tips on finding a good conservator, see "Not Just Any Old Conservator Will Do" on page 53.)

Caution: Avoid using cleaning solvents of any kind on cameos. Don't confuse cameos with painted ivory pieces, which may be about the same size and, like cameos, usually depict a woman's face. Cameos are carved, while painted ivory is, as the name indicates, a painting. If you mistakenly rub a watercolor-painted ivory piece with a damp cloth, you may ruin it.

Cameras

You can buy all kinds of fancy (and expensive) stuff for cleaning your camera, but keeping your tools and your methods simple will cut costs and prevent you from damaging your gear through over-cleaning. "Avoid high-markup items," says Chuck DeLaney, dean of the New York Institute of Photography, the nation's oldest photography school, based in New York City. Four basic tools will arm you for just about any camera cleaning task. These include:

- A sable watercolor paintbrush (number 2, 3, or 4) with a fine point, available at art or hobby stores
- A palm-size, rubber bulb–type ear syringe, available at drugstores
- Microfiber cleaning cloths, available at camera stores: soft cloths with an ultrafine weave that will clean effectively without leaving lint behind; can be machine-washed and reused many times
- Camera lens cleaning fluid, also available at camera stores

You can buy combination blower-brushes at camera shops, but these are much more expensive than a simple ear syringe and sable paintbrush and are less effective. "They have too little blower and too much brush," DeLaney says.

Technique: Start with the exterior of the camera. Look it over carefully to see what is dirty. Always clean your camera under a bright light. Under a dim light, dirt and grime can easily hide in the shadows of crevices. Examine the lens and viewfinder for dust, dirt, grease, or fingerprints. If your camera is an automatic point-and-shoot model with a built-in lens, use the microfiber to wipe the entire exterior, excluding the lens. If the lens is removable, take it off before wiping the exterior. The cloth should get rid of most dust and dirt

HOW I DO IT

Camera Care on the Road

Professional photography assignments have taken Chuck DeLaney all over the world. As dean of the New York Institute of Photography in New York City, he offers some tips for caring for your camera when traveling or shooting outdoors.

Hit the beach with a decoy. A camera's two biggest enemies are excessive moisture and fine gritty sand. If you're going to be taking pictures at the beach, or in places with extreme humidity or dust, leave your expensive camera at home. Instead, take along a disposable camera or an inexpensive, waterproof point-and-shoot model. Even the disposable cameras take fine pictures these days, and an accident or damage won't break the bank.

Rescue it from salt. Should you drop an expensive camera in water, you may be able to save it. If it falls in salt water, remove the camera immediately and submerge as quickly as possible in a container of freshwater. Keep it submerged and take it to a camera repair shop quickly. You want to prevent salt water from drying and leaving corrosive deposits on the delicate parts. If it falls into freshwater, remove the camera from the water, dry it with a towel, then open it and allow the interior to dry with the back open. When it's dry, take it to a camera shop to be checked and relubricated.

Keep cool. Cameras hate heat almost as much as they do moisture and sand. Don't stick a camera or film in the glove compartment of your car, where the summer sun beating down raises temperatures to intolerable levels. Cameras sitting in the sun also can become too hot to handle. Keep them shaded whenever possible.

Skip the flashy cases. Whenever possible, use an old, beat-up looking case to hold your camera supplies, especially when traveling. "One that just says 'Steal me' is a big mistake," DeLaney says. "Those buffed aluminum bags say, 'Come and get it.'"

along with oils from your fingers and face. For heavier grime, you may dampen the cloth slightly with water.

In cleaning the lens, make sure not to scratch it by rubbing a speck of sand or dirt across it. Your first step involves the blower. Holding the tip about one-eighth inch from the lens, blow off any loose dust or dirt. Then use the sable brush to flick away stubborn dirt lodged in crevices. Once the dust and dirt are gone, wipe the lens with the microfiber cloth. For stubborn grime, you may breathe lightly on the lens to create a haze, then wipe. If that fails, try a couple of drops of lens-cleaning fluid on the cloth.

Once you're satisfied that the exterior is clean, make sure that there's no film inside and open the camera. Most cameras are well-sealed, and the interior should require light cleaning only. "Once you're inside the camera, the key word is *gentle*," DeLaney says.

Use the blower and the brush to gently clear away dirt and dust from the film chamber and the take-up reel (which rolls the film as it's used). Clean the back of the lens in the same way that you clean the front. Don't forget to wipe the pressure plate with the cloth or brush. This plate is attached to the camera door and presses the film in place. Blow or brush away dirt and dust from the trough where the door fits into the back of the camera.

Speed tips: A good waterproof camera cover (or even a plastic bag) will help prevent major cleaning jobs by keeping dust and dirt away from your camera and by blocking out moisture.

In a pinch: As a low-budget alternative to microfiber cloths, you can use sections cut from old T-shirts. Older T-shirts work best because the more times they've been washed, the softer they are. But even the oldest, softest T-shirt will leave some lint behind, which is why microfiber cloths are preferable. If you use a T-shirt, follow up with the blower.

Caution: Never use harsh cleaning solvents or soaps to clean your camera. Avoid using lens cleaners made for eyeglasses. These often leave a coating that is perfectly good for glasses but gunks up a camera lens. Some camera stores sell "canned air" to blow-clean your camera. These should be avoided because the air pressure is enough to damage delicate parts if used improperly, says DeLaney. The simple handheld blower is best.

Can Openers

Paper from labels, metal shavings, and food can get jammed up in the cutting assembly.

Technique: If your electric can opener has a removable cutting assembly, the assembly can be placed in the dishwasher. If it's not removable, use a toothbrush or a light scouring pad and some liquid dishwashing detergent to degunk the cutter. A toothpick is the best tool for removing paper labels that get wadded up in the cutter, says Fay Carpenter, manager of home economics at Black and Decker Corporation in Shelton, Connecticut. Wipe the plastic case with a soft damp cloth as part of your regular counter cleaning.

Caution: Be certain that the opener is unplugged before you begin to clean it.

Carpets

The dirt that you can't see can be even more nettlesome to carpets than visible dirt. Bits of dry soil and other debris love to hunker down in the pile of your carpet, where they go to work trying to ruin your investment. To keep carpets in great shape, you will want to establish a long and intimate relationship with your vacuum cleaner. Modern carpets are designed to reflect light and resist stains, making soil harder than ever to see. That's a positive feature, but it means that you should vacuum regularly even if the carpet does not appear to be dirty.

Technique: The Carpet and Rug Institute, based in Dalton, Georgia, recommends vacuuming entryways daily because this is where outside soil is deposited. If you can eliminate the soil before it spreads to other areas, you can lighten your housekeeping load. If that kind of routine won't fit your busy schedule, it's a good idea to take your vacuum cleaner for a spin at least a couple of times per week. Vacuuming frequently will catch more soil while it is still near the surface of your carpet. Once embedded, it is much more difficult to remove. Under foot pressure, the sharp edges of embedded particles will scar or even shear off fibers, distorting the light reflection and dulling the carpet's appearance. "It's just like scratching glass," says Michael Hilton, the institute's carpet-cleaning expert.

Vacuuming protects more than just your carpet. "Cleaning carpets

Air Out That New Carpet

New carpets give off gases known as volatile organic compounds. These may result from chemicals used to glue the carpet to its backing, dyes, stain-resistant treatments, or other sources. The American Lung Association says that few people become seriously ill from these fumes but that they can cause temporary eye, nose, and throat irritation; headaches; skin irritation; or fatigue.

When you install new carpet, the American Lung Association recommends that you:

- Vacuum your old carpet before it's removed (to cut down on dust and other pollutants being kicked up into the air)
- Ask your carpet dealer to allow the carpet to rest unrolled in a well-ventilated area for at least 24 hours before it's installed
- Ask your carpet dealer about newer, "low-emitting" carpets that have become available with the awareness of indoor air pollution
- Ventilate your room or rooms, if weather permits, by opening windows before and after installation or by using mechanical ventilation systems for two to three days if you have them in your house
- Consider having the carpet installed when family members are likely to be away from the house

regularly cuts down on indoor air pollution," says Leyla McCurdy, director of indoor air programs for the American Lung Association in Washington, D.C. "You want to get rid of dirt particles. If there's activity on a dirty carpet, you make them airborne. Then, you're inhaling them."

Vacuuming frequently is especially important if people with allergies live in the house because it will help protect against allergic reactions to dust mites. Vacuuming won't suck up the mites themselves—they're great at clinging fast to fibers. But it will remove mite droppings and body parts, and that's more important than getting the live ones. "Those are the pieces that become airborne and cause allergic reactions," says Thomas Platts-Mills, M.D., Ph.D., head of the division of asthma, allergy, and immunology at the University of Virginia Health Sciences Center in Charlottesville and director of its Asthma and Allergic Disease Center.

When vacuuming, it's best to use slow steady strokes, both pushing and pulling. Pulling the vacuum cleaner against the grain of the carpet stands the fibers up and exposes embedded soil. Repeat several times over each area. Each stroke removes more particles. Make all of your final strokes in the same direction to leave a uniform ap-

Carpet Stains: Out, Out Darn Spots

No carpet, not even modern carpet designed to resist stains, is entirely stainproof. Your best chance for removing stains is to attend to them as quickly as possible.

Always blot liquid stains with dry, white absorbent cloths or white paper towels with no printing on them. With semi-solids, remove as much as you can with a rounded spoon before using stain-removal procedures. The Carpet and Rug Institute, based in Dalton, Georgia, offers the following methods for dealing with specific stains. In each case, call a professional if your own efforts fail or if the stain seems too serious to handle yourself.

Alcoholic beverages: Mix ¼ teaspoon liquid dishwashing detergent in 1 cup lukewarm water. Blot the stain area with the solution, then rinse thoroughly with warm water. You may have to rinse several times to fully remove the solution. If the stain persists, try blotting it with a mixture of 2 tablespoons household ammonia per cup of water. Rinse thoroughly. Then blot the stain with a solution of 1 cup white vinegar to 2 cups water and rinse thoroughly with warm water.

Banana: First blot the stain with a commercial spot remover such as Carbona Stain Devils, available at supermarkets or discount department stores. Pour fluid onto a cloth rather than directly onto the carpet and blot the stain. Rinse thoroughly. If the stain persists, try the dishwashing detergent solution above, then rinse with warm water.

Cola: The methods are the same as for alcoholic beverages. If those steps fail, try using a spot-removal kit, available from most carpet retailers. Follow the directions carefully. These kits often contain a stain-resisting solution to be applied after using a detergent solution that is also included. Applying the stain-resisting solution before the stain is completely gone may make it permanent.

Egg: Same as for alcoholic beverages.

Fruit, fruit juice, jam, jelly: Same as for cola.

Ice cream or milk: First, blot the stain with a commercial spot remover such as Carbona Stain Devils or K2r, available at supermarkets, hardware stores, or discount department stores. Rinse thoroughly. Next, try the dish-

pearance. A vacuum with rotary brushes is best for loosening soil. Keeping your vacuum cleaner well-maintained increases its effectiveness.

Regardless of how often you vacuum, your carpet should be deep cleaned at least every 18 months, or more frequently if it's in a high-traffic area, by you or a professional cleaner. Always vacuum before deep cleaning. There are several reliable deep cleaning methods, some of which require special equipment that can be rented at washing liquid solution described for alcoholic beverages. Rinse thoroughly. If the stain persists, try blotting it with a mixture of 2 tablespoons household ammonia per cup of water. Rinse thoroughly. Then blot the stain with a solution of 1 cup white vinegar to 2 cups water and rinse thoroughly with warm water.

Iodine: Same as for ice cream or milk.

Ketchup: Same as for cola.

Lipstick or lip gloss: As a first step, blot the stain with some nail polish remover. Be certain to rinse thoroughly. Next, blot the stain with a commercial spot remover such as Carbona Stain Devils or K2r, available at supermarkets, hardware stores, or discount department stores. Rinse thoroughly. Next, try the dishwashing liquid solution described for alcoholic beverages. Rinse thoroughly. If that fails, blot with the ammonia solution described for alcoholic beverages. Rinse thoroughly. Try the solution of 1 cup white vinegar to 2 cups water. Rinse thoroughly with warm water. As a final step before calling a professional, try the spot-removal kit described under cola. Then find out who has been kissing your carpet.

Peanut butter: The first step is to blot with commercial spot remover such as Carbona Stain Devils or K2r, available at supermarkets, hardware stores, or discount department stores. Rinse thoroughly. Next, try the dishwashing liquid solution described for alcoholic beverages. Then rinse thoroughly with warm water.

Note: For more information on spot removal, or for tips on hiring a professional, you can write to the Carpet and Rug Institute at P. O. Box 2048, Dalton, GA 30722.

Caution: Always test cleaning methods on an inconspicuous section of carpet before using them on the stain to be certain that your carpet can withstand the given method or solution. Never use laundry detergent on a carpet. These contain optical brighteners that may dye the fibers. Don't use automatic dishwasher detergent, which may contain bleaching agents. Be sure to rinse thoroughly between each step when removing stains. Different cleaning solutions don't always mix well. Carefully read product labels for proper usage and safety precautions.

appliance rental centers. The simplest methods include dry extraction (brushing in an absorbent cleaner, then vacuuming it out) and dry foam extraction (spreading a layer of foam on the carpet, then vacuuming it out). Dry extraction powders are widely available under brand names such as Host and Capture. Woolite, Shout, and Resolve are some of the major dry foam brands. The dry extraction or foam methods are good medium steps between vacuuming and deep cleaning and should be used as needed.

"I have a white carpet in my great room with a marble kitchen next to it. The marble gets dirty easily, and the soil tracks to the nearest carpet surface," Hilton says. "A three-foot-square area gets especially dirty. I use a dry absorbent compound about once a month. I sprinkle it on, scrub it in with a brush, and vacuum it up."

For more thorough cleaning, you can buy or rent a steam cleaner. They can be found at appliance rental centers and even some supermarkets. They're fairly easy to use, but be certain to follow instructions carefully to avoid overwetting the carpet or applying too much cleaning solution.

Even if you vacuum and deep clean regularly, it's a good idea to call in a professional at least every two to three years, more frequently if you've skimped on your own cleaning routine, says Hilton. Most professionals use hot-water extraction or steam cleaning. "Rotary shampoo" and "absorbent pad" methods involve machines that work something like a floor buffer to whisk soil away and only should be used by a professional. The rotary shampoo machine injects a cleaning solution through brushes. The absorbent pad method lifts soil into a pad. For any deep cleaning, it's best to choose whichever method the manufacturer of your carpet suggests. Some warranties will become void if other methods are used. It's also time to call a professional if your own efforts to remove a spot or stain fail.

Speed tips: A simple floor mat placed at each door to the outside can trap much of the soil that would otherwise find its way into your carpet. But it's important to keep these mats cleaned regularly themselves, if only with a good stiff beating outdoors. Otherwise, the mats will fill with soil just like a sponge with water and will actually become a source of soil spread to your carpet.

In a pinch: Place furniture glides or cups under heavy furniture to prevent depression marks from permanently marring your carpet. Also, move the furniture a few inches periodically. If you already have depression marks, work the pile back into place with a coin, then apply steam with a steam iron held two to four inches above the carpet for a few minutes. But don't allow the hot iron to touch the carpet directly.

Caution: When deep cleaning the carpet yourself, follow all instructions carefully, including the recommended strength and dilution for cleaning solutions. Remove furniture from the room until the carpet is completely dry to avoid furniture stain or rust from bleeding onto the carpet. If the furniture is too heavy to remove, place foil or plastic wrap under and around the legs.

Cleaning solutions that are not completely rinsed from carpet can attract dirt. Use ventilation, fans, and heating and air-conditioning units to help dry carpet. If left wet for more than a full day, mold or mildew may develop.

Vacuuming your carpet is bound to kick up some soil. If you are allergy-prone, wear a dust mask.

Cars

There's no set timetable for washing your car. A lot depends on where and how you drive it and whether it sleeps in a garage or under the stars—not to mention, of course, how finicky you are. Are you a car snob or a car slob? For the former, washing a car is an act of love worthy of endless hours of elbow grease. For the latter, a good hard rain suffices. Wherever you fit on the scale, it's important to remember that cleaning your car regularly can extend its life, boost its resale value, and possibly prevent costly repairs.

Manufacturers offer a dizzying array of cleaning products allowing you to get as detailed in your car cleaning as you wish. But for the average car owner, there are a few procedures you need to know.

Body

Wash your car's exterior as needed, and wax or polished it at least twice a year, or when water stops beading on the surface. Wash it frequently enough to "keep the car from becoming so dirty that cleaning becomes a major job," suggests Danny Cooke, a car maintenance and repair specialist with the American Automobile Association in Richmond, Virginia.

Technique: Automotive supply stores sell soap solutions specially made for cleaning car bodies. These are a good safe bet because they are certain to be effective and gentle, says Cooke. As an alternative, make a solution of mild liquid dishwashing detergent and water. Add enough soap to generate good suds, and add more as needed during the cleaning process to keep the suds going. Before washing, hose the car down thoroughly. This not only will make cleaning easier but also will help prevent dirt and debris from scratching the car.

Using a clean cloth or towel dipped frequently in the suds, carefully wash the entire exterior of the car, moving from top to bottom. Be sure not to neglect the out-of-the-way places. For example, open

HOW I DO IT

My Ugly Old Beauty

As a noted automobile historian, James A. Ward, Ph.D., would be the first to tell you that his turquoise six-cylinder 1965 Chevrolet Biscayne is not a car that serious collectors would fight over. But it was a wedding gift from his parents that year, and so the car has special significance. More than three decades and 180,000 miles later, Ward still drives the Biscayne daily and keeps it in pristine condition. Here's how.

"I don't wash my car more than once or twice a year because I never let it get dirty," says Dr. Ward, a professor of history at the University of Tennessee at Chattanooga. "I keep it in the garage at night and park in a covered space at work. Each morning, I dust the exterior to a shine before getting in. I use special dust cloths from a mail-order company called Kozak in Buffalo, New York, that come impregnated with a special cleaning oil.

"About once a year, I wash the vinyl upholstery with a solution of ammonia and water, applied with a sponge. The rest of the interior, which is also vinyl, gets an application of Armor All, the tire stuff. This keeps the vinyl from drying out.

"Chevrolets from the 1960s have a problem with water collecting under a chrome strip running around the base of the back window. Next time you see a Chevy from that era, look at the back, and you may see duct tape where the area has rusted out. I remove the water with a hypodermic needle inserted under the chrome.

"I'm a saver. I still have the original spare tire and the original windshield washer fluid stored away, though both are too old to use. The Biscayne wasn't exactly the cream of the General Motors crop. It's an ugly car. But I'm ugly, too," Dr. Ward jokes. "I have an affinity for things that look like me. I'm slow but I keep rambling along, just like my Biscayne. You are what you drive."

the doors and wipe down the door posts. This will help prevent corrosion, and will also prevent those annoying dirt marks on your clothes when you brush the posts getting into your car. Lift each windshield wiper and run the cloth along the blade.

One of the most important steps in washing a car, particularly if it's parked outdoors for extended periods, is to remove leaves and other debris that work their way into crevices. Open the trunk and clean out the trough that runs around the edge. The trough diverts water from the trunk interior, but if it gets backed up, you may find yourself with soggy luggage. Do the same for the troughs in your sunroof, if you have one, to prevent water from backing up and dripping on you when you drive.

When you've finished washing, be sure to dry the entire car using soft clean cloths or towels, or a chamois cloth. Don't let the car air-dry, as that may leave spots. Whenever possible, wash the car out of direct sunlight, to avoid having parts of the car dry before you've had a chance to dry them by hand.

Use a liquid or paste auto wax to finish the job. Each type has its devotees, but both work fine. Liquid wax is easier to apply. Either way, carefully follow the instructions on the container. Waxing is for more than just aesthetics—it adds a protective coating and dirt is more likely to slide right off your car.

Speed tips: The most obvious speed tip, of course, is to take your car to a car wash. But there are other timesaving measures you can take. To save time and effort during the buffing stage of waxing, you can buy an orbital power buffer at auto parts stores for less than $100. The professionals use rotary buffers, which spin in an exact circle at high speeds. In inexperienced hands, though, it's easy to mess up a paint job with a rotary buffer. The better choice is an orbital buffer, which rotates in an irregular pattern, more closely representing the hand-polishing motion. Even with an orbital buffer you must use a light touch to avoid damage.

Note: Use a toothbrush to remove excess wax from the nameplate, crevices, and other hard-to-reach spots.

Caution: Bird droppings and tree sap should be cleaned up as quickly as possible. They should come off easily if caught early. Over time, they'll eat into a paint job. Never use harsh detergents or abrasive cleansers to wash your car's body. These may scratch the surface or fade the paint. Never wash a car without wetting it down thoroughly first. If possible, wash the car out of direct sunlight. Wait two to four weeks after having body work done to wax your car. Paint jobs from a body shop may require time to properly cure.

Carpet

When vacuuming your car's carpet, tap the carpet firmly and frequently with the vacuum nozzle to dislodge sand and other gritty dirt that becomes embedded.

Engine

Today's auto engines are governed by sophisticated electrical systems and onboard computers that make cars more reliable than ever before. Unfortunately, their complexity means that weekend tinkering just isn't what it used to be. Dislocate the wrong gadget and you could throw the whole system out of whack. The same goes for cleaning an engine. Unless you're an experienced mechanic, any cleaning you do under the hood should be careful and light.

Technique: The best thing you can do under the hood is to clear out leaves and other debris. "You're not worried about appearance here. You just want to keep the crud out," says Cooke. Debris collects in the cowl area, just below the windshield wipers, where fresh air is sucked into the cabin of the car. This should be removed. Also brush debris away from the water troughs on either side of the en-

How to Spot a Good Car Wash

Sure, there's satisfaction in doing things for yourself, and that includes staring at your own smiling reflection in the shiny hood of the car you just spent hours washing and buffing. Still, there are many times when paying a professional is the best way to go. One of the main reasons that car wash customers cite is convenience, says Tina Gonsalves, spokeswoman for the International Carwash Association in Chicago. "It saves a big hassle," she says.

Professional car washes also are bound to be more thorough than average car owners, says Gonsalves, particularly in cleaning such hard-to-reach areas as the undercarriage, where salt and other corrosive substances can hide unseen.

As a third benefit, professional car washes offer environmental advantages, Gonsalves says. When homeowners rinse their cars off, the dirty soapy water runs untreated into storm drains or the surrounding land. Professional car washes are required under the Clean Air Act to dispose of wastewater into the sanitary sewer system. Increasingly, car washes are recycling and reusing water in a voluntary effort to reduce water consumption.

So, how do you choose a good car wash? Most professional car washes today use "touchless" or "soft cloth" methods that are gentle on your car's finish. Still, the array of choices as you drive in can seem vast. Don't allow yourself to be rushed, Gonsalves advises. "The operator should be able to tell you about every piece of the car wash package," Gonsalves says. "If the operator is not able to explain those things, choose another car wash."

Take a good look at the appearance of the business. If it's dirty, that's a good sign they're less than vigilant in washing cars. If the staff is unfriendly, they may be equally unfriendly to your car. Finally, don't be shy about bringing poor service to the attention of the manager. He or she should be courteous in resolving any questions or problems you have with the way your car was handled.

gine. If your car's radiator (located just behind the grille) is fairly accessible, use a low-pressure garden hose to wash debris away. You may also turn the hose on the firewall, which separates the engine from the passenger compartment.

Caution: Never spray a high-pressure hose directly on the engine. Water could work its way under seals and damage delicate electrical systems. Never dislodge an engine part in order to clean it. Any heavy-duty engine cleaning should be done by a professional.

Tires

Using the same solution for washing the body, scrub tires with a stiff-bristle nylon brush until clean. For whitewalls that have become particularly dirty, you may scrub with a product specially made for cleaning tires or a stronger household detergent or a cleanser such as Comet. This is the only part of the car where such cleansers are recommended.

You may want to give your tires a shine by applying a commercial tire dressing such as Armor All. These products are largely cosmetic. But hey, if the rest of your car is sparkling, why not have tires to match?

Windows

Any spray-on window cleaning solution will do a good job on car windows. You can make your own solution by filling a plastic spray bottle with an ammonia-water solution: 1 tablespoon ammonia per gallon of water, says Cooke. Rub inside and outside windows with clean paper towels. Some car buffs insist that old newspapers are best for wiping windows because they don't leave a lot of lint. Others, such as Cooke, say that it's just a good way smudge your fingers with ink.

On hot summer days, use one of those cardboard sunshades that fit between your window and your dashboard, even if it makes you feel like a prima donna. It'll do more than just keep the driver's seat from singeing your bare legs. A shade will help keep the windshield clean. How? When plastics—such as those used in modern dashboards—get hot, they emit solvents that can leave a haze on the inside glass. To remove that haze, pour some isopropyl alcohol on a clean soft cloth and rub.

Cassettes

You can never watch *The Wizard of Oz* too many times. Which is why keeping your videocassettes and audiocassettes clean is important. Clean cassettes last longer, and they keep your VCR and cassette deck running longer, too. Fortunately, keeping them clean is about as simple as clicking your heels together.

Technique: The outer shell of a videocassette or audiocassette may be wiped with a dry, soft static-free cloth, but there is really no way to clean the tape itself. The best way to keep dust from gathering on tapes is to return them to their cases immediately after using. Cleaning your tape player or VCR with head cleaners (cassettes specially designed to clean inside the machine) will prolong the life of your cassettes and the machine, says Lisa Fasold, spokeswoman for the Consumer Electronics Manufacturers Association in Arlington, Virginia. This is especially important if you rent movies frequently because you are transferring dust from many other VCRs into your own every time you play a rented tape.

Caution: Don't leave videotapes inside the machines. The VCR is always "on," at least to run the clock, and, over time, heat can harm the tape.

Ceilings

You don't walk on them and you rarely even touch them, but still they get dirty. Tiny bits of dirt, dust, and other floating particles attach to a ceiling and make it look dim or dingy. For light cleaning jobs, the dry method is best. Heavy-duty dirt may require a detergent solution.

Technique: For conventional cleaning of smooth ceilings, simply dusting may work fine. "I'm a big believer in lamb's wool dusters," says Cliff Zlotnik, owner of Unsmoke/Restorx, a property restoration and cleaning company in Braddock, Pennsylvania, and a member of the Association of Specialists in Cleaning and Restoration in Annapolis Junction, Maryland. "They remove dust, particulate, and loose soil very effectively." Lamb's wool dusters can be purchased at cleaning supply stores, with extension poles that will reach most ceilings.

If the duster doesn't do the trick, or for ceilings stained by soot, you may need to get on a ladder and rub by hand: Rub grime-darkened areas with a putty wallpaper cleaner or a dry, foam-rubber sponge (available at hardware stores, janitorial supply stores, and paint stores) that is specially designed to rub dirt away from walls and ceilings. Place a drop cloth under the ladder to catch debris.

For more serious cleaning jobs, mix 2 to 3 ounces of a household detergent such as Spic and Span in 1 gallon water, and then rub the ceiling with a sponge dipped in the solution. A drop cloth is essential here because you're bound to drip. To prevent bead marks on the ceiling, dry thoroughly with a clean cloth or towel.

Textured ceilings present more of a challenge. You don't want to rub them, or else you may break small pieces of the ceiling off. And they're too absorbent to use a lot of water on. Dust gently, or vacuum using a brush attachment. You may also try lightly spraying dirty spots with a mixture of hydrogen peroxide and water, using mixture amounts recommended on the container. You don't need to wipe this away. If textured ceilings become seriously stained or dirty, the best option may be to paint over them, using a paint sprayer.

In a pinch: If you can't get to the paint store for a foam-rubber sponge or putty wallpaper cleaner, you may rub the ceiling with a hunk of stale crumbly bread, which will scrub without doing damage. Or pat the area with tape.

Caution: Always use a drop cloth when washing or scrubbing ceilings. Use goggles to protect your eyes from drips. Professional cleaners sometimes use harsh chemicals when cleaning ceilings, but these should not be used by inexperienced cleaners.

Chandeliers

Don't forget to glance upward once in a while during your regular cleaning routine. Chandeliers attract a lot of dust and will shine brighter if attended to regularly.

Technique: For light cleaning, run a feather duster lightly over the chandelier, or use a blow-dryer to blow the dust away from delicate parts. For more extensive cleaning, see listings elsewhere in this book for cleaning the metallic parts (Brass on page 84 and Chrome on page 119, for example). To clean glass or crystal prisms, you may want to remove the individual prisms, being careful not to twist or snap the wires that attach them to the chandelier. Use a spray glass cleaner and a clean soft cloth to wipe them down. Or make your own spray mixture using 90 percent distilled water and 10 percent rubbing alcohol. Distilled water is preferable to plain because it contains fewer minerals that can leave spots.

Speed tips: As an alternative to removing the prisms—a time-consuming task—try giving them the white-glove treatment. Put on a soft, white cotton glove. Then, spray the prisms and gently rub them with your gloved hand. "Cotton gloves allow you to grab the prism without straining the wire loop that attaches it," says Martin L. King, a restoration consultant in Arlington, Virginia, and technical advisor to the National Institute of Disaster Restoration in Annapolis, Maryland. "It's a very efficient way to clean them."

Caution: Be sure to move around the chandelier as you clean it rather than staying in one place and twisting it. Even if you're working on a ladder, reposition the ladder periodically. Twisting the chandelier might unscrew it from the ceiling, causing it to crash to the floor. Place soft blankets on the floor or table beneath the chandelier to prevent prisms from shattering if they drop.

Chimneys

Chimneys get dirty when creosote builds up along the flue—something like cholesterol in a blood vessel. Creosote, which is released when wood burns, rises in the smoke and condenses as it passes the relatively cool walls of the flue. You can slow the process by being sure that the fire has an adequate air supply, so keep the damper and glass doors of the fireplace fully open. There's no way to completely prevent creosote from building up over time, however. Left untreated, creosote can make your fireplace burn less efficiently or even lead to a chimney fire.

Technique: Cleaning a chimney is a messy and potentially dangerous affair. It requires special brushes that are precisely fitted to the size of your flue, and plenty of drop cloths to protect the inside of your home. Depending on the configuration of your fireplace and chimney, it may be possible to sweep from the inside of the house. If not, a trip to the roof is required. In any case, unless you have special experience cleaning chimneys, it's best to hire a competent professional chimney sweep.

Have your chimney inspected once a year and cleaned as necessary. "Most fireplaces don't need to be cleaned every year, but they certainly need to be inspected," says Ashley Eldridge, director of education for the Chimney Safety Institute of America and technical di-

Keep Your Cool during a Chimney Fire

Chimney fires occur when creosote that has built up on the flue ignites. Keeping your chimney clean will help prevent such fires. Fires can be large or small, but they all should be taken seriously, says Ashley Eldridge, director of education for the Chimney Safety Institute of America and technical director for the National Chimney Sweep Guild, both in Gaithersburg, Maryland.

If a fire starts in your flue, first account for everyone in the house and have them leave the house. Then call the fire department. This is a good idea even if you think the fire is small. Chimney fires are difficult to gauge. In serious cases, they can spread to other parts of the house.

Until help arrives, you can try dumping some ice cubes onto the fire in the hearth. This will create steam that may dampen the fire as it rises. If the fire occurs in a wood stove, cut off the draft controls. This will cut the air supply to the fire.

For an open fireplace, some people suggest draping a wet blanket over the opening of the fireplace. If you try this, though, you must be sure you can hold the blanket securely in place. Chimney fires create a powerful draft that could suck the blanket into the fire. Do not try to put out the fire by pouring or spraying water down the chimney. Cold water combined with the heat of the fire can easily cause the flue tiles to crack.

Once the fire has been put out, have a certified chimney sweep inspect the chimney before you use it again. Even if you don't notice any damage, the flue could be cracked.

rector for the National Chimney Sweep Guild, both in Gaithersburg, Maryland.

Even if you leave the cleaning to the professionals, there are steps you can take to keep your chimney cleaner for a longer time, starting with the wood you burn. As a rule, the type of wood is less important than the condition of the logs. A dense wood such as hickory will release more creosote per log than a lighter wood such as pine. But you'll need to burn more pine logs to keep the fire going, so there's no particular benefit either way, Eldridge says.

It's far more important to ensure that the logs, whatever the type, are dry. Moist wood burns less efficiently than dry. The more moist the wood is, the cooler the fire will be. The cooler the fire is, the more slowly smoke will rise through the chimney and the more time there will be for deposits to form on the flue. Freshly cut logs should be aged for a minimum of six months. Even aged logs can get waterlogged if stored improperly. Wood stored outdoors should be stacked on pallets, allowing air to circulate underneath. Cover the

How to Find a Sweep You Can Keep

A shoddy cleaning job could damage your chimney or other parts of your home—and jeopardize the safety of the contractor. Ashley Eldridge, director of education for the Chimney Safety Institute of America (CSIA) and technical director for the National Chimney Sweep Guild, offers the following tips for hiring competent help.

Check certification. Ask if the contractor is certified by the Chimney Safety Institute of America, a national organization that trains and certifies some 1,500 sweeps nationwide. The contractor should be able to show you a CSIA photo ID. Also ask whether the contractor is a member of the National Chimney Sweep Guild, the trade association.

Ask about insurance. Make sure that the contractor carries liability insurance, covering both injury and damage, in case something goes wrong. An uninsured contractor who is injured could turn around and sue the homeowner for medical expenses. If your home or chimney is damaged by an uninsured contractor, you may wind up footing the bill out of your own homeowner's policy. For added assurance, you may ask that the contractor's insurer send you certification verifying the coverage.

Look for experience. CSIA certification means that the sweep knows what he is doing. But one who has been in business for at least five years will be experienced enough to handle just about any situation.

Call references. A reputable contractor should be able to provide good references from past jobs. Also contact the local Better Business Bureau to see if there are any unresolved complaints outstanding against your prospective contractor.

stack with a waterproof tarpaulin. If possible, keep the stack in a sunny place. Allow logs to dry indoors for a week before burning. If you use the fireplace all the time, you may want to add an intermediate stage between the big stack outdoors and your indoor supply. You can buy a rack at most hearth stores that will keep a week's supply of wood within easy reach by your back door. Cover that with a tarp, too.

Another way to slow the creosote buildup is to light fewer fires during mild-temperature days in the spring and fall. Chimneys draw most efficiently when the air outside is much colder than the air inside your home. When the temperatures are closer together, smoke rises more sluggishly, leaving more time for deposits to build.

If smoke seems to be rising slowly or if your fires burn weakly no matter what the time of year or what kind of wood you're using, you may have a design defect in your chimney or the chimney may need cleaning. It's a good time to have a professional take a look.

In a pinch: Those imitation logs you can find at the supermarket have gotten a bad rap because of concerns about the waxy material used to bind them. "Actually, they're quite good," Eldridge says. "The reality is that they burn quite nicely. It's about as close as you can get to a controlled fire." They produce a relatively even flame and are reliable and easy to light.

Caution: Don't attempt to clean your chimney yourself unless you have experience. Avoid burning freshly cut wood, also known as green wood.

China

It's always best to wash china dishes by hand, although newer china will do well in the dishwasher.

Technique: To wash by hand, first place a rubber guard, available at housewares stores, on the faucet to prevent chipping. Place a rubber mat or double-folded towel on the bottom of the sink. If it's a divided sink, drape a rubber mat over the divider. Wash in a sinkful of warm water, using any liquid dishwashing detergent and a nonabrasive pad or sponge. To wash figurines or sculptures, use mild soap and warm water, and gently pat dry with a soft cloth.

When cleaning a figurine or sculpture with a wooden base, you don't want to get it wet. Instead of soap and water, just dust it lightly and often as part of your routine chores.

Speed tips: Most china made within the past 25 years will stand up to washing in a dishwasher. But you need to take some precautions. Each item should be loaded carefully but securely to prevent chipping. Use a mild automatic dishwasher detergent such as Cascade. For machine-washing, powders are preferable to liquids because they tend to be more gentle. Avoid detergents that contain lemon because they tend to cause spotting. Make sure that the dishwasher racks haven't worn through the rubber coating, exposing metal. The metal could chip the dishes or leave rust stains. Use the china setting if your dishwasher has one. If not, use a normal cycle. Allow china to cool to room temperature before unloading.

In a pinch: If you have no plate protectors (quilted pads that are sold in department stores), paper towels will do the trick.

Caution: When placing china items in a dishwasher, make sure that they are separated from metal objects that could chip them during washing. China that is 25 years old or older should always be hand-washed. Avoid abrasive cleaners when hand-washing china.

"When storing your china, always use plate protectors between the pieces to prevent scratching," says Alice Kolator, spokeswoman for Lenox, the china and crystal manufacturer in Lawrenceville, New Jersey.

Chocolate Stains

When chocolate melts on your clothes, not in your mouth, quick action is your best hope for coming out clean.

Technique: Milk chocolate and dark chocolate are different types of stains. For milk chocolate, first, blot the stain with cold water. If you can't get it out that way, blot with mild laundry detergent and water. Rinse thoroughly with water. If the stain persists, blot it with the detergent and water solution, with a few drops of ammonia added. Rinse thoroughly with water. If the stain persists, try blotting with an enzyme-based detergent such as Tide.

For dark chocolate, perform the first two steps. Rinse thoroughly with water. If the stain persists, then mix some white vinegar with the detergent and water, and blot. Rinse thoroughly with water. As a final step, try blotting the stain with a small amount of hydrogen peroxide.

Note: Rinsing thoroughly with water between steps is necessary to prevent mixing potentially incompatible solutions.

Speed tips: If you don't have the time or the patience to clean a stain slowly and deliberately, your best bet is a dry cleaner. This is also a good idea if the stain is particularly large or stubborn, or if the garment is one you adore. "If they're precious items, items of value, take them to a dry cleaner," says Jane Rising, instructor in the education department at the International Fabricare Institute in Silver Spring, Maryland.

In a pinch: If the stain happens at work or someplace else where you can't get to cleaning supplies, flushing immediately in cold water may do the trick.

Caution: Be sure to test any cleaning method on a small obscure corner of the fabric before attacking the stain, even if you've used the method before, to make sure that the colors and the fabric can withstand the cleaning. If you can't completely remove a chocolate stain, don't just decide to "live with it." An incompletely cleaned stain may well attract insects. If your methods fail, it's time to get professional dry-cleaning help.

Chrome

Chrome, found in everything from bathroom fixtures to decorative car parts, is not a solid metal like aluminum or steel. Rather, it's the result of a plating process. That's why cleaning must be gentle. Pitted or otherwise damaged chrome is difficult or impossible to repair and must be replaced.

Technique: For routine cleaning, use a spray glass cleaner and a soft clean cloth. "You don't want to use anything abrasive because it will eventually wear through the surface," says Randy Robinson, owner of Robinson's Chrome in Hughson, California, which makes customized chrome and metal products. Chrome can be brought to a shine (and protected) with an application of carnauba wax, available at automotive stores. Before applying the wax, clean the chrome with a solution of ¼ cup liquid dishwashing detergent to 1 gallon water. Wash with a soft cloth and dry. Then wax according to the product's directions.

In a pinch: As a substitute for commercial window cleaner, you can fill a spray bottle with club soda or a teaspoon of baking soda mixed with a quart of warm water. These are slightly less effective than the commercial cleaners but work nicely for routine jobs, Robinson says. To remove tough spots such as paint or tar, apply some paint thinner or lacquer thinner sparingly to a cloth and wipe the spot. To add a shine to chrome fixtures, try rubbing them with a little toothpaste.

Caution: Never use gritty abrasive cleansers on chrome. Over time, these will wear down the plating. Once that happens, the chrome is a goner.

Cleats

The best time to clean muddy athletic cleats is right after a game. The longer they sit, the tougher the mud will be to remove.

HOW I DO IT

A Mud Story

Lambeau Field, home of the 1996 Super Bowl champion Green Bay Packers, has witnessed some of the greatest games in National Football League history. But when bad weather turns that hallowed shrine into a muddy mess, assistant equipment manager Tim O'Neill and others on the Packers' equipment staff must keep players' cleats free of mud and turf from the opening kickoff to the final gun.

"Dry games and really wet games usually aren't a problem," O'Neill says. "When it's raining hard, the mud slides right off. It's the in-between weather that causes the problems. A day or two after a rain, the ground is wet enough to be muddy but dry enough that it cakes.

"Most of the players have cleats on the bottom of their shoes that are $5/8$ inch or $3/4$ inch long. It doesn't take more than one play for cleats to get gunked up, so we roam the sidelines constantly throughout the game. One or two swipes with a putty knife or wire brush usually does the trick. When the defense is on the field, we'll take care of the whole offensive line at once.

"During time-outs, we run onto the field with 'cleat boards,' which are molded boards with plastic or rubber spikes sticking out. Players wipe the bottoms of their shoes on the cleat boards, just like a doormat.

"Nobody's going to confuse cleaning cleats with throwing the winning touchdown or returning a kickoff 99 yards, but it's exciting to be part of the action, and you really feel that you're doing your part. A little thing like clean cleats can make a difference in a game."

Technique: If your cleats have gotten really covered, the best thing to do is hose them down in the yard. Don't be shy about hosing the upper part of the shoe as well. "They're dirty and wet to begin with, so a little more water isn't going to hurt them," says Scott Maslen, footwear test manager for Adidas International in Portland, Oregon. To remove lighter patches of mud or dirt (or to complete the job after hosing), brush the cleats with a stiff-bristle nylon brush.

Many cleated shoes, and most golf shoes, have removable cleats or spikes. Since they don't always wear evenly, individual spikes should be replaced as needed. Uneven cleats may warp the shoe and change its fit.

Speed tips: To keep cleats degunked during muddy games, keep a putty knife handy on the sidelines. Run the blade down the bottom of the shoe to get rid of caked mud.

Caution: Never use detergents, which could damage the leather or synthetic upper portion of the shoes. Wet shoes should be allowed to air-dry completely before wearing again. Do not attempt to speed the drying process by placing them near a radiator or other heat source because this could warp the shoes, especially if they're leather.

Clocks

Hickory dickory dock, don't mess with the insides of your clock. Modern timepieces with automatic movements hardly require cleaning at all. Mechanical clocks, which *do* require periodic cleaning, should be cleaned by professionals. So confine your own efforts mainly to keeping the outside looking good.

Technique: The best tool in cleaning the exterior of a clock is a clean soft cloth. Rub the clear glass, plastic, or acrylic piece covering the face gently to wipe away dirt without scratching. If the covering is glass, you may use some spray window cleaner, but be certain to spray this onto the cloth rather than directly onto the clock.

Rub the rest of the exterior with a clean cloth. If the case is made of wood, you can use a spray-on cleaner and polish, like Endust, on the cloth. Again, spray onto the cloth rather than onto the clock. Most brass on a clock will be covered with lacquer, meaning that it only needs the soft cloth.

About the most you'll have to do with a battery-operated clock is change the battery as needed. Since the movement is usually stored in a compartment inside the clock, it is unlikely to get dusty. "Very seldom does the consumer have to deal with cleaning or repairing the movement," says George Gibson, horologist and manager of clock services for Bulova Corporation in Woodside, New York. If it is dusty, Gibson adds, you can wipe the outside of the movement with a soft cloth sprayed with a little dust-remover. Grandfather clocks and other mechanical clocks should be cleaned and inspected by a professional every two to three years.

Caution: Don't use Windex or other glass cleaners on acrylic or plastic face covers, as these may damage the surface. Never spray cleaners directly at the clock; you don't want the solution getting into the wrong places.

Coffee Grinders

If you've been assuming that coffee doesn't go bad, you're probably less than vigilant about cleaning your coffee grinder. That's a mistake. "Coffee can actually go stale," says Diane Bannister, supervisor of consumer services for Salton Housewares, a manufacturer of coffee grinders, based in Mount Prospect, Illinois. "If you put new beans in with the old ones, it'll give your coffee a bitter taste."

Technique: For routine cleaning of the exterior, wipe the grinder down with a soft damp cloth. If greater cleaning is needed, you can wipe with a cloth dipped in warm soapy water. Then go over the entire surface with a cloth dampened with plain water.

After each use of the grinder, wipe the interior parts with a clean damp cloth to remove residue from ground coffee beans. Use a pipe cleaner to clean residue from crevices and hard-to-reach places in the grinding mechanism.

Speed tips: If your coffee grinder has a removable grinding mechanism, this can be lifted out and washed in the sink with warm soapy water. Rinse thoroughly and allow to dry before replacing. Or, stick it in the dishwasher.

Caution: Never submerge the coffee grinder itself in water. Never use cleaning solutions on the inside of your coffee grinder that you wouldn't want to put in your mouth. At best, these could ruin the taste of your coffee. At worst, they could harm you. Avoid using abrasive pads or cleanser on the exterior. These could mar the surface.

Coffeemakers

Mineral deposits in water can clog a drip coffeemaker. The brewing mechanism should be cleaned thoroughly about once a month, or more often if you use it all the time or if the water in your area is hard. The harder the water, the more deposits.

Technique: After each use, the filter basket and the glass carafe and lid should be cleaned with hot sudsy water or placed in the top rack of the dishwasher. If the parts appear faded from the dishwasher, rubbing them with a soft dry cloth should restore the shine. Wipe the coffeemaker and the heating pad with a soft damp cloth. "It's easy to do when you're wiping off the counters, and it will keep the coffeemaker looking nicer for a longer time," says Fay Carpenter, manager of home economics at Black and Decker Corporation in Shelton, Connecticut.

To clean the brewing mechanism, pour a quart of white vinegar into the carafe, then fill to the 10-cup level with cold water. Pour the mixture into the water reservoir as though you were about to make a pot of coffee. Place a fresh paper filter in the basket and turn the machine on. When about half of the mixture has brewed into the carafe, turn the machine off and let it sit for 15 minutes. Pour the mixture back into the reservoir and this time let all of it brew. Before making coffee again, brew a carafe of plain water.

Caution: Be sure that the coffeemaker has been turned off, unplugged, and allowed to cool before you wipe it down. Never use abrasive scouring pads; scratches will weaken the glass of the carafe and mar other parts.

Coffee Stains

 EMERGENCY ACTION
If you spill coffee on yourself at work or some other place where you can't get to cleaning supplies right away, flush the stain immediately with cool water. That's the first step in conventional cleaning of a coffee stain anyway, and it may be all you need to do.

How you take it affects how you take it out. Coffee with milk or cream, because it contains animal products, becomes a "protein-based" stain that requires a different treatment than black coffee.

Technique: For black coffee on fabric, blot the stain with cool water. Rinse thoroughly with water. If the stain persists, try blotting with some mild laundry detergent and water. Rinse thoroughly with water. Still there? Blot that stubborn stain with detergent and water, this time mixed with a few drops of white vinegar. Rinse thoroughly. As a final step, try some hydrogen peroxide. The reason for rinsing thoroughly between steps is to prevent potentially incompatible cleaning solutions from being mixed.

For coffee with milk or cream, use the first two steps for black coffee. Then blot the stain with mild laundry detergent mixed with a few drops of ammonia. Rinse thoroughly. Finally, blot with an enzyme-based detergent, such as Tide.

Speed tips: If you don't have the time or the patience for a thorough cleaning job, it's a good idea to take the garment to a dry cleaner you trust. This is especially recommended if the garment is old or prized.

Caution: Never put a garment into the dryer until you're sure that the stain is gone. "Tumble it and it may be impossible for you to get the stain out," says Jane Rising, instructor in the education department at the International Fabricare Institute in Silver Spring, Maryland. Be sure to test any cleaning method on a small obscure corner of the fabric before attacking the stain, even if you've used the method before, to make sure that the colors and the fabric can withstand the cleaning.

Coins

If you come across an old coin in the attic or basement that you think might be worth a mint, you may be tempted to give it a good cleaning before showing it to an expert. Don't! "Inexperienced coin cleaners often lower the value of a coin more than they raise it," says J. P. Martin, a coin-preservation expert with the American Numismatic Association, a nonprofit educational organization for the study of coins, medals, and memorabilia, in Colorado Springs. If the coin really is rare and valuable, cleaning away dirt and oxidation may actually lessen its value.

Note: If you're not sure if your coin is too valuable to wash, contact the American Numismatic Association at 818 North Cascade Avenue, Colorado Springs, CO 80903-3279.

Technique: After you have consulted an expert, or if the coin is not especially valuable but you just want to spiff it up, swab it with some acetone-based cleaner such as nail polish remover, using a cotton ball or swab. Or soak the coin in a bath of acetone until clean.

Speed tips: Rubbing alcohol is somewhat easier to use than acetone. It's not quite as effective but may do the trick for some jobs.

Caution: Avoid all abrasives and acid-based cleaners, as they may damage the surface of the coin. These include tarnish removers, baking soda, and toothpaste. Avoid using any abrasive cloth. Stick to cotton balls and cotton swabs.

Combs

Most combs are made of plastic, nylon, or other material that stands up well to a good bathing.

Technique: Before washing a comb, first pull off any hair that is attached to it. Then soak the comb in your sink in a sudsy bath of warm water and mild liquid dishwashing detergent for 10 to 20 minutes, or until there are no more oily deposits and residue from hair gel, styling creams, and such. Then rinse the comb in clear water and lay it on a towel to dry.

If you have a scalp condition such as dandruff, cleaning the comb may be a bit more complicated. "The white flakes sometimes adhere to the teeth, especially with fine-tooth combs," says Rebecca Viands, executive vice president of the Potomac Academy of Hair Design and a commissioner of the National Accrediting Commission of Cosmetology Arts and Sciences, both in Falls Church, Virginia. You can solve

A CLEAN STORY

Keeping Combs Clean: The Story of Barbicide

As barber poles go the way of cigar-store Indians, a more enduring symbol of the tonsorial art has emerged: Barbicide, the blue comb-and-scissors disinfectant in the tall glass jar.

Invented more than 50 years ago by Maurice King, a chemical engineer from Brooklyn, New York, the ubiquitous sterilizing liquid is now sold to barbers and beauticians around the globe at a rate of 18,000 gallons a month. A jar of Barbicide even stands in the Smithsonian Institution in Washington, D.C.

Early in his life, King developed a healthy skepticism of barbers' practices. As a teenager suffering from scalp sores, he endured the painful pricks of many a dirty comb. Later, appalled that barbers cleaned combs and brushes only by running water over them, he set out to create his germ-busting concoction. The key to his breakthrough was a new type of disinfectant, an ammonium compound strong enough to kill germs but mild enough for everyday use.

King decided to dye the concoction blue because of the color's freshness and purity. The idea for the tall glass jar with the liftable platform came from soda fountain straw holders.

And then there's the name.

Because of his aversion to barbers, King called his creation Barbicide—which does *not* refer to the killing of germs—as a secret joke.

this problem by running the bristles of an old toothbrush through the comb while you soak it, Viands says.

In most cases, especially if you are the only one using the comb, the above methods should suffice. If you want extra sanitizing, rub the teeth with a little rubbing alcohol.

Speed tips: Since combs, brushes, and curlers all do well in a warm soapy bath, you can save time and water by washing all of these items together.

In a pinch: In rare cases you might want to take extra steps to disinfect a comb—say, for example, you have combed a child's hair to remove lice eggs, but you don't want to discard the comb. Soak it for about 15 minutes in a 10 percent solution of liquid household bleach and water. Then rinse thoroughly with plain water.

Caution: If you are washing a metal comb, be sure to dry it thoroughly after washing it to prevent rust.

Comforters

Most comforters are easily cleaned in a washing machine and dryer—once you find washing machines and dryers big enough to handle them, that is.

Technique: Whenever possible, closely follow the cleaning instructions on your comforter's label. As a general rule, most comforters with a printed cotton cover and synthetic or down filling are machine washable. Because of their bulk, these items should be washed separately from other items in warm water on the gentle cycle, then machine-dried. Be certain that your washing machine and dryer are big enough so that the comforter fits easily in without cramming. If not, take it to a coin-operated laundry that has king-size appliances.

In a pinch: If the cleaning label has been torn away but you know where the comforter was purchased or who made it, contact the store or the manufacturer for instructions. If not, you may want to discuss your options with a professional cleaner. Comforters made from heavy upholstery-type fabric should be dry-cleaned, but dry cleaning may damage the colors of other comforters.

"Generally, printed fabrics should not be dry-cleaned," says Joan Garrison, manager of consumer relations for the bedding and linens company Fieldcrest Cannon in Kannapolis, North Carolina.

Caution: Never cram a comforter into a washer or dryer. In a washer, the comforter will clean unevenly. In a dryer, you risk scorching the portions jammed against the barrel while the portions turned inward remain wet.

Compact Discs (CDs)

Dust, fingerprints, grease, and oil can make a CD skip, almost like an old-fashioned vinyl record.

Technique: Holding the disc by the rim and center hole, wipe the surface with a clean, soft, dry lint-free cloth. Instead of wiping in a circular motion—which may leave residue on the disc—use straight strokes from the center of the disc to the outer edge, or vice versa, says Lisa Fasold, spokeswoman for the Consumer Electronics Manufacturers Association in Arlington, Virginia. This is called radial cleaning. For more thorough cleaning, you may want to buy a CD-cleaning kit, available in music stores. You can also buy a CD lens cleaner, which is a disc you insert in the player to clean dust that has gathered on the laser pickup.

Caution: Never use an alcohol-based cleaner or a household cleanser or solvent on a CD. These can damage the surface or destroy the CD altogether.

Computers

Dust is public enemy number one for computers. Keeping the air in your home clean and reducing dust in the computer room will go a long way toward keeping your computer free of costly maintenance and repairs. For general tips, see Air on page 45 and Dust on page 159.

Technique: The keyboard should be cleaned occasionally with a soft static-free cloth dampened with cleaning fluid made for computer cleaning. Both are available at computer or electronics stores. Be sure to apply the fluid to the pad rather than to the keyboard. You can also buy pads that are presoaked. For cleaning lint and dust from between the keys you can buy a small vacuum cleaner for computers that comes with a specially designed nozzle and brush, says Lisa Fasold, spokeswoman for the Consumer Electronics Manufacturers

Association in Arlington, Virginia. For a less expensive alternative, use a cotton swab dipped in cleaning fluid. Use the same fluid and cloth to gently wipe the screen of your computer monitor. Don't use spray window cleaners. These can create a film on the screen that will even attract more dust. In combination with cigarette smoke, this film may yellow the screen.

Speed tips: Dust covers will lessen the need for dusting. You can buy dust covers to fit just about any computer component, from the monitor to the keyboard, to the printer to the disk drive.

Caution: Don't use household cleansers, ammonia, powders, or other abrasives to clean the outside of your computer components. These can scratch or otherwise damage the plastic. Don't use household cleaners on keyboards either. "You never know what's in them that could corrode the circuitry," says Fasold. "Never blow on the keyboard," Fasold adds. "You're blowing water into the keyboard. That could make components rust out."

Concrete

Dust and other airborne pollutants can turn concrete surfaces into victims of grime. "Concrete is not totally maintenance-free," says Mary Hurd, an engineer in Farmington Hills, Michigan, and consulting editor of the trade journal *Concrete Construction*. "People think, 'Oh, we never have to do anything to concrete.'" In fact, periodic cleaning can vastly improve the appearance of concrete and also expand its useful life.

Technique: For light cleaning, scrub the concrete with a dry, stiff fiber brush. A good stiff brushing periodically will go a long way toward thwarting grime. "Once every year or so will probably prevent a buildup," Hurd says.

For stubborn grime or stains, mix trisodium phosphate (TSP), which is available at hardware stores, in a bucket of warm water. Use whatever proportions the TSP container recommends for heavy cleaning. Scrub with a stiff fiber brush.

For old or fragile surfaces, first rub gently with a soft brush. Next, brush with warm water and soap. If the grime or stain persists, add some vinegar to the soap and water mixture.

It's best to attend to paint spills and other stains as quickly as possible. Untreated stains may soak into and become part of the concrete.

HOW I DO IT

King of the Road Spills

Andy Bailey, the top maintenance engineer for the Virginia Department of Transportation's 50,000 miles of highways, has cleaned his share of nasty fuel spills on concrete.

"The biggest immediate concern is fire. But spilled fuel can also damage roads, pollute the environment, and pose a safety hazard for drivers, so cleanup has to be done quickly.

"The first thing we do is spread sand or other absorbent over the entire area. Then a truck-mounted machine called a vactor sweeps and vacuums the sand and fuel. The next step is to blast the stain away. We used to use sandblasters, but for environmental reasons we've switched to waterblasters, which kick up a lot less dust.

"The problems are even worse on asphalt. Because asphalt is an oil-based product, diesel fuel left over time will act as a solvent and deteriorate the road. Sometimes the only option is to resurface the area."

Caution: Don't use metallic brushes. They may leave metal particles in the concrete that will rust. Always test-clean a small obscure section of the concrete with whatever method you're planning to use. This way you'll be sure not to make a big noticeable mistake. Read product labels carefully for proper usage and safety precautions.

Containers—Plastic

You finally finish off the leftover spaghetti sauce and you rinse out the plastic container. Uh-oh. Foods high in carotenoids (carrots, tomatoes, sweet potatoes) may be great for the body, but they can sure stain.

Technique: Rubbermaid Consumer Services in Wooster, Ohio, recommends Dawn liquid dishwashing detergent for cleaning their plastic food storage containers. Soak containers that have a greasy film in hot soapy water, remove any residue with a dishcloth, and rinse. To remove any adhesive residue from stickers, use vegetable oil or peanut butter. Stains may be removed by soaking in a solution of 1 tablespoon liquid chlorine bleach per cup of water. Do not mix detergents with bleach, advise experts at Rubbermaid. As a general rule, you can help prevent stains by rinsing containers after each use in cold water, followed immediately by warm sudsy water. To remove stubborn odors in food containers, Rubbermaid suggests placing a slice of lemon in the container, cover, and refrigerate for 6 to 12 hours. Then wash with warm suds. Store containers unsealed to allow air to circulate.

Coolers and Jugs

Stains and mildew are the big enemies to coolers. But since they carry food and drink, you must be careful how you conduct the battle.

Technique: To clean the outside of a plastic or composite-material cooler or jug, mix a weak solution of a household cleaner that doesn't contain bleach, such as Spic and Span and warm water, adding ½ cup cleaner to 1 gallon water. Use a clean soft cloth or sponge dipped in the solution to wash the outside surfaces. Stronger cleaning solutions or abrasive cleansers may cause the exterior color to fade.

The inside will require a different approach. "Don't ever use anything inside a cooler or jug that you wouldn't put in your mouth," says Sandy Hobbs, a consumer service representative for the Coleman Company in Wichita, Kansas.

The best material for cleaning the inside of a cooler or jug is baking soda. Sprinkle baking soda liberally onto a wet cloth or sponge, or directly onto the surface, then apply the elbow grease. To remove a stain, mix baking soda with just enough water to create a thick paste. Spread the paste over the stained area. Let it sit for a half-hour. Then rub the area with a cloth or sponge. Your chances of removing any stain are better if you attend to it quickly. Some stains become impossible to remove if not treated right away. "Nothing's going to take that grape juice out after it has sat there for a while," Hobbs says.

For persistent odors, mix 1 teaspoon vanilla extract in 4 cups water and use the solution to wipe the surface with a soft cloth or sponge.

Speed tips: You can save yourself a lot of cleanup time in the long run by preventing mildew from forming in the first place and by taking care of spills and stains quickly. After using a cooler or jug, don't just stick it back on the shelf with the lid closed. Wash it right away and dry the inside thoroughly with a towel. Then let the cooler or jug sit for two days with the lid off. After that, you can replace the lid and store it.

Caution: Avoid harsh cleaners or abrasives on the exteriors. Don't use chemical cleansers or bleach on the interiors. Never use a chemical mildew remover. Remember, if you wouldn't put it in your mouth, don't put it in your cooler or jug.

Copper

Methods for cleaning copper objects are the same as for bronze, which is an alloy of copper and tin. Left unpolished and unlacquered, it quickly becomes tarnished through oxidation.

Technique: General cleaning of copper objects is easy and should be done gently. The main thing you want to avoid is scratching the surface. For routine maintenance, just dust with a soft dry cloth such as an old T-shirt. If grime from the air has built up on the piece, dampen the cloth with water before rubbing the copper surface. (For tips on treating lacquered and unlacquered copper, see Bronze on page 89. For tips on cleaning copper pots and pans, see Pots and Pans on page 304.)

Unlacquered copper will have to be polished to maintain its shine. Commercial brass polishes such as Brasso work well.

Speed tips: To add a quick shine to bronze or copper buttons and other small pieces, try rubbing them with a little ketchup.

In a pinch: You can make your own polish by mixing 1 table-spoon salt with 1 tablespoon flour, says James W. McGann, vice president for quality at Virginia Metalcrafters in Waynesboro, Virginia, which creates all the brass and bronze pieces used at Colonial Williamsburg. Stir in 1 tablespoon white vinegar. Apply the paste with a soft damp cloth, rub gently, rinse, and wipe dry with a dry soft cloth.

Caution: Never use harsh cleansers or abrasive pads to clean copper. These could scratch the metal. Handle pieces as infrequently as possible. Oils from your fingers can leave permanent marks. If you have a copper piece that you think may be valuable or historically significant, don't polish it until you've had it examined by a professional conservator. If you use moisture when cleaning a copper piece, dry it thoroughly afterward with a soft dry cloth to prevent spots from forming. Don't use spray waxes or polishes. They'll just dull the shine.

Cork

People didn't have much use for cork until the sixteenth century, when they figured out it was great for stopping up glass bottles. These days you can find it any number of places in the home. Your cleaning approach depends on whether the cork is sealed.

Technique: "Cork floors are almost always going to be sealed, in which case you're dealing with the sealant rather than the cork," says Martin L. King, a restoration consultant in Arlington, Virginia, and technical advisor to the National Institute of Disaster Restoration in Annapolis, Maryland. They can be mopped using whatever cleaning materials are appropriate for the sealant, King advises. Untreated cork, including many walls, is quite porous and should not be exposed to much water. Instead, try a dry method such as rubbing the cork with a putty wallpaper cleaner or a dry, foam-rubber sponge (available at hardware stores, janitorial supply stores, and paint stores). This sponge is specially designed to rub dirt particles away from walls and ceilings. Common kitchen sponges shouldn't be used because they will smear dirt instead of rubbing it away. Cork walls may be lightly sanded to remove spots, but be sure to try this on a small area first to be certain that you don't damage the cork or wind up with unsightly patches where you sanded.

In a pinch: If you can't get to the paint store for a foam-rubber sponge or putty wallpaper cleaner, you may rub cork with a hunk of stale crumbly bread, which will scrub without doing damage, or pat the area with tape.

Caution: Even when washing sealed cork floors, don't overdo it with the moisture. If you're mopping, for example, don't pour the water from the bucket directly onto the floor. Never use bleach on untreated cork, which will create a spot.

Cotton

It's comfortable. It's cool. It's durable. It leaps tall washing machines in a single bound! "Cotton is a strong rugged fiber. It's very resistant to alkali, which means that it can stand up well to laundry detergent," says John D. Turner, Ph.D., senior chemist for Cotton, a cotton growers trade group based in Raleigh, North Carolina. Optical brighteners in modern detergents help make colors in cotton fabric bolder. Since just about any laundry detergent will work, your main concerns when washing cotton are shrinkage and discoloration of the fabric.

Technique: When washing cotton fabrics, it's always best to follow the instructions on the manufacturer's care label. The old rule about washing whites separately from colored laundry is a good one, even if the colored laundry has been washed many times before. "There's always some that bleeds off," Dr. Turner says. A white shirt washed repeatedly with colored items will gradually darken. "You don't see it until you buy a new white shirt and lay it down beside the old one," Dr. Turner adds.

Shrinkage

Many people assume that shrinkage occurs when the cotton fibers themselves shrivel as a result of heat in the drying process. Actually, only a fraction of the shrinking process takes place within the fibers. About 95 percent occurs when the weave is mashed and compacted during washing and tumble drying. So don't assume that low heat or air-drying will prevent your new cotton trousers from shrinking. Fortunately, shrinking only occurs once per garment.

The best way to avoid the problem altogether is to buy the increasingly common preshrunk garments. If you have a garment that is not preshrunk and that you desperately don't want to shrink, you can prevent it. But the process is laborious and must be repeated with each washing. First add ¼ cup laundry detergent to a tub of water. Then let the garment soak while gently pushing it up and down in the water. Refill the tub with plain water and repeat the process to rinse. Remove the garment dripping wet. Lay it on a towel and blot it with a second towel. Then pull the garment to its original form, tugging gently on the sleeves or trouser legs. Let it dry in a ventilated room.

Ironing

Cotton can withstand a hot iron. Iron garments while still moist, or spray them with a mist sprayer. This will lubricate the fibers, and they'll respond better to ironing.

Stains

For tips on removing specific stains, see individual listings of stain types elsewhere in this book. As a rule, though, you have the best chance of removing a stain if you attend to it immediately. A dry stain, particularly one that has been tumble dried, may be impossible to remove. If you can't attend to the stain right away, at least try to keep it wet until you can. Always test stain-removal methods on a small section of the garment to make sure that you don't damage it.

Caution: Never leave a hot iron facedown on the fabric for more than a few seconds. Even the most heat-resistant fabrics may scorch. Cotton is vulnerable to acids, which may destroy the fabric. Avoid spilling harsh acids such as battery acid or sulfuric acid on cotton. Even milder acids such as vinegar and fruit juice should not be allowed to linger.

Counters

You want clean kitchen counters for two important reasons: They're a highly visible feature of the kitchen, and they're the site of much of your food preparation. So your cleaning methods should be aggressive enough to get rid of potentially harmful bacteria but careful enough that you don't damage the surface.

Technique: Each time you handle food on a counter, wash the counter afterward with hot soapy water and a clean cloth or sponge. Liquid dishwashing detergent works fine. "It's the sudsing action that lifts the debris," says Bessie Berry, manager of the U.S. Department of Agriculture's Meat and Poultry Hotline in Washington, D.C. Then rinse the counter with clear water and pat dry with clean paper towels.

Each time you handle raw meat, poultry, or fish, take sanitizing an extra step. First, carefully wash the surface to remove debris. Mix 1 teaspoon liquid chlorine bleach per quart of water. Pour enough on the counter to cover it, and let the solution sit for a minute. Then rinse thoroughly with clear water and pat dry. Or use one of the commercial antibacterial products. Read the label for instructions on how to clean kitchen counters.

To keep counters looking good, wipe up spills as soon as possible. How you deal with stains will depend on what type of surface you have. For polished or laminated surfaces (a thin surface layer over a wood base), avoid using any type of abrasive cleanser or pad that could scratch them. "You dull the finish. You dull the sheen. You just take away from the beauty of the product," says Nick Geragi, director of education and product development for the National Kitchen and Bath Association in Hackettstown, New Jersey.

Some counters are nonporous, with a matte finish. These allow you to scour away stains and burn marks with powdered cleansers such as Comet or to use scouring pads such as Scotch-Brite. To ensure a uniform appearance, you might want to scour the entire surface of the counter after taking care of a spot. The Nevamar Corporation, a manufacturer of decorative surfaces, based in Odenton, Maryland, recommends using a wet Scotch-Brite pad on the surface, then cleaning thoroughly with soap and water and letting it dry.

Corian is a particularly tough counter material. It is stain-resistant because it is nonporous, and will stand up to the kind of scouring that will dull plastic laminate. So use of abrasive pads and powdered cleansers is fine. Because Corian, made of acrylic and natural materials, is solid all the way through rather than a thin layer, you can even rub out burns and scratches with fine sandpaper.

For details about cleaning other specific countertop materials, see Butcher Block on page 94, Plastic Laminate on page 301, Stone on page 366, and Tile—Ceramic on page 389.

In a pinch: Burn marks on laminated or polished surfaces are likely to be permanent. If the burn mark is especially noticeable, consider having the affected section removed and replaced with a section of butcher block or glass.

Caution: Never place hot pots or pans directly on counter surfaces. Harsh acidic cleaners such as oven, toilet, and drain cleaners, should be kept away from counters. If they do spill onto a counter, wipe them immediately. When using the bleach-water solution to sanitize a counter, make only enough for the single use. Don't try to save it. The chlorine evaporates and the solution weakens.

Crayon Marks

Yes, you want your budding Edward Hopper or Georgia O'Keeffe to create lasting works of art. You just don't want them on the furniture, walls, and carpeting.

Technique: Binney and Smith, which has been supplying children with crayons since 1903, found that the auto part cleaner/lubricant WD-40 is effective for removing crayon marks from many surfaces. "WD-40 is a penetrating agent that gets between the crayon material and the surface," says Patrick Morris, a spokesman for Binney and Smith in Easton, Pennsylvania. "It makes the crayon easier to remove."

To get crayon off brick or concrete, for example, spray the

stained area with lubricant and brush with a stiff brush. Then re-spray and wipe with a soft cloth. For crayon marks on smooth surfaces such as glass, porcelain, metal, unwaxed vinyl floors, painted walls or painted wood, tile, or marble, spray the surface with WD-40 lubricant and wipe away with a soft cloth. If the stain persists, use a sponge to wash the surface with a mixture of warm water and liquid dishwashing detergent. Work in a circular motion and rinse. In all cases, stains should be treated as soon as possible.

But beware of using lubricant on fabric, warns Jane Rising, instructor in the education department at the International Fabricare Institute in Silver Spring, Maryland. "I can't get it rinsed out, and it leaves a residual odor," she says. Instead, Rising says, try pretreating the stained area with a laundry prewash spray, then running the garment through the hottest water that is safe for that type of fabric. If the stain doesn't go away, blot the stain with a generally available spot remover, such as Carbona Stain Devils or Energine.

Caution: Test-clean a small obscure portion of the surface before cleaning the entire surface. This will help prevent damage to the surface during the cleaning process. Never mix spot removers with water because the two will not dissolve into each other. Let the kids make the crayon stains; you clean them up. Having the offender work on his own stain may be tempting, but it's not a good idea for small children to handle cleaning supplies, especially chemicals.

Crystal

The lead in crystal gives it sparkle, brilliance, and clarity. It also makes the glass soft. Crystal should always be washed by hand. "Putting it in a dishwasher regularly will cause tiny scratches that will cloud up over time," warns Alice Kolator, spokeswoman for Lenox, the china and crystal manufacturer in Lawrenceville, New Jersey.

Technique: To wash by hand, first place a rubber guard (available at housewares stores) on the faucet to prevent chipping. Place a rubber mat or double-folded towel on the bottom of the sink. If it's a divided sink, drape a rubber mat or towel over the divider. Wash using any liquid dishwashing detergent and a nonabrasive cloth or sponge. Hold glasses by the bowl rather than the stem, to avoid dropping.

In a pinch: To remove dried-on food or stains that won't simply soak off, try rubbing with a little baking soda.

Caution: Avoid abrasive cleansers, even for dried-on food. Do not overfill the sink with items that could chip or break.

Cupboards

Keeping your cupboard clean and well-organized not only will make cooking easier and more pleasant but also will reduce your chances of harboring insects or rodents. Household pests require three main things: food, water, and a cozy place to live. A dirty kitchen cupboard, with crumbs, moisture, and dark recesses, is like a dream come true.

Technique: Clean your cupboard at least twice a year, during your spring and fall cleaning. The more often you do it, the easier it will be to remove any grease that has built up on it.

Starting at the top and working a shelf at a time, remove all of the food and other items. Pull up any old paper or shelf liners, and wipe down all surfaces.

Use a sudsy sponge or an all-purpose kitchen cleaner and a sponge on plastic, plastic laminate, and similar surfaces. Rinse by wiping it down with a clean moist sponge or cloth. For wood, either dust with a lightly dampened cloth or use a spray-on cleaner and polish, like Endust. Wipe dust off cans and jars with a lightly dampened cloth.

Make sure that the shelves have a chance to dry before you replace the cans and other items. "If you fill the shelves before they dry, they might stay moist and lead to bacteria growth and bad odors," says Michael Beglinger, executive chef at Deutsche Bank in New York City. If you use shelf liners, lay down fresh ones. For shelves that hold glasses, consider putting down mesh mats, which are available at housewares stores. "It keeps glasses steady and raised off the surface a bit," Beglinger notes.

Speed tips: To cut down on dust—and the amount of time that must be spent removing it—keep the cupboard door closed as much as possible.

Curlers

A warm soapy bath will make your plastic curlers so clean that you can almost convince yourself they're new—and those curls came naturally.

Technique: Soak conventional plastic curlers in your sink in a sudsy solution of mild liquid dishwashing detergent and warm water for 10 to 20 minutes or until all oils and residues from hair styling products are gone. Then rinse with clear water.

Velcro curlers that roll up are increasingly popular among do-it-yourself hair stylists because they don't require pins to stay in place. But if they are easier to use, they are also harder to clean. "The downside is that hair sticks to them," says Rebecca Viands, executive vice president of the Potomac Academy of Hair Design and a commissioner of the National Accrediting Commission of Cosmetology Arts and Sciences, both in Falls Church, Virginia. "It's like picking out one hair at a time." Viands suggests soaking these curlers in the same warm soapy bath, then running a comb over the Velcro hooks to remove what hair you can. Beyond that, don't sweat it. "If you're the only one using them, it's just your hair," Viands says.

Speed tips: Since combs and brushes can also be cleaned in a warm bath, save time and water by soaking all of these items at the same time.

Caution: When cleaning conventional curlers, you can soak the metal pins along with the curlers. But be sure to dry them thoroughly afterward to prevent them from rusting.

Curling Irons

Get as wild as you like when you're putting that curling iron to use—that's your business. But when it comes to cleaning them, the simplest cleaning method is also the best.

Technique: Unplug your curling iron and allow it to cool before cleaning. Then wipe it down with a soft damp cloth. Hair-care products are water-soluble, so even a curling iron gunked up with hair spray or mousse should come off relatively easily with this method.

Caution: Avoid using any abrasive cleaners that could scratch or mar the surface of the curling iron. Never clean it while it is plugged in. Never immerse a curling iron in water.

Curtains

Think of your curtains as more than just pretty window dressing. They become a part of the airflow system in your home, filtering dust out of air moving in and out of windows. Cleaning helps prolong the curtains' life expectancy, which is about five years for lined curtains, four years for unlined curtains, and three years for sheers.

Technique: Always clean matching draperies at the same time. "You can use your vacuum cleaner to get the dust off them," says Maria Ungaro, program director of the Window Coverings Manufacturers Association in New York City. Once a month, vacuum them where they hang using a dusting brush or upholstery attachment. Work from top to bottom, taking care to clean the tops and hems, where dust tends to gather. Hold the curtains taut from below and reduce the vacuum pressure if possible to avoid sucking the fabric into the nozzle. If necessary, attach an extension tube to reach the top of the curtain.

At least once a year, wash your curtains—either in a washing machine or at a professional dry cleaner, depending on the material. Follow the curtains' washing instructions, which should be found on a flap inside the hem. If you machine-wash them, tumble until damp and hang to lessen the wrinkling and the need for ironing.

Speed tips: If curtains are not heavily soiled, instead of washing, simply freshen them by tumbling them in a dryer set on "Air-Fluff" with no heat.

In a pinch: If you don't have time to go over each curtain with the vacuum cleaner, simply beat them lightly or use a feather duster to get the dust out.

Cushions

On the couch, you want to be at ease—and not sneeze. The best strategy for cleaning cushions is to remove accumulated dust regularly so it won't stain when ground in or moistened. Dust also harbors microorganisms, like dust mites, which can cause allergies.

Technique: Remove dust—and dust mites—from cushions about once a month by vacuuming with the appropriate attachments, like an upholstery brush and crevice tool, says Rajiv Jain, laboratory manager for the Association of Specialists in Cleaning and Restoration in Annapolis Junction, Maryland. If you don't have a vacuum cleaner with attachments, gently brush away the dust using a soft-bristle brush.

If your cushions need washing, follow the upholstery manufacturer's suggestions, usually found on a tag attached to the cushion. If there is no tag, try to determine what type of fabric covers your cushions. Some fabrics should not get wet, while others, like nylon, can be cleaned using small amounts of soap and water. To remove stains on dry-clean-only fabrics, blot with a spot remover, like K2r or Carbona Stain Devils. Read product labels carefully for proper usage and safety precautions.

Prevention tip: Use armrest and headrest covers to protect those areas against buildup of greasy soil from skin and hair.

Here are some general cleaning tips, according to cleaning experts.

- Promptly scrape off excess solids or blot up spills using a clean white cloth.
- Do not remove the fabric cover from the cushion because it may be difficult to properly fit back on.
- Always pretest a cleaning solution in an inconspicuous area before using it to make sure that colors won't bleed.
- Never soak the cushion, either in water or in solvent. Moisture trapped inside the cushion can attract dirt.
- For soap-and-water cleaning, mix up a solution of 1 cup cool or warm water and ½ teaspoon mild liquid dishwashing detergent. Whip up a head of suds, and work small amounts of those suds into the soiled area using a clean white cloth. Rinse by blotting with a damp cloth. Let the cushion dry in the air or sun.

Caution: Don't vacuum down-filled cushions if they are not lined with down-proof ticking. Instead, brush them to avoid sucking out the feather quills.

Cutlery

Your main goal is to remove food particles from cutlery. But since bacteria do not grow on steel for very long, it doesn't take much work. So let's cut to the chase.

Technique: Wash all fine cutlery by hand, using liquid dishwashing detergent and a nylon or vegetable scrubber or pad. Do not use steel wool because it can scratch the smooth surfaces. Don't soak knives, especially wooden-handled ones. "Bacteria does not survive long on steel, but water can seep between the handles and the blades and encourage bacteria growth," says Jim Economos, vice president of operations at Imperial Schrade Corporation, a U.S. cutlery manufacturer in Ellenville, New York. Water seepage also leads to deterioration of the bond between handles and blades, and excess water can warp wooden handles. Wipe cutlery dry as soon as possible.

What about washing cutlery in the dishwasher? "Anybody who makes good knives for a living will tell you to never put them in the dishwasher," Economos says. "They bounce around in there and can scratch other utensils, in particular, plastic cooking spoons and spatulas." The knives can also damage other knives.

Caution: To avoid cutting yourself when washing knives, wipe them from the back of the blade diagonally toward the tip.

Cutting Boards

Cutting boards are the perfect home for microorganisms. Whether you use wood or plastic, cleaning cutting surfaces is especially important for health reasons.

Technique: After each use, scrub the board vigorously with a

Cutting Boards: The Wood versus Plastic Debate

With all of the conflicting reports about bacteria growth, it's hard to know just which surface is safer. For many years, conventional wisdom held that nonporous plastic was less hospitable than wood to dangerous contaminants, like *Salmonella* from raw chicken. But a 1993 study done by University of Wisconsin scientists turned that thinking on its head. Trying to find a way to make wooden cutting boards as bacteria-free as plastic, they discovered that 99.9 percent of the bacteria they placed on wooden boards disappeared within three minutes, while none disappeared on the plastic ones.

Problem solved, right? Wrong. After conducting its own studies, the U.S. Food and Drug Administration's Center for Food Safety and Applied Nutrition is sticking with plastic. Its experts found that while bacteria may die on the surface of wood, microorganisms become trapped in the deep cuts common on wooden cutting boards and are hard to remove by washing. On the other hand, they say, these harmful pathogens are easily washed off plastic.

The bottom line is that whichever you choose, clean and sanitize it well, especially after cutting raw meat, says Bessie Berry, manager of the U.S. Department of Agriculture's Meat and Poultry Hotline in Washington, D.C.

scrubber or brush and soapy water. The friction ruptures the cells of microorganisms, and the detergent helps lift and remove the debris that may harbor pathogens. Rinse and air-dry or pat dry with clean paper towels. After each time you use a cutting surface to chop chicken, beef, fish, or any other meat, sanitize it by flooding the surface for a minute with a solution of 1 teaspoon chlorine bleach per quart of water. Rinse it well immediately afterward and dry. These steps are especially critical if you're going to reuse the board for cutting other foods that aren't going to be cooked. "You want to remove any bacteria left by the perishable product," says Bessie Berry, manager of the U.S. Department of Agriculture's Meat and Poultry Hotline in Washington, D.C. "The bleach kills the pathogens that cause people to become ill—*Salmonella, Listeria, Escherichia coli, Staphylococcus.*" Do not store the chlorine solution for future use; because chlorine evaporates, mix up only enough for one application. Because of sanitizing ingredients in automatic dishwasher detergent, machine-washing plastic cutting boards is a safe alternative. Wooden boards, however, warp in dishwashers.

Decks

If you remove the dirt, mildew, and tannin stains from your deck regularly, the wood will last longer and look new longer. The job doesn't take long, so you can get right back to your chaise lounge.

Technique: Occasionally sweep or hose foliage and other large debris off your deck. The longer that decaying leaves and sticks sit on the wood surface, the more chance they have to stain the wood.

Twice a year, give your deck a light scrubbing using a solution of warm water and a few squirts of liquid dishwashing detergent. Scrub with a stiff-bristle brush, preferably one with a long handle. "There are deck brushes that have broom handles so that you don't have to do this down on your hands and knees," says Charlie Jourdain, vice president of technical and inspection services for the California Redwood Association in Novato, California.

Once every two years or so, give your deck a more thorough cleaning. You have a couple of choices: using a two-step scrubbing process or power-spraying the deck.

The scrubbing process is generally less expensive than renting a power sprayer or hiring a professional to do the spray job. And

HOW I DO IT

Quick Deck Maintenance

Bob Hanbury knows his way around a deck. He's a remodeler and the former host of *House Calls*, a home-repair call-in radio show in Newington, Connecticut. Here's what he has to say about cleaning decks.

"If you don't clean the debris that collects in the gaps in your deck, you're going to have a problem with the wood. It's like tooth decay. You want to make sure that the joints are open and clean so that the sun and air can get in there and keep the wood as dry as possible. If it's pressure-treated wood, it can darken it and cause mildew. And if it's not, then the wood can actually rot.

"A high-pressure water sprayer is a quick way to clean out the gaps—up against the house, around the posts and steps, wherever debris can accumulate. But if you're not careful, you can take the finish off the wood. I use an air compressor and nozzle, which is much safer. A leaf blower might do the same thing.

"My mother bought a pressure sprayer. The first time she used it, it was so powerful and had such a concentrated bead that she cut grooves into the wood."

power-spraying can damage a wood deck. But the downside to the scrubbing process is that it involves using chemicals—trisodium phosphate, liquid household bleach, and oxalic acid. When used correctly, none will hurt your lawn or other yard plants.

First, the two-step scrub: Begin with a solution of 1 cup trisodium phosphate (available at hardware stores), 1 cup liquid household bleach, and 1 gallon water. Mix it up, scrub it around your deck using a deck brush, and rinse it off using a garden hose.

Note: A phosphate-free alternative to trisodium phosphate is a product that contains sodium metasilicate, such as TSP-PF, available at hardware stores.

The bleach takes care of any mildew. The trisodium phosphate helps remove surface soil and sticky substances. "You're left with a pretty clean, mildew-free deck," Jourdain says, "but you may still have some darkening and discoloration as a result of weathering and the accumulation of tannins on the surface of the wood."

To remove these stains, clean with oxalic acid or a deck cleaner. Both are available at hardware stores or stores that sell wood deck supplies.

To clean with the oxalic acid, dissolve ½ cup of the crystals in a gallon of hot water, using a plastic bucket or some other nonmetallic container. Apply the solution to the deck using a mop or sponge. Do not scrub. Just coat the wood, let it sit for 20 to 30 minutes, and then rinse it well with the garden hose. The diluted runoff will not harm the plants around the deck.

To clean using a power sprayer, either rent one at an equipment rental shop and do it yourself, or hire a professional. Keep in mind that power-spraying can damage wood decks. "I've seen a number of cases where it has caused excessive erosion on the surface of the wood," Jourdain says.

If you decide to spray your own deck, here are some tips for preventing damage.

- Don't use too much pressure. "Many rentable power sprayers offer water pressure of 3,000 psi (pounds per square inch) or higher," Jourdain says. "I recommend the minimum pressure needed to accomplish the goal—usually 800 to 1,200 psi."
- Use a 45-degree nozzle instead of a needle or pinpoint nozzle.
- Hold the nozzle at an angle, 12 to 18 inches away from the deck's surface.
- Do not concentrate the nozzle in one area for more than a split second.

Caution: When using bleach, trisodium phosphate, or oxalic acid, wear goggles, rubber gloves, and other protective clothing.

When using oxalic acid, remove any potted plants and cover any other plants that could be splashed with the solution. It can burn foliage. (The solution you rinse off the deck will be diluted enough not to harm surrounding plants.)

When operating a power sprayer, use protective eyewear.

Always read the instructions for proper use and safety precautions.

Deodorant Stains

You had the best intentions in using deodorant—making the world safer for sensitive noses. But what you get in return is a dingy eyesore on your clothing. Depending on the type of deodorant you use, some stains can be worse than others. All, however, will eventually yellow and turn permanent if left untreated.

Technique: For washables, apply a liquid laundry detergent (or a paste made from a granular detergent and water) directly onto the stain. Lay the garment on a hard surface and pat the stain lightly with the back of a spoon. "You're trying to get in between fibers and inside fibers because that's where the stains are," says Ann Lemley, Ph.D., chairman of the department of textiles and apparel at Cornell University in Ithaca, New York. Don't rub the material together; that will abrade the fibers. Next, wash as directed either in a machine or by hand in the hottest water safe for the fabric. If your garment is bleachable, first try a color-safe bleach and then a chlorine bleach, both of which work against deodorant stains.

Dry cleaning works very well on deodorant stains; consider it even for clothing you normally would not take to the cleaners. "You'd be amazed," says Dr. Lemley. "Hand-washable silks get a lot of these kinds of stains. If once a year you dry-clean them, it works like magic."

Note: Before using cleaning solutions, always test them on an inconspicuous section of the stained item.

In a pinch: Blot using cotton balls and a spot remover, like Carbona Stain Devils or K2r, available at supermarkets, hardware stores, or discount department stores. Blot from the inside of the garment to push the stain out. Wear protective rubber or latex gloves, and use these products in a well-ventilated area.

Caution: Always rinse out one cleaning solution before trying another. Mixing chemicals, especially ammonia and chlorine bleach, can create noxious fumes. Always read the product label for proper use and safety precautions.

Diapers

If you have chosen cloth diapers over disposables—a terrific way to recycle and save landfill space—good for you. Now there's the small matter of cleaning them.

Technique: Solid wastes are difficult to remove from white diapers. Most mothers make the mistake of using liquid household bleach, which, if not rinsed completely, can irritate babies' skin. "It also eats your diaper up," says Matthew Gerwitz, plant manager of the Dy-Dee Diaper Service in Rochester, New York. "Using bleach, you're going to get six weeks out of your diaper rather than six years."

First, scrape as much of the solid waste as possible into the toilet. Then, by pausing your washing machine during the agitation cycle, let the dirty diapers soak in hot water and a delicate baby-clothing detergent containing protease enzymes, which help break up solids. Complete the wash cycle and run one more complete hot-water wash cycle with the same detergent.

Speed tips: Separate diapers soiled with solid waste from those that are urine-stained only. The same mild detergent easily removes urine after a single wash cycle.

Dish Drainers

Think about it: The job of the dish drainer is to hold clean, drying dishes. A dirty dish drainer simply defeats the purpose. And since it is exposed to moist areas in the kitchen, a dish drainer is a potential breeding ground for bacteria.

Technique: Once every couple of weeks, soak the drainer in a sink or dishpan filled with hot water, a tablespoon of liquid household bleach, and a squirt or two of liquid dishwashing detergent. Clean off any deposits with a sponge soaked in the solution. "The bleach has wonderful germicidal properties," says Marry Keener, assistant director of facilities management at the University of Arizona in Tucson and a member of the technical advisory committee for *Executive Housekeeping Today* magazine. "It will kill any bacteria, mold, or mildew and leave the drainer visibly clean."

In a pinch: Put the drainer in the sink and spray it down with hot water to remove soil. Dry it well with a dry cloth afterward.

Caution: Wear protective gloves when cleaning with the bleach and hot water. Always read the product label for proper use and safety precautions.

Dishes

You want dishes to be sanitary, to be spotlessly clean, and to make it through the washing process in one piece. Plus, since you have a lot on your plate these days, you want to keep this daily chore from consuming too much precious time.

Technique: From a cleanliness standpoint, machine-washing your dishes has a definite edge. But that's not always possible or practical. Here's how to do a top-notch job, whichever route you take.

Hand-Washing

Fill the sink or a dishpan with water as hot as you can stand. "It kills bacteria and cuts grease better," says Kari Kinder, assistant director of food and beverage at the renowned Culinary Institute of America in Hyde Park, New York. While the water is running, add one or two squirts of liquid dishwashing detergent to produce a thick layer of suds. Wear rubber gloves to protect your hands against hot water, to minimize nail damage, and to give yourself a better grip when washing breakable pieces. Begin by cleaning the least-soiled pieces—typically glassware and flatware—followed by plates and bowls, then serving dishes, and finally pots and pans. Depending on your preference, you may clean the dishes underwater or out of the water using a variety of scrubbers: plastic mesh, metal mesh, rough-surfaced sponges and cloths, fine steel wool pads, and brushes. Just make sure that the scrubber is not too abrasive for the item you're cleaning. Change the dishwashing solution if it gets too greasy or too cool or if the suds disappear.

Next, fill a clean basin or sink with hot rinse water and dip the soapy dishes, or stack them in a drain rack on top of a drain tray and spray them with hot water. Be sure to rinse the inside of all bowls, cups and glasses. Air drying is easiest, but wiping with a clean, dry dish towel will remove spotting and filming.

Using a Dishwasher

Loading the dishwasher correctly is important. Most new dishwashers do not require prerinsing. If you plan to load dishes into the machine and wash them later, use the rinse-hold cycle. In terms of positioning, your main goal is to allow the machine's sprayers to get to the heavy soil. "Depending on how the wash arms in your dishwasher spray, your machine could actually miss the face of the plates," notes Kinder. Although you should consult your machine's manual for its optimum dish placement, here are some general tips.

- Place the soiled side of dishes toward the center or source of the water spray.
- Don't let large items shield small ones.
- Keep cups, glasses, and bowls bottoms up.
- Do not crowd flatware in its basket.
- Make sure that delicate items are secure so that they don't topple and chip or break.
- Don't overload the machine, which prevents proper water circulation.

Water temperature should be at least 130°F. To check it, place a food thermometer in a glass in the kitchen sink and let the hot water run until the temperature stabilizes. (Hint: Before turning on your dishwasher, clear the cold water out of the line by running the hot water in the kitchen sink for a minute or so.)

The only detergent you should use in the dishwasher is automatic dishwasher detergent. This tip may sound too simple to mention, but it's important. Those blue or green granules might look just like laundry detergent, but they are specially formulated to create a minimum of suds. Other detergents and soaps can inhibit the washing action or even overflow, damaging the machine and the floor around it. Make sure the detergent dispenser is clean and dry before adding detergent. Otherwise, granular detergents can get caked in the dispenser. Never sprinkle or pour detergent directly onto flatware or other metals. It could cause spotting or pitting.

Hard water contains minerals that can cause spotting and filming on dishes. The average water hardness is from 61 to 120 milligrams of calcium and magnesium per liter. To find out if the water in your area is hard, contact your water utility or your county Cooperative Extension Service. If your water is hard (above the average rating) and causes spotting, either increase the amount of dishwasher detergent or use a rinse agent, like Jet-Dry, to cause the water to sheet off and evaporate more quickly.

To improve dishwasher efficiency, avoid bathing, running the washing machine, and other activities requiring continuous water use while the dishwasher is running. Insufficient water pressure can leave dishes dirty.

Speed tips: Make sure that you scrape and rinse dishes thoroughly before hand-washing. Otherwise, food will end up in your wash water, making grease removal more difficult. Add a capful of vinegar to the dishwater in your sink or dishpan to reinforce the detergent and help it cut grease better. "As far as drying," says Kinder, "hot water definitely speeds things up because it beads up and steams off." Or use a rinse agent, like Jet-Dry, in your dishwasher to help water sheet off dishes and dry more quickly and without spots.

Caution: Do not put stainless steel and silver flatware in the same dishwasher basket. Direct contact between these metals can cause permanent damage to the silver. And because the blades of many silver-plated knives are stainless steel, point all of the blades in the same direction when loading them in the flatware basket.

Dishwashers

Dishwashers do a good job of cleaning themselves while they clean your dishes, so keeping them in good shape is fairly straightforward.

Technique: For general cleaning of the exterior, a clean, damp sponge is the best bet. "You don't want to use anything too harsh," says Eugene P. Krausz, supervisor of the quality engineering lab for Whirlpool Corporation in Findlay, Ohio. If more than plain water is required, add a dab of liquid dishwashing detergent to the sponge. Then rinse the sponge and go over the exterior again to remove the detergent. For caked-on grime, use a glass cleaner, but be sure to spray the cleaner onto the sponge rather than directly onto the dishwasher. Otherwise, liquid could work its way into the console and damage the electronics. Or, more likely, the cleaner will work its way into crevices between controls. Once there, it will be hard to remove and will attract grime.

The inside of the dishwasher is pretty much self-cleaning. Inspect the area where the lower inside lip of

Colossal Cleanups

A Not-So-Little Rascal
The number of dishes washed each day at the Rascal House in Miami Beach, a top-ranked restaurant that serves 1.5 million customers a year: 18,000 to 20,000

the door meets the washer from time to time for signs of discoloration. This can happen if the water in your area is particularly hard and leaves mineral deposits or if you habitually use too much automatic dishwasher detergent. The detergent will accumulate in spots and eventually cause discoloration. (Tip: Don't just automatically fill the detergent compartments all the way when you wash a load. Try filling them halfway for starters, and adjust from there according to need. You'll know if you've used enough if your dishes come out clean.) If discoloration does occur, rub the area with a damp sponge sprinkled with the same automatic dishwasher detergent you use for regular loads.

Speed tips: Occasionally, mineral deposits from hard water may discolor the rest of the interior casing of the dishwasher. When this happens, run your dishwasher through a regular cycle using an automatic dishwasher detergent like Glisten or Glass Magic, which contain citric acid. In case you cannot find either one, Krausz suggests an alternative: Place a clean cereal bowl containing ½ cup white vinegar in the upper rack of your empty dishwasher. Run it on a regular cycle without detergent. The acid in the vinegar should take care of the problem. If you still have discoloration, use more vinegar, says Krausz.

Caution: Never clean the inside of a dishwasher using any type of detergent not specifically made for automatic dishwashers—not even the liquid dishwashing detergent you use at the kitchen sink. "Any other detergent will suds up all over the place," Krausz says. "You'll wind up with a kitchen full of suds."

Don't use any abrasive cleansers or scouring pads on any part of your dishwasher, inside or out. And remember, if you use a spray cleaner on the exterior, never spray the cleaner directly at the dishwasher.

Disposals

In medieval times, you could just pitch your table scraps to a pack of semi-domesticated mutts. Vets frown on that nowadays. The beauty of the in-sink garbage disposal is that it conveniently grinds and discards food waste that might otherwise sit in your kitchen's garbage container, smelling and attracting insects. But unless you clean the disposal itself, food residue can grow rank, creating bad odors and possibly health risks.

Technique: To cut down on buildup, only grind small amounts of waste at a time and make sure to run the disposal each time you put waste in it.

Colossal Cleanups

Keeping Ronald Busy

The amount of trash the average McDonald's restaurant produces a day: 238 pounds

Run the disposal for a few seconds after grinding to make sure that it is empty of food. Once every week or so, after finishing the dishes in the evening, fill the sink about one-third full with lukewarm water and mix it with ½ cup baking soda. Turn on the disposal and pull out the stopper. The mixture will flow through the disposal and help remove odors. At least once every two weeks, flush the garbage disposal by stopping the sink, filling it halfway with cold water, then letting it drain while the disposal runs. "Grinding citrus peelings will help deodorize the disposal," says John Merrill, a doctor of architecture and housing specialist with the University of Wisconsin Cooperative Extension Service in Madison. Occasionally grind ice cubes, fruit pits, or cooked chicken bones to break up grease deposits on rotors. Do not, however, use steak bones or turkey bones, which are too big and too hard and can injure the motor. Always have the water running while your disposal is on.

Caution: Do not use harsh, drain-cleaning chemicals on disposals. They may harm the machine.

Dolls

There are many different types of dolls, from antique porcelain ones to lifelike babies. Some have hair. Most have clothing of some sort. Cleaning them is a matter of removing soil and stains without harming fabric, chipping the paint, or doing other damage.

Technique: The most common doll material—and the easiest to clean—is the rubbery vinyl used since about the 1960s to represent skin. Before you clean the vinyl, remove the doll's clothes.

Clean vinyl with a nonabrasive, nonbleach cleanser. Nonbleach formula Soft Scrub works well, as does a paste of baking soda and water. Using a clean white cloth, gently rub the cleanser on the vinyl until it is clean. Rinse by wiping it off with a clean damp cloth. Avoid overscrubbing painted-on features like eyes, lashes, and mouths. They could rub off.

Some dolls have vinyl arms, legs, and heads, but their bodies are cloth and are stuffed with a fill material. "You can ruin the cloth if you try to spot-clean it," warns Susan Fritz, co-owner of Denver Doll Hospital, a doll-cleaning and restoration business. "If you get the cloth body wet, it leaves yellow water rings." Instead, have a professional doll cleaner dismantle, unstuff, and clean the doll. Look for a

HOW I DO IT

Getting Dolled Up after a Bath

Susan Fritz is co-owner with her mother of Denver Doll Hospital, a doll-cleaning and restoration business. Here's how she puts the finishing touches on a freshly shampooed doll.

"We treat doll hair just like a person's hair," Fritz says. "If a doll had curly hair to begin with, we set it after we wash and comb it. We use perm rollers since they're so small. One of our drawers here looks like it belongs in a beauty shop. It's loaded with different sizes of perm rollers, perm wrapping paper, and hairpins.

"In the late 1940s, there was a doll on the market called the Toni Doll, sold by the same company that makes Toni home perm kits. She came with perm rollers, perm solution—which was sugar water—wrapping papers, the whole bit. Little girls could set the doll's hair. She was hugely popular. Today, she's a collector's item."

doll restorer in the yellow pages, or ask the owner of a shop that sells dolls for a recommendation.

Composition dolls, which typically date back to the early twentieth century, are also tricky to clean without damaging. Usually made of sawdust, chipped wood, and glue, composition dolls deteriorate and their painted surfaces blister when exposed to water.

"Water on a composition doll is deadly," says Fritz. Try rubbing gently with a white vinyl eraser, available at art and office supply stores. Do not rub with a pencil eraser, which is too abrasive. And be careful not to rub away any of the doll's painted features.

Some of the oldest antique dolls are made of bisque porcelain. Because it has been fired, you can clean it with water—but very carefully. Wipe it gently with a cloth dabbed with a nonabrasive, nonbleach cleanser. Avoid overwetting, and do not get any cloth parts wet. Even though the painted-on features are generally fired as well, take extra care with them.

Most doll clothing, unless it is old or deteriorating, is easy to clean. "It's like normal clothing, just smaller," Fritz says. "Some people are afraid of washing doll clothes, but if you treat them the same way as your own clothing, only more gently, they will be fine."

If the cloth is washable, first test for colorfastness by wetting a corner of the material and squeezing it between the folds of a white handkerchief. If it bleeds, use cold water. If not, use lukewarm water. Soak the clothing for an hour or less in a solution of 2 tablespoons of laundry detergent and 1 gallon of water.

Rinse the clothes by soaking them in clean lukewarm water. Empty the rinse water and repeat the process until there is no soap residue left in the water. To dry them, gently roll the clothes up in a towel. Then, lay them flat on the towel and let them air-dry. If the clothes are wrinkled, carefully iron them on a low setting, using starch, as necessary.

Caution: "When washing the clothes of older dolls, liquid household bleach is a no-no, even with white clothes," Fritz says. Old fabrics are usually delicate. The bleach can deteriorate them even further.

If the clothes are made of silk, taffeta, velvet, or some other nonwashable fabric, take them to a dry cleaner. You might get a funny look, but the cleaner should be able to handle the job. Otherwise, send them to a professional doll cleaner.

Most doll hair, like most doll clothing, is washable. Use any standard shampoo. "Wash it the same way you would wash a small child's hair," Fritz says. Do it beside a sink, and try to only wet the hair. Avoid getting the bodies wet. Do not use a conditioner; it leaves a residue, attracts dirt, and can damage the synthetic hair. Once you have finished, comb the hair and reset it, if necessary, using small perm rollers. "You can let the hair air-dry," says Fritz, "but if you're in a hurry, a blow-dryer on a low setting is fine."

Doormats

Doormats serve an important function—to catch dirt and sand from shoes so that it does not get tracked through the house, where it can scratch floor finishes and abrade carpet and rug fibers. Besides, why welcome someone to your home with a dirty mat?

Technique: Clean doormats as often as possible. If you let them go, they fill up with soil and stop doing their job.

"There are many different varieties of doormats," says Marry Keener, assistant director of facilities management at the University of Arizona in Tucson and a member of the technical advisory committee for *Executive Housekeeping Today* magazine. "If it is an exterior mat, chances are that you can simply hose it off because it is already exposed to the elements."

For mats that can't handle the hose, vacuum the dirt and dust up with a carpet attachment. Try to use a vacuum cleaner with a good beater bar. That helps the machine suck up deeply deposited particles. "I vacuum the one by my back door because my dog brings grass onto it," Keener says.

Doors—Aluminum, Wood

A doorway is like a funnel inside your home. Not only does it get all the people traffic through that one little space but it's also part of your home's airflow system. All of this makes a door vulnerable to dust, grease particles, and smudges.

Technique: Wood is one of the most common door materials and is relatively easy to clean, especially if it is painted or finished with a coating of polyurethane or varnish.

Dust wood doors regularly to prevent particles from adhering to the surface. Clean them, when needed, using a cloth lightly dampened with a solution of warm water and a couple of squirts of liquid dishwashing detergent. Work from the top down. Rinse the solution completely from the door using a cloth dampened only with water.

If your doors are made of raw wood with a penetrating finish (in other words, if they are not protected by a surface coat, such as paint or polyurethane), simply dust them with a lightly dampened cloth, and then apply boiled linseed oil or tung oil, both available at hardware stores, says Douglas Gardner, Ph.D., associate professor of wood science at the School of Forestry and Wood Products, Michigan Tech University in Houghton. Work on a small section at a time. Use a clean cloth to rub in the oil in the direction of the grain until the wood absorbs no more. Fold another cloth into a pad and rub the area until it is dry.

Clean aluminum doors the same way as surface-finished wood doors: Dust them with a damp cloth, and then wash them with a detergent solution or a spray-on, all-purpose cleaner. "You're usually just removing dust particles that are clinging due to the accumulation of oil or pollution," says Marry Keener, assistant director of facilities management at the University of Arizona in Tucson and a member of the technical advisory committee for *Executive Housekeeping Today* magazine. "The all-purpose cleaner does a good job at cutting the grease."

If your aluminum door has a screen, remove it occasionally and spray it clean with the garden hose. Use a nylon or vegetable scrubbing brush to remove any heavy deposits.

Caution: When applying linseed oil, wear rubber gloves and work in a well-ventilated area. Always read the product label for proper use and safety precautions.

Down—Comforters, Jackets, Pillows

Down is a delicate—and expensive—gift from nature. It's one of our best insulating materials. Caring for it is relatively simple but important.

Technique: Clean down items twice a year: once during the wearing season and again before they are put in storage, says Jane Rising, instructor in the education department at the International Fabricare Institute in Silver Spring, Maryland. Most down- and feather-filled comforters and jackets are machine washable. The safest advice is to follow the care and cleaning instructions of the manufacturer.

If there are no instructions, wash in warm water on a gentle cycle and tumble dry on a gentle cycle, according to the American Down Association in Sacramento, California.

Down items must be tumble dried to fluff up completely, says Rising. And they must be dried thoroughly to avoid mildew. That can take up to several hours in the home dryer, she says.

Because down has a distinct odor when wet, wash down-filled items separately from other laundry to avoid transferring the smell. Treat down items like delicates; use a mild detergent and avoid those with enzymes. And never use liquid household bleach, which can break down the organic material that gives down its loft, or insulating quality. To help distribute the down and feathers evenly while drying, which improves loft, dry the down along with a couple of clean tennis balls. Once or twice a year, air out things filled with down outdoors in the shade to keep them fresh.

Down pillows are the exception to these rules. Unless the manufacturer gives you specific instructions to do otherwise, you shouldn't attempt to machine-wash a down pillow, according to Rising. "The down itself is not always the main problem. It's actually the pillow covering that causes turmoil in your washer. Most pillow coverings are made of

The Ins and Outs of Down

Down is the soft undercoating of waterfowl. It is made up of light, fluffy filaments growing from a quill point but, unlike a feather, without a quill shaft. Every ounce of down has about two million of these filaments, which interlock and overlap, forming a protective layer of nonconducting still air. Despite its delicate nature, down stands up fine to washing. After all, the ducks and geese that grow it spend a good part of their time in the water.

water-souble material that can break down in the washing machine and allow the down to leak out of the pillow," says Rising.

The safest way to clean your pillow is to take it to a dry cleaner who is experienced in cleaning down, recommends Rising.

In a pinch: To freshen and remove humidity, place down-filled pillows, comforters, and jackets in a dryer on low heat for about 10 minutes.

Drains

You want drains to be speedy, one-way thoroughfares. Maintaining clean drains not only allows you to continue using sinks and tubs but also keeps water from backing up in the sink, a potential health hazard since bacteria and other contaminants breed in those dark moist recesses.

Technique: "Drains often get clogged because of slow buildup, and the problem suddenly becomes acute because you clean your hairbrush or something," says John Merrill, a doctor of architecture and housing specialist with the University of Wisconsin Cooperative Extension Service in Madison. In bathtubs and sinks, remove hair and lint from the drain strainers whenever you clean the bathroom. Avoid pouring grease down kitchen sink drains; it builds up on the walls of the pipes, eventually clogging them. Dr. Merrill suggests using a water-activated biological cleaner, as opposed to a chemical-based cleaner, once every month or two as a preventive measure. Some health food stores carry a product called Earth Enzymes Drain Opener. "These cleaners set up a bacterial culture in the drain that eats soap scum and grease and keeps hair masses from forming," he says. "They're an alternative to harsh cleaners. As far as I know, they're completely safe and biodegradable," he says. What they won't do is clear the drain if it stops up completely.

For clogs, start with a plunger (also known as a plumber's helper). First, fill the problem sink or tub with water and immerse the plunger sideways to capture as little air under the bell as possible. Plug the overflow, usually found above the drain on tubs and underneath the lips of sinks, with a rubber ball or damp cloth so that it does not weaken your suction. Also, the plunger has to fit completely over the drain to work correctly. Move the plunger up and down a few times over the drain to build up the suction, then pull it away quickly. Try it a few times until either it works or it's clear that you're having no impact at all.

Remember the volcano your kid built in science class? To create the eruption, he probably poured vinegar onto baking soda hidden in the crater. If plunging fails, try the same mixture as a nontoxic alternative to drain cleaners. Bail out as much water as possible from the clogged drain, then pour ¼ to ½ box of baking soda down the drain. Add ½ cup white vinegar, cover the drain tightly for a few minutes, then flush with cold water. The acidic vinegar reacts violently with the basic soda, creating pressure and eating away at the scum lodged in your drain. (For a variation on this technique, see "Formulas for a Clean Home and a Clean Planet" on page 34.)

In a pinch: Pour boiling water down drains regularly to keep them free of debris.

Caution: If you just can't stay away from a commercial drain-cleaning chemical, follow directions carefully. If the drain remains clogged after use, call a plumber immediately; the water backing up in the sink will now be contaminated with dangerous toxins. Whatever you do, don't use a plunger after unsuccessfully using a drain cleaner. You're just asking for a toxic splash in the face.

Drawers

Removing drawers means putting them back. Since refitting the drawer roller into the runner can be a hassle—and most drawers these days come on runners—this is one of those cleaning jobs that usually gets done only partially or gets skipped altogether.

Technique: The easiest way to clean your drawers is with a hand vacuum or a vacuum cleaner brush attachment, says Marry Keener, assistant director of facilities management at the University of Arizona in Tucson and a member of the technical advisory committee for *Executive Housekeeping Today* magazine. Remove the contents of the drawer and then suck up the dust and debris. That's as much of a cleaning as most drawers need.

If, however, your drawer needs a more thorough cleaning—to remove a spill, for example, or during your spring cleaning overhaul—wipe the inner surface with a sudsy sponge, says Keener. Rinse by wiping with a damp sponge. Dry the drawer completely before replacing the contents.

Driveways

Like the exterior of your house, your driveway is important because it's part of the first impression people get of your home. A poured concrete or asphalt slab is also a big expense. You want it to look good and last for a long time.

Technique: Basic cleaning of driveways is relatively simple. "Use a broom and a water hose," says Ross Bentsen, education director of the Asphalt Institute in Lexington, Kentucky. Sweep away large debris. Hose off dirt and other small particles. That goes for any hard-surface driveway: asphalt, concrete, or brick.

Driveways also get stained, collect stuck-on grime, and foster the growth of algae and moss. Every once in a while, you should give it a good scrubbing with a stiff-bristle brush and a warm-water solution of mild dishwashing detergent. For heavier soil, first try adding ammonia to your detergent solution. If that doesn't work, use a solution of trisodium phosphate and warm water, available at most hardware stores. Follow the manufacturer's recommendations for determining what strength solution you need.

Scrub with a stiff-bristle nylon or vegetable brush. Do not use a metallic brush. Tiny filaments can break off and stain the concrete when they rust. Be sure to rinse the driveway thoroughly after cleaning.

If oil leaking from a car has pooled up on the driveway, use an absorbent material to soak it up. Hardware stores sell bags of pellets made expressly for picking up oil and grease from concrete. It looks and acts like cat litter. In fact, in a pinch, cat litter does the same thing. Follow up by scrubbing with the detergent solution mentioned above. If the oil has soaked into the driveway, it might not come out.

To remove more deeply imbedded grime from your driveway, rent a high-pressure water sprayer from an equipment rental company. These are relatively easy to use and are a safe alternative to the use of toxic concrete-cleaning chemicals.

Caution: Wear protective eyewear when using a high-pressure sprayer, and protective eyewear, rubber gloves, and other protective clothing when using trisodium phosphate. Always read the product label for proper use and safety precautions.

In a pinch: High-pressure water sprayers typically rely on a jet of water of 800 pounds per square inch or greater. But your garden hose will do a good job of prying up surface grime, too, if you fit it with a flat fan-pattern nozzle and turn the water on full force. It's much easier than scrubbing.

Dust

Think of every speck of dust you wipe up as the gunk that *didn't* make it into your lungs. Dusting is not simply getting rid of that unsightly layer that builds up on household surfaces. By removing dust, you improve indoor air quality, which is important, considering that the respiratory symptoms of asthma (which affects approximately 15 million people in the United States) are often provoked by dust or other airborne allergens.

Technique: Dust from the top down, using on most surfaces a soft cloth, lightly dampened to help it pick up more particles. (For

Where Does Dust Come From?

"Anything and everything makes up dust," says Claudia Ramirez, former executive vice president of the Association of Specialists in Cleaning and Restoration in Annapolis Junction, Maryland. That can include minute soil particulates, fabric fibers, shed skin, animal dander, insect parts, smoke and ashes, pollen and plant spores, fungi, bacteria, dust mites—you name it. Some particles originate inside; others migrate in through windows, doors, and air vents and can increase in quantity if there is nearby construction work.

Sounds horrible, doesn't it? It can be, especially if you have asthma or allergies, or if certain parts of your house act as a breeding ground for the bacteria and other tiny critters floating around in the air. Take mildew, for example. It originates as a fungus present naturally in dust. When this fungus finds a hospitable location to dwell—a dark moist basement, for instance—it quickly settles in and begins munching on cotton, leather, and other organic materials.

Other microbiological beings, like dust mites, for example, live off the dead skin and hair particles they share dust space with. They hole up in upholstered cushions and bedding and wreak havoc among those who are allergic to them.

HOW I DO IT

The Masked Avenger

Claudia Ramirez is well aware of what she calls the LGTs, or little growing things, that live in the dust that circulates through our homes. As former executive vice president of the Association of Specialists in Cleaning and Restoration in Annapolis Junction, Maryland, part of her job has been to study indoor air–quality issues. Here's how she combats harmful biological agents in her home.

"I dust regularly," Ramirez says. "In the bathroom, where I have carpet, I run the exhaust fan to minimize moisture. I don't want to provide a breeding ground for them. I have allergies, so if I'm doing a big cleaning, I put on a dust mask—the kind you get at the hardware store—because I know it will filter out a lot of the allergens."

draperies and upholstery, use a feather duster or vacuum using a brush attachment.) Go over hard surfaces—bookshelves, tables, chairs—and other items, like picture frames, books, stereo components, and knick-knacks, until everything from the floor up is dust-free.

Next, vacuum hardwood floors using a brush attachment, says Carol Seelaus, a speed-cleaning instructor at Temple University in Philadelphia and owner of Somebody's Gotta Do It, a professional cleaning service. Don't use a broom or a dust mop, she adds; they only spread the dust around and embed the particles in cracks and crevices. If the floors are covered in carpet or rugs, vacuum them—daily for heavily trafficked areas and at least once a week for other areas. For rugs vacuumed weekly, flip them at least once a month and vacuum the backsides. For rugs in heavily trafficked areas, vacuum the backsides once a week. Use a quality vacuum cleaner with a good filter system and a rotating beater bar for stirring up particles.

"Today's technology means better multistage filtering systems on vacuum cleaners," says Claudia Ramirez, former executive vice president of the Association of Specialists in Cleaning and Restoration in Annapolis Junction, Maryland. These exhaust filters keep the finer dust particles that aren't caught by the vacuum bag from kicking back out into the air. But it's important to always clean or replace the filters. "It's like the dryer," she says. "After a while, the dryer doesn't like working with an inch of lint on its filter." Also, don't wait for the vacuum bag to fill completely. It removes dust from the air more efficiently if you empty it when it's between one-half and two-thirds full. After every third emptying, turn nondisposable collection bags inside out and sweep off excess lint and dirt. That way, it does not overwork the machine, and it does a much better job of collecting dust.

Your air-conditioning and heating systems do more than just heat and cool the home. They also circulate and filter air. To cut down on the amount of dust in your home, it's important to keep their filters clean. Ramirez jokingly calls the old fiberglass filters used in heating and air-conditioning systems boulder-catchers. They miss the smaller particulates, which tend to set off allergies or are loaded with potentially harmful living organisms.

A better choice is one of the electrostatic or pleated panel filters available today, says Cliff Zlotnik, a professional duct-cleaning instructor and owner of Unsmoke/Restorx, a property restoration and cleaning company in Braddock, Pennsylvania. No matter which filters you have, clean them regularly—in general, once a month—and replace them when they wear out. Those simple steps will also make your heating and air-conditioning more efficient, saving energy costs and increasing the life span of the equipment.

Don't forget the air conditioner drain pan. "It's moist, dark, and warm from the coils—a wonderful little breeding ground for microbiological agents," Ramirez says. Clean it regularly by removing it from the unit, draining the excess water, and washing it with a sponge or cloth in a mild soap and water solution.

Speed tips: To cut down on static electricity, which helps dust cling to objects, moisten a cling-free dryer sheet and wipe over plastic surfaces.

Egg Stains

 **EMERGENCY ACTION**
Rinse or blot away egg with cold water.

So a waiter slid a plateful of over-easies right into your lap? Don't fret. It's a protein-based stain and not that tough to get out. As with all stains, however, you should attack it as soon as possible to increase your chances of removing it entirely.

Technique: Scrape away any excess egg. For washables, first soak the stained item in cold water to remove as much of the egg as possible. The older the stain, the longer you should soak it—up to several hours.

"Then pretreat it," says Ann Lemley, Ph.D., chair of the department of textiles and apparel at Cornell University in Ithaca, New

York. "That's the trick with most food stains." Begin by mixing ¼ teaspoon clear liquid dishwashing detergent and several drops of ammonia with ½ cup warm water. Apply it directly to the fabric, then lay the garment on a hard surface and pat the stain lightly with the back of a spoon. This allows the solution to get in between the fibers, where stains hide. Don't rub the fabric together; that will abrade the fibers. Next, wash as directed either by machine or by hand in the hottest water safe for the fabric. If the stain does not come out completely, follow the same pretreatment procedure, but this time with a liquid laundry detergent containing enzymes (or a paste made from a granular detergent and water). Apply it directly to the stain, pat, then wash.

For fabrics that cannot be washed, either have them professionally dry-cleaned or blot them with a clean white towel and a spot remover, like Carbona Stain Devils or K2r, available at supermarkets, hardware stores, or discount department stores. Blot from the inside of the garment to push the stain out. Read the label before using these products, and use them in a well-ventilated area while wearing protective latex or rubber gloves.

For carpets and rugs, first blot with the detergent and ammonia solution using a clean white towel. Then rinse by blotting with a clean towel and water. Do not blot with laundry detergent because it often contains optical brighteners that can bleach carpet and rug dyes. Instead, if the first solution doesn't work, blot with a solution of 1 cup white vinegar and 2 cups water.

Note: Before using cleaning solutions, always test them on an inconspicuous section of the stained item.

In a pinch: In the case of washable clothing, skip to pretreat step two: Apply an enzyme detergent directly to the stain, then wash.

Caution: Always rinse out one cleaning solution before trying another. Mixing chemicals, especially ammonia and chlorine bleach, can create noxious fumes.

Erasers

Most Americans learned the art of cleaning chalkboard erasers at an early age when, caught chewing gum or talking in class, they were made to stay after school and beat the chalk dust out of them.

Technique: Clapping erasers together still works, as long as you do it outside. If you'd rather not choke on chalk dust, or if the weather's too nasty for eraser clapping outside, there's a hands-off way to get the task done inside. To remove dust from eraser felt, eraser manufacturers toss the material into large commercial dryers, and you can do the same thing at home, says Charles Barnowski, vice president of sales at the Boston Felt Company in East Rochester, New Hampshire. Put your erasers in your clothes dryer and run them on the "Air-Fluff" or "No Heat" cycle for 5 to 10 minutes. The tumbling action loosens the chalk dust, which is captured by the dryer's filter system or blown out the exhaust vent. "Of course, don't put anything else in the dryer with the erasers," Barnowski says.

You can also vacuum the dust off them. Make sure that your vacuum cleaner bag or filter catches the fine dust and doesn't kick it back into the room.

Eyeglasses

Is your vision getting blurry? The answer might be right in front of your nose. Body oils and dirt constantly build up on eyeglasses. Regular cleaning will improve your vision and make glasses last longer.

Technique: Once a day, wash the lenses—front and back—in warm soapy water using a soft cloth. Before rubbing with the cloth, run water over them to remove large particles. A mild liquid dishwashing detergent is best; bar soap is fine, too. Blot them dry with a soft cloth. Never use abrasive materials or cloths. And avoid cleaning the lenses dry. "The problem is that small particles, perhaps not even visible to the eye, might be present on the lens surface and may scratch the lens as you move the cloth across it," says Stephen Miller, O.D., director of the Clinical Care Center of the American Optometric Association in St. Louis.

Once a month, clean the frames in soap and water. If they are really dirty, carefully scrub the nosepiece and hinges with an old toothbrush. You want to make the frames last at least as long as the lenses do.

In a pinch: "Cleaning them with a handkerchief is certainly an option if you don't have another choice," says Dr. Miller. Be careful, though. First, blow on them to get off as many of the loose dust and dirt particles as possible.

Fabric—Old

Found some clothing treasures in Grandma's attic? Watch your step. When you clean soils and stains on old fabric, your biggest concern is dry rot, which begins as water damage and eventually deteriorates fabric from the inside out. "The fabric may look okay," says Claudia Ramirez, former executive vice president of the Association of Specialists in Cleaning and Restoration in Annapolis Junction, Maryland. "But the minute you put stress on it, it begins crumbling."

Technique: When it comes to cleaning antique dresses, rugs, and other old fabric, the cardinal rule is simple: Be careful. If there is ever a time to seek professional cleaning help, even beyond a dry cleaner, this is it. Because of dry rot, you may ruin an heirloom, like an old wedding dress or an antique quilt, when trying to clean it. A professional, on the other hand, might be able to repair or restore the fabric, then clean it. For a fresh spill on old fabric, simply blot it with a clean white cloth; if the stain remains, contact a professional textile cleaner. (For a referral in your area, write to the Association of Specialists in Cleaning and Restoration at 10830 Annapolis Junction Road, Suite 312, Annapolis Junction, MD 20701-1120.)

Fans—Ceiling, Exhaust, Floor

By their nature, fans attract dirt. As air passes through them, particles attach themselves to the blades and other parts. Remove this grime and you have a better-looking, and more efficient, appliance.

Technique: Dust window fans and floor fans regularly to cut down on buildup. Run the vacuum cleaner brush attachment over both sides of the fan grille to remove loose particles. To dust the blades and inner parts, use compressed air or a blow-dryer. Cleaning the blades keeps the fan running smoothly.

Two or three times a year, remove the grilles (if possible) and clean them with a garden hose and a nylon or vegetable brush. Wipe down blades and other plastic parts with a cloth and a little all-purpose cleaner. Spray a bit of lubricant, such as WD-40, at the base of the blade shaft.

Likewise, dust exhaust fans regularly using whatever method works best—a vacuum cleaner or a damp cloth. If possible, remove the fan covers twice a year or so and wipe down the blades and other nonelectric parts with a cloth dampened with a little all-purpose cleaner.

Range hoods collect cooking grease and require a more extensive cleaning. Wipe them down weekly with a sudsy sponge to reduce grease buildup. Every few months, soak the removable, nonelectric parts in a sink or dishpan filled with warm water and a few squirts of liquid dishwashing detergent. Gently scrub grease deposits with a sponge or plastic mesh scrubber. Wipe down the permanently installed parts with a damp sudsy sponge. Do not use steel wool. It can scratch stainless steel, enamel, and plastic.

If your range hood is a ductless one, replace the filter with a new one every three to four months. Or wash the filter as recommended by the manufacturer.

Ceiling fans gather just as much gunk as other fans, sometimes more when they are exposed to rising smoke from cigarettes, fireplaces, or kitchens. Unfortunately, ceiling fans can be difficult to clean. Dangling from a 10-foot ceiling, they make a formidable foe for any dust warrior.

Long-handle brushes designed to clean both sides of a fan blade at once are available. The brush head is shaped like a thin U and the fan blade fits in the slit. You can buy them at home supply stores or wherever they sell ceiling fans.

Dust your ceiling fan monthly. Then, two to four times a year, give it a more thorough cleaning. Wash the blades and housing with a damp cloth and an all-purpose cleaner or a solution of warm water and a couple squirts of liquid dishwashing detergent. Dry them well. Otherwise, they'll pick up more dust.

Caution: Unplug and turn off all fans before cleaning. Do not get any type of cleaning solution into the motor of a fan.

Fiberglass

Not all that glistens is rock hard. Work carefully when cleaning fiberglass, which you find in fixtures, windowpanes, and one-piece showers, tubs, and sinks. It scratches easily, and once its finish is gone, it stains easily, too.

Technique: Clean molded fiberglass using a nonabrasive sponge or cloth and either an all-purpose cleaner or a tub-and-tile cleaner, says Mary Meehan-Strub, Family Living agent at La Crosse County University of Wisconsin Cooperative Extension. Scouring powders or other abrasives will dull, scratch, and discolor the surface and make it vulnerable to staining. Rinse well and dry with a soft cloth.

Since abrasives can't be used, wipe molded sinks and tubs dry after each use to avoid mineral and soap deposits. If these deposits do occur, use baking soda as a gentle abrasive. Apply a paste of baking soda and cool water, leave for an hour, then rub off, rinse, and dry. For stubborn stains and deposits, apply cloths soaked in an all-purpose cleaner and let them stand for at least one hour. Rinse with a clean sponge.

Fireplaces

Because of the nature of what's happening inside a fireplace—and the porous quality of brick—you have to be realistic about how clean-looking you can get it. "Some people expect their fireplaces to look brand new, and that's just not going to happen," says Ashley Eldridge, director of education for the Chimney Safety Institute of America and technical director for the National Chimney Sweep Guild, both in Gaithersburg, Maryland. Keeping the fireplace working efficiently is your main goal. That means removing ash on a regular basis.

Technique: Remove the ashes from your fireplace when the pile gets as high as the fire grate or andirons. But for maximum efficiency, leave an inch-thick layer of ash. It insulates the floor, helping the firebox retain heat and keeping coals burning longer. To remove ash, wait at least two days after your last fire to make sure that all the coals are cool. Set aside the fire screen, andirons, and grate. Using a fireplace broom and shovel, sweep up the ashes and put them in a metal bucket—preferably one with a lid to keep the ashes from floating out. Immediately empty the bucket outdoors away from the house, in a metal trash can with a lid. If the fireplace has an ash pit, open it and sweep the ashes into it (then empty the ash pit from the clean-out door, usually located in the basement or outside the house). Do not vacuum the ashes. Most vacuum cleaners designed for home use will not pick up the finest ash. Instead, they suck it up and shoot it out into the air.

Once a year, give your fireplace a thorough cleaning. Make it part of your annual spring cleaning—after the fire season has ended—and do it first so that the dust it stirs up does not fall on already-clean surfaces. Begin by sweeping up all the ashes. Scrape creosote from the firebox walls using a stiff-bristle wire brush. You can buy them at hardware stores and fireplace-equipment stores, says Eldridge. Use a soap solution of ½ cup liquid dishwashing detergent per gallon of lukewarm water to wash the brick. Apply the solution with a sponge or cloth and scrub with a stiff-bristle fiber brush. (When scrubbing with both the wire brush and the fiber brush, wear protective eyewear.) Rinse the surface with a sponge or cloth and clean water.

For glass doors on enclosed fireplaces, use either a commercial glass cleaner, like Windex, or a homemade solution, like a squirt of liquid dishwashing detergent in a bucket of warm water or 1 cup vinegar per gallon of water. Let the glass cool before cleaning. Spray or sponge the cleaner on, and then wipe it off with newspaper to avoid leaving lint. Scrape off thick gunk deposits using a razor blade. For an old-fashioned chimney sweep's trick, take a moist cloth and lightly dip it in the fluffy ash that sits on top of the ash pile. Rub the ash on the dirty window in a circular motion. "It polishes the glass like a jeweler's rouge," Eldridge explains. Wipe it clean with a paper towel.

Use the same soap and water solution and fiber brush to clean fireplace accessories, like andirons, pokers, and shovels. Then wipe them clean and dry with a cloth. Remove rust or soot deposits from iron or steel tools by rubbing gently using a very fine (#000) steel wool. Then polish by rubbing with a superfine (#0000) steel wool. For brass surfaces, rub on a brass cleaner using a lint-free cloth.

At least once a year, hire a professional to inspect your chimney. Based on the thickness of the buildup, he can determine whether it needs cleaning. This is a necessary safety precaution against the buildup of creosote, gummy resin deposits that can cause dangerous chimney fires. For a referral in your area, contact the National Chimney Sweep Guild, 16021 Industrial Drive, Suite 8, Gaithersburg, MD 20877.

In a pinch: You can't expect to remove all the black coloring from the brick inside the fireplace. "Sometimes it's easier to clean the residual deposits from the surface of the brick, and then paint it all black. Then at least it's uniform," says Eldridge. Use a high-temperature (1,200°F minimum) paint, and be sure to leave the damper open for good ventilation while painting, says Eldridge.

Caution: Wear a dust mask when removing ashes from the fireplace. When sweeping ashes, be extremely careful to avoid still-hot coals. Wait at least two days after your last fire before cleaning ashes. Put them in metal containers only.

Fireplace Screens

Since the fireplace is the centerpiece of many rooms, it is important to keep the fireplace screen that covers it clean and presentable.

Technique: Make cleaning the fireplace screen part of your regular household cleaning routine. To remove dust, vacuum each side with the vacuum cleaner brush attachment.

Once or twice a season (or when necessary), use a cleaning solution of ⅛ cup liquid dishwashing detergent per quart of water to remove caked-on dirt. Gently scrub the screen with a soft-bristle fiber brush. Rinse by wiping the screen with a wet lint-free cloth. Dry thoroughly with a lint-free cloth to avoid rusting. Polish brass sections with a brass cleaner and a lint-free cloth.

Speed tips: To prevent creating extra messes that you'll have to clean up, lay the screen on its side on a drop cloth—in the garage or on a deck, not in the middle of your living room.

In a pinch: After dusting the wire mesh, paint it black using a high-temperature (1,200°F minimum) satin spray paint. Do it outside on a drop cloth or similar ground cover. Spray one side from all angles, let it dry, and then flip the mesh and spray the other from all angles.

Fishing Gear

Clean gear simply makes you fish better. "If you're fishing in salt water, removing salt from your gear is your most important goal," says Mark Sosin, host of *Mark Sosin's Saltwater Journal*, a television program on the Nashville Network, and author of more than two dozen books and countless magazine articles. "But even in freshwater, dirt gets tracked into boats and finds its way into reels." Keeping equipment clean means smoother-spinning reels and other performance benefits, plus added years of use.

Technique: After each time you use your rod and reel, wash them with lukewarm water and liquid dishwashing detergent. Mix the solution in a bucket until sudsy, and then use a sponge or cloth to wipe off all dirt, fish slime, and salt. "You must have detergent to take salt off," Sosin emphasizes. "The detergent floats the salt. If you just rinse it with water, a salt residue remains." Either let the gear air-dry or dry it with a soft cloth. Then apply a coat of demoisturizing compound, like WD-40, by spraying it on a cloth and wiping the cloth over the metal parts. Never spray it directly on the reel. Too much can get sticky and actually attract dirt.

Most rods made today use foam rubber in the handle, but if you have a rod with a cork handle, gently scrub the cork with steel wool to remove dirt and discoloration.

To remove salt and other grime, soak lures in the same bucket of soapy water used to clean the rod and reel, rinse them, then dry them off. Even though most are made of plastic, that will help keep the metal hooks from rusting.

Spray the metal parts of a tackle box with a demoisturizing compound regularly. At least a couple of times a year—more if you fish often—

HOW I DO IT

The Ultimate Casting Call

Mark Sosin makes his living as a sport fisherman. The author of more than two dozen books and countless magazine articles, Sosin is the host of *Mark Sosin's Saltwater Journal*, which ran on ESPN for 12 years and is now on the Nashville Network. "I depend on my tackle. We have big dollars flowing when we shoot our television show, and if the tackle fails, that's a very costly mistake.

"To get the salt and grime off my rod and reel, I use one of those car-washing mitts. I dip my hand in liquid dishwashing detergent and water and run it over the whole thing. I then rinse off with freshwater. It's quick, and if there are any sharp edges, my hand is covered."

lubricate the inside of your reel with a spray or a light oil.

In a pinch: "If I'm traveling, and I don't have the facilities to properly wash my rod and reel," says Sosin, "I just take them in the shower and wash them off with a washcloth."

Fish Ponds

"You want to reduce the organic debris that accumulates in the pond, in order to maintain the pond's natural balance of life," says Keith Folsom, co-owner of Springdale Water Gardens, a mail-order supplier in Greenville, Virginia. "Excess debris causes pond pollution, turning the water pea-soup green and creating odors." The organic wastes also give off nitrogen, which is toxic to fish.

Technique: Remove leaves, sticks, and other debris from the pond periodically, especially in the fall. This makes an annual cleaning easier.

Clean your pond once a year, in the spring or fall when the tap-water temperature is cooler and better-suited for fish. Clean on a cool, cloudy day so that your pond plants don't dry out, advises Folsom.

Begin by filling a holding tank for fish—a five-gallon bucket, an aquarium, or a kiddie pool—halfway with tap water. Use a commercial dechlorinating agent, available at pond supply stores, to dechlorinate the tap water. Fill the holding tank the rest of the way with water from the pond. Use a siphon or pump to make the transfer easier. This mixture helps ease the transition for the fish from a dirty pond to a clean pond.

Using a net, transfer the fish to the holding tank. Keep the holding tank in a shaded area. Place a screen over the container to keep the fish from jumping out.

Continue draining the pond, releasing the nutrient-rich water around the plants in your yard. Gently pull up plants and set them aside in the shade. Cover floating plants, like water lilies, with wet newspaper and plastic to keep them moist.

Note: Plastic alone will cause them to overheat quickly.

As the water level drops, scrub the sides of the pond with a nylon brush. Rinse where you have cleaned by tossing water up onto it and letting it fall into the pond. The sediment will collect at the bottom, once the pond is empty.

Finally, scrape up the silt that has settled to the bottom. Remove it with a shovel, and spread it around the garden as mulch.

After cleaning your pond, dump half the water from the holding tank where you've stored your fish back into the pond. This helps inoculate the clean pond with beneficial bacteria.

Mulm's the Word: An Organic Tip for Fish Ponds

Sometimes squeaky-clean is not the best kind of clean. Take fish ponds, for example. "You don't want to clean your fish pond so that it's spotless," says Keith Folsom, co-owner of Springdale Water Gardens, a mail-order supplier in Greenville, Virginia. "You want to maintain some of the natural bacteria that have grown on the side of the pond."

"Organic waste, known as mulm, settles on the bottom of fish ponds. The beneficial bacteria consume nitrogen given off by the mulm, helping prevent the growth of algae, which needs the nitrogen to thrive. It keeps your water from turning green and protects your fish since the nitrogen can be toxic to them. It's a good way of controlling the quality of your water without relying on chemical means."

Bottom Feeders: Ridding the World of Scum

Remember the Scrubbing Bubbles from that popular TV commercial? The ones that attacked the dirty tub with the cleaning zeal of Marines on inspection day? Think of pond scavengers as real-life scum-busters.

"A combination of snails, mussels, and tadpoles help strike an ecological balance in your fish pond," says Keith Folsom, co-owner of Springdale Water Gardens, a mail-order supplier in Greenville, Virginia. They feed on the organic wastes given off by fish and plants, reducing algae growth and keeping the water clear.

Japanese snails, which graze the muck on the bottom and sides of the pond, are one of the best pond scavengers because they do not overpopulate or escape the water. Tadpoles and mussels filter suspended algae from the water.

A good rule of thumb is to stock one scavenger per square foot of pond surface.

Next, refill the pond with tap water and dechlorinate it. To help the fish adjust to the temperature difference, fill the holding tank with tap water, and wait 20 to 30 minutes. Again, empty half of the water into the pond, and refill the holding tank with tap water. Repeat this procedure until the water temperature in the holding tank is the same as that in the pond.

If your pond is filtered, clean the filtration equipment, following the manufacturer's instructions. Usually, this is simply a matter of spraying the filter element down with a hose. If soap and water is required, make sure that you rinse the filter completely before you replace it.

Speed tips: Keep scavengers like snails or mussels in your fish pond. They help keep it clean, making the year-end cleaning quicker and easier. When cleaning, transfer the snails and mussels to your holding tank before cleaning the pond. Replace them once you have finished.

In a pinch: Using a plastic rake, carefully rake up organic debris from the bottom of your pond. If you use mussels or snails as scavengers, be sure to pick them out of the debris and return them to the water.

Caution: Do not clean your pond more often than once a year. The beneficial bacteria need that time to grow.

Don't attempt to remove fish when the water level in the pond is still high. Chasing them can bruise them. Instead, let it get low enough so that the fish have trouble escaping your net.

Fixtures—Bathroom, Kitchen

Soap scum and grease love to dull a faucet's shine. And when left on the fixture, they foster bacteria growth like a petri dish. You want to get rid of this layer of gunk before it strengthens its hold against future scrubbing.

Technique: Clean faucets, knobs, shower heads, and other fixtures regularly, using an nonabrasive all-purpose cleaner or a tub-and-tile cleaner, like Comet Bathroom Cleaner, and a sponge or soft cloth. Never use abrasive cleaners or scrubbers in the bathroom. Spray it on, let it sit for a few seconds while the cleaning agents work on the scum, and then wipe it off. The cleaner should do most of the work. Clean cracks and crevices with a soft brush. Rinse by wiping everything down with a clean wet sponge or cloth.

Simplify your chores by using one product instead of several. "The commercial spray scum removers like Tilex Soap Scum Remover these days are almost magic," says Jim Brewer, executive housekeeper at the University of Texas at Arlington and a technical advisor to *Cleaning and Maintenance Magazine*. "You're trying to remove three things—oil, soap, and mineral deposits—plus the occasional mildew. People used to clean fixtures at least twice, but the new products are composites. They take all three things off as well as the mildew." While using any cleaning product, it's important that you ventilate the room well by opening the door and windows and turning on the exhaust fan.

Speed tips: Clean bathroom fixtures with your damp towel after showering, when they are slightly moist. Do it often and scum will not have a chance to build up.

Caution: "Rule number one is to never combine any cleaning products because they may contain reactive ingredients such as ammonia or chlorine," says Brewer. "Ammonia and chlorine make a mustard gas, a toxic chlorine gas, if they're combined. I nearly killed myself mixing those chemicals once. I was sick for weeks." Never sniff the bottle to see what's in it, and be sure to read the label completely for proper usage and safety precautions.

Flatware

If dinner guests notice your flatware at all, you want it to be because it shines so brilliantly. Smudgy forks, knives, and spoons won't do. So follow this cutting-edge advice.

Technique: Wash all flatware after use. When you're washing by hand, make it one of the first things you clean, along with glasses. Or, if you do it last, change the dishwater. Let the utensils presoak to loosen caked-on food. Wash them in hot soapy water using a sponge or cloth—never anything abrasive, even on stainless steel. Abrasives will dull the finish of metals. Rinse flatware with hot water. Place it handles-down in a silverware basket to air-dry, and try to leave as much room as possible for air circulation between each piece.

When loading the dishwasher, also place flatware handles-down. "That way, when water drips off of them, it doesn't leave stains on the bowl of the spoon, the tines of the fork or the blade of the knife," says Kari Kinder, assistant director of food and beverage at the renowned Culinary Institute of America in Hyde Park, New York. Never sprinkle automatic dishwasher detergent directly onto flatware before washing. That can cause pitting.

When machine-washing, do not place silver or silver-plate flatware next to stainless steel flatware. The steel will tarnish the silver. For the same reason, make sure that all silver knives are situated with their blades up. Even if the handles are silver, the blades are often stainless steel.

For that extra shine—in preparation for a dinner party, for example—polish flatware with a soft cotton cloth after it has dried.

Floors—Brick, Concrete, Hardwood, Terrazzo, Vinyl

Floors suffer. They hold up our monstrous dressers, pianos, and couches. They bear our shuffling, running, and stomping. And, unless you live in a space station, they catch virtually everything that spills. Still, we expect them to maintain their composure and good looks.

Not only does keeping your floors clean make them look better but also dirt and grit can scratch floors. So clean floors also last longer.

Technique: Vacuum or sweep all types of floors regularly—daily in high-traffic areas—to keep grit to a minimum. Do not use abrasive cleaners that will scratch floors.

Brick

Sealed brick is easier to keep clean than unsealed brick. Regardless of the surface, vacuum or sweep it regularly, and damp mop periodically with plain water. For cleaning heavier soil, mop with a

Cleaning Floors the Old-Fashioned Way

How's this for a housekeeping tip? Empty your spice shelf onto the floor. British author Hannah Glasse, in her *Servants Directory*, published in 1760, recommended the following method for cleaning floors: "Take tanzy, mint, and balm; first sweep the room, then strew the herbs on the floor, and with a long hard brush rub them well all over the boards, till you have scrubb'd the floor clean. When the boards are quite dry, sweep off the greens, and with a dry bubbing brush dry-rub them well, and they will look like mahogany, of a fine brown, and never want any other washing, and give a sweet smell to the room."

moderately strong alkali solution, like Spic and Span or another cleaner that contains trisodium phosphate. Rinse the floor well to remove all of the cleaning solution.

Concrete

Poor lowly concrete. Common in garages and basements, it tends to be forgotten when it comes to upkeep. But it needs regular cleaning, just like finer floors. In fact, a simple scrubbing every once in a while will dramatically enhance the appearance of your concrete.

Sweep your concrete floor regularly. Wash it when needed by mopping or scrubbing with a squirt of liquid dishwashing detergent in a bucket of warm water. For heavier soil, use trisodium phosphate, available at most hardware stores. Follow the manufacturer's recommendations for determining what strength solution you need.

"Scrubbing is, unfortunately, often necessary, and you may have to apply it more than once," says Mary Hurd, an engineer in Farmington Hills, Michigan, and consulting editor of the trade journal *Concrete Construction*. Scrub with a stiff-bristle nylon or vegetable brush. Do not use a metal brush. Tiny filaments can break off and stain the concrete when they rust. Be sure to rinse the floor thoroughly after cleaning with a solution.

Caution: Wear protective eyewear, gloves, and long sleeves when using trisodium phosphate. Always read the product label for proper use and safety precautions.

Hardwood

Most wood floors are protected by a sealer, which penetrates the wood pores, and a coating of polyurethane, shellac, or varnish. Others are covered only by wax. As with all floors, vacuum or sweep often to keep dirt from grinding into the floor's finish. Wipe up spills and mud immediately using a damp cloth. Avoid wetting even well-sealed floors too much. Dry them with a clean towel.

Do not wax a urethane finish. The wax prevents future recoating, which is how you renew a dulled finish without stripping, sanding, and refinishing the floor. Likewise, choose cleaning products carefully. "If a customer just picks up something that says 'Hardwood Floor Cleaner,' it's usually a diluted solution of mineral spirits and wax," says Daniel Boone, technical director of the National Wood Flooring Association in Ellisville, Missouri. "It may look good on the floor, but using it would mean they could never recoat the floor and would void the manufacturer's warranty for a new floor."

Instead, Boone suggests, use a cleaner recommended by the manufacturer of your floor or your floor's finish. "If you use Brand A wood floor finish, then you want to use Brand A cleaner or what Brand A recommends for that specific finish," he says.

If you don't know the type of finish or its manufacturer, use a general cleaner, like Woodwise Floor Cleaner, available at wood flooring distributors or warehouse-style home supply stores.

For wax finishes, do the same. Use a wax recommended by the maker. Never use a water-based cleaner. It can stain the wood white.

To remove white water spots on a wax-finish floor, rub gently and in a circular motion with an extra-fine (#000) steel wool and a small amount of mineral spirits. Be sure that the area in which you are working is adequately ventilated. Then apply additional wax to the area and buff.

Caution: Read product labels completely for proper usage and safety precautions.

Terrazzo

Terrazzo is a mixture of cement and small bits of marble and granite. Because the cement is porous, it tends to absorb stains and is often coated with a penetrating sealer. Some modern forms of terrazzo, made with synthetic resins such as urethane or epoxy in place of the cement, do not stain as readily.

Sweep or vacuum regularly. Damp mop using a cleaner that is as close to neutral as possible—those which are neither acid nor alkaline. Try something mild, like Murphy Oil Soap, suggests Dick Bray, technical services manager for the Wood Floor Covering Association in Anaheim, California. In general, avoid all-purpose cleaners, detergents, and wax removers. With a wet mop, apply the solution and allow it to sit for several minutes. Then mop up the dirty solution, changing the rinse water often. This helps remove all soil and also does away with unsightly mop lines.

If your terrazzo floor contains stubborn dirt, consider renting an electric scrubbing machine from an equipment rental company. Use a stronger solution of the neutral cleaner.

Caution: Never use petroleum-based cleaners, like Endust or Pledge, for dust-mopping terrazzo. The oil can penetrate the surface and cause permanent staining. (Murphy Oil Soap is okay because it is made from vegetable oil.)

Vinyl

Most residential vinyl flooring today is what is known as no-wax flooring. Whether it comes in sheet or tile form, it is usually protected by a polyurethane-type coating that has a built-in shine. To help your floor keep that shine, however, clean it regularly.

For a lightly soiled floor, sweep or vacuum first, and then mop with a sponge mop using warm water and a no-rinse floor cleaner, following label directions. Clean one section of the floor at a time. Rinse the mop in a sink or second bucket before placing it again into the warm water and cleaner. That will keep the wash water cleaner. Be sure to wring out the mop thoroughly at every step. Rinsing is usually not necessary after a light cleaning. To be sure, follow the product manufacturer's recommendations.

If your floor requires a thorough cleaning, begin by sweeping or vacuuming loose debris. Then apply a heavy-duty cleaner, such as a polish remover specifically recommended by your floor's manufacturer. Mop the entire floor, wringing the mop occasionally. Next, using a clean mop and bucket of fresh cool water, rinse the floor to eliminate any remaining cleaning solution. Avoid one-step "mop and polish" products, liquid dishwashing detergents, and oil-based cleaners. They leave a residue that can attract dirt and dull your floor, says Brian Quigley, director of consumer affairs at Congoleum Corporation, a vinyl flooring maker in Mercerville, New Jersey.

Eventually, all finishes lose some of their shine as the no-wax coating dulls. Wear and tear may cause dulling of the shine in some floors. You can renew it by applying a manufacturer-recommended acrylic floor polish, which will help protect the floor against surface abrasions. For best results, apply polish very thinly, following label directions.

Spot-clean spills or scuffs as they occur to prevent them from becoming permanent. Use a clean cloth or paper towel dampened with floor cleaner. Lighter fluid, applied gently with a clean cloth, is suggested for difficult scuff marks or adhesives. Lighter fluid is a flammable solvent, however, so use it cautiously and following information on the label.

Flowers— Artificial, Dried, Silk

You want them to look as beautiful as, well, fresh-cut flowers from the garden. However, "the trouble with silk and other artificial flowers is that, because they are permanent, they collect dust and spider-webs," points out Louise Wrinkle, a veteran horticulture judge for the Garden Club of America in New York City.

Technique: Dust the flowers from time to time using a can of compressed air or a blow-dryer set on the lowest, coolest setting. Be gentle with dried flowers, which are often brittle and can shed. If you find that yours are shedding, take them outside to dust them.

In a pinch: Simply shake or ruffle silk flowers to remove dust. Or if they're delicate, gently blow on them.

Licking the Competition

Flower shows may not offer much in the way of thrills, chills, and excitement, but they can be competitive. And, it turns out, cleanliness counts in the judging. Here's how *The Daffodil Journal*, published by the American Daffodil Society, recommends preparing a winning blossom.

"Thoroughly clean all dirt from the bloom. Use a cotton swab, moistened in your mouth with saliva. Saliva will pick up dust particles better than water.

"Check the back of the flower to see if the spathe (a leaf at the base of the bud) became wet and stained the back of the petals. The only effective way to remove the stain is to lick it off. For those of you saying, 'Yuck,' it's only plant juice, for heaven's sake, and no different from eating your asparagus."

Foam Rubber

Dust, body oil, and perspiration accumulate on foam pillows, cushions, and mattresses. These things harbor microorganisms, like dust mites, which can cause allergies. Take away their dinner and those microorganisms will go away.

Technique: There are different types of foam rubber—some washable, some not. Before you clean for the first time, always read the product care label.

If your foam rubber is a single piece, remove dust and dust mite droppings and body parts by vacuuming it with the appropriate attachment, like an upholstery brush.

As for washing single-piece foam, generally speaking, you should soak it first in cool water. If there are oily stains and perspiration in the foam, pretreat it with a commercial product, like Biz, or apply a liquid laundry detergent (or a paste made from a granular detergent and water) containing enzymes. Look for enzymes in the list of your detergent's ingredients.

Next, fill a sink, tub, or basin with warm water and a few squirts of liquid dishwashing detergent, enough to create a nice sudsy bath. Wash the foam by pushing down on it, releasing and pushing down again. Rinse the same way, using clean water. Empty the rinse water and refill the basin with clean water. Repeat this process until there is no more soap residue.

To dry foam rubber, gently squeeze out as much water as possible, blot with clean towels, and then let it dry in the sun or at room temperature. "The center of the foam rubber can take a while to dry," says Rajiv Jain, laboratory manager for the Association of Specialists in Cleaning and Restoration in Annapolis Junction, Maryland. "But foam usually has a good network of capillaries, and water will eventually evaporate."

If you have the kind of foam pillows that are filled with many small fragments of foam rubber, never take them out of their cover. They are hard to manage and can deteriorate easily. You can wash most types of these pillows in the washing machine. Use cold water, which is safer on the synthetic filling. Tumble dry on low heat or dry them in the sun on a patio chair.

Speed tips: Use an electric fan to speed up the drying process.

Caution: Never use solvents on foam rubber, and never tumble it dry on high heat. Both can damage it.

Food—Lettuce, Root Vegetables, Spinach

If you're going to put it in your mouth, you *really* want it clean. So you want to remove not only the big stuff—dirt and grit—but also any pesticide residue or bacteria clinging to the surface of your fresh vegetables. Even though the veggies themselves do not nurture the growth of pathogens, like meats do, the debris on them very well could, says Bessie Berry, manager of the U.S. Department of Agriculture's Meat and Poultry Hotline in Washington, D.C. Here we address a few vegetables that are famous for needing extra cleanup help.

Technique: To clean lettuce, spinach, and other greens, first clean out your sink or a similar-size basin and fill it with cold tap water. Separate the leaves from the stalk, put them in the sink, and swish them around. The dirt lifts off and sinks to the bottom, and the cold water crisps the greens. Dry in a lettuce spinner, available at kitchen supply stores, or by blotting with paper towels or a clean dishcloth.

"You don't need to run water over each leaf," says Elizabeth Aquino, a freelance chef and graduate of the New York Restaurant School in New York City. "That's a waste of water and a waste of time."

If your greens are really dirty, repeat the procedure after emptying and rinsing the sink and refilling it with freshwater.

Clean root vegetables—carrots, beets, radishes—by scrubbing them under running water with a vegetable brush.

Speed tips: "You don't have to thoroughly clean root vegetables that you're going to peel," Aquino says. Save your energy. Simply rinse them under tap water and peel. If you're cooking the vegetables, roast them in the oven first to make peeling easier.

Food Graters

As with all food-preparation implements, you want to clean off all food residue to avoid bacteria growth and the mixing of flavors.

Technique: Clean graters with a nylon or vegetable scrub brush and warm soapy water. Stroke inside and outside surfaces with the "grain" of the grater, not against it, which will damage the bristles of the brush. The brush fibers work much better than a sponge or scrubbing pad. They get down into the nooks and crannies of the grater to remove stuck-on particles. Dry the grater completely before putting it away.

Speed tips: Surfaces used for grating hard cheeses, ginger, and citrus rinds—the finest side of a box grater—tend to be hardest to clean. To make this task easier, wrap the grater with plastic wrap, grate, and then remove the plastic. "For example, when you're grating lemon rind for a cake batter, all the zest sticks to the plastic wrap and not the grater," says Michael Beglinger, executive chef at Deutsche Bank in New York City. "It makes holes where the grater tips poke out, but the plastic wrap does not rip apart or shred into the food."

Food Grinders

Now you know why the tough chores are called a grind. The most difficult parts of a meat grinder to clean are the dies, the interchangeable pieces that determine the thickness of the food you're grinding. With a meat grinder, for instance, "it's just plain hard to get the meat out of those little holes," says Michael Beglinger, executive chef at Deutsche Bank in New York City. You want to remove any residue to avoid bacteria growth.

Technique: Disassemble the grinder and flush the parts with very hot water. This gets rid of most food particles.

A common way to clean the holes in the die is to poke the meat or other food particles through with a toothpick, but this is time-consuming. "One trick is to fold a sponge in half, soak it with water and press the die on it fast and hard," Beglinger says. That pushes the particles out of the holes. "It works especially well on the really fine dies that are hard to clean."

Next, clean all the pieces in warm soapy water using a nylon or vegetable scrub brush and let them air-dry.

Speed tips: To make it easier to clean a meat grinder, grind a piece of bread after you have finished grinding your meat. As soon as the bread starts coming out, stop. This gets all the meat out of the die. The bread flushes more easily when rinsed with hot water.

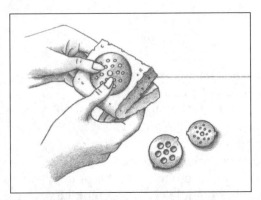

To remove food particles from the small holes of a food-grinder die, press the die down on a wet, folded sponge.

Food Processors

"Most food processors have safety precautions that make cleaning tough," says Michael Beglinger, executive chef at Deutsche Bank in New York City. Any way you slice it, the key is cleaning your food processor right away to remove food before it sticks to hard-to-reach places or dries up and is then harder to clean.

Technique: Begin by reading the manufacturer's recommended cleaning instructions. Generally speaking, you should disassemble your machine and wash the removable parts in warm soapy water. Clean the blades, bowls, and other parts as soon after you use it as possible. Wipe down the base with a sudsy sponge or cloth. Rinse it by wiping with a clean moist sponge. Do not scrub with steel wool or other harsh scouring cleaners. That could scratch the appliance's surface and dull its appearance.

If the food in your processor does dry out and stick, soak the nonelectric parts in warm soapy water. Scrub with a small nylon or vegetable brush to remove residue.

Speed tips: Put the removable parts in the dishwasher. (Read the instructions first to make sure that the parts are dishwasher-safe.) To be safe, put the parts on the top rack. They might melt if they are exposed to the heating element below.

Caution: Unplug your food processor before cleaning. Do not try to sharpen the blades of your food processor unless the manufacturer recommends it. Most have been permanently sharpened by the maker. Food processor blades are extremely sharp, so handle them with care.

Fountains

A trickling fountain is a serene addition to any backyard, until white or green discoloration gets your blood pressure up. "Scale, the white mineral deposits caused by hard water, and algae are the main issues when it comes to fountains," says Keith Folsom, co-owner of Springdale Water Gardens, a mail-order supplier in Greenville, Virginia. Sticking to a cleaning routine will help prevent either from taking hold.

Technique: Both scale and algae build up over time. The more you prevent their buildup, the easier it will be to clean your fountain.

To prevent algae, use a commercial algae treatment, available at water-garden and fountain suppliers. Typically applied a few drops at a time once a month or so, these inhibit algae growth without the use of chlorine or other harsh chemicals.

You can buy a similar commercial treatment for inhibiting scale. It works the same way to keep scale from forming on your fountain, fountainhead, and filters. You use 2 to 4 ounces for each 10 gallons of water.

If you want to not use the commercial products, clean your fountain as needed, usually once a week. "For scale and algae, vinegar is one of the best cleaning agents you can use," Folsom says. Empty the fountain and, using a one-to-one solution of vinegar and water, scrub the surfaces with a nylon brush. "The vinegar will neutralize alkaline mineral deposits, plus it has good cleaning qualities." Rinse well by spraying the fountain with the garden hose.

Clean the pump and filter weekly as well. Remove the filter and spray it with the garden hose. If not, algae, especially the filament-shaped kind, can clog it. Wipe down the exterior of the pump with a wet cloth. If the pump has mineral deposits, wipe it down with the vinegar solution and rinse with clean water. If you need to scrape algae or mineral deposits out of the intake valve, use the bottle brush supplied with your pump kit, or use a wooden stick, like a Popsicle stick. Metal can scratch the surface.

Caution: To avoid the risk of shock, always unplug your pump before cleaning it.

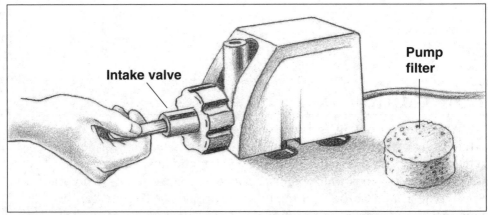

Pump filter

Intake valve

Remove your fountain pump's filter and spray it with the garden hose. Scrape algae or mineral deposits out of the intake valve using a rounded wooden stick or a narrow nylon brush.

Fur

Furs are literally dust magnets. "Furs build up a certain amount of static electricity and attract dust and pollutants in the air, especially when the humidity is low," says David Datlow, a Washington, D.C.–based fur cleaner since 1936. "The dust dulls the sheen and becomes abrasive, causing fine hairs to break." Regular cleaning of your furs removes these harmful particles and leaves the furs looking shiny and new.

Technique: Have your fur professionally cleaned at least once every other year; once a year is even better. It needs conditioning to keep it soft and fresh. Take it to a furrier, never to a dry cleaner, unless the dry cleaner sends furs out to be cleaned by a furrier. To remove dirt and oils, furriers typically tumble furs in a drum with a sawdustlike material that has been soaked in a specially formulated chemical solution. Then they apply silicone and comb the furs, a process called glazing, to bring out their luster and make them soft and fluffy.

For spills, simply blot and dab with a clean white towel. Never rub. Then, immediately take the fur to a professional cleaner. Time and heat can cause stains to seep into the hide of the fur. "Let's assume for a minute that a woman is wearing a $20,000 mink coat," Datlow says, "and she accidentally knocks a cup of hot coffee onto it. If the coffee penetrates the leather, the heat of that liquid will cause that skin to shrink. All skin has a natural moisture content, but unlike living creatures, whose skin can heal itself, a fur simply dries up."

If fur gets wet, shake it out and hang it on a broad-shouldered hanger, away from direct heat and sunlight, to dry.

Furnaces

Cleaning heating systems has very little to do with improved looks. It's strictly a practical matter, but one with many benefits. Regular cleaning and professional tune-ups cut heating costs, breakdowns, and repair costs; extend the life expectancy of your heating system; and reduce the amount of carbon monoxide, smoke, and other pollutants emitted.

Technique: There's actually not much that the average homeowner—without the help of a professional—can do to clean a furnace. The main thing is replacing the filter on forced-air systems. Unrestricted air flow is essential for efficient heating. As dust collects on filters and air registers, blowers must work harder, which raises bills and can lead to blower failure. Widely available (at hardware stores and discount stores, for instance), filters are inexpensive and easy to install. Follow your furnace manufacturer's instructions for choosing the right size filter.

"To do it by the book, clean filters once a month," recommends John Morrill, director of operations for the American Council for an Energy-Efficient Economy in Washington, D.C., and co-author of *Consumer Guide to Home Energy Savings*. "But as a homeowner who has had a forced-air system, I must honestly say that I've never done it once a month myself."

More realistic advice is to replace filters at least twice a year, in the fall and in the spring. If you have pets or if there are smokers in the house, do it more often. "Anything that can circulate in the air and make the house dirtier will end up in the filter," Morrill says.

For the same reasons that you need to replace the filter, you should also regularly clean the heat registers throughout the house and the return-air grille. Vacuum the outside of the grilles during your normal vacuuming routine. Twice a year, remove the covers and vacuum both sides of the grille as well as the inside of the duct. That keeps the air flowing freely.

Along with changing the filter, have your furnace inspected by a trained professional regularly. A complete tune-up includes an efficiency test, a thorough cleaning, and the appropriate modifications. It typically costs $60 to $120 and can reduce your heating bill by 5 to 10 percent. "As good as a tune-up is for saving energy, it's also good for the longevity of the equipment,"

Your Filter or Your Life

Here's an incentive to keep your furnace filters clean. If a fresh filter isn't pulling dirt out of the air, your lungs will have to do the job.

"Human lungs are excellent filters," says John Morrill, director of operations for the American Council for an Energy-Efficient Economy in Washington, D.C., and co-author of *Consumer Guide to Home Energy Savings*. "I always tell people they should replace their furnace filter regularly—at least twice a year—because if it gets full, there's all this crud lingering in the air. Sooner or later it will end up in your lungs. You don't want your lungs to capture what a two-dollar throwaway filter can."

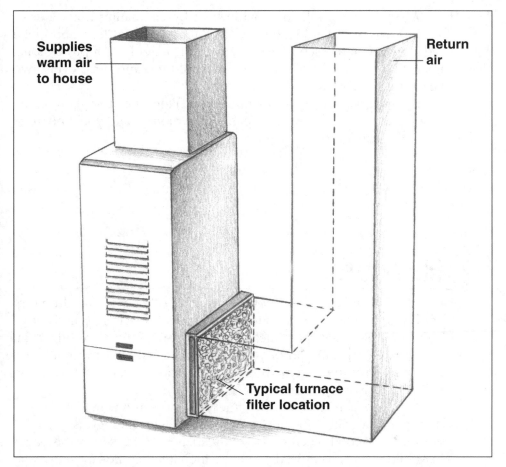

Supplies warm air to house

Return air

Typical furnace filter location

Replace furnace filters at least twice a year, in the spring and fall. They're inexpensive and easy to install.

says Morrill. "And it's a safety check to make sure that there's proper combustion and no blocked flues or potential carbon monoxide leaks."

Follow the manufacturer's recommendations for check-up frequency, or ask the dealer who installed the system. In general, have oil-burning units and heat pumps inspected once a year and gas-fired units and electric furnaces once every two years. The company that sells you oil or gas probably has trained technicians who can give your equipment a tune-up. If not, ask them to recommend an independent company that provides this service.

Note: Make sure that the technician replaces the filter, or do it yourself. Often, the professionals consider this a homeowner's job and fail to do it, even during a "complete" tune-up.

As for boilers, which provide heat by circulating hot water or steam through radiators, there is no filter to clean. Clean and bleed radiators regularly (see Radiators, page 311) and have a professional inspect the boiler—once a year if it is oil-fired and once every two years if it is gas-fired.

Speed tips: Buy a 10-pack of furnace filters and store them in the basement or attic. You will probably save money, and you'll be more likely to change them as needed.

Furniture

Chairs, dining tables, bookshelves, and other pieces of furniture are big investments, and you want them to last a long time (knock on wood). So keep them clean them as part of their upkeep. "You can increase the lifespan of your furniture by taking care of it," says Nancy High of the American Furniture Manufacturers Association in High Point, North Carolina.

Furniture comes in a wide variety of styles and is made of many different materials, including aluminum, chrome, glass, marble, wicker, and wood. Each of these materials is addressed in the pages that follow. For more details, see the individual entries for those materials elsewhere in this book.

While there are more complicated cleaning challenges, your main task with furniture is dusting. A general, but important, dusting tip is to always use a 100 percent cotton cloth, like an old T-shirt or a cloth diaper. Synthetic fibers will create minute scratches that are visible in good lighting and that build up over time. Paper towels are a no-no, too.

Aluminum

Dust aluminum furniture by wiping with a moist cloth. Clean it, if necessary, by wiping with a solution of warm water and a mild liquid dishwashing detergent and a cloth. Never use alkaline cleaners, like ammonia, trisodium phosphate, or even baking soda. (That means no ammonia-based window cleaners, like Windex.) They discolor aluminum.

If the aluminum surface is discolored, wipe it down with a one-

to-one solution of vinegar and water. (Pretest first on an inconspicuous area.) The acid in vinegar will help restore the aluminum's shine.

Caution: Do not use abrasive cleaners, such as scouring powders
or steel wool. They will scratch or dull the surface. Be sure to read
the product label completely for proper usage and safety precautions.

Chrome

Chrome is the shiny metal plating applied to utensils, furniture,
and other household items. It is easy to clean but susceptible to
scratching.

Dust chrome regularly with a damp cloth. For heavier cleaning,
wipe with a sponge or cloth and an all-purpose cleaner.

Caution: Never scour with steel wool or other abrasives, including powdered cleaners like Comet.

Glass

Clean glass tabletops and bookcase doors using newsprint and a
glass cleaner, like Windex, or a solution of ¼ cup vinegar to a quart
of warm water mixed in a spray bottle. Unlike paper towels and
many types of cloth, newsprint will not leave behind traces of lint.
(But be careful if you get newspaper ink on your hands—you could
leave smudges around the house.)

Be sure to clean the underside of glass tabletops, which also get
dirty. If the glass in your furniture is framed by wood, spray the
cleaner directly onto the newsprint and wipe the glass down. Otherwise, you might damage the wood.

Caution: Carefully peel off wax, paint, and other stuck-on substances with a razor blade. Do not use a putty knife, which can
scratch the glass.

Hardware

Fixtures on furniture are often made of brass. These days, most
hardware on new furniture is coated with a surface finish, like lacquer. All you need to do is dust it with a lightly dampened cloth.

Untreated brass hardware, however, will tarnish. Polish it occasionally using a brass cleaner, like Brasso. Do it every year or two, or
more often if you're motivated to. But do it right: Remove the hardware before polishing it, so that you will not damage the surface of
the furniture. Lay the hardware out on the floor or a counter in the
order that it came off to make replacing it easier.

Lacquer

Lacquer is a type of hardwood finish, like shellac. But it can also mean a style of furniture that originated in Asia. "When people talk about lacquer from a fashion standpoint, they are usually referring to wood furniture with a black or red high-sheen finish," says High.

This type of furniture typically has an extremely durable polyester finish that does not need polishing with furniture polish. Simply dust and clean it with a lightly dampened cloth.

Marble

Marble has a highly sensitive surface. So dust marble furniture often with a lightly dampened cloth to keep tiny particles of grit from scratching it. Never clean marble with furniture polish or oil. "Marble is nothing more than a sponge," says Fred Hueston, director of the National Training Center for Stone and Masonry Trades in Longwood, Florida, and author of *Marble and Tile: Selection and Care of Stone and Tile Surfaces*. By soaking into marble, these substances will cause staining.

For heavier cleaning, use a sponge or soft cloth and a neutral cleaner, like Murphy Oil Soap or a liquid dishwashing detergent, mixed with warm water.

To remove stains on marble, use a poultice, which will draw the stains out. For oil stains, mix ½ cup bleached flour, a small squirt of liquid dishwashing detergent, and just enough warm water to make a paste that has the consistency of peanut butter. Spread it over the stained area, cover it with plastic wrap, and tape down the sides with masking tape. Let it sit overnight. Remove the plastic, let the poultice dry, and scrape it away. For food stains (coffee, tea, and juices, for instance), substitute hydrogen peroxide for the detergent. Rub ink, crayon, or nail polish stains with a cotton ball dipped in an acetone-based nail polish remover. (Don't mix the nail polish remover into the poultice.)

Caution: Lemon, vinegar, other substances containing acid will eat into the polished surface of marble. Remember that many bathroom cleaners contain acid. Check the label for proper usage and any safety precautions. And avoid using abrasive cleaners because even the finest grit can dull marble surfaces.

Rattan and Wicker

Most rattan and wicker is coated with one of the same hard-surface finishes used to coat wood furniture. If so, simply dust it by vacuuming regularly with a brush attachment or wiping it down with a lightly dampened cloth. Once every six weeks, polish it with a spray-on furniture polish like Pledge. Spray it directly onto a clean cloth and wipe the surface. This way, you avoid getting the polish into hard-to-reach cracks.

If your wicker is painted, vacuum it regularly and wipe it down with a lightly dampened cloth. Do not use furniture polish.

Upholstery

A good place to begin is with upholstery, a common feature in many different types of furniture. Vacuum it weekly, using the vacuum cleaner upholstery attachment.

"Upholstery takes the most abuse in a living area and is most overlooked when it comes to cleaning," says High. "People fail to realize that there's as much dust on upholstery as on the wood furniture, floor, and other places where you can see it."

Because dust contains microscopic abrasives, like silica, it can damage upholstery if left to be ground in by squirming sitters. And the fabric of upholstery typically wears out sooner than the wood or other materials of your furniture. Regular vacuuming should do the trick.

Wood

Before you clean your wood furniture, you need to know what type of finish it has. Most wood furniture, especially if it is relatively new, has a hard finish, be it lacquer, shellac, varnish, or polyurethane. Some pieces, however, have what is called a soft, or oiled, finish.

To determine the type of finish on a piece of furniture, rub a few drops of boiled linseed oil, a type of linseed oil available at hardware and paint stores, into the wood. If it soaks in, the wood has an oil finish. If it beads up, the wood has a hard finish.

To clean soft-finished furniture, dust it regularly with a lightly dampened cloth. Once or twice a year, or if the wood dries out, apply boiled linseed oil. Using a clean cloth, rub in the oil in the direction of the grain until the wood absorbs no more. Fold another cloth into a pad and rub the area until it is dry.

If your soft-finished wood needs a deeper cleaning, apply kerosene or mineral spirits the same way you would the boiled linseed oil. Follow up by applying the boiled linseed oil.

Dust hard-finished wood at least once a week using a nonwax

spray, like Endust. Avoid dusting with a dry cloth. Not only does dry-dusting spread rather than remove dust but also it can scratch fine surfaces because of the minute abrasives dust contains.

Once every four to six weeks, apply a spray-on wax polish, like Pledge, to hard-finished wood furniture. "I don't recommend doing this more frequently because your furniture doesn't need it and you don't need the extra work," High says.

Read the product labels and choose the appropriate product for the type of finish on your furniture. For furniture with a high shine, choose a high-luster wax; for pieces with a flatter finish, choose a low-luster wax.

You don't have to worry about wax buildup. These spray-on polishes contain mild solvents so that as you apply a new coating of protective wax, you also strip old wax. For detailed furniture or pieces with a lot of hardware, spray the product directly onto the cloth instead of to the furniture to avoid getting it into cracks and crevices.

Once or twice a year, or for sun-damaged or dried-out wood, apply an oil, like Old English Furniture Oil, to the wood. Never saturate the wood with the oil. "This gives life back to tired wood," says Trish Bullock, customer service manager of Bassett Furniture Industries in Bassett, Virginia.

While it may be temptingly handy, do not wipe your dining-room table down with your kitchen dishcloth, Bullock says. "The traces of detergent on it can damage the wood finish," she says. Clean up dried food with a damp cloth, and then follow up by using a furniture polish.

To repair water marks, like rings left by sweaty glasses, rub the area lightly with wood oil, like Old English Furniture Oil, and a cotton cloth. Repeat a few times, if necessary. Do not let the oil sit on the spot, and do not repeat too many times. Otherwise, the white mark will turn black.

If no furniture oil is available for repairing water marks in wood, try mayonnaise instead. Wipe the mayonnaise over the spot with a clean cotton cloth, and then wipe it off.

For yellowing on white-finished wood furniture—caused by tobacco smoke, sunlight, or anything else—use a smoker's tooth polish. Because it contains mild abrasives, avoid rubbing it in. Just wipe it on and wipe it off. Follow up by wiping down the wood with a furniture polish.

If your furniture has odors, like mildew or smoke, wipe it down with a solution of one part vanilla to two parts water. Use only a lightly dampened cloth, and follow up by wiping down the wood with a furniture polish.

Buff out surface scratches. "If you scratch the surface of your car, you wax it out," Bullock says. "You can do the same for wood furniture." Using a cotton cloth, rub briskly with a furniture polish or oil. Do not rub too briskly, however, or you might cause what are known as buffer burns.

If your regular polish doesn't correct the slight imperfections, try a furniture paste wax.

For deeper scratches and dents, use a wax fill stick, available at hardware and paint stores. Rub it in and buff with a clean cloth. Avoid using touch-up markers and stains. "Fill sticks go on like crayons," Bullock says, "so if you mess up, you can wipe it out of the scratch and start over." There are a variety of fill-stick colors. Be sure to buy one that matches the color of your wood. Try calling the manufacturer of your furniture. Most keep matching fill sticks in stock.

In a pinch: If you can't get your hands on a wax fill stick, try paste shoe polish instead. Make sure that the polish matches the color of the furniture: brown for walnut, cordovan for mahogany, or tan for oak. Apply it with a cotton swab or toothpick, and then buff with a clean cloth.

Caution: When working with linseed oil or kerosene, wear rubber gloves and work in a well-ventilated area.

Garden Tools

Leave the mud and dirt in the ground, not on your metal garden tools. Soil holds moisture, which causes rust and shortens the tools' lifespan. Rust is also bad for another reason, explains Fred Hicks, past president of the American Nursery and Landscape Association in Washington, D.C., and president of Hicks Nurseries in Westbury, New York. "In time, rust causes pitting. Dirt sticks to a shovel or spade that is pitted, and that puts extra drag on the tool as it goes in and out of the soil." In essence, dirty tools make you work harder.

Technique: After using garden tools, wipe the mud off them with a cloth before putting them away. Spray them lightly with a lubricant/rust protectant, like WD-40. This is especially important for cutting tools, like shears and pruning saws, and for tools that won't be used for a while. It is essential for people with damp sheds or garages and in colder weather, when condensation tends to build up on surfaces. Before using digging tools, if the soil is relatively dry, work the tool in and out of the ground a few times. The sanding action will remove the light film of rust, leaving it smooth and in good shape.

Keep wooden handles smooth, clean, and dry. Use a solution of mild soapy water and a cloth to remove soil. "If they get wet and dry, wet and dry, the wood starts to get rough," Hicks says. If it starts to splinter or if the wood grain rises— a sign of impending splintering— rub the wood with a fine-grade sandpaper. "It's like your baseball bat," Hicks says. "You don't do much to a bat but keep it clean and dry. The perspiration that soaks into the handle is probably the best thing for it because it puts that little bit of oil and moisture in there." Oil is okay for wooden handles, but avoid products that leave a sticky residue, which collects dirt. Boiled linseed oil, available at hardware stores and paint stores, works well. Wipe it on with a cloth, and then let it soak into the wood and dry.

After using garden sprayers, remove any excess solution. Flush them with water, and then pump a solution of water and liquid dishwashing detergent through to remove the remaining residue. (If you can't resist spraying with toxic chemicals, at least follow your local guidelines about discarding the wash water. Even though you will have diluted your solution even more, be careful about where you empty the sprayer.) Again, flush with water. Clean the outside with soapy water and a cloth or brush. No matter how carefully you clean a sprayer in which weed killer has been used, there's always the danger of lingering chemicals. Therefore, if you use a sprayer for a weed killer, label it clearly, and use another one for nontoxic spraying. Also, be sure not to use the same sprayer for weed killer and insecticides you may spray on your plants. Any weed killer residue left in the sprayer can kill your plants as well.

Speed tips: With most tools, you can just hose them off to remove the dirt and mud and let them drip-dry.

In a pinch: If there's ever a time you can slack off, it's during June,

July, and August. "It's the middle of the summer, the sun is out, it's dry. That's not when your tools rust, so cleaning them after every use is not as critical," says Hicks. You're probably using the tools more, too, which helps keep rust from building up on them.

Caution: Remember that there is a nontoxic solution for most weeds and pests. But if you must use dangerous chemicals, be careful cleaning up after yourself. When cleaning sprayers used for toxic substances, never let the chemicals come in contact with your skin. Always wear protective gloves, like those made of rubber or latex, safety goggles, and a mask over your nose and mouth.

When working with linseed oil, wear rubber gloves and work in a well-ventilated area. Always read product labels for proper use and safety instructions.

Glass

Because they're nonporous, "doing windows" is actually easy. And they should be cleaned regularly because, believe it or not, glass can stain. "Acid rain and other chemicals reacting with window glass can cause discoloration and can even etch it," says Jim Brewer, executive housekeeper at the University of Texas at Arlington and a technical advisor for *Cleaning and Maintenance Magazine*. Exterior glass that has not been cleaned for several years will probably not sparkle the way it once did.

Technique: Clean glass with a solution of one squirt of liquid dishwashing detergent in a bucket of warm water or with 1 cup vinegar per gallon of water. Ammonia-based commercial window cleaners have a tendency to streak, a condition that is especially noticeable in bright sunlight. To avoid leaving traces of lint, wipe away the liquid using a squeegee or newsprint. (If you get ink on your hands from the newspaper, be careful not to smudge the window frames.)

When cleaning vertical glass surfaces, like windows, start at the top and clean down. Apply the cleaning solution with a sponge or soft cloth, and then scrub caked-on grime with a long-bristle vegetable brush. If you're cleaning windows inside, put a towel on the windowsill to catch drips.

When cleaning glass tabletops, use newsprint instead of a squeegee. Make sure to clean the underside of the glass, which also gets dirty.

No Streaking on This Campus

Marry Keener is assistant director of facilities management at the University of Arizona in Tucson and a member of the technical advisory committee for *Executive Housekeeping Today* magazine. After tending to the 35,000 students at Arizona, here's how she cleans her own glass. "I don't use glass cleaner because I don't like ammonia, which streaks. Some glass cleaners say not to use them with direct sunlight. Here, we have direct sunlight 365 days a year. I use a mild solution of liquid dishwashing detergent. It's designed to clean the finest china and doesn't streak, is not abrasive, and doesn't harm your hands or anything else. It has wonderful soil-releasers.

"I use a squirt in a bucket partially filled with warm water. A little is better than making up real heavy concentrations. I use a squeegee to clean without leaving lint. Nine out of 10 professional window washers use liquid dishwashing detergent. It's wonderfully economical."

Carefully peel off paint and other stuck-on substances with a razor blade. "Paint is held on by a vacuum, and a razor blade will actually get under the edge of the paint and pop it off," Brewer says. Do not use a putty knife, which has a duller blade and can damage the glass.

Speed tips: When you are using a squeegee to clean glass, keep a couple of cloths handy. "You have two back pockets," notes Brewer, "one for a cloth to wipe the squeegee with and the other for one to wipe up the corners of the glass."

Glassware

People take it pretty personally when they find smudges on the glasses or cups they're using. "Stains seem to cling to glasses," says Kari Kinder, assistant director of food and beverage at the renowned Culinary Institute of America in Hyde Park, New York.

Technique: Glasses are usually the least-dirty items in your dish stack. When you're washing by hand, clean glassware first. Or, if you do it last, change the dishwater first. Clean glasses in hot water, which helps cut grease. Use a soft sponge, never an abrasive scrubber. Your rinse water should be as hot as is safely possible so that it beads up and steams off, leaving less of a film. If your wash water is greasy, rinse glasses with running water.

Air-dry glasses upside down in a rack on the counter. The rack is essential for avoiding the "greenhouse effect"—the fogging up of glasses from a lack of air circulation. "Fogging leads to film residue," Kinder says. "You want that clear crisp look that comes from proper drying."

If you get a lime buildup on your glassware after washing it in the dishwasher—usually a sign of hard water—try a rinse agent, like Jet-Dry. Rinse agents help water sheet off during the drying process and are typically available either as a tablet that hangs on the dishwasher rack or as a liquid that you add to a dishwasher's automatic dispenser at the beginning of the wash cycle. The less water that remains on your glasses, the less chance they have to spot and streak.

In a pinch: When it comes to washing glasses by hand, air-drying is preferable to towel drying because towels can get greasy and breed bacteria. If you're pressed for time or counter space, however, dry glasses with a soft clean towel.

Gloves—Baseball

Baseball is a grimy game—if you're doing it right. "A ball glove is going to get dirty and messy," says Carrie Fischer, communications manager of the Wilson Sporting Goods Company in Chicago. "That's the nature of the game." So after a day of diving catches, your goal is to remove the dirt and mud from your glove and keep it supple.

Technique: Brush away dry dirt and other debris with a stiff-bristle leather brush, available at leather and shoe stores. If your glove gets muddy, let the mud dry. It's easier to brush off that way. Do not use water to clean a baseball glove.

If your glove gets wet, let it dry at room temperature. Never place it near a radiator, hearth, or other heat source to dry. The heat will cause the leather to stiffen and crack. "Some people say that you're supposed to dry wet gloves in a microwave oven," says Fischer. "We do not recommend that."

To clean stains from leather, try a leather cleaner, available at leather and shoe stores. Follow the manufacturer's instructions for use.

Speed tips: "The best way to break in a glove—and keep it soft and pliant—is continual use," Fischer says. "If you don't have much time, we recommend lanolin." Rub shaving cream containing lanolin into the leather, and then shape it by pounding your fist or a baseball into the pocket.

Gloves—Fabric, Leather, Rubber

For such a common item, gloves are uncommonly tricky to clean. "Gloves are not just one large flat surface," says Jay Ruckel, production manager of LaCrasia Gloves, a glove factory in New York City. "And you're not only cleaning dirt off the outside but also dealing with your own body dirt and oils, which can stain from the inside out." Add to that the fact that many gloves are made of leather, a sensitive and hard-to-clean material, and you have a challenge on your hands, so to speak.

A CLEAN STORY

City of Gloverly Love

Sometimes it pays to let your fingers do the walking—out of town. Jay Ruckel is production manager of LaCrasia Gloves, a glove factory in New York City, tells this story about a glove-cleaning bargain.

"Back in the early 1980s, Joan Collins was using a pair of our gloves for a cover shot for *Vanity Fair* magazine. They were very expensive gloves, about $650 wholesale. They came back to us looking like all the orange makeup used for the photo shoot had been wiped off with the gloves.

"I knew that in Gloversville, New York, there were many glove makers—at least a couple hundred—so I called information and asked for a Gloversville dry cleaner.

"I sent the gloves to a cleaner called Robison and Smith. They cleaned the gloves and sent them back with a note that read: 'During the process of cleaning, we noticed that your fox-fur cuff was sewn on ever so crookedly. We took the liberty of removing it and putting it back properly. Please find enclosed herewith our bill for cleaning, cuff removal, cuff replacement and shipping. Total: $9.75.' Ever since then, I tell people to forget looking for professional glove cleaners in New York City. Go to Gloversville."

Technique: We'll begin with washable gloves, those made of natural and synthetic fabrics, rubber, and washable leather. Many work, gardening, golf, and driving gloves are made of washable substances. Read the gloves' care label to make sure that you can get them wet.

The secret to efficiently washing gloves is to do it with the gloves on your hands. That way, it's easier to flatten out the creases and to get in between the fingers. Wash them with a mild detergent solution—a couple of squirts of a liquid dishwashing detergent in a sink filled with cool to lukewarm water. Then remove the gloves and rinse them in clean water. Empty the water and refill, repeating the process until there is no soap residue in the water.

To dry the gloves, roll them in a clean dry towel. Unroll them, blow into them as you would a balloon to recover their shape, and lay them out flat at room temperature. Do not squeeze or wring them. Never dry them on a radiator or near a heater. If you must iron them, do it between the folds of a clean towel.

Many gloves are made of unwashable leather or suede. There's not a lot the average person can do to clean leather. It's easy to damage the finish. Try using a commercial leather-cleaning product, like Lexol pH, available at leather and shoe repair shops.

If you spill a potential stain-causing substance on your leather gloves, the first thing you should do is blot it up with a clean white towel.

If it's a greasy stain, lay the glove out flat, sprinkle cornstarch on the stain, and let it stand overnight. It might absorb some of the oil.

Keep Your Gloves in the Dark

"When it comes to leather gloves, preservation and care are as important as cleaning," says Jay Ruckel, production manager of LaCrasia Gloves, a glove factory in New York City. Protecting them from direct light, he says, is essential.

"I have some fuchsia gloves that are incredibly faded just from hanging under a fluorescent light for six months. Half the glove is an off-white, and the palm is still a strong fuchsia. I like to keep those around as an example to show people.

"We normally think that only sunlight fades leathers, but interior lighting does the same. They used to make glove boxes and linen and silk envelopes. Some of the bureaus from the nineteenth century would have little glove drawers on top on either side of the mirror.

"You should protect your gloves from the light because correcting that discoloration is difficult. But don't use plastic bags. Leather has to breathe, and plastic just strangles it."

Another method is to place a clean white piece of tissue paper on the greasy spot and run a warm iron over it. Put the iron on the lowest heat setting for cotton. Replace the tissue several times with new tissue until there are no more traces of the stain on the tissue.

For a stain on suede, blot what you can and let the remainder dry for a couple of days. Try to restore the nap by rubbing gently with a soft brush or a dry kitchen sponge. By bringing back the nap, you might eliminate the stain.

For leather discoloration, look for a commercial leather spray like Nu-Life Color Spray, which comes in a variety of colors and is available at shoe repair shops. Choose the one that best matches the original color of your gloves, and then follow the manufacturer's instructions. Be sure to use in a well-ventilated area and always read product labels for proper use and safety instructions. For suede, mask stains and other discoloration in a similar way by rubbing lightly with a colored chalk that matches the original color of the suede.

For stubborn stains, take your gloves to a professional leather cleaner. But choose wisely. Most leather cleaning today is done by wholesalers who pick up from cleaners. If you use a dry cleaner, make sure it sends leather goods out to a leather specialist. Some dry cleaners try to clean the leather themselves—to avoid paying a wholesaler—and they could end up damaging it. For a professional leather cleaner referral in your area, contact the Leather Apparel Association, 19 West 21st Street, Suite 403, New York, NY 10010.

In a pinch: If your leather or suede gloves are wrinkled, take them off and put them on your knee. Pull the fingers tight, stretch them to their natural length, and gently rub your palm over the gloves. "The heat of your palm is almost like a gentle iron," Ruckel says.

Caution: Always test your cleaning solution or method on an inconspicuous part of the gloves.

Gold

Gold does not tarnish the way silver does. However, when gold is less than 24-karat, or pure, the copper, silver, nickel, and other metals alloyed with it can tarnish and smudge. For example, says Julie Livingston, a New York City–based retail training consultant to the World Gold Council, "some people get black marks on their ears when they wear 14-karat gold earrings." And any gold, regardless of its purity, picks up oils from your skin and dust and dirt from the environment. Here's how to keep gold looking the way it should—shiny and beautiful.

Technique: Remove dirt and discoloration by swishing your gold item around in a solution of equal parts water and an all-purpose cleaner such as Mr. Clean. To clean crevices and intricately detailed jewelry, like a link bracelet, scrub lightly with a soft toothbrush. Rinse the item with warm water, and then dry it with a soft chamois cloth.

In a pinch: Just use a drop of mild liquid dishwashing detergent and lukewarm water. Apply with a soft toothbrush or soft cloth and rinse with water. Then dry with a chamois cloth. Or you can simply polish your gold with a dry chamois cloth.

Caution: Gold's worst enemy is chlorine. Repeated exposure can deteriorate gold. Never clean with chlorine, and remove gold jewelry before using chlorinated pools and hot tubs. Do not clean with toothpaste, even though some jewelers recommend it. Certain toothpastes contain harsh abrasives that can sand gold to a matte finish.

Golf Clubs

Messy clubs make for a messy golf game. "Dirt or mud on a club affects the way the ball comes off the head," says Tony Miller, president of Raven Golf, a club manufacturer in Milwaukee. "You'll notice that the professionals on TV wipe their clubs off after every hit."

Technique: If you aren't dedicated enough to clean your clubs after each hole, at least do it following each game. It's a simple technique: "We don't use any kind of special cleaner on clubs," says Eric Pedersen, assistant professional at the Augusta National Golf Club, home of the Masters Tournament, in Georgia. "Just liquid dishwashing detergent, water, and a brush or towel."

Don't get leather grips overly wet. Use only a slightly damp cloth to wipe away dirt and grime. Dry the clubs afterward with a clean dry towel.

Speed tips: Put a moist towel in your golf bag before you play. That will make it easy to clean dirt and mud off the club heads as you round the links.

Gore-Tex

You probably do your job better when you're nice and clean. The same goes for your Gore-Tex, that waterproof/breathable membrane made by W. L. Gore and Associates that is found in outerwear. Cleaning dirt from the membrane improves both of its functions.

Technique: Gore-Tex itself is machine washable. If the outer shell is washable as well, wash on a regular, warm-water cycle using any type of standard laundry detergent. Dry on medium heat until completely dry. If the outer shell contains leather or some other non-washable fabric, follow the instructions on the garment's cleaning tag. Gore-Tex can also be safely dry-cleaned. If the outer shell is a water-resistant nylon, however, multiple machine washings or even one trip to the dry cleaner will remove its water-repellent coating, which helps the Gore-Tex membrane do its job. If this happens, re-coat the outer shell with a spray-on water repellent, available at most camping and outdoors stores.

Graffiti

Unless you want "the word" to spread, remove graffiti as soon as possible. That way, you not only prevent it from soaking into porous surfaces but also discourage other graffiti vandals. "They don't get a chance to admire their work," says Frances Quill, director of car appearance and chemical materials for the New York City Transit Authority, which manages the graffiti-plagued New York subway system. "A wall with graffiti often attracts more people to put graffiti on it."

Technique: Since graffiti is usually in the form of paint, the most common approach is to use a chemical paint remover or solvent, such as Super Strip or Graffiti Remover, available at paint and wallpaper stores. Most of these also lift marks made by felt-tip pens, lipstick, and other substances. To use methylene chloride, a strong but common solvent, carefully brush it on, wait 2 minutes and rinse with water while continuing to brush. Because of concerns that methylene chloride may be carcinogenic, Quill prefers alkaline pastes like Peel-Away 1 that contain a caustic, such as potassium hydroxide or sodium hydroxide. It's available at paint and wallpaper stores. While Quill suggests following the manufacturer's instructions, here's how

A CLEAN STORY

Painting the Town

In 1970, a Greek-American teenager sprayed "Taki 183," his nickname and street address, or "tag," on hundreds of subway cars and walls throughout New York City. Though not the first example of spray-paint art, it was copied by many teenagers and quickly led to a graffiti epidemic that has afflicted New York ever since.

To combat graffiti vandals, New York officials have adopted many creative solutions. They experimented with solvents, like Klout and DWR (Dirty Word Remover), which either didn't work or were so corrosive that the subway car manufacturers threatened to void their warranties unless its use was stopped, according to the *Encyclopedia of New York City*. They coated the cars, plus monuments and public facilities, with Hydron 300, a Teflon-like substance that wipes clean (but that proved too expensive to use). They even passed a bill that outlawed carrying open spray paint in public without a permit.

Today, most of New York's subway cars are stainless steel, which is graffiti-resistant. But the vandalism continues, mainly in the form of tags scratched in the cars' Plexiglas windows.

it typically works. Rub the paste on and let it sit for 5 to 10 minutes until it bubbles up; wipe or scrub it off; then rinse the surface with water and apply a neutralizer, like Peel-Away Neutralizer, usually sold separately. Repeat two or three times if one application does not remove the graffiti.

Two other methods for removing graffiti are waterblasting and sandblasting, both of which work better on brick, stone, and concrete than on wood. Only the finest-grade sandblasters work on metal without damaging the surface. You can usually rent waterblasting machines at a small-equipment rental agency. For sandblasting, however, you should hire a professional. (Look in the yellow pages under "Sandblasting.")

No matter which method you choose to remove the graffiti, first try it out on an inconspicuous test patch since it may alter the surface appearance.

Speed tips: If you anticipate a graffiti hit on a particular surface, apply an antigraffiti coating or sealer, such as Graffiti Barrier, also available at paint and wallpaper stores. As a preventive measure, this will save you cleaning time in the future, especially when it comes to porous surfaces, like brick and concrete, and painted surfaces that can be damaged by graffiti-removing chemicals. Among the best coatings are the aliphatic urethanes, which do not yellow and resist abrasion and the paint solvents used to remove paint. There are other coatings, like acrylics and epoxies, but acrylics dissolve when paint solvents are applied to graffiti and epoxies tend to yellow and discolor.

In a pinch: "If you can find the paint that matches, painting over graffiti is generally the cheapest and easiest way to deal with it," Quill says.

Caution: Always wear rubber gloves and long sleeves when working with paint-removing chemicals. If you'll be scrubbing the chemicals with a brush—or if you're sandblasting or using a pressure steamer—wear protective goggles. Do not inhale the fumes of toxic chemicals. Always read product labels for proper use and safety instructions.

Grass Stains

EMERGENCY ACTION
Blot with rubbing alcohol. If the colors might bleed, dilute the alcohol with two parts water.

Grass is a tough stain, one that is especially common on the knees of children's jeans. But it's not unbeatable, especially if it is fresh.

Technique: Using a clean white towel or cotton ball, blot with rubbing alcohol, then rinse thoroughly. To find out if the color might bleed, first use the clean white towel with alcohol to blot an inconspicuous corner of the stained garment. If the color of the fabric comes off onto the white towel, or if the fabric is acetate, dilute the alcohol with two parts water. If alcohol does not work, try a color-safe liquid household bleach. If that doesn't work, try a chlorine bleach, but only if your garment is bleachable.

"Bleach will take it out, without question," says Ann Lemley, Ph.D., chairman of

Colossal Cleanups

A Presidential Trim

The amount of time it takes eight workers to mow the White House lawn's 18 acres of grass: eight hours the department of textiles and apparel at Cornell University in Ithaca, New York. If it is washable, follow up by washing with regular laundry detergent and the hottest water safe for the fabric.

Caution: Always rinse out one cleaning solution before trying another. Mixing chemicals, especially ammonia and chlorine bleach, can create noxious fumes. Always read product labels for proper use and safety instructions.

Gravy

EMERGENCY ACTION
Rinse or blot away gravy with cold water.

Relax. You may have really embarrassed yourself at the dinner table, but a gravy stain looks worse than it actually is. "Even though gravy usually contains some grease, which can be tough to get out, it is still categorized as a protein stain," says Jane Rising, instructor in the education department at the International Fabricare Institute in Silver Spring, Maryland. That means for washable fabrics, simple water-based solutions should do the trick.

Technique: Scrape away any excess gravy. If the item is washable, soak it first in cold water to remove as much of the stain as possible. The older the stain, the longer you should soak it—up to several hours. Start with a solution of ¼ teaspoon clear liquid dishwashing detergent, several drops of ammonia, and ½ cup warm water. Apply it directly to the fabric, then lay the garment on a hard surface and pat the stain lightly with the back of a spoon. This allows the solution to get in between the fibers, where the stains hide. Don't rub the material together; that will abrade the fibers. Next, wash as directed either by machine or by hand in the hottest water safe for the fabric. If the stain does not come out completely, follow the same pretreatment procedure, but with a liquid clothes detergent containing enzymes (or a paste made from a granular detergent and water). The enzymes eat away at protein-based substances like gravy. Apply it directly to the stain, pat, then wash.

For fabrics that cannot be washed, either have them professionally dry-cleaned or blot with a clean white towel and a spot remover, like Carbona Stain Devils or K2r, available at supermarkets, hardware stores, or discount department stores. Read the labels before using these products, and use them in a well-ventilated area while wearing protective rubber or latex gloves. Blot from the inside of the garment to push the stain out.

For carpets and rugs, first blot with a white towel and a spot remover. If that doesn't work, try blotting with a solution of ¼ cup clear liquid dishwashing detergent and 1 cup lukewarm water. Then rinse by blotting with a clean towel and water; blot dry with a fresh towel. Do not blot with laundry detergent because it often contains optical brighteners that can bleach carpet and rug dyes. Instead, if the two solutions don't work, try blotting with a solution of 2 tablespoons ammonia and 1 cup water. Again, rinse by blotting and dry.

In a pinch: In the case of washable clothing, skip to step two: Apply an enzyme detergent directly onto the stain, then wash.

Caution: Always thoroughly rinse out one cleaning solution before trying another. Mixing chemicals, especially ammonia and chlorine bleach, can create noxious fumes. Always read product labels for proper use and safety instructions. Before using cleaning solutions, always test them on an inconspicuous section of the stained item.

Grease Stains

EMERGENCY ACTION
Remove excess grease with a paper towel, being careful not to spread it. Next, blot with a paper towel dabbed with an acetone-based nail polish remover. Do not, however, use it on acetate. It will dissolve the fabric.

Petroleum-based products act as soil magnets. So petroleum jelly, hand lotion, and engine grease and such can ruin clothing and carpets if left untreated. Your goal here is to remove these stains—and to do it as soon as possible.

Technique: The best substance for removing greasy stains is spot remover. Either have the fabric professionally dry-cleaned or clean it yourself with a spot remover, like Carbona Stain Devils or K2r, available at supermarkets, hardware stores, or discount department stores. Read the labels before using these products, and use them in a well-ventilated area while wearing protective rubber or latex gloves. Lay the stain facedown on a soft absorbent cloth. Apply the spot remover to another clean white cloth, and then blot from the inside of the garment to push the stain out. As the spot remover dissolves the grease, the cloth beneath catches it. For carpets, always apply the spot remover to the towel, never directly onto the carpet. Otherwise, it can soak into the carpet backing or pad and attract more dirt.

In a pinch: If you don't have any spot remover in the house, use an acetone-based nail polish remover. Don't use it on acetate fabric. "It dissolves acetate," says Rajiv Jain, laboratory manager for the Association of Specialists in Cleaning and Restoration in Annapolis Junction, Maryland. "The stain will be gone, but so will the fabric."

Caution: Before using cleaning solutions, always test them on an inconspicuous section of the stained item.

Grout

Unlike the smooth steel fixtures and tile you find elsewhere in the bathroom, grout is rough and porous, a sticking place for soap scum and dirt. Remove this layer of grime before it becomes a permanent resident.

Technique: Clean grout regularly, using a gel or foaming bathroom cleaner, like Comet Bathroom Cleaner, and a long-bristle vegetable brush. Do not use abrasive cleaners or scrubbers. Even nylon or short-bristle brushes can wear down the grout over time. Spray on the cleaning compound, let it sit for a few seconds while the cleaning agents work on the scum, and then scrub it off. Clean hard-to-reach cracks and crevices with a soft toothbrush. Rinse by wiping everything down with a clean wet sponge or cloth.

"Always let the cleaning agent do your work," says Jim Brewer, executive housekeeper at the University of Texas at Arlington and a technical advisor to *Cleaning and Maintenance Magazine.* "If it takes to much handwork, it's the wrong product because it's not breaking down the dirt. Too much scrubbing tends to rub dirt into pores." Instead of scrubbing harder, for heavy soil, repeat the application.

Speed tips: Clean grout soon after you shower, while the grout is still moist.

Caution: Be careful about using ammonia or ammonia-based products when cleaning grout because many bathroom cleaning products contain chlorine. When combined, these two chemicals create a potentially fatal gas. Always read product labels for proper use and safety instructions.

Gum

Chewing gum is fine in its proper place—your mouth—but once you spit it out, it has a nasty habit of sticking around. Here's how to get it out of most textiles, including loose-fiber carpets and rugs.

Technique: Heat the gum with a blow-dryer set on "high" for 30 to 90 seconds, being careful not to bring the heat closer than six inches to the synthetic fibers. It is possible to melt some carpet fibers with high temperatures. Remove as much of the warm, softened gum as possible by picking at it with small squares of plastic film, cut from a sandwich baggie or other bag. (The gum sticks to the plastic and not your fingers.) Reheat the gum and pick at it with fresh squares of plastic several times to get most of it off. Then rub about ½ teaspoon of extra-strength deep-heating muscle rub, like Ben-Gay, into the remaining gum.

"Between the heat and the sliminess of the Ben-Gay, or equivalent rub, you're breaking the actual bonds between the gum and the fabric," says Claudia Ramirez, former executive vice president of the Association of Specialists in Cleaning and Restoration in Annapolis Junction, Maryland.

Again, heat it for 30 to 90 seconds and pick at it with a fresh plastic square. Next, blot the area with a solution of 1 teaspoon mild liquid dishwashing detergent in 1 cup warm water. Blot the area with a clean dry white toweling; then blot with water and repeat with a dry towel. Allow the fabric to dry. If a slight stickiness remains, carefully reheat the area with the blow-dryer and remove the last gum traces with a plastic square.

In a pinch: A quicker, if less thorough, way to remove chewing gum stuck in carpet, fabric, or other materials is to freeze it with an ice cube, then crack it off once it is brittle.

Caution: Before using cleaning solutions, always test them on an inconspicuous section of the stained item.

Guns

They don't call it a "clean" shot for nothing. "Rifles and most handguns have a twisting microgroove cut into the bore. If these grooves load up with lead or copper deposits, you don't get the optimum accuracy out of the round," says Paul Judd, president of Kleen-Bore, a gun-care products company in Easthampton, Massachusetts, and member of the National Shooting Sports Foundation in Newton, Connecticut. So your main goal in cleaning guns is to remove powder and metal buildup from inside the action and the bore and to wipe away rust-causing moisture. These steps are paramount for reliability, accuracy, and safety and to maintain resale value.

Technique: Clean your gun inside and out immediately following each use using the following tips from Judd. To start, make sure that the gun is unloaded by opening the action and checking that the chamber or chambers are empty and that there are no shells in the magazine. Clean from the breech end (that is, the rear of the barrel), whenever possible. With shotguns, you can usually open or remove the barrel; with rifles, open the breech or remove the bolt; with handguns, open the cylinder; and with semi-automatics, disassemble the slide and remove the barrel (for this procedure, follow instructions in your manual). If you have to clean from the muzzle end, try not to push debris into the action. Using a nylon brush (toothbrush-style) and a product like Formula 3 Gun Conditioner, clean and lubricate the action. Then do the same to the bore using the proper length cleaning rod with a cotton mop or patch attached to the end. Apply the cleaning fluid directly to the patch and run the rod in and out 5 to 10 passes. Then do the same using a bore brush (nylon or bronze) to loosen stubborn deposits. Make sure that the patches, mop, and bore brush are the correct size for the gun you are cleaning.

Finally, wipe down the stock and all metal parts using a silicone-impregnated cloth, available at gun stores, or with a cloth and an oil-based liquid.

If you are a frequent shooter, at least once a month precede the above technique by scrubbing the bore, action, and chamber to remove plastic buildup, lead, copper, and powder deposits. Use a bronze brush and a strong bore solvent. After swabbing the bore with solvent, let the gun sit for 30 to 60 minutes for maximum effectiveness. There are solvents made especially for stubborn powder deposits, lead, and copper such as Kleen-Bore's No. 10 Solvent or Copper Cutter. If you have to clean from the muzzle, be sure to protect it from wear by using a muzzle guard.

In a pinch: If you're in a situation where you can't thoroughly clean your gun after a shooting session, at least wipe down the outside with a silicone cloth and some kind of oil-based product. "Use anything to take off the fingerprints, which can be very acidic and cause rust," says Judd. "Then clean the bore later—as soon as you can."

Caution: Always check to make sure that your gun is unloaded before cleaning it. Before your next shooting session, it is always a good idea to check that the bore is clear of any obstructions before loading.

Gutters and Downspouts

Want to know if your gutters need cleaning? Look for discoloration on the lip of the gutter, says Bob Hanbury, a remodeler and the former host of *House Calls*, a home-repair call-in radio show in Newington, Connecticut. "That means that they're clogged and water is spilling over the side." Unfortunately, it also means that you're in for a big dirty job. Naturally, you'd be better off preventing such gutter backups by cleaning regularly. So spend a little time in the gutter now and then.

Technique: Clean your gutters at least twice a year—once in the spring and once in the fall. "In the spring, you have flowers and pollen falling off the trees, and in the fall, dead leaves," Hanbury says. Depending on how heavily wooded your yard is, you might have to clean them more often, especially in the fall.

Check your gutters by climbing up on a ladder. If the gutters have backed up, the best way to clean them out is to reach in and scoop up the sticks and leaves with your hands. Wear work gloves to protect your hands from sharp objects. Hose the gutters out once you have removed the gunk.

Also, shoot the hose down the downspout to clear it of sticks and leaves. If it clogs, try using a hose bladder, also available at hardware stores. Attach it to the end of the hose and insert the bladder as far into the clogged downspout as possible. As it fills with water, the bladder expands several inches. It then opens to emit a powerful stream that helps dislodge the debris. If this doesn't work and you just can't unclog the downspout, you might have to remove the downspout from the side of the house and work on the shorter sections on the ground. Or, call a plumber. He can use his drain snake to unclog it.

Speed tips: Consider using gutter guards or hoods. Quality hoods prevent debris from jamming the gutter. "Cheap, or poorly installed guards, however, can actually lead to quicker clogging," says Hanbury.

In no time, leaves can cover mesh screens that simply lie flat over the gutters. Shop wisely and use common sense.

Caution: Be careful getting to the gutters. "Know how to use a ladder properly," Hanbury says. Stabilize it on the ground. Attach it to the gutter so that you won't fall backward and the wind won't blow the ladder over. If your roof is pitched, don't try to clean the gutters while standing on the roof above them.

Hair Dryers

Keeping your hair dryer free of dust, hair, and lint is a breeze.

Technique: Unplug the hair dryer. As needed, wipe the exterior with a damp cloth to remove dust. For stubborn dirt, wipe with a sudsy cloth or sponge, and then rinse by wiping with a clean damp one. Never clean the inside of a hair dryer.

Remove lint and hair from the front and rear grilles—the intake and exhaust areas—using a soft dry brush. An old toothbrush works well. Do not use water or soap to clean the grilles, unless the grille is removable, says Nancy Drake, a product manager at Sunbeam Corporation in Delray Beach, Florida.

Clean any attachments, like a volumizer or diffuser, in warm soapy water the same way you would clean a comb or brush. Use hand soap or mild liquid dishwashing detergent. If they are matted with hair, let them soak for a while. Scrub gently with soapy water and a brush. Dry them completely with a soft towel before using.

Caution: To avoid shock, always make sure that the hair dryer is unplugged when you clean it. Never submerge a dryer in water.

Hammocks

Hammocks, especially those kept outdoors, collect airborne dust and harbor mildew when they are moist. Keeping your hammock clean prolongs its life and prevents you from getting dirty when you decide to kick back in it for a nap.

Technique: Lay your hammock on a nonabrasive surface, like a tarp. Hose it down and then scrub it using a soft-bristle brush or cloth and a bucket of warm soapy water. A mild liquid dishwashing detergent works best; use a squirt or two. Hose the soap off, turn the hammock over, and repeat the process. Again, hose it down. Never use any type of bleach. Bleach can deteriorate the hammock's fibers.

Next, hang it in the sun to dry. "The rot gets in when it stays wet," says Douglas Orians, vice president of sales and marketing for the Pawleys Island Hammock, manufactured by the Hammock Source, Pawleys Island, South Carolina, whose knotless, spreader-bar hammock design was developed more than 100 years ago by a South Carolina riverboat captain. "A white hammock hung outdoors will never be perfectly white again," he admits. "But the sun will help to bleach it naturally."

Speed tips: When you first buy your hammock, spray it with two light coats of a commercial water-repellent compound, like Scotchgard Heavy-Duty Water Repellent. That will protect the fibers and make cleaning easier.

Handbags

Like luggage, handbags can take a lot of abuse. Unlike luggage, however, they are often made of leather, which is hard to clean without damaging.

Technique: If your handbag is not made of leather, chances are that it is fabric or some type of synthetic material, like vinyl or nylon, which can usually be cleaned with a little water. Never get your bag too wet. Instead, spot-clean by blotting with a damp cloth. For stubborn stains, blot with a sudsy cloth, and then rinse well with a damp cloth.

Most handbags, however, are made of some form of leather, be it full-grained or patent leather, suede, or an exotic skin. Unfortunately, there's not a lot that you can do to clean leather. Try using a commercial leather-cleaning product like Lexol pH, available at leather and shoe repair shops. Wipe the cleaner off with a damp cloth and then apply a conditioner such as Lexol Conditioner. If the leather is light tan, test the conditioner on a small inconspicuous area for color.

For patent leather, use regular Pledge, says Henry Goldsmith, associate professor in the accessories design department at the Fashion Institute of Technology in New York City. Spray it on and wipe with a clean white cloth. Do not use Lemon Pledge. It leaves a film, Goldsmith says.

Polish alligator bags with a paste car wax, such as Simoniz. Apply it lightly with your fingers, and then buff it with a clean white cloth. "I used to make alligator bags that retailed for $3,000 to $6,000," says Goldsmith, a former handbag manufacturer. "A good simonizing paste really protects the bag and makes it shine."

How you clean the inside also depends on what it's made of. Most interiors are safe to wipe down with a lightly dampened sponge or cloth. Either open the bag as far as it will open or carefully pull the liner inside out. Do not use water if the liner is made of silk. Instead, simply shake out any dust and debris and wipe the liner with a dry cloth.

If you spill a potential stain-causing substance on your leather bag, the first thing you should do is blot it up with a clean white towel.

If it's a greasy stain, lay the bag out flat, sprinkle cornstarch on the stain, and let it stand overnight. It might absorb some of the oil. Another method is to place a clean white piece of tissue paper on the greasy spot and run a warm iron over it. Put the iron on the lowest heat setting for cotton. Replace the tissue several times with new tissue until there are no more traces of the stain on the tissue. "Leather is porous," Goldsmith says. "This technique will pull some of the stain out but not all. And it will remove wrinkles."

For a stain on suede, blot what you can and let the remainder dry for a couple of days. Try to restore the nap by rubbing very gently with a brass brush for suede, or fine sandpaper. By bringing back the nap, you might eliminate the stain.

For leather discoloration, look for a commercial leather spray, like Nu-Life. "It's like spray paint for leather," says Goldsmith. It comes in a variety of colors. Choose the one that best matches the original color of your bag, and then follow the manufacturer's instructions. For suede, mask stains and other discoloration by rubbing lightly with colored chalk that matches the original color of the suede.

For stubborn stains, take your bag to a professional leather cleaner. But choose wisely. Most leather cleaning today is done by wholesalers who pick up from cleaners. If you use a dry cleaner, make sure that it sends leather goods out to a leather specialist. Some dry cleaners try to clean the leather themselves—to avoid paying a wholesaler—and they could end up damaging it. For a professional leather cleaner referral in your area, contact the Leather Apparel Association, 19 West 21st Street, Suite 403, New York, NY 10010.

Caution: Always test your cleaning solution or method on an inconspicuous part of the handbag.

Hard-Water Deposits

Hard water contains minerals—namely, calcium and magnesium—that build up over time on sinks and fixtures. Unless you're interested in growing your own personal stalagmites, stay on top of this. The longer you allow these deposits to stand, the harder they are to remove.

Technique: Dissolve hard-water deposits on metal or porcelain enamel with a solution of 1 cup white vinegar per quart of water. Apply the solution with a sponge or soft cloth, and then rinse thoroughly with water, says Kay Weirick, director of housekeeping services at Bally's Las Vegas Hotel and a member of the technical advisory committee for *Executive Housekeeping Today* magazine. Or you can use a commercial preparation, such as Lime-a-way or Lime Buster, available at some hardware stores, supermarkets, and discount department stores. Read the label because it may not be appropriate on some metals. Follow the product label carefully for proper use and safety precautions.

Speed tips: Repair leaky faucets and clean sink and tub basins regularly to avoid stubborn hard-water buildup. A little prevention can save you time and effort in the long run.

Hats—Felt, Leather, Straw

Dust is your hat's primary enemy in terms of appearance. It can turn to mud if a drop of water hits it. "Any time a hat gets wet, you have possible stain problems," says Scott Bengel, plant manager at Hatco, in Garland, Texas, the makers of Stetson and Resistol hats, and a division of Arena Brands.

Technique: Dust hats regularly using a clothes or hat brush. It must be soft-bristle; otherwise, it might scratch the surface. When dusting felt or suede hats, always brush with the nap, not against it.

If something stains your hat, first blot up as much of the substance as possible using a dry cloth. Never use water to clean a fine felt, leather, or straw hat. There are commercial hat stain removers, either spray-on foams or sprinkle-on powders. Both work by absorbing the stain. Ask for them at hat or western retail stores.

For problem stains, you may need the service of a professional hat cleaner. If you can't find a hat cleaner, try a shoe repair shop. Cobblers sometimes clean hats.

In a pinch: If you stain a felt hat, blot as much of the substance as possible using a clean dry towel. Let the stain dry. "Once it's dry," says Bengel, "you can try to cover it up." Gently work colored chalk into the stain to try to match it. If it's too light, use a bit of graphite pencil to mix in with the chalk. "You want to come up with a color that blends the stain into the color hat you have," he says.

Heating Units

Unless they sit for a long period of time or in a very dirty environment—with a lot of airborne grease—portable heaters will not get very dirty. You should, however, keep them free of dust, which helps them work more efficiently.

Technique: Don't take it apart. Heater manufacturers strongly discourage consumers from disassembling their heaters in order to clean them. It is potentially dangerous and, in many cases, will void the manufacturer's warranty for the product.

Instead, to dust small ceramic heaters or heaters with coils, blow compressed air through the grille—from both sides, if possible. This removes any accumulated particles on the heating element and reduces the chance that dust bunnies will collect and clog a vent or filter. Do it at least twice a year—before and after the heating season, advise small-heating-appliance experts.

You can also periodically clean the heater's grille with a vacuum cleaner brush attachment. In addition, use a damp cloth to wipe down the outside casing. If the heater has a removable filter—like the foam filter in most air conditioners—wash it once or twice a season with warm soapy water. Let it dry completely before replacing it.

In a pinch: No compressed air? Use a blow-dryer instead.

Caution: Always turn off and unplug your portable heater before cleaning it.

High Chairs

As with other items that come into contact with food—and high chairs most certainly do—you want to wipe up spills as soon as possible to keep the food from sticking. Keeping high chairs clean helps prevent the growth of bacteria, a potential health threat to your child.

Technique: Clean the high chair with a sudsy sponge or cloth immediately after your child has eaten. Use a liquid dishwashing detergent, preferably one containing antibacterial agents.

Lay a wet cloth over stuck-on food for a few minutes, and then wipe it off once it has loosened. Rinse by wiping down with a clean moist sponge.

Periodically follow the regular cleaning by sanitizing the high chair tray and any other areas that come into contact with food and child. Wipe them down with a fresh 10-to-1 solution of water and chlorine bleach. Let the solution sit for a minute or two, and then rinse it off by wiping with a clean moist sponge, suggest infection-control specialists.

Also, periodically clean any seat padding or covers. Just wipe down vinyl padding. If the padding is covered in a washable fabric, consult the care label for washing instructions.

Once or twice a year, take your high chair outside, hose it off, and give it a good scrubbing with a bucket of sudsy water and a soft nylon brush. Rinse it with the hose, and let it dry in the sun. Or put it in the shower to scrub and rinse off. Let it air-dry.

Speed tips: When it's humid outside, put the high chair in a shaded area on a porch or in the yard and let it sit for a few hours. The moisture will loosen stuck-on food and make wiping it off easier.

Hoses

Good news: "Hoses are pretty much maintenance-free," says Fred Hicks, past president of the American Nursery and Landscape Association in Washington, D.C., and president of Hicks Nurseries in Westbury, New York. The better you take care of them, however, the longer they will last.

Technique: When your hose gets muddy, lay it out on a clean surface, like a driveway or patio, and spray it down. (Talk about self-cleaning!) Then wipe it with a cloth. In the winter, remove water from inside the hose to keep it from freezing, which can damage the hose's interior lining. Pick up one end of the hose and raise it hand over hand until you've drained all of the water. Whenever possible, keep your hose in the shade. Over long periods of time, ultraviolet rays break down the plastic resins, creating cracks and leaks.

In a pinch: "In the winter, I coil my hose up and put it in the basement to keep it from freezing," says Hicks.

Hot Tubs

Above all, keep your hot tub sanitized. "If you don't sanitize the water, bacteria can grow in the tub," says Jeff Kurth, director of the Spa Council for the National Pool and Spa Institute, headquartered in Washington, D.C., and chief executive officer of Marquis Spas, in Independence, Oregon. "Pseudomonas, bacteria that cause a skin rash, are common in hot tubs that aren't cleaned properly."

Technique: One of the most important hot tub cleaning duties is treating the water with chemicals, like chlorine and bromine. When deciding quantity of chemicals and how often to use them, follow the manufacturer's instructions for your particular hot tub.

Clean the filter on a regular basis. "Hair, fibers, body oils, and other soils get trapped in there and cut down the rate at which the water flows through the filter," says Kurth, "which can starve the pumps and lead to bacterial contamination." Most portable hot tubs feature cartridge filters, made of nonwoven polyester, Dacron, or treated paper. Clean these once a week by spraying them with a garden hose, and replace them once a year.

For sand and diatomaceous earth (DE) filters, typically found on larger more permanent hot tubs, you should reverse the water pump on the hot tub once every week or two to agitate the filter bed and remove debris. Follow your hot tub manual for more specific instructions on exactly how often to backwash these filters as well as when to replace the sand or earth.

Drain the hot tub at least three or four times a year—once a month if you're using it heavily. Most tubs are made of cast acrylic, which is easy to clean. Wipe the shell down using a soft cloth or sponge and a solution of warm water and mild detergent, like liquid dishwashing detergent. Do not use abrasive cleaners or scouring pads. Rinse detergent before refilling.

Humidifiers and Vaporizers

Ignore your humidifier, and bacteria, mold, and fungi will thank you. They just love to be left alone in a moist environment like that, says Bill Staples, director of consumer sales at Emerson Air Comfort Products in Hazelwood, Missouri. Regular cleaning will retard such growth. Cleaning humidifiers and vaporizers also removes mineral deposits left by hard water, and that will extend the life of your appliances.

Technique: If you use a portable humidifier with a one- or two-gallon tank, empty the tank every day and refill it with fresh tap water. For larger portable humidifiers, change the water as recommended by the manufacturer.

At least once a week clean all surfaces that come into contact with water, using 1 cup undiluted vinegar, Staples suggests, or follow your machine's instructions. Use a nylon or vegetable brush to loosen deposits and a wire pipe cleaner to clean the intake tube. Let it sit for about 20 minutes. Rinse with warm clean water. Be sure to follow your manufacturer's instructions.

To disinfect the humidifier, use 1 teaspoon chlorine bleach in 1 gallon water and wet all surfaces. Allow the solution to sit for 20 minutes, sloshing the liquid around every few minutes. Rinse with water until the bleach smell is gone. Follow the manufacturer's instructions for how often you should disinfect the unit. At the end of the season, follow the cleaning and disinfecting instructions and make sure that your machine is dry before you put it away.

Consider using a bacteriostat or bacteriocide in evaporative humidifiers. These products, sold at home supply stores along with the humidifiers themselves, help prevent bacteria from growing inside water that sits in the machine. Most are liquids that you add straight to the water, making them easy to use. They also control odors caused by mold and mildew. "Sometimes," Staples says, "people don't know that there's anything wrong with their units until they smell a musty odor."

Follow the same routine for cleaning vaporizers. Also, periodically disassemble the heating element, following the manufacturer's instructions, and wipe clean the heating element. To clean mineral deposits off the heating element, soak it for several hours in a container of undiluted white vinegar. Be sure not to wet the wire or electrical connection points. Use an old toothbrush to scrub off deposits. Rinse and dry the heating unit well, and reassemble it.

If you have a central humidifier attached to your heating or cooling system, be sure to clean the filter and the evaporator tray. Begin by reading the manufacturer's cleaning instructions.

In general, however, to clean the filter, first shut off power to the heating or cooling system and turn off the humidifier's water supply. Remove the cover and lift out the filter drum. Take the filter pad off its frame and soak it in a solution of 2 quarts white vinegar per gallon of water for several hours. This should remove any waterborne mineral deposits. Rinse it thoroughly with water, and wring it until it is almost dry.

Remove the evaporator tray and soak it in the vinegar solution for a few hours. Wipe off any deposits with a cloth soaked in the solution. Rinse the tray thoroughly, and then wipe it dry with a clean cloth. When you reassemble the humidifier, turn on the water supply before turning on the power.

Speed tips: "You can wash some parts of the small tabletop units in the dishwasher if the instructions state that it's okay to do so," Staples says. Do not wash fan motors or other electrical parts. To make sure that the plastic basin and other plastic parts don't melt, put them on the top rack, away from the heating element.

Caution: To avoid possible shock, be sure to unplug the humidifier before cleaning. Wear rubber gloves when cleaning with the bleach solution.

Ice Equipment

Cleaning your ice-making equipment is a matter of taste—literally. Many ice-makers themselves do not require cleaning, says Martha Reek, a senior home economist with the Whirlpool Corporation in Evansville, Indiana. However, free-standing ice-makers need regular cleaning. It's important to follow the manufacturer's directions carefully no matter what type of ice-maker you have. In every case, what does need cleaning is the pan that collects the ice and even the ice itself. Even if your freezer is empty, ice that sits too long in the ice bucket can take on the flavors of food in your fridge—onion and garlic, for instance—because cold air circulates through both compartments. "Fresh ice just tastes better," says Reek.

Technique: Purge ice regularly if you do not use it up. "If your ice begins to take on funky shapes, that means it has been in there way too long and you need to throw it away," Reek explains.

Every six months or so, remove the pan that holds the cubes and wash it in the kitchen sink with warm soapy water. Dry it thoroughly, and then put it back in the freezer. Do the same with ice cube trays. Empty, wash, and dry them; refill them with freshwater; and return them to the freezer.

Tip: If you need a quantity of ice for a picnic or a party, save it in a sealable plastic bag to keep odors out.

Ink

 EMERGENCY ACTION
Blot with rubbing alcohol. If the colors might bleed, dilute the alcohol with two parts water. To test for colorfastness, dab a drop or two of alcohol on the inside of a seam or hem, using a cotton swab.

This is one of the toughest stains to remove. Sometimes all you can hope for, especially in the case of felt-tip pen ink, is minimizing the spot.

Technique: For ballpoint pen ink, blot with a cotton ball or white cotton cloth soaked with rubbing alcohol. If colors might bleed or the fabric is acetate, dilute the alcohol with two parts water. If it is a washable garment, rinse out the alcohol with cold water, then wash in the hottest water safe for the fabric. If it is a carpet or rug, blot clean with a white towel and water.

If that doesn't work, try blotting with a solution of ½ cup warm water, ¼ teaspoon liquid dishwashing detergent, and several drops of ammonia. Finally, after rinsing the ammonia completely, try a 10-to-1 solution of water and chlorine bleach, but only on fabrics that are white or colorfast. (Reminder: Ammonia and chlorine react to create noxious fumes, so make sure that all the ammonia is rinsed out of the fabric before trying the bleach solution.) If the stain remains, try a 4-to-1 solution. "There's a certain point at which you must decide what's worse—a permanently stained garment or a bleached garment," says Ann Lemley, Ph.D., chairman of the department of textiles and apparel at Cornell University in Ithaca, New York. "Sometimes you have to make those choices."

For felt-tip pen stains, blot with an all-purpose cleaner, like Fantastik. Rinse with cold water or, in the case of carpets, blot with a wet towel. Repeat until as much of the stain disappears as possible.

Note: Before using cleaning solutions, always test them on an inconspicuous section of the stained item.

Caution: Always rinse out one cleaning solution before trying another. Mixing chemicals, especially ammonia and chlorine bleach, can create noxious fumes.

Iodine

Iodine was once a staple in many home first-aid kits. "My mother used to use something called Argyrol, which had iodine in it," remembers Ann Lemley, Ph.D., chairman of the department of textiles and apparel at Cornell University in Ithaca, New York. "She would drop it down my throat when it was sore. It was awful." One place where you'll find iodine these days is in the water-purification tablets used by campers. Though not as common, it still creates a deep, dark stain when it spills on fabric.

Technique: For washables, Dr. Lemley suggests applying a liquid laundry detergent containing enzymes (or a paste made from a granular detergent and water) directly on the stain. Lay the garment on a hard surface and pat the stain lightly with the back of a spoon to force the solution into the fibers. Avoid rubbing the material together, which abrades the fibers. Next, wash as directed in the hottest water safe for the fabric. If that does not work, rinse and follow the same patting procedure but with a solution of 2 tablespoons ammonia per 1 cup water. If that fails to remove the stain, rinse and try a vinegar solution—1 cup white vinegar per 2 cups water.

For fabrics that cannot be washed, either have them professionally dry-cleaned or blot them with a white towel and a spot remover, like Carbona Stain Devils or K2r, available at supermarkets, hardware stores, or discount department stores. Blot from the inside of the garment to push the stain out. When using these products, wear protective rubber or latex gloves and use them in a well-ventilated area.

For iodine stains in carpets or rugs, first try a spot remover. Never pour the spot remover directly on the stain. Instead, put it on a clean white towel and blot the stain repeatedly. If that doesn't work, blot with a solution of ¼ teaspoon liquid dishwashing detergent and 1 cup lukewarm water. Rinse by blotting with a clean white towel moistened with water, then dry with a fresh towel.

Note: Before using cleaning solutions, always test them on an inconspicuous section of the stained item.

Caution: Always rinse out one cleaning solution before trying another. Mixing chemicals, especially ammonia and chlorine bleach, can create noxious fumes. Always read and follow the product label carefully for proper use and safety precautions.

Iron—Wrought

Wrought iron is a commercial form of the metal that's both tough and malleable. It does have an Achilles' heel, though: rust.

Technique: If you simply need to remove soil or bird droppings, wipe your iron with a damp cloth or scrub with a nylon brush and wipe it dry.

To remove rust, use a wire brush or medium sandpaper. Then scour it with a fine-grade steel wool, like #00 grade. "The steel wool will remove a very thin layer of iron and make it look like new," says Rajiv Jain, laboratory manager for the Association of Specialists in Cleaning and Restoration in Annapolis Junction, Maryland.

To protect your wrought iron from future rust, treat it with a rust-prohibitor, available at hardware stores.

In a pinch: For light rust on wrought iron, rub with silver polish.

Irons

If the surface of your clothes iron is dirty, you risk staining your clothes permanently since heat seals in stains.

Technique: Always keep your iron dry between uses. This will help you avoid rust, which can ruin clothing. Empty your iron while it's hot. That way, the heat will dry out the cavity. Then, before putting it away, allow the iron to cool.

To remove melted plastic and fabrics, heat at a low setting until the material softens, unplug the iron, and scrape off with a piece of wood, like a wooden spatula or half a clothespin. "Don't use anything made out of metal, because that can scratch the surface," says Cindy Hupert, a product manager at Sunbeam, a manufacturer of irons in Delray Beach, Florida. To remove any remaining residue, let the iron cool and then rub the surface with a paste of baking soda and water. Clean the paste off with a moist cloth.

If your iron is coated with a nonstick soleplate, rub it gently with a nylon mesh pad and suds.

For taking off melted polyester, rub with a cotton ball dabbed in acetone or nail polish remover.

If mineral buildup from the water supply clogs your steam iron, poke the spray nozzle hole with a fine needle. To clean mineral deposits from the steam vents on the bottom of the iron, fill the iron with a solution of one part white vinegar and three parts cool water. Set it on the hottest steam setting, and place it on a flat wire rack (such as a cooling rack for baking) over a heat- and moisture-resistant surface. Stay with the iron while it's hot. Let the iron steam until it is empty. If your iron shuts off automatically after 30 seconds when motionless in the down position, you may have to move it periodically until it's empty. To avoid further mineral buildup in steam irons, use only distilled water.

If lint clogs the steam vents, try steaming it free. Fill the iron with water and let it steam until it is empty, as explained above. Remember, never leave a hot iron unattended.

Speed tips: To quickly remove melted-on plastics or other substances, heat your iron on a low setting until the material softens, and then iron over an old cloth or some other piece of throwaway fabric. "The residue will transfer from the surface of the iron to the surface of the cloth," says Hupert.

Caution: If you are using acetone or nail polish remover to remove melted polyester from your iron's surface, do not get it on the iron's plastic parts. It can eat them away.

Jewelry

"Once mined and worn, gems are exposed to hardships and chemicals they never experienced underground," writes Fred Ward, a gem expert in Bethesda, Maryland, in his book *Gem Care*. Body oils, airborne pollutants, soap scum, and other substances dull the luster of jewelry and can cause permanent damage to what are some of our most valuable possessions.

Technique: Do not overclean. Most jewelry does not need cleaning after each use. The exceptions are softer gems, like turquoise, amber, and especially pearls, all of which should be wiped down with a chamois cloth after each use. Because these gems are porous, substances like perspiration, perfume, cosmetics, and hair spray can stain them. For this reason, always apply makeup, perfume, and hair spray before putting on pearls and other soft gemstones, and try to wear them against clothing and not your skin. Their porous quality also means that certain cleaning fluids can stain them. Every once in a while, wash pearls and other soft gems in lukewarm water and soap, creating very light suds with a white bar soap and gently cleaning the gems with a soft cloth. Anything harder, like a toothbrush, could scratch them. Do not let the gems soak. Rinse them in clean water and dry with a chamois cloth.

Crystalline gems, like diamonds, rubies, garnets, and emeralds, do not absorb moisture and should be cleaned periodically to enhance their luster. "While cleaning them, the only thing you need to be concerned with is that you use something softer than they are to rub with so that you don't scratch them," says Ward. Clean them several times a year, depending on how often you wear them. For all crystalline gems, except diamonds, the safest combination is warm soapy water and a soft toothbrush. Rinse them to remove the soap, and then let them air-dry. "Diamonds are magnets for soap and grease, which make them look dull," Ward explains. Clean diamonds in a one-to-one solution of lukewarm water and an all-purpose cleaner such as Mr. Clean, using a soft toothbrush. Or place your diamonds in a shot glass of straight vodka for a half-hour, brush with a soft brush, and rinse under running water. Make sure that there are no absorbent gems, like pearls, on the piece of diamond jewelry you plan to clean in this solution. If there are, simply use warm water.

Ultrasonic cleaners, which loosen debris by vibrating at thousands of pulses per second, work safely on diamonds and a few other gems. But soft stones, like amber and pearls, can crack in ultrasonic cleaners. Ask your jeweler before using this method.

How Hard Can It Be?

Hardness of minerals is measured using the Mohs scale, developed in the nineteenth century by a German named Friedrich Mohs. Diamonds, the hardest substance known to man, rate 10. Talc, at the opposite end of the scale, rates 1.

Because substances of higher Mohs ratings can scratch those of lower ratings, knowing the hardness of gemstones and precious metals is important in deciding how to clean jewelry. For example, some people, including jewelers, recommend using toothpaste to clean gold. "But certain toothpastes have sand in them," says gem expert Fred Ward of Bethesda, Maryland, author of the *National Geographic*'s gem series for 14 years and author of *Gem Care*, "giving them a hardness close to quartz. They can damage softer gemstones and sandpaper gold, silver, and platinum to a matte finish."

Here's a list of how some common substances rate in the Mohs scale.

Substance	Hardness
Talc	1
Amber	2–2.5
Silver	2.5
Gold	2.5–3
Pearl	2.5–4.5
Coral	3–4
Malachite	3.5–4
Platinum	4–4.33
Glass	5–6
Turquoise	5–6
Opal	5.5
Rhodonite	5.5–6.5
Nephrite jade	6–6.5
Tanzanite	6–7
Zircon	6–7.5
Jadeite	6.5–7
Peridot	6.5–7
Quartz (includes amethyst and citrine)	7
Garnet	7–7.5
Tourmaline	7–7.5
Aquamarine	7.5–8
Emerald	7.5–8
Topaz	8
Ruby	9
Sapphire	9
Diamond	10

In a pinch: Simply wipe jewelry with a soft moist cloth to remove body oils, makeup, and dust.

Caution: Do not use ultrasonic cleaners to clean emeralds. Even though they are hard crystalline gems, they can crack when exposed to ultrasonic vibrations.

Juice Stains

A stain that comes from a plant—whether it's from juice or anything else—is called a tannin stain, says Jane Rising, instructor in the education department at the International Fabricare Institute in Silver Spring, Maryland. That includes grape, prune, tomato, citrus, and other types of juice. Tannin stains are easier to remove from some fabrics than other fabrics. "When you're dealing with polyester," she says, "a juice stain can look horrible, but it will probably come out easily." Cotton can be more difficult. While some juices, like grape juice, stain worse than others, attack them all the same way.

Technique: If it's a washable fabric, begin by blotting with a clean white towel and warm water. Continue until you don't see any more of the juice coming out on the blotting towel.

Next, pretreat the stain before washing the item. Begin by mixing ¼ teaspoon clear liquid dishwashing detergent with ½ cup warm water. Apply it directly to the fabric, and then lay the garment on a hard surface and pat the stain lightly with the back of a spoon. This allows the solution to get in between the fibers, where stains hide. Don't rub the fabric together; that will abrade the fibers. Next, wash as directed either by machine or by hand in the hottest water safe for the fabric.

If the stain does not come out completely, follow the same pretreatment procedure but, this time, with a solution of 1 tablespoon vinegar and ½ cup warm water. Again, wash as directed.

For fabrics that cannot be washed, either have them professionally dry-cleaned or blot them with a clean white towel and a spot remover, like Carbona Stain Devils or K2r, available at supermarkets, hardware stores, or discount department stores. Blot from the inside of the garment to push the stain out. Use aerosol spot removers in a well-ventilated area while wearing protective rubber or latex gloves. Follow all product labels carefully for proper use and safety precautions.

For carpets and rugs, first blot with a clean white towel and water. Next, blot with a white towel dipped in the liquid dishwashing solution. Then rinse by blotting with a clean towel and water. If the first solution doesn't work, blot with the vinegar solution. Do not blot with laundry detergent because it often contains optical brighteners that can bleach carpet and rug dyes.

As a last-ditch effort, try blotting with hydrogen peroxide. But be careful: It will cause color dyes to bleed and fade.

Caution: Always rinse out one cleaning solution before trying another. Mixing chemicals, especially ammonia and chlorine bleach, can create noxious fumes. Read and follow label instructions carefully for proper use and safety precautions. Before using cleaning solutions, always test them on an inconspicuous section of the stained item.

Ketchup Stains

Ketchup is one of our most popular condiments. Unfortunately, the stain it leaves is also one of the toughest to remove.

Technique: Scrape away any excess ketchup. For washables, first soak the stained item in cold water to remove as much of the ketchup as possible. The older the stain, the longer you should soak it—up to several hours.

Then pretreat it before washing it. Begin by mixing ¼ teaspoon clear liquid dishwashing detergent with ½ cup cold water. Apply it directly to the fabric, and then lay the garment on a hard surface and pat the stain lightly with the back of a spoon. This allows the solution to get in between the fibers, where stains hide. Don't rub the fabric together; that will abrade the fibers. Next, wash as directed either by machine or by hand in the hottest water safe for the fabric.

If the stain does not come out completely, follow the same pretreatment procedure but, this time, with a solution of 1 teaspoon ammonia and ½ cup cold water. Again, wash as directed. If that fails, try a liquid laundry detergent containing enzymes (or a paste made from a granular detergent and water). Apply it directly on the stain, pat, and then wash.

For fabrics that cannot be washed, either have them professionally dry-cleaned or blot with a clean white towel and a spot remover, like Carbona Stain Devils or K2r, available at supermarkets, hardware stores, or discount department stores. When you use these products, wear protective rubber or latex gloves and work in a well-ventilated location. Blot from the inside of the garment to push the stain out.

For carpets and rugs, act immediately. If the stain is fresh, you may be able to remove it by blotting the stain with plain water and paper towels. If not, then blot with a solution made from ¼ teaspoon liquid dishwashing detergent per 1 cup of lukewarm water (use a clean white towel). Then blot with a clean towel and water. If the first solution doesn't work, blot with an ammonia solution made from 2 tablespoons of ammonia per 1 cup lukewarm water. Do not blot with laundry detergent.

"If the stain just won't come out, try blotting with a 3 percent solution of hydrogen peroxide," says Rajiv Jain, laboratory manager for the Association of Specialists in Cleaning and Restoration in Annapolis Junction, Maryland. It is available at drugstores. But be careful: It might alter the dyes in the fabric or carpet.

Caution: Always remove one cleaning solution before trying another. Always read product labels for proper use and safety precautions. Before using cleaning solutions, always test them on an inconspicuous section of the stained item. Don't make the solutions any stronger than specified, and use them as sparingly as possible.

Kettles

These hefty pots, usually made of cast iron, were once as common as cooking lard was. Today, olive oil has replaced the animal fat, and fancy, lightweight alloys have replaced the cast iron. Still, some people are rediscovering the joys of cooking with kettles, especially with the increasingly popular Dutch ovens. In terms of cleaning, your main goal is avoiding rust by keeping the cast iron well-seasoned.

Technique: When at all possible, just wipe the surface clean with a dry paper towel. If that doesn't cut the mustard (or grease), use boiling water and a brush. If you need to scour the kettle, first use a plastic scouring pad. And if you have to, contrary to popular belief, you *can* scrub cast iron with soap and water and even scour it with steel wool to remove stuck-on food or rust. But you must re-season the surface after heavy cleaning. After washing, dry it, lightly coating with a no-stick spray like Pam, and wipe it with a clean paper towel to remove the excess grease. Never store your kettle with the lid on.

Cleaning Kettles the Old-Fashioned Way

Billie Hill recalls how her grandparents used to clean and season their large wash kettle. "Back then they only used pure lard to coat their pot. Cast iron rusts when it comes into contact with water. Since they were using the kettle to wash clothes, they put lard on the outside, too," says Hill, who is customer service manager at the Lodge Manufacturing Company in South Pittsburg, Tennessee, where she has worked for almost 50 years.

"Next, they would heat the kettle over a fire in the yard. Because their pot had only three short legs, they would stand the pot on flat stones or bricks over the fire. The pores of the iron would open up when heated and absorb the grease. Then, once the fire had died down, they would wipe the grease up onto the sides with an old mop. The lard on the outside charred the pot to a degree, but that just gave it a nice blackened look.

"Later, it would be ready to wash clothes in. They would boil water inside the pot, and then add the clothes and old-fashioned lye soap. The clothes didn't get greasy because the pot only had a thin coating. Plus, the soap took care of any excess grease.

"When she finished washing clothes, my grandmother would wipe the pot down with a greasy cloth, dry it, and wait for the next wash day."

To season a small kettle—one that will fit inside your oven—begin by washing it with hot soapy water, rinse, and dry. Melt a dollop of solid shortening, like Crisco, in a pan on the stove. Remove from the heat and put a small cloth, about the size of a washcloth, into the melted shortening. Apply melted shortening to both the inside and outside of the kettle and the kettle lid.

Next move the bottom rack of your oven to the lowest slot and place a baking sheet wrapped in aluminum foil on it to catch the grease. Preheat your oven to 350°F. Put your kettle upside down on the rack above it. Heat for an hour. Turn the oven off and let the kettle cool completely.

"Cast iron works like a vacuum," explains Billie Hill, customer service manager for the Lodge Manufacturing Company, makers of cast-iron cookware for more than a century, in South Pittsburg, Tennessee. "When the pores get hot and open up, they suck up a minute amount of grease and no more." You will need to re-season it after cooking beans or acidic foods or if you had to scour with metal pads.

You can also season small kettles on gas or charcoal grills. "You get the grill heated up, put the pot in there, and let 'er cook," says

Hill, who has worked at Lodge for almost 50 years. "It'll smoke and it'll smell, but it's outside so it doesn't matter."

Make sure that the kettle is upside down so that the grease will carbonize properly. Feed a charcoal grill with enough coals so that it cooks for an hour or more. The result is a well-seasoned kettle that is also blackened, the way kettles should be. Leave it on the grill until the coals die down and the kettle cools.

Speed tips: Clean a cast-iron kettle while it's still warm from cooking. Stuck-on food will be easier to remove then.

In a pinch: If your entire kettle does not need re-seasoning, simply wipe a little shortening on the inside and heat it upside down for 30 minutes in a 350°F oven.

Caution: To avoid oven fires, make sure that you catch all dripping grease with an aluminum foil–covered baking sheet. Never use liquid dishwashing detergents to wash cast iron.

Knickknacks

Knickknacks are for display, right? So naturally you want them dust-free and looking their best.

Technique: Knickknacks come in a variety of shapes and sizes and are made of many different materials. Most need only regular dusting.

"You can wipe the majority of things with a damp cloth," says Marry Keener, assistant director of facilities management at the University of Arizona in Tucson and a member of the technical advisory committee for *Executive Housekeeping Today* magazine. "These days, so many surfaces are protected with plastics, vinyls, and paint. Wood is protected with polyurethane."

Use a dry cloth for objects that cannot get wet—unfired pottery, for example, or something that has been hand-painted.

For soft-surface knickknacks, like small pillows and dolls, you also want to remove accumulated dust. They don't necessarily need to be washed; in fact, water can ruin many of these items. Instead, put them in the dryer and tumble for 5 to 10 minutes on the "Air-Fluff" setting, which uses only cool air. (Make sure that they contain no hard or breakable parts.) This will loosen the dust and transfer it from the item to the dryer's filter.

Speed tips: Put glazed pottery, glass, and similar items in the dishwasher and run it on the fine-china cycle. "I let the dishwasher do the work for me," Keener says. The fine-china cycle is typically more delicate and shorter than other cycles.

Labels—Removing Decals, Stickers

Removing that old sticker from the back of your car can be a pain in the bumper. The same goes for decals and such on windows, walls, and other surfaces. Your goal is to get rid of the decal and all of the dust-gathering adhesive without harming the surface on which it is stuck.

Technique: Warm ½ to 1 cup vinegar. Fold a pad of cloth large enough to cover the decal. Soak the fabric in the warm vinegar and apply it to the decal. Hold it there for a few minutes. Once the sticker is saturated, it should peel off easily, says Kay Weirick, director of housekeeping services at Bally's Las Vegas Hotel and a member of the technical advisory committee for *Executive Housekeeping Today* magazine.

Acetone, available in hardware stores, is the main ingredient in acetone nail polish remover and is good for removing old adhesive stains. Dab a cotton ball with acetone, and paint it over the decal. But avoid using acetone to remove decals stuck on painted surfaces. The acetone will remove the paint.

Speed tips: To help the vinegar soak in better, make slits in the decal with a blade—but only if that won't hurt the surface that it's on.

Attach the vinegar-soaked cloth to the decal using masking tape, and go about your business. Come back after a few minutes and the sticker should be saturated.

In a pinch: For removing labels from glass, metal, or some other surface that can withstand heat, first saturate the label as described and then briefly direct warm air from a blow-dryer set on medium toward the label. The label should peel off easily.

Caution: To make sure that your removal method will not damage the surface containing the label, test it on an inconspicuous area first.

Lace

Cleaning lace is no tea party. Lace is fragile because of its structure, and you don't want to damage it or distort its shape. Also, a lot of lace trim, like the glossy kind you see on wedding dresses, is made of rayon. When wet, rayon can lose up to 70 percent of its strength.

Technique: Begin by reading the care labels. If your lace is a dry-clean-only type, then do not wash it. Water could shrink the lace dramatically.

If your lace is washable, the best way to wash it is to soak the lace in warm water and a mild liquid dishwashing detergent, like Ivory Liquid or Palmolive. "Water is a wonderful solvent," says Jane Rising, instructor in the education department at the International Fabricare Institute in Silver Spring, Maryland. "A long soak will take out a lot of things." Avoid scrubbing or other aggressive tactics.

For machine washable lace, such as table linens, wash on a gentle cycle in a net bag or a pillowcase with the end tied. The bag will protect the lace by reducing the potential for snagging.

Dry lace by hanging it on a line out of direct sunlight or laying it on a clean white towel on a flat surface. The flatter you dry it, the easier it will be to press it. Tumbling lace in a dryer leaves it impossibly wrinkled.

"When you're ironing large lace items, use a table covered with a towel," advises Rising. "With an ironing board, you'll end up with puckers in between sections because you're never going to get it totally flat." Set your iron temperature based on the fiber content of the lace. To reduce stretching and distortion, gently move the iron in a circular motion, rather than the traditional back and forth.

Speed tips: "Sometimes with large lace items, it's better to have a professional clean it," Rising says. The large presses used by cleaners are best because they come straight down on the fabric. "It will save you time and hassle, and you'll probably be happier with the results."

Caution: Do not try to clean antique lace. Have a professional fine-textile cleaner do it—not your corner dry cleaner. Look for a specialty cleaner in the yellow pages. Wedding-dress cleaners are often familiar with lace and other fragile fabrics.

Lamps—Electric, Hurricane

Lamps, because they are illuminated, show grime more than most things. Keeping them clean not only improves their looks but also helps them shine brighter.

Technique: There are countless varieties of lamps, made from many different materials—porcelain, blown glass, wood. Cleaning methods will vary, depending on the material from which your lamps are made. Dust them regularly, using either a plain dust cloth or, for detailed designs, a soft-bristle brush.

For heavier cleaning, begin by unplugging the cord, removing the shade, and unscrewing any lightbulbs, says Kay Weirick, director of housekeeping services at Bally's Las Vegas Hotel and a member of the technical advisory committee for *Executive Housekeeping Today* magazine. Fill a kitchen sink with suds using warm water and liquid dishwashing detergent. Place the lamp on the counter next to the sink. Lay it on a towel so that it won't slip. If the base is washable, wipe it with the suds using a cloth or sponge, without getting the cord wet. Rinse the cloth or sponge and wipe away the suds. Dry the lamp with a clean cloth. If the lamp has a reflector bowl, wash and dry it by hand like you would a dish.

If the lamp is not washable, simply wipe it down with a cloth lightly dampened with plain water and dry it.

To wash the cord, wring most of the liquid from a sudsy sponge and fold it in half. Pull the cord between the two layers of the folded sponge, and then wipe it dry.

Clean the bulbs by wiping them with a damp sudsy sponge. Rinse by wiping with a clean sponge. Dry with a cloth. Do not let the metal neck get wet.

For hurricane lamps and other types with glass globes or chimneys, remove the globe and wash it in deep suds. Scrub inside the chimney using a bottle brush. Rinse the glass with hot water and wipe it dry. Wipe the lamp base with a wet sponge. If you'd like extra-sparkling glass, add a few drops of ammonia or vinegar to the rinse water.

Caution: Don't let the cord or socket of the lamp get wet.

Lamp Shades

Lamp shades can be tricky. For one thing, they show dirt because they are so well lit. They also come in many different—and often tough-to-clean—styles. One thing is for sure: If you dust them on a regular basis, dirt won't have as much of a chance to set and stain, and the shades will require deep cleaning less often.

Technique: Dust shades regularly with a clean soft cloth or with the brush attachment of a vacuum cleaner.

Clean shades that are laminated, coated in plastic, or made of parchment or fiberglass with "dry" suds. Put ¼ cup mild liquid dishwashing detergent into a bowl, and add just a little warm water. Whip the mixture with an egg beater to make suds that look like whipped cream, or cover the bowl and shake it a few times. With a cloth or sponge gently rub a little of the suds on the shade. Don't rub or moisten any glued-on bindings or frills. Rinse the shade immediately by wiping it with a clean damp cloth, and then wipe it dry, says Kay Weirick, director of housekeeping services at Bally's Las Vegas Hotel and a member of the technical advisory committee for *Executive Housekeeping Today* magazine.

For shades made of silk, rayon, or nylon, dip the entire shade into a tub or sink filled with mild lukewarm suds (liquid dishwashing detergent is best). Scrub gently, if necessary, with a cloth or sponge. Empty and refill the basin with clean lukewarm water. Dip the shade again to rinse. Repeat the rinse with clean water, if necessary. Tie a string to the middle of the frame, and hang it over the bathtub or from an outdoor clothesline to drip-dry. Do this right away to avoid rust on the metal frame, which could stain the material.

Caution: Do not wash linen, cotton, or hand-painted shades or shades with glued-on trim or other parts in water. Don't try to spot-clean a fabric shade. The flame-resistant solution on it will leave a yellow stain if it gets wet.

Lattices

You typically find lattices in the garden, often exposed to the elements. The trick is cleaning them without injuring the bushes or vines trained on them.

Technique: Clean plant-covered lattice in the dormant season, when vines and plants are at their thinnest. "If possible, clean after you've pruned," says Fred Garrett, coordinator of the landscape gardening program at Sandhills Community College in Pinehurst, North Carolina. "Then, even more of the lattice is exposed."

To clean dirt and debris from a lattice, spray it with a garden hose. Use a nozzle that channels the water into a tight stream. If you must scrub it, use a nylon brush and a mild vegetable-oil soap, like Murphy Oil Soap, which won't harm nearby plants. Be sure to rinse all soap residue off the lattice. It can lead to fungus growth.

Speed tips: Rent a low-pressure power sprayer at an equipment rental shop. This will speed up the process. But be careful: Don't use any soap or chemicals, only water; and don't hold the jet too close to the lattice or for too long in one spot.

Laundry

In the United States, 35 billion loads of wash are done each year—1,000 new loads every second. Indeed, laundry is such a common chore that many people take it for granted. Yet there's more to washing clothes than just filling the machines, turning a dial, and pressing a button. A certain amount of preparation will help clothes get cleaner and last longer.

Follow these suggestions from the Soap and Detergent Association in New York City, and it'll all come out in the wash just fine.

Machine-Washing

By law, garment manufacturers are required to stitch care labels into garments sold in the United States. They are your best guide on how to care for your clothing. Always read the labels before washing. Don't overload the machine. Overloading can cause tangling and prevents clothes from circulating freely.

A few tricks of the laundry trade can save you time and money. First, sort your

Colossal Cleanups

A Washer Workout
The amount of dirty clothes generated by the average American each year: more than a quarter ton

clothing into washer loads that keep similar items together. To prevent lighter clothing from picking up bleeding colors, sort articles by color, keeping whites, darks, and medium colors together. Next,

Is Your Water Hard or Soft?

Soft water makes cleaning easier. Hard water, however, contains minerals—primarily calcium and magnesium—that react with soap and form a curd. This curd leaves a white film on clothes, stiffens fabric, and builds up on the inside of the washing machine. That is why detergents, which react less with hard water, are used for laundry instead of soap. Even though detergents do not form a curd, they are not as effective in hard water as they are in soft water.

What are the signs of hard water? There are several: Soaps and shampoos do not lather well, there is a noticeable ring around your bathtub, fabrics feel stiff, or a white residue forms around faucets and drains. To determine the hardness, or mineral content, of your area's water, contact your water company or the nearest Cooperative Extension Service. You can find your local branch by looking in the government offices section of the phone book. Then, if your water is hard, add a commercial water softener or detergent booster, available at most supermarkets, when you wash clothes, or add slightly more detergent to the wash than the label recommends. According to the Soap and Detergent Association in New York City, here's how the different degrees of hardness are usually defined. The numbers indicate milligrams of minerals (usually calcium and magnesium) per liter:

Soft: 0 to 60
Moderately hard: 61 to 120
Hard: 121 to 180
Very hard: More than 180

separate heavily soiled pieces from lightly soiled ones to avoid dirt transfer. Then separate delicate fabrics and loose knits from tougher fabrics, and separate items that produce a lot of lint such as chinelle robes, new towels, or flannels. Finally, mix together large and small items and distribute them equally to balance the load while washing. A typical load might contain one or two twin sheets, a few pillowcases, two to four shirts and blouses, plus underwear and socks.

If you have a new brightly colored item that you think might bleed when washed, or if the label says "wash separately," wash it alone or with similar colors for the first few times.

Once your laundry is sorted, prepare it for washing by checking pockets. One pen, tube of lipstick, or stick of gum can ruin an entire load of clothes. Close zippers and other fastenings to prevent snagging, and tie strings and sashes to avoid tangling. Take off any non-washable items such as belts, and treat stains.

Stain Removal

For stains, follow a few general rules before washing. First of all, deal with the stain right away; the longer you wait, the more a stain can soak in, making it harder to clean. Identify the source of the stain, then follow one of the recommended stain-removal methods in this book. Never rub a stain, which can spread it or damage fibers. Instead, blot patiently using a clean white towel. If you are using a stain-removing solution, pretest it on a hem or other out-of-the-way part of the fabric. After washing a stained item, check the stain before you put the garment in the dryer. "Stains get set by heat," says Ann Lemley, Ph.D., chairman of the department of textiles and apparel at Cornell University in Ithaca, New York. If the stain is still there, try again to remove it. If it won't come out, let the garment air-dry, rewash it, or try the dry cleaners—even for a piece of clothing you wouldn't ordinarily dry-clean. Be sure to tell the dry-cleaner attendant the stain-removal methods that you have already tried.

Detergents

Several factors determine how much detergent to use: load size, soil conditions, water volume in washer, and water hardness. Detergent box instructions are usually based on the following conditions: five to seven pounds of clothing, moderate soil, 17 gallons of water in a top-loading washer or 8 gallons in a front-loader and moderately hard water. You may need to use more than the recommended amount of detergent for larger loads, heavy soil, harder water, or larger-capacity washers. For softer water, smaller load sizes, lighter soil, or smaller-capacity machines, use slightly less. But too little detergent can lead to poor soil removal and redepositing of soil on clothes.

You can cut down on lint, and soften clothes, by using a fabric softener or dryer sheet. "They cut down on static, so the lint will not be attracted to the fabric," explains

HOW IT WORKS

They Gobble Pills

Do you ever wonder about the bold promises printed on the front of laundry detergent containers? For example, "Makes clothes look brand new!" Most people think that it's just marketing hype. But Ann Lemley, Ph.D., chairman of the department of textiles and apparel at Cornell University in Ithaca, New York, confirms that there is scientific truth to their claims. Most machine washable clothes are made from cotton, she explains, which is a natural fiber containing cellulose. "Some detergents contain cellulose-dissolving enzymes that take the little pills off cotton clothing," Dr. Lemley says. "That makes the clothes look new. It's amazing. And because they're slow-working, they don't eat away the rest of the fabric."

Jane Rising, instructor in the education department at the International Fabricare Institute in Silver Spring, Maryland. "It's similar to using a hair conditioner: If you don't, your hair is full of static electricity; use a hair conditioner, and you're back under control."

When you load the washing machine, add your detergent and any other additives such as water softeners or detergent boosters first. Then fill the tub and, finally, add your clothes. Your machine needs room to agitate the clothing properly, so fill the tub loosely. Set the water level to match your load size and the temperature to match the composition of the load. In general, wash whites, colorfast, and heavily soiled clothing in hot water (106° to 122°F/41° to 50°C). Wash non-colorfast, permanent press, nylon, acrylic, and other man-made fibers and moderately soiled items in warm water (87° to 105°F/31° to 41°C). You can also do washable silks and washable woolens at this temperature. Check the care label first to make sure that they are washable. Wash extra-sensitive colors and lightly soiled items in cold water (65° to 86°F/18° to 30°C). Rinse in cold water.

Machine-Drying

Properly dried clothing looks better and requires less effort to keep wrinkle-free. First of all, make sure that the dryer lint filter is clean. Clogged lint filters increase drying time, which increases energy costs. A clogged filter also causes more lint to collect on clothing. Also combat lint with a dryer sheet or use a fabric softener in the rinse water, which reduces static electricity on clothes.

Before placing an item in the dryer, shake it out lightly to unwad it. As with the washer, don't overload the dryer; clothes will take longer to dry and will wrinkle more easily. Dry like garments together—towels in a load, permanent press in another, and so forth. Dry delicates, like lingerie, separately. Many synthetics—acrylic, nylon, polyester, polyolefin—require a low temperature setting. Read the labels and follow instructions. To avoid wrinkles, remove items from the dryer as soon as it shuts off, then fold or hang them immediately. Straighten fabric lines and creases and brush out wrinkles. Close clasps and button buttons. This will cut down on the amount of ironing needed.

Ironing

Keep your iron and ironing board clean to avoid staining what you iron. Sort items that need to be ironed according to the amount of heat needed. Silks and synthetics should be ironed at low temperatures, while cottons and linens require higher temperatures. To

Tag Translation

Here's a guide to the clothing care symbols that manufacturers use in garments sold in North America. They were introduced in 1997. You will find four basic symbols in washable clothing—wash, dry, bleach, and iron—with elaboration that provides specific instructions for each category. Temperatures will vary slightly depending on your home equipment. For easy reference, photocopy this guide and post it in your laundry room.

WASH

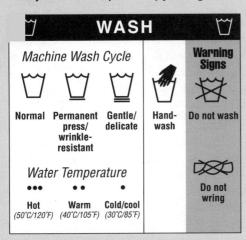

Machine Wash Cycle

| Normal | Permanent press/ wrinkle-resistant | Gentle/ delicate | Hand-wash | Do not wash |

Water Temperature

| Hot (50°C/120°F) | Warm (40°C/105°F) | Cold/cool (30°C/85°F) |

Warning Signs

Do not wash

Do not wring

BLEACH

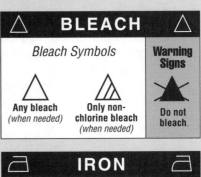

Bleach Symbols

| Any bleach (when needed) | Only non-chlorine bleach (when needed) |

Warning Signs

Do not bleach.

IRON

Iron— Dry or Steam

| Iron | High |
| Medium | Low |

Warning Signs

Do not iron

No steam

DRY

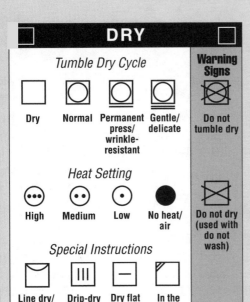

Tumble Dry Cycle

| Dry | Normal | Permanent press/ wrinkle-resistant | Gentle/ delicate | Do not tumble dry |

Heat Setting

| High | Medium | Low | No heat/ air | Do not dry (used with do not wash) |

Special Instructions

| Line dry/ hang to dry | Drip-dry | Dry flat | In the shade |

Warning Signs

DRY-CLEAN

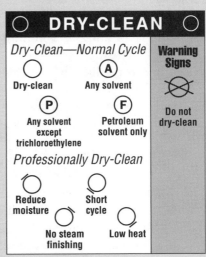

Dry-Clean—Normal Cycle

| Dry-clean | Any solvent (A) |
| Any solvent except trichloroethylene (P) | Petroleum solvent only (F) |

Professionally Dry-Clean

| Reduce moisture | Short cycle |
| No steam finishing | Low heat |

Warning Signs

Do not dry-clean

SOURCE: *Produced by the Federal Trade Commission as part of Project CLEAN*

The Phosphate Debate

Not long ago, most laundry detergents contained a compound called phosphate, a "builder" used to increase the efficiency of the detergent's soil-removing qualities, especially in hard water. Nontoxic phosphate also makes plants grow. But that led to a problem. When wastewater laced with detergent runs into lakes, ponds, and streams, it causes something called eutrophication, or a spurt in plant growth that reduces the oxygen supply for fish.

Some environmentalists argue that phosphates in detergent should be banned. Indeed, in some areas there are now laws against producing and selling detergents containing the compound. As a consumer, you should check labels to find out if the detergent you use contains phosphates. To make your laundry come out whiter, softer, and brighter without phosphates, follow these recommendations from Maytag Consumer Education in Newton, Iowa.

- Use a heavy-duty liquid detergent. These do not contain carbonate, a phosphate substitute that tends to leave a residue and may cause color loss, stiffness, and dinginess in white clothes.
- Use the hottest water that is safe for your laundry load.
- Predissolve granular detergent in hot water before adding it to the wash load.
- Add $\frac{1}{3}$ to $\frac{1}{2}$ cup of a nonprecipitating water softener or conditioner, such as Calgon or Spring Rain.
- Pretreat stains and spots, soak garments before washing, or both.
- Use bleach whenever possible.
- Use soft water.

keep wrinkling at a minimum, iron collars, cuffs, sleeves, and other small areas first and larger areas last. Do not iron stains; contact with a hot iron—like dryer heat—will set the stains. To prevent the fabric you are ironing from getting shiny, buy a pressing cloth at fabric stores or make your own from a single layer of an old sheet. Put the cloth on top of item you are ironing and iron over the pressing cloth.

Hand-Washing and Drying Fine Fabrics

Carefully follow the instructions on the manufacturer's care tag. Wash in warm or cold water, depending on the instructions, then rinse in cold water. Use a light-duty laundry detergent or a liquid dishwashing detergent. Follow label instructions for how much to use. To make sure that the fabric is colorfast, test it by applying a cotton swab dipped in the detergent solution to an inconspicuous section of the garment, like the seam, If the color runs, be sure to wash the fabric separately. Allow powdered detergent to dissolve completely before adding clothes. Carefully wring out excess water and roll the garment in a dry towel. Then unroll it and lay it out flat, away from direct sunlight. To avoid damaging the fabric, do not rub while washing or wring while drying.

Speed tips: Pretreat or presoak stains; you stand a better chance of removing them in one wash cycle. When you are drying clothes, don't add wet items to a partially dried load. With some dryers, you can take advantage of residual heat by reloading the dryer as soon as a cycle is finished. (This won't work if your machine has a cooldown cycle programmed in.)

Laundry Troubleshooting

Here are some typical laundry problems and ways to solve them.

Overall grayness or yellowing: Increase the amount of detergent you use. Increase wash water temperature or use a bleach, if possible.

Blue stains: These stains can be caused when the blue coloring in detergents and fabric softeners does not disperse or dissolve. If caused by a detergent, add 1 cup white vinegar to 1 quart water in a plastic container; soak the item for one hour, then rinse. If caused by fabric softener, rub stains with bar soap, then wash.

Rust stains: Use a commercial rust-removing product recommended for fabrics, such as Whink Rust Stain Remover, which is available at hardware stores. Read the label for safe use. Wear heavy-duty household rubber gloves when you use these products, avoid contact with your skin and eyes, and use only where there is adequate ventilation. Do not use chlorine bleach, which may intensify discoloration. To prevent the problem, try a "nonprecipitating" water softener or conditioner, like Calgon or Spring Rain, in both wash and rinse waters. They prevent iron from depositing on your clothing and are available in supermarkets or discount department stores. Rust in the water supply or from rusty pipes or water heaters sometimes taints wash loads. Run the hot water for a few minutes before starting the wash cycle to clear the lines. Drain the water heater occasionally.

Caution: Always read product labels for proper use and safety precautions.

Detergent residue or stiff harsh fabrics: Add 1 cup white vinegar to 1 gallon warm water in a plastic container; soak item and rinse. In the future, add the detergent to the water first, let it dissolve, then add clothes. Or switch to a liquid laundry detergent.

Lawn Mowers

With lawn mowers, your most important task is removing the grass from underneath the mower deck. But there are a few other things to keep in mind as well.

Technique: Scrape off caked-on grass clippings after each use of your walk-behind power mower. "When you're working with fresh grass, a quick cleanup probably doesn't take more than a minute or two," says Ed Cole, service and support manager for Toro Company's consumer products in Bloomington, Minnesota. Use a wood shim or plastic scraper rather than something made out of metal. Sharpen the end of a wooden dowel to get into crevices. To access the area under the mower deck of gas-powered mowers, turn the mower off, remove the spark-plug wire (and the key from the switch on electric-start models), and roll the mower onto spread-out newspaper. Tilt the mower 30 degrees in any direction, and then prop it on something like a cement block or a log. "Don't turn it on its side, because leaking fuel can damage the engine," Cole says. An even safer alternative is to run out as much fuel as possible while mowing the grass before you do this. For electric mowers, unplug them and remove the key before you start.

Because the walk-behind models are often mulching or recycling mowers, which cut grass into finer bits, grass is more likely to stick to them than to riding mowers. Therefore, it's not necessary—nor is it practical—to clean below the mower deck on riding mowers and small tractors after each use. Instead, do it several times each season—more after it rains and in the spring and fall, when the grass tends to be wet. You'll have to remove the mower housing from the machine.

A bit of spray from a hose will help remove grass clippings from underneath your walk-behind mower. Put the mower on a flat surface and remove the grass catcher. Start the engine. Shoot the water onto the ground just in front of the right rear tire (or the side opposite the discharge chute).

When doing so, carefully follow the manufacturer's instructions. Sharpen the blades a couple of times each season as well—more often if your yard contains sandy soil, which can dull blades more quickly. Plan to sharpen blades and scrape caked-on grass at the same time. If your riding mower is a mulcher, however, inspect it after every use and clean it as needed, suggests Cole.

Once a season, give your mower a complete washdown, but don't use too much water. Water can damage certain engine parts and, on riding mowers, the control panel, lights, and other electrical elements. Set your garden hose nozzle for a fine mist, rather than a direct jet. Never use a pressure sprayer to clean a lawn mower. Remove caked-on dirt and grass from the exterior using a soft cloth and mild soapy water in a bucket. When you've finished washing a mower with water, let it run or drive it around for a few minutes to spin the water off of all belts and pulleys.

Also regularly clean the air filter on lawn mowers. While you should follow the manufacturer's instructions, most air filters need cleaning after every 25 hours of use—more frequently in dusty conditions. If your mower's air filter is a foam filter, remove it, wash it in a bucket filled with mild soapy water—liquid dishwashing detergent works best—and let it dry completely. Most require you to distribute a teaspoon or so of oil throughout the filter. Again, follow the manufacturer's instructions on the type of oil and amount.

Engine oil gets dirty, too. Follow the manufacturer's instructions for changing oil.

Speed tips: "Human nature being what it is, most people want to get to the refrigerator and get that beer after they finish cutting the grass," says Cole. "But cleaning the mower is much faster and easier if you do it when the grass is fresh rather than waiting two weeks and trying to take it off when it's like hardened concrete."

In a pinch: You can do a quick exterior cleaning with a leaf blower. To remove grass clippings from underneath your gas-powered walk-behind mower, put it on a flat surface near a garden hose and remove the grass catcher. Start the engine. Hold a running garden hose at hand level and direct water onto the ground just in front of the right rear tire (or the side opposite the discharge chute). The rotating blade will draw water under the deck and wash out the clippings. Do not use too much water. Let the mower run for a few minutes to dry out belts and pulleys, says Cole.

Don't do this if you have an electric mower. They are light enough to tip over and clean with wooden shim or plastic scraper as described earlier.

Leather

Most leather goods are made of three basic skins—lamb, cow, and pig—and are finished in a variety of ways, from a soft-nap suede to a tough full-grain leather. Cleaning leather, therefore, varies greatly. The only bit of advice that applies to all leather is this: Be careful. Leather can be delicate, and the risk of damaging it if you don't know what you're doing is high.

Technique: There is not much the average consumer can do to clean leather apparel, like jackets, vests, and pants. Usually, when you spill a potential stain-causing substance on, say, your leather coat, you should simply blot it up with a clean white towel, and then take it to a professional leather cleaner. "Forget what the waiter says about using seltzer," says Ralph Sherman, a professional leather cleaner in Roselle, New Jersey, and board member of the Leather Apparel Association in New York City. "Seltzer is good with a little chocolate syrup and milk—when you're making egg creams—but on leather it's no good. You have to be careful about using unproven home methods."

For greasy stains, you may stand a chance. Lay the garment out, sprinkle cornstarch on the stain, and let it stand overnight. Like ab-

SCRUB THIS APPROACH

Five Important Don'ts for Leather Care

1. Don't rub or scrape a stain without testing your technique on an inconspicuous area, like a hem.

2. Don't ever put pressure-sensitive labels, such as "Hello, my name is Joe," on suede or leather garments. "You go to a party, someone slaps that on your garment, and it's ruined," says Ralph Sherman, a professional leather cleaner in Roselle, New Jersey, and board member of the Leather Apparel Association in New York City. "Leather has oil in it. The oil combines with the pressure-sensitive adhesive, and they become as one."

3. Don't get perfume or hair spray on a suede or leather garment. They contain alcohol and other chemicals that will run colors.

4. Don't store suede or leather at home in a plastic bag. "The bag is like a greenhouse," Sherman explains. "All kinds of harmful things build up in there—moisture, mildew, particles from your house's heating system."

5. Don't use heat to dry a wet suede or leather garment. That dries it to a crisp and can cause it to shrink. Hang it on a broad hanger, if appropriate, and dry it at room temperature. If you press the garment, never use steam.

sorbents used to soak up oil from a driveway, the cornstarch might soak up the oil.

For a stain on suede, blot what you can and let the remainder dry for a couple of days. Try to restore the nap by rubbing gently with a soft brush or a dry kitchen sponge. By bringing back the nap, you might eliminate the stain.

When you have leather apparel professionally cleaned, clean matching garments at the same time since the process can cause a slight variation in the color and texture of the leather.

Choose a leather cleaner wisely. Most leather cleaning today is done by wholesalers who pick up from cleaners. If you use a dry cleaner, make sure that it sends leather goods out to a leather specialist. "Most dry cleaners are ethical and won't try to clean a suede garment," says Sherman. "But you have to be careful. Some of them try to clean the leather to avoid paying a wholesaler, and they could end up damaging it."

For a professional leather cleaner referral in your area, contact the Leather Apparel Association, 19 West 21st Street, Suite 403, New York, NY 10010.

When it comes to leather hiking boots or work boots, you have a little more leeway. Clean the dirt off them after each use by scrubbing them in lukewarm water with a long-bristle nylon or vegetable brush. Dry them at room temperature, never near heat, which can cause them to shrink and grow brittle. Condition them occasionally with a commercial boot cleaner/conditioner, like Nikwax, available at outdoor stores and some shoe stores.

Speed tips: To remove sweat and moisture from leather hiking boots, the quickest way is to remove the footpad, if possible, and stuff single sheets of newspaper in them. Replace the newspaper daily until the boots are dry.

Light Fixtures

Sure, you could keep switching to higher-watt bulbs. But why pay all that extra expense when a quick cleanup of your light fixtures will cast a bright new light on everything—without raising your utility bill? Apart from everyday dust buildup, you want to remove the insects that are attracted to the lightbulb and die in the fixture.

Technique: First, remove or unplug the fixture. Dust fixtures as often as possible using a dry cloth. After dusting, wipe them down with a damp cloth or sponge and either an all-purpose cleaner, a glass cleaner, or a squirt of liquid dishwashing detergent mixed in a bucket of lukewarm water. "Most of the insects drawn to lights are moths, whose wings carry a fine dust," says Marry Keener, assistant director of facilities management at the University of Arizona in Tucson and a member of the technical advisory committee for *Executive Housekeeping Today* magazine. "The key is getting rid of that dust before you wipe it down with the damp cloth. Once it gets wet, it streaks and smears and is really hard to remove." Rinse by wiping the fixtures with a clean moist sponge or cloth. Since most light fixtures are made of either glass, plastic, brass, or some other scratchable material, do not use abrasive cleaners or scrubbers.

Speed tips: Remove dust and insects using a vacuum cleaner brush attachment.

Linen

Ah, linen! It's wonderfully absorbent and strong, and it breathes. But this product of the flax plant has its disadvantages as well. It wrinkles easily and is not as simple to care for as cotton, another natural fiber.

Technique: Some linen items are washable, while others are dry cleanable only. Be sure to check the manufacturer's care label. Generally speaking, dry-cleaning is recommended for drapery linens, upholstery linens, and decorative linens as well as fine linen apparel. Handkerchiefs, napkins, and some linen apparel can be washed in warm water by hand or machine. Wash colors in cold water. Use a mild laundry detergent and only oxygen-type bleaches such as Clorox 2, when appropriate. Chlorine bleach can cause yellowing.

"Linen fiber has a natural pectin—like the pectin that makes gelatin solidify—and if you wash it out, it makes the fabric softer," says Pauline Delli-Carpini, director of operations for Masters of Linen, North America, a trade association in New York City. "It becomes a personal statement, whether you want crisp, crisp linen or you want something soft and drapey."

Another reason for choosing dry cleaning is to save on ironing time because linen is a notorious wrinkler. As for why it wrinkles, Delli-Carpini says, "if you look at one linen fiber, it's inelastic—unlike, say, a wool fiber, which has lots of curls in it." Some of the newer permanent press and stain-resistant finishes—65 percent linen, 35 percent polyester—make washing easier and reduce wrinkling.

If you do wash linen, dry it in a machine on low or delicate, on a line, or by rolling it in terry towels. But always remove it before it gets bone-dry to avoid drying the creases into the fabric. Plus, a hot iron glides more smoothly over damp cloth. Do not wring out linen. Here are some other ironing tips.

- For dark-color linen, iron on the "wrong" side so that the fabric does not get shiny.
- Clean the soleplate of your iron for smoother ironing and to avoid staining linen.
- Iron linen until wrinkle-free but not dry, and then hang it to let it dry completely.
- Minimize creasing and bunching when ironing large tablecloths by hanging them over a table adjacent to your ironing board.
- Remove linen from the dryer before it is completely dry and iron it immediately.
- Put linen items in a plastic bag in the refrigerator or freezer for 6 to 24 hours before ironing. "When you pull the fabric out and start ironing, the contact between the hot iron and the cool makes it glide faster and more smoothly," Delli-Carpini says.
- Spraying on sizing, like Magic Sizing, with also make your iron glide more smoothly.

Linens

"Your linens represent a substantial investment," says Marry Keener, previously an executive housekeeper who once oversaw the washing of 2.5 million pounds of laundry per year at the Loews Ventana Canyon Resort in Tucson, Arizona. You want it to be fresh and crisp for each use and to remain that way as long as possible.

Technique: First, check the label to determine the recommended cleaning method. Most bed and bath linens are made of cotton or a cotton-polyester blend and are machine washable.

Launder them frequently—once or twice a week. "When most people check into a hotel, they expect their sheets to be washed once a day," says Keener, currently assistant director of facilities management at the University of Arizona in Tucson and a member of the technical advisory committee for *Executive Housekeeping Today* magazine. That's overkill, she admits, but washing them every fourth or fifth day keeps them sanitary and bright.

Pretreat stains as soon after they occur as possible. Use a commercial stain spotting agent or a simple bar of hand soap. The soap is economical and will remove most stains, even some of the toughest. So keep a bar handy in your laundry room. Wet the stain with cold water—hot water can set stains—and then rub the bar directly onto it and toss the sheet or pillow case in the washer.

If you have silk sheets, chances are that they are made of washable silk, or they are actually satin sheets. Satin sheets resemble silk sheets, but they are made of synthetic material, not natural silk from a silkworm. In either case, wash them in cool water on a gentle cycle. Tumble dry on low heat. But before you wash them, be sure to read the label instructions.

Dry-clean silk bedspreads twice a year or so. You can machine-wash many types of bedspreads. Follow the care label instructions carefully. "Because of the sheer volume of the material," Keener says, "most washers won't hold bedspreads for beds larger than full size." Make sure that whatever you put in your machine will be fully covered with water and will agitate properly. If your bedspread won't fit in your washer, make a special trip to a Laundromat that has extra-large machines. Or, send it to be dry-cleaned. Once or twice a year, it's worth it.

If someone has been ill in the family, wash all of their linens, including the bedspread, afterward to avoid the potential spread of germs.

In a pinch: To freshen up a tired bedspread without giving it a complete washing, tumble it for 5 to 10 minutes in a dryer set on "Air-Fluff." The cycle will loosen dust and other particles and will transfer them from the spread to the machine's filter. Toss in a dryer sheet to give the spread a fresh smell. Or hang the spread on a clothesline on a sunny breezy day. The sun's ultraviolet rays will kill bacteria, and the breeze will remove surface dust.

Lint

Like potholes and taxes, lint is one of life's inevitable irritants. "The fibers in loosely twisted yarns, like fuzzy sweaters, can break off—and create lint," explains Jane Rising, instructor in the education department at the International Fabricare Institute in Silver Spring, Maryland. "Can you stop it? No. It's like dust bunnies under the bed. But you can reduce lint buildup." And, she adds, there are ways to remove lint once it rears its fuzzy little head.

Technique: To clean lint from fabric, hand pat with masking or transparent tape, or use a lint roller or lint brush.

More important, however, is the prevention of lint. Here are some tips for reducing lint on laundry.

- Make sure that all tissues and other papers are out of your clothes' pockets before washing.
- If your washer has a lint filter, clean it before each cycle.
- Use a fabric softener or dryer sheets.
- Separate heavy lint shedders, like blankets, chenille, sweaters, and towels.
- Do not overload washer or dryer.
- Separate dark- and light-color items.
- Clean the dryer filter before each use.

Speed tips: Using a fabric softener—in the washing machine—or dryer sheets—is the quickest and easiest way to cut down on lint.

Litter Boxes

Cleaning the litter box—and doing it thoroughly—is important not only for the health and well-being of your cat but also for cutting down on one of the worst household odors.

Technique: If you use the traditional clay-type litter, scoop out solids daily and dump out everything every five to seven days. Using a liquid dishwashing detergent or a very mild household cleaner, like vegetable oil–based Murphy Oil Soap, wash and rinse the box in warm water. "The plastic box holds on to smells, so don't use anything with a high perfume level because you could actually keep the cat away from litter box," advises Jacque Schultz, director of Companion Animal Services for the American Society for the Prevention of Cruelty to Animals, in New York City. If, instead of a clay-type litter, you're using scoopable litter—the kind that coagulates when it gets wet—scoop the clumps daily and add more litter at least every other day to make sure that urine is not pooling on the bottom. When it starts looking or smelling bad, dump it all and wash the box.

Finally, Schultz advises against litter box liners. "Most cats scratch through them, and urine seeps underneath and builds up," she says.

Speed tips: If you live in an apartment or don't have access to an outdoor hose and wash area, simply clean the litter box in the bathtub, after first removing all solids and litter. Clean and rinse the tub afterward.

Caution: Store harmful cleaning products in a safe, out-of-the-way place so that your pets don't chew on them.

Louvers—Doors, Jalousie Windows

Louvered doors and windows can add a handsome design touch to your home and help out with air flow. But their shape creates a cleaning nightmare—scores of hard-to-reach nooks, crannies, and corners. "It's very time-consuming to clean each window individually," says Clint Sargeant, production coordinator of the J. J. Swartz Company, a remodeling and fire restoration firm in Decatur, Illinois. Unfortunately, sometimes that's your only option.

Technique: Before cleaning wooden door louvers, you must first know how the wood is finished. If it has been coated in a surface finish, like lacquer or polyurethane, dirt will come off easier. The coating protects the wood from the moisture and prohibits dust from penetrating the wood pores. To clean hard-coated louvers, simply wipe them with a lightly dampened cloth. Be sure not to use mineral spirits or kerosene on hard-coated wood.

Follow up by wiping the wood down with a commercial furniture polish, like Pledge. To avoid wax buildup in hard-to-reach cracks and crevices, spray the product onto a cloth, not directly onto the louvers.

If the wood is not coated with a surface finish but, rather, has a penetrating stain or oil finish, dust with a lightly dampened cloth. "On this type of wood, the dust can sink into the wood," Sargeant says. Dust these as often as possible to prevent the soil from penetrating.

To clean these unfinished wood louvers, use a cloth moistened with boiled linseed oil, or a solvent like mineral spirits (both available at hardware stores) or kerosene, available at gas stations. Read the labels for proper use. Be sure to use these products in a well-ventilated room. Test your solution first on an inconspicuous area. Then, rub the cloth over the surface, turning it occasionally as it picks up the dirt and grime. Once you have cleaned the entire surface, you may need to wax the area to restore the shine. Use a product suitable for wood surfaces and buff, if required.

Regardless of the type of wood finish, there are hard-to-reach spots on louvers. To get to them, wrap your cleaning cloth around a putty knife or old butter knife and work it in between crevices.

Jalousie windows pose the same problem. Instead of one smooth pane to clean, the surface is broken up into small slanting bars. You might have to clean them one at a time. If so, open them enough so that you can insert your hand between the panes, and clean with either a commercial glass cleaner, like Windex, or 1 cup vinegar per gallon of water. To avoid streaking, wipe away with crumpled sheets of newspaper or a squeegee.

Speed tips: If possible, clean your jalousie windows from the outside with an all-purpose cleaner and a garden hose. Spray the cleaner on. Loosen stubborn debris using a small nylon brush. Then, close the window and rinse the glass louvers by spraying them with the hose.

In a pinch: Dust louvers with a clean long-bristle brush, like a paintbrush.

Caution: Always read product labels for proper use and safety. Test any cleaning product in an inconspicuous place first.

Luggage

In a sense, luggage is meant to get dirty. Its job, after all, is to protect what's inside—clothes, camera gear, or golf clubs. But proper care helps luggage last longer and look better, which can be important in public places like airports and gyms and on golf courses.

Technique: It is best to spot-clean most luggage. For garment, tote, and duffel bags and hard suitcases made of synthetic materials and canvas, first try a moist cloth and a simple detergent solution—warm water and a squirt of liquid dishwashing detergent. Do not soak the luggage; rather, dab and lightly rub the soiled spots.

To clean scuff marks—the kind left by black airport conveyor belts—use an all-purpose cleaner, like Fantastik. Spray it on a soft cloth or sponge, and then wipe the surface with the cloth. "I've never had to deep clean it any more than that," says flight attendant Sharon

B. Wingler, the Chicago-based author of *Travel Alone and Love It*. (Wingler's travel tip: Black luggage hides scuff marks, making cleaning less necessary. "All of my bags are black," she says.)

Aluminum Luggage

Use a solution of warm water and a mild liquid dishwashing detergent and a cloth. Never use alkaline cleaners like ammonia, trisodium phosphate, or even baking soda. They discolor aluminum. If the aluminum surface is discolored, wash it with the detergent solution mixed with a dash of lemon juice or vinegar. (*Note:* Pretest first on an inconspicuous area.) The acid in those substances will help restore the aluminum's shine.

Do not use abrasive cleaners, such as scouring powders or steel wool. They might scratch or dull the surface.

Leather Luggage

Leather is sensitive to water and cleaning chemicals, so be careful when you're faced with a dirty leather bag. First, follow the recommendations of the manufacturer. Try a leather cleaner, available at luggage stores or shoe repair shops. Before using it, however, test it on an inconspicuous area to make sure that it does not cause the leather dyes to bleed or affect the texture of the hide.

For fine leather luggage or especially difficult-to-remove stains, you may want to contact a professional leather cleaner. Choose wisely. Most leather cleaning today is done by wholesalers who pick up from cleaners. If you use a dry cleaner, make sure that it sends leather goods out to a leather specialist. For a professional leather cleaner referral in your area, contact the Leather Apparel Association, 19 West 21st Street, Suite 403, New York, NY 10010.

Golf Bags

Most golf bags these days are easy to clean. "It rains on golfers every once and a while, or it's early in the morning and you lay the bag down in the grass. That's why the vast majority of bags are made with synthetic materials," says Ron Reczek, production manager at All-American Golf, a maker of bags and other golf equipment in Joliet, Illinois. He suggests spot-cleaning with a terry towel and a solution of warm water and a squirt of mild liquid dishwashing detergent. Use a stiff-bristle toothbrush for scrubbing the nooks and crannies.

"Not too many people use leather—even the professionals. It's so expensive," says Reczek. For leather trim, however, use a leather cleaner, available at most luggage or shoe stores.

Speed tips: Using a thin-tipped attachment, vacuum the dirt and grass out of your golf bag's pockets. Also, put a damp towel stored in a plastic bag in your golf bag before you play. That will make it easy to clean dirt and mud off the bag as you round the links.

Lunch Boxes

Rye or whole wheat? Lettuce or tomato? Mustard or mayonnaise? Okay, for cleaning purposes the only question you really have to answer is this: Metal or plastic? Fortunately, lunch boxes made from either are easy to clean.

Technique: Wipe your plastic lunch box or the liner of your insulated lunch bag down with a moist cloth or sponge after use. If you have a metal lunch box, periodically polish it with a liquid car wax and a cotton cloth. Use cotton swabs to get into the crevices.

"In terms of cleaning, there's not a lot of difference between a lunch box with graphics on it and a Cadillac," says Allen Woodall, co-author of *The Illustrated Encyclopedia of Metal Lunch Boxes* and creator of the Lunch Box Museum in Salem, Alabama. "The wax pulls all the dirt out," he says. "It cleans and waxes at the same time."

If your lunch box has a lot of dirt or rust, use the mildest automobile rubbing compound available. Because it is an abrasive compound, use it sparingly and work it in gently.

Macramé

Unless you let your dog drag it around the backyard, cleaning macramé is simple—usually just a matter of keeping it free of dust.

Technique: Dusting your knotty artwork might not seem easy, but you can easily remove accumulated particles from most macramé items by tumbling it on the "Air-Fluff" setting of your dryer. This cool-air cycle loosens the dust particles and transfers them from the macramé's surface to the dryer's filter. Do it for 5 to 10 minutes or until the macramé is clean.

If your macramé is stained, spot-clean it only, first using a damp cloth, and then trying a solution of 1 cup water and a few drops of liquid dishwashing detergent. Most macramé is made of heavy nylon cord and will come clean relatively easily. Machine-washing macramé is not recommended, unless the manufacturer's instructions explicitly say so. It might unravel or shrink.

"I've seen some macramé that is made of imported fibers," says Marry Keener, assistant director of facilities management at the University of Arizona in Tucson and a member of the technical advisory committee for *Executive Housekeeping Today* magazine. "We're not really familiar with some of the products coming from around the world. You launder something like that, and it can disintegrate."

In a pinch: Instead of tumbling your macramé on "Air-Fluff," try vacuuming it. This might remove the dust, especially if it is a large piece.

Makeup Stains

Grease is a major ingredient in lipstick and other cosmetics. When removing most makeup stains, therefore, you first want to attack that grease, then deal with nongreasy residue.

Technique: The best substance for removing greasy stains is spot remover, says Ann Lemley, Ph.D., chairman of the department of textiles and apparel at Cornell University in Ithaca, New York. Have the item professionally dry-cleaned or clean it yourself with a spot remover, like Carbona Stain Devils or K2r, available at supermarkets, hardware stores, or discount department stores. Wear protective rub-

HOW I DO IT

A Makeup Cure, Bar None

Before she became the assistant director of facilities management at the University of Arizona in Tucson, Marry Keener was director of housekeeping at the fashionable Loews Ventana Canyon Resort in Tucson, where she oversaw the washing of 2.5 million pounds of laundry per year—with plenty of makeup stains. Here's her personal tip for removing these difficult stains from washable fabric. "One of the best methods of pretreatment for makeup stains is bar soap. You don't need to wet the spot first. Just rub it with a bar that has had a chance to soften up in its dish, and then wash the item as instructed. It's a lot cheaper than the commercial spotting agents, and it takes off mascara and lipstick like you wouldn't believe."

ber or latex gloves, and use these products in a well-ventilated area. Lay the stain facedown on a soft absorbent cloth. Apply the spot remover to another clean white cloth, and then blot from the inside of the garment to push the stain out. As the spot remover dissolves the grease in the makeup, the cloth beneath catches it.

To remove the last traces of the stain, says Dr. Lemley, blot with a solution of ¼ teaspoon clear liquid dishwashing detergent and ½ cup cold water, using a clean white towel. Then wash the item as directed. If that does not remove the stain completely, follow the same technique but use a solution of 1 teaspoon ammonia and ½ cup cold water. Again, wash as directed.

For carpets, always apply cleaning solutions to a towel, never directly onto the carpet. Otherwise, it can soak into the carpet backing or pad and attract more dirt.

Note: Before using cleaning solutions, always test them on an inconspicuous section of the stained item.

Caution: Always rinse one cleaning solution before trying another. Mixing chemicals, especially ammonia and chlorine bleach, can create noxious fumes. Always read the product label for proper use and safety precautions.

Marble

Talk about walking on eggshells! "Marble is a wonderful thing, but it is a pain to take care of," says Kay Weirick, director of housekeeping services at Bally's Las Vegas Hotel and a member of the technical advisory committee for *Executive Housekeeping Today* magazine. For a stone, it's fragile and porous. It's important to keep marble clean, but it is equally important that you not damage its beautiful surface.

Technique: To keep tiny particles of grit from scratching the surface of marble floors, dust them often with an untreated dust mop. Because marble is porous, a treated dust mop can cause staining.

Clean marble with a sponge, soft cloth, or mop and a neutral cleaner, like Murphy Oil Soap or a liquid dishwashing detergent, mixed with warm water.

"To remove stains in marble, you have to wick or suck them back out of the stone," says Fred Hueston, director of the National Training Center for Stone and Masonry Trades in Longwood, Florida, and author of *Marble and Tile: Selection and Care of Stone and Tile Sur-*

SCRUB THIS APPROACH

Hold the Vinegar!

You can sprinkle vinegar on a salad. But if you pour it onto a marble floor, it'll eat that gorgeous stone for lunch. Fred Hueston, director of the National Training Center for Stone and Masonry Trades in Longwood, Florida, and author of *Marble and Tile: Selection and Care of Stone and Tile Surfaces*, debunks a commonly held marble-cleaning myth.

"There's an old tale that says that vinegar and water is the greatest thing for marble. It's not. Absolutely never, ever use vinegar and water on marble.

"It began with ceramic-tile installers, who have branched over into the field of marble tile and brought a lot of their practices with them. For years they have recommended vinegar and water as a cleaner, which is fine for tile but not for marble. Vinegar is acidic and eats away at the surface of marble. It's one of the most common questions we get here at the training center: 'Can't I just use vinegar and water? That's what the installer told me.' "

faces. The best way is with a poultice. For oil stains, mix ½ cup bleached flour, a small squirt of liquid dishwashing detergent, and warm water into a paste that has the consistency of peanut butter. Spread it over the stained area, cover it with plastic wrap, and tape down the sides with masking tape. Let it sit overnight. Remove the plastic, let the poultice dry, and scrape it away. For food stains—coffee, tea, juices—substitute hydrogen peroxide for the detergent. Rub ink, crayon, or nail polish stains with a cotton ball dipped in an acetone-based nail polish remover. (Don't mix the nail polish remover into the poultice.)

Speed tips: Sealing marble surfaces with a penetrating sealer, available at hardware and home supply stores, facilitates cleaning. "A stone sealer does nothing to alter the appearance," says Hueston. "It works on marble like a water seal works on a wood deck."

Caution: Lemon or anything else with any acidity will eat into, or etch, the polished surface of marble. Be wary of bathroom cleaners. They often contain acid. Check the label: Federal law requires the product to list all acid ingredients. Also avoid using abrasive cleaners. Even the finest grit can dull marble surfaces.

Mattresses and Box Springs

Think of it as sleeping with the enemy. Your bed collects dust and dander and harbors microscopic dust mites, all of which are major causes of allergies. Keeping your mattress and box spring clean not only helps them last longer but also improves the health conditions in the room where you spend at least one-third of your time.

Technique: Vacuum mattresses and box springs twice a year. Use an appropriate attachment, not the carpet sweeper. "Put a fresh bag in beforehand as a test," says Marry Keener, assistant director of facilities management at the University of Arizona in Tucson and a member of the technical advisory committee for *Executive Housekeeping Today* magazine. "You'll be surprised at how much dander and lint are in there."

If you use a plastic mattress cover, wash it in the washing machine or wipe it down using a sponge and a mild solution of liquid dishwashing detergent. "If someone in the home is ill, clean it with a disinfectant, like Lysol," Keener suggests. "That helps prevent the spread of viruses and bacteria from family member to family member."

You should also turn your mattress twice a year—each time you clean it—to distribute the wear. Alternate which way you turn it: side-to-side one time, and then end-to-end the next.

If you're cleaning up after a bed wetter, blot up as much of the urine as possible using a clean white towel, and then extract the rest using a wet vacuum–style carpet cleaner with an upholstery attachment. If you do not have access to one of those machines, blot with wet towels and sponge in a little vinegar to neutralize the odor. Blot again using wet towels, and then dry the mattress in the sun. The sun's rays also kill bacteria.

Speed tips: To facilitate cleaning up after a chronic bed wetter, use a plastic mattress cover. After an accident, simply wipe up urine with a sponge or cloth, and then follow up with a disinfectant such as Lysol.

Microwave Ovens

Microwaves are a zap—er, snap—to clean, especially if you do it regularly.

Technique: Wipe up spills as they occur, especially those around the door seal. To remove caked-on food, fill a bowl halfway with water and boil it for two to three minutes at the microwave oven's highest power, says Cindy Cook, a trained home economist at the Michigan State University Extension in East Lansing and manager of its Home Maintenance and Repair Database on the Internet. Wipe away stains loosened by the steam.

To remove odors, clean the interior with a solution of 1 table-spoon baking soda to 1 cup warm water, rinse, and dry. Never use abrasive pads or powders on a microwave oven.

Mildew

Mildew is like the monster in a horror movie: It seems to spring out of nowhere. Indeed, it is a living organism, the by-product of a destructive fungus that feeds on cotton, wood, paper, leather, and other organic materials. Mildew exists in the air in a dormant state. Dampness, darkness, and warmth cause it to multiply rapidly, often in less than 72 hours. When allowed to flourish, mildew causes dis-coloration, a musty smell—the result of its digestive process—and ir-reversible deterioration of fibers. Overcoming this household fiend is a matter of preventing its growth and then effectively cleaning the items it attacks. Since you're referring to this section, you probably already have mildew, so we'll start with the latter.

Technique: Treat mildew immediately to avoid serious damage to whatever it has latched on to. "Mildew is not just something on the surface," says Martha Shortlidge, a home economics program leader and cooperative extension agent with the Cornell Cooperative Ex-tension in Valhalla, New York. Left to grow, mildew eats away at the organic fibers of things like cotton and wool rugs, clothing, and books, causing permanent damage. When you discover mildew, first brush off the surface growth outdoors to avoid scattering the spores. Then, let the items dry in the air and sun. Follow the care instructions of the particular item you're cleaning. Send nonwashables to a dry cleaner and launder washables promptly with plenty of hot suds, which should remove light stains. To remove stains from golf bags, canvas awnings, and other nonwashables, wipe them with a solution of 1 cup hot water and ¼ teaspoon liquid dishwashing detergent, using a white cotton cloth. When possible, use liquid household bleach in the wash. Bleach not only whitens mildew stains but also kills any remaining spores.

"Mildew is usually a symptom of poor ventilation," explains Shortlidge. To prevent mildew, keep your home clean and moisture-free. Use fans to ventilate the house and basement. But be careful not to pull air inside on really humid days; you might actually increase the moisture level. Poor housing design—an incorrectly graded slope that brings rainwater into the basement, for example—is often a cause of moisture problems, which you may need to address.

Other tips: Before storing clothes, remove grease or soil, which provide food for mold to develop. Even synthetic fibers that are mildew-resistant can attract the fungus if they are wet and soiled. Don't let damp or wet clothing lie around, especially in dark places like a clothes hamper. Either wash them immediately or hang them to dry. In closets, hang clothes loosely so that air can circulate around them; avoid storing items in garment bags. Store shoes and leather goods on a shelf instead of on the floor. During hot, humid weather regularly check the clothes in your closets for mildew.

Note: Before using cleaning solutions, always test them on an inconspicuous section of the stained item.

Caution: Always rinse out one cleaning solution before trying another. Mixing chemicals, especially ammonia and chlorine bleach, can create noxious fumes. Always read the product label for proper use and safety precautions.

Mirrors

You want that face staring back at you from the mirror to look as good as possible, right? You don't need streaks and lint sullying your image. Fortunately, cleaning mirrors, like cleaning glass, is pretty straightforward. So let's reflect for a moment on the best and quickest strategies.

Technique: Clean mirrors with a solution of 1 cup vinegar per gallon of warm water or a squirt of liquid dishwashing detergent in a bucket of water, says Jim Brewer, executive housekeeper at the University of Texas at Arlington and a technical advisor to *Cleaning and Maintenance Magazine*. Ammonia-based window cleaners have a tendency to streak, a condition that is especially noticeable in bright sunlight. To avoid leaving traces of lint, wipe away the liquid using a squeegee or newsprint.

When cleaning vertical glass surfaces, like windows, start at the top and clean down. Apply the cleaning solution with a sponge, soft cloth, or spray bottle, then scrub caked-on grime with a long-bristle vegetable brush.

Carefully peel off paint and other stuck-on substances with a razor blade. Do not use a putty knife, which has a duller blade and can damage the glass. •

Mites

Yikes—the unseen enemy! There are many kinds of mites, from those that invade your houseplants to the microscopic dust mites that live off discarded human skin and are a major cause of allergic reactions in humans.

Technique: Spray mite-infested plants with a solution of insecticidal soap, available at most home and garden centers. These relatively nontoxic substances contain potassium salts, sodium salts, or certain fatty acids. "Insecticidal soap is one of the least toxic treatments available," says Jerry Giordano, a horticulture consultant with the Cornell Cooperative Extension in Valhalla, New York. Typically, you mix it with water and use a standard spray bottle or pump-up pressure sprayer to apply it. Because of its makeup, the soap only works when mixed with soft water. To test your solution, mix a small batch and let it sit for 15 minutes. If a scum or "curd" of soap forms on the surface, use a water softener and remix.

Be sure to thoroughly clean the undersides of leaves, where the mites may also live. Treat when and where infestation appears, not as a preventive measure.

Dust mites, which you can't see, thrive in moist, warm conditions and live in dust, often in mattresses, carpets, and upholstered furniture. Get rid of them by avoiding overhumid conditions and keeping dust to a minimum. Vacuum carpets and upholstered furniture often, and empty the vacuum bag after each session.

In a pinch: Instead of spraying houseplants with an insecticidal soap solution, simply wash the plants with soapy water and a soft brush or cloth, says the Cornell Cooperative Extension. Use 2 teaspoons of a mild dishwashing detergent in a gallon of water. Or spray them with a jet of clean water to knock mites off.

Caution: When using insecticidal soaps, watch your plants for signs of phototoxicity, an adverse reaction. Symptoms are yellow or brown foliage spotting, "burned" tips, and yellow or brown scorching on the leaf edges. If symptoms occur, stop using the soap. Always read the product label for proper use and safety precautions.

Motorcycles

Like cars, motorcycles are a big investment. And like their four-wheel counterparts, they collect dirt, grease, grime, and bug gunk on the road and in the driveway. So cleaning motorcycles is essential, not only for helping them look their best but also for keeping their shells, frames, and engines in top working order.

Technique: How often should you clean a motorcycle? Well, how often do you ride? And where do you park—outside or in a garage? As a rule of thumb, clean weekly if you ride your bike heavily or if it's subjected to the elements. If you only ride on weekends and park in a garage, a good wash once a month is sufficient.

A complete cleaning is a several-step process. Begin by wetting the motorcycle with a garden hose. Do not spray it directly, but rather sprinkle the water on gently. Never get water in the exhaust pipe or in the carburetor. That could cause engine damage.

Spray the wheels and spokes, engine, and other areas where grease has collected with a commercial degreasing compound, like S100 Total Cycle Cleaner, available at motorcycle supply stores. "That gets in between the cracks, where we can't get, to take out some of the excess grease and brake dust," says Eladio Gonzalez, a mechanic at Brooklyn Harley-Davidson in New York City. Let it sit for 5 to 10 minutes while it loosens the grease, and then wipe it down with a wet cloth.

HOW I DO IT

The Brown Badge of Honor

Oliver Shokouh is the owner of Harley-Davidson of Glendale in Glendale, California, and founder of the Love Ride, an annual celebrity motorcycle event that raises money for muscular dystrophy. Here's what he says about cleaning bikes. "A lot of people think of their motorcycles as works of art. They like showing them off to friends. They're motorheads, and they're proud of their motors. But there are some people who spend more time cleaning than riding the bikes. I like riding long distances, and when I'm on the road, my bike gets pretty dirty.

"I took my bike up to Alaska. When I got there, I loved the way it looked. The dirt was like a sign of experience. People knew I hadn't trailered the bike. But I had to clean it.

"I used a high-pressure cleaner, like the ones at a self-service car wash. You have to be careful. The pressure can be too intense. It can strip the paint and stripes right off. But after my Alaska trip, it really needed it."

Next, using a soft cloth or sponge and a bucket of warm water with a few squirts of liquid dishwashing detergent in it, wash off the degreaser, along with any grime and stuck-on bugs. Never use anything abrasive. That can ruin the painted or chrome finish. Dry the bike completely using clean dry towels. Water left standing can rust exposed metal parts.

Once the bike is dry, clean and glaze the chrome with a special metal-cleaning product, like S100 Spray Wax or Mothers Mag and Aluminum Polish, also available at stores where motorcycles are sold. Wax the tanks, fenders, and other painted surfaces with a rub-on car wax.

Speed tips: "Once I've washed a bike," Gonzalez says, "I bring it in the shop and use the air hose to blow-dry the bike completely so that nothing will rust." You can use a leaf blower to do the same thing, he says, as long as you do it in a dust-free area.

In a pinch: Simply follow the first couple of steps: Wet the bike, spray on the degreaser, wash it with soap and water, and dry it. This will remove bug gunk and other grime before it has a chance to stick too much. Then, once every few washes, follow up with a detailed polishing.

Caution: Always read the product label for proper use and safety precautions.

Mud

"Mud is just wet dirt," says Jane Rising, instructor in the education department at the International Fabricare Institute in Silver Spring, Maryland. When you clean mud from fabric, you want to clean it without smearing it.

Technique: "Most people put water on a mud stain right away, hoping to remove it," Rising says, "but that only makes more mud." Instead, first brush away as much of the mud as possible using a soft brush or a dull blade.

Next, if the fabric is washable, pretreat the stain. Begin by mixing ¼ teaspoon clear liquid dishwashing detergent with ½ cup warm water. Apply it directly to the fabric, and then lay the garment on a hard surface and pat the stain lightly with the back of a spoon. This allows the solution to get in between the fibers, where stains hide. Don't rub the fabric together. That will abrade the fibers. Next, wash as directed either by machine or by hand in the hottest water safe for the fabric.

If the stain does not come out completely, follow the same pre-treatment procedure, but this time apply a paste made from a granular laundry detergent and water directly to the stain. Let it sit for a while, then wash as directed. For red clay or other stubborn mud stains, instead of water, make the paste with the detergent and ammonia. Again, wash as directed.

For fabrics that cannot be washed, either have them professionally dry-cleaned or blot with a clean white towel and a spot remover, like Carbona Stain Devils or K2r, available at supermarkets, hardware stores, or discount department stores. Blot from the inside of the garment to push the stain out. Wear protective rubber or latex gloves, and use these products in a well-ventilated area.

When it comes to carpets and rugs, "it's a lot easier to remove dirt than mud," says Claudia Ramirez, former executive vice president of the Association of Specialists in Cleaning and Restoration in Annapolis Junction, Maryland. Let the mud dry, and then lift up as much as you can with the handle of a spoon or a dull knife. Vacuum the rest. If a residue remains, blot with the liquid dishwashing solution using a clean white towel. Then rinse by blotting with a clean towel and water. Do not blot with laundry detergent because it often contains optical brighteners that can bleach carpet and rug dyes.

Note: Before using cleaning solutions, always test them on an inconspicuous section of the stained item.

Caution: Always rinse out one cleaning solution before trying another. Mixing chemicals, especially ammonia and chlorine bleach, can create noxious fumes. Always read the product label for proper use and safety precautions.

Musical Instruments

Clean instrument, clean sound. Keeping a musical instrument clean is essential for maintaining its integrity. A horn caked with gunk or a clarinet with saliva-soaked key pads will sound different from a clean one. And cleanliness prolongs the life of these expensive devices. Still, most professionals agree that you should never overclean your instrument.

Here are techniques, organized by type of instrument, for keeping your musical equipment as fit as a fiddle.

Strings

Keep string instruments—from violins and cellos to guitars and zithers—clean with a soft dry cloth, preferably one made from chamois. Wipe off perspiration and buff away fingerprints. It doesn't take much more than that. (In fact, cleaning solvents, especially alcohol-based products, can ruin the thin coating of varnish covering most string instruments.) After playing bow instruments, dust off the rosin that accrues beneath the strings near the bridge and wipe away any perspiration. At least once a year, have fine instruments professionally cleaned. Call your local symphony orchestra or school bandleader for a professional referral.

Brass

When it comes to brass instruments, like trumpets, French horns, and tubas, cleaning the inside is more important than cleaning the outside. Like a sink drain, the lead pipe and the valves collect layers of scum—usually a combination of lint, saliva, and dust. "When stuff

HOW I DO IT

Once Over, Lightly

As principal cellist for the New York Philharmonic in New York City, Carter Brey knows a thing or two about upkeep. For instance, he plays a cello made in 1754 by the famed instrument maker Giovanni Battista Guadagnini. Here's how Brey cleans his cello.

"When it comes to cleaning string instruments, which are often pieces of incredibly valuable Italian furniture from the seventeenth and eighteenth centuries, the less done, the better. Sometimes people take the furniture parallel too far and try using something like Lemon Pledge. You go out on stage to play, and it smells like a lemon grove. I think the conservative approach is the best. Whenever I finish playing, I dust off the rosin that accrues beneath the strings near the bridge. After a strenuous performance under hot lights, you can find yourself dripping sweat onto the instrument. The varnish coating is hydrophilic, or water-absorbent, and the salt from sweat can eat into the varnish, so I wipe that off, too.

"Once or twice a year I take it to a specialist—one of these guys who maintains very old fragile instruments—and he gives it a professional cleaning. He uses xylene, a compound that is perilously close to alcohol, which will immediately ruin the fine old Italian varnish from an instrument. When xylene is used by a professional, however, it will not hurt the instrument. He usually puts some on a cloth, very quickly passes it over the instrument and then immediately polishes it off."

builds up, you are effectively changing the inside diameter and measurements of the tube, and that changes the way it plays," says Warren Deck, principal tuba player with the New York Philharmonic in New York City. After each use, make sure to empty all water and saliva from inside the horn before putting it in its case. Otherwise, your instrument is susceptible to an interior deterioration known as red rot. Every three or four months, flush the instrument with water, filling the bell and letting it run out of the mouthpiece. Then remove the lead pipe, if possible, and clean it with a "snake"—a brush on the end of a flexible wire (sold at most music stores)—by running it in and out like a pipe cleaner. Again, flush with water. Remove the valves and all tuning slides and run the snake through the slides and remaining tubes. To clean the oily buildup on the valves, dilute a pinch of mild scouring powder, such as Comet, with water and rub with a moistened cotton or paper cloth. Finally, dry the instrument thoroughly with a cotton towel to avoid water spotting.

Cleaning the exterior of the brass instrument is more a matter of personal taste. "My horns turn green with patina, and I just let them," admits Deck. "It takes six to eight hours to polish a tuba, and in two weeks it looks like you never did anything to it." For those who prefer a shiny instrument, he suggests a brass cleaner, like Brasso. Over time, however, repeated cleanings with such abrasives thin the metal, which can also change the sound. An alternative is to have it dipped in a nonabrasive cleaning solution at a professional brass-repair shop.

Speed tips: Flush the larger brass instruments, like tubas and French horns, with a garden hose or in the shower. (You sing in the shower, so why shouldn't you include instrumentation?) Just make sure that you dry them well to avoid water spotting.

Woodwinds

Avoiding extreme temperature and humidity changes will keep a wood instrument from cracking, says Jonathan Watkins, a professional bassoonist and woodwind expert in New York City. Removing interior moisture is an important goal in cleaning woodwind instruments. Oboes and clarinets are the woodwinds that are most likely to crack over time due to changes in temperature and humidity. The key pads on all woodwinds—made out of a variety of materials, including leather, cork, Gore-Tex, and even fish skin—fit so precisely on the key holes that even the slightest swelling or disfiguration due to water absorption can break the seal, hurting the sound quality. Therefore, swab inside moisture on all woodwind instruments immediately after each use.

For flutes, thread a cotton handkerchief through the needlelike eye of a flute swabbing rod, available at music stores, and run it in and out of the flute several times, until it is dry. Be careful not to scratch the bore. For saxophones, clarinets, oboes, and bassoons, first remove the mouthpiece and wipe it down with a dry cloth. Then feed a weighted cloth—called a drop swab, also available at music stores—through the instrument's bigger end and pull it through the smaller end. To clean the pads, gently place a piece of glueless cigarette rolling paper under the pad on the key hole and press the key up and down a few times. To clean the mouthpiece, wash with lukewarm water and a mild solution of liquid dishwashing detergent and water. Never use hot water to clean a mouthpiece.

Polish the exteriors with a chamois cloth. Silver polishing cloth works well on flutes, says Watkins. But resist the temptation to use silver polish because of the chance that it will get under the keys and onto the pads.

Caution: Remember that water can help deteriorate the key pads on all woodwinds no matter what the instrument is made of.

Pianos

Dust the exterior regularly the way you would fine wooden furniture. Use a soft cloth and, depending on the finish, possibly a spray-on furniture polish. Spray polish on the cloth, not directly onto the piano, being careful not to get the spray on the tuning pins. To cut down on interior dust buildup, keep the various parts of the piano closed when the piano is not in use. Once a month or so, make two or three passes across the keys with your vacuum cleaner's crevice attachment. Then, clean any smudges off of the keys with a window cleaner, like Windex. Again, do not spray directly onto the keys but, rather, onto a cloth.

Once every couple of years, your piano needs a thorough cleaning. Cleaning an upright piano is easier than cleaning a grand piano. If either is too complicated, you can always call a professional to come to your house and service the piano. Ask for referrals from local orchestras and school music departments, or friends who have a piano. If you have an upright piano, you could clean behind the foot pedals by removing the bottom panel, says Ira King, owner of Tri-Arts Piano Tuning in New York City. Look underneath the key bed for a spring that releases the panel, but be careful; the panel can be heavy. Then vacuum the area with the crevice attachment and the brush attachment. To replace the panel, carefully fit it into the wooden pins on the bottom edge and ease the panel back into posi-

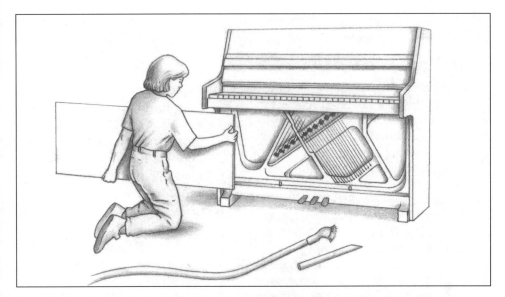

Remove the piano's bottom panel and vacuum behind the foot pedals with a brush attachment. Look underneath the key bed for a spring that releases the panel. Be careful; these panels can be heavy.

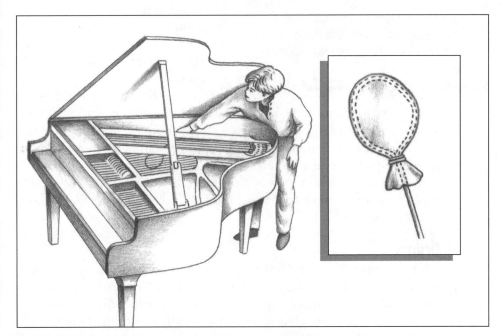

Use a cloth-wrapped coat hanger to dust the horizontal soundboard on a grand piano. Spray the cloth lightly with furniture polish. Reach in from the bass end, taking care not to scratch the soundboard.

A CLEAN STORY

Wolfgang Amadeus Mousezart

Ira King, owner of Tri-Arts Piano Tuning in New York City, has been cleaning and servicing pianos for almost 30 years. He has seen some strange things in his day. Here's one of them.

"Mice love pianos. It's an ideal place for them. It's dark and nobody goes there, there's a lot of wood for them to chew on, and if the piano isn't played much, all the better. Once I was looking at an old spinet—a very short upright piano—and I removed the keys and found a couple of dead mice. Now, when I open the bottom of an upright, I sometimes wonder if a mouse is going to run out. My advice for keeping mice out of your piano is the same as for any place. Just keep the house clean and set traps if you see any signs of rodents."

tion, says King. Be sure that the spring or latch that holds the panel is back in place.

Because the key bed on a grand piano is difficult to access, have a professional clean it, says King. The soundboard, too, is hard to get to but not impossible to clean. It is horizontal and collects dust, which should be wiped off at least once a year. Unravel a wire coat hanger, make a palm-size loop in the end by bending and twisting the wire, then spread a soft cotton cloth over the loop and tie it off. Spray the cloth lightly with furniture polish. Using the wire as an extension, reach in from the bass-string end and wipe away as much dust as possible, taking care not to scratch the soundboard with any exposed metal.

On both upright and grand pianos, once a year vacuum the dust off the hammers with the brush attachment. Carefully run it front to back, not side to side, because you might break a hammer. To get to the hammers in an upright piano you will need to open the top lid of your piano and remove the front panel. Don't try to do this yourself, warns King, because the panel is quite heavy. Either enlist the help of a friend or, ideally, consult a professional.

Drums

Dust drums as needed using a clean dry cloth, says Nodar Rode, owner of the Manhattan Drum Shop in New York City. If you don't play your drums often, keep them covered with a clean bedsheet. Once a year, give them a thorough cleaning. Replace the heads when they begin to lose flexibility or no longer sound good, says Rode. Begin by removing the heads and all the hardware from the actual drum itself. Using a clean soft cloth, moistened with water, gently wipe away dirt and grease. Carefully rub stubborn spots with a one-to-one solution of window cleaner and water. Thoroughly rinse off any residue with a clean damp cloth. Dry the drums completely with a clean dry cloth. Be careful when cleaning these delicate instruments, says Rode. Consult a professional if your drums are very old or excessively dirty.

Once you have removed the hardware from the drum, says Rode, gently loosen the dirt on it with superfine (#0000) steel wool and a squirt of WD-40 (either on the steel wool or on the hardware itself). The WD-40 should help reduce any possible scratching, he adds. Then scrub the hardware with a regular sponge in a solution of warm water and a squirt of liquid dishwashing detergent. Do not wash the springs. To avoid rust, says Rode, dry first with a towel and then with a blow-dryer on a cool or warm setting, making sure to remove all moisture from inside the casings. Let the pieces cool completely before touching them. Lubricate the parts by rubbing the threads and insert points with petroleum jelly. If you keep your drums in a moist or humid area, clean and lubricate the hardware about once every two months to prevent rust.

Dust cymbals as needed with a clean dry cloth, says Rode. New cymbals are usually covered in lacquer, which protects the cymbals from tarnishing. Because many solvents dissolve this coating, avoid heavy-duty cleaning. If they need cleaning, call a professional for further advice.

Mustard

EMERGENCY ACTION
Rinse or blot away mustard with cold water.

Don't let mustard's light color fool you. It's one of the toughest stains around. "It has disperse dyes, the kind used for dying polyester," explains Rajiv Jain, laboratory manager for the Association of Specialists in Cleaning and Restoration in Annapolis Junction, Maryland. "These dyes impart color by dispersing into the fiber structure."

Technique: Scrape away any excess mustard. For washables, first soak the item in cold water to remove as much of the stain as possible. Then pretreat it by mixing ¼ teaspoon clear liquid dishwashing detergent and ½ cup warm water. Apply it directly to the fabric, then lay the garment on a hard surface and pat the stain lightly with the back of a spoon. This allows the solution to get into and in between the fibers, where stains hide. Don't rub the material together; that will abrade the fibers. Next, wash as directed either by machine or by hand in the hottest water safe for the fabric. If the stain does not come out completely, follow the same pretreatment procedure but, this time, with a solution of one part vinegar and two parts water. Never use ammonia or any other alkaline substance, which can darken a mustard stain. "It might not all come out," Jain says. "It depends on how much was spilled and when." The bigger and older the stain, the harder it will be to remove.

For fabrics that cannot be washed, either have them professionally dry-cleaned or blot the stain with a clean white towel and a spot remover, like Carbona Stain Devils or K2r, available at supermarkets, hardware stores, or discount department stores. Blot from the inside of the garment to push the stain out. Wear protective rubber or latex gloves, and use these products in a well-ventilated area.

For carpets and rugs, first blot the stain with the detergent solution using a clean white towel. Then rinse by blotting with a clean towel and water. Do not blot with laundry detergent because it often contains optical brighteners that can bleach carpet and rug dyes. Instead, if the first solution does not work, try blotting with a solution of one part white vinegar and two parts water. Rinse by blotting with a towel and water, then dry with a fresh towel.

Note: Before using cleaning solutions, always test them on an inconspicuous section of the stained item.

Caution: Always rinse out one cleaning solution before trying another. Mixing chemicals, especially ammonia and chlorine bleach, can create noxious fumes. Always read the product label for proper use and safety precautions.

Needlework

You want to clean needlework without harming it, of course. That means dusting, and then seeking professional help for anything more involved.

Technique: During your normal cleaning routine, vacuum the dust off of needlepoint pillows and other needlework. The brush attachment works best.

Don't clean needlework with water. In the case of a spill, blot up as much of the substance as possible using a clean white towel. Then have the work professionally cleaned, says Marry Keener, assistant director of facilities management at the University of Arizona in Tucson and a member of the technical advisory committee for *Executive Housekeeping Today* magazine.

In a pinch: Take needlepoint pillows outside and gently beat the dust out of them.

Nylons

The world is cruel to nylons—when you wear them and when you toss them in the wash, too. You want to clean them without snagging, running, shrinking, or stretching them.

Technique: Put nylons in a tightly sealed mesh laundry bag and wash them on a gentle permanent press cycle using regular laundry detergent. "If you don't use a mesh bag, they get tangled up with the stem of the machine," says Dorothy Cummings, wardrobe mistress for the New York City Ballet. Pretreat stains, especially makeup, by rubbing in a little mild bar soap, like Ivory or Dove.

Remove the nylons from the bag and tumble dry at a low temperature. For best results, remove them from the dryer after about 15 minutes and hang them to dry completely.

Speed tips: To minimize static electricity and make handling your nylons easier, use a dryer sheet when drying.

Odors

Sniff, sniff. Phew! What's that odor? Most nose-offending scents are caused by spills—either from the spill itself or bacteria growing on the spill. Other common odors are caused by pet accidents, cooking certain foods, mildew, and skunks. The bigger a spill or pet accident and the longer it remains untreated, the more difficult it is to remove the smells.

Technique: "There are two main ways of handling odors," says

Beating Odors the Old-Fashioned Way

Isn't canned freshness a contradiction in terms? Many commercial air fresheners either coat your nasal passages with an undetectable oil film or diminish your sense of smell with a nerve-deadening agent. Here are some time-tested recipes for odor-eating alternatives, says Cindy Cook, a trained home economist at the Michigan State University Extension in East Lansing and manager of its Home Maintenance and Repair Database on the Internet.

Ventilation: This is as simple as opening windows and doors in the house as often as possible. It helps dry up and clear away the sources that cause odors. (Of course, if it's very humid out, don't ventilate.)

Vinegar: Boil a solution of 1 tablespoon white vinegar and 1 cup water to eliminate unpleasant cooking odors. When cutting onions, rub vinegar on your hands before and after slicing to reduce odors.

Celery: This is another remedy for onion odor on hands. Cut a celery stalk and rub the ends on your hands before and after handling onions.

Cinnamon and cloves: Mix these spices together in a cheesecloth bag and boil the bundle. The bag makes cleanup quick and easy.

Vanilla: Moisten a cotton ball with pure vanilla and place it in a small saucer. Place the saucer in the car (while it's standing), in the refrigerator, or throughout the house to remove odors. (Keep it out of the reach of children, however. Vanilla has a high alcohol content.)

Borax: To prevent the growth of odor-producing molds and bacteria, sprinkle $\frac{1}{2}$ cup borax in the bottom of the garbage can.

Rajiv Jain, laboratory manager for the Association of Specialists in Cleaning and Restoration in Annapolis Junction, Maryland. "The easy way out is to mask the smell with something like perfume. The best way, however, is to remove the source of the odor."

Dave Heberly agrees. He is technical service director at Steam Way International, a carpet-cleaner manufacturer in Denver that provides education to professional carpet cleaners, including seminars on odor control. "If you find a dead mouse, do you run to the grocery store and buy something to spray on it, or do you just throw it away?" he asks. "Even when the source of the odor is not so easy to remove, you have to get rid of it first."

Pet Urine

This is one of the most common odor sources. If pet urine seeps into carpet and carpet backing, urine can smell for long periods and can draw pets back to urinate on the same spot. It is also a breeding ground for bacteria, which give off their own particular odors.

First, absorb as much of the pet urine as possible using white cloths or paper towels. Then blot the area with a white towel soaked in a solution of 1 teaspoon white or colorless liquid dishwashing detergent in 1 cup lukewarm water. Soak up as much as possible using a clean towel. Next, blot the area with a solution of one part white vinegar to two parts water. Again, use a towel to soak up as much as possible. Cover the area with several white terry towels, place something heavy on them, and allow the area to dry for at least six hours.

Cooking Odors

"If you leave a four-pound chicken on the stove, and it cooks down to nothing," says Heberly, "you'll end up with four pounds of burned meat on your walls, carpet, and ceiling." Those particles give off odors.

The same thing occurs—albeit to a lesser degree—when you cook with strong-smelling foods like fish, onions, and garlic. To remove the source of cooking odors, clean kitchen surfaces. Disinfect with a commercial cleaner, like Pine-Sol.

Heat rises and, in its effort to seek equilibrium, is drawn to cool areas. Concentrate cleaning energy, therefore, on high areas, metal surfaces (faucets, towel racks, door handles, hinges), and areas around windows and doors.

Smoke

Treat smoke the same way you would cooking odors. Try to wash away the smoke residue left on the surfaces of the affected room. Wash or dry-clean rugs, draperies, and other fabric. If you're cleaning up after a more serious smoke odor problem, such as a house fire, you'll probably need to

HOW IT WORKS

The Science of Smell

Odor occurs when substances, usually organic, give off molecules that float through the air and find their way into your nasal passages. Higher temperatures make substances more volatile and, therefore, increase smells given off. Higher humidity increases odors, too, by slowing the molecules' rate of evaporation. There are six main odor qualities: fruity, flowery, resinous, spicy, foul, and burned.

The sense of smell is thought to be 10,000 times more sensitive than taste. For example, scientists have found that humans can smell ethyl mercaptan, an odor-causing substance in rotten meat, even in traces as scarce as $1/400$ milligram per liter of air.

Hunger heightens the sense of smell. Pain does, too, probably as a way of alerting the body to dangerous stimuli in the environment. And because pain endings are found on the nerves in the nose, certain odors, such as ammonia, can actually cause physical discomfort.

Rocket Science Meets Home Ec

Paintings damaged by smoke are hard to clean because most solvents used to remove smoke can also dissolve many types of paint. But NASA scientists working as consultants for Cleveland Museum of Art conservators have developed a cleaning method for smoke-damaged art that is out of this world.

The technique uses single-atom oxygen, known as atomic oxygen, says Sharon Rutledge, a research engineer at NASA's Lewis Research Center in Cleveland. Atomic oxygen is abundant in the upper reaches of the atmosphere, where ultraviolet rays split normal oxygen, O_2, into individual atoms. These single atoms of oxygen aggressively seek out something with which to bond. This is a problem for satellites in orbit around the earth because the bonding reaction slowly erodes many materials that are typically used on a satellite's exterior surface.

In their experiment with smoke-damaged art, the scientists split oxygen molecules in a vacuum chamber and then exposed paintings damaged by an oil fire and a furniture fire to the atomic oxygen. The atoms bonded with the carbon-based residue, creating carbon dioxide, carbon monoxide, and water. The canvas damaged by oil smoke came clean in an hour, and the one damaged by furniture smoke came clean in 23 hours—with no apparent harm done to the paintings, says Rutledge.

call a professional odor-removal company. To remove stubborn smoke smells, professionals use a variety of techniques, including treatment with ozone gas, which oxidizes the odor molecule and renders it virtually fragrance-free. For a professional referral in your area, contact the Association of Specialists in Cleaning and Restoration at 10830 Annapolis Junction Road, Suite 312, Annapolis Junction, MD 20701-1120.

Refrigerator Odors

To keep refrigerator odors at bay, give your refrigerator a regular and thorough cleaning according to the manufacturer's instructions, says Martha Reek, a senior home economist with the Whirlpool Corporation in Evansville, Indiana. Keep all foods covered to prevent odor transfer. And discard old unusable foods before they start to smell. As a preventive measure, place a small opened box of baking soda in your refrigerator and another in your freezer to absorb food odors. Replace them with new boxes every few months.

For especially bad smells, says Reek, spread a medium-size box of baking soda or organic based activated charcoal, available at aquarium supply stores, into a shallow pan and let it stand on a refrigerator shelf for a few days. Or do the same with freshly ground coffee in a cereal bowl.

Note: Freshly ground coffee may cause ice and ice cream to take on a coffee flavor. To avoid this, discard these items or seal them in a plastic bag.

If you're about to junk your refrigerator because of ghastly odors—the kind caused by rotten and forgotten meat—try the following first, says Reek. Empty your refrigerator and clean it thoroughly according to the manufacturer's instructions. Pack each shelf with crumpled newspapers. Set a cup of water on the top shelf or sprinkle the papers lightly with water, and let it stand for five to six days while the refrigerator is running. Replace the newspaper every two days. The refrigeration system will pull moist air across the newspaper surfaces, which will absorb odor molecules. It's inconvenient, but it works. So arrange for a backup refrigerator.

Mildew

When you discover mildew, first brush off the surface growth outdoors to avoid scattering the spores. Then, let the items dry in the air and sun. Follow the care instructions of the particular item you're cleaning. Send nonwashables to a dry cleaner, and launder washables promptly with plenty of hot suds. To remove mildew from golf bags, canvas awnings, and other nonwashables, wipe them with a solution of 1 cup hot water and ¼ teaspoon liquid dishwashing detergent, using a white cotton cloth. When possible, use chlorine bleach in the wash. Bleach kills any remaining spores.

To avoid mildew, ventilate your house well and control moisture. If you can't pin down the source of a mildew odor, check the evaporation pan under your refrigerator, if it has one. It's warm, dark, and dank under there—the perfect mildew-growing conditions.

Skunk Odor

Neutralize the skunk funk on a dog by washing the dog with tomato juice or vinegar. For decks, driveways, and other hard surfaces harboring a skunk smell, mix a quart of 3 percent hydrogen peroxide, ¼ cup baking soda, and 1 tablespoon liquid dishwashing detergent. Put it in a plastic spray bottle, and spray it on the surfaces. Leave the solution for a few minutes, and then hose it off.

Speed tips: If you have a heavy-duty vacuum cleaner—like a Shop-Vac, capable of picking up liquids—use it to remove urine and other odor-causing liquids from carpet and rugs as soon as possible. First, mist the stain with water to dilute it, and then suck as much as possible up with the vacuum. Repeat the process as many times as needed.

Oil Stains

 EMERGENCY ACTION
Remove excess oil by blotting with a paper towel, being careful not to spread it. Next, blot with a paper towel dabbed with an acetone-based nail polish remover. Do not use it on acetate. It will dissolve the fabric.

Oil is a tough stain, plus it is like a magnet for dirt. Remove oil stains as quickly as possible.

Technique: The best substance for removing oily or greasy stains is dry-cleaning solvent. Either have the item professionally dry-cleaned or blot with a clean white towel and a spot remover, like Carbona Stain Devils or K2r, available at supermarkets, hardware stores, or discount department stores. Lay the stain facedown on a soft absorbent cloth. Apply the spot remover to another cloth, and then blot from the inside of the garment to push the stain out. "It's important to have something underneath because what you want to do is send the stain somewhere else," says Ann Lemley, Ph.D., chairman of the department of textiles and apparel at Cornell University in Ithaca, New York. "As the spot remover dissolves the oil, you want to drive it away." For carpets, always apply the spot remover to a towel, never directly onto the carpet. Otherwise, it can soak into the carpet backing or pad and attract more dirt. Wear protective rubber or latex gloves, and use these products in a well-ventilated area.

Note: Before using cleaning solutions, always test them on an inconspicuous section of the stained item.

In a pinch: If you don't have any spot remover around the house, use an acetone-based nail polish remover. Do not, however, use it on acetate fabric. It dissolves the fabric.

Caution: Always rinse out one cleaning solution before trying another. Always read the product label for proper use and safety precautions.

Ovens

There's nothing worse than trying to scrape off spilled food that has attached itself like igneous rock to the inside of an oven. The secret—at least with most ovens—is getting to the grime quickly, preferably just after it spills. And generally speaking, the more often you clean your oven, the easier it will be to remove the food and grease.

Of course, preventing spills in the first place will save you a lot of grief. If you think a pie or casserole might bubble over, place a piece of foil that is just slightly larger than the cooking dish on a rack below. (Do not place foil directly on the entire bottom of the oven or cover a rack entirely with foil. You might cause an uneven distribution of heat.) "All those drippings will fall right onto that foil," says Beth McIntyre, a home economist for Maytag Appliances in Newton, Iowa. "It saves an extreme amount of cleanup."

In terms of cleaning, there are three basic types of ovens: conventional, self-cleaning, and continuous-clean. Each has its own requirements.

Conventional Ovens

A quick and easy way to clean standard ovens that are lightly soiled is to fill a small glass bowl with ½ cup ammonia, place it in the oven, and close the door. Do not turn on the oven. "The fumes will help loosen the baked-on food," McIntyre says. Let it stand overnight. Be careful when you open the oven door. Ammonia fumes can irritate eyes. Stand back and let the air clear a few minutes before wiping the loosened crud from the oven with paper towels or newspaper.

Note: If you have a gas oven with a continuous pilot light, extinguish the pilot light before putting ammonia in your oven.

If your oven is moderately to heavily soiled, that method probably won't get all the grime. You'll need more intensive measures. Wash the oven with a scrubber, like a nylon mesh ball, dipped in warm soapy water. Rub the surface gently and then rinse it with a sponge or cloth. Avoid scouring with steel wool, which can scratch the surface. That will help food cling to it and make it harder to clean the next time.

Commercial oven cleaners work well on standard ovens. However, they are strong and should be used with care. "Depending on how burned on the food is, it could be next to impossible to remove everything with just ammonia and soapy water," McIntyre points out.

Oven cleaners can damage other nearby surfaces that come in

contact with the product. Protect these areas with layers of newspaper or other materials, and wear protective gloves. Follow the manufacturer's instructions carefully.

Wash removable racks and broiler pans by hand, soaking them first in soapy water and then scrubbing them with a plastic scrubber. Add a little ammonia to the water to loosen food while you scrub.

Clean glass doors by wiping them with ammonia. Wait a few minutes, and then wipe them with a moist sponge. If the gunk is heavy, scrape it off with a windshield ice scraper or a single-edge razor blade. Do not, however, scour the glass with steel wool.

Caution: Never spray commercial oven cleaner on a hot oven. It can become even more caustic and can corrode surfaces. Likewise, never spray oven cleaner on oven lights, electric elements, or gas pilot lights. (It's best to turn off the pilot light when using spray oven cleaner.)

Self-Cleaning Ovens

Self-cleaning ovens have a cycle during which the oven gets hot enough to disintegrate food spills and other soil. Oven models and brands vary. First and foremost, follow your oven manufacturer's directions.

To prevent food from being baked on, preclean the areas not exposed to the high heat during the self-cleaning cycle: the frame around the oven opening and the edge of the door outside the gasket. (*Caution:* Never clean the gasket with anything. Even water can corrode it, breaking the heat seal.) Use hot water and liquid dishwashing detergent or a paste of baking soda and hot water on harder-to-clean areas. Rinse well with water mixed with a little vinegar to remove all residue. Reclean these areas after you run the cleaning cycle.

To avoid etching or discoloration of the oven finish, wipe up food spills that are high in acid, like tomato sauce, fruit, or milk products. The porcelain enamel inside your oven is acid-resistant but not acid-proof.

Remove the oven racks and broiler pan before starting the cleaning cycle. Wash them by hand, soaking them first in soapy water and then scrubbing them with a plastic scrubber. Add a little ammonia to the soaking water to loosen food while you scrub.

When the cycle is finished, wipe out the small amount of fine ash left inside with a damp cloth.

Caution: Never use chemical oven cleaner in a self-cleaning oven. If residue remains, it can be changed by the high heat into compounds that etch the porcelain enamel.

Continuous-Clean Ovens

These are made with a rough, porous interior surface designed to resist stains and partially absorb grease. It also spreads spills out so that they oxidize more easily when the oven is hot. Keep in mind, however, that these ovens do not typically get squeaky-clean.

To help the oven catch up with accumulated grease and food, occasionally wipe out the inside of the oven with a nylon pad and plain water.

Wash the oven racks and broiler pan by hand, soaking them first in soapy water and then scrubbing them with a plastic scrubber. Add a little ammonia to the soaking water to loosen food while you scrub.

Sugar spills are the hardest for a continuous-clean oven to remove, so take precautions against fruit-cobbler boil-overs and other such spills.

If large spills do occur, they can seal the surface, preventing the oven's continuous oxidation process. While the oven is still slightly warm and the spill soft, blot up the food using paper towels or a sponge. Don't rub because the particles could clog the oven's pores.

Once the oven is completely cool, spray the spill with an all-purpose spray-on cleaner, like Fantastik. Work it into the porous surface by scrubbing gently with a nylon-bristle brush or nylon net pad. Let it stand 15 to 30 minutes, and then scrub the softened soil gently with the nylon brush or pad. Rinse the area thoroughly with cold water and a sponge, being careful not to let water run down into the burner assembly on gas ranges.

Speed tips: Are your oven racks really dirty? Put them in a heavy-duty plastic trash bag, add ½ cup household ammonia, and tie the bag up tightly. Let it sit overnight. When you open the bag, stand back and let the air clear for a few minutes before removing the racks. Then hose the racks down outside or rinse them in the sink.

Note: Ammonia can discolor racks with a high nickel content. Check with the manufacturer and ask if yours contain nickel. If you're unsure, test first by applying ammonia to an inconspicuous area.

Caution: Never apply all-purpose cleaners to a hot oven. Be sure to rinse away all cleaner residue. When heated, they can leave a chalky, hard-to-remove stain.

Never use oven cleaners or powdered cleaners on continuous-clean ovens. They will clog the pores. Likewise, never use any metal pads or abrasives. They can wear off the coating.

Paint

No need to change clothes, you thought, for a tiny little touch-up paint job. And now you've speckled your favorite dress shirt. You've just had a brush with paint stains, one of the toughest types to clean. But attacking paint stains before they have dried will improve your chances of removing them completely.

Technique: If possible, lay the stain faceup on white paper towels on a flat surface. Blot with a paper towel dabbed with a generally available spot remover, such as Energine. Use the spot remover in a well-ventilated area. After you have removed all you can by blotting, turn the stain over onto fresh towels and drop a few drops of the liquid onto the back of the stain with an eyedropper. This should force loose particles into the paper towels. "At that point, you've probably gotten rid of the plastic component," says Jane Rising, instructor in the education department at the International Fabricare Institute in Silver Spring, Maryland. If not, try the same technique using acetone, the main ingredient in one type of nail polish remover, available in drugstores and hardware stores. Be careful because acetone dissolves acetate fabric.

To remove the last traces of the stain, blot with a solution of ¼ teaspoon clear liquid dishwashing detergent and ½ cup cold water, using a clean white towel. Then wash the item as directed. If that does not remove the stain completely, follow the same technique but with a solution of 1 teaspoon ammonia and ½ cup cold water. Again, wash as directed.

For carpets, always apply cleaning solutions to a towel, never directly onto the carpet. Otherwise, it can soak into the carpet backing or pad and attract more dirt.

Note: Before using cleaning solutions, always test them on an inconspicuous section of the stained item.

Caution: "Do not reach for the paint thinner," Rising warns. "Paint thinners are not colorless liquids. You might get the paint stain out, but then you have another stain."

Always rinse one cleaning solution before trying another. Mixing chemicals, especially ammonia and chlorine bleach, can create noxious fumes. Read all product labels carefully for proper usage and safety precautions.

Painted Surfaces

Walls and other painted surfaces collect dirt and grime like magnets. "Dogs rub up against walls, and children wipe greasy fingerprints on them," says Kay Weirick, director of housekeeping services at Bally's Las Vegas Hotel and a member of the technical advisory committee for *Executive Housekeeping Today* magazine. "How you clean painted walls depends on what type of paint was used."

Technique: First, remove loose soil by dusting or vacuuming the surface.

No matter what type of paint you have, always test your cleaning solution first on an inconspicuous area. Wipe it on and let it dry before inspecting. If the paint is gloss or semigloss, use an all-purpose cleaner or a solution of liquid dishwashing detergent and warm water. Start at the bottom and work up so that your cleaning solution does not run down the dirty wall and cause hard-to-remove streaks. Rub gently using a sponge or soft cloth. Rinse by wiping with a clean moist sponge or cloth. Dry the area with clean towels.

Try to avoid touch-up painting. Even if you have the matching paint color, touch-ups of paint older than a year tend to look splotchy.

If it is flat paint, try removing small marks with a white vinyl eraser, available at art and office supply stores. Water can remove and stain flat paint.

Painting Equipment

The key to cleaning up after a painting job is to do it sooner rather than later. The more the paint has a chance to dry, the harder it will be to remove. Let the chore slip and you may have to buy new brushes or rollers the next time you pop open a paint can.

Technique: The first consideration when it comes to cleaning painting equipment—buckets and pans, brushes and rollers—is the type of paint that you're using.

Water-based paint is much easier to clean than oil-based paint. For rollers, begin by scraping the excess paint back into the original can using a crescent-shape scraper, often found on 5-in-1 painters tools. Then wash the roller in warm soapy water until it is free of paint.

Wash brushes used with water-based paint in warm soapy water until free of paint. Use a paintbrush comb, available at hardware and paint supply stores, to clean between bristles. Pans and buckets come clean easily when washed with soapy water.

For cleaning oil-based paint off equipment, first remove any excess paint. In the case of rollers, again use the crescent-shape scraper. Next, use a brush and roller cleaner, like Kwikeeze, available at paint supply and hardware stores. "These products work better than the typical paint thinner," says Jim Westerman, president of the Carbit Paint Company in Chicago, "and they work on all types of paint."

Pour the cleaner in an old paint-free paint can or coffee can. Let the brush or roller soak for a while, and then rub and scrape the paint off. "Because brush and roller cleaners don't evaporate very quickly, they're reusable," Westerman says. The paint eventually settles to the bottom, and you can pour off the pure solvent for use later. Give the brush or roller a final rinse in clean paint thinner. Wrap it in aluminum foil and tightly seal the ends for storage.

Clean buckets and pans used with oil-based paint with the brush and roller cleaner. Or, just remove excess paint and let the rest dry. Keep pans clean in the first place by covering them in aluminum foil. Throw the foil away when you're finished.

Speed tips: Holding your brush head-down inside an empty bucket or can, with the handle between your two palms, spin it to remove excess paint and paint solvent. Holding it in the can keeps paint from splattering. Do the same with rollers by using a roller spinner, available at paint supply stores.

In a pinch: When you're planning to reuse a brush that has been used with oil-based paint, save yourself the trouble of a complete cleaning by simply standing it on its bristles in a half-inch of brush and roller cleaner. Then cover it with plastic wrap. "Through capillary action, the solvent will rise and keep the brush from drying out for a day or two," says Westerman. Do same with a roller by dipping it in the solvent and wrapping it tightly with aluminum foil.

Caution: When cleaning painting equipment with solvents, such as a brush and roller cleaner or paint thinner, use protective eyewear.

Petroleum-based solvents are very flammable and dangerous to breathe. Ventilate the work area well. Keep the solvent away from open flame (like pilot lights) and sparks. Carefully read product labels for proper usage and safety precautions.

Paintings

Unless you have been trained as a conservator, there's not much you can do to clean paintings. Because materials vary greatly, what works on one painting might cause irreparable damage to another. Your main goal is avoiding a buildup of dust.

Technique: Dust oil paintings as part of your regular cleaning routine—but only paintings that won't be damaged by dusting. "Even dusting can dislodge loose flakes of paint, break off the tips of brushstrokes, or damage the surface of a fragile painting," cautions Julie Barten, a conservator with the Guggenheim Museum in New York City. Use a very soft brush, like a wide squirrel mop brush, available at art supply stores.

Some paintings are coated with varnish, which can discolor with age. Do not try to clean or remove the varnish. You might injure the painting. For any stain or discoloration you're not sure of, call a professional art conservator. For a referral in your area, contact the American Institute for Conservation of Historic and Artistic Works at 1717 K Street NW, Suite 301, Washington, DC 20006.

Paneling

To properly clean paneling, you must first identify it. There is real wood paneling, which comes in a variety of different wood species and finishes, and there is hardboard paneling, which features a baked-on plastic coating made to look like wood. While the faux-finish style is relatively easy to clean, you must be careful cleaning real wood paneling. Like wood furniture, it is sensitive to many cleaning materials and techniques.

Technique: Dust both types of surfaces regularly as part of your normal cleaning routine.

To clean hardboard paneling, wipe it down with a sponge or

cloth dampened in a solution of warm water and a squirt of liquid dishwashing detergent. Rinse by wiping it down with a clean damp sponge or cloth.

If the wall is very dirty, use a stronger solution, such as an all-purpose household cleaner whose label says it is safe for painted walls. Test it first in an inconspicuous area to make sure that it does not damage the finish. Rinse the paneling thoroughly by wiping with a clean damp sponge or cloth. Do not use any solvents on hardboard paneling. It may strip the finish.

For paneling made from real wood, try to get by with the dusting alone. "It's best to try to avoid water as much as possible when you're cleaning real wood," says Douglas Gardner, Ph.D., associate professor of wood science at the School of Forestry and Wood Products, Michigan Technological University in Houghton.

If the paneling needs a heavier cleaning, however, you can use a spray-on product like Endust or Pledge. A nonemulsified polish like Pledge is clear and will remove grease and wax. An emulsified polish, which is milky-white, will clean water-soluble dirt as well as grease. Use a nonemulsified polish on old fragile wood to avoid damaging the finish. Or use a lightly dampened cloth and a neutral cleaner, like Murphy Oil Soap. Follow the manufacturer's instructions for mixing the solution. Again, pretest the cleaner on a small inconspicuous area first.

Speed tips: To dust paneling, especially that with detailed carving, use a vacuum cleaner brush attachment.

Patio Furniture

Patio furniture is made for the outdoors, which means that it can handle a good hose-and-scrub cleaning. If you do it regularly, you'll keep dirt, tree sap, and other grime from taking over. You'll save yourself a major cleaning job, and you'll have more time for your magazines and umbrella drinks.

Technique: Clean patio furniture at least twice a year. Spray it with a garden hose, and then wash it with a nylon brush and a bucket of warm water with a few squirts of liquid dishwashing detergent.

Avoid using steel wool and other abrasives on patio furniture. Most surfaces scratch easily. Some plastics and vinyls are even coated with special finishes that protect the furniture from ultraviolet rays.

You don't want to remove these. Scrub joints and crevices with an old toothbrush. Rinse suds by spraying with the garden hose. Dry the furniture with clean towels or by leaving it in the sun.

Apply automotive wax or polish to most nonwood surfaces—painted metal, anodized aluminum, plastic, and vinyl. This helps protect the surface from the elements and gives it a nice long-lasting shine. "It's just like your automobile," says Mary Lou Heltemes, customer service supervisor at Homecrest Industries, an outdoor furniture manufacturer in Wadena, Missouri. "If you don't wax it, the frame finish will oxidize and dull." Always read product labels to make sure that they are recommended for your particular material.

Here are general tips for materials found in most types of patio furniture.

Aluminum

Although aluminum does not rust, it can discolor and corrode slightly when exposed to pollutants in the air and rain. This condition, known as oxidation, can cause pitting, which looks like fine grit stuck to the surface and does not come off easily.

Never use alkaline cleaners—like ammonia, trisodium phosphate, or even baking soda—on aluminum. They discolor it. If the aluminum surface is discolored, wash it with a one-to-one solution of vinegar and water. (*Note:* Pretest first on an inconspicuous area.) The acid in vinegar will help restore the aluminum's shine.

Do not use abrasive cleaners, such as scouring powders or steel wool. They might scratch or dull the surface.

Coat your aluminum patio furniture with automotive wax or a silicon spray to protect it from corrosion and pitting.

Cushions

Most outdoor furniture cushions these days are covered with water-resistant and sunproof materials. Generally speaking, you should clean these the same way you would the furniture and dry them by standing them up in the sun. However, always follow the manufacturer's recommended cleaning instructions.

In the case of mildew, you'll want to deep clean the cushions. Fill a clean garbage can (or some other large container) with a solution of 1 cup liquid chlorine bleach and 1 cup powdered laundry detergent to 3 gallons warm water. (Double the solution, if necessary.) Soak the cushions for at least two hours, and then scrub them with a nylon brush. Do not use bleach on cushions covered in colorful fabrics. It will cause the colors to fade and bleed.

It is essential to rinse the cushions thoroughly with cold water.

Otherwise, the mildew can return. "One way to do it is to take them to a self-service car wash," Heltemes says. "They have good water pressure and a drainage system, too." Dry the cushions completely by allowing them to sit in the sun for several days. (*Note:* This deep cleaning is only if recommended by the cushion manufacturer.)

To keep mildew off cushions, especially those with bright prints that cannot be bleached, clean them more often than normal. Mildew grows on organic materials, like cotton, leather, and paper. "Because most of the cushion materials are synthetic, the mildew feeds off foreign substances, like pollen, dust particles, or juice that your kid spilled," Heltemes says.

Speed tips: Use a leaf blower to help dry wet cushions.

Pencil Marks

It's time to get the "lead" out. "Pencil is basically graphite, which has layers," says Rajiv Jain, laboratory manager for the Association of Specialists in Cleaning and Restoration in Annapolis Junction, Maryland. "Since the stain is on the surface, you must use regular me-

HOW IT WORKS

Pass Me That Basketball, I Made a Mistake

Think of erasers as the other way to dry-clean, says Jim Weissenborn, chief executive officer of the General Pencil Company in Redwood, California.

"Through adhesion, erasers pull substances like pencil graphite off surfaces," says Weissenborn. "If you really wanted to, you could erase with a rubber ball, like a racquetball or basketball—anything that's abrasive. For years, erasers, like the pink kind you used in school, contained rubber and pumice. The old gray typewriter erasers had loads of pumice because they had to take the typing ink out of the paper. Actually, what they did was remove half of the paper. But more and more erasers these days are made out of plastic or vinyl, without the pumice. They don't dig in as much. They actually remove whatever is on the surface of the paper or wallpaper, without hurting the material. There are even erasers for taking pencil out of fabric."

chanical means, like surfactants." In other words, there are no chemical solutions that dissolve it.

Technique: For pencil marks in fabric, blot with a white towel and a solution of 1 teaspoon liquid dishwashing detergent and 1 cup lukewarm water. Don't rub the stain. That could smear it. Wash as directed.

If it's a pencil mark on a wall, use the same soapy solution but scrub gently with a sponge. "The sponge has just enough 'tooth' to pull the stain off," says Jim Weissenborn, chief executive officer of the General Pencil Company in Redwood, California, which has been in his family since 1889.

For nonwashable surfaces, gently erase pencil marks using a white vinyl eraser, available at office and art supply stores. Avoid using normal pink pencil erasers, which tend to be abrasive. A white vinyl eraser will work on painted surfaces, wallpaper, and even fabric.

Perfume

What pleases the nose may not please the eye. "Perfumes contain oils that can oxidize and become very difficult to remove," says Jane Rising, instructor in the education department at the International Fabricare Institute in Silver Spring, Maryland. "They also contain alcohol, which can damage color." The sooner you attack a perfume stain, the better.

Technique: Pretreat the stain before washing the item. Begin by mixing ¼ teaspoon clear liquid dishwashing detergent with ½ cup warm water. Apply it directly to the fabric, and then lay the garment on a hard surface and pat the stain lightly with the back of a spoon. This allows the solution to get in between the fibers, where stains hide. Don't rub the fabric together. That will abrade the fibers. Next, wash as directed either by machine or by hand in the hottest water safe for the fabric.

If that doesn't remove the perfume completely, try rubbing alcohol. But be careful because alcohol can cause dyes to bleed. Lay the stain facedown on an absorbent white cloth. Apply the alcohol to another cloth or cotton ball, and then blot from the inside of the garment to push the stain out. If colors bleed or the fabric is acetate, try diluting the alcohol with two parts water.

For carpets, always apply the solvent to a towel—never directly onto the carpet. Otherwise, it can soak into the carpet backing or pad and attract more dirt. Rinse by blotting with a clean white cloth soaked in water.

Note: Before using cleaning solutions, always test them on an inconspicuous section of the stained item.

Caution: Always rinse a cleaning solution before trying another. Mixing chemicals, especially ammonia and chlorine bleach, can create noxious fumes. Carefully read all product labels for proper usage and safety precautions.

Perspiration

"Sweat equity" is fine if you're improving your house. But don't let it build up in your clothes.

"Perspiration contains chloride salts, which can damage both color and fiber," says Jane Rising, instructor in the education department at the International Fabricare Institute in Silver Spring, Maryland. "It starts out acidic and becomes alkaline with age, and alkalis can damage silk and other fibers." Perspiration also attracts clothes moths. Your goal is to remove perspiration stains as soon as possible.

Technique: If you have washable items with stubborn sweat stains, soak them for several hours in a solution of warm water and a pretreatment product containing enzymes, like Biz. Keep the water warm while soaking. Next, wash as directed either by machine or by hand in the hottest water safe for the fabric.

Take dry-clean-only garments, especially silks, to be cleaned as soon as you can.

Note: Before using cleaning solutions, always test them on an inconspicuous section of the stained item.

Pests—Bugs, Fleas, Rodents, Spiders

The number one strategy for controlling household pests is a preventive tactic—general cleanliness around your home. Sometimes, even despite your best efforts, worrisome little critters will work their way inside. And that calls for directed hand-to-hand (hand-to-feeler?) combat.

Technique: Reduce potential habitats and food sources for household pests by picking up clutter, keeping the house free of moisture and food particles, moving woodpiles away from your home, and keeping plants well-pruned and gardens free of debris. Many creatures like to live and breed in dark undisturbed areas. Be sure to clean under furniture, around baseboards, and in furnace air ducts, closets, food storage nooks, and pet resting areas. Clean mildew; book lice and other insects feed on it.

Blocking potential thoroughfares into your home from the out-

SCRUB THIS APPROACH

Pests Shrug Off Sonic Solutions

You've probably seen them advertised on TV—plug-in gadgets that emit a high-pitch whine beyond the range of the human ear. They're billed as a miracle cure for roach and rodent infestation. They're small, nontoxic, and tuck neatly out of sight below the kitchen cabinet. There's only one problem. Research doesn't show that they work, says Roger Gold, Ph.D., professor of urban and structural entomology at Texas A&M University in College Station.

"Cockroaches don't have the neurocapabilities to hear a lot of the sound," says Dr. Gold. As for what they *can* hear, "the cockroaches habituate to it fairly quickly. They just tune it out."

Dr. Gold began studying this type of pest repellent in the late 1980s, when the Federal Trade Commission asked him to test the units for a court case it filed against a manufacturer. In one test, he put the device in a four-foot-square box with an exit hole and a horde of roaches. He then measured the number of insects that fled the box when the sound device was on and when it was off. There was no difference. In fact, he laughs, "because they generate a little bit of heat, we found that the devices themselves became pretty good harborage after a while."

He has since tested many different makes and styles, including units that emit microvibrational and magnetic fields. Scientific testing has not been able to prove that they work, says Dr. Gold.

"The first indication there may be a problem is when the package says, 'Will affect rats but not the family's pet mouse or gerbil,'" warns Dr. Gold. "There are some pretty darn shrewd marketers out there. One company offers a warranty for the first 30 days and then says that the device takes 60 days to work."

doors is also an important measure. Seal cracks around the house. Use well-fitting screens. Keep doors closed. You'd be surprised at how quickly bugs can take advantage of an open threshold. To attract fewer insects to the vicinity of your home, use yellow bulbs for porch and outdoor lighting.

Fleas

Flea control can keep you hopping. It's not a one-time thing, and it involves more than just treating a flea-infested pet. Fleas can live and breed all over your house, hiding in carpets and dark places. "Fleas are tough and adaptable creatures," says Mary Beth Leininger, D.V.M., past president of the American Veterinary Medical Association in Schaumburg, Illinois. "Not only have they been around for millions of years but also I think they'd probably even survive a nuclear holocaust."

Treat pets and premises simultaneously. To know when to begin your flea-control efforts, you need to monitor your pets for fleas throughout the year by using a specially manufactured flea comb available at pet stores. Focus the combing around the neck and base of the tail where most fleas congregate. Keep a wide container of soapy water nearby to drown any captured fleas. When the number of fleas begins to increase significantly, you need to start your flea-control program. Choose washable pet bedding and clean it weekly. Vacuum carpets, upholstered furniture, and floors weekly (more often if flea populations are high). Although vacuuming is very effective at picking up adult and egg-stage fleas, it is less effective at pulling flea larvae out of carpeting. When infestations are severe, you may want to treat your carpets with a borate powder, such as Fleabusters' Rx for Fleas Plus, available at pet supply stores. Sprinkle the powder evenly over the carpet, rub it in using a broom, and then vacuum. These products are not toxic to mammals but are very effective against fleas, says Tanya Drlik, integrated pest-management specialist at the Bio-Integral Resource Center in Berkeley, California, a nonprofit pest-management organization that advocates nontoxic alternatives.

Note: Wear a dust mask and goggles when applying flea-control powders. Read all product labels carefully for proper usage and safety precautions.

Shampoo your pets, with a product that contains pyrethrium or some other flea-killing substance, but be sure that they are safe for your animal. Don't put too much stock in flea collars, says Dr. Leininger. People tend to rely on them solely, even though their effectiveness is limited. The new prescription-only flea-control products, used once a month, are much more effective against fleas both on the pet and in the environment. Ask your veterinarian which is the best product for your situation.

"Do not try to combat fleas by spraying insecticide around the perimeter of your house or spraying your entire yard," says Drlik. "Spot-treat only those places where you find large accumulations of fleas."

A safe pesticide alternative is insecticidal soap, available at most home and garden centers, says Drlik. It contains potassium salts, sodium salts, or certain fatty acids that kill insects and their larvae on contact. Typically, you mix it with water and use a standard spray bottle or pump-up pressure sprayer to apply it. Because of its makeup, the soap only works when mixed with soft water. To test your solution, mix a small batch and let it sit for 15 minutes. If a scum or "curd" of soap forms on the surface, use a water softener and remix. Treat when and where infestation appears, not as a preventive measure. And because the soap can kill many types of insects—some beneficial—don't spray the whole yard. Spray only where pets rest and other potentially infested areas.

Speed tips: Verify flea hot spots by walking through your house and yard wearing white tube socks. The movement and the warmth of your body draws the fleas to you. As they jump onto your feet and ankles, their dark bodies show up against the white socks.

Cover your pet's bedding with a washable blanket. When you want to remove flea eggs, simply lift the cover and toss it in the washing machine.

Caution: If you have cats or small children, be especially careful about the flea-fighting product you choose. Ask your vet what's safe. "Vets are equally concerned about the safety of the products pet owners use as well as the products' effectiveness," Dr. Leininger says. "Often people will pick up something from the garden supply store without realizing that it might be dangerous." Carefully read product labels for proper usage and safety precautions.

Ants

There are many species of ants and many different behavior patterns, so there is no one-size-fits-all solution. If you find that you have an ant problem, begin by calling your county cooperative extension office and identifying the ant. The extension can then give specific suggestions for attacking the invading army.

"Carpenter ants nest in wood, while pavement ants nest in soil under sidewalks, driveways, or under the concrete slab under your house," says Jeffrey Hahn, an entomologist with the University of

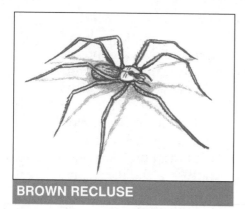

BROWN RECLUSE

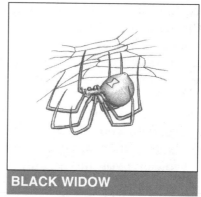

BLACK WIDOW

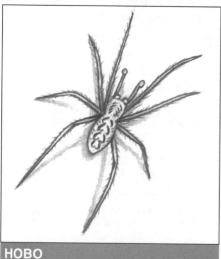

HOBO

Three dangerous spiders: the brown recluse, usually found in southern and midwestern states; black widow spiders, found throughout the United States; and the hobo spider, usually found only in the western states. Kill them by hitting them with a broom or rolled-up newspaper, by stepping on them, or by vacuuming them up. If you need to identify a spider, place the remains in rubbing alcohol.

Minnesota extension service in St. Paul. "Some ants take bait; others do not. Food sources differ. Different ants may be active at different times of the year."

Spiders

Spiders are beneficial because they cause no damage to your belongings but feed on the insects that do. Still, it can be disconcerting to see a large, black eight-legged creature emerging from beneath the kitchen cabinets. And a few species in this country—the black widow, the brown recluse, and the hobo spider—bite with a venom that is strong enough to make humans very sick.

If you encounter a spider, cover it with a glass or cup, and then slide it onto a piece of paper. Lift the glass and paper and take the spider outside, away from the house. If you must kill the spider—if you think it might be poisonous, for instance—do it manually rather than using a toxic insecticide. Step on it (with shoes on, of course), swat it with a broom or a rolled-up newspaper, or vacuum it up and discard the vacuum bag.

Remove spiderwebs and discourage future construction of them by cleaning places where walls meet ceilings, especially in corners. Crush spider egg sacks to stop a potential passel of spiders from hatching. Caulk and seal cracks around the house. Move outdoor debris and piles of wood away from the house. "You're not going to stop them, but you reduce their opportunity to get in and multiply," Hahn says.

Cockroaches

Like most pest control, beating roaches is a multistage effort. "Roaches need food, shelter, and water," says Drlik, "and if you can reduce any of those, you're going to have fewer roaches."

Begin by filling and caulking cracks in walls and cleaning thoroughly. Wipe down surfaces. Vacuum crumbs. Make sure that things stay clean, especially overnight. For example, if you can't do the dishes one night, put them in soapy water so that the cockroaches can't get to them.

Next, do a little sleuthing, using sticky traps, to try to determine

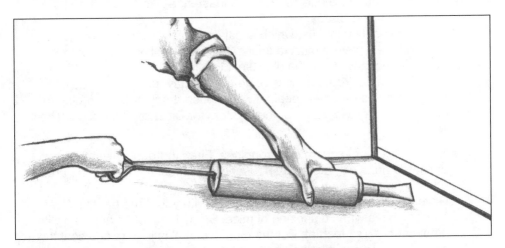

Use a garden dust applicator to blow boric acid into cracks and crevices and around the motor of your refrigerator. Brush any powder that remains after application into the crevices and cracks. Read and follow all instructions on the boric acid label.

where the roaches live and feed. Follow up by lightly dusting the roach thoroughfares and dens with boric acid, a widely available powder that kills roaches yet, if used correctly, is safe for household use. Apply it into cracks and crevices and around the motor of your refrigerator. "They like to live in engine compartments where it's warm," Drlik says. The roaches walk over the boric acid and then ingest it while cleaning themselves.

Attack hard-to-reach nests using roach baits. A wide variety are available at grocery and hardware stores. The idea is that foraging roaches pick up the deadly bait, and then pass it on to other roaches once they return home.

Speed tips: Apply boric acid with a garden dust applicator, a small metal or plastic canister with a pump or a plunger usually found in garden supply stores, hardware stores, or mail-order catalogs.

Dangerous Mouse Droppings

The next time you're cleaning house and discover a rodent den—be it occupied or abandoned—think twice before sweeping up any pellets left behind. The Centers for Disease Control and Prevention, in Atlanta, found that mice are one of the most common carriers of a rare disease called Hantavirus pulmonary syndrome. The virus is mainly transmitted to people when they breathe in air contaminated with the virus. This happens when fresh rodent urine, droppings, or nesting materials are stirred up and become airborne. Since 1993, the disease has killed more than 60 people in the United States.

Symptoms of Hantavirus, which escalate quickly, include fever, dizziness, headaches, severe muscle aches, fatigue, vomiting, and stomach pain. Among those who get the disease, half die.

But don't panic. Your chances of getting Hantavirus are slim. Still, here are some tips for safely dealing with mouse droppings, according to Thomas Skinner, press officer of the Centers for Disease Control and Prevention.

- Never sweep or vacuum dry droppings. First, thoroughly wet the contaminated area with a general household disinfectant. Before the area dries, mop or wipe up the droppings.
- Never touch a dead mouse or droppings with your bare hands. Wear rubber gloves when disposing of mice. Spray the mouse and trap with a household disinfectant. Put the mouse in a plastic bag, and seal the bag before tossing it in the trash.
- Disinfect gloves with a household disinfectant or soap and water before taking them off. After taking off the gloves, thoroughly wash your hands with soap and water.

Caution: When applying boric acid or other roach powders, wear a dust mask and goggles. Do not swallow it, and avoid eye contact. Brush any powder that is visible after application into the cracks and crevices. Wash your hands afterward. Do not spread it in areas where small children or pets might ingest it. Avoid contamination of food and water. Carefully read all products labels for proper usage and safety precautions.

Rodents

Rodents are like thieves. If there is little for them to take—be it valuables or crumbs—and if entry to your house is difficult, they'll pick an easier target. The two most important steps in controlling mice and rats, therefore, are sanitation and sealing. Follow the same advice for preventing spiders, roaches, and other pests—caulk cracks, clean up debris, move woodpiles away from the house, and keep the kitchen clean and crumb-free.

If you need to rid your home of the critters, however, the time-tested snap-back trap is still one of the most effective for killing rodents without using poisons, advise experts at the Cornell University Cooperative Extension in Valhalla, New York. Bait them with peanut butter, which is hard to steal without triggering the trap, and place them out of sight and out of the reach of children and pets. Glue traps can cause mice to die slow deaths, and if you get to the mouse before it has died, you have to deal with getting rid of one very unhappy critter.

Pet Hair

Apart from simply looking bad, pet hair on furniture and carpets is a breeding ground for dust mites, microscopic insects that feed on the hair and can cause allergic reactions.

Technique: You can't beat a vacuum cleaner for sucking hair out of carpets and rugs. "People who have a lot of pets—like breeders—love Electrolux vacuum cleaners because they seem to be the sturdiest," says Jacque Schultz, director of Companion Animal Services for the American Society for the Prevention of Cruelty to Animals, in New York City.

Speed tips: Use a lint brush for quick hair removal from clothes and fine fabric. Or try a handheld vacuum. Not only is it easier than

HOW I DO IT

The Brush-Off

As director of Companion Animal Services for the American Society for the Prevention of Cruelty to Animals, in New York City, Jacque Schultz works with cats and dogs every day. Then when she gets home at night, she has a handful of friends waiting—two Italian greyhounds and three domestic shorthair cats. Here's one way she keeps pet hair off the furniture.

"There are these little rubber nubby-type brushes used for grooming cats," Schultz says. "But I've found that if you go over furniture with them, it does the same thing—it balls the hair up into clumps. They only cost a few dollars, and most pet supply stores have them. The one I have has worked very nicely on my cats' scratching post. With all the rounded edges and half circles for them to sleep in, it's difficult to run even a handheld vacuum cleaner over it adequately. A couple of passes with this rubber brush and I have all the hair loose."

lugging a full-size vacuum out of the closet (the thought of which is sometimes enough to kill cleaning motivation) but also it is great for upholstery and getting into those hard-to-reach crevices.

Pet Urine and Excrement

When you gotta go, you gotta go—and that applies even to house-trained dogs and the most domesticated cats. The key in cleaning up after them is to do it as quickly as possible to prevent staining, discoloration, and odors.

Technique: Urine is more problematic, especially on carpets and fabrics, because it can cause dyes to bleed and fibers to deteriorate. First, absorb as much of the pet urine as possible using white cloths or paper towels. Then blot the area with a white towel soaked in a solution of 1 teaspoon neutral white or colorless liquid dishwashing detergent in 1 cup lukewarm water. Soak up as much as possible using a clean towel. Next, blot the area with a solution of one part white vinegar to two parts water. Again, use a towel to soak up as much as possible. Cover the area with several white terry towels, place something heavy on them, and allow the area to dry for at least six hours.

As an alternative, first, clean up urine or watery excrement with paper towels. "Then, saturate the spot with an enzymatic odor neutralizer, such as Nature's Miracle, sold at pet stores," says Jacque Schultz, director of Companion Animal Services for the American Society for the Prevention of Cruelty to Animals, in New York City. These contain living bacteria that eat the waste's protein base. They typically call for keeping the spot moistened for about eight hours, but you should follow the directions on the particular product you purchase. Afterward, clean the area by blotting with a towel soaked in water, and then blot dry with a towel.

For excrement, pick up solid deposits as quickly as possible using a plastic sandwich bag or tissue paper and discard. Clean the area with the same detergent solution used to clean urine, and blot dry. Rinse the area with water and blot dry again. Follow up with a disinfectant or one of the many odor removers available at pet supply stores. For less-than-solid solids, follow one of the procedures described for cleaning urine, then follow up with the disinfectant.

Note: Before using cleaning solutions, always test them on an inconspicuous section of the stained item.

Caution: Store cleaning products in a safe out-of-the-way place so that your pets don't chew on them. Read product labels carefully for proper usage and safety precautions.

Colossal Cleanups

Just Call Them Slobbopotamuses

The amount of time it takes San Diego Zoo keepers to clean the 980-square-foot sleeping area of two hippos: two to three hours, which is five times longer than it takes to clean up after just about any other zoo animal

Pewter

Although pewter does not tarnish as much as silver, over time it still develops a layer of corrosion that can be cleaned.

Technique: Simply polish it with a flannel cloth. "On the whole, I don't do much to pewter," says Ellen Salzman, an objects conservator at the Metropolitan Museum of Art in New York City. "I think the nature of the material lends itself to a more modest shine." On older pieces that patina is desired and may even add value.

If, however, the pewter has been sitting for a long time and is covered in a stubborn layer of tarnish, use a mild silver polish diluted with water to make it less abrasive. "Generally, you can feel if something is too abrasive. If you can't feel the grit, it's mild enough," Salzman explains.

Photographs

Simple mishandling is one of the leading causes of injured photos. "There's a reason that you should hold the prints by the edges," says Peter Halpert, an independent curator in New York City and contributing editor of *American Photo* magazine. "Your hands naturally carry oils, and when you rub them over your face and your hair, they pick up more oil." The oils and salt will eventually react with the photographic chemicals and cause color distortion and fading.

Technique: Color prints are very sensitive. They cannot be safely cleaned with water or a solvent. Instead, buff fingerprints and other stains with clean dry cotton. Do not use an eraser because it can

HOW I DO IT

Focus on Prevention

Because photographs are so sensitive and fragile, prevention is just as important as cleaning, says Peter Halpert, an independent curator in New York City and contributing editor of *American Photo* magazine. Here are a few strategies that he uses to keep from having to clean his prints and negatives.

"I never put prints in those photo albums with self-sticking pages, the kind that have the glue backing," Halpert says. "The glue seeps into the papers. It's the worst thing you can do to your family treasures, or even your fun snaps.

"I use the old system that everyone's grandmother had of tucking the photos into four little corners and pasting those corners onto black acid-free paper. That's the best thing that you can do for photos.

"I also separate the pictures from atmospheric conditions as much as possible. Humidity can cause the emulsion of one print to stick to another print. If that happens, and you pull them apart, it will damage the photos. I'm not talking about things that necessarily have great artistic value, but they may have a great deal of sentimental value."

abrade the surface and remove the glossy sheen.

Most contemporary black-and-white prints are made from gelatin bromide, which can be cleaned carefully with a solvent. Look for a film-cleaning solvent that does not contain a lubricant at your local photo laboratory. Moisten a cotton ball and gently wipe across the fingerprint. Although the fingerprint impression may not come off, this will remove the damaging oily residue. The same applies to black-and-white gelatin prints dating back to the 1920s, but treat older photos with even more care. Anything before that era should be cleaned by a professional. (For a photography conservator referral in your area, write to the American Institute for Conservation of Historic and Artistic Works at 1717 K Street NW, Suite 301, Washington, DC 20006.)

If your photos get wet, the best way to dry them is to carefully hang them on a line using clothespins. Prevent moisture, dust, and other atmospheric substances from harming photos by putting them in photo albums with acid-free paper and storing the albums in boxes. Do not store the boxes in damp basements or near heaters. Do not stack photos together in a shoe box.

The Low-Sodium Résumé

On his way to becoming one of this country's most respected photography conservators, José Orraca worked at the George Eastman House International Museum of Photography and Film in Rochester, New York.

"It was often said at the George Eastman House," says Orraca, "that when you applied for a job in the research laboratory at Kodak, the last thing they would do in the interview process was put your fingers on a piece of metal. If the metal did not rust, you were more likely to be hired. The reason is that some of us have more natural body oils and salts than others, which rust metal and can damage photographic materials."

Pictures and Frames

The whole point of display objects like framed pictures is to keep them looking their best. So make sure that any cleaning you do will not harm the frame's finish or what is under the glass.

Technique: Dust pictures and frames regularly to avoid dirt buildup. Use a feather duster or soft-bristle brush.

For harder-to-remove soil, wipe with a slightly moistened cloth. Use a solution of warm water and mild liquid dishwashing detergent, if needed, taking care to wring the cloth well to avoid wetting the frame too much.

"Be careful of shellac and other finishes," says Kay Weirick, director of housekeeping services at Bally's Las Vegas Hotel and a member of the technical advisory committee for *Executive Housekeeping Today* magazine. "Something like Windex can remove a fake brass finish." Avoid wetting antique or especially fragile or ornate frames. Simply keep them free of dust.

Never spray glass cleaner directly onto the glass. It might hurt the frame or run between the glass and frame and ruin the matting or picture. Instead, wipe the glass carefully with a cloth moistened with the mild detergent solution. "In the old days, we used vinegar and water and newspaper," Weirick says. That still works for cleaning glass, as long as you apply it carefully and avoid making ink smudges.

Speed tips: For hard-to-reach nooks and crannies, blow air over them by squeezing an empty plastic bottle with a small nozzle—an old shampoo bottle, for example.

Pilling

Your favorite sweater has broken out with a rash of minuscule pom-poms. This pilling is caused by short fibers that stick out of the fabric. The fibers fray and form ugly little balls. "Those little fuzz balls are really grounded into the fabric," says Darcy Crocker, quality control supervisor at the Wool Bureau in New York City. "Has your dog ever come home with burrs in its fur? Pilling is similar."

Technique: The best way to clean up large pills on a garment is to remove them manually, either with your fingers or with a depilling device. To get rid of the small pills that form on cotton fabric, simply wash the clothes in a laundry detergent that contains enzymes (check the list of ingredients on the box). The enzymes eat away at the cellulose of the exposed fibers, leaving the garment looking fresh and new.

Crocker recommends a product called d-fuzz-it, which resembles a lint brush but has a coarse-grade sandpaper facing. When you brush it over the garment, the brush picks the pills off. Another type of device is the battery-operated pill remover. It looks like an electric shaver and works much the same way. A rotating blade clips the pills and draws them into a compartment in the handle. When it's full, you

Pilling: Know Thine Enemy

By understanding the nature of those annoying balls of fuzz that collect on clothing, you stand a better chance of defeating them.

"To make yarn—regardless of whether it is polyester, rayon or wool—you spin fibers together," explains Darcy Crocker, quality control supervisor at the Wool Bureau in New York City. "When you wrap them around one another, some fiber ends protrude." The arm of your jacket brushes against your side, abrading the protruding fibers. They fray and join together, forming balls. "That's what causes pilling," she says.

Then the pills slowly work the fibers out even more and grow into even bigger pills.

"The shorter the length of the fibers, the more chance there is for the garment to pill," Crocker says. Silk is a continuous filament and does not pill. Wool, on the other hand, is a notorious piller made from fibers that are only ¼ inch to 4 inches long. A worsted wool suit, made from long wool fibers that are well-combed and tightly woven, does not pill as much as a Shetland wool sweater, which contains short fuzzy fibers.

To combat pilling, you must either depill or try to prevent it, which isn't easy. Look for garments, like silk, worsted wool, or cotton, that are made from longer, more tightly woven fibers. Or try to reduce the amount of abrasion you subject a garment to. If your favorite dress has a tendency to pill, don't wear it quite as often. And try to wear nonpilling items when doing active things.

In other words, "don't play touch football in your favorite wool sweater," says Crocker.

simply open it up and discard the pile of pills. Fabric and department stores sell both types of devices.

"Don't do it too roughly," Crocker warns, "or do too much at once." When you pull pills, you also pull fibers, which can thin out your garment.

In a pinch: "If you have a large area of pilling but you don't have a lot of time, defuzz it randomly," Crocker says. "Pick off one here and one there to reduce the overall appearance."

Pillows

Here's a thought that will keep you awake at night: "Most people don't realize how much dead skin our bodies slough off," says Marry Keener, assistant director of facilities management at the University of Arizona in Tucson and a member of the technical advisory committee for *Executive Housekeeping Today* magazine. You want to remove that dander to keep pillows fresh and clean-smelling.

Technique: Clean pillows at least twice a year. You can machine-wash most fiber-filled pillows. Use cold water, which is safer on the synthetic filling. Tumble dry on low heat, or dry them in the sun on a patio chair.

Don't clean down-filled pillows at home, recommends Jane Rising, instructor in the education department at the International Fabricare Institute in Silver Spring, Maryland. "Many pillow coverings have natural starches that hold the fill in place," she says. "Washing them causes the starches to break down, and the down can begin to leak from the pillow." Your best bet for pillows is to take them to a dry cleaner who is an expert in cleaning down, says Rising.

Once or twice a year, air out down pillows outdoors in the shade to keep them fresh.

In a pinch: To freshen and remove humidity, place down-filled pillows in a dryer on low heat for about 10 minutes. "A lot of the dust and dander will be trapped in the lint filter," says Keener.

Place Mats

It's usually easy to clean place mats. After all, they were made for catching spilled food.

Technique: You can wash most cloth place mats in the washing machine on a normal cycle. Tumble them dry, remove them promptly from the dryer to reduce wrinkling, and then iron, if necessary.

Some place mats are made of silk, but it is usually washable silk. While you should follow the instructions on the care label, generally speaking, you can wash such silk in a washer on a cool-water cycle. Tumble them dry on a low-heat setting.

If you have plastic or vinyl place mats, simply wipe them down after use with a moist sudsy sponge. Rinse with a clean moist sponge.

Every once in a while, disinfect plastic-coated place mats. Food spills make them vulnerable to bacteria growth. Use a kitchen cleaner that contains a disinfectant. Or sponge it off with a bleach solution—1 teaspoon chlorine bleach per quart of water. Let the bleach solution sit for a few minutes before you rinse it off.

Plants

Cleaning plants is not like scrubbing bathroom tile. You want to keep plants looking dust-free and fresh—but rough treatment would grind them into pulp.

Technique: The bathtub is a convenient place to clean houseplants. First, put each plant's pot in a plastic bag and tie the bag loosely around the stem. This keeps the water from splashing dirt out of the pot and onto the plant and tub. Next, put the plants in the bathtub and let the shower run over their leaves for a few minutes.

"They get sprayed from overhead just like they're out in the rain," says Louise Wrinkle, a veteran horticulture judge for the Garden Club of America in New York City.

When the weather is nice, take plants outside and spray them with the hose. Be careful, however, about leaving them outside. The sudden change from inside to outside—and vice versa—can harm some plants.

In a pinch: Dust plants where they stand using a can of compressed air or a blow-dryer set on its lowest coolest setting. Do not blow plants with heavy gusts of hot air.

Plastic Laminate

Often referred to by the popular brand name Formica, plastic laminate was designed to be easy to clean. Hey, someone's watching out for you after all!

Technique: Wipe up spills with a moist sponge. Clean with a soapy sponge or a grit-free all-purpose cleaner—never anything abrasive. "Use a germicide on kitchen countertops because that's one of the main places germs are," says Kay Weirick, director of housekeeping services at Bally's Las Vegas Hotel and a member of the technical advisory committee for *Executive Housekeeping Today* magazine. She recommends reading the labels of kitchen-cleaning products and choosing one that specifically says that it sanitizes or kills germs.

To remove stains, such as mustard, grape juice, or coffee, sprinkle baking soda on a soft damp cloth and rub gently. For more stubborn stains, dampen the stained area and spray or sprinkle with a cleanser containing bleach, such as Comet with Bleach. Let it stand for about 10 minutes, and then rinse it off with clear water. If it stands longer, it may bleach the color out of the plastic.

Do not cut on plastic laminate. Soil gets into cracks and causes stains and breeds bacteria.

Plywood and Particleboard

As with other wood products, the cleaning method for plywood and particleboard depends on the finish. Either way, they do not pose a big cleaning challenge.

Technique: Most plywood and particleboard used in the home is covered in some type of surface—either vinyl or a plastic laminate, like Formica. Clean these water-resistant finishes with a moist cloth and warm sudsy water or an all-purpose cleaner.

For raw wood surfaces, try to avoid cleaning with water. Dust periodically with a dry cloth. If you must wipe away soil or residue, use a cloth lightly dampened only with water, and dry the wood quickly. Use a dry cloth or ventilate the room well. Otherwise, the moisture could seep into the porous wood or particleboard and cause warping or thickness swells.

Polyester

Polyester is relatively easy to clean because its fibers do not absorb water-soluble stains. "Oil stains in polyester are another ball game," says Jane Rising, instructor in the education department at the International Fabricare Institute in Silver Spring, Maryland. "Stains with grease or oil, even body oils, are hard to remove because the polyester absorbs them."

Technique: Always read care labels first. Most polyester can be machine-washed. Other types, however, like coated polyester draperies should be dry-cleaned only.

For machine washable polyester, wash on a cool- or warm-water cycle using regular laundry detergent. "The danger in washing polyester in hot water is that it wrinkles terribly," Rising explains.

Tumble dry at a low temperature and remove the articles as soon as the tumbling cycle is complete. If ironing is needed, use a cool to moderately warm iron. Look for a polyester setting on your iron.

For most stains, including light oil-based and perspiration stains, pretreat with a spray-on stain remover, like Shout. Or apply a liquid laundry detergent (or a paste made from a granular detergent and water) directly onto the stain. Lay the garment on a hard surface and pat the stain lightly with the back of a spoon. Don't rub the material together. That can abrade the fibers. Next, wash as directed either by machine or by hand in the hottest water safe for the fabric.

For stubborn oily or greasy stains, have your polyester item dry-cleaned.

Porcelain

Because porcelain is delicate, cleaning it requires know-how and a gentle touch.

Technique: For soap scum, light rust stains, and mold growth on porcelain surfaces—sinks, tubs, toilets, and some appliances—use an all-purpose household cleaner, a nonabrasive tub-and-tile cleaner, or warm water and plain baking soda. Scrub with a cloth or sponge, rinse, and dry. Avoid harsh scouring agents and scrubbers. They can scratch the surface and cause it to stain. Never use steel wool on porcelain.

For valuable vases, cups, and other objects, which often can't be submerged, use a solution of warm water and a few drops of a mild liquid dishwashing detergent. Dip a cotton cloth, ball, or swab into the solution and wipe it across the surface. To clean hard-to-reach areas, try a soft toothbrush. "Do it the same way the dentist tells you to brush your teeth," says Ellen Salzman, an objects conservator at the Metropolitan Museum of Art in New York City, "slowly and carefully as opposed to sawing back and forth." Never use metal, which can scratch porcelain. Bamboo skewers and wooden toothpicks are good for safely cleaning gunk out of cracks and crevices.

For those impossible stains, especially the ones that adhere to cracks and other rough spots where the glaze is gone, try hydrogen peroxide, but only as a last resort. And be careful. Rather than removing the stain, hydrogen peroxide bleaches it, so make sure that all paint and gilding is securely fired on. Lay a cotton poultice soaked in a 5 percent solution of hydrogen peroxide along the stained area. Cover it with cellophane to keep it moist. Check it after 10 minutes to make sure that it is not damaging the porcelain surface. Repeat this procedure until the stain is bleached. Afterward, soak the object in water or wipe it clean with a moist cotton cloth.

If you have a valuable porcelain heirloom that needs cleaning, consider hiring a professional. For a referral in your area, contact the nearest museum and ask for the objects conservation department. Or write to the American Institute for Conservation of Historic and Artistic Works at 1717 K Street NW, Suite 301, Washington, DC 20006.

Speed tips: "Spit works very well," says Salzman. "Saliva has an enzyme called amylase that aids in the cleaning process." Just spit on a cotton cloth or moisten a swab in your mouth, and wipe it across stains.

Pots and Pans

Ignore your pots and pans and they'll get back at you. "Any food left in a pot will absorb a soap flavor and will affect the next thing you cook," says Kari Kinder, assistant director of food and beverage at the renowned Culinary Institute of America in Hyde Park, New York. "And it can breed bacteria." It's also important to clean pots and pans thoroughly to remove grease from the outside surface. Otherwise, when heated that residue can cause a nasty, hard-to-remove carbon buildup.

Technique: Generally speaking, you should wash pots and pans by hand. Don't forget to clean the greasy bottoms of pots and pans. For burned-on food, bring a solution of water and ¼ teaspoon liquid dishwashing detergent to a boil in the dirty pan. Simmer until soil loosens.

Aluminum

Automatic dishwasher detergent and minerals in water can discolor aluminum finishes. Washing by hand helps avoid dulling of the sheen. Remove discoloration in pots by boiling a solution of 1 to 2 tablespoons cream of tartar or lemon juice to each quart of water for 10 minutes. Loosen lime scale—deposited by waterborne minerals—from teakettles by boiling a one-to-one solution of water and vinegar. Let the solution stand in the teakettle for several hours, and then rub with steel wool. Do not store water or moist foods in aluminum because the moisture can pit the metal.

Brass and Copper

To remove tarnish from brass or copper, sprinkle on salt and a little vinegar or lemon juice, rub, rinse, and dry. Or rub gently with a paste made from flour, salt, and vinegar or lemon juice. The acid in the vinegar and lemon juice gives the metal a bright shine. "Don't use abrasive cleaners like Brasso," warns Kinder. "We have actually had to replace pots here at the Culinary Institute because students scrubbed away the brass."

Enamelware

This cookware is usually made from metal covered with porcelain enamel. Soften burned-on food by presoaking it in warm soapy water. Scrub with a nonabrasive scrubber, like a nylon net ball. Avoid using scouring powders or steel wool. As a mild cleaning powder, try baking soda.

Iron

One of the biggest issues with cast-iron cookware, like skillets, is avoiding rust. Store iron pots and pans in a dry place. Never leave the lids on because condensation can cause rust. Iron cookware needs to be seasoned occasionally to avoid rusting. To season it, clean it in hot soapy water, dry it, and then coat it lightly with shortening or vegetable oil and heat at 200° to 300°F in the oven for 30 minutes. Let the skillet cool, and wipe off the excess fat with a paper towel. After use, gently clean the pan in hot sudsy water (without heavy scrubbing), rinse, and dry it. (Hint: To get iron pans really dry, heat them briefly over a stove burner.) Finally, wipe them with a thin coating of oil before storing. Never scour with harsh powders or steel wool. To loosen cooked-on food, boil a solution of 2 teaspoons baking soda per quart of water. If the pot does rust, scrub it with steel wool, clean in hot sudsy water, and re-season.

Nonstick

Once these surface coatings are scratched, they lose their nonstick quality. Avoid using abrasive cleaners, such as steel wool and

The Pots and Pans Problem-Solver

Pot type	Problem	Cleaning substance	Technique
Aluminum	Discoloration	1 to 2 tablespoons cream of tartar or lemon juice per quart of water	Boil for 10 minutes
	Lime scale (in teakettles)	One-to-one vinegar and water	Let stand for several hours, and then scrub with steel wool
Brass/copper	Tarnish	Paste made from flour, salt, and vinegar or lemon juice	Rub gently
Enamelware	Stubborn stains	Baking soda	Scrub gently
Iron	Cooked-on food	2 teaspoons baking soda per quart of water	Boil for a few minutes to loosen
Nonstick	Lingering flavors (like onion or garlic)	1 tablespoon vinegar or lemon juice per pan	Let soak, and then wash with soapy sponge full of water
	Stubborn stains or cooked-on food	3 tablespoons oxygen bleach per cup of water	Simmer for 15 to 20 minutes
Pyrex	Burned-on foods, especially sugar and starch	Squirt of liquid dishwashing detergent, 1 tablespoon baking soda, water	Let soak and then clean with nonabrasive scrubber

scouring powders. Instead, wash in hot soapy water using a sponge, rinse, and dry. For hard-water stains or baked-on food in a nonstick pan, simmer a solution of 3 tablespoons oxygen bleach (also called all-fabric bleach) and 1 cup water for 15 to 20 minutes. Wash the pan thoroughly, rinse, and dry. For lingering garlic, onion, or other flavors in a nonstick pan, mix 1 tablespoon vinegar or lemon juice into a full pan of water. Let it soak, wash with a soapy sponge, then rinse and dry.

Pyrex

Wash this sturdy glass cookware in the dishwasher or by hand in warm soapy water. For baked-on food in casserole dishes and other bakeware of glass or glass-ceramic material, soak in a solution of liquid dishwashing detergent and water to loosen soil. For burned-on sugar or starchy foods, add a little baking soda to the presoak solution. Then scrub using a mild product like baking soda. Do not use metal scouring pads, which may scratch the surface. To remove greasy stains, use ammonia or a cleaner that contains ammonia, such as Soft Scrub. For coffee and tea stains, soak in a solution of 2 tablespoons automatic dishwasher detergent per quart of warm water.

Speed tips: It's common sense, but it's worth reiterating. Scraping and presoaking pots and pans greatly speeds up the process.

Use a nonstick spray, like Pam, before cooking. These typically spread a thin layer of vegetable oil or lecithin on the pan and are especially useful on old pans whose nonstick surface is worn partially off.

Pottery

Cleaning glazed pottery is a fairly simple task. Unglazed pottery requires a different technique and a gentle hand.

Technique: If the pottery is well-glazed, then simply clean it with warm water, a mild liquid dishwashing detergent, and a gentle sponge or vegetable brush, like you would everyday china. "The less fired the pottery, the more fragile it is and the less water you should get on it," says Ellen Salzman, an objects conservator at the Metropolitan Museum of Art in New York City. "It can start to break apart. If it's chipped, pieces of the glaze can fall off."

Clean fragile pottery like you would porcelain. Dip a cotton cloth, ball, or swab into a solution of warm water and a mild liquid dishwashing detergent, then wipe it gently across the surface. If there are parts that are not fired at all, roll the cotton over them rather than rub it back and forth. Or give them a gentle dry cleaning by lightly rubbing stains with a white vinyl block eraser, available at stationery and art supply stores. Do not use a pink pencil eraser, which is too abrasive and can leave behind damaging residue.

Speed tips: Because it contains the enzyme amylase, saliva is a good cleaning compound. "Sometimes I think I went to school for four years to learn how to clean with spit," laughs Salzman, referring to how often she uses this simple technique. Just spit on a cotton cloth or moisten a swab in your mouth, and wipe or roll it across stains.

Pressure Cookers

Pressure cookers are basically pots with a screw-on, tightly sealed top and a valve for letting steam escape. So cleaning them is much like cleaning any other pot, except you must also clean the valve and the gasket around the rim of the top.

Technique: Begin by cleaning your pressure cooker like any other pot—with warm soapy water or in the dishwasher. Don't forget to clean any grease on the bottom. For burned-on food, bring a solution of water and ¼ teaspoon liquid dishwashing detergent to a boil in the dirty pan. Simmer with the top off until the food loosens.

Remove the valve from the top, take it apart, and clean the parts with warm soapy water and a kitchen scrubber. (If it is unclear how to take the valve apart, read the manufacturer's instructions.)

"The valve should not be difficult to clean," says Michael Beglinger, executive chef at Deutsche Bank in New York City. "Steam is all that passes through it." Still, you want to wash and dry it completely before storing the pressure cooker.

Also remove the rubber gasket from the pressure cooker's lid. Clean it in warm soapy water, and clean the surface of the lid underneath the gasket. Let them both dry completely before replacing the gasket.

Quilts

Quilt cleaning is no simple Sunday chore. There are several key issues: the type and strength of the fabric, the colorfastness of the dyes, the type of fill, and the quilt's age and condition. You want to clean your quilt but not at the risk of ruining it, especially if it is old or has sentimental value.

Technique: If your quilt is treasured or fragile, avoid cleaning when possible, or if you must clean it, have it cleaned by a professional cleaner who is experienced in cleaning fabrics for museums. Quilt appraisers do not recommend dry-cleaning quilts. Often, wedding-dress cleaners clean quilts and other fragile textiles. If you must dry-clean a quilt, ask that fresh solvent be used. Certain types of quilts, such as wool, silk, and combination quilts (such as crazy quilts), should be dry-cleaned only if they are so soiled that you cannot enjoy them, says Nancy O'Bryant, a national expert on quilt care from Austin, Texas, and a contributing author in *The Quilters Ultimate Visual Guide*. For really valuable pieces, contact your local museum's conservation department for advice.

Even cleaning newer quilts can be tricky. First, look for a care label and follow the instructions. If it has no label, proceed carefully.

Begin by testing for colorfastness. Use a clean white handkerchief and a solution of liquid dishwashing detergent and warm water. Dip a corner of the handkerchief in the solution, wrap a color patch from the quilt around it, and squeeze for about a minute. "If there is any color transfer, you should not continue," says Jane Rising, instructor in the education department at the International Fabricare Institute in Silver Spring, Maryland. "It means that you can't clean the quilt without causing damage." If there is no color transfer, continue until you have tested each of the different colors and different pieces of fabric.

If it passes the colorfastness test, you must next consider the integrity of the fibers. Age and exposure to light, moisture, and atmospheric gases can cause fabrics to deteriorate. "Since we have three layers of goodies here—the top of the quilt, the fill and the back—it could be that one or all have lost enough strength so that it comes apart like tissue paper when it's wet," Rising warns.

Another concern is the quilt's fill, which will vary depending on its age and where it was made. Since the fill is on the inside—and presumably you don't want to tear open your quilt to get to it—the more you know about the origin of the quilt, the better. For example, older quilts are often filled with cotton batting that was never completely cleared of sticks and other cotton-plant residue. This residue can bleed when wet, leaving brown spots. Other quilts contain wool batting, which can shrink when washed with high heat and heavy mechanical action.

If you decide that it's safe to clean your quilt, line a clean bathtub with a sheet. Fill the tub up with 6 to 10 inches of warm water, and add several squirts of mild liquid dishwashing detergent. Fold the quilt and lay it flat in the tub. Using a clean plunger, agitate the water, not the quilt. Let it soak for five minutes, and then agitate the water some more. Do not scrub the quilt or put any tension on it because the stitches might pop. The combination of warm water, detergent, and mild agitation should remove much of the surface soil.

To rinse the quilt, empty the tub and refill it with clean water. Continue agitating the water. Empty the tub and repeat this cycle until there is no longer any soap residue. Carefully lift the sheet up with the quilt in it to move it to a flat drying area.

Do not wring the quilt to remove the water. Instead, roll up the folded quilt and push gently. Unroll it and repeat this drying process several times.

For a speedier method, you can use the tub of your washing machine to "hand-wash" your quilt, says Becky Herdle, a quilting expert and instructor in Rochester, New York, and a contributing author in *The Quilters Ultimate Visual Guide.* Spin the water out after the soaking and gentle agitation. Spinning pushes the quilt against the walls of the machine, but it doesn't agitate. Rinse several times to get the soap solution out.

Finally, place it somewhere—away from direct sunlight—to dry. Do not hang a quilt on a clothesline. The stress and weight of the wet quilt can be too much for the seams. To dry, first place a sheet outdoors on a clean, dry flat surface, such as the lawn or a deck. Then lay the quilt on top and cover with another sheet to protect it from debris, insects, and fading. If you must dry the quilt indoors, lay it on top of a clean plastic sheet. Direct a fan slightly above it to help speed drying.

Most quilts can be vacuumed, which removes quite a bit of dirt. Use a screen made from a square of fiberglass or nylon screening (two by two feet square) with the edges covered with duct tape so that they don't snag the fabric. Place the screen over one section of the flat quilt. Use old pantyhose or several layers of cheesecloth or similar material to cover the opening of the upholstery attachment of your vacuum cleaner or of a handheld vacuum. Use the lowest setting on the machine. Hold the screen firmly and move the vacuum over the screen and the quilt. Vacuum both sides of the quilt in this manner.

Caution: When washing a quilt, do not use water hotter than 89°F. High temperatures can cause the fill to shrink.

Rackets

You don't play dirty, of course. But your choice of courts will affect how easy it is to come clean after your game. "Generally speaking, you're not going to be playing tennis in the rain or in any other conditions where you'll get your racket dirty," says David Sparrow, a former equipment editor for *World Tennis* magazine and now senior editor at *Men's Journal* magazine in New York City. That goes for most racket sports. "The exception is tennis on clay courts."

Technique: Wipe dust and clay residue from racket heads with a lightly dampened cloth. "You'll tend to get clay in the grommets and spaces around the rim of the racket—especially if you're the type of player who digs on shots," says Sparrow, who was a U.S. Open ball boy in the 1980s. Use something pointed, like a nail file or a letter opener, to remove it. (Hint: Use the same sharp tool to scrape the clay out of the soles of your tennis shoes.)

Wipe the grip with a dry cloth to remove dust and dirt. Moisture can alter the tackiness of the leather or synthetic material. If you use an overgrip, like many players these days do, simply replace it occasionally.

Speed tips: If you play tennis on clay courts, use protective head tape to keep the clay from getting into the grooves and holes in the frame. That'll save you time in the long run.

Caution: Never get racket strings wet. Moisture can ruin them, especially if they are made of real animal gut.

Radiators

Trying to heat your home with a dirty radiator is like driving your car around with a trunkload of bricks all year. It's wasting energy. "The layer of dust that collects on radiators acts as an insulator," says John Morrill, director of operations for the American Council for an Energy-Efficient Economy in Washington, D.C., and co-author of *Consumer Guide to Home Energy Savings*. It keeps the radiator from doing its job—to radiate heat—as efficiently as it can. Regular cleaning, therefore, can help you get the most for your heating dollar.

Technique: Vacuum radiators and hot-water baseboards as part of your regular vacuuming routine. Use a brush attachment on top of the radiator and a long thin tube to get in between and behind the pipes. "The baseboards radiate heat, but they also work by convection," Morrill says. "Air circulates underneath them, is heated, and flows upward, which is why it's important to keep them clean." It is also important to keep the area around all types of radiators free from clutter and other objects so that heat will be well-distributed.

Bleed hot-water radiators (as opposed to those that circulate steam) a couple of times each heating season. "This lets trapped air out to ensure that the radiators are full of circulating hot water instead of air bubbles because there's not a lot of heat in air bubbles," explains Morrill. Using a radiator key, available at hardware stores, slowly open the small valve near the top of your radiator. Hold a heat-safe cup under the valve. When all of the air has escaped, water will trickle out. Retighten the valve.

If your radiator is rusty, put on some protective goggles and scrape the rust off with a wire brush and sandpaper. The rougher the rusted surface, the heavier-grade sandpaper you'll need. If there's no evidence of a leak, just follow the directions given here for painting. To prevent future rust, make sure that there is no rust residue. If there is, the metal can continue rusting even after it has been painted. Next, treat the metal with a rust-resistant primer, or paint, like Rust-Oleum. Use a spray can to coat the hard-to-reach areas. This is a project to do during a time of year when your heating system is not in use.

In a pinch: While it's best to vacuum your radiators year-round, it's most important during the winter months, when the radiators are in use.

Caution: Be careful when bleeding or cleaning your radiator. The water can be very hot.

Rayon

Rayon fibers may be man-made, but they're actually organic in origin—spun from cellulose extracted from tree pulp. Because of the many different rayon blends and treatments, how you clean it depends on the particular garment.

Technique: As a general rule, rayon should only be dry-cleaned. Even to remove small stains, it is best to dry-clean the whole garment. Because rayon is highly absorbent—even more so than cotton—it tends to ring and spot when it gets wet, so dabbing food spills with a moist dishcloth can worsen the situation.

"There are some garments on the market that have been resin-treated, which means that the fiber is not as liquid-absorbent," says Roman L. Horne, a technical service representative with the Lenzing Fibers Corporation in Lowland, Tennessee, one of the few rayon-makers in the United States. If a rayon garment has been resin-treated, it may be washable. Always read the clothing tag for washing instructions. If the fabric is washable, it usually means that you should wash on a gentle machine cycle or by hand. If washing by hand, gently squeeze mild lukewarm or cool suds through the fabric and rinse in lukewarm water. Do not wring it dry or stretch it while wet. Smooth or shake out the article and place it on a rust-free hanger to dry. Or, simply lay it out flat to dry. Iron the inside of the garment while it is still damp with an iron set at moderate. If you must iron the exterior, use a press cloth.

In a pinch: Because of possible chemical residues, it's best to let a professional dry-clean rayon. But keep your own spot removers, like Carbona Stain Devils or K2r, available at supermarkets, hardware stores, or discount department stores, around the house for emergency stains. Blot using the spot remover and a clean white cloth. Always check for colorfastness first on an inconspicuous area. If the spot forms a ring, take it to professional dry cleaner.

Caution: When using a spot remover, always read and follow product label carefully for proper use and safety precautions.

Records

Remember records—those grooved platters of black vinyl? They're virtually historical artifacts now, but many people are hanging on to them, and keeping them dust-free is the best way to extend their play, advises Bobbie Enke, manager at Sam Goody's Music store at the Plymouth Meeting Mall in Plymouth Meeting, Pennsylvania.

Technique: To avoid smearing perspiration and oils onto the surface, only touch the outer edges of records. Before you play a record, lay it on the turntable and clean it with a cloth-pile brush and special cleaning fluid that is available in a kit from electronics stores. The fluid should not contain silicone, which can actually help dust adhere. Or you can try the following method, suggests Enke. Dampen a lint-free cloth, like a diaper, in 2 quarts warm water in which you have dissolved a dab of mild liquid dishwashing detergent. Wring out the cloth until it's almost dry. Wipe the record in a circular motion with the cloth, says Enke. When you are finished playing the record, slide it back into its inner dust sleeve and slide the dust sleeve into the album cover so that the sleeve's opening is not facing out.

Recreational Vehicles (RVs)

Keeping your recreational vehicle clean helps protect your investment, and it improves the quality of life on the road.

Technique: First, there is the exterior. To get the road grime off, wash the RV like you would a car—using a hose, a soft brush or old cotton cloths, a bucket, and a squirt or two of liquid dishwashing detergent. Do it about once a month, less if the RV is parked for long periods of time. To clean hard-to-reach high spots, use a stepladder or a long brush, like the ones for washing windows and house siding.

"Whenever possible, we wash our RV right in the campground," says Ron Hofmeister, co-author with his wife, Barb, of *An Alternative Lifestyle: Living and Traveling Full-Time in a Recreational Vehicle.* "We carry a small aluminum ladder with us wherever we go."

Scrub the bugs and other debris off the grille and windshield using a gentle dish scrubber. Never use steel wool, which can damage the finish. Finally, don't forget to clean the roof. Usually, there is a ladder leading up the back. Be careful of your footing, and don't do it on a windy day.

If washing the outside of an RV is like washing a car, cleaning the interior is more like cleaning your house—except that it's much more cramped. "We stock multipurpose cleaners," Hofmeister says. "You don't want to carry five different bottles around. We use the same mild liquid dishwashing detergent for dishes and cleaning the RV and other things." Pack a handheld vacuum cleaner for cleaning the carpet and upholstery. Do it more often if you're parked at a campsite surrounded by dirt rather than grass or concrete.

Speed tips: Once or twice a year, put a coat of wax on your RV. That makes it much easier to clean.

In a pinch: If you're on the road, hire a professional once in a while. "Since a lot of RVers are seniors trying to enjoy themselves, it makes sense," Hofmeister says. Handymen advertise on campground brochures and bulletin boards. "They usually charge about $1 a foot to wash an RV. Once," he adds, "we called up a professional carpet

HOW I DO IT

Technique Changes with the Landscape

Ron and Barb Hofmeister, co-authors of *An Alternative Lifestyle: Living and Traveling Full-Time in a Recreational Vehicle*, spent much of the 1990s criss-crossing the United States in their recreational vehicle (RV). Here are Ron's thoughts on how location affects cleaning:

"Normally, you should wash the outside of your RV once a month, but it depends on where you are. Barb and I were down in South Padre, Texas, last winter, where the salty air drifts in from the Gulf of Mexico. I hosed the RV down every other day. It also depends on whether you're moving or sitting still. If you're moving, you're going to get dirty quicker. Sitting still, I'd give it a wash every three to four months.

"Other parts of the country can be a problem, too. In Florida during May and November, there are the lovebugs. They commit suicide on your windshield while they're mating. They're hard to get off, and because they're highly acidic—birds won't even eat them—they can hurt the paint. I use a cloth scouring pad with a little bit of detergent to remove them, but never steel wool. That'll scratch your paint."

cleaner. He came out to the RV park and cleaned it for $30. Of course, we don't have a whole lot of carpet."

Refrigerators and Freezers

Cleaning your refrigerator and freezer is important for many reasons. Wiping up spills and removing old unusable foods before they start to smell cut down on bad odors. And dusting condenser coils helps the machines run more efficiently, saving you money and lessening the chances of compressor failure, which can amount to several hundred dollars to repair on most refrigerators and freezers.

Technique: Give your refrigerator a thorough cleaning according to the manufacturer's instructions about once a month. A good time to do it is just before shopping, when the food supply is lowest. Get rid of spoiled food. Take out all removable parts—shelves, drawers, egg trays—and wash them with warm soapy water, preferably using a mild liquid dishwashing detergent. Wipe down the inside walls with a solution of 2 tablespoons baking soda to 1 quart warm water. Rinse thoroughly and dry. Wipe off jars, bottles, and other containers. "If you use the meat pan regularly, and juice leaks into it out of the meat packages, clean that out more often—basically, once a week or before you buy more meat," says Martha Reek, a senior home economist with the Whirlpool Corporation in Evansville, Indiana. Clean other compartments weekly, too, for safe storage. Then clean the folds in the gasket seal around the door with warm soapy water, rinse well, and dry. If your refrigerator has removable drain plugs, take them out and squirt warm water through the drain using a turkey baster.

The baking soda solution will help remove odors, but plastic walls and hard-to-clean crevices can absorb smells and sometimes require further effort. "Maybe a power outage occurred while you were on vacation," says Reek, "and the food in your refrigerator sat for a week." Spread a medium-size box of baking soda or a couple of inches of activated charcoal, available at aquarium supply stores, into a shallow pan and let it stand on a refrigerator shelf for a few days. Or do the same with freshly ground coffee in a cereal bowl.

Note: Freshly ground coffee may cause ice and ice cream to take on a coffee flavor. Discard these items or seal them in plastic bags to avoid an unwanted coffee taste.

If problem odors are making you consider replacing your refrigerator, try the following first. Empty your refrigerator and clean it thoroughly according to the manufacturer's instructions. It helps if you have another refrigerator to use as a backup. Pack each shelf of the smelly one with crumpled newspapers. Place a cup of water on the top shelf or sprinkle the papers lightly with water, and let it stand for five to six days while the refrigerator is running. Replace the newspaper every two days. It's inconvenient, but it works. How? The refrigeration system will pull moist air across the newspaper surfaces, which will absorb odor molecules.

Defrost freezers when the ice is approximately ¼ inch thick. This helps the motor work more efficiently. Remove the frozen items and either store them temporarily in a cooler or wrap them in several layers of newspaper to insulate them. Turn the freezer control knob to "off" or "defrost." Then let the freezer sit until defrosted. To speed up the process, place pans of hot water in the freezer. Don't chip off the ice with a sharp tool. It could damage the freezer compartment. Get rid of the melted defrost water, then wipe down the compartment with the baking soda solution, rinse, and dry. Wipe off any moisture before returning frozen goods to the freezer.

Cleaning the refrigerator or freezer's condenser coils is even more important to your appliance's well-being. Dust that collects on them acts as an insulator, causing the compressor to work harder to cycle refrigerant through the cooling system. At least twice a year—twice as often if you have pets—dust them using your vacuum cleaner's crevice attachment or a soft long-fiber bottle brush. Unplug the refrigerator before dusting. Determine what type of condenser your appliance has—a static condenser mounted on its back or a fan-cooled condenser mounted below. If the condenser is mounted below, remove the front grille cover, typically held in place by spring clips, and run the vacuum across it until the dust is gone. If it's on the back, pull the refrigerator out until you can access it fully, then vacuum up the dust.

When you put the refrigerator back in place, make sure that there is enough room in back for it to "breathe"—it needs proper air circulation to work efficiently. (Check your manual for the manufacturer's suggested amount of air-circulation space.)

Finally, if your refrigerator has a removable condenser drip pan—sometimes found beneath the appliance—wash it with warm soapy water. This kills any bacteria growing there and prevents other microscopic life forms from homesteading.

Speed tips: If you see a spill, clean it up. Regular spot-cleaning will save you time during thorough cleanings.

In a pinch: "If you don't have time one month for the thorough cleaning, use the swipe and wipe method," says Reek. Getting up spilled foods and liquids, keeping foods covered, and purging old foods will cut down on odors.

Caution: Before you clean the condenser coils on a refrigerator or freezer, unplug the appliance to avoid possible shock. Be sure to read and follow the manufacturer's instructions for cleaning and maintaining your refrigerator and freezer.

Resins

If you've ever raised a tree-climbing kid, you know all about resin. It's the sticky sap that some plants—most notably pine trees—produce to help them withstand rot and weather. It is not soluble in water, which makes washing resin out nearly impossible. A stronger solvent is required, says Ann Lemley, Ph.D., a chemist and chairman of the department of textiles and apparel at Cornell University in Ithaca, New York.

Technique: First, gently scrape off any large deposits of resin.

A CLEAN STORY

A Christmas Miracle

Ann Lemley, Ph.D., a chemist and chairman of the department of textiles and apparel at Cornell University in Ithaca, New York, explains how the perfect solution for cleaning tree resin just hit her out of the blue. "I was carrying my 11-foot-tall Christmas tree out of the house when this huge glob of tree resin dropped into my hair. I thought, 'What a pain—this isn't going to come out with shampoo.' Then I used my chemist's logic and grabbed some rubbing alcohol. Like dissolves like, and resin is similar in content to alcohol. The alcohol took the resin right out."

Then blot with rubbing alcohol, but only if the fabric is colorfast. Lay the stain facedown on a soft absorbent cloth. Apply the alcohol to another clean white cloth, and then blot from the inside of the garment to push the stain out. As the alcohol dissolves the resin, the cloth beneath catches it. For small stains, soak a cotton ball or swab in alcohol and blot the stain. When cleaning resin from carpets, always apply the alcohol to a towel, never directly onto the carpet. Otherwise, it can soak into the carpet backing or pad and attract more dirt.

Note: Before using cleaning solutions, always test them on an inconspicuous section of the stained item. Always read and follow the product label carefully for proper use and safety precautions.

Rugs

Many people think rugs are merely decorative. Yet rugs also act as filters, trapping dirt and dust and keeping it out of the air you breathe. Cleaning them regularly, therefore, is also more than a matter of cosmetics.

"A rug is kind of like a sinkful of dirty dishes," says Claudia Ramirez, former executive vice president of the Association of Specialists in Cleaning and Restoration, in Annapolis Junction, Maryland. "When you run out of space, things start spilling over."

Technique: One of the biggest causes of rug damage is dry soil, which makes up 90 percent of the trash your rug collects. (In fact, an excessively soiled rug can contain up to one pound of dirt per square yard.) The grains of soil cut away at the fibers and eventually wear them thin. The best way to keep a rug clean is by vacuuming correctly and regularly—daily for heavily trafficked areas and at least once a week for other areas. Use a quality vacuum cleaner with a good filter system and a rotating beater bar for stirring up particles. Look for HEPA (high-efficiency particulate air), HEPA-type, or electrostatic filter systems on a vacuum cleaner. Terms such as rotating brush or power head indicate a rotating beater bar on the machine. For area rugs vacuumed weekly, flip them at least once a month and vacuum the backsides. For area rugs in heavily trafficked areas, vacuum the backside once a week. To pick up hard-to-remove ground-in soil, run the vacuum against the nap of the rug. Make six to eight overlapping strokes over the dirtiest areas.

When it comes to spot-cleaning, a few major rules apply. First, blot; don't rub. When the fibers are wet, the chance for distortion of fibers increases greatly. "Think about when your hair dries funny," Ramirez says. The same thing happens to a rug—it ends up looking disheveled. And when blotting a large stain, work from the edges in. People have a tendency to dive right in and tackle the stain's center, or darkest part, but that only spreads the substance even more. The stain's tendency is to wick outward; you should contain it and work inward. If the spot has soaked all the way through a rug that is not tacked down, put another white cloth beneath and work from one side, forcing it down through to the other side. Finally, have patience. If mere blotting only pulls a portion of the stain, try blotting with the following cleaning procedures in the order indicated until the stain is removed, suggests the Association of Specialists and Cleaning and Restoration.

- First, use a small amount of spot remover. Follow the directions carefully.
- If that doesn't work try a mixture of 1 teaspoon mild dishwashing detergent that doesn't contain any strong alkalis or bleaches with 1 cup lukewarm water. Rinse by blotting with a clean white towel moistened with water. Do not overwet.
- Still no luck? Make a cleaning solution with 1 tablespoon household ammonia and ½ cup of water. Blot to rinse as above.
- Follow this with ⅓ cup white vinegar and ⅔ cup water, which neutralizes the ammonia. Blot to rinse as above.
- As a last resort, prepare a solution of powered enzyme laundry detergent (that does not contain optical brighteners) and water following directions on the detergent label. Allow the solution to remain on the stain for the time recommended on the detergent label. Blot to rinse and remove the detergent. Discard any leftover solution.

Do not overwet wall-to-wall carpeting—excessive wetting can cause the fabric backing to shrink. Sometimes this shrinkage can even cause tears in the carpet.

For many nonoil-based stains on water-treatable cotton and wool rugs, a good solution to begin with is ¼ teaspoon clear dishwashing liquid and 1 cup warm water. Pretest by dabbing a cotton swab soaked in the solution on an inconspicuous area. Try it on the various colors—if any dye bleeds onto the swab, do not continue; rather, contact a rug-cleaning professional, who might be able to set the dyes or control the bleeding. (For a referral in your area, write to the Association of Specialists in Cleaning and Restoration at 10830 Annapolis Junction Road, Suite 312, Annapolis Junction, MD 20701-1120.) If there is no dye transfer, blot the shaded area with a white cotton towel soaked in the solution. When the stain is gone, blot with a clean towel and water to remove detergent residue, which attracts dirt and dust if left to dry.

Cotton rugs or wool rugs with lengthwise cotton yarns often shrink or ripple when treated with water. When spot-cleaning with water, never pour the solution directly onto the stain; always blot with a presoaked towel. By overwetting you also risk soaking the underlying cushion. Moisture that sits in a rug mat may wick back up later—and bring with it other soils that you didn't know were down there.

Dirt is a lot easier to get out than mud. That means if your kids track mud over your Oriental runner in the hallway, let it dry first. Then lift up as much as you can with a dull knife or the handle of a spoon and vacuum the rest. If there is still a residual effect, like a

SCRUB THIS APPROACH

Rug-Cleaning Myths

A well-known household advice columnist once recommended cabbage as a rug cleaner. Shredded and worked into a carpet or rug, the cabbage was said to act as an acidic poultice, yet one that was mild enough not to cause the dyes to bleed. Today, experts shy away from techniques that leave behind fodder for bacteria and fungi.

Another myth warned *against* cleaning carpets and rugs at all. Many people, including carpet and rug retailers, believed that cleaning a rug caused it to get dirty faster. Of course, that's not true—unless, perhaps, you clean it with cabbage.

slight shading where the mud was, use the aforementioned detergent solution.

Deep clean your rug every 12 to 18 months, either by hiring a professional or doing it yourself. If you use a wet method, like shampooing, remove the furniture from the room beforehand. Or, to prevent rust or other stains from leaking into the rug, place plastic food wrap under and around the legs of chairs and tables. Follow all instructions carefully. Never exceed the recommended solution strength.

When you are finished, remove all shampoos, detergents, and moisture, which cause dirt to stick to the rug. Follow the instructions on the product label for proper use and safety precautions. Send higher-quality rugs, such as Orientals, out to a professional for in-plant cleaning. (For either an on-site or in-plant rug cleaner, look under "Carpet and Rug Cleaners" in the yellow pages of your phone book.)

Speed tips: Well-maintained vacuuming equipment improves vacuum-cleaner efficiency and speeds up the cleaning process. Don't wait for vacuum-cleaner bags to fill completely; replace or empty them once they are one-half to two-thirds full. After every third emptying, turn nondisposable collection bags inside out and sweep off excess lint and dirt. Before each use, make sure that the vacuum-cleaner filter is free of lint and dust.

In a pinch: If your time is limited, make vacuuming the heavily trafficked areas a priority.

Caution: Beware of commercial spotting products that contain optical brighteners, sometimes referred to as blueing or whitening agents. These are actually fluorescent or ultraviolet dyes that cancel out the yellowing that can occur as a result of old stains or age. They make a rug look clean, but overapplication can actually bleach out color. With repeated use, the dyes will even turn yellow.

Rust

Rust is almost like a living creature. "If you leave any little bit of rust on something, it will continue to spread," says Bob Hanbury, a remodeler and the former host of *House Calls*, a home-repair call-in radio show in Newington, Connecticut. Rust, which is the oxidation of metal, even "grows" after you've coated it with paint. Your main goal, therefore, is to get the rusted surface down to the bare metal, where there's no rust at all, and then to treat it to prevent more rusting.

Technique: Removing rust depends on what has rusted and how bad the problem is. For light rust, rub with a fine-grit sandpaper. "The more corrosion, the heavier the paper you'll need," Handbury says. "Begin with the finest paper you can—100 or even 200 grit—and if that doesn't do the job, switch to a heavier grade, like 60 or 80 grit." Because of its strong cloth backing, emery paper will also work well on metal.

For light rust, you might also try Naval Jelly, a commercial rust remover that is available at most hardware stores.

For really heavy, bumpy rust, scrape with a wire brush, or use a wire wheel on an electric drill. "The wire wheel digs a lot better than if you are just using elbow grease," says Clint Sargeant, production coordinator of the J. J. Swartz Company, a remodeling and fire restoration firm in Decatur, Illinois. "It even removes some of the surface metal so that you can be sure that you have gotten every bit of the rust."

Follow up by sanding until the metal is shiny. Feather the edge so that the repair will look neat when you paint it.

Mask deep rust holes in thick metal surfaces using a fiberglass repair kit from an auto supply store. Clean and sand the rusted area. (If possible, drill a few small holes in the affected area to help anchor the fiberglass filler.) Using a putty knife, apply the filler to the rust hole. Once it has dried, sand the surface flush before priming and painting.

After all the rust residue is gone, prime the metal with a rust-prohibitive primer, such as Derusto, and then paint it. If you don't prime it first, new rust can cause your paint layer to pop and blister. Some paints for metal come with built-in primer. Be sure to read and follow all safety instructions on the product label. Be sure that there is lots of ventilation where you use these products. Wear gloves and eye protection with shields when applying the paint.

Caution: When scraping rust with a wire brush or a wire wheel on an electric drill, wear glasses or goggles to keep rust and metal bits from injuring your eyes. Also, wear heavy work gloves. Otherwise, Sargeant says, "the wheel can jump and nick your hand."

Rust Stains

The most common rust stains appear around the drain in porcelain sinks and on clothing because of iron particles in the water.

Technique: To remove the brown rings around faucets and other light rust stains, rub with a sponge and lemon juice or white vinegar. Rinse with water. If that doesn't work, use a cloth to rub with a little kerosene. Rinse well with soap and water.

For tougher stains—on clothing, vinyl flooring, and concrete driveways—use a 5 percent solution of oxalic acid, such as Bondex, available at hardware stores. To create this solution, mix 6 ounces oxalic acid powder with a gallon of warm water. Apply the solution to the rust stain using a cloth, let it sit for five minutes, and then rinse it well with water. Repeat the process if necessary.

Caution: Oxalic acid is a skin and eye irritant in both crystal and solution form. Wear long sleeves, rubber gloves, and protective eyewear when using. Read and follow the product label carefully for proper use and safety precautions.

Chlorine bleach does not remove rust stains. It makes them darker. "Bleach is an oxidizing agent, so it oxides the rust further," says Rajiv Jain, laboratory manager of the Association of Specialists in Cleaning and Restoration in Annapolis Junction, Maryland. Hydrogen peroxide does the same thing. "On rust-stained textiles it will eat away the fabric."

Sandboxes

A sandbox is one of the few things that can be considered clean and still be filled with dirt—or, more precisely, sand. Cleaning it, then, simply means removing debris and wiping down the sides.

Technique: To wash plastic sandboxes, mix up a 10 percent solution of hot water and bleach, says Lorraine Pickruhn, owner of For Babies Only, a childcare center in Wausau, Wisconsin. Add a few squirts of liquid dishwashing or laundry detergent to the mixture. Scrub the surface with a nylon brush. Use rubbing alcohol to remove crayon and ink stains.

Rake up sticks and other large pieces of debris. For smaller debris, says Pickruhn, either sift the sand using an old kitchen strainer.

Prevention tip: Keep your sandbox covered as much as possible to keep cats and other animals from using it as a giant litter box.

Scissors

Clean scissors cut better and more precisely. Most scissors these days are made of stainless steel, and cleaning them is a snip—er, snap.

Technique: Simply wipe down stainless-steel scissors with a damp cloth or sponge. If they are sticky, oily, or covered with stubborn soil, wipe them down with a sudsy sponge.

If your scissors are not stainless steel, you must dry them completely after wiping them down. Otherwise, they can rust, which can ruin their cutting precision. Spray them with WD-40 or some other rust protectant and lubricant. Open and close them several times to work the lubricant down into the joint, says Cam Wiegmann, manager of Henry Westpfal, a New York City–based scissors sales and sharpening business founded in 1874.

If your scissors do get rusty, rub the rust away gently with a non-soapy steel wool pad. The finer the pad, the better. Be careful not to rub the cutting edge—you might dull it. Afterward, spray the scissors with WD-40.

Do not try to sharpen scissors yourself. Take them to a professional—either a hardware store that can sharpen scissors or a fabric shop.

Caution: Do not put scissors in the dishwasher. The heat might affect the temper or plastic handles.

Screens

Think of screens as air filters that stand between your living space and the outside. "Frankly speaking, most people never clean their screens," admits Charlie Brakefield, a marketing director of Phifer Wire Products in Tuscaloosa, Alabama. They should. While keeping bugs, birds, and large airborne debris out of your house, screens are exposed to the elements and collect a lot of dust and dirt in the process.

Technique: Clean your screens at least once a year. If they are the type with the vinyl-coated fiberglass mesh—commonly referred to as plastic screens—do it more often. Because of static electricity, they collect more dirt.

Remove the screens from the window frames. Usually, that involves lifting two loop latches at the bottom of the frame, pulling the bottom out, and then sliding the screen out of two U-shape grooves at the top. Dust the screens' mesh and frames with a soft-bristle brush or cloth. Mix up a sudsy solution of liquid dishwashing detergent and hot water in a bucket. Lean the screens against something outside—the side of the house or a railing. Wet the screens by spraying them with a garden hose. Scrub the grime off each side of the screen mesh with a soft-bristle nylon brush dipped into the sudsy water. Wash the frame with a sponge or cloth dipped into the suds. Rinse the screens with the hose. Wipe the excess water away with a clean cloth, and then stand the screens up to air-dry.

HOW I DO IT

Garden-Variety Cleaning

Marry Keener is the assistant director of facilities management at the University of Arizona in Tucson and a member of the technical advisory committee for *Executive Housekeeping Today* magazine. Here's how she cleans screens on her aluminum doors.

"I use the garden sprayer—the kind that looks like a jar and attaches to the end of a hose—with a few drops of liquid dishwashing detergent. This works wonders. Detergent has special surfactants that release clinging soil, particularly if it's bound by any kind of oil, like air pollution and kitchen grease. The combination of the water pressure and the detergent makes cleaning them easy."

Before replacing the screens, clean the grooves that hold them in place. Scrub the dirt from inside the grooves using a toothbrush dipped in the soapy solution. Rinse the grooves with a cloth or sponge, then dry them with a cloth. As long as the screens are down, you might as well wash the windows and window frames.

Speed tips: To make it easy to keep track of which screens fit which windows, number each frame, then give the same number to the matching screen. (Scratch the number in a corner of the screen that will be hidden once it is replaced.) Put the screws or nuts that accompany the screen in a bag and write the same number on it.

In a pinch: Hose the screens down in place (with the windows closed, of course). "Most of the airborne contaminants that collect on a screen are on the outside," Brakefield says.

Sewing Machines

A clean machine sews better and lasts longer. So keep moving parts free of lint and other debris.

Technique: At the end of every sewing session, clean the lint out of the shuttle area with a small, semistiff-bristle nylon brush. Remove the retaining ring, the shuttle hook (if you can), and the bobbin. If there is a removable throat plate, take that off as well and clean beneath it.

Then, unless your machine is self-lubricating, put a drop or two of oil onto the moving parts when putting them back into the machine. (Follow the manufacturer's instructions for oiling your particular model.) "The standard three-in-one type oil is not good," says Richard Hartmann, a technical-support manager for Brother International Corporation in Somerset, New Jersey, maker of sewing machines since 1954. "It gums up when the machine sits in the closet for a while. I use WD-40, or some other silicone-based lubricant." Do not spray the lubricant directly onto the machine, which could damage the motor or electronic components. Instead, spray a little bit on a cloth, and then wipe the cloth on the moving parts.

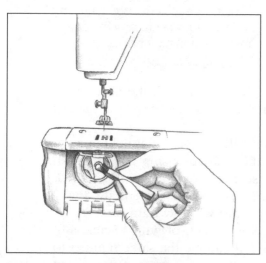

At the end of every sewing session, clean the lint out of the shuttle area with a small, semistiff-bristle nylon brush.

Keep the exterior shell free of dust with a lint-free cloth. Although all sewing machines were once made of metal, most machines these days are plastic. "Benzene and other harsh chemicals are strictly a no-no," says Hartmann. A mild all-purpose household cleaner works well to remove fingerprints and other rubbed-on grime. Again, spray it on the cloth, and then wipe the cloth on the machine.

Speed tips: If the machine

has not been cleaned in a while and is caked with dust, inside and out, use a blow-dryer (set on cool) or a hose attached to the exhaust outlet of your vacuum cleaner to blow the dust away.

In a pinch: Keep a can of compressed air handy. When you don't have time to clean the shuttle area, just give it a quick blast of air to remove any lint or leftover thread.

Caution: Before cleaning, unplug the machine. "You don't want to sew your fingers together," Hartmann says. If your wall outlet is hard to reach, simply remove the cord from the machine. Most connect there as well.

Shades

With window shades, a little light dusting will go a long way. Do it regularly, and you'll delay the need for a big cleaning job down the road.

Technique: Dust shades with a feather duster or with a vacuum cleaner attachment, like a wand or soft brush. "Do it once a week, unless you're in some place that's really dusty. Then you might have to do it more often," says Kay Weirick, director of housekeeping services at Bally's Las Vegas Hotel and a member of the technical advisory committee for *Executive Housekeeping Today* magazine.

Clean vinyl shades once or twice a year using a sponge or soft cloth and an all-purpose cleaner or solution of ¼ cup vinegar and 1 quart warm water.

There are many different types of fabric shades. Some can be washed and ironed. Others must be dry-cleaned. Read care labels or call the manufacturer for care instructions. Be careful when trying to spot-clean shades. Before cleaning, always test cleaning solutions on an inconspicuous section of the shade.

Sheds

An estimated 65 million U.S. households took part in gardening activities in 1996, according to the National Gardening Association in

Burlington, Vermont. This is one reason that sheds have become a backyard fixture. The other is that we can't fit one more thing in the garage. From a cleaning standpoint, sheds don't need sanitation and sparkle; they need to be orderly and free of clutter. The average shed measures about 10 feet by 8 feet—giving you 80 square feet of floor space and nearly 300 square feet of wall space for storage. Your goal is to have a designated place for everything as well as some room to maneuver.

Technique: Maintain the exterior of the shed according to its building materials. If it has windows, wash them once a year. If it has siding, wash it down with the hose every spring. If it has a wood floor, sweep it with a broom regularly, and paint it to protect it from dirt, oils, and chemicals.

Generally, prefabricated metal sheds are maintenance-free. Wood structures, on the other hand, may require painting after several years and are prone to uninvited visits from curious creatures. Check wooden sheds in fall and spring for holes along the roof and foundation where little critters could squeeze in to snack on seeds or nest in your potting soil.

"Have a place for everything and everything in its place," says Linda Joan Smith, author of *The Potting Shed.*

To maximize use of limited space, map out a storage plan on paper and follow these tips.

- Store grass seed, garden seeds, and birdseed in sealed airtight containers that cannot be penetrated by animal teeth or spilled over.
- Hang Peg-Board, hooks, and shelves to utilize vertical storage space for small tools and implements. But don't put them too close to the door, where you're likely to knock things down coming in and out of the shed.
- Leave enough floor space to perform simple maintenance chores, such as changing the string line on a trimmer.
- Store potting mixes in sealed plastic bins to keep soil moist and workable. The bins also stack nicely.

Speed tips: To find what you need fast, rotate equipment with the seasons. Large items like lawn mowers and snow throwers can trade positions, depending on the time of year.

In a pinch: Need extra storage? The space above and between the trusses can be used to hold lightweight seldom-used items.

Caution: Storage sheds are attractive play areas for children. Keep sharp objects securely out of reach. Install a locked cabinet for lawn and garden chemicals to avoid accidental poisoning of children or pets.

A CLEAN STORY

Americans Now Dig Their Garden Sheds

The utilitarian beginnings of today's popular backyard sheds date back nearly 1,000 years. The first garden sheds were built in the Middle Ages, when the monasteries of Europe kept extensive gardens and needed a place to store tools, according to Linda Joan Smith, author of *The Potting Shed*.

In America, potting sheds became popular in the late 1800s when Victorian gardens were all the rage. By the early twentieth century, however, the romantic potting shed had been relegated to just a toolshed as Americans got away from elaborate English gardens and began just growing lawns. Today, the role of the backyard shed is evolving again as gardeners are looking at sheds as more than storage areas. "It's no longer just a place to keep the lawn mower. It's a place where gardeners spend time," says Smith.

If you have a pool, never store pool chemicals in the same shed with lawn and garden supplies. Keep them in a separate storage shed designated solely for pool chemicals. Or dedicate a separate cabinet for them in your garage. Mark the area clearly with a sign that indicates its contents. Granulated pool chemicals are extremely flammable, so make sure that you rinse containers thoroughly before disposing of them.

Shells

When you pick up a shell on the beach, clean it as soon as possible. Remove any decaying flesh which, besides smelling unpleasant, could discolor and ruin the shell. Many beautiful specimens have been tossed away because the collector didn't realize that the meat had to be cleaned out of the shell.

Technique: Freezing is one of the easiest ways to clean a shell. But you have to be patient because the freezing and thawing process is gradual and takes four days to effectively clean the shell and prevent it from cracking, according to R. Tucker Abbott in the book *Kingdom of the Seashell*.

Place your mollusks in a plastic bag, tied shut, in the lower part of your refrigerator for a few hours. Then transfer to the freezer for two to three days. To thaw, place the bag back in the lower part of the refrigerator for 12 hours or so, and then soak it in cold water. When completely thawed, which usually takes about 24 hours, the meats of most univalves can be removed by pulling on them in an unwinding corkscrew fashion, using a fork or a bent safety pin.

Once the flesh is removed from the interior, clean the exterior of shells by brushing with warm soapy water. Shell exteriors can also be cleaned by soaking them overnight in full-strength bleach. To give shells a brighter color, sparingly apply a coat of baby oil.

Speed tips: Clean new shells in less time by boiling in freshwater or salt water. Because rapid temperature changes will cause minute cracks in the surface of shiny shells, start with warm water, not hot water. Boil bivalves, such as clam shells, for 1 to 2 minutes and univalves, such as snails, for 6 to 10 minutes. Let the pot stand for an hour to bring the temperature down slowly. You may add small quantities of cold water to speed up the cooling process. Once cool enough to handle, follow the procedure outlined above for removing meat from the shell.

Commercial shellers dump live smelly shells in a solution of one part water to one part chlorine bleach to dissolve the flesh.

In a pinch: If you discover the specimen of a lifetime while on a trip to a remote island paradise but don't have access to a freezer or a stove, bury the specimen in a bucket of dry sand with the open end of the shell pointing down. The decaying matter will drain out without harming the shell.

Caution: Do not soak shells in plain water to clean them. Decaying animal matter circulating in the water will remove the natural color from the shell.

Using muriatic acid, a hydrochloric acid often used to clean up mortar spills on brick, is not recommended. Even a mild 10 percent solution is corrosive enough to damage shells.

Shoes

In the 8,000 steps that each one of us takes in an average day, our shoes take a beating. But whether it's your finest leather dress shoes or a $10 pair of canvas sneakers, shoe care professionals recommend applying a protective water and stain repellent to the up-

MONEY-SAVERS

Five Steps for Making Your Shoes Last Longer

Give them a day off. Never wear the same shoes two days in a row. Let them have a day to dry out from the perspiration from your feet. This also allows footwear to spring back into shape and decompress from a day of wearing.

Invest in cedar shoe trees. Using shoe trees can double the life of your shoes by allowing them to retain their shape. Cedar shoe trees have an added benefit over plastic. Their unique wicking action absorbs the perspiration deposited in your shoes each day and the acids and salts that accompany it, according to the Shoe Service Institute of America in Baltimore. Don't forget to remove the trees after a day or so to allow for air circulation.

Polish new shoes before wearing them. Brand-new, just-out-of-the-box leather shoes are especially prone to scuffing and scratching, so protect them with polish.

Do daily maintenance. Brush or wipe all shoes after each wearing.

Replace heels at the first sign of wear. Worn heels not only can ruin your shoes beyond repair but also can affect your posture.

pers of all shoes when they are new. "This puts a protective layer between the dirt and the shoe," says Mitch Lebovic, editor of *Shoe Service* magazine in Baltimore.

Athletic

Technique: Remove laces and inserts and rinse shoes with water. Use a sneaker shampoo or any neutral cleaner, such as liquid dishwashing detergent, and a soft brush to remove dirt. Rinse and allow to air-dry stuffed with absorbent white paper towels. Use a cedar shoe tree to reshape the shoe.

If shoes are scuffed, apply shoe whitening product to restore the color. Dusting with baby powder after you polish will prevent it from rubbing off.

The biggest problem in caring for athletic shoes is controlling odor. Each foot has 125,000 sweat glands, which deposit up to $\frac{1}{4}$ cup sweat into each shoe every day. The foam construction of athletic insoles provides an ideal breeding ground for odor-causing bacteria. Lebovic suggests using over-the-counter products that will counteract the odor-causing bacteria, such as Dr. Scholl's Odor Destroyers Deodorant Spray. Such products also are available as powders and insoles. But read the label to be sure that you're not buying a product that will simply mask the odor.

In a pinch: To get scuffs off white leather, rub with nongel toothpaste, rinse, wipe, and let dry.

Caution: Shoe manufacturers advise against placing athletic shoes in the washer. The agitation breaks down the adhesives of the shoe and damages the leather. When cleaning, do not use solvents, harsh abrasives, or bleach on shoes.

Canvas

Technique: You can throw old-fashioned canvas sneakers in the washer; however, shoe-care experts say that this isn't the best way to get them clean. It ruins their shape and often doesn't do the job of removing the dirt thoroughly. If canvas shoes are sealed properly when they are new, says Lebovic, dirt can essentially be sponged off. Upholstery cleaner works well to lift dirt from the fibers. Spray on and sponge off. For white rubber soles, use whitewall tire cleaner. Always allow shoes to air-dry. The heat of the dryer will shrink them.

Speed tips: Use putty-type wallpaper cleaner, available at home center stores, to lift dirt off canvas shoes.

In a pinch: Spray starch or an ordinary fabric protector, like Scotchgard, will protect your canvas shoes from dirt.

Leather

Technique: A good pair of men's leather shoes can be resoled seven times if you take care of the uppers properly. Follow this four-step process recommended by the Shoe Service Institute of America in Baltimore for cleaning and maintaining leather shoes.

1. Clean. Remove loose dirt from the shoe with a soft brush. Clean with a cream leather cleaner.

2. Condition. Once the leather is clean, apply a conditioner, which prevents cracking and puts oil back into the shoes to make them last longer.

3. Polish. Polishes renew pigments and cover scuffs, provide shine, and protect and condition the leather. They come in three forms: liquid, paste, and cream. Liquid is easiest to apply but has the least staying power. Pastes provide the best coverage and a superior shine, but are not available in a wide variety of colors. Creams offer a happy medium between the other two. Apply polish in circular motions. Buff with a cloth. Apply a second coat and buff with a second clean cloth. For an all-out gleaming shine, apply an additional coat of paste wax with a wet cloth. Let shoes dry and buff.

4. Weatherproof. Mink oil, beeswax, and silicone are some of the choices available for weatherproofing sealants. While polish provides some sealing qualities, if you work in a wet, muddy, or oily environment, you should weatherproof your shoes.

In a pinch: If your shoes get soaked from the rain, the best thing to do is put in shoe trees and allow them to air-dry at room temperature. Never put them near a heat source. It will dry and crack the leather.

Caution: Never polish leather shoes before you have cleaned them. If you do, the polish will embed the dirt in the grain of the leather.

Shower Stalls

If you stick to a simple weekly cleaning routine and follow a few daily preventive measures, you'll keep those three shower-polluters—soap scum, mildew, and hard-water deposits—out of your bathroom for good.

Technique: Remove soap and shampoos from shower. Spray shower walls, fixtures, floor, and the curtain or door thoroughly with an all-purpose cleaner. "Let the cleaner do the work for you," says Margaret Dasso, owner of the Clean Sweep, a professional cleaning service in Lafayette, California, and co-author of *Dirt Busters*. Dasso recommends using Tilex Soap Scum Remover. Working from top to bottom, wipe the shower with a nylon scrubber pad. Use a toothbrush or grout brush on any stubborn stains or buildup. Rinse with warm water and dry with a soft cloth. Shine chrome fixtures with rubbing alcohol and a dry cloth. (See Hard-Water Deposits on page 212, Rust on page 321, and Soap Scum on page 348 for specific cleaning techniques.)

To retard the formation of soap scum and mineral deposits, finish off by applying a coat of lemon oil furniture polish to the entire shower area. Pour lemon oil polish onto a cloth and rub evenly over shower walls.

Speed tips: Use a sponge mop reserved strictly for shower cleaning to avoid kneeling and bending.

Rinse the shower after each use to prevent soap film and hard-water deposits from forming. Before you dry off after a shower, dry the shower itself, the doors, and chrome fixtures with a squeegee or

MONEY-SAVERS

Your Secret Weapon against Mildew

You don't need costly specialized cleaners to get rid of black grimy mildew growing in your shower. Household bleach works just fine and will kill mildew in minutes, says cleaning pro Margaret Dasso, owner of the Clean Sweep, a professional cleaning service in Lafayette, California, and co-author of *Dirt Busters*. But avoid these common mistakes when working with bleach.

- Never use full-strength bleach on tile showers. It will erode the grout. The Clorox Company recommends using a solution of about ¾ cup bleach per gallon of water.
- Don't skip the rinse cycle when working with bleach. Bleach residue will damage the grout.
- Wear old clothes, and use care not to let bleach solution splatter onto carpets or towels.

chamois. This one-minute job will save you tons of time and aggravation by preventing mildew, soap scum, and hard-water deposits. The benefits are twofold. Not only will your shower look cleaner but also it will actually be cleaner since keeping it dry also prevents germ growth. Germs will begin to die after two hours on a dry surface, while a wet surface provides a breeding ground for bacteria colonies.

If you can't bring yourself to squeegee in the nude, simply leaving the shower doors or curtain open after use will help to prevent mildew by allowing air to circulate. Let the shower curtain hang loosely enough that it doesn't trap moisture in the folds.

In a pinch: If you don't have lemon oil furniture polish, any type of furniture polish or car wax can be substituted.

Caution: Avoid slips and falls. Do not apply wax or polish to the shower floor.

Shutters

Once they get really dirty, there's no easy way to clean shutters. Essentially, each one of those of pivoting little louvers that look so charming on your window has to be cleaned.

Technique: It takes a lot of water and scrubbing to reach all the cracks and crevices of shutters, so, if possible, remove the shutters from the window—they should lift right off the hinges—and work at a towel-lined countertop or table. Spray the entire shutter with all-purpose cleaner, taking care to reach all the crevices. Let the solution soak for a few minutes before cleaning each slat. Working from the top to the bottom, scrub each louver with a terry towel or grout brush. "You need a little brush of some sort because as soon as you spray the shutters, all the dirt is going to flow to the cracks and crevices," says Carol Seelaus, a speed-cleaning instructor at Temple University in Philadelphia and owner of Somebody's Gotta Do It, a professional cleaning service.

Spray loosened dirt and cleaning solution away with clean water. Dry with a clean cloth. Dry hard-to-reach areas by applying a clean absorbent cloth wrapped around a wooden spoon handle.

Speed tips: Keep shutters well-dusted and you won't have to scrub, says Seelaus. The longer dust and dirt are allowed to sit on a surface, the harder it is to just suck it up in the vacuum. Once a month, dust front and back sides of the louvers with a canister vacuum. Using the dust brush attachment, go up and down the shutter as well as side to side to vacuum dust in hard-to-reach areas. City dwellers should dust more frequently.

In a pinch: Use an old toothbrush in place of a grout brush. If you don't have a wooden spoon, use a small plastic or wooden ruler instead.

Siding

Do you want to give your house a face-lift and maybe avoid a paint job in the bargain? Clean the siding. Dirt from pollution, dust, pollen, trees, and even rain accumulates on siding, especially on the underside. If a chalky look on your aluminum siding is your only complaint, a good scrubbing may eliminate the need to call in the housepainters.

If the siding is only lightly soiled, even a heavy rain may remedy the problem. But in most cases you'll have to clean it every year or so, especially if you live in an urban or wooded area.

Technique: Start at the bottom and work up to the top, says the Vinyl Siding Institute in Washington, D.C. For light soil and surface dirt, spray a section of siding with the garden hose and then lightly scrub with a long-handle, soft-bristle brush. Be sure to scrub the underside where dirt tends to build up. Follow with a second rinse to

The Dark Side:
Getting Rid of Mold, Mildew, and Moss

Mold, mildew, and moss are most likely to appear on the sides of your house where there's high humidity and little sunlight—the north side of the house in particular. Mildew and mold may appear as black spots on the surface of the siding, while moss will show up as patches of green.

To remove it and discourage new growth of this dirty plant matter on aluminum and wood siding, scrub with the following solution recommended by PPG Coatings, a Pittsburgh manufacturer of the factory finishes applied to aluminum siding: 1/3 cup laundry detergent, 2/3 cup trisodium phosphate, 1 quart liquid household bleach, and 3 quarts water.

Using medium pressure, scrub with a soft-bristle brush and rinse well with clear water. Follow the proportions exactly—a stronger concentration of ingredients could damage the painted finish on the siding.

Do not use solutions containing bleach or organic solvents on vinyl siding. They could damage the surface. Instead, the Vinyl Siding Institute in Washington, D.C., recommends using a solution of 30 percent vinegar and 70 percent water, or an all-purpose nonabrasive cleaner such as Fantastik.

remove the dirt loosened by the brush. Work in sections that are the size of a comfortable arm's reach.

If you live in an area where heavy industrial deposits dull the siding, scrub with a solution of household detergent and water, then rinse with the garden hose.

Speed tips: Skip the scrubbing and use a pressure washer to clean the siding in minutes instead of hours. Pressure washers, which connect to your garden hose, remove dirt with water that is propelled at a pressure of 1,000 to 2,400 pounds per square inch. You can pick one up at a rental store for less than $75.

In a pinch: If you don't have time to scrub the entire house, spot-clean the areas that are dirtiest. Look for soiled areas on a shady portion of the house, smoke residue around the chimney area, or dirt splatters around the base of the house.

Caution: If it's necessary to use a ladder to clean the house, wear nonslip shoes.

Cleaners containing organic solvents, such as chlorine bleach, liquid grease remover, nail polish remover, or furniture polish, can mar the surface of vinyl siding.

Silk

Silk has been a symbol of elegance and beauty since it was discovered 4,000 years ago. It is the strongest of all natural fibers. A filament of silk is stronger than a like filament of steel, according to the International Silk Association in New York City. So it seems strange that when these fibers are woven, they create a fabric known for its delicacy—a fabric that in some forms will wrinkle and pucker at the first drop of water. Many of us shy away from silk garments, believing that they have to be dry-cleaned (and silk is the most expensive fabric to dry-clean, aside from suede and leather).

But this is not always the case. In response to consumer demand, manufacturers are producing garments from many types of silk that can be laundered at home. Before you buy a garment, find out what type of silk it is. Spun silk, the fabric most often used for lingerie, and untreated crepe de chine, which has a soft flowing texture, are natural silks and can be hand-washed, according to the International Silk Association. On the other hand, chemically treated silks, such as taffeta and treated crepe de chine can be damaged by water and should be dry-cleaned.

The labels on many items of silk clothing say "Dry-Clean Only," even though some may be safe to wash. If you don't know whether to plunge that $80 blouse into a basin of water, test the garment for colorfastness. If the color runs or changes, do not hand-wash the item. How do you know if your garment is colorfast? Dab a cotton swab moistened with cool water on a small inside corner of a seam, says the International Silk Association. Then press the spot on a white cloth or paper towel using a warm iron. If the silk doesn't leave a color, it can be washed.

Technique: The International Silk Association recommends the following method for hand-washing silk. Make a thick suds in lukewarm water with mild white soap flakes. Gently agitate by squeezing suds through the silk. Don't scrub; silk fibers will abrade easily. Rinse two or three times in tepid water until the water is clear. Roll the garment in a bath towel to remove as much water as possible, and then hang it indoors to dry away from strong sun or heat until it is damp-dry.

Only soak natural silk for three to five minutes, and "washable" silk no longer than two minutes. Alkalies such as soaps, shampoos, detergents and even toothpaste can cause color change or loss in silks, according to the International Fabricare Institute in Silver Spring, Maryland.

MONEY-SAVERS

Storing Silks to Make Them Last

It's beautiful and it's expensive, so naturally, silk is an investment that you want to last.

"Silk is supremely lasting," says the International Silk Association in New York City. "The beautiful fabrics remaining to us from ancient days attest to silk's almost uncanny resistance to aging."

Follow these tips to get lasting wear from your silk.

- Always hang silk on padded hangers and cover with plastic. The continuous fibers of silk can be damaged by folding.
- Never use mothballs. Silk will absorb the odor, and it's impossible to wash out.
- Store silk away from light, which will damage the fibers and cause dyes to fade.

Press silk garments with an iron on the lowest setting while the garment is still damp. Always press silks on the "wrong" side with a low iron. Finish seams and collars on the right side with a pressing cloth to protect the fabric.

Spots and stains are best left to a professional dry cleaner.

Speed tips: Washable silk can be safely laundered in most home washers on the gentle setting in warm water with a nonalkaline detergent or mild soap, according to the International Fabricare Institute. Hang it right away to reshape and prevent wrinkles.

In a pinch: Localized areas of color loss caused by spot-cleaning can sometimes be remedied by treating the area with steam. Hold the spotted area over steam from a teakettle, or mist it lightly with a steamer for three to five seconds, says the International Fabricare Institute. But be careful not to get the fabric wet. Color should be restored within 30 seconds.

Caution: Regardless of the type of silk, experts recommend dry cleaning for very fine garments such as evening dresses, bright multicolored silks, embroidered silk, and those with a raised pattern. Here are other cautions about cleaning silk.

- Alcohol can cause fabric dyes in silk to bleed. Allow perfumes, hair sprays, and other toiletries containing alcohol to dry before you dress. Spills from alcoholic beverages should be removed as soon as possible by a professional dry cleaner.
- Salts from perspiration can severely weaken and stain silk. If you perspire heavily, wear dress shields with silk garments. Clean perspiration-stained garments as soon as possible.
- Never use chlorine bleach on silk. It will cause permanent damage to the fabric.

- Test crepe de chine for colorfastness on a small piece of hem or cuff. Untreated crepe de chine is safe to wash, while chemically treated crepe de chine will streak in water. Most labels won't tell whether the fabric is treated or untreated.
- Printed silk has a clarity and depth that other fabrics cannot match. Bleeding and dye migration is a common problem, however. Never wash light-colored silks with bright-colored silks. Always test multicolored garments for colorfastness before laundering. And don't allow them to remain in a damp or wet condition for prolonged periods.
- Dry and store silks away from any light source to prevent fading.

Silver

The villain here is silver sulfide. If that's too much of a mouthful, just call it by its common name: tarnish. It's the black film that forms when silver comes into contact with sulfur in the air, the carbon in rubber, or even the acids and salts in certain foods.

Technique: Using your silver regularly will help keep tarnish at a minimum. The best way to clean silver is the old-fashioned way—with a good-quality, antitarnish silver polish and a soft cloth, says Robert M. Johnston, a consultant in Baltimore who has worked in the silverware industry for more than 50 years. Silver is the most reflective of all metals, and buffing with silver polish produces a rich luster that enhances the beauty of the piece and retards the development of tarnish.

Apply polish with a soft damp cloth or a sponge. Rub vigorously to remove tarnish. You will see the cloth turn black as tarnish is removed. Polish thoroughly and rinse right away with soap and warm water. Dry with a soft towel to avoid water spots.

When storing silver for an extended time, seal it from air and moisture, protect it from bumps and scratches, and remember to check it at least once a year for signs of tarnishing. Store it in flannel antitarnish bags, which are available at jewelry stores, to prevent the silver from oxidizing. Then place it in zippered plastic bags. This is the most important step in storing your silver because it isolates the metal from environmental factors that cause tarnish and corrosion, according to J. A. Wright and Company in Keene, New Hampshire, manufacturers of metal polishes.

SCRUB THIS APPROACH

Skip the Dip

You've seen it hyped on infomercials. A coal-black silver teapot is dipped in an instant cleaner and—voilà!—it comes out gleaming. According to experts, though, instant chemical cleaners should not be used on fine silver.

"Most dips are a chemical process that eats away at the top of the silver. Repeated use will erode the finish," says Robert M. Johnston, a consultant in Baltimore who has worked in the silverware industry for more than 50 years.

And don't bother with electrolytic cleaning—a process that uses an aluminum plate or foil and a combination of boiling water, baking soda, and salt to lift tarnish off the silver, according to Johnston. The process tends to dull the finish and may remove antique shading.

Speed tips: If you use your silver frequently and rotate place settings, you will only need to polish it once or twice a year. Less polishing will spare the thin coating on silver plate from being rubbed away by too-frequent polishing. Cleaning cloths impregnated with rouge are good for touch ups, but not if the piece is heavily tarnished.

In a pinch: "If you have guests at your front door and a speck of tarnish on your silver serving spoon, you can usually buff it out with toothpaste," says Johnston. Apply it with a damp cloth and rub the spot. "This is good if you're in a bind but is not really a very efficient way to clean anything more than a spot here or there."

If you don't have flannel antitarnish bags, it is acceptable to store your silver in zippered plastic bags alone. Just make sure that the bags are protected from bumps and abrasions. Do not use plastic cling wrap, which can stick to the silver and can be tough to remove.

For black spots that are etched in, take the piece to a silver repair shop or a jeweler to be buffed.

Caution: Chemical dips contain thiourea, a cancer-causing chemical. The colorless and odorless chemical can be absorbed through your skin, so wear protective gloves if you choose to use these products. And completely rinse silver, countertops, and sink to remove any traces of the chemical. Besides being harmful for you, chemical dips can also damage the finish of your silver, says Johnston. Also keep these tips in mind.

- Wash silver that has come in contact with mustard, salt, or ketchup right away to prevent pitting and tarnishing.

- Don't wrap silver in newspaper or rubber bands. Both contain carbon, which reacts with the silver, turns it black, and eats into the surface if left on the piece.

Sinks

Chances are that when you think of household germs, you think of toilets. In turns out, though, that sinks—in particular, kitchen sinks, not toilets—are one of the most germ-ridden areas of the house. A University of Arizona study found that bacteria tend to be concentrated in the sink, its drain, and the sponge or dishcloth. Germs that you expect to find on a toilet rim, such as fecal coliform, were seldom found there. But in the kitchen, they were everywhere. The smooth surface of a sink is a landscape of nooks and crannies from a microbe's perspective. The trick to cleaning is to knock them loose and discourage them from remultiplying.

Technique: Ordinary scrubbing with a disinfectant will dissolve food particles and remove clinging microbes. Using a new or sterilized sponge, scrub the sides and bottom of sink. (Hint: You can sterilize your sponge in the dishwasher or by soaking it for five minutes in a solution of ¾ cup bleach in 1 gallon water.) Follow up with a sanitizing rinse with a similar solution of diluted household bleach, which will destroy even the most tenacious hangers-on. Let the solution stay wet in your sink for five minutes. For stains, porcelain and stainless steel can tolerate light abrasive cleaners such as liquid cleansers or baking soda.

Speed tips: For a quick cleanup, spray the entire sink with a disinfectant cleaner and wipe it off with a paper towel.

In a pinch: Rinse sink with plain water and dry with paper towels. Whenever bacteria find a site harboring moisture and food, they will set up housekeeping and grow, says Edmund A. Zottola, Ph.D., professor emeritus of food microbiology at the University of Minnesota in St. Paul. Resident bacteria can only survive a few hours on a dry surface.

To remove stains from a porcelain sink, fill it with warm water and add a few tablespoons of chlorine bleach. Let the solution stand for an hour and rinse. If the stain persists, line the sink with paper towels, saturate them with chlorine bleach and let soak for a half-hour. Wear gloves and make sure that the area is well-ventilated when using this technique.

Caution: Don't use abrasives on cultured marble, fiberglass, or plastic, which will scratch the sink and cause it to become porous and prone to stains and germ growth. Always read product labels for proper use and safety precautions.

Skis

Okay, sometimes you *want* things to go downhill in a hurry. Keep your skis clean, and they will.

Technique: Wipe off surface dirt with a damp cloth. If the snow was sparse and they're muddy, hose them off. Stubborn spots and old wax can be removed with a base cleaner, available at ski shops, says Bret Williamson, rental and repair shop supervisor at Killington Ski Resort in Killington, Vermont. In a well-ventilated area, spray the cleaner on the skis and wipe them with a clean cloth. Let them air-dry for a few minutes.

Binding mechanisms on today's skis are sealed and no longer need cleaning or lubrication. In fact, don't put anything on them at all, says Williamson. Ski manufacturers grease and lubricate the bindings in the factory. Products like WD-40 or silicone sprays can break down the grease and destroy lubrication.

All other maintenance is best left to a trained technician.

In a pinch: To prevent maintenance headaches, like rust, wipe your skis completely dry after using them.

Caution: Always read product labels for proper use and safety precautions.

Skylights

If you want to let the sun shine in, skylights need to be cleaned once a year or so. If neglected, skylights—in particular, the Plexiglas bubble type—can be permanently damaged by droppings from trees, the growth of mildew or moss, and even ordinary rain and airborne dirt that can bind to the glass after it bakes in the sun for a period of time. "Let it go long enough and you'll have to replace it," says Karen

J. Blough, who, as owner of Blough's Cleaning Services in Reading, Pennsylvania, has been washing skylights since 1989.

While fingerprints aren't usually problem on skylights, interiors need to be cleaned as well since they develop a dirty film from cooking, fireplaces, and dust in the home.

Technique: Inside, move any furniture out of the way and lay a plastic cloth under the skylight to catch any drips. Because they're most frequently installed in vaulted ceilings at an angle, skylights can be difficult to reach. Use a professional-quality washer-and-squeegee tool (available at janitorial supply stores) attached to an extension wand. Use a six- or eight-foot stepladder under the skylight to reach it with the extended squeegee. Climb the ladder and remove the screen, if necessary. Clean the screen with a vacuum or brush. Dip the tool in a solution of ¼ cup sudsy ammonia and a squirt of liquid dishwashing detergent in 1 gallon water, and squeeze out the excess. Apply the solution to the skylight with firm even strokes. Squeegee off. Wipe around the edges with an absorbent cloth draped over the end of your extension wand to remove any drips.

Outside, place a ladder at the lowest point on the house and climb onto the roof. With a handheld squeegee, use the same ammonia solution and cleaning technique. Rub any stubborn spots with a nylon scrubber. Mop up any drips with a soft cloth.

Plexiglas bubble skylights should only be cleaned with soft cotton cloths to avoid scratching.

Speed tips: New windows have a protective film on them from the manufacturer and may need a stronger ammonia solution if it's a first-time cleaning. "Otherwise you'll get streaks and may end up cleaning it two or three times," says Blough. She recommends adding small amounts of ammonia or detergent to the solution until the glass comes out streak-free.

If you can reach the exterior surface of your skylight with a garden hose, give it a quick spray if you happen to be watering the flowers or washing the car.

In a pinch: If you don't have a strip washer, apply cleaning solution with a sponge mop. Make sure that it's clean and free of soap residue.

An old broom handle can usually be used to extend the reach of your squeegee.

Caution: Use care when climbing ladders and cleaning windows on the roof. Avoid loose or flowing clothing, and wear shoes with nonskid soles. It's a good idea to wear safety glasses to protect your eyes from cleaning solution drips.

Slate

Slate is a hard dense rock formed from compressed shale or clay. Usually a medium gray, it has a tendency to split into long thin planes, which are then cut for use as roofing shingles, floor tiles, and billiard tabletops. Slate is an extremely durable easy-care material that looks best when allowed to develop its own lustrous patina without being coated with waxes or shiny sealants.

Technique: Slate should be protected from stains with a stone impregnator, which chemically closes the pores of the stone and hardens the surface. Like water filling a sponge, the impregnator fills the porous cells of the stone so that stains will not penetrate. Apply the product in two coats with a long-bristle brush, as if you were painting it on the slate. Wait 5 to 10 minutes between applications. Remove any excess with a clean, dry terry towel.

Regular cleaning should include frequent dust mopping or vacuuming to remove dirt particles, which dull and scratch the surface. Damp mop occasionally with a neutral no-rinse cleaner designed for stone. These cleaners provide a conditioning action, which is important to maintain the natural beauty of the stone. Commercial cleaners, which are typically found on the grocery store shelves, have a pH between 8 and 9 and are designed for glazed tiles and vinyl flooring. They are too harsh for slate and, over time, will dull and discolor the natural luster of the stone.

Speed tips: "An entrance mat is the most basic requirement for any stone floor. Without it, even the best maintenance system will be unsuccessful," says Detlev Wolske, president of HMK Stone Care Sys-

SCRUB THIS APPROACH

With Slate, Keep It Simple

People often put wax or shiny coatings on slate floors. But in the long run, this approach is going to make the floor look worse, not better, says Detlev Wolske, president of HMK Stone Care System in San Francisco.

Waxes and surface coatings do not adhere well to slate and will rub off quickly from ordinary foot traffic. The floor will look good initially, but after a week or so, scratches will begin to show where the coating has chipped off.

If you want a shinier floor, mopping with a neutral, no-rinse stone cleaner and occasional buffing will develop a natural scratch-resistant luster.

tem in San Francisco. The entrance mat collects dirt and grit from the bottom of shoes and prevents them from scratching the floor. The less dirt and grit on the floor, the less you have to clean.

In a pinch: Plain water can be used to damp mop your floor occasionally. It won't leave a dulling film on the stone, although the chlorine, minerals, and salts in ordinary tap water are capable of staining a stone floor over time.

Caution: It's an old trade secret that's good to know: Don't use vinegar on slate floors. It will dull the floor overall.

Sleeping Bags

Sleeping bags are filled with either goose down or a synthetic down imitator. Down bags will need to be cleaned more often to keep the fill fluffy and insulating.

Technique: Clean only when necessary. Although they're made for roughing it in the great outdoors, they aren't cut out for the rigors of a normal household washer with an agitator. Take them to a Laundromat and wash in warm water on the gentle cycle in a front-loading, oversize commercial washer. Down bags should be washed with a mild detergent, according to the American Down Association in Sacramento, California. Run the bag through a second cycle without detergent to thoroughly rinse. Dry on a warm gentle setting. Be patient. Down bags dry slowly. If not dried thoroughly, a down bag will mat down and mildew.

Speed tips: To keep cleaning to a minimum, sleep with a folded sheet inside the bag and keep it off the bare ground. When camping, shake it out hard every day and hang it to air out. Store sleeping bags outside their stuff sacks to avoid overcompression of their fill. Spot-clean stains and spots before resorting to the washing machine.

In a pinch: A sleeping bag can be washed in a bathtub if a commercial Laundromat is not accessible. Care must be taken when handling the wet bag so that you do not rip the interior baffling. Be sure to rinse it thoroughly.

Caution: Do not dry-clean sleeping bags. The solvents will strip down feathers of their natural oils and are very toxic. If a care label insists on dry-cleaning, air the bag out for at least a week before sleeping in it again.

To avoid rips in the baffling, gently transfer wet bags to the dryer rolled in a ball.

Sliding-Door Tracks

A buildup of dirt and debris makes rough sliding for your door. And that's not all: It also attracts and holds water and moisture, which can damage the tracks of the slider or the door itself. To have a smoothly operating door, remember to clean the bottom and top tracks of the slider.

Technique: Vacuum any loose dirt out of the track, and spray with an all-purpose cleaner. Let it soak for a few minutes, then wipe loosened grime with a cloth. If your fingers are too big to get into the grooves comfortably, try wrapping a piece of cloth around a wooden spoon handle and run it back and forth along the tracks. You may have to repeat the process a few times to get sparkling results. Once clean, run the door back and forth a few times to dislodge any additional dirt from the glides or wheels. Then give the tracks a final wipe.

Speed tips: Clean regularly with the dusting or crevice tool of the vacuum cleaner, according to Caradon Doors and Windows, a sliding glass door manufacturer in Norcross, Georgia.

Caution: Lubricate the tracks after cleaning with a good silicone spray lubricant, which does not attract dirt and trash. Keep in mind that only a light coating is needed.

Smoke

 EMERGENCY ACTION
If there's a fire in your home, or if you don't know the source of the smoke, get everyone out and call the fire department. If there is no fire, open windows and doors to air out the house immediately. This will quickly lower odor levels and reduce the amount of smoke residue and the amount of cleanup necessary.

When the fire is out and the air has cleared, the filth that's left behind is called smoke residue. And while the dirt and damage will be most prevalent where the fire occurred, it usually permeates the whole house, requiring cleaning of clothing, drapes, carpeting, and upholstery to eliminate the foul odor. Depending on what has burned, the residue may be dry particles, smeary flakes, or even sticky liquids. Protein fires, such as a forgotten pot roast in the oven, leave a clear residue with a yellowish, pinkish cast and are typically characterized by their obnoxious odor.

Smoke and soot are often mistakenly lumped together as one problem. Smoke, however, is far more difficult to clean up since it is driven by heat, says Martin L. King, a restoration consultant in Arlington, Virginia, and technical advisor to the National Institute of Disaster Restoration in Annapolis, Maryland. It permeates fibers and invades closed areas. Unless you're attempting a minor cleanup, smoke cleanup is best left to professional restoration specialists. Even the smoke from a closed fireplace flue can cause enough damage to warrant professional attention.

Colossal Cleanups

So That's Where the Day Goes!

The amount of time the average two-career couple spends doing housework each week: 23 hours

Laundry

Shake loose particles from items. Soak or spray stains with pre-treater. Wash in the hottest water allowable for fabric and detergent. Add ½ cup washing soda to the load to cut through the oily residue.

Speed tips: Masking tape can help remove surface spots and residue from fabric.

Caution: Do not take smoked garments to an ordinary dry cleaner. Improper cleaning may permanently set stains and odors. Find a dry cleaner who is knowledgeable, and only take one or two things to be cleaned initially and see how they turn out.

Upholstery and Carpets

Carpets and upholstery can be shampooed or cleaned with a powdered cleaner such as Host or Capture (available at home centers), says King. Inaccessible smoke odor and residue trapped in the carpet padding and furniture stuffing materials, however, is likely to persist. Airing it out will help, but often the only solution is to have carpet and upholstery professionally cleaned and deodorized.

Caution: Avoid using upholstered furniture that has been damaged by smoke residue until it has been properly cleaned or restored. Using the furniture will further embed the residue in the textile fibers. Toxicity of the residue is also a concern if it is ingested by children or pets, says King.

Walls and Ceilings

Because of the numerous types of smoke residue, the Association of Specialists in Cleaning and Restoration in Annapolis Junction, Maryland, advises that you seek professional help to clean walls, ceilings, and other absorbent surfaces so that the appropriate cleaner can be used to neutralize odors. Cleaning smoke-damaged walls is a long tedious process, says King. If you only have an isolated amount of smoke damage, however, you can use the following technique to clean walls and ceilings.

Technique: Remove smoke with dry sponges (a specific type of smoke-cleaning sponge available at janitorial supply stores). Then wash with a solution of degreaser, such as Formula 409, and water. Dry with a cloth.

In a pinch: If smoke film or odor persists, repainting or refinishing may be required.

Smoke Alarms

If you keep in mind that the piercing shriek of a smoke alarm could save your life someday, it makes sense to give it some cleaning attention now and then.

Technique: The manufacturer of First Alert smoke alarms recommends that you gently vacuum the accumulated dust from the cover with a handheld soft brush attachment once a month. Make sure that the perforated sensing chamber isn't blocked by lint. Test the unit after vacuuming by following the manufacturer's instructions.

Caution: Don't use water, cleaners, or solvents on the unit because they may damage it.

Soap Scum

Do you have any insoluble precipitates lurking in your shower? No, don't call the vice squad. Insoluble precipitates are what you get when soap combines with mineral salts found in hard water, such as calcium and magnesium, says the Soap and Detergent Association in

New York City. Of course, those of us who have attempted to scrub, scrape, and dissolve this tenacious gray film from the bathtub, the shower walls, or even clothing just call it soap scum.

Technique: You can purchase one of the numerous cleaners on the market specifically formulated to dissolve soap scum or use a variety of home remedies for ridding tile, showers and bathtubs from the dull gray film. Shower tile and doors can be cleaned by wiping on lemon oil furniture polish with a clean soft cloth. Allow it to soak a few minutes—longer if the film is severe. Then wipe clean with a dry cloth or paper towel. You may need to use a plastic scrubber in areas where there is a heavy buildup of residue. Lemon oil also retards future soap-scum buildup. For the shower curtain, rub a sponge soaked in white vinegar over the curtain to dissolve soap film. It will also kill mold and mildew.

On your laundry, soap residue makes fabrics feel stiff and shows up as white streaks or spots. To remove residue, add 1 cup white vinegar to 1 gallon warm water in a plastic container. Soak the item and rinse. To prevent future residue from forming, add a water-softening agent to your washer or use liquid laundry detergent. Make sure that textiles are adequately rinsed before drying.

Speed tips: The best way to save time cleaning up soap scum in the bath or shower is to prevent it from forming in the first place. "Try changing brands of soap," says Margaret Dasso, owner of the Clean Sweep, a professional cleaning service in Lafayette, California, and co-author of *Dirt Busters*. Some brands, such as Zest and Ivory, cause less film.

Clean a soap-scummed shower curtain in the washing machine. Fill the washer with warm water and equal parts of detergent and baking soda. Add the shower curtain and two large terry towels (the towels will help to rub the scum off the curtains during the washing process). Add 1 cup of vinegar to the rinse cycle. Remove the shower curtain before the spin cycle and hang to dry.

In a pinch: There are several household items that cut through soap film. Soap is alkaline, and acidic products such as vinegar or lemon juice will dissolve it.

Caution: Be sure to follow warnings on commercial soap-scum dissolvers. They may irritate the skin, eyes, or nose.

Soil

EMERGENCY ACTION
If it's dry, brush or shake off as much of the soil as possible before laundering. If it's in the form of mud, let it dry before attempting to clean it. Trying to remove soil when it's wet will embed it further into the fibers. Once dry, most of the soil can be removed with a vacuum or a dry brush.

You'll find five basic types of soil dotting the backyards of America—sand, limestone, clay, silt, and peat. While scientists can't say for sure that Georgia clay has more staining power than Mississippi River silt, in general, soils composed of finer particles, such as clay and silt, stain more readily than coarse granular soils like limestone. "Smaller particles penetrate deeper into the fibers," says Beth McIntyre, a home economist for Maytag Appliances in Newton, Iowa. Regardless of the soil type, your cleaning technique is the same.

Technique: Brush unpenetrated dirt off the surface. Soak in cold water for a few minutes to loosen dirt particles. Then pretreat with a paste made of granular detergent and water. "Granular detergents remove soil and mud better than liquid detergents," says McIntyre. Launder in the hottest water possible for the fabric. All-fabric bleach can be added to boost the cleaning action of the detergent. Check to make sure that the stain is removed before drying sets it.

Speed tips: Items do not need to be soaked for hours at time. Most of the cleaning action occurs in the first half-hour, according to McIntyre. Use the presoak cycle on your washer to save time and effort. The 20- to 30-minute cycles on washing machines provide an adequate soaking time.

In a pinch: If stain persists, instead of water, make the paste with the granular detergent and ammonia, says Jane Rising, instructor in the education department at the International Fabricare Institute in Silver Spring, Maryland. Wash as directed above. (If the detergent contains chlorine bleach, don't mix it with ammonia. Toxic fumes can result.)

Caution: Use extra care when making a pretreat paste from granular detergent that contains all-fabric bleach. The bleach may fade the fabric, so only allow pretreat pastes of this type to sit on the stain for 5 to 10 minutes. Always read product labels for proper use and safety precautions.

Soot

- **Change your furnace filter. (Save the old one to show to the service technician.)**
- **Vacuum soot particles from upholstery, drapes, carpeting, and floors. Use the brush attachment with long soft bristles. The brush may have to be cleaned repeatedly during the cleaning process. Do not allow the metal vacuum tube to touch surfaces. It could cause the soot to smear and stain.**
- **Tape double layers of cheesecloth over air registers with masking tape to prevent further soot deposits.**
- **Cover upholstery with clean sheets.**

Soot is a combination of oil and carbon, usually deposited in the form of fine homogeneous dust caused by unburned fuel from a malfunctioning furnace. Smoke and soot are often mistakenly lumped together as one cleaning problem. Smoke, however, is heat-driven and pushes its way into even closed-off places, such as drawers, while soot travels through the air currents and settles on surfaces. One way to tell them apart is that soot has no odor.

"Soot can accumulate because it does not have an obnoxious odor like smoke does," says Martin L. King, a restoration consultant in Arlington, Virginia, and technical advisor to the National Institute of Disaster Restoration in Annapolis, Maryland. Soot also tends to be evenly distributed, while smoke damage is concentrated near the source of the fire.

Technique: If the problem occurred as a result of a furnace malfunction, cleanup may be covered under your homeowner's insurance policy, and your best bet may be to have a cleaning restoration specialist tackle the job. There's not much room for error when dealing with soot; an oily smear easily becomes a permanent stain.

Remove as much soot as possible from all surfaces through dry methods such as vacuuming. In places where a vacuum does not reach, try blowing the soot out with compressed air.

Once vacuumed, clean hard surfaces, such as wood furniture, countertops, sinks, appliances, light fixtures, hardwood and resilient floors, and windows with a towel dipped in a solution of degreaser and warm water. Use a lifting motion as you clean, not a circular rubbing motion.

You probably should leave walls and ceilings to a professional.

"The average individual does not have the skills or patience because it's a long and tedious process," says King. "They might start out okay, but then they start looking for shortcuts." If you're determined to do it on your own, use dry sponges, which are available from janitorial supply stores.

Textiles are difficult to clean. Everything should be vacuumed or shaken out first. If it's washable, pretreat any stains and wash in the warmest temperature possible, preferably hot water. Adding ½ cup washing soda, a strong alkaline which boosts the water's cleaning ability, to the load can help battle the grease. Carpets should be vacuumed first and cleaned with a powdered cleaner such as Host or Capture, which are available at home centers.

Speed tips: When you're working with only a three-inch dust brush attachment on a vacuum cleaner, the task can seem endless. On large areas, a feather duster works well to lift soot off and push it to the floor where it can be quickly swept up.

In a pinch: If you don't have cheesecloth to tape over your air registers, any lightweight cloth that permits air circulation, such as handkerchiefs, will do. You want to prevent more soot from blowing into the house until the air ducts are cleaned.

Caution: Do not attempt to clean the following items. They should be cleaned by a professional restoration specialist, says King.

- Electronics (computers, televisions, and stereos need interior cleaning)
- Walls and ceilings
- Duct system
- Artwork
- Pianos and organs

Spiderwebs

The average spider takes 30 to 60 minutes to completely spin its web, according to *The Gale Book of Averages*. So theoretically, if you have spiders, you could de-web your entire house, only to find it rewebbed in less than an hour.

Technique: The best mechanical device for cleaning up spiderwebs is the vacuum, but any type of dust wand will usually do the trick to snare the spiderwebs from the corners of your walls and ceilings. Use care not to press too firmly and stain your ceiling or walls with any dirt or bug carcasses enmeshed in the web. Instead, lift up and away from surfaces. Shake or vacuum the webs from the duster.

Speed tips: Fewer spiders means fewer spiderwebs. General sanitation, both indoors and outdoors, is essential in controlling spiders. Clean up all woodpiles, rocks, trash, compost piles, old boards, and other debris, which attract spiders. Keep crawl spaces, basements, and porches as dry as possible.

Caution: When handling live spiders, wear gloves to avoid being bitten.

Spills

Spill cleanup is the emergency-room duty of the cleaning world. Unlike regular cleaning, when you're trying to sparkle, sanitize, or even beautify, cleaning up spills and the unexpected mess they make is essentially damage control. You can prevent 90 percent of the spots and stains from liquid spills if you take immediate steps to absorb the mess, according to the Association of Specialists in Cleaning and Restoration in Annapolis Junction, Maryland.

Technique: Every spill is different—from candle wax on your tablecloth, to vomit on your carpeting, to a broken toner cartridge in your office, to a plate of spaghetti in your lap. So you need to know some basic techniques that prevent spills from becoming stains.

The time to take care of a spill is immediately after the mishap. Always remove as much of the spillage as possible before attempting any stain-removal techniques.

• If it's dry, keep it dry. Dry spills such as flour, sugar, or toner should be cleaned as thoroughly as possible by first using dry methods such as a vacuum cleaner, broom, or a dustpan and brush. Using water to clean up dry items will only liquefy the mess and make it harder to clean up and more likely to penetrate fibers and cause an annoying stain.

• Soak it up. Liquid spills should be blotted up with clean, white absorbent material such as paper towels, napkins, or tissues. The more of the spillage that's absorbed right away, the less residue is left to create a stain.

• After absorbing as much as of the spill as possible, sponge water-based spills such as coffee, tea, fruit juice, soda, milk, blood, or egg with clear water to remove residual spillage, which will eventually cause staining. If water does not remove the spill completely, a specific stain remedy will be necessary.

How to Beat the Drinks Jinx

Spilled drinks can come back to haunt you.

Beverages containing sugar are often the culprits when a brown discoloration appears days, weeks, or months after a spill on carpet or upholstery. Why? Because the liquid, containing colorless sugar, remains in the fibers after the spill is cleaned up. After exposure to air, the sugar causes insoluble brown stains.

To prevent this kind of damage from spilled coffee, tea, fruit juice, or soda, immediate action is necessary. Put a half-inch thickness of white absorbent towel on top of the spill and weight it down. As the stain is wicked into the towel, replace it with fresh material. When you have absorbed as much of the spill as possible, the Association of Specialists in Cleaning and Restoration in Annapolis Junction, Maryland, recommends blotting with small amounts of the following solutions until you remove the stain. Keep a supply of clean, white absorbent towels handy. You'll need a clean one to apply each solution in the order indicated below and to blot and rinse excess solution between applications.

- A commercial spot remover or alcohol
- 1 teaspoon mild (nonalkaline and nonbleach) liquid dishwashing detergent mixed with 1 cup lukewarm water
- 1 tablespoon household ammonia and ½ cup water
- ⅓ cup white vinegar (to neutralize the ammonia) and ⅔ cup water
- A paste of powdered enzyme detergent and water

Always spot-check in an inconspicuous area to make sure that the fabric is colorfast, says Wm. (Bill) R. Griffin, president of Cleaning Consultant Services in Seattle. And refer to the instructions that came with your carpet or upholstery to be certain that you won't void the warranty by attempting to clean it yourself.

Be conservative with water. The Association of Specialists in Cleaning and Restoration warns against overwetting, which can cause carpet and upholstery to shrink. After you have eradicated the stain, blot away any lingering solution with a towel. Weight it down and allow it to dry for at least six hours, changing the dressing frequently. (Keep in mind that some stubborn stains may need professional attention.)

- Spills such as paint, oil-based paint, or grease should be blotted with spot removers, such as K2r or Energine (available at supermarkets, hardware stores, or discount department stores), instead of water.
- When working with carpets and upholstery, use small amounts of water and blot the area frequently to prevent discoloration from overwetting stuffing or backing materials. Blot from the outside edge and work your way toward the center to prevent the spill from spreading.

- Start with the mess, then work on the stain. When you spill a combination of liquid and solids, like a nice hearty bowl of minestrone soup, you have a combination mess. Spilled solids, such as food, should be lifted off first with a spoon or spatula. After you have removed as much solid matter as possible, soak up the liquid part of the mess with absorbent white towels and follow the tips for liquid spills.

Speed tips: A wet-dry vacuum cleaner will make quick work of wet, dry, and combination spills. They are especially useful in extracting liquids from carpeting and upholstery. One-gallon wet vacuums are available at hardware stores for small jobs. Clean and dry the equipment when you are finished with it.

In a pinch: If you don't have any cleaning tools handy, pull out your wallet. A credit card works great for lifting and scooping messes up and off surfaces.

Stainless Steel

An alloy of iron, chromium, and occasionally other metals, stainless steel is practically immune to rust and corrosion. It can stain, however—especially when exposed to high heat—and must be cared for.

Technique: Even though stainless steel resists corrosion, it is vulnerable to scratching. "Try to keep abrasives away from your stainless steel," says Kari Kinder, assistant director of food and beverage at the renowned Culinary Institute of America in Hyde Park, New York. "They will scratch and dull its shine."

Wash stainless-steel utensils and cookware in hot sudsy water or in the dishwasher. Wipe down stainless-steel sinks with a sudsy sponge or cloth. Brighten stainless steel by polishing it with a cloth soaked in vinegar. Rinse and buff items dry to remove water spots, which are caused by minerals in the water, a condition known as hard water.

Water that has more than 60 milligrams of calcium and magnesium per liter is considered hard. If you have hard water and spotting is a major problem, increase the amount of dishwasher detergent that you've been using by one extra teaspoon for each 20 milligrams per liter of water hardness over 60. To find out the hardness of the water in your area, contact your water utility or your county Cooperative Extension Service.

Rub burned-on foods with baking soda or a paste made of ammonia, water, and a mild nonchlorinated scouring powder.

How to Keep That Stainless Steel, Well, Stainless

With stainless steel, rust isn't a problem, and for the most part, neither are stains. Manufactured in different grades, the finish can be as shiny as a mirror or brushed. Here are a few tips from cleaning experts to keep your stainless looking its best.

Dry spots away. Washing in hot soapy water keeps pots and utensils clean. But make sure that you dry it right away with a cloth since stainless steel tends to water-spot.

Say goodbye to the blues. You can remove some of the blue discoloration that appears when stainless steel is overheated by scrubbing brushed surfaces with a mild abrasive cleaner like Bon Ami and polishing shiny surfaces with a cream silver polish.

Shine on. Surfaces that don't come in contact with food, such as appliance fronts, can be rubbed with lemon oil to shine and protect from fingerprints.

Discolorations caused by overheating are almost impossible to remove. Try rubbing them lightly with steel wool and a mild scouring powder. Otherwise, never use steel wool on stainless steel flatware.

Caution: Ammonia and chlorine, when mixed, cause noxious fumes.

Stains

Dealing with stains is a confusing maze of do's and don'ts for many of us. There are dozens of stain remedies, yet no universal rule applies to all stains. A remedy that works on one stain will set another. A good example is ordinary bar soap. It's great for getting out fabric softener stains but will set a fruit stain.

"It's not just the stain; it's what it's on and how long it has been there," says Carol Seelaus, a speed-cleaning instructor at Temple University in Philadelphia and owner of Somebody's Gotta Do It, a professional cleaning service. With the exception of mud and Play-Doh, stains that are treated right away are much more likely to be removed completely than stains that have had a chance to dry and penetrate the fabric or surface. This is the first rule of stain removal—act quickly.

But when it comes to stain removal, quickly is a variable term. Depending on the stain, you could have minutes, hours, or even days before it sets. Drinks like red Hawaiian Punch are some of the worst stain offenders, says Margaret Dasso, owner of the Clean Sweep, a professional cleaning service in Lafayette, California, and co-author of *Dirt Busters*. But if you treat it in the first few minutes, you may be able to remove the stain. The folks who make Hawaiian Punch suggest rinsing clothing immediately with cold water, then soaking the item in an enzyme prewash, such as Biz. Wash it in the hottest water allowable for the fabric. Check to make sure that the stain is gone before machine-drying. On carpets, flush the spill with club soda and blot with clean white towels. With greasy salad dressing, you still need to act quickly, but you have a few days until the oils oxidize and permanently darken the fabric.

Technique: For the best results, follow these general rules for stain removal.

First, try to identify the stain. "You're miles ahead if you know what you have on it," says Beth McIntyre, a home economist for Maytag Appliances in Newton, Iowa. Look at the color of the stain. Look at the surface. Is it soaked in or crusted on? Crusty stains that turn white when scratched are often sugar-based. If you can't identify the stain specifically, try to learn if it's a protein stain, a greasy stain, a water-soluble stain, a waxy stain, a chemical stain, or a combination stain. Certain stains can be set by the wrong treatment. If you can categorize the stain, proceed with an appropriate treatment.

Wait before you wet. Remove as much of the stain as possible before wetting it with water or cleaning solvent, which will immediately start to dissolve the stain and spread it to other fibers. So blot away liquids and scrape or lift away as much solid residue as possible.

Be wary of heat. The heat of the dryer or even hot water can set stains, so stick to cool or

---

The Seven Deadly Stains

Watch out! These stains don't just work their way into the fibers; they permanently deface and discolor furniture, carpeting, flooring, upholstery, and clothing, says Carol Seelaus, a speed-cleaning instructor at Temple University in Philadelphia and owner of Somebody's Gotta Do It, a professional cleaning service.

1. Acids (tile cleaners, toilet-bowl cleaners, urine, vomit)
2. Benzoyl peroxide (acne medication, age-spot remover)
3. Bleach (automatic dishwasher detergent, chlorine)
4. Hair dyes
5. Herbal teas
6. Liquid plant food
7. Strong alkalis (drain cleaner, lye, oven cleaner)

Your Stain-Fighting Tool Kit

Be prepared. Keep these tools and cleaners on hand, advise cleaning experts.

Absorbents: Cornmeal, cornstarch, or talcum powder; can be sprinkled on a grease stain, allowed to sit to absorb it, and brushed or vacuumed to remove.

Ammonia: Use the plain kind when you need a mild alkaline solution. Use with caution. Never mix chlorine bleach and ammonia. This can cause dangerous fumes.

Bar soap: Rub on fabric softener stains to remove them.

Chlorine bleach: A powerful tool for removing stains if the fabric can tolerate it.

Denatured or isopropyl alcohol: Useful for removing stains on water-sensitive fabrics. Check for colorfastness first.

Digestant: Contains enzymes that eat tough protein stains such as food, vomit, and blood. Can be purchased in pure enzyme form from some health food stores or as a laundry presoak, such as Biz. Use warm water. Don't mix with other chemicals. Enzymes are sensititve. Also, you may need to apply several treatments.

Laundry pretreaters: Available in sprays, liquid, gels, and sticks. Different types work better on different stains.

Neutral detergent: A liquid dishwashing detergent works fine. Use a clear one that has a pH of 7. Mix a light solution of 2 or 3 drops in 1 cup water. Opaque or colored ones may contain dye or skin softeners.

Spot remover: A spot remover, such as Energine, Carbona Stain Devils, or K2r (available at supermarkets, hardware stores, or discount department stores), is good for removing oily stains from fabrics that can only be dry-cleaned. It can be used on most fabrics and will not set stains. Watch for flammability.

3 percent hydrogen peroxide: Provides a mild bleaching action for fabrics that can't tolerate chlorine bleach. Allow time for it to work.

Water: A spray bottle filled with water at room temperature is your best tool. "Most stains are water-soluble," says Carol Seelaus, a speed-cleaning instructor at Temple University in Philadelphia and owner of Somebody's Gotta Do It, a professional cleaning service. "Nine times out of 10, water will do the trick."

Use it to flush the stain and to rinse solvents from the fabric or stained surface.

White vinegar: Good for stains that call for acid or to neutralize alkaline stains. It will also neutralize smoke odor.

warm water when working on an unknown stain. After laundering, allow stained items to air-dry until you're sure that the stain has been completely removed.

"Anytime a stain is washed, not noticed, and dried, it is very difficult to remove because the dryer heat sets the stains," says McIntyre. The heat of the dryer will set sugar stains, protein stains, and a host of other stains. The iron will permanently set perspiration stains and bring out a lovely shade of yellow-brown in old sugar stains. There are exceptions, though. Grease and soil stains should be washed with hot water.

Lift the stain out. Never rub a stain. Rubbing abrades textile fibers and carpeting and drives the stain further into the surface. Use the following methods to effectively pull stains from some fibers and surfaces.

- Blot fresh stains with clean white cloths.
- Flush with cool or warm water, or with an appropriate cleaning solvent.
- Soak in cool water.
- Freeze the stain and peel or pick off.
- Tamp with a flat-bristle brush to break up stain particles so that they can be lifted off by cleaner. Tamping is a vertical striking motion, not a back and forth scrubbing motion.

Check the colorfastness before treatment. In an inconspicuous place, such as a seam or hem on clothing or a hidden corner on carpeting or furniture, test your fabric for dye bleeding. Apply cleaning solution or pretreater. Let it soak for a few minutes, then blot with a clean white cloth. Look for dye on the cloth or lightening on the fabric. Silk is extremely prone to dye migration. Commercial stain pretreaters may make neon dyes bleed.

Pretreat stains. This can be done using a commercial prewash stain remover, such as Shout or Spray 'n Wash, or by making your own from a liquid laundry detergent, a paste of water and granular detergent, bar soap, or a laundry additive, such as borax.

Be persistent. It may take more than one try to get the stain out. If you see some lightening of the stain on the first attempt. Try again.

Toss it in the washer. Always launder washable items after treating to remove residues of both the stain and the stain remover.

Speed tips: To save yourself time and aggravation when dealing with a stain, remember the first rule of thumb: Deal with it right away. It also helps to:

- Know where to look for stains. On clothing look at collars, underarm areas, elbows and knees, cuffs, and seams.
- Mark the spot. If you don't have time to attack a stain until laun-

> # HOW IT WORKS
>
> ## The Chemistry of Laundry Pretreaters
>
> Laundry stain pretreaters help you soften up the enemy before the battle even begins. They're available in aerosol and pump sprays and liquid, gel, and stick form. They work by suspending stains in the fabric so that they can be washed away.
>
> But pretreaters are not created equal when it comes to stain removal. Although they are marketed as a general, cure-all stain solution, pretreaters are stain-specific, says Beth McIntyre, a home economist for Maytag Corporation in Newton, Iowa.
>
> Liquids and sprays are derived from petroleum distillates and work best on oily and greasy stains.
>
> "We have found that grease removes grease better. Grease takes grease out," says McIntyre. The liquid and spray forms should be applied a few minutes before laundering. It is important to remember that these products should not be allowed to dry out or else they lose their stain-removal power.
>
> Gels and sticks, on the other hand, are enzyme-based and work well on protein stains, such as blood, grass, baby formula, dairy products, eggs, and chocolate, says McIntyre. Sticks can be applied up to a week before laundering.
>
> Do not use pretreater for spot removal on items that cannot be laundered, such as upholstery, carpeting, or dry-cleanable items.

dry day, mark it with a piece of masking tape or a Post-it Note before putting it in the hamper.

- Use the soak cycle on your washer, recommends McIntyre. Soaking does not need to take hours and hours to be effective. The 20- to 30-minute cycle provides an adequate amount of cleaning action.
- Wash it on laundry day. If you don't have time to wash it now, laundry stain sticks do a pretty good job on most stains, says McIntyre. As long as it's not a grease or oil stain, a stick is effective. Keep one next to the hamper and train everyone in the household to use it.

In a pinch: If you just can't figure out what kind of stain it is, McIntyre recommends soaking the item in cold water for 30 minutes to loosen the stain, then applying a pretreater such as a paste made from granular detergent and water, and then laundering the item in warm water.

Caution: For the sake of your family's health as well as your clothing:

- Never mix chemicals together. They can give off toxic fumes. The classic example is chlorine bleach and ammonia.
- Work in a well-ventilated area, and don't smoke when working with chemical spotters. They're flammable.
- Prevent accidental poisoning. Keep cleaning chemicals in their original packaging stored out of the reach of children.
- Wear gloves when working with all cleaning solvents. Chemicals can be absorbed through the skin.
- When using any bleach (chlorine or oxygen), treat the entire item. That way, if the color is affected, at least it will change evenly.

Stairs and Steps

Because they are awkward to clean, stairs and steps are often neglected. How you clean them depends on whether they are carpeted or bare and whether they are located inside or outside.

Carpeted Stairs

An excessively soiled carpet can hold up to one pound of dirt in each square yard. On carpeted stairs embedded dirt tends to be concentrated in the center and front of the tread where people walk. To suck up dirt and soil, the vacuum cleaner is the tool of choice, preferably one with a beater bar. Use it at least once a week for best results.

"Make sure that the carpet gets agitation so that dirt can vibrate its way to the top," says Mary Nuosce, consumer education manager for the Hoover Company in North Canton, Ohio.

A small handheld vacuum with a beater bar will provide the agitation and grooming action needed to suction dirt from the center as well as all the hills and valleys of a staircase. On carpeted stairs it doesn't matter whether you start at the top or the bottom—whichever works into your cleaning routine best. But you should work it into your routine at least once a week.

Use six to eight overlapping strokes against the nap of the carpet to vacuum high-traffic areas and three or four overlapping strokes at the edges and risers, where dust, pet hair, and lint accumulate.

Outdoor stairs that are carpeted should be vacuumed or blown clean to remove leaves and debris. Embedded dirt can be hosed using a top to bottom, side to side cleaning action. Always remember to move the dirt away from the house.

Speed tips: If you are pressed for time, it is better to vacuum only the heavy-traffic areas rather than trying to give everything a quick once-over. Take off your shoes at the door. Sweep sidewalks and driveways to prevent tracking in soil.

In a pinch: If you don't own a handheld vacuum but have a canister vacuum, try removing the metal wands and attaching the carpet agitator directly to the nozzle. This gives you the power of a regular vacuum without the unwieldy awkwardness of negotiating a set of stairs with a full-size vacuum. "This way you can see what you're doing," Nuosce says.

The handheld flat upholstery attachment is also an effective alternative.

Uncarpeted Steps and Stairs

Unlike carpeted stairs, dirt tends to collect along the edges and corners on a hard-surface staircase, while the centers of the treads remain relatively clean. "A canister vacuum is the most effective tool for reaching the dirt that's trapped in all the cracks and crevices," says Carol Seelaus, a speed-cleaning instructor at Temple University in Philadelphia and owner of Somebody's Gotta Do It, a professional cleaning service. Use a floor brush or crevice tool attachment.

On outdoor steps sweep the steps clean from top to bottom with a broom, then spray them with a garden hose to remove fine particles. Remember to sweep dirt away from the house.

Sweep at least once a week or more often in wet weather and dusty climates.

Speed tips: The worn areas of outdoor wooden steps can really begin to absorb mud and stains. Save yourself some time and cleaning effort by applying deck enamel or a clear sealant.

In a pinch: If you don't have a canister vacuum, a handheld dust brush works well because the fine soft bristles tend to snare more dirt than a broom. Work from top to bottom, sweeping directly into a dustpan at the edge of the tread.

Caution: To avoid injury, don't hose down steps when there is a chance that the water could turn to ice.

Stamps

Among stamp collectors, "cleaning" in its purest sense refers to the removal of a postmark for fraudulent reuse, which is illegal. However, cleaning can also refer to the process of removing the backing envelope from the stamp itself.

Technique: To remove canceled postage stamps, cut the stamp from its envelope leaving a small border of paper around the stamp. Soak it in a bowl of tepid water. "Take the baby test. If it feels too hot for your wrist, it's too hot for the stamp," says Carol Cervenka, secretary-treasurer of the International Society of Worldwide Stamp Collectors in Caddo Mills, Texas, who has collected stamps for more than 50 years. Once the bond between the envelope and stamp is dissolved, carefully remove the stamp from the water bath with your fingertips. (Clean hands are a must.) Dry it facedown on plain white paper towels. (The dye from colored paper towels can migrate to the stamp and ruin it.) If you notice the edges of the stamp beginning to curl, place it between two paper towels and weight it with a book. Curling sometimes occurs with stamps from foreign countries.

Stamps have a tendency to mildew because of the sucrose-based gum on the back, so allow stamps to dry thoroughly overnight. Loose stamps can then be stored in a small container, such as a cigar box, until you are ready to mount them. Use a desiccant, such as the packets of silica found in vitamin bottles, to keep the container moisture-free. Handle dry stamps with stamp tongs, not your fingers, which can transfer skin oils that will later discolor the stamp. Tweezers aren't recommended because they have an abrasive inner surface that can tear the stamp.

Speed tips: Wait until you have several envelopes collected and save time by cleaning in volume.

In a pinch: To salvage stamps that have been damaged by mildew, prepare a tepid water bath of 2 gallons water, a scant teaspoon of bleach, and a few drops of liquid dishwashing detergent. Soak for 30 minutes. Carefully agitate water to remove loosened dirt. Rinse in a second container filled with clean tepid water. Do not rinse under running water, as this may further damage the stamp. Follow the drying method outlined above.

Caution: It is a federal offense to intentionally remove the cancellation mark on a postage stamp. Do not soak stamps in order to remove the cancellation mark.

Never soak stamps attached to brightly colored greeting card envelopes, especially red ones. The dye from these envelopes can bleed into the water bath and tint the stamp. Some airmail envelopes containing the red and blue striped border may also bleed. To avoid dye damage, use a stamp lifting product available from stamp dealers. If you must soak these stamps, soak each one separately.

Steel

Because it is so prone to rust, steel is usually coated with a protective finish. Its exterior coating determines how you should clean it. Steel appliances often have an enamel finish. Vinyl coated steel is used in items like dishwasher racks or appliance trim. In general, you'll need to guard against scratches and punctures, which would allow the steel to come in contact with moisture and rust. Rust can form in just four hours.

Technique: Clean surfaces with a nonabrasive all-purpose cleaner, such as Formula 409, and a sponge or soft cloth. Rinse with a separate sponge dipped in clean water, and dry with a soft cloth. You can also clean and protect appliances and cabinets with a painted or baked enamel finish with a creamy liquid kitchen wax, according to the Soap and Detergent Association in New York City. Wm. (Bill) R. Griffin, president of Cleaning Consultant Services in Seattle, suggests Jubilee. Apply wax to a damp cloth and rub onto the finish. Work in small sections, cleaning about one square foot at a time. This is necessary so that you can buff each area with a dry cloth while the wax is still moist. Appliances should only be waxed three or four times per year to avoid wax buildup.

Speed tips: Hardened spills on stove tops may need to soak in a cleaning solution for 15 minutes to remove without scratching the protective finish. Save yourself time by cleaning up spots and spills when they happen with plain water or a spray of all-purpose cleaner.

In a pinch: If rust develops at the site of a scratch on a painted finish, you may be able to repair the damage. Remove rust with sandpaper or a rust remover such as Duro Naval Jelly. If the steel is still in good condition, touch up the spot with a dab of appliance paint or enamel paint.

Caution: Never use abrasive cleaners, such as steel wool or powdered cleansers on coated steel finishes. It could scratch the surface and eventually cause the steel to rust. It's okay to use a white scrubbing pad.

Stereo Equipment

Your ears will tell you when it's time to clean your stereo equipment. Dirt, dust, and oxides gradually collect on the sensitive parts of your audio system and erode the sound. Telltale signs are crackling when the volume knob is adjusted, muffled or distorted sound, weak or dropped signals from the left or right speaker, or the compact disc (CD) player skipping tracks. You can have your audio system sounding as good as new by investing a few dollars and a few minutes.

Technique: Periodically dust the stereo components. Use a nonmetallic brush to loosen dust and a vacuum cleaner to remove it. "Don't move around any parts, such as wires or resistors. From the way they look, you say, 'Why is this thing sticking up in the air?' But moving them around can loosen connections and cause problems that you never had before," says Dave Barnes, service manager for Crutchfield, a mail-order audio equipment distributor in Charlottesville, Virginia. "As far as dust buildup, the only thing that's truly harmful is dust on the optic laser of the CD player."

But steer clear of manually cleaning the lens of the CD player; it can be damaged easily. You can clean lenses safely and effectively on single CD players by purchasing a commercial CD cleaner, which has a brush fused to its playing surface, for about $10.

Don't forget about the wires that deliver the sound to your system. About once a year unplug and wipe down all jacks and cables with denatured alcohol.

If you hear a crackling sound when you adjust the volume, you probably have a buildup of dust and dirt on the carbon tracks in the knob housing. Turn the unit off and unplug it. Remove the cover from

SCRUB THIS APPROACH

Don't Gum Up the Works

It makes audio service technicians shake their heads sadly—the common misuse of aerosol lubricants on stereo systems, says Dave Barnes, service manager for Crutchfield, a mail-order audio equipment distributor in Charlottesville, Virginia.

"It makes a mess out of stuff," he says. Sometimes a tape player or turntable runs slowly or appears to be sticking. Thinking that they'll just get things moving a little better, a person sprays a silicone-based cleaner or lubricant into the system.

"That ruins the felt drive clutches and impregnates the rubber, causing it to slip and swell," Barnes says. His advice is to stay away from aerosol lubricants. Unplug your unit and remove the outer cover. Use a vacuum cleaner reversed to blow air out instead. If you can't remove the dust by vacuuming, try blowing it out with compressed air. Wipe the rubber and clutch pads with a cotton swab moistened with a small amount of denatured alcohol.

the component and any shrouding around the knob until you can see where it meets the circuit board. There should be a hole visible. Spray a small amount of light silicone cleaner into the hole. It will remove the dust and prevent further buildup. Turn the knob back and forth about four times. Turn the unit on with the volume at a minimum level to see if the crackling has disappeared. Repeat the process if it hasn't. If you don't have a silicone cleaner, denatured alcohol will remove existing dirt, but it won't provide the protective coating to repel dust. This procedure can be used to clean all your function knobs—balance, bass, treble, tape monitor, and auxiliary. "When you have one dirty knob, you probably have a mess of them," says Barnes.

If the jacks on your equipment are badly corroded, rub them with fine sandpaper.

Even if you don't play records like you used to, don't ignore your turntable. It's a good idea to replace your needle after every 30 hours of use. A dull needle can damage your records, especially as they become brittle with age. It's a good idea to buy more than one replacement because you may not be able to find it in a few years. Store your vinyl records in an upright position (never leaning) away from sunlight. Use a velvet brush to clean them.

Speed tips: Keep covers and doors closed on stereo equipment to avoid dust buildup. Dirt on tapes, CDs, and records get deposited in your components. Store them in their jackets or cases to keep them clean and dust-free.

Caution: Make sure that the system is off and unplugged during cleaning, especially when you're removing the jacks. You don't want to send a damaging blast of noise through your speakers as you reconnect them.

Be sure to check with your manufacturer to make sure that opening the unit will not void the warranty.

Stone

Stone is being used in an increasing number of American homes for floors, counters, and walls. "Stone is becoming more affordable because of improving technology in the stonecutting industry," says Fred Hueston, director of the National Training Center for Stone and Masonry Trades in Longwood, Florida, and author of *The Stain Removal Guide for Stone*. Granite, marble, limestone, slate, and sandstone are easy-care durable materials that will last a lifetime if cared for properly.

Technique: The first step in maintaining a stone surface is to protect it from stains by sealing it with an impregnator, which is available from a floor-care specialist. Like water filling a sponge, the impregnator fills up the pores of the stone so that stains cannot penetrate.

New surfaces should be cleaned with a stone soap, allowed to dry thoroughly, and sealed. On older surfaces, make sure that all stains are removed prior to sealing. Once the stain is sealed in, it will never come out.

To Clean Stone, Go Deep

You need more than a scrub brush to remove a stain from stone. You may scrub it away only to have it resurface days later.

"What most people don't realize is that the stain has permeated into the pores of the stone," says Fred Hueston, director of the National Training Center for Stone and Masonry Trades in Longwood, Florida, and author of *The Stain Removal Guide for Stone*. "You have to put something on the stain to draw it out."

Stain removal for stone requires making a poultice, a paste which is applied to the stained area, allowed to dry, and scraped off.

"Drying is very important. If it's not allowed to dry, it will not wick or draw the stain out of the stone," says Hueston.

Poultice Formulas

Ink, tea, coffee, wine, fruit and most food stains (excluding oil): Mix white bleached flour with hydrogen peroxide to form a paste the consistency of yogurt.

Cooking oil, copper stains: Mix white bleached flour and ammonia into a paste.

Mildew, algae, mold: Form a paste combining household bleach and flour. This works well on grout that has embedded stains.

Directions

Apply the poultice over the stained area, overlapping by at least one inch all around. Cover with plastic wrap and allow to sit for 12 to 24 hours. Remove plastic and test for dryness. If it is not thoroughly dry, allow it to dry uncovered. Once dry, scrape with wooden spoon or similar dull instrument and examine the area.

Don't give up after one try. If you see some improvement, try again. It may take two to five applications to completely remove some stains.

Sealers can be sprayed on or wiped on. Hueston recommends using a lamb's wool applicator to wipe the impregnator on because it doesn't streak.

Depending on the level of use, the stone can be resealed every six months to five years. "From practical experience, I think it's a good idea to go on a once-a-year basis," says Hueston.

If in doubt, Hueston says, you should perform the water absorption test. Drop several drops of water on the surface. "If you see signs of absorption (darkening of the stone) in under one minute, it's time to reseal."

Ordinary maintenance of stone floors should include daily dust mopping or vacuuming to remove scratchy grit and weekly damp mopping or scrubbing with a stone soap. Wipe countertops clean with nonabrasive cleaner after each use.

For tips on stone care, send a self-addressed stamped envelope to the National Training Center for Stone and Masonry Trades, 941 Longdale Avenue, Longwood, FL 32750.

Speed tips: Save steps by including your stone walls and floors in your vacuuming routine to remove excess dirt and dust. Frequent vacuuming will lessen the need for mopping. Prevention and cleaning frequency are key. Use exterior walk-off mats. Take off your shoes at the door, recommends Bill R. Griffin, president of Cleaning Consultant Services in Seattle.

In a pinch: If you don't have stone soap, use a mild vegetable-oil soap, like Murphy Oil Soap.

Caution: If you live in an area where it freezes in the winter, experts advise against sealing exterior stone. If stone is sealed improperly with water trapped in it, freezing will destroy the stone. Allow exterior stone to weather and develop its own patina.

Stoves

When *Woman's Day* magazine surveyed 1,000 women to find out the household chores that they absolutely hate, cleaning the stove came up number one. So if degreasing little knobs and scouring petrified food from once-shiny surfaces is a dreaded task in your house, take heart; you have lots of company. Since there are hundreds of different models in use, it makes sense to consult your owner's manual for any specific instructions. But basically, cleaning a stove—

whether it's gas or electric—involves the same tasks: taking it apart, cleaning it, and putting it back together.

Technique: Make sure that all parts of the stove are cool. Remove control knobs and grates and soak them in hot soapy water. Clean with a nylon scrub pad or toothbrush and rinse well. Soak drip pans in a strong solution of automatic dishwasher detergent, says Margaret Dasso, owner of the Clean Sweep, a professional cleaning service in Lafayette, California, and co-author of *Dirt Busters*. Clean the stove top and backsplash with a degreaser, like Ultra Mr. Clean Top Job, and white nylon scrubber. If it's not a sealed cooktop, don't forget to clean the area underneath the burners, where all the drips flow. Clean the underside of the stove top with a degreaser and white nylon scrubber. Rinse with a sponge. When all areas are clean, finish off with by polishing with window cleaner. Replace knobs, grates, heating elements, and drip pans.

Speed tips: Don't give food a chance to fossilize on your stove surfaces. Wipe spills up as soon as they occur. Or include a quick spray and wipe with all-purpose cleaner in your daily kitchen cleanup routine.

Clean drip pans in the dishwasher. Prior to cooking, remove drip pans and lightly spray them with nonstick vegetable spray; cleanup will be easier.

In a pinch: If you don't have a commercial degreasing solution on hand, make your own degreasing spray cleaner with these ingredients suggested by "green"-minded cleaning experts. Mix ½ teaspoon washing soda, 1 teaspoon borax, ¼ to ½ teaspoon liquid dishwashing detergent, 3 tablespoons vinegar or 2 tablespoons lemon juice, and 2 cups hot water. Spray and let soak on greasy area for several minutes before rinsing.

Caution: Harsh abrasives, green scrubbing pads, and steel wool will cause scratches on all surfaces.

Stuffed Toy Animals

Every year toy manufacturers flood the market with more than 110 million stuffed animals. When faced with a treasured collection of dusty, matted, stained critters as big as nature's own wild kingdom, many parents have faced the dilemma: Do I clean them or do I trash them? If you opt for cleaning, there are three basic techniques. Which method you use is determined by the age, construction, and stuffing materials.

Technique: Read the tag to see if the stuffed animal is machine washable. Some can be machine-washed in cold water on the gentle cycle. To protect the animal's "fur" and your washer should the animal disintegrate in the wash, place it in an old pillowcase tied shut before washing. Use mild laundry detergent. After washing, put it in the dryer on "Air-Fluff" for 5 to 10 minutes, then allow it to air-dry.

For collectible stuffed toys, toys with unknown stuffing contents, or toys with no care instructions, cleaning should be restricted to the surface of the animal. Saturation of the toy with water or other cleaners could cause an array of complications—from split seams to lost appendages. To clean, vacuum to remove surface dust and dirt, says Marjorie Merritt Darrah, owner of Mary Merritt's Doll Museum in Douglassville, Pennsylvania. Apply foam upholstery cleaner, or make your own with an electric mixer with 2 cups warm water with a squirt of liquid dishwashing detergent. Mix at medium speed until it foams. Using a circular motion, apply foam to the toy with a dry brush. Using a spray bottle, rinse with clear water. Alternately spray the animal with water using the "spray" or "mist" setting and blot with clean cloth. Continue this procedure until the animal is thoroughly rinsed. Wipe the surface with a dry white terry towel. Then allow to air-dry, and brush with hairbrush to fluff.

Speed tips: To dry shampoo your furry friends, rub cornstarch into the fur and vacuum.

In a pinch: Place the stuffed toy in the dryer on "Fluff" or "Air" setting for a few minutes to freshen.

Caution: Don't use harsh upholstery cleaners on toys that will be handled by young children who might want to put the toy in their mouths.

Suede

A simple preventive maintenance routine is the key to protecting your suede from looking flat and shiny.

Technique: Suede shoes and garments should be brushed with a plastic- or rubber-tipped suede brush after each wearing. Suede tends get shiny when it is dirty, and brushing fluffs up the nap, loosens and releases dirt, and restores the rich texture of the suede.

Remove spots and oily stains immediately before they have

chance to penetrate the leather. You can use solvent-based cleaners (similar to dry cleaners) that are specially formulated for suede. Oil-absorbing blocks, which abrade the leather to bring back the nap and remove the stain, are also available at some shoe repair shops and some supermarkets.

Speed tips: The key to saving your time and saving your suede is preventive maintenance. Before you wear your suede shoes or clothing, always protect them with a water and stain repellent designed specifically for suede. "That way when you do encounter stains from day-to-day wear, they will be much easier to take off," says Mitch Lebovic, editor of *Shoe Service* magazine in Baltimore. "As soon as you notice that water is no longer beading up, treat again."

In a pinch: Use a terry towel or an old toothbrush to brush suede. A gum eraser or fine sandpaper can be used in place of stone to remove dirt and stains.

To restore the color to faded suede, pass it quickly through the steam of a teakettle. Be careful not to let condensation form.

Caution: Suede and water don't mix. If suede becomes wet, allow it to dry away from heat sources, then brush to remove water spots. If spots remain, have the garment professionally cleaned.

Leather cleaners are formulated for the smooth finish of leather. Do not use them on suede. They will mat down the nap and ruin it.

Swimming Pools

Algae never get the day off, so neither do you. To keep your pool water clean and clear, and to protect your investment, pool cleaning has to be an everyday task.

Technique: To remove airborne dirt and debris, clean the pool surface every day with a leaf skimmer. Neglected surface dirt will eventually sink to the bottom and become more difficult to remove. Clean surface skimmer baskets daily to maintain proper circulation in your filtration system. Chemical levels should also be tested.

"Just like your teeth, you should brush your pool every morning," says Tom Griffiths, Ph.D., manager of aquatic facilities at Pennsylvania State University in University Park and author of *The Complete Swimming Pool Reference* and *The Swimming Pool Book*. "I can't emphasize brushing enough." Run the pool brush around every surface area under the water line, pushing dirt toward the main drain. The benefits of brushing are twofold. It fluffs up surface dirt so that it can

HOW IT WORKS

Does Chlorine Make You See Red?

The stinging stench and burning eyes that most people associate with overchlorinating is really caused by low levels of chlorine in the pool, according to Tom Griffiths, Ph.D., manager of aquatic facilities at Pennsylvania State University in University Park and author of *The Complete Swimming Pool Reference* and *The Swimming Pool Book.*

Chlorine does three things to keep the water quality high: It disinfects, it oxidizes the water and burns up any organic matter, and it stays in the water to protect. "It has staying power. That's the beauty of chlorine," Dr. Griffiths says.

Simply stated, when there's too little chlorine in the pool, there's too much organic matter—skin oils, hair, perspiration—in the pool. The nitrogen in organic matter combines with chlorine to form a gas called chloramine. The unmistakable nose-burning bleach odor is caused by the chloramine gas, not chlorine. When the levels of chlorine are adequate, your pool will not have an odor.

One option that Dr. Griffiths recommends is keeping your chlorine levels at two to three parts per million to avoid the formation of chloramines.

be caught by the skimmers, and it loosens submerged dirt so that it can go down the drain. In southern climates where algae growth is a huge problem, everyday brushing (which takes less than five minutes) can discourage algae growth by giving the chlorine a chance to oxidize additional organic debris.

Once a week, vacuum the bottom of your pool. This also should be done immediately after inclement weather. Wipe the scum line off with a suitable pool cleaner. Clean and backwash the filter to ensure good water clarity and to preserve your pool equipment.

Speed tips: Automatic vacuums are affordable and can save you hours of cleaning time every month. Run the vacuum whenever the pool is not in use.

Place a thermal blanket on your pool when it's not in use. It reduces the amount of dirt in the pool, conserves your pool chemicals, and in the long run, saves energy and cleaning time.

In a pinch: If you are out of chlorine and you can't get to the pool store, use regular liquid household bleach from the grocery store. Distribute a gallon at a time evenly in the pool until your chlorine level is where you want it. Always keep three to five gallons of household bleach on hand in your pool storage area.

Note: This method should only be used as a last resort. Household bleach is not a good substitute to use regularly.

Caution: Never store pool chemicals with other household products. Pool chemicals, such as calcium hypochloride, are extremely flammable and react violently to even a small handful of foreign material, such as fertilizer. In general, don't store any pool equipment with garden or garage supplies. Dirt and oils from lawn mowers and tools could transfer to the equipment and end up in your pool. Keep all pool supplies in a separate storage shed or dedicate a separate cabinet for them in your garage. Mark the area clearly with a sign that indicates its contents. And be sure to rinse containers thoroughly before disposing of them.

Tablecloths

It's inevitable. Even the most careful diners eventually slop greasy gravy, dribble candle wax, or slosh red wine onto the table linens. Don't panic, advises Elizabeth Barbatelli, president of the Laundry at Linens Limited, a Milwaukee-based mail-order laundry that specializes in cleaning heirloom-quality linens. You don't need to whisk the tablecloth out from under your guests in quick-jerk magician fashion. "It takes about three weeks for a stain to set," says Barbatelli.

Technique: Prior to washing, treat and remove any known stains on the tablecloth. (See Stains on page 356 or specific stain listings.) Then determine whether the tablecloth (or napkins or place mats) can be machine-washed or needs to be laundered by hand.

For new items, read the care label instructions. For other items, follow these recommendations outlined by Michele Durkson Clise in her book *The Linen Closet: How to Care for Your Fine Linens and Lace*. Antique whites made of cotton or linen that are not trimmed in lace can be machine-washed in hot water on the gentle cycle using plain laundry soap without any additives such as bleach or blueing ingredients. Lacy or fragile items, containing embroidery or cutwork should be washed by hand in Liquid Tide or Orvus, which is available at most quilting stores, a nondetergent cleanser frequently used on antique textiles. Place items in a net bag or white pillowcase tied shut with colorfast material.

For heavily soiled items it is essential to presoak first in cold water, then in hot water to loosen stains and dirt.

Whether washing by machine or by hand, make sure that there is enough room for the water to adequately circulate around the cloth in order to wash effectively. A bathtub or utility sink is a good choice.

Rinse thoroughly in hot or cold water three times or until suds are no longer visible. Poor rinsing can leave a residue, which may scorch during ironing or turn yellow over time.

Sturdy table linens can be dried on a low-heat setting in the clothes dryer. However, air drying is preferred because it preserves the shape and dimensions of linens. For easier ironing, give it a quick shake before hanging. If linens are going to be stored for several months, put them away unstarched and not ironed. Roll them in clean white cloths or acid-free tissue until ready for ironing.

Speed tips: For quicker results once it's time to get the ironing board out, season your table linens. The process of sprinkling your tablecloth with hot water, rolling it up, and setting it aside for several hours—or seasoning—makes the linen fibers much more pliable and easier to iron. Lay table linens on a clean countertop or table. Sprinkle evenly with hot water to prevent a blotchy finish. Roll up in a clean white cloth for an hour or more. Putting the tablecloth in the refrigerator for several hours makes ironing even easier. Iron within a day to avoid mildew growth.

In a pinch: If you don't have a spray bottle to season your linens, use a whisk broom or your fingers. Dip in the hot water and shake fine drops over the linen.

Caution: Handle wet linens carefully. When line-drying, never hang a tablecloth by the corners. It could stretch or tear from the weight of the water. Instead, fold it over the clothesline and secure with clothespins. Also, storing table linens on bare wood shelves could cause yellowing.

Tape Players

Is your tape player emitting a pronounced hiss? Has the sound gotten muffled. Those are sure signs that a tape deck needs to be cleaned, says the Consumer Electronics Manufacturers Association (CEMA) in Arlington, Virginia. The dirt, dust, and oxide that build up inside the player cause these problems. As tapes move through the machine, bits of the oxide particle coating can flake off the tape and stick to the heads and tape path mechanism. Ordinary dust can also damage heads, decks, and tapes. Dust can build up in automobile and portable tape decks even more than home decks. Dirty capstans are the leading cause of problems in car decks, according to CEMA.

If you ignore the problem, eventually the player will start to eat

Clean Tapes, Clean Tape Player

Keeping your tapes in top-notch condition will keep your tape deck cleaner. Follow these tips, according to the Consumer Electronics Manufacturers Association.

- Keep tapes in their cases when not in use.
- Eject tapes after playing if your player doesn't do it automatically.
- Keep cassettes away from heat when not in use.
- Avoid storing cassettes on top of the TV, stereo speakers, or anyplace where a magnetic field can partially erase high-frequency sounds.

your tapes. But investing just a few minutes and a few dollars can keep your sound sparkling.

Technique: Isopropyl (rubbing) alcohol is the universal audio cleaning agent. But the kind you get in the drugstore is diluted and not very effective. Your best bet is to buy it in concentrated form at an electronics store, where it's typically labeled as a cleaner/degreaser.

Using a cotton swab dipped in alcohol, gently clean recording and playback heads, the capstan, the rubber pinch rollers, and any tape guides. Use enough cleaner to dissolve all the buildup, but take care not to drip it all over the tape player's interior. CEMA recommends that you clean your tape deck after every 15 to 20 hours of playing time.

Vacuum the cabinets, exterior, and ventilation grille of the tape player often to remove dust. Both plastic and metal exteriors should be cleaned by wiping with a cloth moistened with water or all-purpose cleaner. Don't use paper towels; they can scratch the plastic.

Speed tips: Popping in a tape head–cleaning cassette can be a time-saver. However, it will not clean the player as effectively. Some miss the capstan and the roller entirely, so only use them occasionally. Use a non-abrasive cassette—preferably the type that uses a cleaning solution. The dry cleaners clean by grinding dirt away and can eventually damage your tape player, says Gary Leiby, owner of Electronic Hardware Repair in Allentown, Pennsylvania.

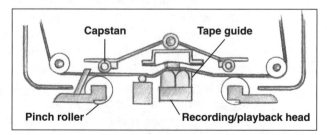

Here's a look at the interior of a typical tape player. Use a cotton swab dipped in alcohol to gently clean the capstan, pinch rollers, recording and playback heads, and tape guide.

Excess Magnetism: The Invisible "Dirt"

An invisible kind of contamination can build up in tape players—excess magnetism. Because the playback heads rub against magnetic cassette tape, they can eventually become magnetized. In addition to causing a distinctive hissing sound, magnetized heads can also erase music from your tapes. To prevent this from happening, use a demagnetizer at least once a year, says the Consumer Electronics Manufacturers Association in Arlington, Virginia.

There are two types: wand demagnetizers, which generate their own magnetic field to neutralize the one on your tape head, and cassette-type demagnetizers, which utilize a filament brush and a field-discharge chip to demagnetize heads. Electronics retailers sell both types.

In a pinch: Ordinary isopropyl alcohol can be substituted. However, since it is diluted, it is not as effective at dissolving built-up gunk and dirt.

Caution: Alcohol is extremely flammable. Do not smoke while using alcohol-based cleaners or use them near an open flame.

Tapestries

Over time, airborne dust and pollution can soil and discolor tapestries and other textile wall hangings, such as quilts and rugs. Textile conservators recommend using extreme caution when cleaning wool tapestries, particularly if a piece is valuable. "It's easy to do this wrong," says Marlene Eidelheit, director of the Textile Conservation Lab at the Cathedral of Saint John the Divine in New York City. Once wet, the heavy fabric is prone to tears and stretching if it is not supported evenly on all sides. A general rule of thumb is that if the piece is bigger than your bathtub, do not attempt to clean it at home. Seek the services of a qualified dry cleaner or a textile conservator.

Technique: To avoid tears and stretching, it is crucial to keep the piece flat during the cleaning process. This can be accomplished by placing the piece on a rigid frame with fiberglass or nylon screening (available at larger hardware stores), which can be immersed in your bathtub. Start by vacuuming the loose dirt and particles from the tapestry with the handheld brush attachment. Do not drag the brush or else you may abrade the fabric. If the piece is very delicate, place a section of nylon hosiery or fiberglass screen over the end of the vacuum tube. Next, it is essential to test for colorfastness. Using an eyedropper, drip tepid (about 80°F) spring or distilled water on each color, especially all shades of red. Blot with blotting paper or clean white cloth such as muslin or sheeting to see if the color bleeds. Repeat the procedure with a detergent solution using roughly 1 tablespoon laundry soap to 4 gallons water. Because many commercial soap products contain additives including brighteners, which can leave a dirt-attracting residue behind, textile conservators use a pH-balanced anionic surfactant cleaner called Orvus, available at most quilting stores or by mail from University Products, P. O. Box 101, Holyoke, MA 01041. If it fails the colorfastness test, seek professional help to clean the piece.

Lay the tapestry flat on a screen and immerse in spring or distilled tepid water for 10 minutes to loosen the dirt. Gently clean by placing a very soft sponge in the detergent solution and rolling it over the surface of the tapestry. If you have a handheld shower, rinse with a gentle spray of lukewarm water and then drain the tub. Repeat the spray-and-rinse process until no soap bubbles are visible in the tub. To clean the reverse side, roll the piece onto a sturdy tube covered in plastic at least four inches in diameter, available at home centers, and unroll on the screen with the reverse side facing up to avoid tearing or stretching. Repeat the rinse process with spray of lukewarm water or by filling and draining the tub until soap bubbles are no longer visible. The final rinse should be done with purified spring water or distilled water, which is free of mineral deposits and pollutants that could break down the fibers.

Remove the tapestry and screen to a clean flat surface for drying. To expedite drying, roll the tapestry in a double thickness of clean white muslin or sheeting towels. Unroll it and place back on the screen to dry. You may use a fan to speed the drying process, but never try to help things along by placing the piece in the clothes dryer.

Speed tips: Cleaning a tapestry the right way is an arduous process, and skipping any one of the steps to save time

A CLEAN STORY

Stumbling Upon an Industry

Legend has it that in a Paris bar in the late 1800s, a drunken man knocked a lamp onto a beautiful tapestry. As the spilled kerosene flowed over the tapestry, it immediately turned brighter and cleaner. And so began the process of dry cleaning. Needless to say, this approach is not recommended at home.

could result in ruining a fine piece of art. A twice-a-month sweep of the vacuum, however, can prevent the buildup of dust and soil that requires a soap-and-water cleaning. "Vacuuming is one of the most underestimated preventive measures," says Eidelheit. You can tell if the tapestry is clean by doing a blotting test with water after vacuuming. Drop a few drops of spring or distilled water onto the tapestry and blot with plain white muslin or sheeting cloth to see evidence of dirt.

Caution: Water-soaked fibers in a tapestry are extremely fragile during the cleaning process. Do not fold the piece or pick it up by the edges, which could cause it to tear or stretch.

Tar

 EMERGENCY ACTION
Freeze with ice cubes until the tar becomes brittle, then carefully scrape with a plastic spatula. If ice is not available, gently pull as much tar off the surface as you can.

Remember that tar was made to be tough. When you try to remove a tar stain, keep in mind that you're up against a construction material highly valued for its imperviousness to water and its ability to stick where stuck.

Technique: After you've scraped as much tar as possible from the surface, treat the underlying stain as soon as possible. There are several methods. Before you begin, test a small part of the fabric for colorfastness. For a fresh stain, the Soap and Detergent Association in New York City recommends placing the stain facedown on paper towels and sponging it with white kerosene. Replace the paper towels frequently to absorb as much tar as possible and to avoid transferring the stain. Apply stain pretreater and launder the article in the hottest water possible with regular laundry detergent.

For a hard dry stain, apply petroleum jelly to soften it, then sponge with cleaning solvent.

Speed tips: The quickest way to get tar out is to act quickly. Old stains are nearly impossible to remove.

In a pinch: Try nonbutane lighter fluid to loosen and remove the tar stain. Test for colorfastness first. Use in a well-ventilated area away from heat or flames.

If you still can't get the stain out after several tries with kerosene or lighter fluid, apply and reapply laundry pretreater to keep the stain wet for 20 minutes. Follow with a rinse in warm water.

Caution: Do not apply water to the stain until you have removed as much as possible with solvents. Water tends to set tar and make the stain even worse. Do not launder until the stain is completely gone. Always read the product label for proper usage and safety precautions. Tar stains are some of the most difficult to remove without permanent damage to fabric surfaces, according to Bill R. Griffin, president of Cleaning Consultant Services in Seattle.

Tarnish

When it develops on a bronze statue, tarnish is called patina and is considered a beautiful part of the aging process. But on most metals regular removal of tarnish is recommended to prevent it from becoming embedded in the finish.

Tarnish is the discoloration that occurs when metals react with salts, acids, and even the oxygen in the air. Over time, tarnish will progressively dull and darken brass, silver, copper, and gold. On aluminum, which reacts with salt in the air, tarnish shows up as a white crust.

Technique: To keep your metals gleaming, wash and polish them regularly. Use a commercial polish formulated for the specific metal, or mix your own polish from household ingredients. (Also see specific entries for individual metals.)

There are four basic cleaning methods that naturally bring a shine back to metal.

- Abrasion, which combines a granular ingredient with elbow grease
- Soaking in an acidic solution
- Applying an alkaline paste, which is rubbed onto the surface, allowed to dry, and then rinsed off
- Submerging the item in an acidic solution

Pantry staples like lemon juice, vinegar, salt, cream of tartar, baking soda, toothpaste, and olive oil are the basis of various homemade metal polishes. Apply polishes or pastes with a sponge, cloth, or soft brush.

For brass and copper, which need a stronger abrasive than silver, mix 2 teaspoons salt, 1 tablespoon flour, and enough vinegar to make a paste. Vigorously apply the paste with a sponge and dry. Rinse in hot water and polish to a shine with a dry towel.

Although different metals require varying degrees of abrasion and rubbing, you can use an effective all-purpose metal cleaner. Rub some soft-grade blackboard chalk into a damp rough cloth and polish the surface. It will remove dirt and grease, yet it won't scratch.

Speed tips: Opt for the submersion method of cleaning if you want to save some time and elbow grease. Stains on aluminum, for instance, can be removed by stewing the metal piece on low heat for an hour or so in a water bath that contains an acidic ingredient, such as 2 halved tomatoes, 2 or 3 halved lemons, or 1 grapefruit cut in quarters, plus 1 to 2 cups freshly cut rhubarb.

In a pinch: The acidic qualities of lemon juice used full strength will remove tarnish on brass, bronze, and copper. The white of its rind will polish chrome.

Caution: Baking soda or washing soda are not recommended for cleaning aluminum.

Taxidermy

Keep dirt and dust from accumulating on your mounted trophies by following a few preventive measures. Display your stuffed creature away from sunlight or else your black bear may end up looking like a polar bear. A climate-controlled room free of the airborne impurities of smoke (either fireplace or cigarette), kitchen fumes, and humidity from bathing and laundry is the best location for your display.

Technique: At least once a month, remove dust from the fur using a one-inch artist's brush. Carefully stroke in the natural direction of the fur.

Eyes, teeth, noses, horns, and other hard surfaces can be cleaned with a lightly dampened (not wet) cloth or with an antistatic cloth (the kind used to clean photographs). Be careful because water and moisture can stretch the skin or fur of preserved animals.

While the most common cleaning concern for your mounted treasures is dust, pests that feed on the organic matter of the animal can be a problem since arsenic is no longer used in the preservation process. Museums regularly freeze their taxidermy to kill any bugs or larvae. You, too, can use your freezer (if it's large enough) to get rid of infestation. If you've inspected your trophy and found evidence of infestation (such as bits of wings or shed insect larval casings), Catharine Hawks, a conservator in private practice in Falls Church,

A CLEAN STORY

Happy Tails to You, Trigger

A star in his own right, Trigger appeared with Roy Rogers in 188 movies and television episodes. Although he died in 1965, the golden palomino legend isn't just a celluloid memory. You can visit all 15½ hands of Trigger, who is mounted at the Roy Rogers–Dale Evans Museum in Victorville, California.

"Never call him stuffed. He's mounted," says Roy Rogers Jr., president and executive officer of the family-run museum. After his death at age 33, Trigger's hide was stretched over a fiberglass mold that details his physical structure down to the last muscle and vein.

Over 100,000 people a year trek to the desert to visit him, so he has to look good.

"The mounts in the last few years are a lot easier to take care of," says Rogers. About once a year, he wipes Trigger's coat down twice with alcohol. "This removes airborne contaminants that could discolor the fur and keeps a sheen to the hair."

The mane and tail are gently shaken free of dust, which is swept up with an ordinary vacuum cleaner held about three inches away. To protect Trigger's coat from skin oils, Rogers wears gloves during the cleaning process.

As manager of the family museum, Rogers takes care of everything else, too, including 200 other mounted creatures and thousands of items of memorabilia. "I do a little bit of everything. If the toilet overflows, they call me for that also. And I wear gloves when I'm doing that, too."

Virginia, recommends placing the taxidermy in the freezer. First, remove all the food from the freezer and put the taxidermy in a sealed plastic bag to avoid contact with any moisture, which could damage the fur or skin of the animal. Freezing is most effective at –4°F for a minimum of one week. If your freezer doesn't go that low, extend the freezing time. If your freezer only goes to 14°F, you may need up to 30 days of freezing to kill all stages of any insects. To properly measure the temperature of your freezer, put a candy thermometer in a glass of water into your freezer.

Speed tips: You can also blow dust off with a blow-dryer on a cool setting.

In a pinch: If you don't have an artist's brush, use any soft-bristle clean brush or a feather duster. Remember to clean in the direction of the nap, never against it.

Caution: Wear rubber or disposable surgical gloves when handling all taxidermy to avoid transferring skin oils onto the piece, which will act as a dust magnet. If you have a pre-1970s mounting that was preserved with arsenic, don't clean it by hand. The only safe way to clean mounts with arsenic is with a vacuum with a HEPA (high-efficiency particulate air) filter. The HEPA-filtered vacuum doesn't redistribute dust into the air. Electrolux makes HEPA-filtered vacuums, but you might find it more reasonable just to hire a professional conservator to care for your pre-1970s mounting. Call your local museum and ask them to recommend someone.

Don't brush or wipe birds with anything. You will ruin the feather patterns.

Telephones

Because we get up close and personal with the telephone every time we use it, skin oils, hair preparations, dirt, and plain old germs accumulate on it. So we really ought to try to keep them a little cleaner than we do.

Technique: A cloth soaked in ordinary rubbing alcohol will cut through dirt on plastic telephones. It will also serve as a disinfectant. Be sure to put the alcohol on the cloth, not the telephone, and wipe clean. Remove dirt between push buttons with a cotton swab dipped in alcohol, says William Ruhe, owner of Atlantic Telephone and Data Services in Whitehall, Pennsylvania.

The metal battery charger buttons on the base of cordless telephones should not be wet down with cleaner. Instead, rub clean with the tip of a pencil eraser, says Ruhe.

Speed tips: Don't neglect the coils of your telephone cord. Extra-long, walk-around-the-kitchen-while-you-talk versions can get particularly dirty from dragging on the floor. To clean, disconnect it from the base and handset, and then pull it through a folded cleaning cloth that has been generously sprayed with all-purpose cleaner.

In a pinch: If you don't have rubbing alcohol on hand, any spray-on disinfectant or all-purpose cleaner will also work.

Caution: Never spritz cleaner directly into the receiver holes or onto the button area. Plastic telephones are easily scratched by abrasive cleaners. Stick to soft cloths.

Televisions

The average American watches about three hours of television a day. And the more that it's on, the dirtier it gets since heat and static electricity generated by televisions make them natural dust magnets.

Technique: Dust accumulates on the entire television, not just the screen. Clean your television once a week with an antistatic dust cloth, says Carol Seelaus, a speed-cleaning instructor at Temple University in Philadelphia and owner of Somebody's Gotta Do It, a professional cleaning service. Polish the glass screen with a cloth or paper towel dampened with window cleaner. Be sure to reach all the nooks and crannies around knobs and buttons where dust can get stuck. And don't neglect the back of the television, where dust bunnies nest in the jumble of cables and wires that connect the VCR, video games, and cable television to the electronic command station. Wood cabinets can be polished with furniture polish.

Speed tips: If fingerprints aren't a problem, you can get a dust-free television by vacuuming. A few swipes with the dust brush attachment of a canister vacuum while you're cleaning the rest of the room should do the trick.

In a pinch: If you don't have an antistatic cloth, any cloth dampened with a window cleaner like Windex will pick up dust just fine.

Cleaning for Couch Potatoes

Armed for a night of couch-bound relaxation, you have the remote in one hand and a bowl of popcorn in the other.

"Everyone I know has popcorn in their couch and grease on the remote," says Carol Seelaus, a speed-cleaning instructor at Temple University in Philadelphia and owner of Somebody's Gotta Do It, a professional cleaning service.

Remote controls fall into the same category of cleaning neglect as doorknobs and telephones—frequently touched and hardly cleaned.

Next time you're planted in front of the tube for an evening, take a bottle of rubbing alcohol, a couple paper towels, and a few cotton swabs and clean your remote.

Alcohol evaporates quickly, so it's the best cleaner to use on electronic items. There's less chance of getting them wet. Dip the swabs in the alcohol to clean the buttons and in between. Dampen the paper towel to clean the plastic casing. Never pour the alcohol directly onto the remote, or you may find yourself having to walk across the room to change channels from then on.

Make sure that it's damp because a dry cloth will only scatter dust.

Caution: Never poke anything into the ventilation openings of a television for cleaning or any other reason. Never spray cleaner or polish directly onto the television. The wetness could seep into the electronic parts and ruin the set. Never clean the television while it is turned on.

Tents

Whether they're nylon or canvas, tents are made to shrug off dirt from the great outdoors. But keep in mind that you're communing with nature, not wallowing in it. If you neglect to clean a tent, the accumulated dirt will eventually wear out the nylon fibers.

"Anyplace you have dirt, that's where your tent is going to wear out," says Eric Hagerman, associate editor for *Outside* magazine. Dirt will also provide organic matter for the growth of mildew, which causes an irreversible loss in fiber strength, staining, and odor. In the right conditions—dampness, darkness, and warmth—mildew can begin to grow within 72 hours. To prevent mildew growth and premature wear, you should clean and dry the tent after each outing.

A CLEAN STORY

Taming a Wild Candy Bar

The nylon dome tents used by Canyon Explorations, of Flagstaff, Arizona, are set up and taken down an average of 100 times a season along the Colorado River in the Grand Canyon. Sand is the primary cleaning problem. It abrades the fabric and clogs the zippers, but for the most part can just be shaken out. Forgetful campers cause the outfitter's stickiest cleaning situations.

"Two or three times a year, we'll have a tent come back that's all gooey and messy," says Mark Piller, operations manager. The problem is melted chocolate candy bars left in the tents in the heat of the sun.

To clean up the mess, scrape away as much of the chocolate residue as soon as possible. Heat and age will set the stain. Sponge with a solution of one capful liquid dishwashing detergent in a bucket of warm water to lift the particles out of the tent fabric. Liquid detergents will work better on a greasy stain like chocolate. Rinse the soap off the tent thoroughly and make sure that it's dry before storing it.

Technique: When you come home from camping, set up the tent one more time—in the garage, basement, or yard. Sponge it down with warm soapy water (Dawn dishwashing detergent works well) followed by a sponge rinse with clean water. Blot up the excess moisture with old towels. "Leave it pitched until it's bone-dry—not the least bit damp," says Hagerman. Putting your tent away while it's wet, or even damp, invites the growth of black smelly mildew. So does storing the tent in a humid area, such as a basement. Even if the tent seems dry, the floor is probably still damp. When it's dry, roll it up loosely and store it in a breathable sack, such as a pillowcase.

"If you store it in your stuff sack, you're promoting mildew growth," says Hagerman. Store the sack in a cool dry place.

Once a year at the end of the camping season, coat all seams with a waterproof sealant. Inspect zippers and spray any sticky ones with silicone.

Speed tips: Use a fan to speed up drying time. Or hang the tent outside over two clotheslines.

In a pinch: If you don't have time to sponge-clean the tent, at least hang it up to dry thoroughly before putting it away.

Caution: Don't use solvents or abrasive cleaners. They can damage the water repellence of the fabric. Don't wash tents in an automatic washer. It will tear the seams and screens to shreds.

Thermos Bottles

Cleanup of freshly used Thermos bottles is no problem. But the one that rolls around in your car for three weeks before making its way to the kitchen sink presents the challenge. Ask anyone who has tried to clean the dried-on goo from the bottom of a one-quart Thermos.

Technique: On all three types—glass, stainless steel, and plastic—a swish of dishwashing detergent and hot water will remove fresh food and drink residue. Rinse well, and turn the bottle upside down to dry fully before storing. Store the bottle with cup and stopper removed to discourage odors and bacteria growth.

To clean dried-on residue, fill the bottle with hot water and a few tablespoons of baking soda and allow to soak for several hours, says the Thermos Company, based in Batesville, Mississippi. If odors are a problem, soak in a solution of hot water and lemon juice or vinegar. On stainless-steel and plastic bottles a brush may be used.

A CLEAN STORY

From the Lab to the Lunch Box

Patented in Germany in 1903, the household vacuum bottle was invented 10 years earlier—not for keeping your chicken soup hot but as a science apparatus for storage of vaccines. The winning entry in a contest to name the new household contraption was Thermos, the Greek word for heat. Though the original glass and metal design has remained handy for the past 100 years for keeping things hot or cold, two other types of vacuum bottles are also popular—stainless steel, which are sturdier and more expensive than glass, and plastic, which are only effective for keeping things cold, according to the Thermos Company in Batesville, Mississippi.

Hard-water buildup and coffee stains can be removed with the coffeepot cleaner Dip-It, or by filling the bottle with water and dropping a couple of denture tablets in it (soak for up to eight hours, then rinse).

Speed tips: For light dirt, fill stainless-steel bottles with boiling water, allow to soak for five minutes, and rinse.

In a pinch: Don't throw a broken glass Thermos away. You can replace broken glass liners. Write the manufacturer at Thermos Company, 355 Thermos Drive, Batesville, MS 38606 to order a replacement liner.

If mildew is a problem, soak the cup and stopper in a mild bleach solution or liquid dishwasher detergent.

Caution: Don't use bleach on stainless-steel bottles. It breaks the weld, and the bottle will no longer hold heat.

Glass bottles are fragile. Do not clean with a brush or any other cleaning tool. And do not remove the base of the liner.

Do not put Thermos bottles in the dishwasher. And avoid immersing the entire bottle since water could seep between the bottle and the insulating liner.

Ties

If you wear neckties, you're probably aware of their unmatched stain-snaring capabilities. Dangling down the length of your torso, a tie is in perfect position to catch, drag, and dip its way through all kinds of messes. The problem is that there's no easy way to clean them. Even professional dry cleaners have a hard time cleaning ties so that they look presentable afterward. Part of the problem is what they're made of—about 75 percent of the ties sold are silk, a fabric that stains easily, abrades easily, and is prone to dye bleeding. The

Three Crucial Questions for Your Dry Cleaner

Neckwear experts generally do not recommend taking a tie to a regular dry cleaner. Although they usually are able to remove the stain and clean the tie, they run into problems during the pressing process.

"You just can't put a tie under the press and wham it. The roll gets pressed flat, the fabric shines, and the tie just doesn't look the same," says Gerald Anderson, executive director of the Neckwear Association of America in New York City.

Ties require hand-finishing techniques to restore their shape and appearance after cleaning. Andy Tarshis, president of Tiecrafters, a New York City–based mail-order dry cleaner specializing in neckties, has blotted sloppy stains off ties that have been knotted around some of the most famous necks in the world, including former president Richard Nixon. He recommends asking a dry cleaner the following questions before handing over your fine neckwear.

1. How do you press your ties? Or, how should a tie be pressed? "You want to make sure that the person at the counter knows that the tie is not supposed to be flat," says Tarshis. Look for answers that include references to softly rolled edges and a symmetrical triangle at the bottom of the tie.

2. Do you clean a lot of silk? Or, do you clean a lot of ties? If the dry cleaner is not used to working with silk, they probably won't try anything out of the ordinary to remove the stains. The problem is that the majority of stains on ties are combination food stains that take expertise and a certain degree of risk taking to remove, says Tarshis. If in doubt, offer the dry cleaner an out: This is a very expensive tie; are you sure you want to take it?

3. Do you ever open up the ties to finish them? After a tie has been cleaned, sometimes the lining balls up. To properly finish the tie, expert cleaners will open up the tie and straighten the lining. If they say, "Why would you want to do that?" then they don't clean a lot of ties.

Try to word your questions to elicit an explanation, not just a yes or no response. "If any of these questions don't make sense to the dry cleaner, you may get someone who is not used to doing ties," says Tarshis.

MONEY-SAVERS

Keep Your Ties in Tip-Top Shape

With neckwear sporting higher and higher prices, it pays to take some extra care to keep your ties looking good, says Andy Tarshis, president of Tiecrafters, a New York City–based mail-order dry cleaner specializing in neckties. Proper care starts when you take them off your neck.

- Always take the knot out of your ties.
- Remove your tie by reversing the tying procedure. No matter how convenient it seems to slip the small end out of the knot, remember that doing so will stretch the tie out of shape and significantly reduce its longevity. The reversal of steps allows the fibers of the material and lining to untwist.
- Hang ties to help ease out the wrinkles. A rack designed for storage works better than a hanger, where ties can slip and twist.
- Avoid choking your tie knot. It twists the lining.
- Cut loose threads. Pulling can damage the tie.

other cleaning difficulty stems from how they're constructed. Ties are cut on the bias so that they'll recover their shape after being knotted all day. "Aside from the shoelace, it's the only piece of apparel we tie in a knot all day and expect to recover," says Gerald Anderson, executive director of the Neckwear Association of America in New York City. Fabric cut on the bias, however, tends to pull and distort very easily.

So what do you do the next time you drip salad dressing on your favorite tie? You have three options: spot-clean the stain yourself, take the tie to a dry cleaner that specializes in cleaning ties, or toss it in the rag bag.

Technique: Ties made of wool, cotton, or polyester respond well to spot-cleaning techniques. Before attempting to remove a spot, test for colorfastness in an inconspicuous area, such as the back of the tie. Do not attempt to rub away stains. It causes fabric abrasion and color loss. Blot the stained area with a cleaning solution appropriate for the type of stain (see Stains on page 356). Work from the outside of the stain toward the center to prevent it from spreading.

Silk ties are best left to a professional.

To remove wrinkles, always steam a tie with a handheld steamer or similar device to preserve its rolled construction. Ironing flattens the edges of the tie, compresses the layers and can ruin the natural luster of the fiber.

In a pinch: To remove water spots on silk ties, rub the mark against another area of the tie until it disappears. "The idea is that you're rubbing silk against silk, so the fabric won't abrade," says Andy Tarshis, president of Tiecrafters, a New York City–based mail-order dry cleaner specializing in neckties. The company's address is 252 West 29th Street, New York, NY 10001.

Caution: The alcohol in cologne and toiletries will discolor silk ties, so apply before putting on your tie.

Tile—Ceramic

Ceramic tile is an extremely durable, low-maintenance surface. Used on walls, floors, and countertops, most tiles have a glazed glassy finish that protects the baked clay from stains and moisture. Unglazed tiles, such as quarry tile, may require additional care, such as more frequent cleaning and occasional sealing. But for the most part, tile is virtually carefree, requiring no waxing or floor finish. Most cleaning and maintenance headaches are related to the grout that holds it all in place (see Grout on page 205).

Technique: Sweep loose dirt with a broom or vacuum. Mop regularly with clear water or a mild soap solution. Change the water frequently—as soon as it gets cloudy—or you'll have streaks. If you use a soap solution, rinse with clear water or else your tile will have a dull sticky film. Walls and countertops should be wiped regularly with a damp cloth or sponge and all-purpose cleaner. In kitchen

How Does Your Tile Rate?

You won't have to clean as often if you buy a high-rated tile, advises *Consumer's Research Magazine*. Most American tile manufacturers use a 1-to-5 rating scale for their floor tiles, with the highest rating indicating the most durable. However, you may find the 1-to-4 rating system used by European tile-makers more prevalent since most of the tile sold in the United States is imported.

Lower ratings may save a few dollars, but in the long run they add up to more hours swishing the sponge mop. The potential for scratches, chips, and breaks increases with lower numbered tiles, which are often fired at lower temperatures. This means that even small bits of gravel tracked in on shoes can scratch a low-grade finish and eventually lead to cracking.

areas, a dose of antibacterial cleaner used regularly will disinfect countertops and prevent the spread of germs. (See Mildew on page 256 and Soap Scum on page 348 for tips on how to clean tile walls in showers.)

Stubborn dirt from spills and drips can be cleaned with a brush or nylon scrubber.

Speed tips: "Some tile floors streak no matter how carefully you rinse them," says Margaret Dasso, owner of the Clean Sweep, a professional cleaning service based in Lafayette, California, and coauthor of *Dirt Busters.* A quick swish of a large bath towel will fix the problem. "Just step on the towel with both feet and boogie around a bit," says Dasso.

Ventilating the bathroom is one of the easiest ways to cut on cleaning time for mildew-prone bathroom tile. Install a ventilation fan or simply open a window after showering.

In a pinch: If you crack a tile and don't have an extra to replace it, use one that you remove from an inconspicuous place, such as a closet.

Caution: Never use abrasive cleaners or scouring powders. They can scratch the finish.

Tile—Vinyl

The vinyl tile on your floor could be solid vinyl, which often has a soft resilient feel, or vinyl composition tile, called VCT, which is made of mineral fillers bound to a thin layer of vinyl. Care and cleaning of either vinyl tile is essentially the same as vinyl sheet flooring, but there are precautions to be aware of when cleaning VCT, some of which, if it was made prior to the mid-1980s, may contain asbestos.

Technique: To preserve the shine and finish, use the mildest cleaning method possible to make the floor clean again. Vacuum or sweep frequently to remove dirt before it has a chance to grind into the finish and abrade the shine. If a light damp mop with plain lukewarm water fails to remove the dirt, clean with a solution of warm water and a detergent recommended by the tile's manufacturer. Follow label directions for proper amounts. Use care not to let water stand on the tiles, as it may loosen the adhesive backing.

Rinse well with cool clear water no matter what the cleaner says about not rinsing.

Speed tips: Mopping with plain water when possible will preserve the shine and save you from having to rinse.

Caution: Unless you are sure beyond a doubt, assume that VCT contains asbestos. If your floor is in good shape, leave it alone. Just keep it waxed and don't use an abrasive cleaner on it, which can remove the protective coating, says Ken Giles of the Consumer Products Safety Commission in Bethesda, Maryland. If the floor must be replaced, hire a professional to do the job, says Giles.

Causes and Cures for Yellowing

If your white or light-colored vinyl tile has yellowed, one of these reasons may be the cause.

- Too much sunlight. Hang window treatments to prevent further yellowing.
- Asphalt residue from driveway and road surfaces tracked in on feet reacts with vinyl and can cause permanent yellowing. Prevent it by using a doormat to wipe feet.

Tin

A soft crystalline metal with a silvery-white luster, tin is used as a thin, protective coating on pans and utensils and for decorative items. Tin darkens with age, which is beneficial on ovenware items since the dark color absorbs heat better, according to the Michigan State University Extension in East Lansing.

Technique: Wash tin in warm sudsy water and dry thoroughly. Do not use sharp tools or harsh abrasives, which may scrape off the thin plating and expose the rust-prone base metal. Remove rust by rubbing tin with superfine (#0000) steel wool dipped in vegetable oil.

Speed tips: Coat decorative tin items with a thin coat of paste wax containing carnauba or lacquer to help prevent rust. Waxed tin is also easier to dust.

In a pinch: Baking soda and water will remove food from tin without scratching.

Toaster Ovens

Most toaster ovens have a continuous-cleaning coating that keeps the interior looking good, but the rest of the oven parts require regular cleaning to remove crumbs, greasy fingerprints, and food splatters.

Technique: Empty the crumb tray regularly to avoid a fire hazard, and wipe up any food spills with a damp cloth. Baked-on crud can be removed with a nylon scrubber. The wire rack and the oven tray can be cleaned with a nylon scrubber and warm sudsy water, says Joanne Nosiglia, product manager for cooking at Black and Decker Household Products in Shelton, Connecticut. Clean the glass door with a nylon pad and sudsy water. Do not use spray glass cleaners. Exterior chrome and plastic should be cleaned with a damp sponge or cloth. Stubborn spots can be removed with baking soda, but avoid harsh abrasives, which will scratch the finish.

It's important to dry all parts of the oven thoroughly prior to use.

Speed tips: You'll save time in the long run if you wipe up spills, splatters, and crumbs after each use. A drip of melted cheese, which wipes away in seconds today, may form a fossilized crud that adheres to the oven with the tenacity of superglue after continued use of the appliance.

Save time and elbow grease by washing the wire rack, glass door, and drip tray in the dishwasher.

Caution: Make sure that the oven is unplugged and cool before cleaning any part. Avoid dripping water or cleaners inside the oven or poking around with utensils, which could damage the elements or heat sensor.

Toasters

Ever since the Egyptians started baking bread in 2600 B.C., people have been making toast. For more than 4,000 years, the family toaster was a skewer that held a piece of bread over an open fire. With the arrival of electricity around the beginning of the twentieth century, inventors began seeking convenient ways to enjoy a slice of toast. The first pop-up toaster for the home, the Toastmaster, introduced in 1926, solved that problem but created another—how to clean the crumb-filled contraption.

Technique: Unplug the toaster and allow it to cool. Hold the toaster over the trash can or sink and empty crumb tray. Use a thin brush to clean out stubborn crumbs. Wipe the tray with a damp cloth or sponge, and dry it completely before closing. How often you need to empty the crumb tray depends on how often you use the toaster. If you use it every day, appliance manufacturers recommend that you clean it once a week.

Clean the outside of chrome toasters with a damp sponge and baking soda or a cloth dampened with window cleaner. Lightly rub stubborn stains with dry superfine (#0000) steel wool. Wipe plastic-sided toasters with mild liquid dishwashing detergent or baking soda and water. Do not use abrasive cleaning products, which could scratch the finish.

Speed tips: If your toaster regularly sits out on the counter, give it a quick wipe with a damp sponge or cloth while you're wiping up your countertops or cleaning fingerprints off the refrigerator.

In a pinch: Clean stubborn crumbs with a pipe cleaner if you don't have a brush handy.

Caution: Always unplug the toaster before cleaning it. To remove a piece of stuck toast from the toaster, first unplug it. Then, move the toaster carriage up and down while turning the toaster upside down and right side up until the toast gets dislodged, says Joanne Nosiglia, product manager for cooking with Black and Decker Household products in Shelton, Connecticut. Always be careful not to insert utensils into the toaster, for they will damage the fine wires, which do the toasting. Do not spray cleaners directly onto the toaster.

Toilets

It's not as bad as a root canal, but there are few household chores more thoroughly reviled than cleaning the toilet. "Most people are revolted by the idea of cleaning the toilet," says Kent Gerard, a cleaning consultant from Oakland, California. "They pinch their noses and get through it as quickly as possible."

Maybe that's why the manufacturers of toilet-cleaning products are always trying to show us a lighter side to toilet cleaning. Remember the startled housewife of the 1970s discovering a miniature speedboat floating in her toilet tank? Bobbing around in a sea of crystal blue toilet water, the Ty-D-Bol man—clad in his nautical duds—assured us that the repugnant task of cleaning the toilet could be solved by using an automatic toilet-bowl cleaner. He wasn't totally off base. In-tank toilet-bowl cleaners help sanitize the bowl, prevent stains, and can even stretch out the time between cleaning. But they're no substitute for regular scrubbing with a brush and some liquid cleanser such as Comet or Ajax with bleach.

The good news is that toilets aren't as dirty as you think. "The toilet is probably a safer place to eat a sandwich than the countertop," says Charles Gerba, Ph.D., professor of microbiology at the University of Arizona in Tucson, who has done several studies on household germs.

Technique: To thoroughly clean a toilet bowl stained by hard water, rust, or just plain neglect, you should drain the water out of the bowl. You can do this two ways. Force the water out by thrusting a plunger into the neck at the bottom of the toilet bowl, or turn off the water valve and flush the toilet. Bacteria and germs cling the sides of the bowl and set up housekeeping in the pores of the porcelain. To kill germs and open pores for a deep cleaning, pour boiling water in the toilet bowl and allow it to drain. "Like cleaning your skin, the hot water will open the pores of the toilet bowl, so you can get it clean," says Gerard. Using a small brush and liquid cleanser containing bleach, scrub the toilet bowl and under the rim where rust and mineral stains are likely

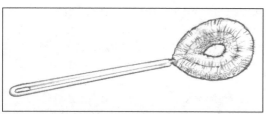
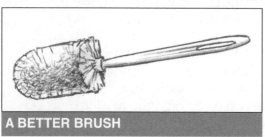

A BETTER BRUSH

The metal wire in a traditional oval-shape brush (top) can cause black scratch marks in the toilet bowl. A better choice is a round toilet brush (bottom) with nylon bristles attached to a plastic handle.

to build up. After you're done scrubbing, turn the water valve back on and flush once the tank is filled with water.

The best way to clean a toilet, according to Bill R. Griffin, president of Cleaning Consultant Services in Seattle, is with liquid cleanser, a white scrubbing pad, and a gloved hand. Further, he stresses the importance of doing it at least twice a week for best results.

Most of the germs that we come in contact with are on the toilet itself, so spray the entire fixture with disinfectant cleaner—the lid, the top and bottom of the seat, the rim of the bowl, around the hinges where billions of microbes like to accumulate, the base, the tank, and the handle. Allow the disinfectant to do its germ-killing work for a few minutes and then wipe dry with a clean cloth or paper towel. Beware of sponges, which could reinfect your sanitized toilet with their own thriving colony of germs.

Speed tips: If you're going away for the weekend, pour a cup of household bleach into the toilet, close the lid, and flush it when you come home. This is a good way to get rid of old built-up stains. "Letting it soak for a couple of days in bleach water does wonders for some stains," says Gerard.

In a pinch: Even if you don't have any toilet-bowl cleaner on hand, you can effectively get rid of germs in the bowl. When you flush, some bacteria cling to the sides and remain in the bowl. You can remove almost all of the bacteria from the toilet bowl by just scrubbing the sides with a brush and flushing, according to Dr. Gerba.

If you live in a hard-water area, your toilet will develop a raised ring at the water line from mineral deposits. If acid toilet bowl cleaner and brushing have failed to remove it, try using a pumice stone. Wet the stone in water and rub it on the ring. Make sure that the stone stays wet as you work your way around the bowl. Only use a pumice

Keep a Lid on Those Germs

If you want to keep your bathroom from being contaminated by a layer of airborne bacteria and viruses, close the lid when you flush.

"When you flush, the toilet spews a fine mist of whatever is in the bowl," says Kent Gerard, a cleaning consultant from Oakland, California, and advocate of lowering the lid.

Studies conducted by Charles Gerba, Ph.D., professor of microbiology at the University of Arizona in Tucson, show that when you flush, the toilet shoots out an invisible mist of tiny germ-infested water droplets that get all over everything. You can get infected with diarrhea or hepatitis A by touching the surfaces where the bacteria- and virus-laden spray lands—like your toothbrush, for example—or by inhaling the invisible mist into your respiratory tract.

Closing the lid is one way that you can prevent the mist from being propelled into the room. But Dr. Gerba advises that you keep the lid down until the toilet is used again. The germ-laden mist remains airborne in the bowl for some time after the flush, Dr. Gerba says. Opening the lid too soon will only draw aerosol up and out of the bowl—and usually directly into your face.

If you don't feel like hanging a sign in your bathroom that says, "Close the lid when you flush," automatic toilet-bowl cleaners—such as Ty-D-Bol or 2000 Flushes—are an effective way to reduce the number of bacteria that are propelled from the bowl during flushing.

Six Dirty Little Secrets about Toilets

1. The dirtiest part of the toilet is the bottom of the toilet seat. Second place goes to the base and the floor surrounding the toilet.

2. The average person uses the toilet seven times a day.

3. Older toilets need to be cleaned more frequently than new ones. "The older a toilet is, the more porous it is to stains. The older it is, the more you need to clean it," says Kent Gerard, a cleaning consultant from Oakland, California.

4. In public rest rooms, the first stall is most likely to have the fewest bacteria and the middle ones are likely to have the most because more people use them.

5. Women's rest rooms are dirtier than men's rest rooms. The floor of the stall and the hot-water tap were the most frequent sites for bacterial contamination, while the top side of the toilet seat, which nearly half of all women either wipe or cover before using, ranked as one of the least contaminated areas in public rest rooms.

6. The cleanest public toilets are found in national chain restaurants; the worst are found in gas stations.

stone on white, vitreous china toilets. It will scratch the finish on colored, enameled, or plastic fixtures. Pumice is a last resort. Regular cleaning is the better approach.

Caution: Do not spray cleaners on the seat or rim at the same time you are cleaning the bowl with an acid toilet-bowl cleaner. Toilet-bowl cleaners often contain hydrochloric acid, which could cause a dangerous chemical reaction if inadvertently mixed with other cleaners. To avoid the possibility of a noxious mixture, use acid toilet-bowl cleaners either before or after disinfecting the seat and rim. If used prior to cleaning the seat area, be sure that the acid cleaner is flushed and thoroughly rinsed away. In most cases, regular twice-weekly cleaning will eliminate the need to use harsh acid bowl cleaners, says Griffin.

Automatic toilet-bowl cleaners that contain bleach are great for killing germs, but they are hard on the working parts of the toilet tank—especially those made of rubber.

Toys

Most toys don't come with cleaning instructions. If they do, they're usually long gone by the time hours of play have left their mark. So you usually have to rely on common sense when figuring out how to clean kids' playthings. Rule number one: If it's not washable, don't give it to a child.

Technique: Toddler toys often have to pass the taste test and should be washed regularly to discourage the spread of germs. Most are plastic and can be washed in the sink with warm water and mild liquid dishwashing detergent. Rinse thoroughly and drip-dry on a dish rack. Harsh cleaners and vigorous scrubbing can remove painted facial features and decorative stickers.

Use a damp cloth to wipe off toys that cannot be immersed in water, such as wooden toys, battery-operated dolls, and electronic games. A cotton swab dipped in alcohol is handy for cleaning hand-held electronic toys.

The plastic skin on dolls can be cleaned by gently rubbing with a cloth dipped in cold cream. Board games can usually tolerate a quick wipe-down with a barely damp cloth. Wipe plastic toys with a mild disinfectant solution after use to help prevent the spread of germs to nonfamily guests, advises Bill R. Griffin, president of Cleaning Consultant Services in Seattle.

Speed tips: Many toys manufactured for children under the age of two years are dishwasher-safe. Since these toys often spend as much time in curious little mouths as they do the hands, it's a good idea to use the cleaning capabilities of the top rack of the dishwasher. It saves time, too.

In a pinch: Of course, there's another angle to cleaning toys: gathering them up when they're scattered all over the floor. Straighten up a toy-covered floor with a plastic rake, recommends Margaret Dasso, owner of the Clean Sweep, a professional cleaning service based in Lafayette, California, and co-author of *Dirt Busters.* "It will cut time and fatigue by two-thirds," she says.

Trash Cans

There's nothing like the stench from a dirty trash can on a hot day to remind you that it's time to clean it. The best time, of course, is right after the garbage collectors have emptied the cans.

Technique: Hose metal and plastic cans down on the inside with a high-pressure spray to clean off any chunks of rotting trash. Dump out the water and spray the inside thoroughly with a disinfectant. Allow the disinfectant time to kill the billions of bacteria that are thriving in the moist dark recesses of the trash cans, and then scrub them with a good stiff brush. Rinse the cans and turn them upside down to dry. Any water left in the can will be a breeding ground for germs and odors.

Colossal Cleanups

Weighing In at the Curb
The amount of garbage the typical suburban family of three generates a week: 40 pounds

Speed tips: Sprinkle borax, a naturally occurring mineral containing sodium, boron, oxygen, and water, in the bottom of the can to prevent odors. Borax absorbs moisture, which is why it prevents odors, according to the Dial Corporation in Phoenix.

In a pinch: You can also use a solution of borax and warm water to clean and deodorize the inside of trash cans if you don't have disinfectant. Borax, however, will not kill germs.

Trash Compactors

If your municipality or collector limits the amount of trash that you can dispose of each week, a compactor can reduce your waste volume by 80 percent. Recycling can reduce waste volume by 40 to 50 percent.

Technique: Remove the compactor bucket or drawer, and wipe down the inside of the compactor with disinfectant. It's a good idea to wear rubber gloves because glass shards and sharp debris may be hidden in the recesses of the compactor. Hose down the bucket or drawer outside and scrub with disinfectant cleaner. While you have the compactor apart, change the odor filter, if necessary. Consult your owner's manual for instructions on how to clean the ram (the part that actually compacts the trash). Wipe down the outside of the appliance with all-purpose cleaner.

Speed tips: To keep the compactor clean and free of odors, avoid putting messy wet garbage such as food scraps in it. Save those for the garbage disposal or the compost heap. Also, don't put odor-prone trash such as disposable diapers in it.

In a pinch: If the compactor must be used to dispose of all your trash, place messy items such as food scraps in plastic bags before compacting.

Caution: Make sure that the compactor is in the "Off" or "Lock" position before cleaning. Consult your owner's manual for specific cleaning instructions.

Typewriters

Correcting a few typos can be an exercise in frustration on a dirty typewriter. Dust-encrusted rollers tend to slip, throwing the line spacing off just enough to make your corrections stick out like a sore thumb. "One of the biggest problems that occurs is from normal everyday dust in the air getting down in the machine," says Mark Gebert, service manager for Office Concepts at Rochester Typewriter in Troy, Michigan. Signs that it's time for a cleaning are keys that stick, slow-starting motors, and slow-moving carriages. But with a few basic household items and a can of compressed air, you can have your typewriter working like new.

Technique: Remove typing ribbons, correction ribbon, and daisy wheel (if applicable) before you begin. First, get the dust out. Remove the cover and stand the machine on its back facing you. With a can of compressed air, available at office supply stores, blow dust down and out of the machine. Force air between each key starting from the inside of the machine and working your way out. "The more dust you can get out of the machine, the better," says Gebert.

The roller, or platen, keeps the paper grip tight so that line spacing is even. There are two to four additional small rollers located under the large one. Clean rollers with an alcohol (isopropyl or rubbing) dampened cloth. Move the cloth back and forth along the length of the roller while turning it to clean completely.

Plastic keys should be cleaned with a cloth dampened with all-purpose cleaner. Don't use anything abrasive. It will scratch and mar the keys. And don't spray the keyboard directly.

Ink-gunked type bars will produce poor-quality lettering, so clean them, too. Dampen a small wire brush with alcohol and rub the ink residue off of the metal type. Dry with a lint-free cloth as you go. You may need to pick ink out of the letters with a safety pin. "Anything circular has a tendency to collect ink," Gebert says.

To clean a daisy wheel that is plastic, remove it from the machine and lay it on an absorbent cloth. Spray with all-purpose cleaner and dab clean with a dry cloth.

Speed tips: Keep the dust out in the first place. When not in use, keep your typewriter covered or stored in its case.

In a pinch: If you don't have a can of compressed air, use a blow-dryer. An old toothbrush works fine for cleaning type if you don't have a small wire brush.

Caution: Make sure that the machine is unplugged before you begin cleaning. Stick to routine cleaning. "Don't get into taking the machine apart," advises Gebert. It's not a good idea to use the vacuum to suck dust out. You run the risk of sucking up tiny parts of the machine.

Umbrellas

Both kinds of umbrellas protect you from the elements. But the two basic types—those that block the sun and those that block the rain—require slightly different care and cleaning procedures.

Rain Umbrellas

Technique: If you get mud-splashed while waiting for the bus next to a puddle, hose off your umbrella in the open position to clean it. Stubborn dirt can be removed by sponging on any water-based cleaner, such as ordinary liquid dishwashing detergent that doesn't contain bleach, which will discolor the fabric, advise experts at Totes Isotoner Corporation, a leading umbrella manufacturer based in Loveland, Ohio.

Speed tips: After use, allow your umbrella to dry in the open position to prevent rust from forming on interior hardware. To speed up drying, shake the water from the fabric by opening and closing the umbrella quickly a few times.

Caution: Do not use spot removers on umbrellas. They can remove the silicone water-repellency coating on the fabric.

Sun Umbrellas

Technique: Clean your patio umbrella once a year before storing it for the winter. The festive sun shade that looks so cheerful and fresh in the spring usually accumulates a gray film by fall, caused by dirt from rain, trees, and the air.

You can clean coarse fabric and vinyl umbrellas with a solution of mild liquid dishwashing detergent and water, according to experts at the Michigan State University Extension in East Lansing. Sponge or brush it on, particularly in the folds of the umbrella where dirt tends to collect. Allow it to soak for several minutes and then rinse it with a hose. Dry thoroughly in an open position before storing.

Speed tips: Open sun umbrellas after it rains and allow them to dry in an open position so that dirt will not collect in the folds.

In a pinch: Use an automobile vinyl-top cleaner, such as Blue-Magic Convertible Top Cleaner, on vinyl umbrellas that will not come clean with detergent. Then apply vinyl protector for upholstery or automobiles, such as Armor All Protectant, for a finish that will resist dirt. This is easiest to do if the umbrella can be spread on a large flat surface, such as a driveway.

Caution: Always close a sun umbrella during storms and high winds to avoid damage.

Upholstery

You won't notice the dirt on upholstered furniture until it's really heavily soiled. So adopt a regardless-of-whether-it-looks-dirty approach in your vacuuming routine. If your furniture is dirty enough that it's readily visible, then vacuuming will probably not remove the dirt. You'll have to take cleaning to next level.

Cleaning a piece of upholstered furniture is a complicated task that

How the Pros Clean Up Their Dirty Talk

Professional cleaners are trained to avoid certain words so that they won't alarm customers. But here are some translations so that you'll understand what's going on.

A client's furniture is never *dirty*; it's *soiled*. Testing for colorfastness is done with a *sour* solution, not with an *acid* one.

They never *scrub*, *wash*, or *bleach*; they *clean*, *restore*, or *brighten*.

A qualified professional will *preinspect* your furniture before cleaning to spot potential problems and point them out to you so that they are not held responsible. The Association of Specialists in Cleaning and Restoration in Annapolis Junction, Maryland, says that these are some of the things they look for.

- Color bleeding from previous cleanings or spills
- Color loss
- Deterioration of the foam rubber in cushions, or markings that will bleed through during cleaning
- Loose gimp—the decorative trim strip on furniture edges
- Rips, tears, or frays in fabric, particularly on the welting
- Odor
- Nicks in the wood trim
- Stains from hair oil, perspiration, or shoe polish
- Structural damage or weak joints

What Those Cleaning Code Labels Mean

Furniture purchased in the last few years may have a cleaning code on its label. Look under the cushions for a tag. Some manufacturers have voluntarily adopted uniform standards for furniture cleanability.

W: Use a water-based cleaner.
S: Solvent-based cleaners or dry cleaning are necessary.
W-S: Choose either of the above two methods.
X: Neither water- nor solvent-based cleaning can be used. Only cleaning by vacuuming is recommended.

One of the problems with the codes is that they are based on color-fastness, says Claudia Ramirez, former executive vice president of the Association of Specialists in Cleaning and Restoration in Annapolis Junction, Maryland. The codes don't have anything to do with shrinkage or browning, two of the most common problems with cleaning upholstery, especially natural fibers.

requires patience and skill. Because so many things can go wrong—dye bleeding, shrinkage, yellowing, browning, and water spotting—your best bet is to hire a professional.

There are a lot of unknowns when it comes to upholstery. You don't see what's behind the surface fabric. Stuffing materials may contain color that will wick to the surface if you overwet the upholstery during cleaning. Materials may turn brown or shrink after cleaning.

"The hidden sin can come to the surface," says Claudia Ramirez, former executive vice president of the Association of Specialists in Cleaning and Restoration in Annapolis Junction, Maryland. Sometimes during manufacturing, pens are used to mark cushions. "You may see a number one wick to the surface during the cleaning process," she says.

Upholstery fabrics are often blends of different fibers that react differently to cleaning. So test the fabric in an inconspicuous area before applying any type of cleaning solution. While man-made fibers such as olefin, nylon, and polyester stand up well to wet cleaning, natural fibers such as cotton, silk, linen, and wool are likely to shrink, spot, or bleed.

If you're determined to try your hand at cleaning a piece of upholstery yourself, there are two methods to choose from: hot-water extraction and wet shampooing.

Hot-Water Extraction

Sometimes called steam cleaning, this process extracts soils and residue from fabric with a machine that applies a solution of hot water and special detergent, not steam, to the fabric and then suctions it out.

The method is effective, especially at removing residue from previous cleanings. Before you begin, test your fabric for colorfastness in an inconspicuous area by applying a small amount of water and blotting it with a white cloth. If it doesn't bleed, try the same procedure with the cleaning solution. If there is any color transfer in either test, consult a professional upholstery cleaner.

If the fabric passes the cleanability test, you can proceed with wet cleaning, but be careful not to overwet the fabric, advise experts at the Michigan State University Extension in East Lansing. Overwetting increases the likelihood of discoloration caused by liquid penetrating the colored stuffing materials or wood and wicking to the surface fabric. It also promotes the growth of mildew.

Once the piece is cleaned, open windows and use fans to speed drying. Upholstery should dry within 24 hours.

Wet Shampooing

Use a commercial upholstery shampoo such as Blue Luster, or make your own shampoo by mixing ½ teaspoon liquid dishwashing detergent per quart of warm water and making suds by squeezing a sponge through it, advise experts at the Michigan State University Extension. Test material for colorfastness first, then apply the suds to the fabric with a sponge or soft brush rubbing gently with the grain of the material. Work on a small area at a time, rinsing each area as you go along with a damp sponge dipped in clear water. Avoid soaking the fabric, but be sure to remove all the soap. If you leave a residue, it will attract dirt.

SCRUB THIS APPROACH

Foam Cleaners: A Not-So-Bright Idea?

Some commercial foam upholstery cleaners contain fluorescent brightening agents that make the fabric appear cleaner initially but can yellow with age and exposure to ultraviolet light, according to the Association of Specialists in Cleaning and Restoration in Annapolis Junction, Maryland.

"Brighteners make the fabric look cleaner to your eye; the fabric looks brighter," says Claudia Ramirez, former executive vice president of the Association of Specialists in Cleaning and Restoration in Annapolis Junction, Maryland. "Perception is reality, so if it looks brighter, it's cleaner."

While foam cleaners may remove some of the dirt, they leave a residue that can cause yellowing. If that happens to you, talk to a professional upholstery cleaner.

Speed tips: You can reduce or eliminate the need for costly and time-consuming cleaning procedures if you vacuum your upholstered furniture regularly—weekly for your favorite chair and monthly for any touch-me-not stuff in the living room. Dust doesn't show up on fabric the same way it does on wood furniture, but it's there along with a host of other critters.

"Vacuuming will take the surface soils out before they can damage the fibers," says Ramirez. Regular vacuuming will also take care of your upholstery from a health standpoint. "When you sit in your favorite chair, your body sheds its skin cells. The dust mites feed on them, and their feces and decomposing carcasses serve as allergens," explains Ramirez.

Use a canister vacuum with an upholstery attachment, and change the bag when it's one-half to two-thirds full. Vacuum the entire piece—both sides of the cushions, the back and sides, the arms, and the platform underneath the cushions.

In a pinch: If you don't have a canister vacuum, you can remove dust from upholstered furniture by brushing it.

Spot-clean stains as soon as possible. Scrape away excess spillage. Working toward the center of the stain, sponge with the dishwashing detergent suds solution on wet-clean fabrics or a solvent-based cleaner on dry-cleanable materials. Blot frequently, and be careful not to overwet the area or spotting could occur.

Caution: Cushions may appear to be removable because of their zippered construction. However, you should not remove the covers for cleaning. Shrinkage could occur, making it impossible to replace the cover.

Spot removers are intended for spot-cleaning only. Never try to clean an entire piece of furniture using these products, which could create a dangerous amount of fumes. Read product labels carefully for proper usage and safety precautions.

Varnished Surfaces

Unlike shellac or lacquer finishes, oil-based varnished surfaces will not develop a white ring from moisture. That's what makes it a durable finish for surfaces like dining room tables that are subject to spills and moisture, says Ian Turner, restoration expert for Garrett

Wade Company, a professional woodworkers supply house in New York City.

Technique: To protect the finish, wax twice a year with a good-quality beeswax and carnauba wax blend, such as BriWax, available in home stores. Apply the wax in a circular motion with a soft cloth and allow it to sit for a few minutes. Then buff to a shine with a dry cloth. If you follow this procedure, wax buildup should not be a problem, says Turner. "People get this image of wax that it builds up on layer upon layer. But most of it is wiped off in buffing. Only a very minor layer remains to protect the varnish," Turner says.

To remove fingerprints and light soil, softly wash the surface with a barely damp cloth that has been dipped in a solution of warm water and a few drops of liquid dishwashing detergent and then wrung nearly dry. Buff the surface immediately with a dry cloth.

If the wood finish still seems lackluster after cleaning, gently wipe the surface down with a cloth that has been lightly soaked in mineral spirits. "Sometimes the grain of the wood becomes obliterated by years of dust and wax," Turner says. The mineral spirits will effectively remove dirt and wax without harming the finish.

Speed tips: In between damp-cloth cleaning, which should be done only when necessary, buff the surface with a soft dry cloth to remove dust and restore the shine.

Dust regularly with a feather duster or dust wand attachment of the vacuum cleaner. Use a light touch to avoid scratching. Save a lot of time and elbow grease by using a small electric polisher when waxing varnished surfaces.

In a pinch: If you develop a white ring on a varnished surface, it

What Kind of Finish Is It?

Many surfaces that appear to be varnished may actually contain lacquer or shellac. Here's a quick test recommended by Ian Turner, restoration expert for Garrett Wade Company, a professional woodworkers supply house in New York City, to find out if the surface that you're cleaning is really varnish. Knowing the finish can be important if you're working with a valuable or antique piece of furniture.

In an inconspicuous place, apply a dab of denatured alcohol. If the finish becomes tacky, it contains shellac. In a second inconspicuous spot, apply a drop of acetone (or nail polish remover). If the surface becomes tacky, it contains lacquer. If nothing happens on either spot, your surface is a varnished finish.

may actually be caused by the wax, not the wood finish. Strip the wax using a cloth dipped in mineral spirits.

Use a superfine (#0000) steel wool to remove wax in recesses and other hard-to-reach areas. Be sure to rub with the grain of the wood.

Caution: Avoid using paper towels to clean varnished surfaces—they can scratch the finish.

Vases and Bottles

Dirt that you can't easily reach, like the residue that dries on the sides of vases and bottles, may seem impossible to clean. Before you toss it on the recycling heap, try some of these easy remedies.

Technique: Even if you can't get your hand (or even a finger) down the neck of a vase or bottle, you can scrub it using dried beans, uncooked rice, or sand. Fill the bottle halfway with hot soapy water, add a handful of your chosen scrubbing material, and shake vigorously. This action will remove the dirt. If the container is extra dirty, before you scrub it, let it soak overnight in ammonia water or in a solution of automatic dishwasher detergent and water. Use 1 tablespoon detergent for each cup of water.

To remove stains, let a mixture of 1 cup strong, cold black tea and 3 tablespoons vinegar stand in the vase overnight.

If a vase or bottle is cloudy, it probably has a mineral film buildup on the sides, according to Robert Montgomery, who has unearthed and cleaned more than 250 antique bottles buried in southeastern Pennsylvania. Remove mineral buildup by filling the container with water, adding 1 to 2 tablespoons automatic dishwasher detergent, and soaking it overnight. Or fill it with water and a couple teaspoons of ammonia, or drop in a denture tablet and shake. If these remedies don't work, try using a commercial mineral and lime remover that contains phosphoric acid, such as CLR.

Speed tips: If you don't have a day to soak an encrusted con-

HOW I DO IT

Vase Advice

Louise Wrinkle often brightens her Alabama home with flowers from her own splendid garden, which has been featured more than once in glossy decorating magazines. A veteran horticulture judge for the Garden Club of America in New York City, she offers these tips for keeping cut flowers—and gardening hands—clean and fresh.

"When you fill a dirty bowl with water, it grows algae, which stops up the stems and causes flowers to dry up sooner," says Wrinkle. "To keep bowls and vases really clean, use a denture cleaner, like Polident. Dissolve one or two tablets in a vase half-filled with water. Scrub the inside of the vase with the solution and it will be squeaky-clean.

"I also put three or four drops of liquid household bleach into the water to deter bacteria from growing. I fill an old eyedropper bottle with bleach and keep it on the shelf next to my vases. That way, I don't have to reach under the sink for the big heavy bottle.

"When you're finished cutting flowers, if you have green and brown grunge on your hands, wash them with the denture-cleaner solution. It cleans them and leaves them feeling smooth."

tainer, bottle brushes are the most effective way to get right to the dirt. They are available in dozens of shapes and sizes and are generally sold in hardware stores. "The brushes are flexible and bendable. Get a range of sizes from small to large, bend them to the shape you need for a particular bottle, and then clean," says Montgomery.

In a pinch: Sometimes old bottles develop a milky-white haze that just won't come off. If you want to hide the stain, try an old trick used by bottle collectors. Clean the bottle as well as you can and dry thoroughly. Put several drops of vegetable oil in the bottle and roll it around to mask the cloudiness caused by magnesium and calcium.

VCRs

Because a VCR can play as good as new for 2,500 hours, or four films a week for seven years, one approach to cleaning it is this: Don't bother. If you buy a $200 VCR, the cost works out to about eight cents a day. On the other hand, regular cleaning will extend the life of your VCR, preserve your tapes, and keep your picture sharp. In an age where techno-obsolescence of electronics products is calculated in months instead of years, seven years of trouble-free service may seem like a fair trade-off for cleaning neglect. But for those of you looking for some extra mileage for your investment, here are a few cleaning strategies.

Technique: A VCR has more moving mechanical parts than any other consumer electronics product, according the Consumer Electronics Manufacturers Association in Arlington, Virginia. Most of the dirt and dust particles that build up are magnetic, so they are naturally attracted to your tape heads. If you don't clean them, eventually the dirt will begin to affect your video quality, translating into images full of white streaks, black lines, and snow. "In fact, most video problems with a VCR can be solved simply by cleaning the heads," says Lisa Fasold, spokeswoman for the Consumer Electronics Manufacturers Association.

They should be cleaned after every 20 hours of use with a good head cleaner—more frequently if you rent a lot of tapes. There are three types of head-cleaning tape cartridges on the market: dry, wet, and magnetic-based. All you do is place the cartridge in the VCR, push "Play," and let the head cleaner do its work.

Magnetic cleaning is the safest method. As you play the tape, on-screen video and audio signals tell you when the heads are clean. With wet cleaning cartridges, the ribbon is moistened with a cleaner and then placed in the VCR. As it plays, it swabs away dirt. Just be careful not to use too much cleaning solution. Dry systems, which use abrasion to clean and can wear down the heads, are not recommended.

Although the wet and magnetic cleaners do a good job at cleaning your tape heads, they don't remove dirt that builds up along the tape path. If streaks and snow persist, your VCR may need to be cleaned by a professional.

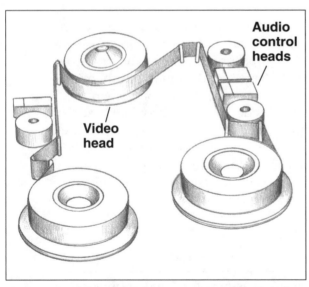

Audio control heads

Video head

Clean audio and video heads in your VCR after every 20 hours of use—more often if you rent a lot of tapes. This illustration shows the inside of a typical VCR and all the places that dirt can build up on the heads and along the tape path.

MONEY-SAVERS

Tape Tactics

The Consumer Electronics Manufacturers Association in Arlington, Virginia, offers the following advice on tape maintenance.

1. Tape used over and over for timed recording and viewing will begin to shed its oxide coating and gum the heads. Discard them after about 200 recording/playback cycles.

2. Keep tapes in their jackets to prevent dust and dirt from accumulating. A dirty tape can transfer particles to the record and playback heads causing poor image quality and possible head damage.

3. Keep tapes away from strong magnetic fields, such as televisions, speakers, and electric motors.

4. Use your tapes at least once a year to prevent the magnetic particles and binder from sticking together. If you don't have time to watch the tape, simply fast-forward it and then rewind it. For longer tape life, store the tape in an upright position like a book with the fully wound spool of tape on the bottom to ease pressure on the hubs.

Don't neglect the outside of your VCR. Dust frequently and wipe with a damp cloth, if necessary.

Speed tips: You'll need to clean your VCR less frequently if you use good-quality tape. Low-quality tape can damage your VCR by shedding particles that clog heads and the tape path. Although letter designations indicate the grade level of tape within a brand, there are no standard designations, so relative quality of high-grade videotape varies from manufacturer to manufacturer. In other words, a bargain store's high-grade tape may not be as good as standard-grade tape from a high-quality supplier. The Consumer Electronics Manufacturers Association recommends buying your tapes from a high-quality, well-known supplier.

In a pinch: If you can no longer tell whether Dorothy is in Kansas or Oz and you don't have a head-cleaner system, cotton swabs and rubbing alcohol should clear up your image. Longer cotton swabs on wooden sticks—if you have them—will work better to reach inside the machine. Dip the swab in alcohol and rub on the audio and video heads to dissolve dirt and particle buildup.

Caution: Do not pour alcohol or cleaning solution directly onto or into the machine.

Velcro

In the laboratory, industrial-grade Velcro products can endure 10,000 "rips" and reclosures. But in the real world of lint, hair, and debris, many of these hook-and-loop fasteners (with the Velcro brand being the most recognizable) lose their sticking power long before they are actually worn-out. The closures on shoes and sandals are especially prone to collecting dirt from floors and carpets, which gets enmeshed in the hook side of the Velcro. The soft, fluffy "loops" side normally is not the cause of the problem. You can regain some, but not all, of its fastening ability by cleaning out the scratchy hook portion.

Technique: The Velcro company suggests taking a clean section of hooks and running it through the contaminated section. It will act as a comb to remove any fibers or debris caught in the hooks. A small piece costs a few cents.

Speed tips: Hold the Velcro on a flat surface and vacuum the hooks for a quick cleanup.

Keep hook and loops securely fastened to prevent lint and dirt from getting trapped in the hooks.

In a pinch: If you don't have an extra piece of Velcro handy, substitute a fine-tooth comb to clean the fuzzed-up hooks.

Caution: Always attach fasteners prior to laundering. This not only protects the Velcro from being clogged with lint but also protects other items in the wash from being snagged by the hooks.

Veneer

To produce a wood product less expensively sometimes a thin layer of fine wood, called veneer, is glued to a base of lesser grade. Cut with giant blades, veneer manufactured today can be as thin as 1/60 inch, while antique veneer cut by hand will vary in thickness. Whether it's thick or thin, you should clean veneer according to the finish that is on the wood, such as shellac, varnish, lacquer, or polyurethane.

Technique: Wax once or twice a year with beeswax, suggests Ian Turner, restoration expert for Garrett Wade Company, a professional woodworkers supply house in New York City. Clean fingerprints and dust with a damp cloth and buff dry with a cloth. Veneer is more susceptible to changes in heat and humidity than other types of furniture. The expansion and contraction caused by temperature and moisture variations can eventually cause veneer to bubble or pop. Position veneer away from heat sources and air conditioners. Do not store in damp areas such as basements.

In a pinch: Small pieces of loose veneer or small blisters in veneer can be reglued. Experts from the Michigan State University Extension in East Lansing offer the following advice: Lay veneer on a flat surface and scrape off the old glue. Do not get the veneer wet. Then scrape the old glue from the base wood or furniture. Put glue on both pieces, put the veneer in place, press the pieces together, and cover with a paper pad. Lay weights on it, making sure that there is pressure on all sections of the newly glued veneer. Use a thin knife blade or hypodermic needle to force wood glue into areas where the veneer is loose but still attached. Then weight the glued area down until dry.

Vents

Airborne dust and dirt that circulates through your home's heating and cooling system will eventually collect on the blades that channel air through the vent.

Technique: Vacuum loose dust with the handheld brush attachment. Wipe with a damp cloth following the pattern of the ridged air channels. Extremely dirty vents, such as those soiled by soot from a malfunctioning furnace, should be vacuumed and removed and then scrubbed with a nylon brush and dishwashing detergent solution. Be sure to dry it thoroughly. Most are made of painted metal and may rust if subjected to prolonged moisture.

Speed tips: Skip the scrubbing by vacuuming air vents regularly when sucking up dirt on floors or along baseboards.

In a pinch: If you don't use a vacuum with handheld attachments, a dusting wand works well to snare dust trapped between the ridges of a vent.

Vinyl

Vinyl made its debut in the plastics market in 1928 when it was commonly used for tablecloths, garment bags, and shower curtains. It's virtually maintenance-free, so in today's plasticized world it is found everywhere—from floors to upholstery. About 20 percent of new homes are now covered in vinyl siding. While it's known for its easy-care properties, vinyl can become hard and brittle over time if you don't take care of it.

Technique: According to experts at the Michigan State University Extension in East Lansing, for light soiling, wash vinyl with a mild cleaner, such as liquid dishwashing detergent, and water. Use a soft-bristle brush to loosen dirt from crevices and textured surfaces. Rinse with clear water and buff dry. The vinyl cleaners, such as Armor All Protectant (sold in auto supply stores), are useful for removing stubborn soil, and the conditioners in these products help to rejuvenate the plasticizers that keep the vinyl soft.

Speed tips: Unlike the leather that it simulates, vinyl does not like oil. Even a buildup of skin oils will eventually cause vinyl to harden. Instead of scrubbing down an entire piece of furniture, spot-clean headrest and armrest areas, where oil tends to collect.

In a pinch: To restore luster to dulled surfaces, the manufacturers of Naugahyde products recommend spraying the surface with a light coat of furniture wax. Allow it to soak for 30 seconds, and follow with a light buffing.

Caution: Some household cleaners and solvents remove plasticizers from vinyl, which will cause it to get harden and crack. Avoid the use of acetone, lacquer thinner, and dry-cleaning fluid to remove spots and stains.

Vomit

EMERGENCY ACTION
Act quickly. Like chlorine bleach, the stomach acids in vomit can permanently change the color of fabric. Scrape and blot up as much of the mess as you can, and then dilute the acids with water, advises Carol Seelaus, a speed-cleaning instructor at Temple University in Philadelphia and owner of Somebody's Gotta Do It, a professional cleaning service. On clothing or washable fabric, flush the spot with cool or tepid water. On carpet and upholstery, sponge with water and blot to remove.

Scientists believe that vomiting is one of our most important adaptive traits. It keeps us from getting sick or even dying from something we've eaten, all of which is small comfort to the poor souls who must clean up a chunky foul-smelling stew of stomach acids, enzymes, and partially digested food.

Technique: After you have scraped the spot and flushed it with water, soak washable items for 30 minutes to an hour in a solution of 1 quart warm water mixed with 1 teaspoon laundry detergent and 2 tablespoons ammonia. Rinse in cool water. If the stain remains, soak the item in an enzyme presoak, such as Biz, to digest the stain and then launder in warm water. If the stain is colored, it may be caused by dye in something you ate or drank. If the fabric appears to have lightened, the stomach acids in the vomit have caused a permanent color change.

On carpet and upholstery, flush with a solution of water and a bacteria/enzyme digester, such as Odormute, available in some pet supply stores, before applying any other cleaning solution. The natural enzyme formula chemically changes the source of the odor to eliminate it, not just mask it. And as anyone who has had the unpleasant experience of cleaning up tossed cookies knows, vomit has a lingering stench. Detergents or cleaning solutions that are applied before the enzyme digestant could set the odor permanently, advise the makers of Odormute.

Speed tips: Remember the kid who threw up in grade school? While everyone ogled the mess, the janitor came into the room and shook a pungent smelling sawdust material on the vomit to absorb the liquid so that it could be quickly swept up.

If vomit occurs on a hard surface, such as a floor, a brown powder substance called Z Goop, available in janitorial supply stores, will absorb the mess so that it can be easily scooped up and thrown into a trash can. Cat litter will also do the trick.

A CLEAN STORY

What Happens When Your Lunch Is Lost in Space?

During the first few days of space travel, 40 to 50 percent of astronauts experience space motion sickness (SMS). Like motion sickness or seasickness on Earth, SMS can cause nausea and vomiting. Unlike Earth-bound motion sickness, with SMS vomiting can come on suddenly and without symptoms.

In the microgravity environment of space, the problem with vomiting is not how to mop it up but how to contain it so that it does not become a floating mess in the tight confines of the space shuttle. Astronauts are armed with airsick bags. But in the event that this method fails, the shuttle is equipped with a vacuum cleaner to snare space messes.

In a pinch: Borax, a naturally occurring mineral used as a laundry booster, can effectively neutralize some odors on carpets and upholstery. After sponging and blotting the area with water, sprinkle with dry borax to cover the entire spot. Allow it to dry, and vacuum. Test for colorfastness in an inconspicuous area by applying a paste made of borax and water.

Caution: Do not use ammonia to clean vomit from silk or wool.

Wading Pools

Whether they are the soft, plastic inflatable type or the rigid, molded plastic kind, backyard kiddie pools are easy to clean when they're empty. But keeping the water clean in them for even a few hours can be a challenge. Within minutes little feet can turn the inviting clear water into a cloudy stew of grass clippings, dead bugs, and dirt.

Technique: After the kids are done for the day, drain the pool promptly and rinse with a hose to remove dirt and grass. Instead of pulling the plug and letting the water drain on the lawn, dip it out with a bucket to water the garden or houseplants.

To make a tool for skimming debris out of a wading pool: Bend a coat hanger into a circle. Snip the legs off an old pair of panty hose, pull the remainder over the wire loop, and tie the fabric at the bottom.

A pool that has been sitting out in the weather may develop a stubborn layer of dirt that can be loosened with a nylon scrub brush and a mild cleaning solution (add ¼ cup liquid household bleach to 1 gallon water). If you have to keep the pool outside, store it upside down or standing on its side so that rain and dirt will not collect in it.

Speed tips: Keep dirt and insects out of the water while it warms up with a lawn furniture cover. Some sizes fit perfectly over a child's wading pool.

In a pinch: Make your own pool skimmer to remove grass and insects that are sloshing around in the water. Bend a wire hanger into a circle and cover with a pair of old panty hose knotted at the bottom with the legs removed.

Waffle Irons

Maybe the thought of scrubbing batter from a zillion nooks and crannies is keeping you from making a delicious waffle breakfast. Well, get out the syrup. All your waffle iron needs is a little seasoning. Properly seasoned grids will develop a nonstick surface that brushes clean in a few seconds.

Technique: After baking waffles, remove crumbs by brushing grids with a soft plastic brush while it's still warm. Do not wash grids or put any water on them, or they will have to be re-seasoned. Allow the iron to cool and wipe any spills or splatters on the outside while they're still fresh, using a damp sponge or all-purpose cleaner.

Speed tips: Proper seasoning of the grid surface is essential for quick cleanups. All waffle irons should be seasoned prior to first use and periodically after that if waffles begin to stick.

Brush unsalted fat or cooking oil on grids and heat until they begin to smoke. Bake a waffle, following the manufacturer's directions concerning time and temperature, to absorb excess fat. (Generally, the waffle is done when the iron stops steaming.) Discard the waffle. You now have a perfectly seasoned waffle iron.

Grids should be re-seasoned if they are washed with soapy water.

In a pinch: If you don't have a soft brush, wipe warm grids with a paper towel or dish towel to remove crumbs.

Caution: Unplug the waffle iron prior to cleaning to avoid burns or electrical shock.

Wagons

How much effort do you put into cleaning and maintaining a child's wagon? It probably depends on whether you own an inexpensive lightweight metal toy or an heirloom-quality solid-oak vehicle complete with air tires and no-tip steering. "A well-made wagon can last generations," says Pete Furlong, owner of the Wagon Man in Springfield, Oregon.

Technique: Wash wood wagons with a soft cloth and a solution of warm water and a mild soap, such as Murphy Oil Soap. Dry thoroughly so that the finish stays intact.

Metal wagons can be cleaned with a car wash solution. Dry and follow up with a coat of polish to ward off rust.

Plastic wagons, especially those left to weather in the yard, can develop a layer of dirt that is literally embedded in the molded texture of the plastic. To lift embedded dirt, use a stiff brush and a capful of liquid dishwashing detergent in a bucket of water.

Don't neglect the handle and wheels. Clean and protect metal handles and rubber tires with a coating of silicone spray, which doesn't attract dirt and dust.

Speed tips: Of course, for a quick cleanup you can always hose them down. Just be sure to dry metal and wood wagons thoroughly. "Most of the grunge and dirt comes from letting them sit outside unprotected," says Furlong. Keep cleaning to a minimum and store wagons in a dry place, such as the garage, house, or even a covered porch.

In a pinch: If you just don't have an inside storage space, turn the wagon upside down to keep rainwater and dirt from collecting in the body.

Wallpaper and Wall Coverings

Although it tends to conceal dirt better than plain painted walls, wallpaper can last 10 years or more, so you'll have to clean it sooner or later. More than 75 percent of the wallpaper sold today is vinyl-coated, which means that it's washable and often scrubbable. Despite its easy cleanability, if you leave dirt on vinyl wall coverings too long the vinyl tends to absorb it.

Technique: Vacuum periodically with a brush attachment to remove loose dust and dirt, especially on textured and fabric covered walls that cannot not be easily washed. Use an upward motion to snare cobwebs; brushing down may cause streaks.

Washable coverings can be cleaned with a sponge dampened in a mild all-purpose cleaner or in ½ cup ammonia mixed in 1 gallon water. Scrubbable papers can be cleaned with the same solution applied with a soft-bristle brush. Be careful not to overwet the seams, or you may find yourself pasting them back down.

Nonwashable papers, such as uncoated papers and flocked and fabric coverings, can be cleaned with a commercial doughlike product called Absorene that is rubbed over the surface. Test behind a piece of furniture to make sure that it does not streak. After cleaning, brush or vacuum stray bits of cleaner from the wall.

Speed tips: Wash the wall in half the time by using a sponge mop reserved for walls only.

Stain Remedies on Wallpaper

Here's how to remove common stains and marks from wallpaper, according to cleaning experts.

Grease
- Blot spot with paper towels and sprinkle cornstarch on the stain. When the grease is absorbed by the cornstarch, remove gently and vacuum.
- Rub with a slice of white bread.

Crayon
- Apply WD-40 to the stain and wipe with a soft cloth. If there's still crayon remaining, add some liquid dishwashing detergent to water. Using a sponge, work in a circular motion to clean the area, and rinse. This is for scrubbable wallpaper. If yours isn't, test it on a small area before starting.

Felt-Tip Marker
- Spray with nonoily hair spray and wipe off.
- Apply rubbing alcohol and blot up.

In a pinch: If you don't have a vacuum, use a clean cloth tied around a broom or mop to remove dust from the walls. Change the cloth when it becomes soiled to prevent streaks.

Walls

Wall-washing rule number one is to start at the bottom and work your way up. "If you start at the top, the dirty water will drip down over the soiled walls and create streaks that are hard to remove," says Kent Gerard, a cleaning consultant from Oakland, California. Essentially, the clean streaks created by dirty water dripped on dirty walls are harder to clean than dirty water dripped on clean walls. "In general, you want to be careful. You want to enforce drip control," says Gerard. To do this, work in small overlapping sections.

Technique: Before washing, dust or vacuum walls to remove loose soil. Most painted surfaces can be cleaned with a mild solution of warm water and liquid dishwashing detergent and then rinsed with clear water.

You'll need two buckets—one for the cleaning solution and one

Before You Open That Paint Can...

Preparing your walls for a new coat of paint? Paint professionals use trisodium phosphate, a powdered cleaner sold in hardware stores, to clean and degloss walls. The alkaline cleaner doesn't disinfect; it smooths and levels the surface of the wall. If you decide to use it to clean your walls for better paint adhesion, be sure to wear protective eyewear, rubber gloves, and a long-sleeve shirt, and rinse the walls thoroughly afterward.

for the rinse water—two large cellulose sponges, and it's a good idea to have two rubber gloves to protect your hands, says the Michigan State University Extension in East Lansing.

Working in overlapping sections manageable for your arm length, apply the cleaning solution to the walls by rubbing gently with a sponge. Semigloss and gloss paints are less likely to be damaged by cleaning than flat latex paint. Rinse with a separate sponge reserved specifically for the rinse water. After you're done with one section, proceed to the next area, making sure that the cleaning edges overlap. When you've done several areas, dry off the excess moisture with a soft absorbent cloth.

If the walls are very dirty, you can use a stronger alkali solution to dissolve the dirt. Add 2 tablespoons ammonia, 1 tablespoon trisodium phosphate (available in hardware stores), or 2 tablespoons powder laundry detergent to 1 gallon warm water, says the Michigan State University Extension. Stronger solutions may remove paint, particularly flat finishes. For greasy walls, dissolve ½ cup washing soda in 2 gallons hot water for your cleaning solution.

Speed tips: In seldom-used rooms or in bedrooms, you can get away with simply dusting and spot-cleaning the walls. Use an all-purpose spray cleaner, such as Fantastik, and wipe dirty areas like light switches and doorways. Test the spray cleaner in a small area before spraying the entire area. If it makes the wall feel tacky, don't use that cleaner.

You can work in larger overlapping sections by using a sponge mop on walls and ceilings. But make sure that it's not the same one that you use on the floor, or your walls could actually end up dirtier than when you started.

In a pinch: In between cleanings, rub smudges away with an art gum eraser (the brown crumbly kind from art stores).

If you have rough plaster walls that shred sponges, clean them with bunched up nylon panty hose.

To remove tape from walls, apply a warm iron over a protective cloth. Press the iron lightly to loosen the tape, and then peel it off slowly.

Caution: Test cleaner in an inconspicuous corner first to make sure that the paint color and finish are not damaged by cleaning.

When using trisodium phosphate, wear protective eyewear, rubber gloves, and a long-sleeve shirt. Always read the label for proper usage and safety precautions.

Watches

When you wear a watch day in and day out, lotion, perfume, skin oil, and perspiration eventually accumulate on your timepiece and watchband. If neglected, the buildup can cloud the crystal and corrode the case plating. In general, the more skin preparations you use, the more often you need to clean your watch.

Technique: Wipe the crystal and watch case with a barely damp cloth. "You have to be very careful. You don't want to get any solution moisture in the movement of the watch," says Gordon Engle, proprietor of Engle's Jewelers in Pottstown, Pennsylvania.

To thoroughly clean the band, remove it by releasing the spring action pins on each side of the case. Fine metal bands can be soaked overnight in a detergent-and-water solution—a couple of drops of Ivory Liquid in a regular-size coffee cup—or washed with a cloth dampened in ammonia. Leather bands can be spruced up by cleaning them with saddle soap, but they also must be replaced periodically. "After being exposed to day-to-day perspiration and dirt, they get to the point of no return," says Engle.

Getting a Watertight Seal Is Worth Your Time

If you're a scuba diver, ask your jeweler to send your water-resistant timepiece to the manufacturer for battery changes, says Gordon Engle, proprietor of Engle's Jewelers in Pottstown, Pennsylvania. When the batteries are changed on a water-resistant watch, the original factory seal is broken. After resealing, the tiny gasket in the watch will not be as effective as before at keeping water out. And if water gets in, the watch will stop keeping time.

"When you're depending on that watch to tell you how much air you have in your tank, it's critical," says Engle, who has been repairing jewelry for more than 40 years. Sending the watch back to the manufacturer ensures a factory-quality seal that will stand up to the rigors of scuba diving. It will, however, take more time and cost more than having your jeweler do the job.

Save any cleaning or maintenance of the interior movement of the watch for the jeweler. Today's quartz watches have very few moving parts and don't require much maintenance beyond a periodic battery change. Windup watches, however, should be serviced and cleaned by a jeweler when their timing becomes sluggish.

Speed tips: For gleaming results with little effort, place a metal watchband in a nylon bag and run it through the washer. "Toss it in with a load of towels and it comes out really nice," says Engle. The ultrasonic cleaning devices used by jewelers have a vibrating action similar to the agitation in a washing machine.

In a pinch: If you don't feel dexterous enough to remove your watchband to clean it, you can prevent dirty buildup by getting in the habit of wiping your watch off with a dry cloth a few times a week. Good times to do it include when you take it off at night or before you shower.

Caution: Moisture will damage the movement of the watch, so use little or no wetness when cleaning. Even water-resistant watches are susceptible; the gasket that provides a barrier to moisture breaks down over time.

Water Beds

On a conventional bed, the oil and skin cells you shed burrow into the fibers of the mattress. But on a water bed, they build up on the surface of the vinyl mattress instead.

Technique: About once a month, sponge the top and the sides of the mattress off. Use a mild soap solution (any hand soap or liquid dishwashing detergent may be used, mixed with warm water). Use one bucket for the cleaning solution and one for the rinse water. Then rinse the mattress so that there isn't a soap residue left on it. Vinyl cleaners and conditioners really aren't necessary, says James Hauser, general manager of Specialized Plastic Sealing, a water bed mattress manufacturer in Carlsbad, New Mexico. The conditioners are applied to the surface to refresh the plasticizer.

"The problem is that vinyl deteriorates from the inside out, not the outside in. The volatile chemicals escape, and eventually, it will harden. It takes 735 years for vinyl to turn back into its natural state," says Hauser. "Vinyl conditioners won't extend the life of your mattress except maybe by a few days."

Take care of the water inside your mattress by adding a conditioner approved by the Environmental Protection Agency that kills

A CLEAN STORY

Bacteria Can Make Waves in the Bedroom

Bacteria don't harm the vinyl of your water bed mattress, but they can cause an odor similar to the stench of rotten eggs.

"It will chase you right out of your bedroom," says James Hauser, general manager of Specialized Plastic Sealing, a water bed mattress manufacturer in Carlsbad, New Mexico. "It kept me out of my bedroom one time for a month."

When the rotten odor started, Hauser suspected that it was a dead mouse. When he finally determined that the smell was coming from the water bed, he drained it and tried twice to deodorize the mattress by refilling it and adding $\frac{1}{2}$ gallon chlorine to the water. He ended up draining it a third time and airing the mattress out for six months to dissipate the odor.

You can avoid this scenario if you make sure to use a conditioner when you fill the bed, especially if you have well water. Conditioners come in liquid, powder, and tablet form and cost from $4 to $30. Hauser recommends using the powder. It's easy to handle and comes in a bottle that you pour directly into the valve.

odor-causing bacteria (available at water bed stores) before you fill the bed. Adding it before the bed is filled will distribute the conditioner throughout the mattress.

Speed tips: Use a mattress pad to extend the life of your water bed and to keep it cleaner.

Water Stains

Exposure to plain old H_2O can damage or stain furniture, walls, carpets, upholstery, and certain fabrics. As with other stains, prompt action can minimize or prevent the damage caused by water.

Wood Furniture

Water rings or white marks on furniture are caused when moisture gets trapped under the finish, giving it a milky appearance. Even the condensation from a hot pizza box can cause discoloration. Water rings usually indicate that the finish contains lacquer; varnished finishes will not ring, says Ian Turner, restoration expert for Garrett Wade Company, a professional woodworkers supply house in New York City.

Technique: Some marks will fade by themselves, so allow the stain to sit for a couple of days to give the absorbed moisture a chance to evaporate. If it doesn't go away on its own, a white mark can usually be rubbed out by using a mild abrasive mixed with a lubricant. Rubbing with the grain of the wood, try one of these combinations.

- Paste wax or mineral spirits and superfine (#0000) steel wool
- A small piece of cheesecloth dipped in hot water containing a few drops of household ammonia; wring the cloth out thoroughly, and lightly rub the spot

Apply a protective coat of wax to the furniture after the mark has been removed.

In a pinch: Make your own rubbing compound from some of these household ingredients. Rub with a mixture of nongel toothpaste and water, then buff. Or rub in a little mayonnaise or salad oil mixed with cooled cigarette or cigar ashes. Let it sit for a while, and then wipe it off.

Caution: Don't be tempted to use stronger abrasives when dealing with water rings. They may scratch or even remove the finish.

Carpets and Upholstery

When carpet or upholstery fibers get overly wet and then dry slowly, dyelike material will dissolve from the backing or stuffing and wick to the surface. Spills, tracked-in rain or snow, floods, and even overwetting by do-it-yourself carpet and upholstery cleaners can cause brown discoloration, which usually goes unnoticed until a subsequent cleaning, says the Association of Specialists in Cleaning and Restoration in Annapolis Junction, Maryland.

Technique: You're going to need a carpet or upholstery professional for this. On synthetic fibers the brown discoloration can usually be removed by professional treatment. On some natural fibers, such as wool and cotton, the staining may be permanent. For the name and location of a certified technician, contact the Association of Specialists in Cleaning and Restoration, 10830 Annapolis Junction Road, Suite 312, Annapolis Junction, MD 20701-1120.

Speed tips: If your carpet or upholstery becomes overwet, take measures to minimize water damage. "The harmful effect of water is sharply reduced by prompt action," says Martin L. King, a restoration consultant in Arlington, Virginia, and technical advisor to the National Institute of Disaster Restoration in Annapolis, Maryland.

Immediately blot as much of the water as possible from the affected area with white paper towels to prevent soaking the backing or stuffing material. To prevent discoloration from wicking to the surface fibers, dry the area quickly. Remove upholstery cushions and prop them up. During the summer, turn on air-conditioning for maximum drying. To speed drying in the winter, alternate heat and open windows.

Ceilings and Walls

Water that leaks through walls or ceilings will leave a brown ringlike discoloration after it dries.

Technique: If a pipe has burst and the ceiling is sagging, punch a small hole in it and place a pan underneath to collect the water.

After the water has dried, try to bleach the stain out by spraying it with a solution of one part chlorine bleach to five parts water, or straight hydrogen peroxide.

If bleaching doesn't work, repaint the area. First apply a coat of sealer such as B-I-N Primer/Sealant, available at any paint store. Follow with a coat of paint to match the surrounding area. If you don't seal it first, the stain will bleed right through the fresh paint.

Speed tips: Dab spots on white ceilings with a little white shoe polish.

Fabric

Water stains occur on fabrics that contain sizing or finishing agents, which give a stiffer feel or a sheen. There are a variety of finishes; some may even have a waxy or plastic feel to them. The water-soluble, starch-based finishes—applied to new fabrics to give them added body—are the most prone to water spotting. When exposed to a drop of water, the sizing is displaced and forms a ring or wavy line where it is deposited. Water spotting often happens with taffeta, moiré, silk, and rayon.

Technique: Launder washables or rewet the entire garment and dry as you normally would. Dry-cleanable fabric can be rewet by passing it through steam from a teakettle spout. Press while the fabric is still damp. If the spot remains, have the garment dry-cleaned professionally.

Wax—Dripped

There are two methods of removing dripped wax—scraping it away or using heat to melt it so that it can be absorbed. Scraping is the best technique for removing wax from hard surfaces such as floors or wood furniture, while melting is the best method to remove it from textiles, such as table linens and upholstery. Colored candles complicate the wax-removal process because they create the potential for permanent dye stain, "Often the dyes used in candles can penetrate the fibers and create a stain," says Elizabeth Barbatelli, president of the Laundry at Linens Limited, a Milwaukee-based mail-order laundry.

Technique: Scrape away as much wax as you can with a firm plastic kitchen spatula. This procedure should remove all but a few traces of wax. To remove the last bits on wood, rub with a cloth dampened with mineral spirits.

Peeling, scraping, or pulling hardened wax can damage fabrics, says Barbatelli. Instead, for white wax, place several layers of clean white paper towels over the wax (and under it if you are working with a tablecloth) and press the towels with an iron at its lowest setting. Change the towels as the wax is absorbed, and keep ironing until all the wax is gone. Sponge wax residue and dye with a small amount of spot remover and blot dry. On carpet and upholstery, blot with a spot remover such as Goof-off, available at grocery stores. On washable items, launder as soon as possible using a laundry detergent, and add a bleach that is safe for the fabric in the hottest water allowed by the manufacturer, says the Michigan State University Extension in East Lansing.

The iron technique above won't work for colored wax. You may have to use bleach. Test the fabric in an inconspicuous area and bleach the entire item in a bleach that is safe for that material.

In a pinch: Plain kraft paper, like that used for paper bags, can be substituted for paper towels.

Before laundering, sponge dye stains with rubbing alcohol to help remove them.

Caution: Candle wax colored with red dye is the most difficult to remove and may require professional treatment. Always read product label for proper use and safety precautions.

Wax Buildup—Floors

Wax buildup is usually most evident in corners where the wax or polish isn't worn away by traffic. A vinyl or tile floor may begin to look yellow, while a wood floor that has been waxed too much may appear scuffed or white. Remove old wax and polish no more than once a year, or after six to eight coats have been applied.

Technique: Unless you're using a floor buffing machine, stripping wax typically takes a lot of time and elbow grease. There are commercial products for removing wax buildup, but a typical formula for removing wax finish from nonwood floors is ¼ cup nonchlorine floor cleaner and 1 cup ammonia mixed with ½ gallon hot water. Sweep or vacuum the floor to remove loose dirt. Apply stripping solution to a small workable section of the floor with a sponge mop and let it sit for 5 to 10 minutes.

The floor will begin to turn cloudy if the wax is softening. Scrub the softened area with a stiff brush, an electric scrubber, or very fine (#000) steel wool pads to lift the wax. You can squeegee the loosened slop into a dustpan and dispose of it. This is quicker than trying to mop it up. It is best to use a wet vacuum, suggests Bill R. Griffin, president of Cleaning Consultant Services in Seattle. Then thoroughly rinse the stripped section with clean water. Let air-dry and then move on to the next section. When done, refinish the entire floor with two or three thin coats of finish instead of one thick coat, says Griffin.

If you still see dark areas after rinsing the floor, or if you can still scrape up wax with the edge of a coin, you probably need to repeat the stripping process.

Wood that hasn't been covered in a surface finish, such as polyurethane, should be waxed with a solvent-based wax, such as paste wax. Never use water or commercial wax removers to strip wax from a wood floor, according to the National Wood Flooring Association in Manchester, Missouri. Instead, use a solvent-type material such as mineral spirits or paint thinner and fine (#00) steel wool. Be sure to rub with the grain of the wood when removing the wax.

Speed tips: Once you have about two coats of wax on the entire floor, wax only in high-traffic areas where it needs it. This way you'll prevent wax buildup from occurring.

On wood floors, try buffing with a floor polisher instead of waxing to restore the luster. Only wax when buffing the floor no longer makes it shine. Use a wet-dry vacuum to suck up the waxy goop as you scrape it off the floor.

In a pinch: If you don't have a squeegee, scoop up softened wax with a Teflon spatula from the kitchen.

Caution: Wear rubber gloves and work in a well-ventilated area when stripping wax because the fumes are strong.

Do not use self-polishing waxes on unsealed wood floors, says the National Wood Flooring Association. Most of these products contain water (which should not be used on wood) and plastic. The shiny coat of plastic will discolor the wood and require harsh chemicals to remove.

Whirlpools

Some people avoid using their whirlpools because they don't want to contend with the chore of cleaning an oversized bathtub with a dozen little jets along the sides. With price tags ranging up to $2,000 or more, whirlpools may just be one of the most expensive ways to get clean. But if you have one, you may as well enjoy it.

Technique: Clean acrylic, fiberglass, and cast-iron whirlpools with nonabrasive household cleaner, such as Comet Liquid Gel Cleaner with Bleach. Wipe down the sides of the whirlpool with a sponge and cleaner. Rinse with clear water and dry with a soft cloth.

Flush the whirlpool system at least twice a month to keep jets clean and functioning properly. You should adjust jets so that there is no air induction (that is, they're not drawing in air—check your manual). Then fill the bath with hot water to about three inches above the highest jets, and add 2 teaspoons of a low-foaming automatic dishwasher detergent such as Calgonite or Cascade and 4 ounces of liquid household bleach such as Clorox. Run the whirlpool for 10 to 15 minutes, and then drain the bath. To rinse it, fill the bath with cold water to three inches above the highest jet, and run the whirlpool for another 5 to 10 minutes. Drain the bath and wipe dry with a soft cloth.

Speed tips: Wipe the whirlpool after each use to prevent the buildup of soap scum. Better yet, enjoy a soap-free soak, and all you will need is a quick wipe of a towel to clean your whirlpool.

In a pinch: If the surface becomes dull, use an automotive-type rubbing compound followed by an application of paste wax.

Caution: Do not use abrasive cleaners on fiberglass or acrylic whirlpools. They will scratch and dull the surface. Always read product label for proper use and safety precautions.

Wicker

Wicker is a catchall term for furniture woven out of a variety of plant fibers. Most wicker is made from rattan, but canes, reeds, sea grasses, willow branches, fiber rush (twisted paper), and synthetic materials are also used.

"Everybody has a different opinion on how to clean wicker," says Joyce Brown-Tickle, owner of Wicker Works in Wilmington, North

Carolina. Some advocate blasting the dirt off with a garden hose, while others say don't even get it wet. Both are right, Brown-Tickle says. It just depends on what type of wicker needs to be cleaned—synthetic or natural fibers. Synthetic, which is excellent for outdoor use, can be hosed down without being harmed. Natural fibers, however, are more likely to crack, swell, rot, or discolor from prolonged exposure to water and direct sunlight.

If you don't know whether a wicker piece is synthetic or natural fibers, look for an indication of where it was made, says Brown-Tickle. If the label says "Made in the U.S.A.," it is most likely manufactured from synthetic materials since nearly all the natural wicker is imported from China and the Philippines.

Technique: When cleaning wicker, use the smallest amount of water possible to get the item clean. Interior wicker made from natural or synthetic materials should be vacuumed first to remove loose dust and dirt. If further cleaning is necessary, mix up a sudsy solution of a capful of Murphy Oil Soap and a quart of water. Using a damp sponge, skim off the suds and apply the suds to the furniture. Use a small brush if needed to reach between the reeds. Wipe off the suds with a clean damp sponge. Be careful not to wet any wooden parts if you are cleaning a piece that is constructed around a wood frame.

Wicker used outside often requires a more vigorous cleaning technique. Scrub synthetic and raw natural wicker with warm water and a brush, and then rinse with a hose. Dry it as fast as possible so that the woven fibers will not swell or rot. Place it in the hot sun or next to a fan.

Extreme wetness will cause painted wicker to swell and the paint will flake off. Clean it with a damp sponge and wire brush to remove the loose paint. Allow it to dry thoroughly, and then repaint.

When the wicker is thoroughly dry, check the surfaces for sharp strands or fuzzy places. Sand them smooth with fine sandpaper. Then give it a coat of spray-on automobile wax.

Speed tips: Vacuum wicker regularly with the brush attachment to avoid dust buildup. Cover tabletops and dresser bureaus with a sheet of glass to prevent dust from getting trapped in the weave. Then all you need is a few sprays of glass cleaner to keep the top—the part of the furniture most likely to collect dust, dirt, and stains—looking as good as the day you bought it.

To speed up drying, wash your wicker on a windy day.

In a pinch: If you don't have a vacuum, a dry paintbrush will clean dust and dirt particles from the weave.

If your wicker chair crackles and creaks when you sit down, it might need some moisture. Dry indoor heat and arid climates dry wicker out. Wipe it down occasionally with a damp sponge to restore moisture to the fibers.

Caution: Wicker needs a certain amount of humidity to prevent it from cracking, but too much will damage the fibers and cause them to rot. Keep natural wicker out of direct sunlight, dew, and rain for extended periods of time.

Windows

The trick to gleaming windows is in the drying, not in the washing. That's why professional window washers may have differing opinions on which cleaning formula works best, but the universal tool of choice for wiping it off is a squeegee. The truth is that unless they are heavily soiled, most windows can be cleaned with sudsy water. Besides costing next to nothing, water doesn't streak—even on a warm day.

Windows dried with a squeegee stay clean longer than windows cleaned with paper towels. Scrubbing with a paper towel builds a static charge on the window that attracts dust. It pays to purchase a good-quality squeegee. The rubber will be pliable and adhere to the window surface better for more effective drying. Ettore makes a professional-quality tool that is sold at janitorial supply houses. Your window cleaning should also include some old bath towels to catch drips, cloths to dry-wipe your squeegee between passes, a window scrubber to apply cleaning solution, and a large plastic bucket.

Technique: If you plan to clean windowsills and window frames,

SCRUB THIS APPROACH

Bad News about Newsprint

Grandma may swear by it, but newspapers can be a problematic choice for cleaning windows. Consumers Union, the publisher of *Consumer Reports*, used newspaper and an effective commercial cleaner to clean heavily soiled windows. They found that newspaper is not very absorbent. A fair amount of rubbing and wiping was necessary to polish a window with it. Not only that, but you and your window can actually end up dirtier after cleaning with it.

The ink-blackened hands left smudges on the window mullions.

THE DOUBLE-HUNG DILEMMA SOLVED

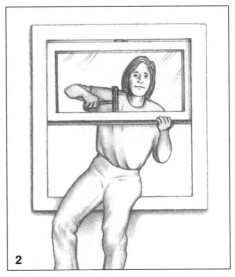

Step 1: Cleaning the outside of a double-hung window can seem like a "can't get there from here" proposition. To start, pull the top of the double-hung window down as far as it will go. Reach out and mop the outside of the window with the scrubber. Working from above, draw the squeegee across and down the window as far as you can go. **Step 2**: Raise both the inside and outside window as far as each will go and finish the bottom of the outside window in overlapping passes.

Step 3: Lower the inside window enough so that you can reach above it and push the outside window to its lowest point. Reach out the window from above, apply cleaner to the top half of the inside window with the scrubber. **Step 4**: Raise the outside window and lower the inside window enough to repeat the scrubbing process on the lower half of the inside window by reaching out and up. Return windows to position in Step 3 to squeegee the top half of the inside window. Repeat movement in Step 4 to squeegee the outside of the lower half of the inside window.

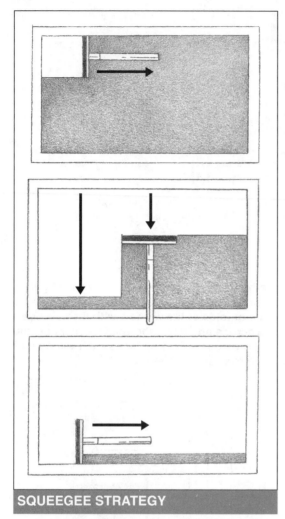

SQUEEGEE STRATEGY

Here's the ultimate no-streak, no-mess plan for using a squeegee on windows. Draw the squeegee across the top of the window to stop the flow of drips. Starting either side, draw the squeegee down to nearly the bottom of the window. Continue the vertical pattern in overlapping strokes to prevent streaks. Finish by drawing the squeegee across the bottom. *Note:* Wipe the squeegee with a cloth between passes.

do it before you wash the glass. Vacuum window frames and windowsills to remove excess dirt. Clean wood or aluminum window frames with a solution of mild liquid dishwashing detergent and warm water. An old toothbrush is useful for reaching into the corners of the mullions. Rinse and dry with a cloth. If your aluminum frames are looking gray and weathered, shine them with a cream silver polish. Window frames with natural wood finishes can be cleaned with a wax instead of soap and water.

Once the window frames and windowsills are clean, you can move on to the glass. Mix up a glass-cleaning solution that suits your preferences—alkaline solutions will remove dirt, vinegar will remove hard-water deposits, sudsy water will prevent streaking on a warm day, and adding several ounces of rubbing alcohol will cut through greasy film. Don't mix alkalis and acids, such as vinegar and ammonia, in the hope of solving two cleaning problems. One will partially neutralize the other so that neither will be fully effective.

Dampen the window scrubber and apply the solution to the window. You want to make the window wet enough to dissolve dirt, but not so wet that it's a dripping mess. Lightly draw the squeegee across the top of the window (this will help stop drips). Then draw it down the window, stopping a few inches from the bottom. In an overlapping stroke, make another vertical pass on the glass. Continue this pattern across the width of the window, wiping the blade of the squeegee with a cloth between each pass. Finish off by drawing the squeegee across the bottom. Wipe any drips around the frame with an absorbent cloth.

When cleaning window exteriors, do the windows on the top floor first. Dirty water may drip from the windowsill onto freshly cleaned glass below.

Speed tips: Always wash windows from top to bottom so that you won't get drips on the ones that you've already done. Use vertical strokes outside and horizontal strokes inside so that you'll know which side the streaks are on.

In a pinch: For small windowpanes where a squeegee just won't fit, use a chamois to dry windows. Rub a clean blackboard eraser over the just-washed window for a quick shine.

If you're thrifty, substitute a fluffy paint roller to apply your glass cleaning solution.

Caution: Ammoniated cleaners are hard on your hands and on the blade of the squeegee. Watch the temperature outside if you plan to clean aluminum window frames. Don't clean if it's below 50°F or if the aluminum is too hot to touch. And avoid the use of abrasive cleaners, which will permanently scratch the finish.

Be careful not to drip alkaline or alcohol solutions on painted or varnished woodwork. It will damage the finish.

MONEY-SAVERS

Three Window-Cleaning Formulas

Make your own window cleaner like the professionals. Commercial "blue" cleaners are costly and tend to leave streaks. Here are alternatives recommended by cleaning experts.

- Plain lukewarm water works just fine if your windows aren't too dirty. And it has two big advantages. No streaks if you're washing on a warm day. And it's practically free.
- Add $\frac{1}{2}$ cup white vinegar to 1 quart cool water.
- Mix $\frac{1}{2}$ cup sudsy ammonia, 1 pint rubbing alcohol, and 1 teaspoon liquid dishwashing detergent (don't use more, or streaking could result), and add enough water to make 1 gallon.

Wine Stains

EMERGENCY ACTION
Sprinkle a red-wine spill immediately with a liberal amount of salt. Allow the salt to absorb the wine, and then rinse in cool water. For white wine, blot up as much of the spill as you can and sponge with cool water, according to cleaning experts.

To prevent wine stains altogether, take these precautions suggested by wine experts. Learn to pour like a wine steward, slowly twisting the bottle neck to the side as you finish pouring so that drips will stay inside the bottle. Instead of laying the cork on your tablecloth, use a dish or ashtray.

Technique: If you can launder a white-wine spill before it has dried, then it is not likely to stain. Rinse the spill immediately. Apply an undiluted neutral detergent such as Liquid Tide and a few drops of white vinegar. Rinse. Launder washables in warm water. Dry cleanables should be taken to a professional if any stain remains.

Depending on the fabric and the age of the spot, red-wine stains can be impossible to remove. If you use the salt and cool water treatment for fresh spills outlined above, apply liquid laundry detergent and rinse in cool water. If the stain remains, apply a paste made from bleach-enzyme laundry soap such as Biz (mix according to package directions), soak for 30 minutes in an all-fabric bleach, and then launder.

For dried stains on durable fabrics, such as a tablecloth, hold the stained area over a bowl and cover with salt. Pour boiling water over the salt until the stain disappears. On other fabrics, soak with a few drops of white vinegar and blot, or try soaking with a solution of hydrogen peroxide (a mild bleach) and a few drops of ammonia. Test your fabric for colorfastness first.

On rugs and carpets, immediately cover the spill with a generous amount of salt. Allow it to dry, and then vacuum.

HOW IT WORKS

What Puts the Red in Red Wine?

The color of wine is not determined by the color of the grape but rather by the length of time that the skins of the fruit remain with the juice. A white wine can be made with red, black, or white grapes, with the skins being removed early in the wine-making process. For rosés—or pink wines—red or black grapes are used, and the skins are removed after one to three days. In red wine making the skins remain for longer periods.

In a pinch: For dried stains on washable fabric, pour club soda through the spot and launder as outlined earlier.

Caution: Avoid vinegar on cotton, linen, rayon, and acetate.

Woodstoves

To keep a woodstove burning efficiently and safely during the heating season, your regular cleaning should include removal of ashes from the firebox and removal of creosote buildup from the stovepipe. "Woodstoves really require very little maintenance," says Carl Harner, owner of Kring's Stoves and Fireplaces, a hearth products retailer in Boyertown, Pennsylvania.

To meet government emission standards, the majority of woodstoves manufactured since 1986 generate less ash and creosote buildup because they burn wood so efficiently. Hard-working stoves that are fired every day through the heating season should be cleaned and inspected every month. An annual inspection—usually prior to the heating season—of exterior surfaces, the doors, seams, and the catalytic converter will determine if any further cleaning or maintenance is necessary.

Technique: If the stove has a built-in ash pan, do not empty it until the pan is full. "Ash will not interfere with the efficiency of the stove, but it does take up space," says Harner. A layer of ashes in any stove acts as an insulator that will help produce a good fire by holding the heat in the coals. If your firebox does not have a grate, a layer of stove bricks, ashes, or sand is necessary to protect and insulate the floor of the box.

Colossal Cleanups

Blanketing the Territory
The amount of ash given off by Mount St. Helens in southwest Washington when it erupted in 1980: 540 million tons, enough to bury a football field to the depth of more than 150 miles

The best way to remove ashes is with a metal shovel. Avoid using a broom since sweeping will send a cloud of fine ashes through the room. Put the ashes in a fireproof container—a heavy metal trash can works well—and take them outside immediately. Hot coals can smolder in a bed of ashes for days.

Five Steps to Seasoned Wood

Green wood can contain up to 50 percent water—much of which will combine with smoke to form creosote in your chimney and stovepipe. It also doesn't generate much heat, so who needs it?

You'll keep your stove clean longer if you burn well-seasoned firewood with a moisture content of about 20 percent. Dry firewood will have cracks at the end that radiate outward and will be a weathered gray. Here's how to make sure that your wood dries thoroughly, according to Carl Harner, owner of Kring's Stoves and Fireplaces, a hearth products retailer in Boyertown, Pennsylvania.

- Cut it and split it into small pieces.
- Stack it. Wood loses moisture from the cut ends, not the sides.
- Store it off the ground.
- Store it under cover with the sides exposed to air.
- Allow it to dry for at least 6 months, but preferably for 9 to 12 months.

When you're ready to shut down the stove during the summer months, you can remove additional residue on the inner walls of the firebox with a wire brush.

A layer of ash can build up on the baffle of the stove, which will restrict air flow and affect your stove's efficiency. If the stove starts to smoke when you open the door, check the baffle—a plate across the top of the firebox—for ash buildup. You can see the baffle either by opening the front doors of the stove and looking straight up or by taking off the stove pipe. A layer of flyaway ash can accumulate here, but there is no danger of smoldering hot coals. So when there isn't a fire in the stove, you can clean the baffle with a vacuum cleaner. Or remove the baffle and brush it clean with a whisk broom.

Even though today's woodstoves emit significantly less creosote than older airtight stoves, creosote will accumulate in stovepipes and the chimney under certain conditions—smoke, water, and low temperatures. "When you burn wood, any unburned hydrocarbons will mix with water and form creosote," says Harner. "It's a highly combustible material. A buildup of creosote definitely needs to be cleaned out." Creosote can have the appearance of black water, a dark sticky goo, or a glazed porcelain enamel. To remove it, dismantle the pipe and take it outside to clean. Hold the pipe over a trash can or drop cloth and use a plastic brush to remove the creosote buildup. Don't use a steel brush—that will score the inside of the pipe, making it more likely to accumulate soot or creosote.

Clean dust from the surface of painted stoves with a vacuum

cleaner or cloth. Avoid using water since the paint used on stoves has virtually no rust-inhibiting characteristics, says Harner. Once a year, retouch with high-temperature paint (1,200°F) or stove polish to prevent rusting and chalking that occurs on matte finishes. (This paint is available from a hearth products specialty retailer.) Rust can be removed with a wire brush, steel wool, or an emery cloth. Porcelain enamel finishes can be cleaned with a damp sponge.

Check the gaskets used to seal the doors. They usually last about two to three years. "Place a dollar bill in the door and close it—while it's not burning," Harner says. If you can easily remove the bill or slide it around the perimeter of the door, then the gasket needs to be replaced. If you can remove it with a slow steady pull, you can get one more season out of the gaskets. But plan on replacing them the next year.

Cast-iron stoves are made with tongue-and-groove plates that are bolted and cemented together. Over time—usually 5 to 15 years—the cement can become brittle and begin to crack from the heating and cooling. "If you neglect to repair the cracks, your stove will be hard to control and burn hot," says Harner. "Or if you have a bad draft, smoke may seep through the cracks."

Coal Stoves: Ashes to Acid, Stovepipe to Dust

Ah, chemistry! The ash from coal contains sulfur dioxide, and by the end of winter the inside of your stovepipe is lined with the stuff. Then comes summer, and lots of moisture in the air. And guess what happens to that sulfur dioxide when it mixes with water—it turns into sulfuric acid, which can eat away your stovepipe in just a year.

So cleaning a coal stove is essentially the same as cleaning a woodstove, with the exception of a few special procedures at the end of each heating season to prevent premature rusting of your stovepipe, says Carl Harner, owner of Kring's Stoves and Fireplaces, a hearth products retailer in Boyertown, Pennsylvania.

Remove the stovepipe and brush as you would a woodstove pipe. Then wash it with a mild solution of soap and water (a dishwashing detergent in the same proportions used to wash dishes would be fine). You can use baking soda to help neutralize the acid. Dry the pipe, and coat the inside with a layer of oil—any kind—to protect it from moisture during the months when the stove is not in use. Moisture is not a problem when the stove is fired.

Or, you can just store the clean pipe for the summer in a dry place, such as an attic.

To test the seals on a cast-iron stove, put a 100-watt light in the stove and close the doors. In a darkened room, any light that shines through the stove will show where there are cracks in the cement seal. If your stove has started to crack, it will need to be dismantled and reassembled with a new application of furnace cement.

If your stove contains a catalytic converter, examine it annually to make sure that all the holes of its honeycomb-type construction are open and unobstructed. Remove any buildup with a soft brush or vacuum cleaner with a brush attachment.

Speed tips: To prevent creosote buildup, burn your stove hot and with well-seasoned clean wood. If the flue temperature falls below 300°F, creosote will begin to form in the stovepipe.

If you have cracks in a cast-iron stove and don't want to dismantle the whole stove, you can patch a cracked area with furnace cement for an interim fix.

In a pinch: Ashes contain an abundance of potash and trace minerals that are good for the soil. If you don't want to throw them in the garbage, after they are extinguished, spread them in the garden. But check the pH of your soil first since ashes are highly alkaline.

Caution: Make sure that the fire is extinguished before cleaning a wood or coal stove. Put ashes in a fireproof container and place the container outside to avoid fire hazard. Creosote is a highly combustible material and should be removed promptly from the stovepipe and chimney.

Woodwork

Woodwork should be cleaned according to the type of finish that is on it—such as paint, varnish, polyurethane, stain—not according to the type of wood it is.

Technique: Dust baseboards weekly in heavily used rooms and monthly in seldom-used areas of the house. Vacuum baseboards with the dust brush attachment while you're doing the floors, or use a lamb's wool duster. Most woodwork has a sealed finish and can be cleaned with water when needed. Wipe it clean with a damp sponge dipped in an cleaning solution recommended by the finish's manufacturer (follow the product directions for proper usage). Then polish dry with a clean towel. Remove black heel marks with a little mineral spirits on a cotton swab, says Colleen Dodson, vice president of Lehigh Valley Hardwood Flooring in Allentown, Pennsylvania.

Speed tips: Before you start washing down the woodwork in a room, take a damp paper towel and wipe it along the baseboard to pick up lint, dirt, and bugs so that they don't get embedded in your sponge and end up in the cleaning solution.

In a pinch: To remove grease and smoke stains from painted woodwork without damaging the finish, use trisodium phosphate (available at hardware stores) according to the manufacturer's directions and be sure to do a thorough clean-water rinse, says Jim Capehart, president of Buss Paint and Wallpaper in Emmaus, Pennsylvania.

Caution: Don't try to clean woodwork when you're washing the walls. Baseboards are usually covered with lint, hair, and dead bugs, which can stick to the sponge and then transfer onto the wall.

When using trisodium phosphate, wear protective eyewear, rubber gloves, and a long-sleeve shirt. Always read the product label for proper usage and safety precautions.

Wool

Wool stays clean longer than other fabrics. Its coiled fibers and their shinglelike structure keep dirt from penetrating the surface, says

Five Basics for Keeping Your Wool in Sheep-Shape

1. Dry-clean sparingly. Once a season is usually sufficient. Wool, like hair, can be burned by overexposure to chemicals. Excessive dry-cleaning will give it a shiny appearance, according to the Wool Bureau in New York City.

2. Give it a breath of fresh air to release odors and wrinkles from the fibers.

3. Empty the pockets to prevent bulgy bumps and sags. Wool has a memory and will take on a new shape.

4. Let it rest 24 hours before the next wearing. This allows the fabric to spring back into shape.

5. Store your wool garments with cedar blocks or in a cedar-lined closet or chest to avoid moths. Clean garments prior to storing; it's the body oils that the moths are attracted to.

Jennifer Morgan, Ph.D., product technologist for the Wool Bureau in New York City. Stains and spills naturally bead up on the surface, while dirt caught in the springy surface hairs can usually be brushed off easily. Ironically, the same characteristics that enable wool to repel dirt so effectively also cause its main laundering problem—shrinkage.

Technique: Wool garments should be hand-washed since agitation can cause the fibers to interlock and shrink. Dissolve a small amount of mild laundry detergent, such as Woolite, in lukewarm water. Immerse the garment and gently squeeze the suds through. Allow the garment to soak for three to four minutes. Using several changes of cool water, rinse thoroughly until no more suds are visible in the water. Gently squeeze the wool to remove excess moisture. Never wring or twist it. Reshape it and lay it on a flat towel to dry.

Speed tips: Brush your wool garment after every wear with a clothes brush to remove surface soil and prevent it from becoming a stain later on. Wool responds well to spot-cleaning. If you find a small spill or stain on a garment, rinse it with cold water or seltzer and blot it dry with a clean white cloth to remove it. Never use paper towels.

In a pinch: To remove wrinkles, hang the garment in a steamy bathroom.

How to Wash a Wool Blanket

Measure the blanket before washing so that you can block it or stretch it to the original shape and size after laundering. Fill the empty washer with warm or cold water—the dirtier the blanket, the warmer the water should be. Add laundry detergent or soap and agitate briefly to dissolve. Stop the washer and add the blanket, distributing it loosely and evenly around the agitator. Soak for 10 to 15 minutes. Restart the washer and advance the control until the agitation stops and the washer begins pumping the water out of the tub. After a 1-minute spin cycle, advance the washer to the rinse cycle and allow the washer to finish automatically.

Set the dryer on the high-temperature setting and preheat three or four dry bath towels, which will be used to absorb moisture from the blanket so that it will not pill in the dryer. Place the blanket in the dryer with the warm towels for about 10 minutes at the same high-temperature setting. Remove while slightly damp to avoid shrinkage. Stretch the blanket back to its original shape and finish drying it on a flat surface or over two clotheslines, says the Michigan State University Extension in East Lansing, a community education program.

Remedy for a Shrunken Sweater

The following soaking method may soften and relax the wool fibers of a shrunken sweater enough to allow reshaping, according to Jennifer Morgan, Ph.D., product technologist for the Wool Bureau in New York City. But before trying this method, test your sweater for felting. Hold it up to your ear and stretch it. If you hear a cracking sound, that means that the shrinkage is irreversible and this method won't help.

If your garment passes the test, here's how to proceed: Add ½ cup hair conditioner to 1 gallon lukewarm water. Dip the sweater until wet. Squeeze conditioning solution from the fibers; do not rinse. Reshape on a flat surface, and let it dry.

Caution: Do not hang wool to dry it. With the exception of woolen blankets, do not dry wool in or near a source of heat. It will shrink. While wool knits, sweaters, and blankets can be laundered at home, dry-cleaning is recommended for tailored garments, such as suits. If a garment label states "Dry-Clean Only," take it to a professional dry cleaner.

Part 3

Tools
and
Materials

Grime-Fighters, Choose Your Weapons

The Ultimate Primer on Cleaning Implements and Chemicals

If you want to clean fast and do it right, it's important to know the tools and materials of cleaning. Most chores call only for the basics—things like an all-purpose cleaner, a white scrub pad, and a disinfectant. But occasionally, making a clean sweep of spills and stains requires slightly more exotic supplies such as spot removers, neat's-foot oil, or hydrogen peroxide.

Brushing up on the tools of the trade will save you money and ensure that you finish the job safely and quickly. And that means that you'll be able to spend more time on family, work, and fun.

For advice and assistance in assembling the following material, we turned to Wm. (Bill) R. Griffin, president of Cleaning Consultant Services in Seattle, which provides literature, videos, software, and seminars about cleaning.

CHOOSE THE RIGHT TOOL

When it comes to cleaning, the old shop master's rule applies: Use the right tool for the right job. The benefits are substantial.

Save time. Let's say that you need to remove adhesive tape or paint from a window. If you try to scrub it, remove it with a cleaner, or scratch it off with a knife, you're in for a long day. But with the right tool—a razor blade in a safety holder—the job will be finished in minutes.

Save money. Choosing the right cleaner sometimes means saving big bucks. For example, if you plan to scrub the mildew from your bathroom tile grout, you could buy an off-the-shelf bathroom mildew cleaner. But that can cost up to 25 cents an ounce. Making your own highly effective mildew-buster will cost just pennies. (Mix 3 tablespoons chlorine bleach with 1 quart water and put it in a spray bottle.)

Prevent damage. Follow this simple rule of thumb: Start with the gentlest cleaning methods and move on to more aggressive approaches only when the gentler means have failed. And always pretest the harsher methods in an inconspicuous spot before starting the job. Using a harsh tool or cleaning substance can damage the very thing you're trying to clean. For example, using steel wool on a stained porcelain sink could scratch the surface. Replacing a sink is much more expensive than using a gentler white nylon scrubbing pad from the start.

Learn the Five Basic Cleaning Chemicals

The cleaning aisle of any supermarket is packed floor to ceiling with a stupefying array of products. But here's a little secret. There are only five basic types of cleaning chemicals. Understand them, and you'll be able to pick the right one for the job and save money in the bargain. Here's a rundown.

Surfactants: These are also listed as surface-active agents on labels. The secret behind the chemical scrubbing power of almost every cleaner on the market, surfactants create what chemists call wetting. Essentially, surfactants lower the surface tension of water on the item, making it flow more smoothly over surfaces and into tiny cracks, crevices, and pores. Once this liquid has penetrated, the other chemicals in a cleaning solution can get in there and break down soils. "Then you can wash away the soil along with the liquid," explains Mahilal Dahanayake, Ph.D., senior manager for household and industrial surfactants at Rhône-Poulenc Corporation in Princeton, New Jersey, which makes the basic surfactant chemicals that go into everything from shampoos and detergents to industrial cleaners and soaps.

Alkalies: Most cleaners contain alkalies, not acids. To understand why, you have to know a little about the pH scale. The scale, which runs from 0 to 14, is a measure of the acidity or alkalinity of a water-based solution. A value of 7 on the scale is neutral. Solutions with a value

HOW IT WORKS

The pH Scale

You don't need a Ph.D. to understand the pH scale. Here's a rundown of a few products and their pH values.

pH	Product
Acidic	
0–1	Hydrochloric, sulfuric, nitric acids
1–2	Phosphoric, sulfamic acids
2.0	Citrus fruit
2.5	Carbonated drinks
3.0	Vinegar
3.7	Red wine
6.5	Milk
Neutral	
7.0	Neutral cleaners
Alkaline	
8.0	Egg whites
9.5	Soap
10.0	Baking soda
12.0	Household ammonia
12.8	Liquid household bleach
13–14	Caustic soda, floor strippers

lower than 7 are acidic; those with values higher than 7 are alkaline. Substances at the far ends of the scale, such as sulfuric acid and caustic soda, are extremely aggressive and corrosive. Here's where all this is leading. Soils made of acids (and all fats and oils are made of fatty acids and glycerol) break down when combined with alkalies. And alkaline soils break down when combined with acids. Since the majority of soils—from hamburger grease to plain old mud—are acidic, most cleaners are powered with alkalies. "Alkalies actually chew up fat and oil molecules, breaking them into smaller particles that become suspended and can be washed away," Dr. Dahanayake says.

Acids: Fewer soils are alkaline, and so fewer cleaners use acidic solutions to do the dirty work. Certain soils—such as lime scale, soap deposits, rust, tannin (from coffee and tea stains), alcoholic beverages, and mustard—are alkaline and need to be attacked with an acidic cleaner. They range in strength from the mildness of a white vinegar and water solution to the harshness of sulfuric acid.

Solvents: The chemistry of solvents is different than that of acids or alkalies. Rather than neutralizing soils, solvents actually dissolve them. Almost all solvents are distilled from petroleum or plant products, and they're mostly used to dissolve oily and greasy soils and substances—everything from grass stains to oil-based varnish. Common solvents include paint thinner and lacquer thinner (derived from petroleum products); acetone; alcohol and glycerin (derived from plants and animals); and some spot removers. Though effective, solvents are often flammable, usually toxic, and also hard on the environment. For that reason, professional cleaners and the manufacturers of consumer cleaning products have been cutting back on using and selling them in the past decade.

Disinfectants: Chemical disinfectants have the ability to kill germs. For the most part, this involves wiping out the germs that smell, cause disease, stain clothes, and spoil food. (Some germs, like the bacteria in your stomach, are necessary for health.) Products sold as disinfectants must be registered with the Environmental Protection Agency before they can be sold. There are three main disinfectants you can buy for home use. The most common kind of cleaning disinfectants are called quaternary ammonium compounds. "Quats," as the professionals call them, can be combined easily with detergents that pack a pH of 9 to 10 without losing their germ-killing power. That's why you'll find them in bathroom and kitchen cleaners like Lysol Antibacterial Kitchen Cleaner.

Don't try to make your own disinfectants at home. Combining chemicals can be tricky. You run the risk of destroying the germ-killing effects of the chemicals. And there's also the very real danger

(continued on page 448)

Cleaning Chemicals: What's in This Stuff Anyway?

Here's a rundown of the common household cleaners, their ingredients, and their uses.

ALL-PURPOSE CLEANERS
Abrasive liquids

Ingredients: Suspension of solid abrasive particles in thickened liquid, and more surfactants than in abrasive powders.
Uses: Cleansing hard surfaces like sinks, tubs, and counters susceptible to scratching by harsher abrasives.

Abrasive powders

Ingredients: Fine particles of minerals such as calcite, quartz, and silica. Also surfactants and sometimes bleach.
Uses: Removing relatively heavy amounts of soil from sturdy surfaces.

Nonabrasive powders and liquids

Ingredients: Surfactants, builders (which soften hard water and keep soil particles in suspension), and alkaline buffer salts. Sometimes disinfectants, ammonia, pine oil, and organic solvents. Usually diluted with water.
Uses: Cleaning large washable surfaces like floors, walls, countertops, and woodwork.

Nonabrasive sprays

Ingredients: Surfactants, builders (which soften hard water and suspend particles of dirt), and organic solvents. No need to dilute.
Uses: Removing greasy soils in small areas like walls around appliances, cooktops, and switch plates.

OTHER CLEANING AIDS
Ammonia

Ingredients: Ammonium hydroxide (ammoniated cleaners usually are mixed with detergent).

Uses: Since it leaves no streaks, good for cleaning glass and shiny appliances and removing buildup from no-wax floors. Also an effective spot remover. Do not use on clear plastic windows.

Baking soda

Ingredients: Sodium bicarbonate.
Uses: Mild abrasive for cleaning softer surfaces like fiberglass. Also good for deodorizing refrigerators, freezers, and pet litter boxes.

Borax

Ingredients: Sodium borate.
Uses: Mildly alkaline water-soluble salt works as a mild abrasive. Add to laundry load to boost cleaning power.

KITCHEN, BATHROOM, GLASS, AND METAL CLEANERS
Bleaches

Ingredients: Sodium hypochlorite (liquid household bleach).
Uses: Removing stains on fabrics and hard surfaces. Kills bacteria, viruses, and fungi.

Disinfectants and disinfectant cleaners

Ingredients: Antimicrobial agents such as pine oil, sodium hypochlorite, quaternary ammonium compounds, or phenols. Disinfectant cleaners contain surfactants and builders (which soften hard water and hold dirt in suspension).
Uses: Cleaning and disinfecting hard surfaces such as floors, sinks, showers, and tubs.

Drain openers

Ingredients: Some openers are formulated to reduce clog buildup. They contain enzymes that digest organic materials. Traditional drain openers (liquid or crystal) contain powerful lyes or acids made of sodium hydroxide or sodium hypochlorite to open the blockage.

Uses: Preventing drain clogs, dissolving drain clogs.

Glass and multisurface cleaners

Ingredients: Surfactants, mild solvents, alcohol (to speed drying), and sometimes ammonia (to prevent streaking).

Uses: Cleaning glass, and cleaning and polishing chrome, stainless steel, and other brightwork.

Hard-water mineral removers

Ingredients: Spray and powder forms contain citric, oxalic, sulfamic, or hydroxyacetic acid. Also include surfactants and organic solvents.

Uses: Dissolving minerals, lime scale, and rust left behind by hard-water evaporation.

Metal cleaners and polishes

Ingredients: Mild abrasive such as kaopolite or hydrous silica and acid such as oxalic, sulfuric, or citric. Some products contain antioxidants to protect against rapid retarnishing, and surfactants.

Uses: Removing tarnish and cleaning.

Oven cleaners

Ingredients: Surfactants and a strong alkali such as sodium hydroxide (lye) or less alkaline salts (used with oven heat).

Uses: Cleaning oven interior and racks.

Toilet-bowl cleaners

Ingredients: Surfactants plus oxidants or acids; disinfecting formulas also contain antimicrobial agents such as quaternary ammonium salts.

Uses: Removing deposits, cleaning, and sometimes disinfecting.

Tub, tile, and sink cleaners

Ingredients: Surfactants and solvents. Some products contain oxidants such as sodium hypochlorite and antimicrobial agents to kill mold and mildew. Some are formulated with alkaline ingredients such as sodium carbonate, sodium silicate, and sodium hydroxide.

Uses: Removing hard-water deposits, soap scum, rust stains, and discoloration due to mold.

FLOOR AND FURNITURE PRODUCTS

Carpet and rug cleaners

Ingredients: Surfactant and a polymer that helps dry the product into a brittle form that can be removed by vacuuming.

Uses: Taking up oily and greasy soils from carpet.

Dusting products

Ingredients: Hydrocarbon oil that attracts dust and sometimes organic solvent and water for stain removal.

Uses: Picking up and holding dust on a cloth or applicator.

Floor-care products

Ingredients: Cleaners contain surfactants and builders (which soften hard water and keep soil particles in suspension). Products that also wax contain particles of polyethylene or carnauba and polymers, such as polyacrylate. Floor strippers contain ammonia.

Uses: Removing soil, stripping, polishing, and protecting surface.

Furniture cleaners and polishes

Ingredients: Silicone fluids, wax, lemon oil, tung oil, and hydrocarbon solvent to remove oily stains and some wax buildup.

Uses: Removing dust and stains, producing shine, protecting against water spots.

of creating toxic or volatile mixtures. Other common disinfectants include liquid household bleach (like Clorox), and some pine oil cleaners with natural pine oil also qualify as disinfectants.

To Master Messes, Get Mobile

It's very easy to put together a cleaning kit that's portable and has the right stuff for swabbing up about 90 percent of household messes. Think of it as the light infantry in your cleaning army, says John Becker, sales manager at Easterday Janitorial Supply Company in San Francisco, one of the West Coast's largest janitorial companies. Your cleaning kit should be neatly packed in an organized box or, better yet, a plastic cleaning caddy, which can be easily picked up and whisked off to the scene of the grime. Becker, who teaches janitors about the tools of their trade, advises them to stock a cleaning kit with three basic strategies in mind. The advice works just as well at home.

Protect yourself. Scrubbing and using cleaning chemicals can be hard on your hands and potentially dangerous for your eyes. So your cleaning kit should include a sturdy pair of rubber gloves and a pair of safety glasses that you can use when necessary.

Stock the basic cleaners. Becker and other experts recommend stocking your kit with just three cleaning products: an all-purpose cleaner (a mild one such as liquid dishwashing detergent or Fantastik), a glass cleaner (like Windex), and a disinfectant cleaner (like Lysol Antibacterial Kitchen Cleaner). To make the kit complete for taking on a bathroom, add a spray bottle with a freshly prepared solution of 1 quart water and 3 tablespoons chlorine bleach, and a good toilet-bowl cleaner (which contains a fairly acidic cleaner and should only be used in the toilet bowl). Do not mix cleaning products.

Carry scrubbers. Your kit should include a sponge with a nylon scrubber backing that's white or tan (which indicates mild abrasiveness that's safe for most surfaces). Throw in a good nylon scrub brush and your basic cleaning kit is complete.

SMART SOLUTIONS

Now it's time to take your cleaning campaign to a new level. Here are some tool-savvy strategies that will help you save time, money, and effort while cleaning around the house.

Find Quick Fixes at Your Fingertips

For generations, common household items—from vinegar and baking soda to cola and rubbing alcohol—have been used in a pinch as cleaners and spot removers. In many cases, they work well. In some cases, you're better off reaching for a good basic cleaner like liquid dishwashing detergent. Here's the real story, and some cautions, on how to use some common household items.

Alcohol: Isopropyl alcohol is a solvent that will remove many types of dye stains from fabric. Be careful, though. It can also make the dye you want to stay in the fabric run. Test it in an inconspicuous place first, especially with silk and acetate.

Cola: In a pinch, the phosphoric acid in cola will clean alkaline soils like those found inside a toilet bowl. But beware: The sugar and caramel coloring can leave stains if left to dry on a surface.

Hair spray: Because it contains alcohol and other solvents and resins, hair spray will dissolve ink. You may wish to use men's unscented hair spray to get stains off vinyl. Cheaper brands of hair spray actually work the best. It is useful as a laundry pretreater for ink stains. But make sure that you launder any fabric after using hair spray. It can stiffen the fabric permanently.

Meat tenderizer: The enzymes "digest" stains from foods such as meat, eggs, blood, and milk, which are made up mainly of protein. Enzymes sold as cleaners work as well or better, and they don't contain the spices and coloring of a meat tenderizer.

Nail polish remover: Nail polish remover contains the solvent amyl acetate and sometimes acetone. Just as it will remove polish from your fingernails, it can also remove it from fabrics. It can also remove model airplane glue. But be cautious: Some nail polish removers contain oil that can leave a stain of its own on fabric. And the solvents will destroy acetate fabrics.

Reach Out for Those Distant Nooks and Crannies

The nice thing about hard-to-reach places is that it's harder for dirt and grime to reach them, too. Still, the dust and dirt circulating indoors will find their way to ceilings, high windows, beams, molding, cracks, and crevices. There are two basic approaches to getting the out-of-the-way soils where they live.

Reach it. Start the attack with a tool that can do the reaching for you. One of the best is the extension wand on your vacuum cleaner. Use the brush attachment to loosen cobwebs and dust and to reach behind furniture and appliances. You can buy extra lengths of extension pipe at a good vacuum repair shop.

Another great reaching tool is the telescoping extension handle available in most hardware stores and janitorial supply stores. This pole extends up to 12 feet and is designed to hold squeegees and brushes.

Climb to it. There are three solid approaches here, with the emphasis on solid. For stretching only slightly beyond your normal reach, use a very sturdy step stool or sturdy, reinforced wooden box. For climbing the higher heights, use a lightweight stepladder. The best choice is a five-foot aluminum model. It's sturdy, lightweight, and high enough to reach eight-foot ceilings but not so tall as to crash into doorways and walls when you're carrying it from room to room. For jobs that require extended time on high, assemble a temporary scaffolding by supporting a sturdy, two-inch-thick plank on the level between the box and the stepladder (or between two stepladders). This allows you to clean the length of an entire room without having to climb up and down a ladder.

Manage Your Machines Wisely

Finally, before we plunge into a complete A-to-Z listing of the individual cleaning tools and chemicals, here are a couple of tips for managing cleaning equipment.

For infrequent jobs, rent. Some cleaning jobs—such as carpet cleaning, pressure washing, and drain unclogging—require special equipment and sometimes special knowledge. In these cases, you should consider renting the equipment rather than owning it yourself. Why? You'll save money and aggravation—not to mention space in your storage areas—by renting, says Griffin. "Unless you can keep a machine busy almost all the time, it's not worth buying it," he says.

Here's a good rule of thumb. If you will use the equipment fewer than six times a year, rent it.

Clean those cleaning tools, too. Of course, cleaning tools need cleaning and maintenance themselves. After all, they get down and dirty with the grime. For some tools, the cleanup should be done at the time of use. So, for example, rinse out buckets, mops, and sponges when you're through cleaning. Launder cleaning cloths and even your favorite cleaning outfits separately; the extra grime they carry should be kept away from your everyday wash. And speaking of laundry, keep your dryer's lint filter clean so that the air inside flows efficiently.

Other tools need regular maintenance. Consider, for example, the vacuum cleaner. The bag must be changed regularly, and you should periodically clean thread and hair from the beater brush (the cylindrical brush that rolls against the carpet) and make sure that it's in good shape.

Tools and Materials, from A to Z

Here's an A-to-Z rundown of everything you will need to know about buying and using household cleaning materials and tools. The uses for these items are described here in general terms. Specific applications are found throughout the preceding A-to-Z listing, "The Dirty Stuff," beginning on page 41.

Abrasive Cleaners

Uses: Abrasive cleaners contain small particles of grit that help dislodge soil from a surface. These particles do the grinding. Most abrasive cleaners—from scouring powder to toothpaste—also contain chemicals that help the cleaning along. Color-coded nylon scrub pads, like Scotch-Brite, are filled with abrasives. Brown and black are the scratchiest; blue and green are slightly less abrasive; red is medium; and white, tan, and yellow pads are the least abrasive. Use the white pads only to avoid scratching surfaces, advises Bill R. Griffin, president of Cleaning Consultant Services in Seattle.

Use abrasives on tougher materials that resist scratching. Sinks, tile showers, tubs, and toilets can be cleaned safely with most modern-formulation liquid scouring cleansers. Still, abrasives can cause microscratches and dull finishes. It's best to turn to abrasives only

How Does Your Cleaning Arsenal Stack Up?

Here's a checklist of the cleaning items every house should have, says Bill R. Griffin, president of Cleaning Consultant Services in Seattle.

- All-purpose cleaner
- Disinfectant cleaner
- Glass and surface cleaner
- Neutral cleaner
- Sponge mop
- Lamb's wool duster
- Kitchen broom
- Rubber gloves
- Bowl caddy and toilet brush
- Carpet spotter (without optical brighteners)
- Spray bottles
- Upright vacuum
- Squeegee
- Abrasive-backed sponge (white)
- Terry towels (white)

after gentler methods fail, and always use the gentlest abrasive first. It's also smart to test abrasives on an inconspicuous spot before tackling the whole job.

Maybe it's the get-tough approach that makes abrasive cleaners a favorite of the military. Powdered cleansers are one of the three basic "cleaning tools" used in the U.S. Marines, says retired Gunnery Sergeant Sylvia Gethicker, formerly stationed at Camp LeJeune in North Carolina (the other Marine standbys are glass cleaner and all-purpose cleaner). Thoroughly rinsing sinks and toilets is an important part of using abrasive powders properly, Sgt. Gethicker says. "If I rub my hand over it and there's a powder residue, that wouldn't be considered clean," she says. "The trick is that you don't use too much and that you rinse well."

How to buy: For tougher jobs, buy liquid cleansers that contain bleach. The differences between brands are minimal, so look for the best price. The liquids also have the advantage of squirting easily into harder-to-reach spots like the rim of a toilet bowl.

Caution: By their very nature, abrasives can scratch and dull even hard surfaces like porcelain or enamel. They will damage mirror-finish stainless steel, fiberglass, laminated surfaces such as Formica, and cultured marble countertops. Use gentler methods first. Also, as with any cleaner that contains bleach, it's important not to mix bleach cleansers with ammonia products because toxic fumes will result.

Absorbents

Uses: Usually made of powdery or granular materials, absorbents work like slow-acting natural vacuum cleaners. When placed on a stain or on a porous material, they absorb the spill so that you can sweep, vacuum, or brush it away.

Use absorbents on fresh stains—especially grease and oil—that are still damp. In many cases, you should blot them and place a dry washcloth or towel over the stain. Then place a book or some other household item on it to hold the towel in place, and leave the absorbents to do their spongelike work for several hours and as long as overnight. Absorbents are often a good first step for eliminating a stain before you resort to stronger methods. They can work on the nastiest messy spills, like engine oil on a driveway or vomit on a carpet. Cat litter or sawdust is a good absorbent for these jobs. For more delicate situations, like pulling up a gravy stain from a dry-clean-only wool blazer, absorbents such as talcum powder or cornstarch can be effective. Salt works for lifting flavored drink mix such as Kool-Aid (and stains from Popsicles or fruit-flavored gelatin such as Jell-O) from carpet and clothes.

How to buy: Commercial preparations are available, but in many cases the household items like talcum powder, cornmeal, and salt work just as well. For bigger, messy cleanups buy regular cat litter (not the clumping kind) or a commercial product like Quicksorb.

Caution: If you use an absorbent outside, be sure to remove it before it gets tracked inside or blown into flower beds (or your neighbor's yard). Be careful using talcum powder and cornstarch on fabric. They're sometimes hard to remove.

Acidic Cleaners

Most cleaners use mildly alkaline chemicals to do the dirty work. That's because most soils are acidic, which is on the other end of the pH scale. Alkalis neutralize acids, and the rest is cleaning history. But a few stains and soils are alkaline, and for those you need cleaners with acid to do the neutralizing. Acid cleaners range from substances as benign as white vinegar to compounds as corrosive and dangerous as sulfuric acid. Always read product labels for proper use and safety precautions. Here's a rundown of the seven most common types of acid cleaners.

Acetic (Vinegar)

Uses: Undiluted, it works to remove mild amounts of lime in coffeepots and teapots, it rinses, and it neutralizes residue of alkaline cleaners.

How to buy: Clear white distilled vinegar is best. Wine and cider vinegars can leave stains.

Caution: Vinegar can weaken cotton, linen, and acetate.

Citric (Lemon Juice)

Uses: As a stain remover, it functions as a mild bleach. It also can remove stains from coffeepots and teapots, but it takes longer.

How to buy: Simply pick up some fresh lemons at the grocery store and squeeze their juice. (By the way, lemons squeezed at room temperature produce about twice as much juice.) You can also buy it in bottled form at the grocery store.

Caution: Lemon juice may tarnish metals.

Oxalic

Uses: A gentler acid for removing rust stains, it has a bleaching effect.

How to buy: See the ingredients on the product label. You can find it at janitorial supply stores.

Caution: It is poisonous if ingested. Always read product labels for proper use and safety precautions.

Phosphoric

Uses: It's a component in toilet-bowl cleaners, tub-and-tile cleaners, lime descalers, metal polishes, and denture cleaners. It's also an ingredient in most soft drinks.

How to buy: Check the ingredients list on the product label. You can also purchase it at janitorial supply stores.

Caution: Phosphoric acid can damage surfaces if not rinsed immediately after use. It's also a mild skin and mucous membrane irritant. It is best to avoid breathing its fumes. Wear rubber gloves.

Hydrochloric

Uses: An ingredient in some toilet-bowl and drain cleaners, it's also used to clean mineral deposits from quarry tile floors and to etch concrete floors before sealing.

How to buy: Check the ingredients list on the product label. You can also purchase it at janitorial supply stores.

Caution: Hydrochloric acid is very corrosive and, at greater concentrations, poisonous. It will damage skin and mucous membranes. Avoid breathing fumes, and wear rubber gloves when using. It also bleaches nylon and dissolves cotton and rayon, so be especially careful using it around carpet. It can also weaken the binders in cement. This is nasty stuff. Avoid using it.

Sulfuric

Uses: An ingredient in some toilet-bowl and drain cleaners, this powerful acid attacks and corrodes most organic substances, nylon, and vinyl.

How to buy: See the ingredients list on the drain cleaner label. You can also purchase it at janitorial supply stores.

Caution: Sulfuric acid is extremely corrosive. It damages eyes and mucous membranes on contact and eats skin in seconds. The fumes released when the acid reacts with organic matter (in drain-pipes) can contain noxious gases, so be sure that the room is well-ventilated. The heat produced in drainpipes is sometimes enough to crack or melt pipes. This is nasty stuff. Avoid using it.

Hydrofluoric

Uses: It is used in rust and lime-scale removers and commercial rust removers.

How to buy: See the ingredients on the product label. You can find it at janitorial supply stores.

Caution: Hydrofluoric acid etches porcelain and glass. It quickly burns skin, so use rubber gloves, goggles, and extra caution. Always read product labels for proper use and safety precautions. This is nasty stuff. Avoid using it.

MONEY-SAVERS

Clean Up with Neutral Concentrates

It may not be fancy, but concentrated neutral cleaner is perfect for most daily cleaning needs—everything from floor mopping to wall washing. This is a cleaning product that has a neutral pH, or a pH around 7. It's safe for most surfaces and fabrics and doesn't leave streaks. And by getting it in its undiluted form, you can save money and save room in your storage closet. Buy it at a janitorial supply store and dilute according to the directions.

Alcohol

Uses: A fairly pure solvent, alcohol is an effective antiseptic (it's what gives hospital waiting rooms their peculiar odor) and also a good cleaner.

Alcohol cuts grease and works well for cleaning the smudges and fingerprints from windows (mix one part alcohol with four parts water and apply with a cloth and rinse clean with a squeegee). It's a common ingredient in many glass cleaners because it dries quickly and leaves no streaks. Alcohol also dissolves body oils and makeup on shiny jewelry (although it will dissolve and damage lacquered metal jewelry). Alcohol works well as a stain remover. It will get rid of grass stains, pencil, some inks, and some dyes. As with all spot removers, be sure to pretest an inconspicuous area of fabric or surface to make sure that the cleaner causes no damage. In a pinch, alcohol will also help dissolve and remove the adhesive of stickers on windows or hard surfaces.

How to buy: Look for denatured or isopropyl alcohol at drugstores. Avoid rubbing alcohol, which can contain dyes, perfumes, and excessive water.

Caution: Isopropyl alcohol is poisonous and flammable. It should be used only in a well-ventilated area and never around open flames (including pilot lights). As a solvent, it can dissolve plastics and adhesives. It can also damage certain fabrics. Don't use it on wool. For silk and acetates, dilute it by half with water. Always read product labels for proper use and safety precautions.

Alkali Cleaners

Because most common messes are acidic (they have a value of less than 7 on the pH scale), the vast majority of cleaners are alkaline. Remember that alkalies neutralize acids. Once neutralized, the soil (be it hamburger grease or a kid's handprint) can be rinsed away more easily.

The variety of alkaline cleaners is mind-numbing. Everything from liquid dishwashing detergent and glass cleaner to caustic lye drain openers and wax strippers can be classified as alkaline cleaners. Manufacturers use various alkaline chemicals as the basis for most of their products. These chemicals include sodium hydroxide and sodium metasilicate (strong alkalies), sodium carbonate (baking soda), and the old standby ammonia, which works especially well as a floor cleaner because it is very effective at removing wax finish. Here's an overview of the spectrum of alkali cleaning products.

pH: 12–14

Uses: The strongest alkalies are effective for heavy-duty cleaning and stain removal.

Products: These chemicals are used in oven cleaners, lye drain openers, automatic dishwasher detergents, wax strippers, degreasers, heavy-duty cleaners.

Caution: Be extremely careful when using these heavy-duty cleaners. Their strong alkalinity can damage skin and mucous membranes, so be sure to wear rubber gloves and safety glasses. They can also damage paint, aluminum, copper, and silk and wool fabrics. Fumes can be caustic, so make sure that the area you are working in is well-ventilated. Wear gloves and safety glasses.

pH: 9–12

Uses: These milder products are excellent for general cleaning and won't damage surfaces and fabrics the way stronger cleaners can.

Products: Laundry detergent, all-purpose cleaners, glass and multisurface cleaners are among the cleaners that contain middle-range alkalies.

Caution: These products can damage delicate fabrics. At the same time, they may not have the cleaning ferocity needed for tougher jobs.

pH: 7–9

Uses: The neutral to mildest alkalies are safe for almost all surfaces and fabrics. They're especially good for light-duty jobs like floor mopping and wall washing.

Products: Liquid dishwashing detergents, neutral cleaners, and mild laundry detergents, such as Woolite, contain these mild chemicals.

Caution: These products may not have the cleaning ferocity needed for tougher jobs.

All-Purpose Cleaners

All-purpose cleaners are the foot soldiers of any household general's cleaning army. They are the first line of offense you should try before resorting to the heavy artillery. Why? An all-purpose cleaner's mildness won't damage most surfaces and fabrics. They come in several formulations and have various attributes—from the relative strength of spray cleaners like Formula 409 or Fantastik to the mildness of a fine fabric detergent like Woolite. Most are mildly to moderately alkaline (because they're cleaning up acidic soils like grease and dirt). And most lack the special attributes required to clean windows and ovens or to remove mildew. Their virtue lies in their versatility. Here's a walk down the all-purpose aisle.

Concentrates

Uses: The basics: washing floors, counters, walls—anywhere that gets some dirt but not built-up grime. Concentrates are cleaners that need to be diluted with water before you use them. Cleaners in this form are cheaper, require less packaging, and are lighter in your grocery bag. One of the safest all-purpose cleaners is plain old liquid dish-

Cleaning Product Do's and Don'ts

Cleaning products are tested, labeled, inspected, and often government-approved, but they can still be dangerous—especially if you try to mix them. Follow these suggestions, says John Becker, sales manager at Easterday Janitorial Supply Company in San Francisco, to avoid becoming a cleaning casualty.

Do:
- Read and follow label instructions.
- Store cleaning products away from food and in a place inaccessible to young children.
- Store products in their original containers. This ensures that the label—with its instructions for use, disposal, and first-aid—will always stay with the right product.
- Put products safely away immediately after dispensing what you need. This limits possible exposure to children and heads off accidental spills.
- Properly close containers, especially those with child-resistant caps.

Don't:
- Mix cleaning products. Stick with the basics and you'll have no need for fancy formulations, whether homemade or store-bought. It's especially important not to combine products containing liquid household bleach (sodium hypochlorite) with products containing ammonia or acids. These mixtures release hazardous gases.
- Reuse empty product containers for another purpose. This can lead to confusion about proper use, precautions, and first-aid treatments.

washing detergent. Another mild all-purpose liquid, neutral cleaner, is available in concentrated form at any janitorial supply store. Many contain pine oil, which in higher concentrations can work as a disinfectant. (Look for the Environmental Protection Agency registration notice on the label, designating it as a disinfectant.) It also smells nice and clean. Products with higher concentrations of ammonia may fall into this category, but they're generally high enough in alkalinity to be considered heavy-duty cleaners.

How to buy: The choices are vast. So stick with a relatively inexpensive brand that works for you. Most of the cleaners contain the same basic ingredients: surfactants, builders and alkaline buffer, and sometimes disinfectant pine oil.

Caution: Don't rely on all-purpose cleaners for effective germ killing. Most don't contain enough disinfectant chemical to do much more than wipe out a few million of the malicious microbes—and that's just scratching the surface.

Spray Cleaners

Uses: Aim these handy cleaners, like Formula 409, at smaller washable areas like soiled switch plates, chrome fixtures, appliances, and nonglass cooktops. (You can get special cleaners for glass cooktops from kitchen appliance stores.) Spray on, then quickly wipe off. Some of the most popular sprays contain alkaline chemicals that push them into the heavy-duty cleaner range. When using a spray cleaner on a surface for the first time—especially painted surfaces—test on an inconspicuous spot first.

How to buy: Mix your own in a quart spray bottle using concentrated cleaner that you can buy in a janitorial supply store, or find a brand off the shelf that works for you.

Caution: Stronger spray cleaners can take the finish off furniture and soften or discolor paint, especially when left on more than a minute or so. When mixing your own spray from concentrate, make sure that you measure the proportions correctly. A too-strong preparation will be harsher and won't rinse as easily.

Ammonia

Uses: Ammonia is one of those basic cleaning chemicals that shows up in lots of products and does many different jobs. Here's a look at three of ammonia's biggest duties in the cleaning world.

General Cleaning

Ammonia cleaners usually come formulated with a detergent to make them sudsy and help mask the strong vapors that ammonia (ammonium hydroxide) gives off. Ammonia helps boost a cleaner's alkalinity, which makes it a decent grease-cutter. Use ammoniated cleaners for no-wax floors, walls, and light-duty bathroom cleaning. The usual mixture is about ½ cup ammonia per gallon of water. Stronger mixtures of ammonia are also effective for stripping wax floors. For bigger degreasing jobs (like range hoods), use a product such as Formula 409. One other hint: Those smelly ammonia fumes can be put to good use. A pan of ammonia left in the oven overnight will make oven cleaning easier. Remember not to turn the oven on and to be careful when opening the oven door because of ammonia's strong fumes.

Window Cleaning

Because ammonia is what chemists call a volatile alkali, it leaves no solid residue as it dries. That's why it's a staple in glass-cleaning products and some specialty cleaners for shiny surfaces. It puts the "free" in "streak-free." You can make your own glass cleaner using a solution of 1 ounce clear ammonia to 1 quart water. Dispense it with a pump sprayer or apply and remove it with a sponge or squeegee.

Spot Removal

Ammonia has a mild bleaching action, which makes it an effective spot remover for many soils, surfaces, and fabrics. To make a spotting solution, combine 1 tablespoon household ammonia with ½ cup water. It will help remove spots caused by a wide range of items, including alcoholic beverages, ink, mustard, and tomato sauce.

How to buy: Versatile clear ammonia is available at janitorial supply stores and grocery stores. At the grocery store and drugstore, read ingredient labels to find cleaning and glass products that contain ammonia.

Caution: Use caution when using ammonia. It is poisonous if swallowed, and the fumes can harm mucous membranes in your nasal passages, eyes, throat, and lungs. So make sure that the area you are cleaning is well-ventilated. Be sure to use rubber gloves and safety glasses when cleaning with ammonia because it can irritate the skin. Never mix ammonia with household bleach products—the combination can cause toxic fumes.

Ammonia takes the wax finish off floors, so don't use it on a

---

Ammonia's Godly Beginnings

The story of the word *ammonia* has more twists than an Agatha Christie mystery.

The name derives from a mythological god of ancient Egypt, Ammon. The chief temple of Ammon was in the desert, about 240 miles west of present-day Cairo. The area contained beds of natural salt containing amazing transparent crystals that were prized as jewels. The salt, which was eventually exported throughout the Western world, became known as "sal ammoniac," which meant "salt of Ammon." Chemists today would call it ammonium chloride.

Ammonia the gas was eventually discovered and routinely created by heating ammonium chloride. In the mid-eighteenth century, three French chemists proposed calling the gas *ammoniaque*. And by the end of that century, the term had been translated into English. Ammonia was here to stay.

waxed floor unless you want to strip it. Dilute it according to directions and wear rubber gloves. Use in a well-ventilated area. Ammonia can also harm varnished surfaces, marble, soft plastic, and leather. Ammonia will darken aluminum pans, so don't soak them in it. It can also alter the color of some dyes, so before using it as a spot remover, test on an inconspicuous spot. Ammonia will cause browning of some upholstery fabrics and natural-fiber carpets and rugs. Always read product labels for proper use and safety precautions.

Baking Soda

Uses: It's named for its ability to make baked goods rise, but that's just the beginning of baking soda's usefulness. Sodium bicarbonate (baking soda's chemical handle) turns out to be an adequate replacement for many household cleaners. And it's finding new converts today, says John Becker, sales manager at Easterday Janitorial Supply Company in San Francisco. "We're going back to the way Grandma used to clean," he says. "She wasn't too bad off using household cleaners like baking soda."

Baking soda is mildly alkaline, gently abrasive, and safe on most surfaces and fabrics. There are three basic cleaning uses for baking soda: It boosts cleaning and bleaching in laundering, works as a gently abrasive cleaner and stain remover on hard surfaces, and can be used as a deodorizer in lots of places.

Baking soda does clean, but it doesn't have the cleaning oomph of a detergent. So experiment with different surfaces and soils to figure out whether baking soda is up to the job. Although baking soda brings out the shine in most metals, it won't shine aluminum surfaces.

Laundry booster: To improve cleaning and help deodorize, add ½ cup baking soda to liquid laundry detergent to help whiten socks and other light durable fabrics. You can also reduce the use of chlorine bleach by using baking soda. Instead of using a full cup of bleach, use ½ cup regular bleach and ½ cup baking soda to boost bleaching action.

Hard-surface cleaning: For light cleaning of kitchen and bathroom surfaces, make a solution of 4 tablespoons baking soda to 1 quart warm water and wipe, using a cleaning cloth. Then rinse. For tougher hard-surface jobs, mix up a paste using equal parts baking soda and warm water. You can also mix up a poultice of baking soda and water that, when left on for an hour or so, will pull stains from china, porcelain, countertops, and other hard surfaces.

Deodorizing: Baking soda absorbs odors in the refrigerator, in carpet, and in pet areas. To deodorize a refrigerator, take the top completely off a box and leave it inside at the back of a shelf. You can also leave an open box in musty closets or storage areas. Change them every three months. For carpets, sprinkle directly on, allow it to sit about 15 minutes, and vacuum. To keep litter box odor to a minimum, sprinkle baking soda in the box before adding the litter.

How to buy: Even name-brand baking soda is quite inexpensive, but store brands and generics are generally cheaper and equally pure, says Becker. Just make sure that the label says "USP," which means that it meets United States Pharmacopeia purity standards.

Bleach

Uses: When people speak of bleach, they usually mean chlorine bleach like liquid Clorox bleach. But there are other bleaches, including hydrogen peroxide (the same stuff you put on cuts and scrapes) and oxygen bleach (nonchlorine "all-fabric" bleaches such as Clorox 2). Ammonia, lemon juice, and white vinegar also can remove specific stains. Why does chlorine bleach seem to get all the attention? It's the most effective and powerful by far.

Used according to label directions, chlorine bleach is a great whitener and brightener for laundry. It's also the bleach that disinfects. Use it only on whites and colorfast fabrics. (If you're not sure about colorfastness, pretest using a solution of 1 tablespoon bleach in ¼ cup water. Using a cotton swab, dab a drop on an inside seam. Wait one minute, then blot dry with a paper towel. If no color comes off on the towel, the fabric can be washed safely in liquid bleach.) Be sure to test all colors and decorative trim. Chlorine bleach removes the color from stains in fabrics and whitens. In addition to gentle beaching action, all-fabric bleaches often have enzymes (to remove stains) and brighteners (to keep clothes looking new). You can also use chlorine bleach to pretreat stubborn stains such as tough baby and toddler stains, says Sandy Sullivan, manager of marketing and environmental communications, and spokesperson for the Clorox Company in Oakland, California. Check for colorfastness and check the label to see if the fabric can be bleached. Soak the whole garment for about five minutes in a solution of ¼ cup bleach and 1 gallon cool water. If it's a two-piece outfit, soak both pieces.

Chlorine bleach works especially well to kill and remove mildew in the bathroom. Dilute it (¾ cup per gallon of water), put it in a spray bottle, and go to work spritzing the tile. Let it sit for three to five minutes, then scrub with a white scrubbing pad. Be sure to rinse all surfaces thoroughly, and ventilate the room well during cleaning. Bleach breaks down quickly, so mix a fresh batch each time and discard any leftover solution.

How to buy: As a cleaning agent, there's little difference between brands of bleaches, so look for the best buy. But if disinfection is important to you, look for the word *disinfectant* on the label, which means that it's registered with the Environmental Protection Agency.

Caution: Never mix chlorine bleach with other household cleaners, especially ammonia. Toxic fumes can result. Read and carefully follow the product label for proper use and safety precautions.

Use chlorine bleach to brighten laundry or remove stains. Never use chlorine bleach on wool, silk, mohair, leather, Spandex, noncolorfast fabrics, or rugs or carpets. Don't use undiluted bleach; always follow the label instructions.

Borax

Uses: Borax is a mildly alkaline, water-soluble salt. This white crystalline stuff appears as an ingredient in some detergents and heavy-duty hand-washing formulations. Borax can be mixed with water and used as a household cleaner. Most often, though, it's added to laundry to boost cleaning power. When you're laundering diapers, borax can help eliminate odors. You can also add a teaspoon or so to automatic dishwasher detergent to increase alkalinity and improve cleaning.

How to buy: The white crystals are incorporated in small amounts in some laundry detergents and many diaper presoak products. Look for it on the label. You can also find pure borax as a laundry additive at grocery stores and drugstores.

Caution: As a household cleaner, borax isn't as effective as detergent or all-purpose cleaner. Some hand-washing formulations can be hard on your skin. Follow the product label for proper use and safety precautions.

Brooms

Uses: Sure, it's incredibly primitive in design, but there's still nothing handier than a broom for efficiently removing debris from smooth floors, patios, and driveways. Brooms are also good for sweeping out carpeted corners and edges before vacuuming.

For relatively small floors, and to prepare carpet for vacuuming, use an angled nylon broom. It can reach into corners better, the split-tip bristles pick up even fine dirt, and the angled end allows more of the broom to come comfortably into contact with the floor.

For outdoor sweeping and for rough surfaces, use a push broom with hard bristles of plastic, nylon, or bassine fiber.

A Stroke of Genius

When you've swept as much hay, sawdust, and horse dung as Pete Cimini and his crew have, you learn a few tricks for making the job easier. One of the best, says Cimini, stable manager for the Ringling Bros. and Barnum and Bailey Circus, headquartered in Vienna, Virginia, is the technique he uses to sweep large areas.

It's simple. Don't start at one side of the large area, sweep a long row, and then trudge back to sweep another long row. Instead:

1. Start in one corner, sweep one long stroke, about the length of your arm.
2. Step sideways to make another long stroke. Continue moving sideways after each stroke.
3. When you reach the other side of the area you're sweeping, step forward one broom stroke and work your way back toward the other side.

"Try it," Cimini says. "You'll save a lot of time by not walking back and forth."

How to buy: For indoor brooms, avoid the type with traditional strawlike bristles—they tend to shed bristles. Instead, look for an angled broom with nylon bristles. They're relatively inexpensive, especially at warehouse home supply stores, so buy several to keep in different parts of your home. Hang a broom by the ring or the hole at the end of the handle so that it doesn't stand on its bristles. For push jobs that require finer bristles, choose a broom with harder plastic bristles around the perimeter of the broom head and softer nylon in the center.

Caution: When using a push broom, remember to switch the handle from your left to your right side every few minutes to avoid strain and fatigue on one side. When practical, use a vacuum instead of a broom. It's better for indoor air quality and does a more thorough cleaning.

HOW I DO IT

Here's the Scoop on Superheavy Sweeping

Maybe you've knocked down an old plaster wall. Maybe you're clearing the debris left by a storm or flood. Or maybe you're staring at the "business" end of an elephant. Push brooms can handle heavier debris, but if you really want to make your life easier for those monstrous sweeping jobs, call in the heavy artillery. Shovel first, then sweep the remainder, advises a man who ought to know—Pete Cimini, stable manager for the Ringling Bros. and Barnum and Bailey Circus, headquartered in Vienna, Virginia. He runs a crew of 20 whose duties include sweeping up after the elephants.

"Imagine a basketball. One healthy load will be a good 25 pounds," he says. "If you try to sweep 25 pounds of manure, you're going to break the broom."

Brushes—Scrub, Wire

Uses: For cleaning an object or surface with a pitted, variable, or meshed surface, a sturdy brush is the tool of choice. The idea is to reach between the cracks and crevices. Use a scrub brush with synthetic bristles to get into the grout between tiles and into the crevices in a range or stove top. On the other hand, wire brushes should be reserved for sturdy hard surfaces, like barbecue grills. They can also be used as a first pass at paint removal.

How to buy: Home supply stores carry scrub and wire brushes. Look for scrub brushes with synthetic or natural bristles, one-piece plastic backings, and comfortable handles. Buy wire brushes with sturdy wooden or plastic handles.

Caution: Make sure that you match the brush to the surface to be cleaned. A too-stiff brush can damage delicate surfaces. A too-soft brush may be damaged by a rough surface. Don't forget to thoroughly rinse scrub brushes after use, before the grime dries on the bristles and makes it harder to use next time.

Buckets

Uses: One of the basic cleaning tools, buckets should be used to hold cleaning and rinsing solutions—separately. A bucket is invaluable for mopping and can also be used to hold a cleaning solution for general household cleaning.

How to buy: Plastic buckets with sturdy handles are best. Metal buckets can dent and corrode. Also, square buckets are more stable and can also more easily accommodate a self-wringing mop.

Caution: Be sure to rinse and dry a bucket after use. Moisture and soil left inside provide a perfect environment for mold and bacteria growth.

Stock an inexpensive caddy with the basic cleaning tools, and store it in an accessible place.

Caddies

Uses: A caddy is like a cleaning ambulance: It rushes needed equipment to the scene of the accident. Keep the basic cleaning tools in your caddy (see "To Master Messes, Get Mobile" on page 448), and store it in a handy place that you can get to easily.

How to buy: Hardware and janitorial supply stores carry caddies. Because they're inexpensive (generally under $10), it's worth having more than one so that your cleaning supplies are never far from the action.

Carpet Sweepers

Uses: A carpet sweeper—a device powered by its own rolling— is fine for quick pickups when you don't want to bother hauling out the vacuum. These lightweight tools use the same rotating brush action of a vacuum, without the suction. They're especially handy in finished basements, recreation rooms, and in areas where children play (and snack).

How to buy: Carpet sweepers are usually available at discount stores and janitorial supply stores.

Caution: Don't rely on a carpet sweeper for regular carpet care. It won't remove the embedded soil. Remember to empty the sweeper and clean the brush regularly. Its efficiency plummets when it gets full.

Chamois

Uses: These absorbent tanned sheepskins are the perfect tool for lint-free drying of everything from cars to windows. You must dampen a chamois before it can be used.

How to buy: Hardware stores and auto supply stores usually have a good selection.

Caution: Make sure that you wash it in warm, mild soapy water after use. Detergents will remove the essential oil. Just gently squeeze until damp, then dry on a flat surface.

Citric Acid

Uses: The substance that gives citrus fruit its zing is also used in some commercial cleaners. But the easiest way to put it to work around the house is to slice open a lemon. The juice can be a natural remover of alkaline stains caused by coffee, tea, and liquor. Mix lemon juice with salt to form a paste and gently blot to remove more stubborn stains, like red wine and rust, from sensitive fabrics. Keep moist, leave on for 5 to 10 minutes, and then carefully rinse.

How to buy: Get fresh lemons or buy concentrate in a bottle at the supermarket.

Caution: Test on small area for colorfastness. Citric acid can tarnish metals.

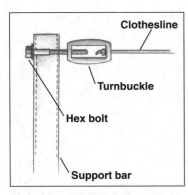

Clothesline

Turnbuckle

Hex bolt

Support bar

Install a metal turnbuckle at one end of your clothesline to adjust the tension.

Clotheslines

Uses: Line-dried clothes just smell fresher than those that come out of a dryer. And line-drying also saves energy. Clotheslines can also be used for hanging doormats, floormats, and rugs for cleaning.

How to buy: Look for a plastic-coated wire, which won't soil clothes and is the perfect size for clothespins. Hardware and discount stores stock them. Also get a metal turnbuckle, which you can attach at one end of the line to adjust the tension.

Clothespins

Uses: The classic use is for holding clothes on a clothesline. But these ingenious devices are also good for holding in place items like rugs, floormats, and shower curtains while you clean them outside with a rug beater, hose, or brush.

How to buy: For most uses, the two-piece wooden clothespins with steel springs will provide the strongest hold and last longest. Buy a bag of 100 or 150 at a drugstore or discount store.

Caution: Don't forget to remove clothespins from the line and store them indoors. Rain and weather can cause the steel spring to rust and the wood to mildew, which can, in turn, stain clean clothes and fabric. To clean wooden clothespins, soak them in warm water with liquid dishwashing detergent for 10 minutes and then rinse. Mix 1 tablespoon bleach with 1 gallon water and soak the clothespins for about 10 minutes, then rinse.

Cloths

Uses: For general light-duty cleaning, nothing beats a soft cloth. Use it for dusting, wiping, and the final shine-up. To get more cleaning surface out of a cloth, fold a hand towel–size cloth several times so that it fits comfortably in your hand. When the surface gets dirty, turn it over. Continue unfolding until all surfaces are dirty, then switch to a new cloth.

How to buy: The key is cotton because it's absorbent. Synthetic fabrics like nylon, polyester, and rayon are engineered not to absorb. Diapers, flannel, and old T-shirts work well. You can also buy squares of cotton at most hardware stores. White terry towels are best since there's no danger that the fabric's dye will come off on what you're cleaning and they are very absorbent.

Caution: Remember to wash your cleaning cloths after use or they'll become dense and gritty with soil and cleaning chemicals. Just throw them in the washing machine with some bleach.

Club Soda

Uses: Since club soda contains a little bit of citric acid, you can use it in a pinch as a spot remover for alkaline spills such as coffee, tea, and alcohol. White vinegar and water is cheaper and more effective.

How to buy: You know—the drinks section at the supermarket.

Caution: Make sure that the fizzy drink you use is plain club soda. Many clear, carbonated waters around today contain sugary flavoring that can stain and soil fabric.

Cola

Uses: The phosphoric acid in drinks like Coke and Pepsi will work as a fairly effective cleaner on things with alkaline soils, such as toilet bowls and whitewall tires.

How to buy: Generic cola is cheapest and has just as much acid as the name brands.

Caution: The caramel coloring and sugar can cause stains of their own. Regular phosphoric acid cleaners are better for all but emergency jobs.

Concentrates

Uses: Just like their diluted cousins, concentrates work for glass cleaning, heavy-duty cleaning, disinfectant cleaning, and where a neutral cleaner is best (light-duty cleaning with minimal residue). Mix the concentrate with water in a spray bottle.

How to buy: Ounce for ounce, concentrated cleaners are much cheaper than the diluted ones you'll find on grocery store shelves. Most janitorial supply stores will sell concentrates to the general public. Find one that will extend its wholesale price to you.

Caution: Make sure that you measure the right amount of concentrate. Excess chemical will leave residue. Also, pour water in the spray bottle first, then add the chemical. This minimizes oversudsing and protects against chemical splashes. Read the product label carefully for proper usage and safety precautions.

Copper Cleaners

Uses: Like brass, bronze, and silver, copper tarnishes. Copper cleaners and polishes remove the tarnish and renew the shine.

How to buy: There are two types: polish and cleaner. Polish usually comes in a cream or paste form. It's better at restoring a high gloss. For cookware and items with lots of details and grooves, choose a rinse-off type cleaner. Both are available at hardware stores, most grocery stores, and at janitorial supply stores.

Caution: It's especially important to remove any green tarnish (called verdigris) from the interior of copper cookware. It's toxic. Wear rubber gloves.

Detergents

Uses: Detergents were developed to do the same job as soap—dispersing and suspending dirty stuff—without forming insoluble "soap curd." You'll use very different detergents to do three different kinds of cleaning: dishwashing by hand, dishwashing by machine, and laundering.

Automatic dishwasher detergent: This detergent is a strong, even harsh cleaner that's usually quite alkaline (12 to 14 on the pH scale). It does an excellent job of helping to sanitize dishes in the dishwasher. It can also be used for a few heavy-duty cleaning jobs, like soaking electronic air filter collector cells from heating and cooling units.

Liquid dishwashing detergent: This is the mildest kind of detergent. It's an almost-neutral cleaner (the pH is slightly on the alkaline side of neutral) and is designed to cut grease and lift soil, then rinse easily. It also makes an ideal light-duty cleaner for any washable surface.

Laundry detergent: Laundry detergent comes in a bewildering array of formulations—with bleach, with enzymes, phosphate, nonphosphate, liquid, and powder. As you might guess, the differences among them are minimal. "They're tinkering at the margins," says Mahilal Dahanayake, Ph.D., senior manager for household and industrial surfactants at Rhône-Poulenc Corporation in Princeton, New Jersey. "Advertising plays a big part." Powders are more effective in preventing minerals such as iron from staining laundry.

How to buy: A little trial and error is the best way to find a brand that works for you. Put a premium on low price.

Caution: When using liquid dishwashing detergent for general cleaning, don't use too much; it will create excessive suds. When using automatic dishwasher detergent for heavy-duty cleaning, use gloves to protect your hands.

Dishwashers

Uses: Not only are dishwashers convenient but also they sanitize dishes more thoroughly than it is possible to do with human hands. Today's models can handle most of the rinsing, washing, and drying that would otherwise have to be done by hand. They often use less hot water than hand-washing, too. Some even come with built-in disposals that chop and grind rinsed-off food particles.

You can also use dishwashers to wash items that you can't put in the washing machine, such as baseball-type caps. Just put the cap in a plastic hat holder (available at home, hardware, and even some grocery stores) and place it in the upper rack. Wash separately on a short wash cycle using cool or warm water.

How to buy: Most major manufacturer's dishwashers work fairly well doing the basic cleaning. Look for a model with heavier-gauge coated wire racks and a quality sound-dampening package. Extra spraying arms ensure more thorough washing. For most families, the economy model with the basic "normal," "light wash," and "rinse only" cycles will do nicely. A booster heater is a handy feature; it will automatically heat incoming water if hot water is in short supply.

Four Steps to Dishwasher Success

Dishwashers can be the ultimate cleaning device, but you have to load them correctly. Follow these guidelines from dishwashing experts.

No rinsing necessary. Other than removing big chunks of food, today's dishwashers will remove most of the food particles from dishes. You'll still need to use elbow grease to prescrub burnt-on soils.

No touching. To allow water to circulate and clean efficiently, all the items should face the same direction and not touch each other.

Don't block the spray. Make sure that dishes and pans don't hang over the edge of the racks or cover the top rack significantly (with a large baking sheet, for example). This will block water circulation and spraying.

Prevent meltdown. Some plastic and rubber items may be warped or damaged by the heat. Check care instructions on these items.

Caution: Be careful about subjecting fine crystal or china, especially that with gold trim, to the rigors of the automatic dishwasher. The harsh detergents can remove the trim and etch and damage these dishes. To avoid etching everyday glassware, be sure not to use excessive detergent, especially if you have soft water. As a rule, use 1 teaspoon detergent per 20 milligrams (of minerals—usually calcium and magnesium) per liter of water hardness. Your water company can tell the hardness rating for your water. Soft water is 0 to 60 milligrams per liter, moderately hard is 61 to 120 milligrams, hard is 121 to 180 milligrams, and very hard is more than 180 milligrams.

Never wash stainless-steel cutlery or flatware together with silver or silver-plated cutlery or flatware. The two metals can react against each other and cause the silver to become pitted or stained. Keep children, especially toddlers, away from door vents. During drying they can emit steam.

Disinfectants

Uses: The purpose of disinfectants is simple: to kill germs. But from there, disinfecting can get complicated because germs—undesirable and harmful microorganisms—are amazingly varied and surprisingly clever. They're also good at what they do: reproducing, causing disease, creating foul odors, spoiling food, causing stains, and destroying fabric. In response, manufacturers have come up with a variety of products designed to disinfect.

Antibacterial cleaners: These are the most popular and common disinfectants. Most of them are formulated with quaternary ammonium compound—"quats," for short—because it combines well with dirt- and grease-fighting chemicals and is also an excellent broad-spectrum germ killer. They're good for cleaning and disinfecting large surfaces, such as floors and counters. Other uses include cleaning toilet bowls, sinks, and tubs.

Fungicides: Fungi produce mold and mildew. They're actually a kind of plant. Fungicides can wipe out these buggers before they create a mess. One of the most effective fungicides is plain old chlorine bleach. Diluted (3 tablespoons bleach with 1 quart water) and placed in a spray bottle, it will kill mildew and at the same time bleach the stain that mildew creates. Disinfectant cleaners that contain quats are another weapon against mold and mildew. They have the power to kill fungus before it grows mold or mildew. Finally, perhaps the best fungicide is adequate light and dry air since fungus thrives in damp dark places.

Germicides: This is just another way of saying "disinfectant." Products that claim to be "germicides" for use on hard surfaces contacted in everyday living, like countertops, refrigerators, and door handles, must also be officially registered as disinfectants with the Environmental Protection Agency (EPA), says Joseph Rubino, director of biological sciences for Reckitt and Coleman in Montvale, New Jersey, the company that makes Lysol brand products. "You can't call it a germicide if it isn't a disinfectant," he says.

How to buy: When buying a disinfectant, look for an official EPA registration number on the label. This means that the product has been properly registered as a germ-killer. The EPA defines a disinfectant as a product that kills 100 percent of the targeted germs on a surface that has already been cleaned of heavy soil. The effectiveness of most disinfectants plummets in the presence of organic matter like food, milk, hair, feces, urine, or dander. Also look for the active disinfectant ingredient—usually quaternary ammonium compound or pine oil.

Caution: Don't try to make your own disinfectants at home. Combining chemicals can be tricky. You run the risk of destroying the germ-killing effects of the chemicals. And there's also the very real danger of creating toxic or volatile mixtures. When using disinfectants, carefully read product labels for proper usage and safety precautions.

Some disinfectants can irritate your skin or eyes. As with any cleaning product, wear rubber gloves when using disinfectants, especially if you have sensitive skin. Also, remember that effective germ killing takes a little time. Leave the disinfectant in contact with the surface for a good 10 minutes, then completely rinse the chemical off with fresh water.

Dry-Cleaning

Uses: One of the most powerful cleaning strategies at your disposal is to take soiled garments to a professional dry cleaner. Not only do they have the equipment and chemicals specifically tailored to cleaning delicate fabrics and tough stains but they usually have extensive training and experience.

Dry cleaners use volatile solvents (mostly perchloroethylene) instead of water. If a garment's label says "Dry-Clean Only"—and most wool and fine fabrics such as silk and rayon do—play it safe and dry-clean. When you take clothes to a dry cleaner, be sure to mention any unusual spots or marks on a garment and how you've tried to remove them.

How to buy: Dry-cleaning is expensive compared to regular laundering, so remember that you don't have to clean most garments after only one wearing.

The best way to find a good dry cleaner is to ask for recommendations from friends. Then, try out the cleaner by taking in only one or two items for cleaning. If that cleaner wins your confidence, you can return with more in the future.

Caution: Perchloroethylene is a strong chemical that is classified by the Environmental Protection Agency as a potential human carcinogen. So minimize your exposure to perchloroethylene. Dry cleaners should remove as much of the chemical as possible. When you pick up a garment, remove the plastic from the garment and let it air out for a day. If you smell a chemical odor, it may not be perchloroethylene but residue from detergents or sizing treatments, for example. But you may want to return the garment for better rinsing, or wait a week or so before wearing a garment that has been dry-cleaned.

Dryers

Uses: Amazingly effective at drying even absorbent items like towels and flannel sheets, dryers can also be used to fluff pillows and comforters and to freshen draperies and bedspreads.

How to buy: Most major manufacturers' dryers work fairly well doing the basic job of tumbling and drying. Look for a dryer with a resilient finish that is warranted against rust. Also look for an easily accessible lint filter and adjustable legs for leveling. The more expensive models will have added features like a larger capacity, electronic controls, sound dampening, and a removable drying rack. Simple time-setting controls are the least expensive, although thermostat and moisture-sensing systems are available, too. The choice of a gas dryer versus an electric dryer depends largely on your local electric rates and the hookups available in your home. Electric dryers gener-

Spin Control: Four Superb Drying Tactics

Here's how to get the best results from your clothes dryer, according to Maytag Appliances consumer information in Newtown, Iowa.

Get the load right. For most home dryers, one washer load is the maximum capacity for one dryer load. Overloading increases drying time and wastes energy.

Remember that the minimum is optimum. Don't overdry. To avoid pressing in wrinkles, take laundry out of the dryer as soon as it's dry. Also, using the "Permanent Press" setting adds a cooldown period to the drying cycle, which decreases wrinkling.

Keep up the good work. When possible, put one load in after another, which allows you to take advantage of the heat remaining in the dryer from the previous load.

Sort your duds. Mixing hard-to-dry items with those that dry more quickly is inefficient. When you unload, the faster-drying laundry will be overdried or the heavier items will still be damp.

ally cost less to buy but are more costly to operate. Gas dryers, on the other hand, require a professionally installed gas line to your laundry area.

Caution: To prevent fires and make drying more efficient, clean the lint screen before each load. Certain fabrics and materials—vinyl, rubber-coated items, laminate fabrics, plastics, and some woolens—should never be dried on a heat setting. You can often dry these simply by tumbling in cool air.

Dust Cloths and Dusters

Uses: The point of a dust cloth is not to just spread dust around but to capture the soil, remove it, and dispose of it. A good dusting tool should attract dust and hold it. It should also be able to reach into the cracks and crevices.

One of the best general dusting tools is a white square of cotton (flannel is excellent) spritzed with a dust remover, like Endust, so that the cloth is moist but not wet. Ideally, dust cloths should be treated, tightly covered, and stored overnight in a plastic bag before using to give the oil a chance to saturate the cloth evenly.

For dusting knickknacks and hard-to-reach places, use a lamb's wool duster. You can also buy electrostatic dust cloths, which use static electricity to attract particles and are available from janitorial supply companies.

How to buy: You can buy aerosol dust remover (like Endust) in the supermarket. It's also available from janitorial supply stores as a liquid that you put in your own spray bottle. Lamb's wool dusters hold dust better than feather dusters. Feather dusters tend to spread dust around and should be avoided. Dusters are available at home supply stores and janitorial supply stores.

Caution: Store treated dust cloths in a plastic bag to avoid leaving oil stains on the surface they come in contact with.

Dustpans

Uses: Dustpans provide a handy way to pick up debris—even the fine stuff like powdery dust and cat hair—after sweeping.

How to buy: For outdoor use, look for the larger heavier models that can handle bigger loads. For indoors, the kind with a rubber lip is best because it allows you to sweep up fine dust. If you want to avoid excessive bending, consider a long-handle dustpan, which is available at janitorial supply stores.

Caution: Make sure that your dustpan is wider than the broom you plan to use with it. Otherwise, you'll sweep some particles and litter around the edge of the dustpan.

Colossal Cleanups

That's a Lot of Champagne Corks
The amount of trash New York sanitation workers collect from Times Square after ringing in the New Year: 45.5 tons

Enzyme Digesters

Uses: Enzyme digesters actually "eat" some spills. They're best for removing organic matter like urine, vomit, blood, and fecal matter from porous surfaces and objects (clothing and carpeting, for starters). You can use enzyme detergents to presoak laundry and also (when mixed up as a paste) as a spotting agent—even on dry cleanables. There are a few enzyme drain openers, which work more slowly but are safer and much less harsh on plumbing fixtures and the environment. They actually contain friendly bacteria that take up residence in your pipes and eat the goopy organic stuff that contributes to drain clogs.

How to buy: You'll find enzyme detergents and bleaches in the supermarket (Biz, for example). You can also purchase bacterial digestive enzyme products that contain proteolytic enzymes for protein stains like meat juice, egg, blood, or milk, and amylolytic enzymes for starch and carbohydrates stains. Bacterial drain cleaners, such as Rid-X Septic System Treatment, are available in supermarkets and home stores.

Caution: Don't use enzyme digestants on wool or silk. The fabric will be eaten right along with the stain. Enzyme drain treatments will help maintain free-flowing pipes, but they don't have the chemical power to clear out a badly clogged drain.

Floor Machines

Uses: These machines have two basic uses. First, floor machines clean and strip floors of soil and finish. Then, when you change from the cleaning/stripping chemicals and pad, the machine will apply a floor finish with woolly or synthetic buffing pads. In years past, the finish was usually wax. But today, floors are finished with a water-based synthetic polymer finish.

How to buy: Using a floor machine is worthwhile, but you probably only need it once a year. So it's better to rent one from your local rental store. If you want to buy, consider scoping out second-hand and thrift stores. You can often pick up one there for a song.

Caution: Floor machines are heavy electrical appliances. Follow the directions that come with the machine. Always unplug before changing pads or chemicals. Wear boots or sturdy shoes when operating.

The swirling pads on a floor machine strip floors of soil and finish. Then the pads are changed for applying a finish. Unplug the machine before changing pads.

Gloves—Rubber

Uses: Gloves to protect your hands should be a standard part of your cleaning kit, especially if you use chemicals any harsher than liquid dishwashing detergent or neutral cleaners. Rubber gloves, usually made of synthetic materials like latex, neoprene, or PVC (polyvinyl chloride), form a barrier between your skin and cleaning surfaces, tools, and chemicals, says John Becker, sales manager at Easterday Janitorial Supply Company in San Francisco. They also allow you to withstand hotter temperatures when cleaning with hot water.

How to buy: Get a pair of gloves that are one size bigger than your hands to make it easier to get them on and off. If you're working with specialty chemicals, make sure that the glove package indicates that the material will protect against those chemicals. Look for these gloves at janitorial supply stores. Buy two pairs at the same time, suggests Bill R. Griffin, president of Cleaning Consultant Services in Seattle.

Caution: Discard gloves with holes—even tiny ones. Liquid will enter the glove and be held against your skin by the glove.

Hair Spray

Uses: Besides holding hair in place, hair spray is a surprisingly effective spotting agent and laundry pretreatment for ink. The effective ingredients are alcohol and volatile solvents and resins.

How to buy: "Try a men's unscented hair spray," recommends Bill R. Griffin, president of Cleaning Consultant Services in Seattle. More expensive hair sprays often contain ingredients that will stain.

Caution: Always test on an inconspicuous place on the garment (or on similar fabric) first. Be especially careful with wool, acetate, and silk. Launder garments after using hair spray as a spotter since it will make the fabric stiff.

Hydrogen Peroxide

Uses: A form of bleach, hydrogen peroxide works well as a spotting chemical on fabric, especially for blood and scorch marks, says Bill R. Griffin, president of Cleaning Consultant Services in Seattle. And, of course, hydrogen peroxide can also be used as an antiseptic.

How to buy: Buy the 3 percent solution sold in drugstores. Buy only as much as you will need right away because its strength decreases when it sits for too long.

Caution: Hydrogen peroxide may be used on most fabrics, even silk, acetate, and wool, which are chlorine-sensitive. But always pretest on an inconspicuous spot first.

Laundry Pretreaters

Uses: Today's washing machines and laundry detergents are good, but they're not good enough to erase extra soils and small stains without pretreating. That's where laundry sticks, sprays, and liquid pretreatments do their work. The liquids (which, technically, include the spray and aerosol varieties) are the most effective at softening and dissolving grease and oil spots, says Bill R. Griffin, president of Cleaning Consultant Services in Seattle. There's a drawback to the liquids, though. You should use them only three to five minutes before washing a garment. That means that the stain may have set in the fabric while it was sitting in the laundry hamper for three to five days.

That's where sticks have the advantage. Although they're not quite as powerful as the liquids, you can make up for that by treating the stain soon after it happens. Then toss the garment back into the hamper for a full laundering later. But it's still best to launder as soon as possible. Don't wait, says Griffin.

How to buy: All the pretreatments perform fairly well. You can buy both the liquids (such as Shout) and the sticks (such as Spray 'n Wash) in grocery and variety stores. Experiment with a few brands and settle on the one or two that work best for the kind of stains you and your family get into.

Caution: Avoid breathing the fumes or getting the spray on your skin or in your eyes. Always read the product label for proper use and safety precautions. Don't use laundry pretreatments on upholstery and carpet, which can't be laundered.

Lemon Juice

Uses: You thought it was just for adding some kick to your tea? As an emergency spotter and occasional cleaning and spotting chemical, lemon juice is hard to beat. Traditionally, homemakers have used it to remove alkaline stains left by liquor, coffee, tea, and other tannins, says John Becker, sales manager at Easterday Janitorial Supply Company in San Francisco. "Today, even professional cleaners are going back to the way Grandma used to clean—with lemon juice, vinegar, baking soda, and salt." Mixed with salt, lemon juice can do a respectable job on even tough stains like wine. As a spot remover, lemon juice, which is citric acid, can knock out stains on fabric (rub lemon juice directly onto the stain) and even on harder surfaces like laminate (make a poultice with baking soda and lemon juice, smear on, and let dry).

How to buy: Simply buy fresh lemons and slice them open for the juice, or buy bottled juice made from concentrate.

Caution: Lemon juice also contains some fruit sugar, which can leave a sticky residue and even stain. It must be rinsed thoroughly after use as a cleaner or spot remover. Test first before using on silk, wool, cotton, linen, rayon, or acetate. Avoid using lemon juice to clean metals; it can tarnish them if left in contact.

Mops—Dust, Wet

Uses: Mops are the perfect solution for light cleaning of flooring. If you are faced with heavy-duty grime on a floor, you will need something tougher than a mop—usually a sturdy scrub brush or a long-handle scrubber with a nylon-pad attachment. When it comes to mopping, though, there are two issues: getting the loose dirt and dust off the floor, and removing the dried-on grime from the surface. Each of those issues involves a different type of mop.

Dust Mop

Dust mops get dust off large floors more completely and more quickly than sweeping, and they grab on to the finest particles. For best results, treat your dust mop with a dusting spray, such as Endust, which makes it attract and hold particles. Shake out your dust mop and give it a light misting of dusting spray after use to restore its dust-catching power.

How to buy: Dust mops, too, are available at home stores. The 18-inch size is convenient for the home.

Wet Mop

For most homes with relatively little flooring—just the bathrooms and the kitchen—a simple sponge mop is usually sufficient. Use it

How the Lakers Mop Up

You may not have to clean a floor as large as the Great Western Forum, where the Los Angeles Lakers play basketball. But you can still use the same mopping technique perfected by the professionals to make floors shine.

Louie Galicia, operations manager for the Lakers, says that this is his tried-and-true drill for perfect mopping.

1. Mop the floor with a good dust mop to remove all the loose dirt.
2. Using a separate bucket for washing and rinsing, mop the floor with a string or sponge mop. Use a mild floor detergent and change the rinse bucket whenever it looks murky.
3. When the floor is dry, go over it once again with a clean dust mop.

"We've been using this method for years and years, and it works wonders," says Galicia.

with a light-duty cleaner, such as a squirt of liquid dishwashing detergent in a bucket. You can also use a sponge mop for applying wax to waxable floors, but it's not ideal. A lamb's wool applicator leaves fewer bubbles in the wax. For mopping large areas of flooring, consider a string mop, which does the job faster. String mops also go into tight corners and clean under cabinets easier than sponge mops.

How to buy: You can buy sponge mops in grocery stores, discount department stores, or home stores. The type with a built-in squeeze wringer works well, but be sure to get one with sturdy hardware.

For home use, try a 16-ounce string mop. They're available at home stores and janitorial supply stores.

Caution: After use, be sure to rinse wet mops thoroughly, then allow them to hang dry by their handles to avoid mildewing.

Oils—Lemon, Linseed, Neat's-Foot, Pine, Tung

Uses: Oils extracted from animals and plants are among the most traditional of cleaners and protectants. Use the right oil for the right job.

Lemon Oil

Lemon oil has a pleasant scent. Used to beautify and preserve dry or bare wood, it can also restore the glow and depth to varnished or sealed wood, polish stainless steel, brighten the finish on laminate, protect ceramic tile from soap scum, and shine anodized aluminum.

Linseed Oil

Used mostly to help condition and seal bare wood, linseed oil is derived from the seed of flax, or linseed. It's especially good for protecting outdoor furniture from the elements. Linseed oil may not be listed on product labels, but it is an ingredient in many paints, varnishes, and stains.

Neat's-Foot Oil

If you know that *neat* is an old-fashioned word for "cattle," then you probably can guess that neat's-foot oil is derived from cattle hooves. This amber-hue oil is used mostly as a leather conditioner—on baseball gloves, saddles, and work boots—keeping the leather soft and supple. Don't use it on items that you want to shine, however, because it leaves a dull finish that is hard to polish.

Pine Oil

A natural resin distilled from pine trees, pine oil is used mostly as an ingredient in all-purpose cleaners. These products have the power to clean, deodorize, and to some degree, disinfect. Only cleaners with 20 percent or more pine oil are effective germ-fighters, though. "Unless they are very concentrated, most pine cleaners are more likely to make the germs smell better than to kill them," says Bill R. Griffin, president of Cleaning Consultant Services in Seattle.

Tung Oil

Extracted from the nut of the tung tree, tung oil penetrates into wood pores and forms a seal against moisture. The oil dries hard but never loses its elasticity. Tung oil is often found as an ingredient in oil-based paints and varnishes, but you can also use it alone as a sealer and protective coating for wood surfaces.

How to buy: Furniture-care oils and finishes are available at hardware and home stores. You can buy pine oil cleaners at grocery and variety stores and at janitorial supply stores. Neat's-foot oil can be found at specialty shoe and luggage shops. Tung oil can be found at home stores.

Caution: Since linseed oil dries slowly, don't use furniture treated with it for a few days. Carefully dispose of cloths used to apply oil such as linseed and tung oil because they can spontaneously combust. Submerge cloths in water and place the container outside of the building. When buying pine oil cleaners, make sure that the ingredients include pine oil. Many are simply scented with pine perfume. Always read product labels for proper use and safety precautions.

Paper Towels

Uses: The uses for paper towels seem endless. Maybe that's why we tend to overuse them. It's best to save them for grabbing in a crisis (such as when spilled purple grape juice on your glass-top coffee table is getting ready to drip onto your white carpet) and for wiping up the kind of sticky messes that would be difficult to clean from a cloth (oven-cleaner residue, range-hood grease, and paint spills, for instance).

How to buy: For absorbent cleaning and wiping, buy the double-ply type without printing (which, in the presence of some cleaners, can bleed onto light surfaces). Also, double-ply towels generally tear at their perforations easier than single-ply ones, so you'll be less likely to rip towels in half. Consider what you use paper towels for. It may be worthwhile to buy a cheap roll for small spills, like iced tea on a countertop, and a quality roll for major jobs, like sopping up spilled motor oil.

Polishes and Waxes

Uses: Polishing and waxing have become less popular in more recent years as we've gotten busier with work and family and as the surfaces we used to polish and wax have gotten easier to care for. Still, if you really want to put a shine on many types of furniture, floors, or cars, you have to haul out the polish or wax and crank up the elbow grease.

Furniture

A good dusting with a dusting spray such as Endust will spruce up most wood furniture. Dusting spray will also protect the wood because dusting with a dry cloth can scratch and dull wood's finish. If the finish does become dull or scratched, waxing or polishing can certainly help.

Products such as Pledge furniture polish contain polishes and cleaners, so they clean and leave a shine behind. Don't use excessive amounts of polish, though. It attracts dust.

Older and antique furniture can benefit from old-fashioned paste wax because it fills in small cracks and scratches. It takes a long time to dry, though, and after applying, it must be buffed.

Floors

Newer vinyl no-wax and laminate floors don't require finish or wax but will benefit from an occasional coat of polish. Just wash them with a product specially made for your type of floor. But linoleum, older hardwood, and cork floors need to be stripped and rewaxed or finished periodically. Most of the "waxes" you can buy at the store today aren't waxes at all but clear polymer finishes, such as Future. These products can be used on no-wax and vinyl floors but not wood or cork. You apply them wet, and when they dry, they leave a shiny hard surface behind. Traditional wood floors that are not sealed with a hard-coat finish can be waxed with special liquid or paste wax for wood floors. Be sure that the wax doesn't include water, which can damage the floor. On wood or laminate floors, use a very well wrung out mop. Excessive moisture will damage the floor.

Car

Automobile finishes are much harder today than they were even 10 years ago, so waxing is not as crucial today. Still, a good waxing will give your car a certain sparkle, and older cars will benefit by having the layer of oxidized paint removed with wax. Today's car "waxes" are as sophisticated as the paints they're designed to clean and protect. They are made of complicated mixtures of wax, silicones, and polymers.

How to buy: Furniture polish and waxes are available at grocery and discount department stores. You'll find more specialized waxes at hardware stores. For waxing nonwood floors, look for a newer polymer finish such as Future. These can be used on nonwax floors. Do not apply any type of coating to laminate floors. For real waxing, you can get liquid wax, which is easier to apply but doesn't offer quite as much protection as paste wax. You'll find products like Future in grocery stores, discount department stores, and home stores. You'll find liquid and paste waxes at home stores. Car waxes and polishes are best purchased at an auto supply or discount department store.

Caution: Be loyal to one brand and type of furniture polish. Switching between types and brands can damage wood's finish. Always read product labels for proper use and safety precautions.

Polishing Cloths

Uses: Polishing cloths have a dual purpose: applying polish and buffing a polished surface. You can use the same cloth for both jobs by flipping or refolding the cloth to expose a fresh buffing surface. Or use two separate cloths.

How to buy: For most polishing jobs—on furniture, metal, and automobiles, for instance—you can use a square of absorbent natural fabric such as cotton flannel or cotton diaper cloth. Special polishing cloths are usually made of a cotton or feltlike material and sold for especially delicate jobs such as instrument polishing. You can also buy polishing cloths already impregnated with metal polish. Look for these in hardware stores.

Caution: Synthetic fabrics such as polyester, nylon, and rayon make poor polishing cloths. They're not absorbent enough. Avoid dyed or printed fabrics; the solvents in some polishes can cause the color to bleed onto the thing you're polishing. Also, don't use cloths with any buttons, clips, or zippers.

Poultices

Uses: A poultice is a paste used for drawing a stain out of hard surfaces such as laminate, unsealed concrete, marble, granite, and other porous stone. You can make a poultice from many different combinations of powdered or granular absorbents and liquid solvents or acids. Typical poultice recipes include baking soda and lemon juice (for stains on laminate), cat litter and paint thinner (for stains on concrete), and chalk or talc with paint thinner or lighter fluid (for stains on porous stone). You place the pastelike mixture on the stain, sometimes more than once, and allow it to dry. Then sweep, wipe, or vacuum it away.

How to buy: Most of the ingredients of poultices—such as cat litter, baking soda, chalk, lighter fluid, paint thinner, and lemon juice—

are available at grocery stores, discount department stores, and home stores. You can also buy commercially prepared poultices from specialty stone-care dealers.

Caution: Be sure to test poultices first on an inconspicuous spot before applying them to stains. If you make a poultice from a volatile solvent, be sure to use it in a well-ventilated area. Also, cover solvent-based poultices for a while with a damp cloth or plastic wrap to keep them from drying out too soon. Always read product labels for proper use and safety precautions.

Pumice

Uses: Pumice stone, which is made from the hardened foam of volcanic lava, is used mostly as an abrasive. It has just the right hardness to scratch off stains and hardened soils from brick, cast-iron cookware, concrete, cooking grills, and toilet bowls.

How to buy: You'll find inexpensive pumice stone at hardware and janitorial supply stores.

Caution: Be sure to use pumice stones wet to protect the surface being scoured. The abrasiveness that makes pumice good for scrubbing hard durable surfaces makes it dangerous on softer materials. Don't use it on laminate, cultured marble, enameled metals, plastics, or fiberglass. If you use it in combination with acid when cleaning a toilet bowl, wear rubber gloves.

Razor Blades

Uses: Razor blades are excellent for light scraping, especially for taking dried paint, candle wax, and stickers off glass and mirrors.

How to buy: Always get the single-edge blades designed to fit in a retractable safety holder. You'll find these at hardware and home stores. For covering large areas, you can buy three- or four-inch blades and holders at a janitorial supply store.

Caution: Obviously, razor blades are extremely dangerous because of their sharpness. When removing paint or stickers from glass, wet the surface, keep your fingers clear, and push a single-edge razor blade under the substance to be removed. Replace blades often; dull blades are unsafe and may scratch the surface. Be cautious using razor blades in extremely cold temperatures—they can become brittle and break. Never use a razor blade to scrape on softer materials like Plexiglas, wood, vinyl, or plastic. It will scratch and even puncture the surface.

Rubbing Compound

Uses: Rubbing compound is used to gently abrade a surface, remove scratches and oxidation, and leave a smooth surface. You can use it to get rid of small scratches on Plexiglas, cultured marble, and fiberglass. Jeweler's rouge or plastic compound would do the job even better, says Bill R. Griffin, president of Cleaning Consultant Services in Seattle.

How to buy: Rubbing compound is available in hardware, discount, and automotive stores. Jeweler's rouge and plastic compound are available through jeweler supply and lapidary supply stores.

Caution: Like all abrasives, rubbing compound does its work by removing a thin layer of the surface being cleaned, so be cautious not to use it excessively or on surfaces with a thin veneer of paint. Test an obscure spot first. Don't rub any harder or longer than necessary or bear down too hard. Rinse frequently to assess your progress. Automotive paint experts do not recommended using rubbing compound, especially on newer clear-coat paints. Since rubbing compounds remove the critical ultraviolet protection layer of these paints, repeated use can cause the paint to prematurely deteriorate, says Michael J. Horvath, an automotive technology expert in Allentown, Pennsylvania.

Sandpaper

Uses: Sandpaper is best used to smooth rough surfaces and erase corrosion and blemishes before you refinish. As a cleaning tool, think of it only as a last resort since sandpaper—even the finest grits—scratches surfaces, making them more porous and more easily soiled in the future.

How to buy: You will find a vast array of sandpaper at hardware and home stores. Discount department stores usually carry a smaller variety.

Two numbering systems are used to describe the size of the grit on sandpaper. The higher the number, the finer the grit. Very fine sandpaper, for instance is designated as 8/0 to 6/0, or 280 to 220 grit. Coarse sandpaper is designated as ½ to 1½, or 60 to 40 grit. The systems vary from one manufacturer to another.

There are three common kinds of sandpaper.

Flint: The cheapest and least durable. It's cream-colored or tan.

Emery: Also called emery cloth or emery paper, this sandpaper is black.

Aluminum oxide: This reddish sandpaper is the most common and the longest-lasting.

Caution: Sandpaper will scratch and damage just about any surface. Use a light hand.

Scouring Powders

Uses: The tough-guy scouring powders of old contained silicate (that is, sand) that could be really hard on surfaces like toilet bowls and bathtubs. Today's scouring powders are much milder. You can use them safely to clean basins, tubs and tiles, matte-finish stainless steel, and baked enamel cookware. You can also use a mixture of scouring powder and water to make a poultice for lifting stains off some hard surfaces.

How to buy: Available in grocery and discount department stores, these products are fairly similar. Some contain bleach.

Caution: Scouring powders can scratch many surfaces. Don't mix scouring powder that contains bleach with other cleaning chemicals, especially those with ammonia. Dangerous fumes can result. Always read product labels for proper use and safety precautions.

Sealants

Uses: Sealants are used as a barrier between the world of dirt and grime and a broad range of absorbent or permeable materials, like carpet, upholstery, and concrete. The basic strategy is to block soil from penetrating and being absorbed. Sealed textiles and surfaces are thus easier to clean and keep clean.

How to buy: For textiles, look for fluorocarbon-type stain repellent such as Scotchgard, available in home and hardware stores. Aerosol sprayers (as opposed to pump sprayers) deliver the most consistent coating. Professional cleaning services can also apply sealants and stain repellents. Protective sealers for wood and masonry are available in home and hardware stores.

Caution: Silicone sealants for fabrics and carpets protect only against water-based stains (not oil-based) and can yellow with exposure to sunlight. Avoid using these products, advises Bill R. Griffin, president of Cleaning Consultant Services in Seattle. Use Teflon- or fluorocarbon-based products. Always read product labels for proper use and safety precautions.

Soap

Uses: Real soap—the stuff made from fats and oils brought into chemical contact with alkalis—is commonly used for bath bars and laundry products like Ivory Snow. Soap gently cleans by lowering the surface tension of water (just like surfactants in a detergent) and by emulsifying oils and fats so that they can be rinsed away.

Soapy Sales: Daytime Dramas Are Big Business

They don't call them soap operas for nothing. Proctor and Gamble, the manufacturer of Tide laundry detergent and Ivory soap, started the country's first soap opera, *Guiding Light*, in 1952. Today, the Cincinnati-based company still produces that show, along with *As the World Turns* and *Another World*.

Hoping to reach an estimated 16 million viewers, mostly women, advertisers spend a total of more than $1 billion each year buying time during the soaps. The average cost of a 30-second spot is $22,000, according to Competitive Media Reporting, a media research firm in New York City. That's $733 gone in the time it takes to say "one-Mississippi."

The popularity of the VCR, however, has advertisers worried. Twelve percent of soap viewers now record their favorite shows and watch them later, which means that they're probably fast-forwarding past the commercials.

How to buy: Buy soaps at grocery stores, discount department stores, and drugstores.

Caution: Unlike detergents, soap combines with the minerals in hard water and can form a bathtub ring.

Solvents

Uses: Chemical solvents, which are derived from plant or petroleum products, have the wondrous ability to dissolve stains and soils. They're also used to thin paint and varnish. Here's a primer.

Acetone: One of the most powerful solvents, acetone is made from alcohol. It can be diluted with water and used to remove nail polish, airplane glue, rubber cement, and grease.

Alcohol: Use denatured or isopropyl alcohol to remove grease and grime from metal objects and glass and as a spot remover for grass stains, inks, and dyes.

Amyl acetate: Amyl acetate is hard to find, but it can do most of the things that acetone does. And it's safe on acetate and other fabrics that are destroyed by acetone.

Mineral spirits: Alias paint thinner, this petroleum distillate is effective for removing lots of oil and grease stains from machine parts, metal, concrete, and hard plastic surfaces. It's good for cleaning up oil-based paint spatters and paintbrushes and rollers used for oil painting. It's found in commercial preparations to remove adhesives and paints.

Turpentine: Distilled from the sap of pine trees, turpentine is an excellent thinner of oil paints, but it's not great for cleaning and degreasing because it leaves a sticky residue.

How to buy: Buy turpentine and mineral spirits at home, hardware, and paint stores. You can find acetone and alcohol at hardware stores, grocery stores, or drugstores. D-limonene, a citrus-based solvent, is considered an organic replacement for petroleum-based solvents. Look for products such as Citrus Strip, which contains d-limonene, in home, hardware, and paint stores.

Caution: Though effective, solvents are often flammable, usually toxic, and also hard on the environment. They can be absorbed through the skin and through breathing the fumes. Some solvents are harmful to silk, acetate, wool, and nylon; they dissolve the fabric. When using solvents, wear gloves and make sure that the area is well-ventilated. Always read product labels for proper use and safety precautions.

Sponges

Uses: Sponges are efficient for cleaning and wiping smooth surfaces, from dinner plates to plate glass to walls. They drip less and hold more cleaning solution and soil than cloths or paper towels. Don't use sponges where bacteria control or food safety are issues, advises Bill R. Griffin, president of Cleaning Consultant Services in Seattle.

How to buy: You can get cellulose sponges at supermarkets, drugstores, and home stores. Natural sponges are harder to find. If you buy the type of cellulose sponge with abrasive backing, make sure that you get one with the correct level of abrasion for the job (white pads are the least abrasive; blue is a bit more abrasive; green is medium; and black is the scratchiest of all). Use the sponges with the white abrasive backing for your household chores, says Griffin. The others will damage almost any surface.

Caution: Make sure that you clean your sponge with mild liquid

The Dirty Little Secret of Sponges

You think of sponges as a cleaning tool, right? But they can easily turn into germ dispensers, smearing nasty microbes all over your kitchen countertops, cabinets, refrigerator handles, and more. The problem is that continually moist cellulose sponges provide just the right environment for colony-forming microbes—a surface to cling to, moisture, and a steady supply of nutrients. The same holds true for cotton dishcloths.

"If there's ever a new life form on the planet, it's going to come from the sponge. There are billions and billions of microbes on them," says Charles Gerba, Ph.D., professor of microbiology at the University of Arizona in Tucson, who conducted a study of 75 dishcloths and 325 sponges from home kitchens and found large numbers of virulent bacteria, including *Escherichia coli* and strains of *Salmonella, Pseudomonas*, and *Staphylococcus*.

The good news is that there's an easy way to sterilize your sponge: Let your dishwasher do the work. You can disinfect sponges in your dishwasher at the same time as you clean your glassware, dishes, and flatware.

You can also sanitize a sponge with household bleach, says Gayle Coleman, R.D., a food, nutrition, and health education associate program leader with the Michigan State University Extension in East Lansing. The Clorox Company recommends mixing ¾ cup bleach in 1 gallon water and soaking your sponges in the solution for five minutes to kill germs. There is no need to rinse.

dishwashing detergent after use, then allow it to dry so that bacteria don't multiply. Because you can't get inside your sponge to sterilize it, Griffin recommends using the antibacterial variety available at most supermarkets. Replace your sponge once a month.

Spot Removers

Uses: Spot removers designed for general use on fabric or carpet come in two varieties: wet and "dry." The wet spotters, such as Whink Instant Spot Remover (for clothes) or Whink Carpet Stain Remover (for upholstery and carpets), are made to get out spots made by such things as cola, fruit juice, and coffee. They are formulated from water-based detergents. The dry spotters, such as Carbona Stain Devils and K2r, are made from solvents and are effective against grease, oil, tar, and other solvent-soluble messes.

How to buy: Spot removers are available in supermarkets, hardware stores, home stores, or discount department stores on the carpet-cleaning shelf. Look for brands such as Afta, Carbona Stain Devils, Energine, K2r, Renuzite, and Thoro. You can also buy industrial brands (usually at lower cost) at a janitorial supply store.

Caution: Depending on the kind of stain, a spill may require specialty chemicals or even professional care. Solvent-based spot removers are flammable and require adequate ventilation. Also, use solvent-based spot removers in small amounts on upholstery and carpet because solvents deteriorate foam, latex adhesives, and carpet glue. Always read product labels for proper use and safety precautions.

Spray Bottles

Uses: Spray bottles make it quick and easy to apply cleaning solution and to get the cleaning stuff into hard-to-reach areas. Also, using a spray bottle, you can dilute your own concentrated chemicals and save money. To keep indoor air quality high, limit spraying, suggests Bill R. Griffin, president of Cleaning Consultant Services in Seattle. Apply products with a cloth whenever possible.

How to buy: You can find decent spray bottles at discount department stores and supermarkets. But for better-quality sprayers and larger-capacity bottles, go to a janitorial supply store.

Caution: When you mix your own concentrated cleaners, make sure that you label the bottles so that anyone using them knows their contents.

Squeegees

Uses: Using a squeegee is the fastest, most efficient way to clean a window or mirror. You can also keep a squeegee handy in the bathroom to quickly wipe down a shower stall after use and thus prevent mildew formation and soap scum buildup.

How to buy: Squeegees are available at home stores. The best-quality squeegees are sold by janitorial supply stores. For home use, the 12-inch size is the easiest to manage, says Margaret Dasso, owner of the Clean Sweep, a professional cleaning service based in Lafayette, California, and co-author of *Dirt Busters.* If you plan to use your squeegee a lot, don't buy one with a built-in applicator sponge. Once the sponge wears out, you'll have to buy a whole new squeegee.

Caution: Don't wipe the blade with a dry cloth when using—it won't slide over the glass surface as easily. Use a damp cloth instead. When the blade wears out, replace it, if possible (you can do that with the better squeegees), or toss the squeegee and buy a new one.

HOW IT WORKS

The Squeegee: Give Your Windows a Shave

Glass-cleaning solution loosens dirt and floats it off the window. The squeegee then dries the window by shaving the dirty water off the surface. But the more solution you put on, the more you have to shave off, so use a damp window scrubber, not one that is dripping wet.

When you scrub a window with paper towels, balled-up newspaper, or a cloth, dirt is wiped around the window and cleaned up a little at a time instead of being lifted off with a few quick strokes.

Steam Cleaners

Uses: Steam-cleaning is one of the most effective ways to deep clean carpet. Also called hot-water extraction, it involves a machine that sprays a blast of heated cleaning detergent into the carpet, which loosens dirt and is then sucked up with a strong vacuum. This method is excellent for removing the tons of dirt and grime that accumulate in your carpet pile over the years.

How to buy: You can rent—or even buy—hot-water extraction equipment at rental supplies and sometimes at supermarkets. But consumer and rental machines are not nearly as effective as the machines used by professional carpet cleaners, and they tend to over-wet the carpet, says Bill R. Griffin, president of Cleaning Consultant Services in Seattle. The best approach is to use a professional who is certified by the Institute of Inspection, Cleaning, and Restoration Certification (IICRC). To find a certified professional in your area, write to the IICRC at 2715 East Mill Plain Boulevard, Vancouver, WA 98661. Include your ZIP code and they'll send you the names of several professionals in your area.

Steel Wool

Uses: One of the toughest nonchemical cleaning tools, steel wool works as an abrasive to remove stubborn stains and gunk. But because it's so harsh, steel wool is generally reserved for times when other methods have failed, and even then you should only use it on surfaces that are very hard or that you don't mind scratching. It works well for scrubbing burnt-on grease from broiling pans and is also effective at removing crud from cast-iron cookware. The very finest grades of steel wool can be used for delicate cleaning tasks, such as removing rust spots from polished metals and wood before repolishing. It's also an excellent way to sand surfaces between coats of paint or varnish.

How to buy: Steel wool is available in home and hardware stores in grades ranging from #0000 (superfine) to #4 (extra-coarse). You can also find steel wool impregnated with soap at supermarkets and hardware stores.

Caution: Steel wool will scratch other metals (including gold, brass, copper, and silver) as well as wood, plastic, paint, fiberglass, and laminate.

Steel wool with the grade of #0000 will not scratch, if used cautiously. This grade will remove hard-water stains and pits from chrome, says Bill R. Griffin, president of Cleaning Consultant Services in Seattle. Use a white scrubbing pad for other surfaces.

Toothpaste

Uses: Because it's a mild abrasive, toothpaste can clean more than teeth. It can be used to gently scrub intricate engraved metal and, mixed with water, will polish away water rings or white marks on wood furniture. It also can be used to clean the grout between ceramic tiles in the shower.

How to buy: Get the plain white paste. Colored toothpastes can leave a stain themselves.

Caution: Just like other abrasives, toothpaste can scratch and dull softer surfaces, especially when rubbed too hard. It's best to test on a small inconspicuous area first. Thin the toothpaste with water. Try baking soda first.

Vacuum Cleaners

Uses: The role of a vacuum cleaner goes right to the heart of the cleaning enterprise: to pick up soil, encase it, and dispose of it. Different types of vacuums have been developed to specialize in certain cleaning situations. Here's a rundown.

Uprights: The most popular type of vacuum, uprights excel at cleaning carpets. With their beater bars and powerful suction, uprights first loosen, then extract the dust and dirt that otherwise would provide enough grit and abrasion to scratch the fibers over time. Most uprights have borrowed some ideas from canister vacuums and come with hoses and attachments that can be used to sweep and suction bare floors and other surfaces.

Canister: Usually more powerful and handier for cleaning stairs, upholstery, and hard-to-reach spots, a canister does its best work on bare floors. Many canisters have borrowed a page from the upright book and come with a power nozzle that will do a respectable job sucking debris from carpet.

Wet-dry: Wet-dry vacuums can pick up dry waste and liquid

messes, too. They're handy to have around if your basement floods, or for cleaning up after construction or floor stripping. A one-gallon wet vacuum is available for quick and easy spot or soil removal.

How to buy: Buying a vacuum can be a complicated undertaking. Look for a reputable dealer, and research consumer information before jumping in. Look for an easy-to-operate on-off switch and a model that allows you to adjust the cleaning height. The cord should be easy to pull out and rewind, and the bag should be easy to replace. Check its weight—and imagine yourself lugging it up and down stairs. Check whether the noise it makes is acceptable.

When you go to try out vacuum cleaners, take along some debris that represents the typical cleaning situations in your home—like pet hair, sand, or cracker crumbs. Also "test-drive" your prospective vacuum cleaner on both carpet and a hard surface, and to see how well it gets into corners and under furniture. Note how wide an area the vacuum cleans. Sure, the bigger the swath, the fewer the strokes. But there's a trade-off: A larger swath means reduced suction and, therefore, less cleaning power. Bill R. Griffin, president of Cleaning Consultant Services in Seattle, recommends a swath of 12 inches or less. Also, when you're shopping for a vacuum, ask the salesperson about each unit's power to move air (expressed as cubic feet per minute, or cfm). A higher cfm means more air movement and better cleaning.

Heavy-duty vacuums, which have sturdier engines and moving parts, are available in janitorial supply stores.

Caution: As a vacuum bag fills, its suction efficiency is drastically reduced. Recent changes in bags allow them to filter smaller soil particles out of the air. These may pack the bag and decrease air movement. Pat the paper bag occasionally to knock soil out and increase air movement through the bag, suggests Griffin. Items that get caught in a vacuum's brush or fan blades may cause the motor to overheat and burn out. Many machines have an automatic shutoff for these situations, but monitor the vacuum and try to turn it off as quickly as possible.

Vinegar

Uses: Also known as acetic acid, vinegar is a cheap and useful household cleaner and spot remover. As a cleaner, it's most effective in counteracting alkaline residue. Use it (½ cup white vinegar per gallon of water) to rinse the alkaline residue left behind by wax strippers and floor cleaners, says Bill R. Griffin, president of Cleaning Consultant Services in Seattle. You can also add it to the rinse water when doing dishes by hand. Use about 1 ounce vinegar in a full sink of water, says Griffin. That helps neutralize and rinse away detergent residue and leaves behind shiny, less-spotted glassware. Wear rubber gloves when rinsing with vinegar, warns Griffin. The acid in it can dry out your skin and fingernails. Straight vinegar also works as a lime deposit remover in coffeemakers, coffeepots, and teapots. Vinegar acts as an acid spotter, neutralizing agent, and mild bleach. Vinegar can be used on stains caused by beer, mustard, and many other common spills.

How to buy: Buy plain white distilled vinegar at the grocery store. Wine vinegar, cider vinegar, and others with plant pigment can cause stains of their own.

Caution: You can use vinegar in a pinch to do some basic cleaning chores like window washing and general cleaning. It's not as effective as a mild detergent, though, because most soils are acid, and vinegar—being an acid—will not neutralize them. As a spotting agent, vinegar shouldn't be used on cotton, linen, or acetate. It can damage the fabric. And always test it on an inconspicuous spot before using it on colored fabrics.

Washing Machines

Uses: Today's washing machines are well-designed and effective for doing that most tiresome of cleaning chores—laundry. Washers basically perform four operations: filling the tub, washing, rinsing, and spinning. And the cycles you choose command the machine to perform some variation of that sequence. Most washers have "Regular," "Permanent Press," and "Delicate" cycles, which is about all that most people need. You can also use the washing machine's spin cycle to remove the water from bulky items you hand-wash, such as synthetic-filled pillows.

How to buy: Most of the machines sold today will do an effective job on your laundry. Still, the choices of models, options, and features can be dizzying. Study consumer publications, and then buy from a reputable dealer. Less-expensive machines are likely to have a smaller tub and just basic controls. They may also lack automatic dispensers for bleach and fabric softener. Electronic touch-pad controls add as much as $300 to the cost without improving performance. Front-loading washers tend to have smaller capacity than top-loaders, and you have to bend over to load and unload them. On the other hand, front-loading washers use less hot water, so they're cheaper to operate.

Caution: Don't put too large a load in a washing machine. That keeps the laundry from circulating and agitating in the tub, and your clothes won't get clean. When washing large items like comforters or sleeping bags, be sure to put a few other pieces of laundry in the machine to help balance the load. Add detergent to the load either as the tub fills with water or after you've loaded the clothes and agitation has begun. If the machine doesn't have an automatic liquid bleach dis-

Colossal Cleanups

That's One Busy Maid Service!

The amount of bedsheets laundered each year by the MGM Grand in Las Vegas, the largest hotel/casino in the world, with 5,005 rooms and suites: more than 29 million pounds

penser, be sure to wait about five minutes after agitation begins to add chlorine bleach. Most machines are designed to stop spinning when you lift the lid. Still, be careful not to reach into a machine until it has stopped spinning completely.

Index

Underscored page references indicate boxed text. **Boldface** references indicate illustrations. *Italicized* references indicate tables.

Underscored page references indicate boxed text. **Boldface** references indicate illustrations. _Italicized_ references indicate tables.

<u>Underscored</u> page references indicate boxed text. **Boldface** references indicate illustrations. *Italicized* references indicate tables.

Underscored page references indicate boxed text. **Boldface** references
indicate illustrations. *Italicized* references indicate tables.

Underscored page references indicate boxed text. **Boldface** references
indicate illustrations. *Italicized* references indicate tables.

Underscored page references indicate boxed text. **Boldface** references
indicate illustrations. _Italicized_ references indicate tables.

Underscored page references indicate boxed text. **Boldface** references
indicate illustrations. *Italicized* references indicate tables.

Underscored page references indicate boxed text. **Boldface** references
indicate illustrations. *Italicized* references indicate tables.

Underscored page references indicate boxed text. **Boldface** references indicate illustrations. *Italicized* references indicate tables.

Underscored page references indicate boxed text. **Boldface** references indicate illustrations. _Italicized_ references indicate tables.

Underscored page references indicate boxed text. **Boldface** references indicate illustrations. *Italicized* references indicate tables.

Underscored page references indicate boxed text. **Boldface** references indicate illustrations. *Italicized* references indicate tables.

Underscored page references indicate boxed text. **Boldface** references indicate illustrations. _Italicized_ references indicate tables.

Underscored page references indicate boxed text. **Boldface** references indicate illustrations. *Italicized* references indicate tables.

Underscored page references indicate boxed text. **Boldface** references
indicate illustrations. *Italicized* references indicate tables.

Underscored page references indicate boxed text. **Boldface** references indicate illustrations. _Italicized_ references indicate tables.

Underscored page references indicate boxed text. **Boldface** references indicate illustrations. *Italicized* references indicate tables.

Underscored page references indicate boxed text. **Boldface** references indicate illustrations. *Italicized* references indicate tables.